Digital Design

Published by Princeton University Press, 41 William Street, Princeton, New Jersey 08540
In the United Kingdom: Princeton University Press, 99 Banbury Road, Oxford OX2 6JX
press.princeton.edu

Jacket image: Cocoloris Co. / Unsplash

Library of Congress Cataloging-in-Publication Data
Names: Eskilson, Stephen, 1964– author.
Title: Digital design : a history / Stephen J. Eskilson, Princeton University.
Description: Princeton : Princeton University Press, [2023] | Includes index.
Identifiers: LCCN 2022055583 | ISBN 9780691181394 (hardback) | ISBN 9780691253244 (ebook)
Subjects: LCSH: Design and technology. | Design—Technological innovations. | BISAC: ART / Digital | ART / Criticism & Theory
Classification: LCC NK1520 .E85 2023 | DDC 744.0285—dc23/eng/20221125

LC record available at https://lccn.loc.gov/2022055583
British Library Cataloging-in-Publication Data is available

Cover Design: Jason Allejandro
Text Design: OoLB

This book has been composed in Untitled Sans
Printed on acid-free paper. ∞

Printed in China
10 9 8 7 6 5 4 3 2 1

Digital Design: a History

Stephen J. Eskilson

Princeton University Press
Princeton and Oxford

Contents

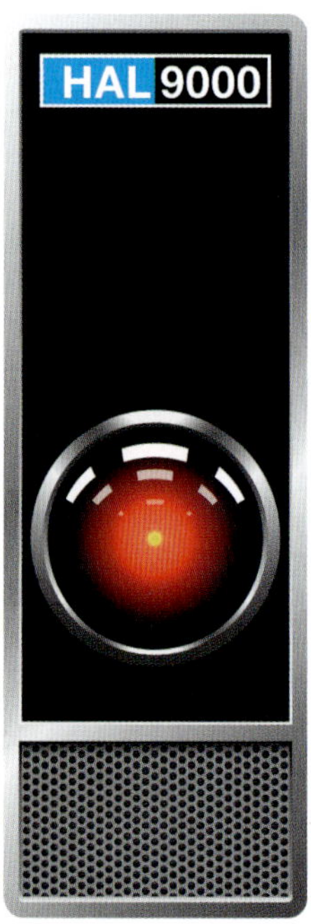

0.1. Illustration of HAL 9000 computer based on Stanley Kubrick's *2001: A Space Odyssey*, 1968

Introduction

> **Dave Bowman: Open the pod bay doors, HAL.**
> **HAL: I'm sorry, Dave. I'm afraid I can't do that.**
> **Dave Bowman: What's the problem?**
> **HAL: I think you know what the problem is just as well as I do.**

This 1968 exchange between astronaut and computer from the Stanley Kubrick film *2001: A Space Odyssey* records one of the earliest and most devastating human–computer conversations ever imagined, crystallizing the sometimes fraught relationship that lies at the core of the digital age: how will people relate to emerging technologies (figure 0.1)? Implicit in the film is the way in which emotion guides our response to the digital. When HAL is shut down in a subsequent scene, stating, "I know everything hasn't been quite right with me, recently," the poignancy of his sorrow outstrips that of many human deaths in cinema.

The interaction between people and computers is mediated by designers. They structure our relationship with digital technology and make it work or, in HAL's case, fail. As Apple

Computer art director Clement Mok has asserted, "Design, in its broadest sense, is the enabler of the digital era—it's a process that creates order out of chaos." In creating this order, digital designers have consistently focused on the future, rarely looking back to consider how their work is rooted in the past. But it is, in fact, the past that haunts nearly every disruptive digital technology.

Take the transformation of recorded music three decades ago, for example, and one can see the complex impact of the digital. In a sense, the shift from analog LP vinyl to digital CDs represented a total disruption, one that beset a multitude of listeners embedded in analog thinking. A widespread urban legend developed, asserting that the sound quality of digital compact discs could be improved by using a green marker to color the edges of the CD. Major news outlets and music aficionados were taken in by this fantasy because they did not understand how digital storage worked. The underlying notion that the laser of a CD player was analogous to the needle burrowed into a vinyl channel was, of course, completely spurious. The technological gulf was too great for many to understand. This technical transition meant next to nothing, however, as listeners continued to relate to music—analog or digital—in myriad ways, just as they had before. The digital does not always transform the cultural. Thus, a central premise of this book is the recognition that the digital cannot be separated from the analog. For all its talk of disruption, the digital is firmly connected to the past.

To fully understand digital design, one needs to grapple with both the future and the past. Take the phrase itself. The term "digital" originated with the Latin word *digitus*, which means fingers or toes—appendages that are the analog gateway into counting. By the seventeenth century, "digital" had begun to refer to numerical notation and any whole number less than ten. Then in the thirties, "digital" became associated with computers and their use of numerical digits. In more recent years, the term "digital" has proved to be a particularly elastic one, as it has expanded to encompass almost all facets of contemporary culture. As computers have come to mediate even the most mundane aspects of daily life, many people have further expanded the term to define human experience in the broadest terms: a digital age.

The term "design" has a much more substantive role in framing contemporary practice. As an English word, it did not become commonplace until the middle of the twentieth century, at which time a slew of practices—industrial arts, commercial graphics, and architecture—were gradually collapsed into the term. Of course, the conceptualization of the word "design" has a much longer prehistory, dating back to the humanist theories of the Renaissance. During the 1400s in Italy, the polymath scholar Leon Battista Alberti famously popularized the Italian word *disegno*, endowing it with multiple meanings. Disegno could refer both to a drawing of something as well as to an overall compositional scheme: these definitions overlapped insomuch as many Renaissance artistic practices relied on drawing to convey a given compositional idea. Importantly, through disegno, Alberti established the idea that the design of a given object was essentially intellectual and not necessarily tied to the execution of the tangible result itself. Mario Carpo has written extensively about this shift and how Alberti reframed architecture from an artisanal process, in which design and execution are performed by the same person, to a cerebral one, whereby a designer plans a building, and workers build it by following drawn instructions. Alberti famously devised a series of standardized production drawings for his planned buildings using a computational methodology. In this manner, architecture became the first modern allographic process in which the design of the work was largely sundered from its execution.

While architecture was first to garner the high status associated with a theoretical design process, the other practical so-called decorative arts languished at the bottom of the hierarchy well into the industrial age. Then, nineteenth-century reformers spent decades vilifying the products of the machine, which were widely derided as aesthetically crude and unsophisticated. Nikolaus Pevsner provides the most important reference points for understanding the process through which the designers of industrial products and mass-produced graphics managed to climb out of this netherworld. Pevsner's canon-forming book, *Pioneers of the Modern Movement from William Morris to Walter Gropius*, first published in 1936, still in many ways defines our understanding of this era. Its luster, combined with its tight focus on certain countries and practitioners, has led to *Pioneers* becoming perhaps the most contested design tome in history. Susie Harries, Pevsner's biographer, has related that Pevsner "said late in his career that whenever he saw his name in print now, it was usually preceded by the word 'not', as in 'not, as Pevsner assumed.'"

Nonetheless, and despite privileging the elite realm of the architect, *Pioneers* did much to establish the notion that machine age designers of all manner of works—from graphics to light fixtures—operated at the same high level as architects. This was especially true by midcentury, when the Museum of Modern Art published a second edition in the United States, now rebranded under Philip Johnson's tutelage as *Pioneers of Modern Design*. At this point, the word "design" became high functioning, as it somewhat collapsed the hierarchy that had separated architecture from the rest. Now, architects were designers, art directors were graphic designers, the industrial arts became industrial design, and so on. At the same time, these varied practices continued to shed their artisanal roots and establish themselves as allographic pursuits with the theoretical dimension separated from the manufacture. As will be elucidated in the pages to come, Pevsner's midcentury conception of design—especially his celebration of the Bauhaus as the core achievement—has played a determinant role in how digital design is perceived today. This newest phase called digital, in which design is married to the binary code, is much more rooted in the past than in the future.

Today, digital design is still an emerging concept; it connotes a slippery discourse, continually contested and evolving. In its narrowest sense, "digital design" is often used as a synonym for "screen-based graphic design." This thought follows logically from the fact that—in contrast to a chair or a building—web design and its brethren are designed, produced, and *experienced* through computers. While this type of digital design rightfully has a high profile, it is by no means the totality of the field. In contrast and at its most capacious, the phrase "digital design" has been used to frame even the most seemingly analog object; curators at the Victoria and Albert Museum (V&A) have asserted that the handcrafted "pussy hat" of activist fame qualifies for the category because word of it circulated online through social media. Considering how social media has colonized so much of people's online lives, this definition might prove too vast for practicality. The current book takes a moderate stance, focusing on phenomena that have a primary debt to the use of computers. As a digital design canon forms, and museums appoint new digital curators and universities new researchers, the still indistinct realm will doubtless acquire a clearer shape.

This book begins with a look at two overarching topics: first, the visionaries and then the machines of the digital era. Chapter 1 explores the way digital culture has been shaped by various analysts. Since the onset of widespread computer use, many people have voiced strong opinions about what this technology means and where it will lead humanity. Although past technological innovations engendered analytic takes, none so reflected the intensity and revolutionary fervor of digital visionaries. The second chapter shifts to a more tangible subject, the hardware that made digital design possible in the first place. Operating systems, graphical user interfaces, and software have all shaped people's ability to interact with evolving technology.

Chapter 3 focuses on one of the most fundamental areas of digital graphic design: type. Some of the most fascinating pioneers of the digital world worked to design typefaces. This chapter also highlights how digital type is embedded in the past, as modernist design is reinterpreted and redeployed by twenty-first-century technology companies. The next chapter delves into the importance of *playing* with computers. From experimental art projects to first-person shooters, much of digital design has sought to create immersive, interactive experiences that are joyfully engaging. Then, chapter 5 turns the reader's attention to the newly minted internet of the nineties, detailing how designers began to navigate this novel virtual space. Digging into another facet of digital design, chapter 6 considers the theories and practices that molded the integration of computers and architecture. From the most esoteric semiotic takes to the pragmatic concerns of construction managers, digital design has revamped our approach to architecture. During this journey, certain buildings and architects have come to define different moments, serving as touchpoints where emerging ideas could crystallize. Chapter 7 adds another layer to the discussion of digital visual communication, detailing how technological changes such as Flash enabled web design to enter a new phase of interactivity. Beyond commerce, art and experimental play again performed a central role in shifting the focus of the design community. While chapter 7 concludes with a case study that reinforces the trajectory of graphic design through to the present, chapter 8 shines a light on contemporary digital architecture at its richest and most dynamic. This chapter also introduces issues of parametric and generative design strategies that are pursued more fully in later chapters. Finally, chapter 9 returns to the issues of industrial design first broached in chapter 2's look at digital hardware, tracing that medium's development into a dominant technological aesthetic rooted in the past.

The book's framing device shifts with the onset of chapter 10, turning from a consideration of siloed realms—architecture, graphic design, and so forth—to the organizing principles of the digital topics themselves. In this way, chapter 10 treats the rise of algorithmic culture and artificial intelligence (AI), trends that have affected varied facets of digital design across all media. From DIY to cryptocurrency, algorithms have repositioned the human–technology relationship in myriad ways. This relationship largely flows through a river of data, and chapter 11 ponders the past and future of data visualization techniques. How we understand and interpret data is in many ways determined by the work of digital designers. Last, chapter 12 explores the consequences of virtual reality, which has led to real-world results while also reigniting the visionary spirit that portends radical change in the future.

In 1968, the AI named HAL cinematically murdered most of the crew of the spaceship *Discovery One*; yet his rampage was stopped by the human ingenuity of Dave Bowman. Nearly fifty years later, Ava, the AI protagonist of the film *Ex Machina*, outwits her human companions, leaving them to die while she blends seamlessly into an urban crowd. Before the murders and her escape, Ava asks her designer, "Isn't it strange, to create something that hates you?" The question has both emotional and existential relevance. As humanity's relationship to machines adds layers and intensifies, the work of digital designers will be embedded in every aspect of society. They will help determine whether digital creations seem to love us or hate us, bringing joy and productivity, or enervation and despair.

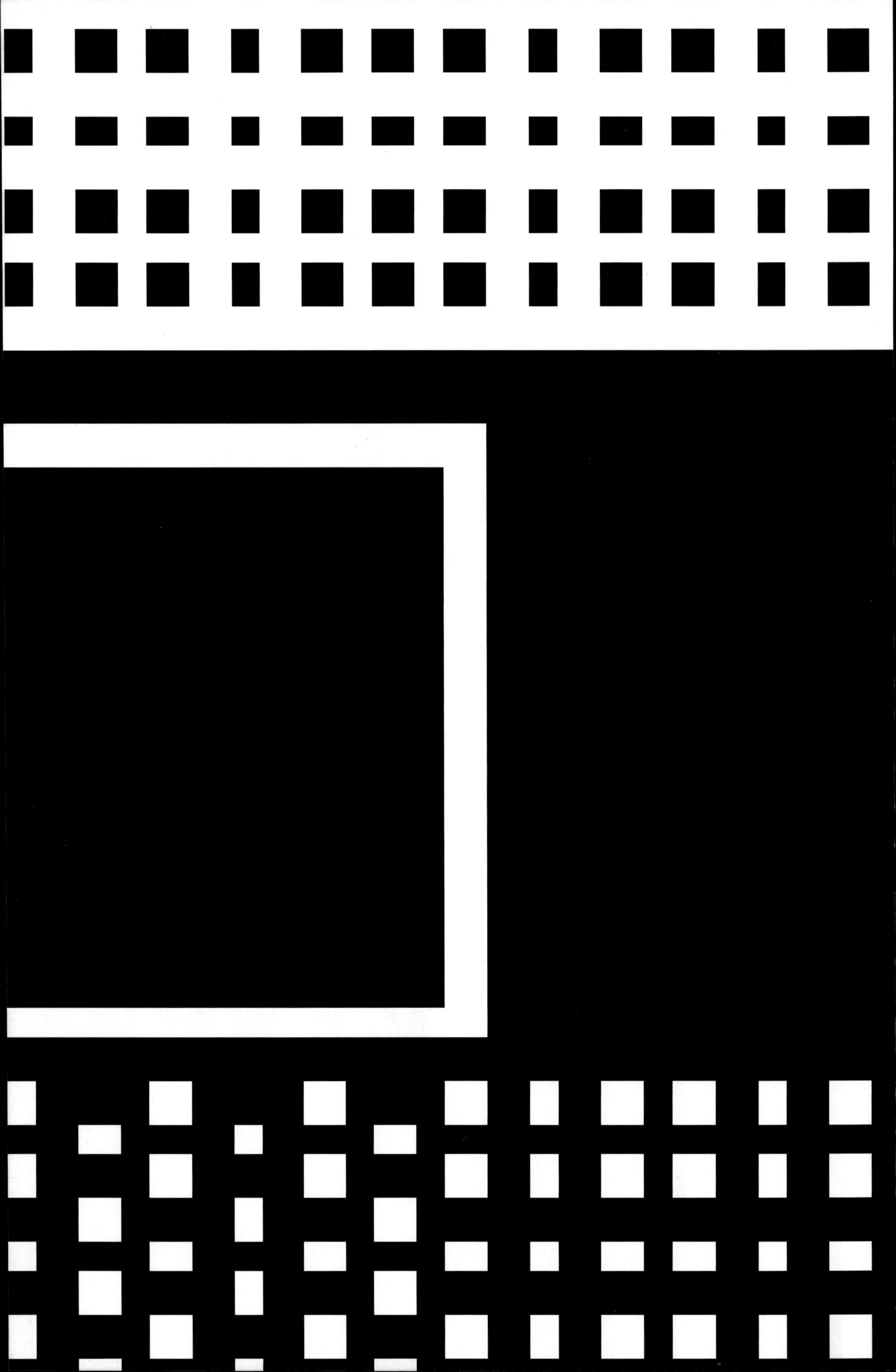

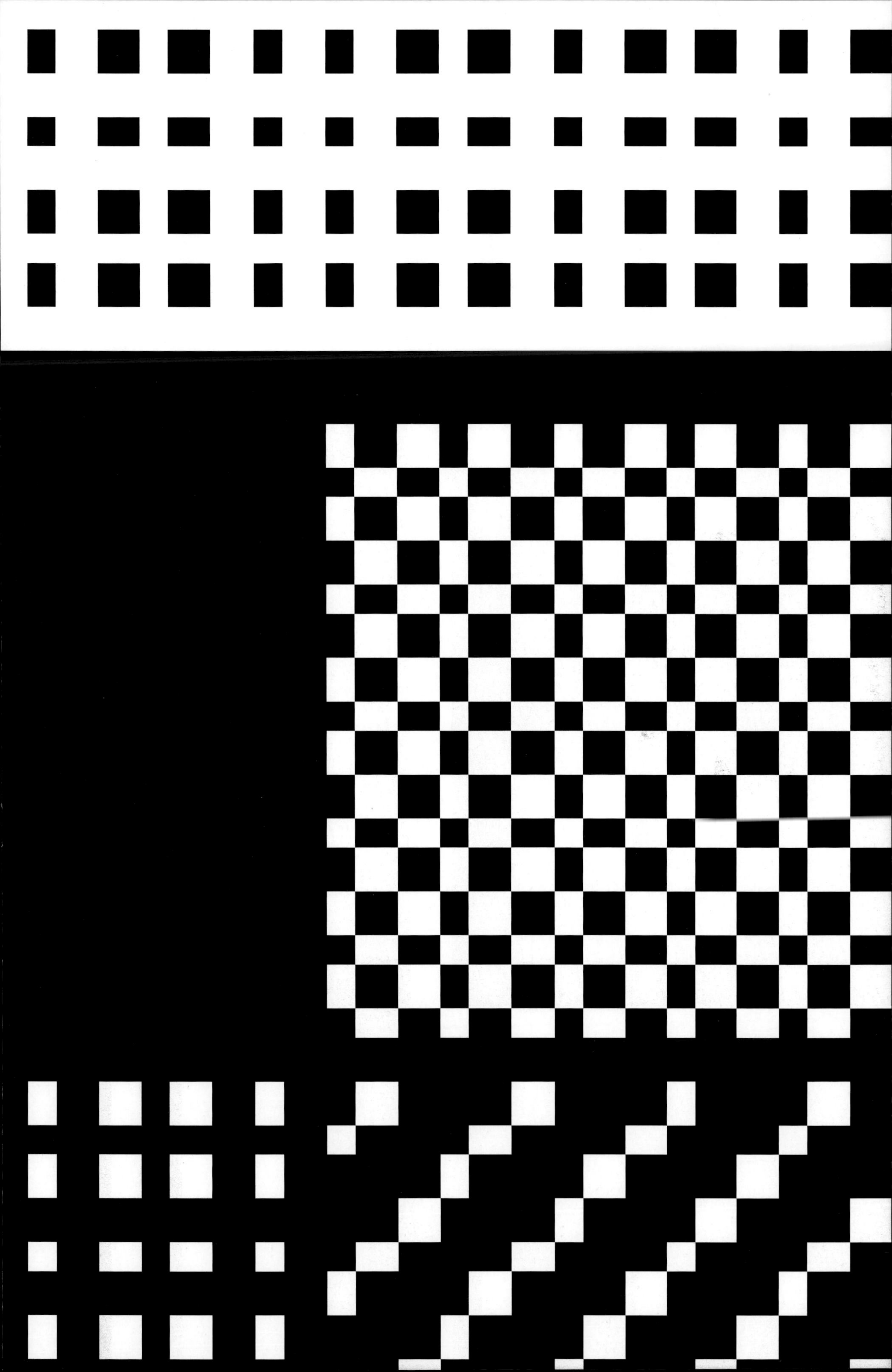

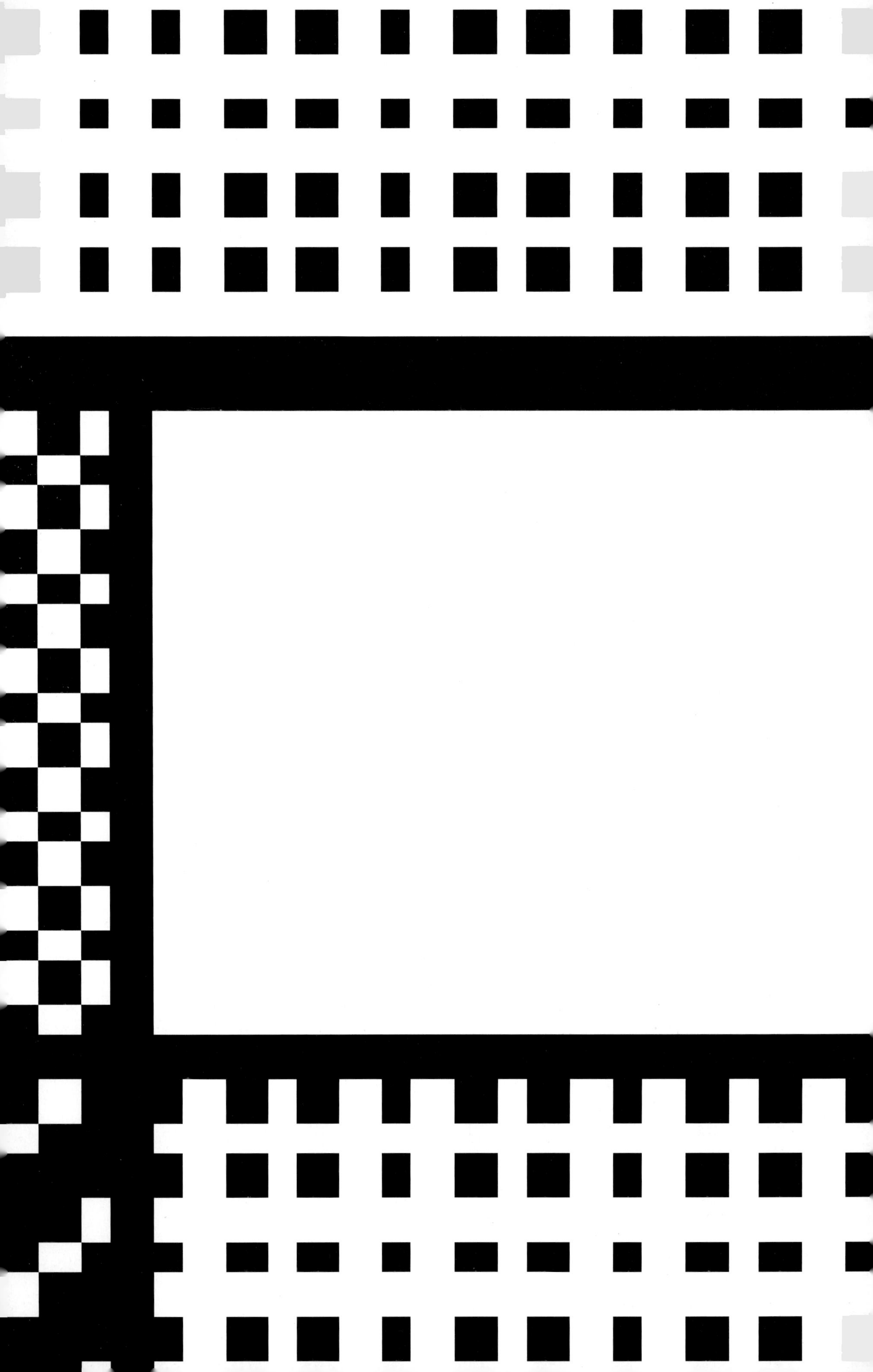

One. The Visionaries

Clement Mok is one of a large cohort of designers who emerged in the nineties as digital visionaries, thinkers who would help humanity process its relationship to new technology. The place of the digital visionary is a profound one, and one with a substantial backstory that still resonates today. Over the past thirty years, digital design's greatest strength—and perhaps also its greatest weakness—has been its visionary nature. Never before has a technological shift been freighted with so much baggage by thinkers both inside and outside the industry. Prophets, gurus, and seers have sought to explain and project what digital design was doing, could do, and would do; they have produced a vast sea of speculation that has both enriched and complicated any understanding of the digital era. This is not to say that no true, material reality underlies this discourse, but rather to acknowledge that contemporary digital design is enmeshed in a matrix that combines past, present, and future in a dense series of layers like a Photoshop project run amok.

The burden of expectations placed on digital designers has been unprecedented. Take, for comparison's sake, the career of another agent of great technological change, Nicolas Jenson. Jenson was born around 1420 in France, where he first worked as a die cutter for coins. As pan-European trade expanded in the fifteenth century, he immigrated to Mainz, Germany, a port city on the Rhine, where he learned the fundamentals of printing with mechanical type amid the nascent industry pioneered there by Johannes Gutenberg. After a decade in Mainz, Jenson moved again, opening a printing and type-designing business in Venice. Over the final decade of his life, Jenson published more than 150 works and was one of the key figures in promoting the roman style of type. Roman type, based on a mash-up of the eponymous imperial majuscule letters and the bureaucratic handwriting of Charlemagne's empire (called Carolingian minuscule), represented the maturing of the printing business as it adopted a lettering style that remains the basis of all writing in the Western world today.

The invention of mechanical printing with movable metal type, an accomplishment in which Jenson played a substantial role, had a transformative effect on European society. Yet, nobody was particularly interested in writing about it, let alone having a metadiscourse. Imagine for a minute if Jenson and his cohort, busy in the 1470s publishing the books we now call incunabula, had been surrounded by printing visionaries proclaiming what the future might bring: Knowledge will circulate outside the realm of the elites! Printing will lead to near universal literacy! The Reformation will upend European Christianity! Enlightenment thinkers will undermine absolute rulers! People will demand just, representative governments! Science and technology will flourish through shared research! You can read it all on a portable digital device!

It would perhaps be hard to concentrate on one's work if the stakes were so high. But this is the world inhabited by many digital designers. If assiduous in following news of the field, they are liable to read every workday a series of breathless predictions about how society will be transformed by technology. Also, the chronology has been mightily compressed: today's visionaries tend not to offer a view of what could happen next century or even next decade, but rather next year or even next month.

The whole character of what visionary even means has changed in the digital era. Compared to the Industrial Revolution of the eighteenth and nineteenth centuries, when a "visionary" was most likely to be lauded for tangible accomplishments, today's prophets and seers may well not have any clear intrinsic relationship to the field. In contrast, eighteenth-century copper coinage magnate Matthew Boulton (1728–1809) is today acclaimed as a visionary for what he actually accomplished not for what he feverishly predicted. In 1775, he partnered with James Watt (1736–1819) to finance Watt's upgrade of the Newcomen steam engine. Steam was the silicon of the Industrial Revolution. As an angel investor, Boulton provided capital and savvy to the task of improving and marketing the machine that functioned as the beating heart of the Industrial Revolution in England. Watt, along with other engineering luminaries such as Isambard Brunel—designer of more than twenty railway lines, steamships, and the like—followed the new technology where it led without promising immediate and complete societal transformation.

When in 1861 the Western Union Telegraph Company completed the first transcontinental information superhighway (or railway?), uniting its East and West Coast networks, the public and the press barely noticed. The telegraph—originally a French neologism meaning "far writer"—had first been devised in the 1700s and gradually expanded around the globe toward the middle of the nineteenth century. Electrical telegraphy had been further facilitated by the invention of the eponymous Morse code, an 1830s messaging system that eventually became a mainstay of telegraphy. While some early telegraphically communicated events—such as the birth of one of Queen Victoria's children—had been cause for public celebration, the creation of the transcontinental link barely raised an eyebrow. The *New York Times* devoted only one single story to it over the entire year (October 26, 1861), and that one remarked on the general lack of enthusiasm. "The work of carrying westward the transcontinental telegraphic line has progressed with so little blazonment, that it is with almost an electric thrill one reads the words of greeting yesterday flashed instantaneously over the wires direct from California." By the 1870s, transatlantic cables had been set down, and soon the world was united by more than 650,000 miles of wires.

The transcontinental telegraph transformed communication on a grand scale, both in practical ways—the end of the Pony Express and the new ability to wire transfer money—and in cultural ones: the post–Civil War development of a national identity, complete with a belief in Manifest Destiny, would have arguably played out much differently without electronic communication. Yes, an occasional pundit asserted that the telegraph would further world understanding. In 1878, for example, an author opined that to "a very remarkable degree the telegraph confederated human sympathies and elevated the conception of human brotherhood. By it the peoples of the world were made to stand closer together." But one must assiduously dig through history to find such blandishments; overall, the telegraph was absorbed into commerce and personal lives without much in the way of superheated commentary. Whither the visionaries? If mechanical printing was the first internet, and the telegraph was the second, then both managed to emerge with little fanfare compared to the digital iteration.

Likewise, twentieth-century industrial transformations flourished without the prognostications of contemporary seers. Influential industrialists such as Henry Ford did much to change the culture of commerce; in Ford's case, he championed franchised dealerships, vertical integration of production, and the twenty-four-hour shift-based assembly line, all of which had enormous impact on manufacturing and society. While he was an oft-quoted architect of many a self-help platitude or conspiratorial aside, as to the view that automobiles would overturn many conventions of Western culture and social relationships, Ford and others had little to say.

Part of the reason for the dearth of speculation on the impact of older technologies came from the lag time that often separated an invention from its widespread implementation, let alone its clear cultural impact. Consider the history of electricity. By the 1880s, electrical generating stations were popping up in major cities, while light bulbs and electric motors were commercially available. Still, for the next three decades, architects continued to rely on light courts and windows paired with gas jets to illuminate their buildings, while factory owners commissioned cutting-edge production facilities committed to centralized steam power. Also ponder the emergence of photography. Invented in the first half of the nineteenth century, it would not play a significant role in graphic design for seventy years. These technological advances were digested over decades, and the changes they wrought came about organically, so they were positively unheralded by today's standards.

Digital Visionaries

When the age of the digital visionary began, it was a combination of the probable and the improbable. With hindsight, the predictable part was the decade of the 1960s. Revered and reviled, the sixties witnessed a slew of micro and macro adjustments to Western culture. From university curricula to war in Southeast Asia, from civil rights to birth control pills, assassinations to flower children, Mexican Olympics to Mai Soixante-Huit, suffice it to say that the decade has earned its reputation as the Lacanian mirror stage of Western society. A new self-consciousness permeated the culture, and an anticipation of a radically different future dominated the discourse. Flux became the new static.

The improbable part of this history was the person whose views came to dominate the technocultural conversation: an unknown and unfashionably middle-aged Canadian English professor named Marshall McLuhan. A frequent publisher of obscure works of cultural criticism, McLuhan had long sought to break out of the academy into the business world, having even founded a consulting business—Idea Consultants—in 1955. Nothing really came of these efforts until 1964, when McLuhan published a new book called *Understanding Media: The Extensions of Man*. Partly a reprisal of his earlier forays into overarching theories of human society, *Understanding Media* situated communication technology at the center of the discussion. But while the subject matter was familiar ground for McLuhan, his take on it represented a radical break with his past work. McLuhan's new stance initiated a turn away from a lifelong tendency toward curmudgeonly pessimism to outright breathless enthusiasm. For McLuhan, what powered this newfound passion was his vision of a world interconnected through electronic media.

McLuhan's central thesis in *Understanding Media* is often boiled down to the oft-quoted aphorism, "The medium is the message." The point here was that in the age of electronic media—radio, televisions, telephones, and computers—the means of transmitting knowledge and culture was more important than the content itself (note that while McLuhan mentions computers in futuristic terms, his clear focus is on radio and television, the dominant electronic media of the day). Like so many of McLuhan's epigrammatic pronouncements, "the medium is the message" sounds insightful and could serve as a counterintuitive discussion starter, but it is, at its core, nonsensical. A moment's thought conjures countless scenarios—pretty much all of them in fact—where the message trumps the medium (orders for nuclear war, anyone?). Also, the clichéd reasoning behind "the medium is the message" begs disbelief in its strangeness. McLuhan asserted that "tribal man"—think of a romantic, natural being who is untutored or distorted by culture—had lived a sensual life in the oral age of rich, face-to-face communication. Next, Gutenberg and Jenson et al. destroyed this harmonious Eden with the invention of mechanical printing and the start of a typographic era that had suppressed the imaginative potential of humanity. Fortunately, this typographic hegemony of the written word was to be replaced by the sensual, even mystical, electronic age. The emerging electronic media would unleash the passionate potential of the global village (another McLuhanism) while restoring magic to the world. Here, there is "blazonment." The key point is not that much of this theory does not seem to make much sense (it requires more tortured explanations to relate, for example, why television represents an aural, not a visual, experience) but that it did not matter that it does not make sense.

"Clear prose indicates the absence of thought," McLuhan once said. One of the great ironies of McLuhanism is that his success and celebrity proved that in some ways neither the medium nor the message was the key to communication. His own medium was originally typographic, not electronic (which should in his own terms trap his readers in a world of desiccated logocentrism), and his message bordered on the incomprehensible. But ever did he communicate. With a little nudge from some astute public relations executives, in 1965 McLuhan's fame accelerated across the media spectrum. In the *New York Herald Tribune*, Tom Wolfe breathlessly intoned, "Suppose he is what he sounds like, the most important thinker since Newton, Darwin, Freud, Einstein, and Pavlov, studs of the intelligentsia game[. S]uppose he is the oracle of the modern times—what if he is right?" Wolfe's essay made the question "what if he is right?" into a mantra, repeating it throughout the piece as he describes McLuhan's various pronouncements made in the company of the intellectual and moneyed elite. McLuhan must have felt such a thrill of jouissance to be wined and dined while throwing out such notions as, "Well, of course, a city like New York is obsolete."

The graphic designer David Carson once admonished, "Don't confuse legibility with communication." This could equally apply to McLuhan, whose cryptic techno-utopian messaging moved and inspired millions of people to embrace an emerging technological society. The details, even the central thesis, did not matter in the end, as it was McLuhan's optimistic attitude that came through. Electronic media were going to make human life better on every possible level; not just materially, but spiritually and emotionally. As Wolfe captured this image, he closed his essay with four words: "serene, the new world." It is the Panglossian aspect of McLuhan's thought that really changed the culture. As noted above, earlier eras of rapid technological change had not shared nearly this degree of visionary speculation: McLuhan truly changed the discourse on technology in a way that has resonated through to the present day and has both burdened and blessed the designers of the digital.

Amid all his offbeat pronouncements, McLuhan did communicate, in my view, what is a central issue driving digital designers: making the computer world warm and relatable. This was in a way McLuhan's core thesis, that the new age would bring harmony and joy to people's lives. Rich emotion would flow through electronic circuits. In *Understanding Media* he opined that this was an organic development: "The aspiration of our time for wholeness, empathy and depth of awareness is a natural adjunct of electric technology. . . . There is deep faith to be found in this new attitude—a faith that concerns the ultimate harmony of all being." Importantly, this new attitude would come about because humanity would not just relate to technology but eventually unite with it. "Rapidly, we approach the final phase of the extensions of man—the technological simulation of consciousness, when the creative process of knowing will be collectively and corporately extended to the whole of human society, much as we have already extended our senses and our nerves by the various media."

Becoming Digital Visionaries

Like so many aspects of the digital world, McLuhan's high stature proved fleeting, and his fame decelerated in the seventies as fast as it had accelerated in the sixties. Beset by critics who were baffled by his obtuse pronouncements and perhaps envious of his high profile, McLuhan disappeared from the world stage. But there would be a reprisal. His strain of optimistic techno-mysticism reemerged in the nineties, and he was rehabilitated as the prophet of the internet age. While McLuhan had gestured toward digital design in his writings, his theories in the sixties had rested more on transistor-age electronics than on the silicon internet. Because he had said so much on such a diverse range of topics, however, some of it stuck. Just as Leonardo da Vinci became credited with "inventing" all sorts of contraptions because he imagined and drew them, so McLuhan successfully "predicted" telecommuting, internet shopping, and the digital matrix as an extension of human consciousness. The rebranded internet-McLuhan of the midnineties (a posthumous figure: the author had died in 1980) became a folk hero of sorts, a man doomed to live before his time. In an introduction to a reissue of *Understanding Media*, the venerable editor of *Harper's Magazine*, Lewis Lapham, summarized the resurgence. "Much of what McLuhan had to say makes a good deal more sense in 1994 than it did in 1964, and even as his book was being remanded to the backlist, its more profound implications were beginning to make themselves manifest."

While on the one hand, digital theory is constantly being refreshed, on the other, many of the tropes of digital design theory were clearly first formulated in the nineties—the era of McLuhan redux. One of the great engines of the visionary nineties was *Wired* magazine. Founded by Louis Rossetto and Jane Metcalfe, the aspirational nature of the project was encoded in its print DNA; the media of the coming digital matrix was paper and ink and available at newsstands. Rossetto and Metcalfe from the start planned a magazine that would cover technology from a cultural angle, akin to the strategy that Jann Wenner had developed for *Rolling Stone* magazine vis-à-vis rock music in the sixties. *Wired* was to be about global cultural change, not just the latest hardware. Designer Barbara Kuhr recounted, "All the computer magazines we'd seen to date had pictures of machines or people sitting with machines. We said, 'No machines. We're taking pictures of you.'" Along these lines, the editors and designers at *Wired* sought to make technology warm and relatable ("Greetings from Burning Man!"), a cultural revolution that would lead to a return of McLuhan's emotionally textured primeval society.

When the first issue of *Wired* appeared in 1993, the debt to McLuhanism was readily apparent. McLuhan was not presented as a figure of the past but was rebranded as the digital visionary of the emerging future. The first year's issues were

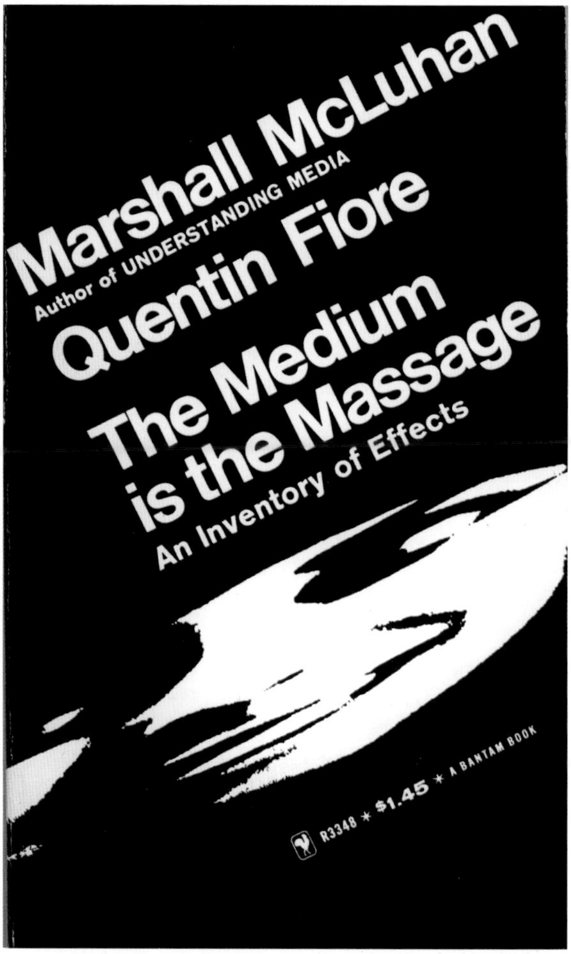

1.1. Cover of Marshall McLuhan and Quentin Fiore's *The Medium is the Massage: An Inventory of Effects*, 1967

replete with articles, quotations, and slogans that invoked the magazine's "patron saint" (as he was listed on the codex), recapturing the sense of awe and wonder (and obtuseness) that had first captured the public's imagination a generation earlier. In fact, the first words printed in the premiere issue of *Wired* were an exemplary McLuhan quote: "The medium, or process, of our time—electric technology—is reshaping and restructuring patterns of social interdependence and every aspect of our personal life."

Another element of *Wired's* coverage that resonates with McLuhanism is the catch-all quality of the magazine's employment of the word "digital." Like McLuhan's references to "electronic media," references to a digital revolution were and still often are acts of leveling, positing homogeneity where it may not exist. This is one of the problems in any attempt to deal with digital design; it can seem as if there is one holistic center that unites all things digital while in fact different media have developed in dramatically different ways. To cite one example, influential theorists of digital architecture in the nineties committed themselves to a very obtuse reading of technology that has no strong parallel in the other design arts. While some broad trends—increases in productivity or a love of curvilinear, futuristic-looking surfaces—appear in multiple mediums, preexisting professional structures often limited dialogue. Of course, part of the anticipated digital disruption involved breaking down these professional silos of practice and concept, but, perhaps unsurprisingly, entrenched institutional and economic forces have proved quite resilient. Likewise, the fragmented, nonsynchronous nature of such fluid change has led to different trajectories in established media while creating new hybrid discourses at every turn.

Insomuch as the nineties digital McLuhan set the tone for so many subsequent digital theorists, his unfailing optimism should not be overlooked as a driver of his success. As Jefferson Pooley has noted, "His exuberant, birdsong prose, Delphic bursts of forced profundity, and Whiggish faith in technological progress fed a hyper-mediated culture hungry for affirmation.... Conference halls won't be booked for corporate executives to listen to gloomy takedowns of US consumer culture." This resolute positivity had partly been responsible for McLuhan's banishment by a consensus of intellectual elites. The French Marxist theorist Guy Debord, founder of situationism, in 1988 wrote perhaps the most stinging rebuttal of this aspect of McLuhan's work (and by extension that of subsequent digital utopians): "The sage of Toronto had formerly spent several decades marveling at the numerous freedoms created by a 'global village' instantly and effortlessly accessible to all. Villages, unlike towns, have always been ruled by conformism, isolation, petty surveillance, boredom and repetitive malicious gossip." Debord's critique points to one of the most easily overlooked aspect of digital visions: rarely, if ever, is there a sense of the digital as something subversive. In Debord's terms, there is little digital *detournement*. Taking the darkest view, digital design represents a new instance of Western colonialism, whereby homogeneity and conformism suffuse global culture anew.

The simplest explanation for the unrelenting optimism about technology is, of course, that dystopic villages do not sell products. Under this rubric, the disinterested doyens of academe are untainted by vulgar mercantilism. The relationship between theoreticians and the market is in fact more nuanced: there is no firewall between the purveyors of technology and the intellectuals of the academy. The editors at *Wired* actually made light of this facet of digital theory in the premiere issue under the heading "Po-Mo Gets Tek-No." This rather snarky paragraph points out that the fashionable acolytes of Michel Foucault and Jean-François Lyotard had started to mine the digital realm. "The recession woke up the post-modernists to the fact that technology, not comparative lit, is where the money is." Downstream we will see that some aspects of digital design, notably architecture, were destined to become enmeshed in poststructuralist discourse while others sidestepped it completely.

Design was at the center of Rossetto and Metcalfe's vision for *Wired*. They intuited that they could only communicate their view of the near future through a holistic integration of concept, text, and image. For this reason, they recruited a graphic design partnership, Kuhr and John Plunkett, at the outset. Plunkett later recalled the designers' debt to McLuhan, especially his 1967 release *The Medium is the Massage: An Inventory of Effects* (figure 1.1). Paradoxically, though *The Medium is the Massage* was a bestseller that represented the apogee of McLuhan's fame, it also met with a harsh critical assessment that signaled the beginning of the end for his "serious" reputation. Importantly, the book was a collaborative project that showcased the design skills of coauthor Quentin Fiore, who provided striking layouts, albeit limited to black-and-white photography. In contrast, Plunkett and Kuhr had the latest six-color printing technology at their disposal and wanted to use it "to make the magazine that McLuhan would look at and say, 'Well, finally!' " In the end, the centrality of design to the digital world was perhaps *Wired*'s greatest contribution to the field. While surely one can say that the editors were only channeling the zeitgeist and not necessarily the first or the best, the fact remains that *Wired* more than any other media outlet fueled the sense that the emerging digital transformation would need to be mediated and structured by design. Although the Day-Glo palette of the early issues would soon prove transient, the core message would remain and continue to resonate.

Wired was also the public launching point for one of the titans of the digerati, Nicholas Negroponte. A graduate of and faculty member at Massachusetts Institute of Technology (MIT) since the sixties, Negroponte was positioned by his intellect and family wealth to become a key voice at *Wired*, as one of its earliest investors as well as an influential essayist. Trained as an architect and a cofounder of the MIT Media Lab (1985), Negroponte had built his reputation as one of the pioneering researchers in computer-aided design, and he shared Metcalfe and Rossetto's enthusiasm for the budding digital revolution. As senior columnist at *Wired*, Negroponte offered a diverse set of topical musings on digital culture to the magazine's readers. In 1995, he published a collection of his early essays for *Wired* in a book called *Being Digital*. Like McLuhan before him, Negroponte's central thesis was that human society was undergoing a material transformation that led to an upheaval of subjectivity. The back cover offered a synopsis: "And this lively, breathtakingly timely book suggests what being digital will mean for our laws, education, politics, and amusements—in short, for the way we live." Inside the book, like many visionaries, Negroponte offered a host of speculative coming attractions, many of which have proved prescient, such as smartphones, while some—"Twenty years from now, when you look out a window, what you see may be five thousand miles and six time zones away"—have yet to come about.

Amid this cohort of utopians, the occasional contrarian would speak up. In 1995, the year Negroponte's *Being Digital* was published, engineer-essayist Clifford Stoll published his now-notorious rant in *Newsweek* magazine regarding what he saw as overblown claims about the internet. "Visionaries see a future of telecommuting workers, interactive libraries and multimedia classrooms. They speak of electronic town meetings and virtual communities. Commerce and business will shift from offices and malls to networks and modems. And the freedom of digital networks will make government more democratic. Baloney. Do our computer pundits lack all common sense? The truth [is] no online database will replace your daily newspaper, no CD-ROM can take the place of a competent teacher and no computer network will change the way government works." The core of Stoll's antivisionary argument centered on the lack of "human contact" in the digital realm, and his basic point remains valid, as digitally mediated interaction continues to be fraught with peril. Zoom call, anyone?

Despite the ruminations of antivisionaries such as Stoll, overall thinkers like Negroponte designed the burden that digital workers must bear: lofty expectations that enthusiastic members of the visionary class posit and that are promoted in the media and hungrily consumed by the mainstream. Negroponte, of course, put this burden on himself. In 1995, he needed to explain in *Being Digital* why he had published in the fashion of Gutenberg, in his parlance, through "atoms not bits." Negroponte explained that this friction came about because digital media had not yet colonized the mainstream and so an old-fashioned book was still the best way to tout the future. This situation, whereby the reality of technological change lagged behind the futuristic plans of the digerati, also at times arose at *Wired*. For example, when journalist John Heilemann was tasked with providing the magazine's political coverage of the 1996 presidential election, he quickly realized that the "first wired election" was not in fact occurring. "As if. At least any illusions I had were shattered early," he reported that November. Heilemann found that the political campaigns were still totally wedded to television and had embraced the web in only the most superficial fashion.

Digital futurism, along with the feeling that radical change has become the new stasis, so embedded in the culture that it thrives even in staid academic discourse, is a trend engaged by the staid historical compendium *Digital Design Theory: Readings from the Field* (2016). The introduction, by Helen Armstrong, is subtitled, "Giving Form to the Future," and is replete with predictions that resonate with the enthusiastic tone of the visionary class. For example, Ray Kurzweil is cited as having predicted that the age of "transhuman intelligence" will begin in 2045 (the arbitrariness of choosing a specific year is striking; why not December 2044?). In direct contradiction to this discourse, the current book will be attuned to seeing the digital present through the past rather than the future. A central premise is that the analog and digital realms are coextensive and continuous; the past haunts the present like DOS buried in Windows 98.

Negroponte and Heilemann—and McLuhan before them—all waded into what has proved to be one of the most problematic areas of visionary speculation: the effect on the polis. McLuhan referred to "global villages," while *Wired* espoused the reign of the "netizen," and Negroponte opined, "As we interconnect ourselves, many of the values of a nation-state will give way to those of both larger and smaller electronic communities." The digital era would not just give us new gadgets but fundamentally reorder society into a utopia of participatory global democracy, fueled by netizens who had all the critical information available on a screen. The interactive nature of coming digital media would prevent people from being manipulated by the powers that be in a one-sided fashion, while the new McLuhan-esque "tribal man" would become a proactive, creative force for good. Not only will machines be warm and relatable, but so will humanity writ large. Old ethno-tribal and nationalist allegiances would break down in the face of a new interconnected age of harmony. Of course, Socrates's fate was not factored in when it came to participatory democracy, and he might have said regarding his end, "As if." Note that this illusory new global utopia was again reliant on the designers of the digital to make it happen, as expectations continued to soar.

In recent years, the situation for digital designers has been further complicated by a new type of dystopian visionary. These thinkers do not just incrementally walk back the utopian futurism of the Panglossian class; rather, they often posit the inverse: in their view the digital world is a treacherous one. Surveillance, disinformation, self-aware AIs, unrecognized deepfakes, identity theft: many fearsome outcomes have been created through digital design. Both virtual and physical shelves today are filled with pronouncements on the likelihood of one or another terrifying possible outcome. Journalist Samuel Woolley's alarmist 2020 book, *The Reality Game: How the Next Wave of Technology Will Break the Truth*, is representative of the work of dystopic visionaries. Woolley argues that misinformation, which he defines as the accidental digital circulation of fraudulent content, and disinformation, the purposeful spread of falsehoods, threaten our social fabric to an unparalleled degree. Likewise, Siva Vaidhyanathan argued in his 2018 book *Antisocial Media: How Facebook Disconnects Us and Undermines Democracy*: "If you wanted to build a machine that would distribute propaganda to millions of people, distract them from important issues, energize hatred and bigotry, erode social trust, undermine respectable journalism, foster doubts about science, and engage in massive surveillance all at once, you would make something a lot like Facebook."

"Alexa, are you going to murder me?" While the depredations of social media may seem to be a manageable threat, the notion of a superconscious digital machine can create a ripple of unease in even the most digitally aware technology leader. For example, Elon Musk has famously railed against AI, telling a government gathering in 2017, "I have exposure to the very cutting edge AI, and I think people should be really concerned about it. I keep sounding the alarm bell, but until people see robots going down the street killing people, they don't know how to react, because it seems so ethereal." Bill Gates has also addressed the challenges wrought by AI, which he feels may someday transform military hardware in dangerous ways. While he sees promise in digital technology's ability to remake public health, he also admits that autonomous weapons systems are a frightening possibility.

Steve Jobs, John Maeda, Clement Mok, Bill Moggridge, Elon Musk: digital visionaries of every stripe always had *Wired*, and they still have TED. Originally founded in 1984 by Richard Wurman and Harry Marks, TED—the acronym stands for technology, entertainment, and design—was destined to become a major driver of digital design theory. Negroponte in fact gave one of the first talks in 1984, naturally titled "5 Predictions." While that first eighties manifestation of TED died on the vine, in 1990 Wurman revived the annual symposia in spectacular fashion. Focusing on short presentations by gurus declaiming the synergistic impact of the digital world to acolytes gathered in a Southern California locale, TED annual conferences brought to the stolid academic format some of the creative frisson generally associated with film festivals or Burning Man. Since the nineties, TED has expanded explosively, adding regional sessions across the globe as a complement to the original venue in Monterey. In 2006, TED became even more pervasive as a selection of talks were uploaded to the internet. Today thousands of TED talks are available for viewing, covering every imaginable technocultural topic. Tens of thousands of people have given one of these eighteen-minute speeches, and many of those have taken on the futurist optimism pioneered by McLuhan. In some ways TED has created a new class of DIY visionary, fueling a process whereby thousands can experience the rush of predicting the digital future.

Like the character Ava in *Ex Machina*, soon the digital hivemind may be able to claim its autonomy and become its own visionary. In November 2022 OpenAI's ChatGPT swept across digital spaces as well as the "real world." This newly released chatbot tech produces startlingly believable texts that may quickly surpass most human written and spoken communication. Chatbots do not plagiarize the internet; they create original interactive conversations. Kirell Benzi explored GPT's ability to replace his own work. He prompted, "10 quotes of Kirell Benzi Ph.D. data artist." The first response gives a sense of the chatbot's fearsome potential: "Data is the new canvas. It is a medium that allows us to create new forms of art and visualizations." A visionary indeed.

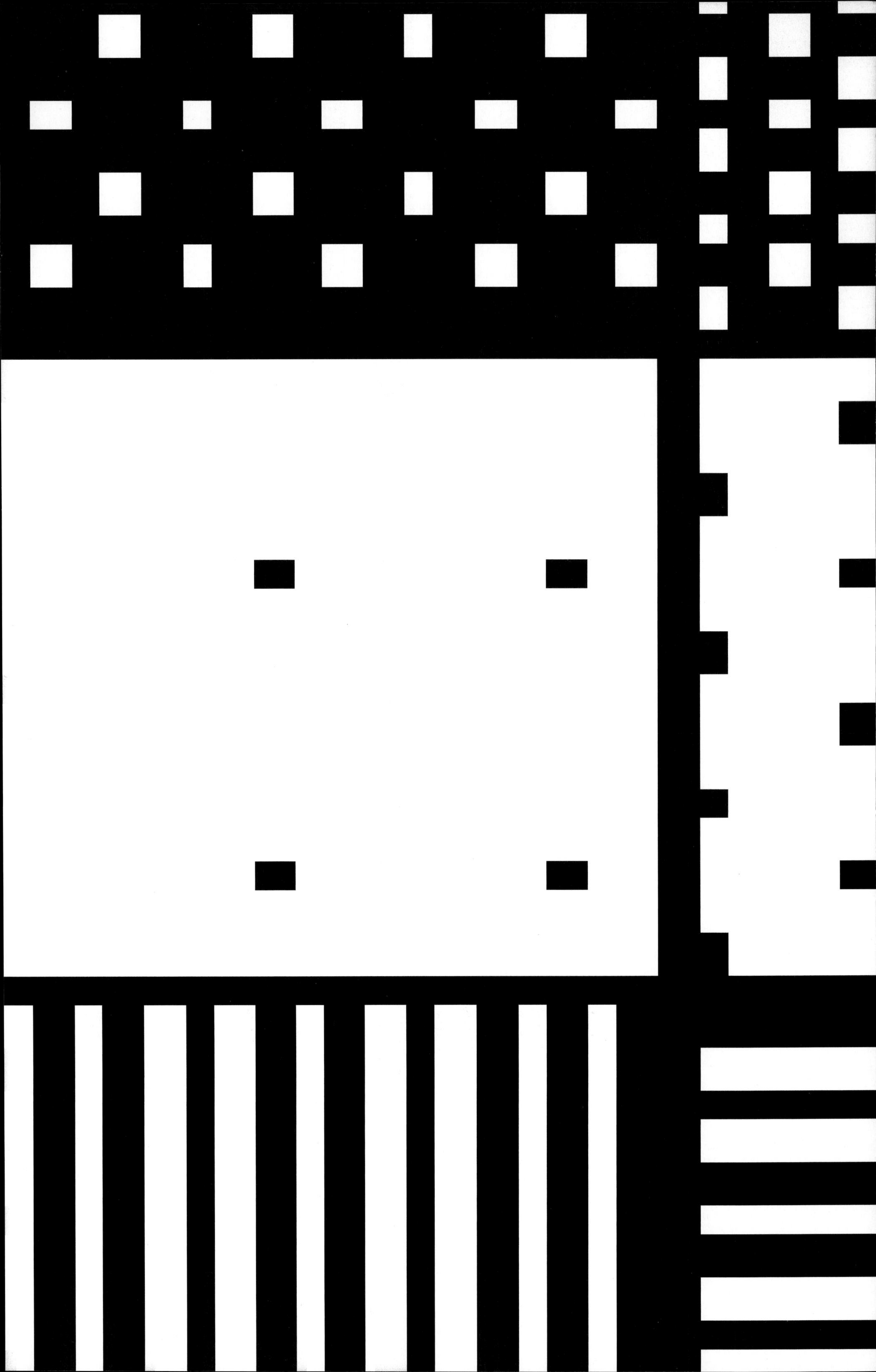

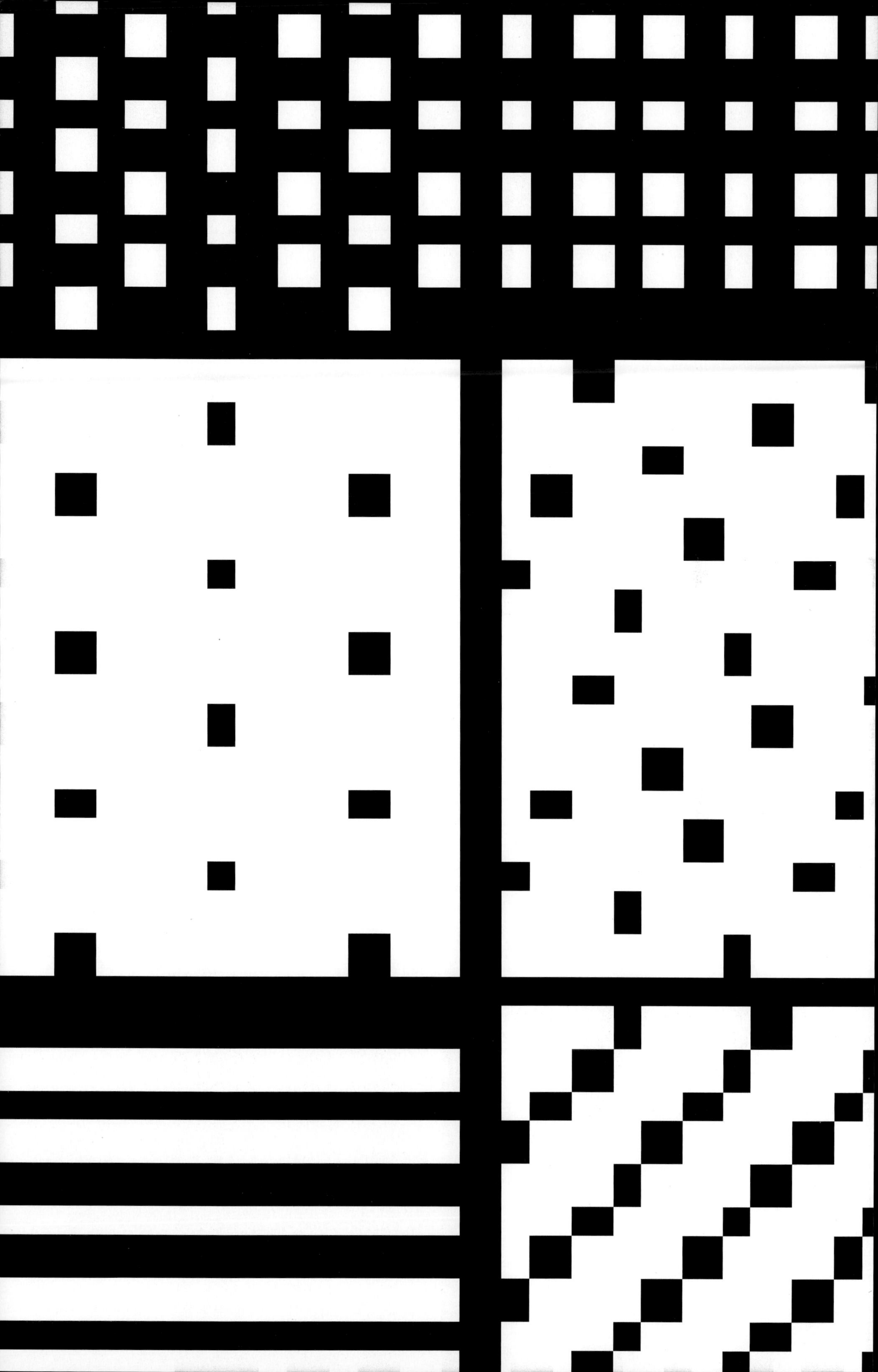

2.1. Citroën DS, designed by André Lefebvre and Flaminio Bertoni in 1955

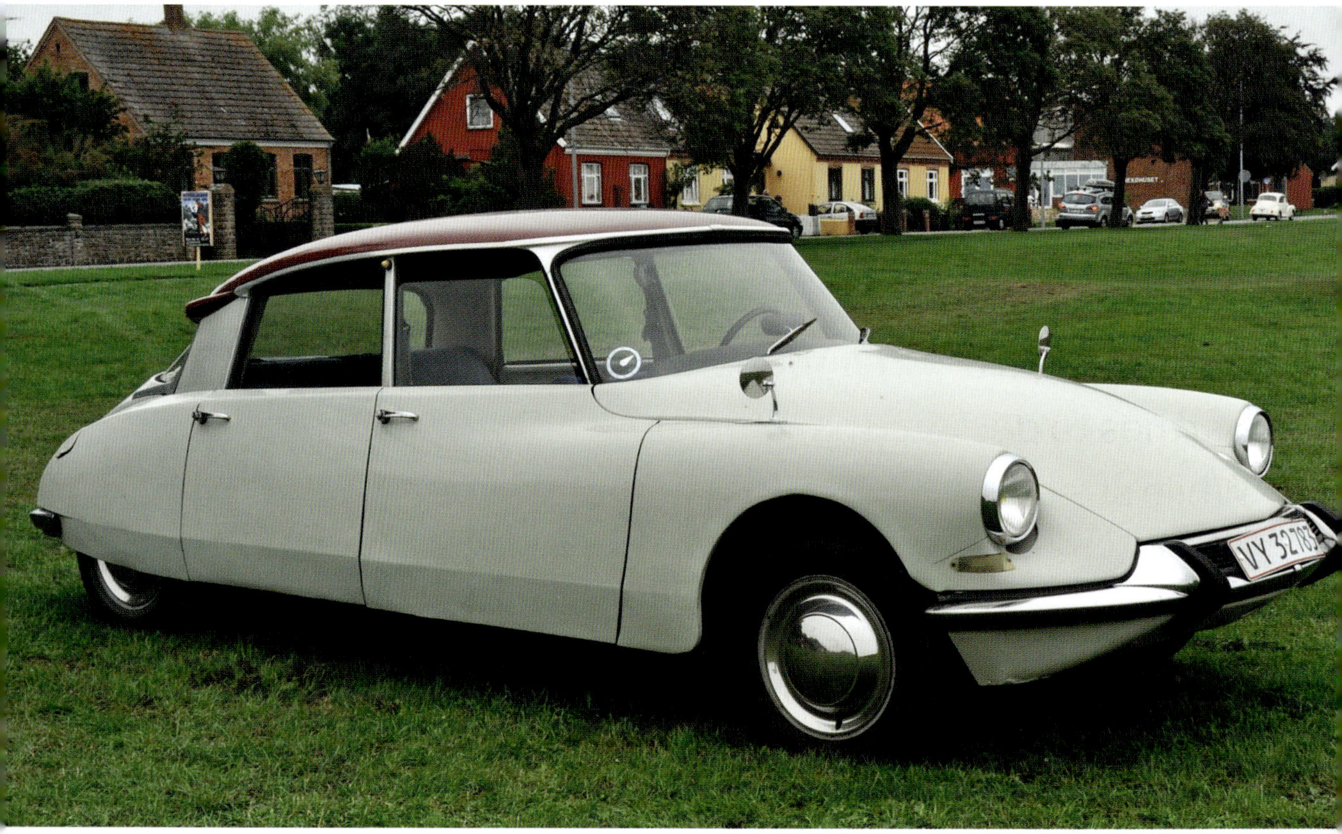

Two. The Machines

Digital design began with the curve. Stamped into sheet metal or arranged as an array of pixels, a series of curvilinear shapes have come to define the digital age visually and conceptually at almost every turn. Perhaps the first digital, or at least computational, curves that broke into the public's consciousness were those that defined the sweeping body panels of the 1955 Citroën DS (figure 2.1). Introduced to wide acclaim at that year's Paris auto show, the sinuous and sleek DS (in French, the pair of letters are a homophone for "Goddess") contrasted starkly with its aggressively box-shaped contemporaries and their toothy grills. Tapering from front to back, the curvaceous DS projected an urbane sophistication that spurred Roland Barthes to declaim that it must have "fallen from the sky." While streamlining had already become a familiar design gesture before the war, the creators of the DS melded the sleek style into the overall form in a dramatic new way; here, streamlining was not ornament or function but a holistic gestalt. The DS backed up its promise of futuristic technology by including several technical advances—

self-leveling suspension and unibody construction (meaning the outer shell is structural)—that testified to the fact that its beauty went below the surface. Over the next two decades, Citroën would sell well over a million and a half iterations of the DS.

As was often the case with early digital work, the curves of the DS were only partially computational, and the design pure analog. The DS had been originally modeled by André Lefebvre, who had experience in aerospace technology and its associated streamlining, and Flaminio Bertoni, a longtime designer for Citroën. Bertoni was a sculptor both at heart and through practice, and the expressive curves of the DS are often compared to the sensuous forms of Bernini and the like. In this way, the curves of the DS look futuristic while embodying the achievements of an artisanal tradition that goes back centuries. The original DS was a three-dimensional clay model created by hand; this trend, whereby digital-looking works belie their true process—Frank Gehry's Guggenheim Bilbao (1997) is an obvious example—has recurred many times through to the present. In a larger sense, this facet of design is indicative of a situation whereby much of the labor, sometimes artistic like Bertoni's and sometimes grueling like that of the armies of coders grinding offstage every day, is hidden behind a gleaming, curving shell or screen.

The flowing unibody curves of the DS had been modeled by hand, but they led to the first digital designs. It became readily apparent at Citroën in the late fifties that the production techniques for creating the curved body panels were much too subjective, with all the tooling and milling referring to an actual physical master model of the car. Each stage of production could introduce human error, as technicians measured and shaped parts through a partly intuitive process. Citroën needed to find a way to express curved parts in equations. While their engineers possessed automated machine tools, especially computer numerical control (CNC) devices, they were unable to use them for curved parts such as those on the DS. With unibody construction, this was more than just an aesthetic issue, as the panels made the car structurally sound. In 1959, Citroën hired a mathematician, Paul de Faget de Casteljau, who was tasked with solving this problem. Over the next several years, de Casteljau developed an algorithm using differential geometry that allowed for the mathematical representation of a curved surface. Importantly, these data could be used to program CNC machines to produce exact copies of a given part without consulting a physical model. An entire automobile's precise specifications could now be stored numerically and transferred between engineers and factories wherever and whenever they were needed.

Of course, many other researchers grappled with this emerging technology. While de Casteljau solved this problem at Citroën, at its arch-competitor Renault, head of design Pierre Bézier accomplished the same task. Like de Casteljau's solution, Bézier based his work on the Bernstein polynomial, creating a system whereby three-dimensional curved surfaces could be mathematically indexed. The basis for vector graphics of all kinds, the Bézier curve still plays an essential role in many aspects of digital design. In another arena, in the United States, Patrick Hanratty at General Electric in 1957 devised one of the first programming languages for machine tools, called Pronto.

As the computational curve first implemented industrially at French automobile companies diffused throughout engineering circles, it changed the way things were made and eventually changed how they were designed. The productivity element should not be overlooked in favor of styling; many of the transformations that define the digital era make things faster or better rather than visually distinct. And these technical advances are often hybrid ones, equally enmeshed in analog and digital. The Citroën DS, to borrow from Nicholas Negroponte, did not start as digital—it became digital as the years went by.

Designing Hardware

At a time when computers did not possess any substantial design capabilities, they had nonetheless revolutionized the industrial world through better automation and efficiency. But running a CNC machine was one thing and designing a car something completely different. As computer science researchers (many of the earliest ones had degrees in electrical engineering) sought to expand the reach of this technology, they naturally turned toward the question of how computers could help people design better. Starting in the fifties, these questions were being asked at a range of institutions, including the US military; technologically focused universities (especially MIT and Stanford University); and corporate-sponsored labs at companies like IBM and Xerox. The large centralized systems of this era required an immense amount of technological expertise to navigate, and their interfaces consisted strictly of computational (punch cards, for example) and, later, simple text inputs. A critical mass of digital researchers, however, would gradually devise strategies to make computers more accessible and relatable.

To design with computers, one first needed to design the right computer. Two threads emerged here: first, the design of the physical machine itself, a factor that only gains prominence as computers are marketed to consumers; and second, the design of the interface, which includes actual objects like the keyboard as well as the screen-based virtual world that enables designers to get to work. Without delving too deeply into the long cast of characters and their incremental accomplishments at an array of research facilities, it is still important to sketch out some of the key moments in the essentially artisanal designs of the early digital age.

Douglas Ross, head of MIT's Computer Applications Group starting in the midfifties, came to the digital world after pursuing degrees in pure mathematics. One of the first programmers, his earliest project at MIT involved creating a programming language for machine tools like those used to build a Citroën. While he continued to work on engineering software, Ross also started to pursue the potential for computers to facilitate the design process. Generally credited with coining the term "computer-aided design," Ross used those words in a 1960 technical memorandum describing his approach to this new area of research. "The objective of the Computer-Aided Design Project is to evolve a man-machine system which will permit the human designer and the computer to work together on creative design problems.... [T]he possibility of having a computer be an active partner to the designer, to accept and analyze his sketches and perform all or a substantial

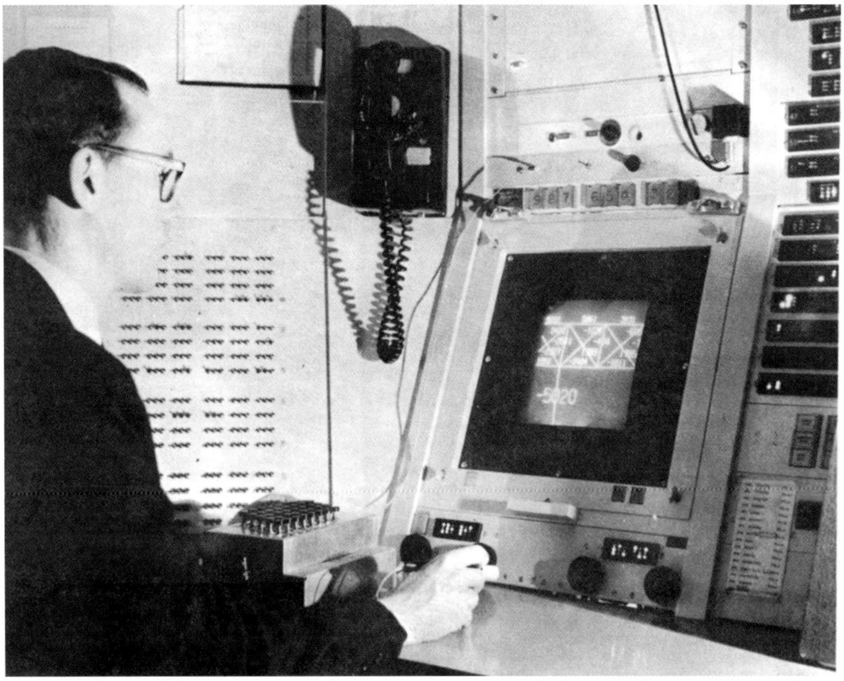

2.2. Digital Equipment Corporation and MIT's TX-2 computer, 1958

amount of the necessary design calculations, does seem reasonable for the near future."

The Massachusetts Institute of Technology was also the site where some of the first research computers were assembled; in 1958 the TX-2 (figure 2.2), one of the first computers to make use of electronic transistors (as opposed to vacuum tubes), became operational. A continual work in progress, the TX-2 was shut down for maintenance and upgrades once per week, in an accelerated version of a process familiar to every smartphone user today. The TX-2 features included an oscilloscope screen with high resolution, plus a light pen and programmable buttons as an interface. While the TX-2 played a role in several early computer experiments, from a design standpoint, its most important achievement was in serving as the platform for "Sketchpad: A Man-Machine Graphical Communication System," as described by the creator, Ivan Sutherland, a PhD student at MIT, in his paper on its design. Sketchpad was a major step in demonstrating the potential of what will become two foci of digital design: computer-aided design (CAD) and human–computer interaction (HCI). Of course, these broad terms overlap, especially insomuch as effective HCI is what makes CAD possible.

In the sixties on the opposite coast, Douglas Engelbart, chairman of the Stanford Research Institute, oversaw a lab that sought to devise new interface strategies while demonstrating the networking capabilities of computers. Largely supported by the military, scientists at the institute created the oN-Line System, or NLS, a suite of projects that together greatly advanced HCI (and should win an award for worst technical acronym). The NLS included hierarchical menus, hyperlinks, video conferencing, and even the first mouse. On December 9, 1968, Engelbart arranged one of the most legendary events in computer history, a demonstration of research that had investigated "principles by which interactive computer aids can augment intellectual capability." Today this session, at which the NLS was presented via video link between Menlo Park (where the lab was located) and San Francisco, is known simply as the "mother of all demos," as it represented the first time that multiple futuristic, yet practical, computing innovations were assembled and demonstrated outside the laboratory environment.

Taken together, Sketchpad and the NLS represented concrete steps toward what would become the centerpiece of digital design: a viable, relatable graphical user interface, or GUI. In combination with the physical mouse that Engelbart devised as an addendum to the keyboard, GUIs are what enable designers to virtually interact with their creations. The next step in interaction design occurred at Xerox's Palo Alto Research Center (PARC), where a number of Engelbart's students congregated in an effort to produce the first personal computer. Bringing aspects of the NLS with them, the team at PARC set to work on the Alto, which was destined to be the first computer with an accessible GUI. The Alto made use of NLS elements—the mouse, hypertext, and text editing—while also offering new features such as a bitmap display with greater definition (72 dpi) and navigable layout software. The Alto's GUI was designed so that what you see is what you get (WYSIWYG), making it much more understandable to the ordinary person.

The Palo Alto Research Center also witnessed the birth of one of the most enduring allegories of all time, the virtual desktop. Credited mainly to Tim Mott, the desktop—really more an office than a desk, complete with trash can, windows, and icons—has become so ubiquitous as to be almost invisible. Although some digital artists have decried how it helped define computers in the public's imagination as staid and uncreative, the metaphor has proved its merit by providing a virtual space that is comfortable and familiar. The Alto was originally released in 1973, and its more commercially minded descendant, the Xerox Star, in 1981. While both machines were aimed at the personal computer user, their abundant memory and high-end graphics made them cost-prohibitive for all but the wealthiest institutions and consumers.

The PC and the Macintosh

In hindsight, 1981 was a watershed moment in computer design, as the focus shifted from expensive, experimental mainframes and workstations, such as the TX-2 and the Alto, toward more economical personal computers aimed at ordinary people in their homes and offices. Earlier, in the seventies, IBM had come to dominate the lucrative market for large mainframe computers, leaving the low-end "personal computer" market to a slew of smaller companies, including Atari, Texas Instruments, Tandy, and Commodore. As the consumer market powered up, IBM decided to join the fray, introducing the 5150 in 1981, known by one and all as the IBM PC; the success of this endeavor—in a few years IBM utterly dominated the market—is obvious by the way the generic letters PC came to refer to IBM systems and their related clones. Of course, one of the legions of small computer companies, Apple, would offer two new models soon thereafter; the Lisa in 1983 and the Macintosh in 1984. Because the early eighties would prove to be a pivot point in terms of later designers' choice in computers and software, it is important to trace the trajectory of how IBM and Apple came to the market and defined their devices.

The conventional wisdom of many people over the last few decades is predicated on the belief that Apple computers are for creative, design-savvy consumers, while PCs running Microsoft software are staid and suboptimal. This reputation was originally formulated in the eighties and was largely based on a comparison of the Apple Macintosh and the IBM PC and their respective operating systems. What is paradoxical about this development is that, starting in the fifties, IBM had become known as perhaps the most design-forward corporation in the United States. In 1956, IBM CEO Thomas J. Watson Jr., partly in response to the remarkable styling of products sold by its Italian competitor Olivetti, hired industrial designer Eliot Noyes to create a corporate design program to modernize and unify the visual culture of the company. Over the next two decades until Noyes's death in 1977, he oversaw a commitment to high design standards in just about every facet of IBM's operations, implementing a program that resonated with the renowned aphorism of the

Deutscher Werkbund, "Vom Sofakissen zum Städtebau." Noyes had in fact studied at Harvard under Werkbund architect and Bauhaus founder Walter Gropius, who had immigrated to the United States and become an influential professor of architecture in 1937.

At IBM, Noyes oversaw a series of legendary corporate identity projects, including architecture by former Bauhaus *jungmeister* and Gropius protégé Marcel Breuer, graphic design by American modernist Paul Rand, and communication exhibits by Charles and Ray Eames. Along the way, Noyes also recruited Isamu Noguchi and Eero Saarinen as part of his stable of creative talents. Noyes's tenure at IBM has become synonymous with the rise of corporate identity, and his continual espousal of the sentiment that "good design equals good business" became a defining leitmotif of an era when global companies committed themselves to styling on a new scale. This era also witnessed the Americanization of Werkbund and Bauhaus design theories, helping establish a reconstituted vision of the latter as promoting simple, clean design styles with universal appeal. Of course, this Americanized Bauhaus had been whitewashed of all the theoretical complexity and radical politics of the 1920s, while the input of Russian constructivist Bolshevik true believers was completely elided. Smooth machine forms were all that remained.

In terms of actual designs, Noyes's name is most closely connected with the styling of the IBM Selectric, the most successful electric typewriter of all time (figure 2.3). Released in 1961 after a seven-year planning process, the Selectric was "very simple," according to Noyes, who noted, "We tried to emphasize the singleness and simpleness of form." This type of reductive invocation of Bauhaus aesthetics will prove to be one of the most lasting carryovers into the contemporary scene. As IBM's signature mass-market product, the Selectric combined IBM's vaunted durability with a deep attention to ergonomic design, the forerunner to today's attention to the intricacies of every click as part of the user experience.

While the Selectric came to dominate the market for analog word processing, Noyes also oversaw the dramatic restyling of IBM's digital business, culminating in the release of the System/360 mainframe computer system in 1964 (figure 2.4). The S/360 was the result of a push to combine all five of IBM's existing large computer lines into one modular, expandable system. In many ways announcing the beginning of the big data era, the S/360 introduced 8-bit processing and openness to third-party peripheral devices in a way that allowed for the continual upgrading and scaling of the machines. Complete with a sans serif logotype by Rand and a Selectric-like smoothly sculpted keyboard interface, the S/360 was rarely seen in person by consumers but was nonetheless a key part of popular culture with its constant presence in mass-media images. Despite Noyes's dedication to "Bauhaus simplicity," both the Selectric and the S/360 were available in a trendy palette of vibrant colors, including iridescent shades of red that resonated with the psychedelic hues preferred in the counterculture.

> 2.3. IBM Selectric Typewriter, designed by Eliot Noyes in 1961

> 2.4. IBM System/360, designed by Eliot Noyes in 1964

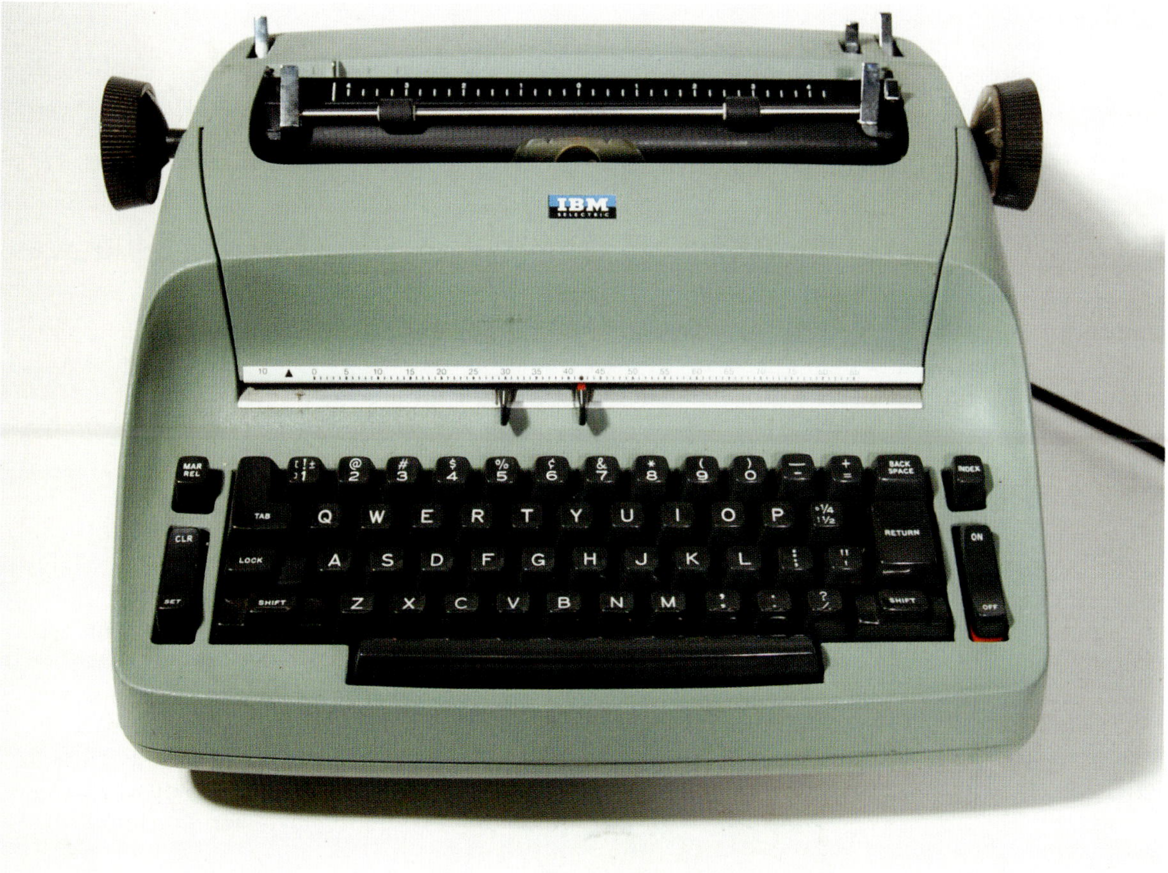
IBM
SELECTRIC

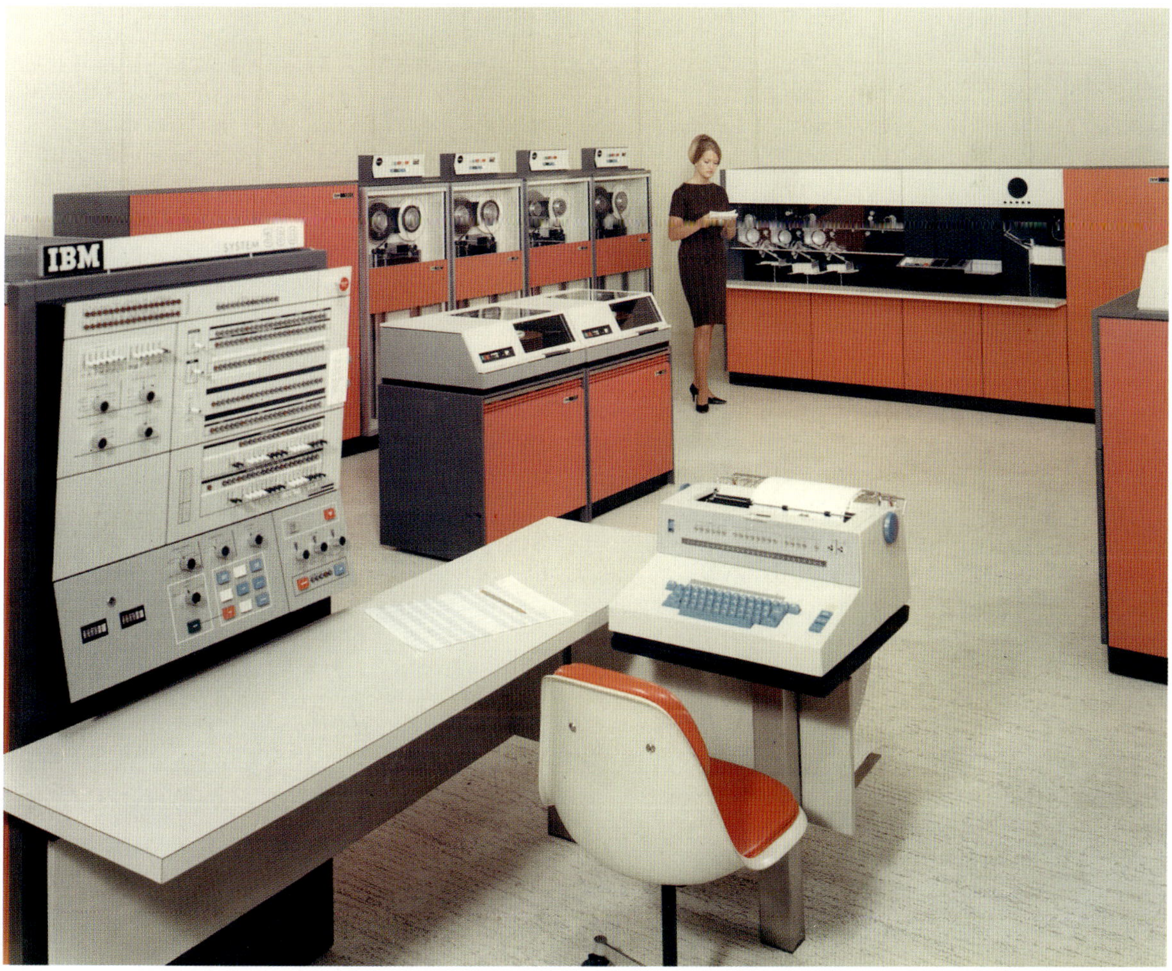
IBM
SYSTEM

In the seventies, through the examples of its products and corporate architecture, IBM must have seemed destined to continually lead the design world; its employment of shrewd styling attracted media attention and created a culture of futuristic styling. But when Noyes died unexpectedly in 1977, IBM's commitment to design-forward thinking almost immediately began to fray. When Charles Eames died in 1978, and IBM lost its other strong design personality, the company appeared to rely on institutional momentum to maintain its culture. A new product under development would soon drastically change IBM's reputation for good design.

The era of digital design did not reach critical mass until the widespread adoption of the desktop computer in the eighties. Although some large firms had used mainframe systems or specialized minicomputers for design tasks, the inexpensive personal computer ushered in an era when digital tools were accessible to the mainstream. At IBM, just as the Noyes era started to fade, executive William Lowe successfully advanced a project called Chess, which culminated in the introduction of the aforementioned IBM PC in 1981 (figure 2.5). Brought to the market by Don Estridge, who had succeeded Lowe at the helm, the IBM 5150 represented a stark departure from the design focus of the S/360. Essentially, the IBM PC was not "designed" in Noyes's sense of the word but cobbled together and encased. Unlike other IBM products, the technology of the IBM PC was almost entirely outsourced from other companies; the mandate of creating a desktop computer with a price around $1,500 (the base model of the 5150 PC actually came in at $1,565) overrode all other considerations. To keep the cost down and accelerate the planning process, the IBM PC was built with a chip from Intel, a text-based operating system from Microsoft (DOS), and an Epson printer. The resulting machine, even when upgraded with floppy drives, expanded memory, and a color monitor that pushed the price close to $3,000, had much less capability than the Xerox Star, for example, but was widely available at a fraction of the cost and soon came to dominate the market.

From a design standpoint, the IBM PC represented an almost antidesign. First and foremost, the boxy, shapeless cabinet with obvious expansion slots on the front had none of the sizzle of the S/360. It looked quite ordinary compared to the stylish Selectric, which it would soon displace (the legendary typewriter was discontinued in 1986). Also, the text-based DOS interface used a clumsy set of commands and, most significantly, lacked a mouse and a GUI. The 5150 likely benefited from the residual impact of the Noyes era, which was imprinted on many consumers; however, the PC was destined to have its own legacy, besmirching the design reputation of IBM and Microsoft for decades to come. In the nineties, in a famous summation of the visceral impact of this nondesign, Apple Computer cofounder Steve Jobs insightfully remarked of Microsoft, a company that rose to dominance based on the adoption of DOS for the PC, that "they don't bring much culture into their products."

Whatever the design limitations of the PC and its interface, one decision made by IBM would have far-reaching consequences for computer design. This was the "open architecture" strategy, whereby the hardware and software specifications of the machine, including the source

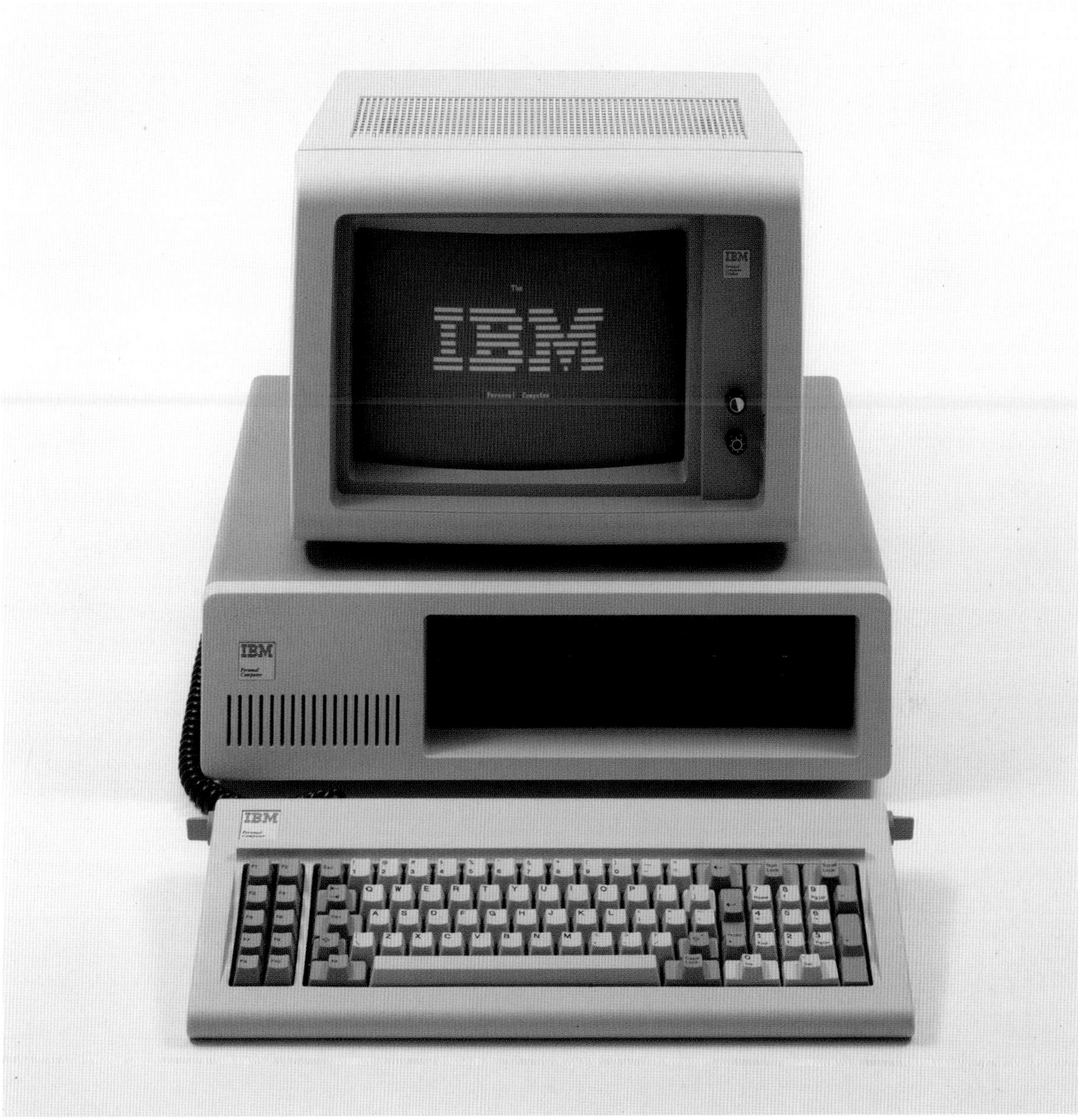

2.5. IBM 5150 PC, 1981

code, were made available to anyone who wanted to develop new software programs or hardware peripherals. Of course, many companies also chose to make their own less expensive "clones" of the PC itself, vastly expanding the PC market.

While IBM's brand recognition and marketing power were largely responsible for the success of the IBM PC, credit should also go to the campaign created by Tom Mabley of Lord, Geller, Federico, Einstein as part of the initial product launch. Mabley based the campaign on Charlie Chaplin's silent film–era character known as the Little Tramp. The Little Tramp had first catapulted Charlie Chaplin to fame decades earlier, his slapstick hijinks becoming a trope of American culture. The character was retired after starring in one of Chaplin's best-known films, *Modern Times* (1936). In this movie, the Little Tramp appeared as a factory worker who becomes overwhelmed by the massive machinery of the industrial age, and in its most famous scene, he struggles vainly to keep pace with a frenetic assembly line that eventually lands him amid a landscape of gears. Promoted as an everyman character who was "profoundly human," the Little Tramp proved to be the perfect spokesman to represent the nonexpert, nonhobbyist consumer who was the intended purchaser of the IBM PC. In myriad formulations, through both television vignettes and a massive print campaign, the Little Tramp made the IBM PC appear relatable and understandable to the novice user. In a slyly plotted inversion of *Modern Times*, some of the advertisements showed a lovably bewildered Little Tramp use the IBM PC to solve chaotic scenes of data

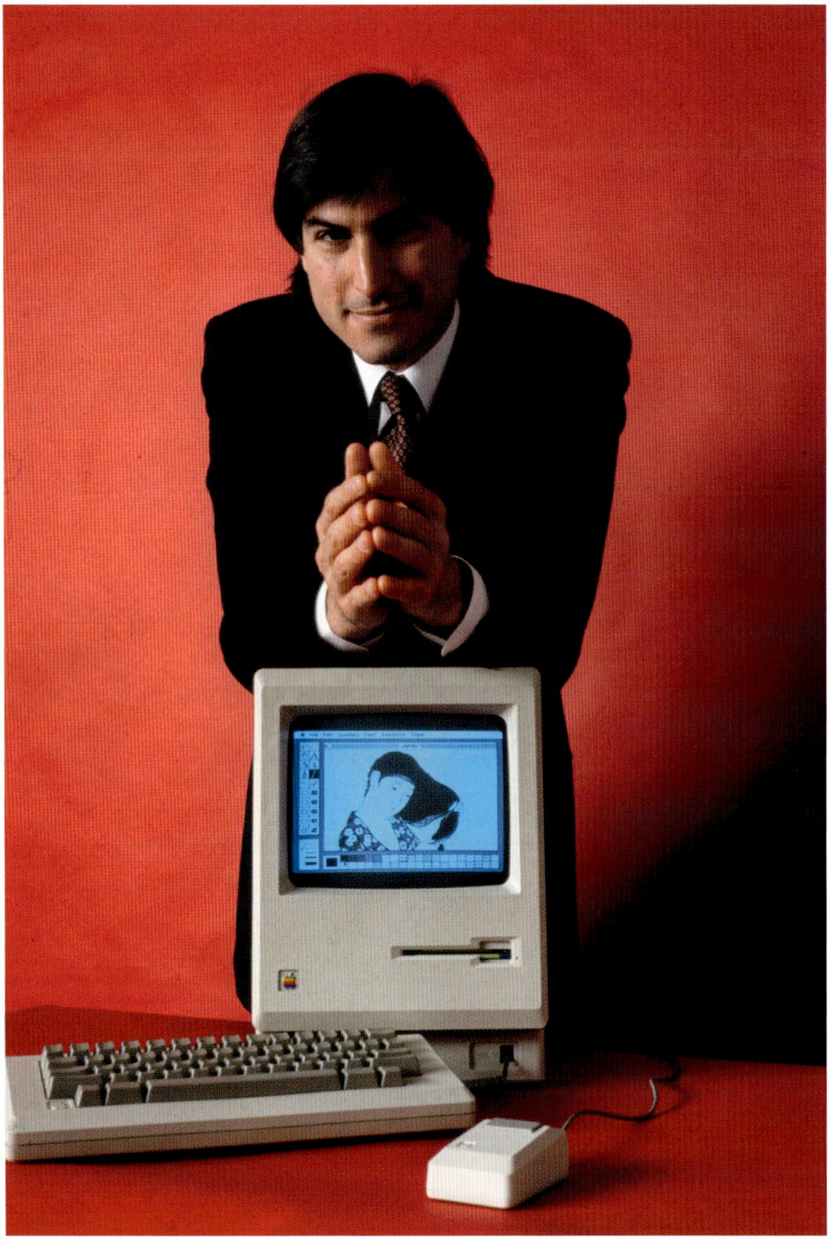

2.6. Steve Jobs and Apple Computer's Macintosh computer, 1984

running amok. Paired with the sheer ordinariness of the PC's design, the Little Tramp successfully brought the computer age into homes, small businesses, and schools, normalizing its use as an everyday experience.

Of course, the IBM PC did not represent the first attempt at making a home computer relatable. That theme had been the impetus of the 1977 release of the Apple II, the first complete system offered by the company. Apple had been founded in 1976, but their first product, the Apple I, had been a kit aimed more at sophisticated users who were able to build out the machine's peripherals themselves. Although overshadowed in the design world by the later Macintosh, the Apple II would generate over 5 million sales during the lifespan of the machine. Importantly, the Apple II showcased the company's devotion to the design of the physical device. Jobs himself famously oversaw the creation of the case by Jerry Manock, who crafted a smooth, minimalist enclosure that appears to have borrowed heavily from Noyes's design of the ubiquitous Selectric typewriter as well as the work of Dieter Rams for Braun (see chapter 9). While the Apple II and the IBM PC both built tremendous market share in the eighties, a new computer from Apple, the Macintosh (figure 2.6), would transform the design world with its user interface (UI).

The external form of the Macintosh showcased the input of a team that included both Jobs and German industrial designer Hartmut Esslinger. The latter had moved his studio to Silicon Valley and established Frog Design after signing a lucrative contract with Apple in 1982. In terms

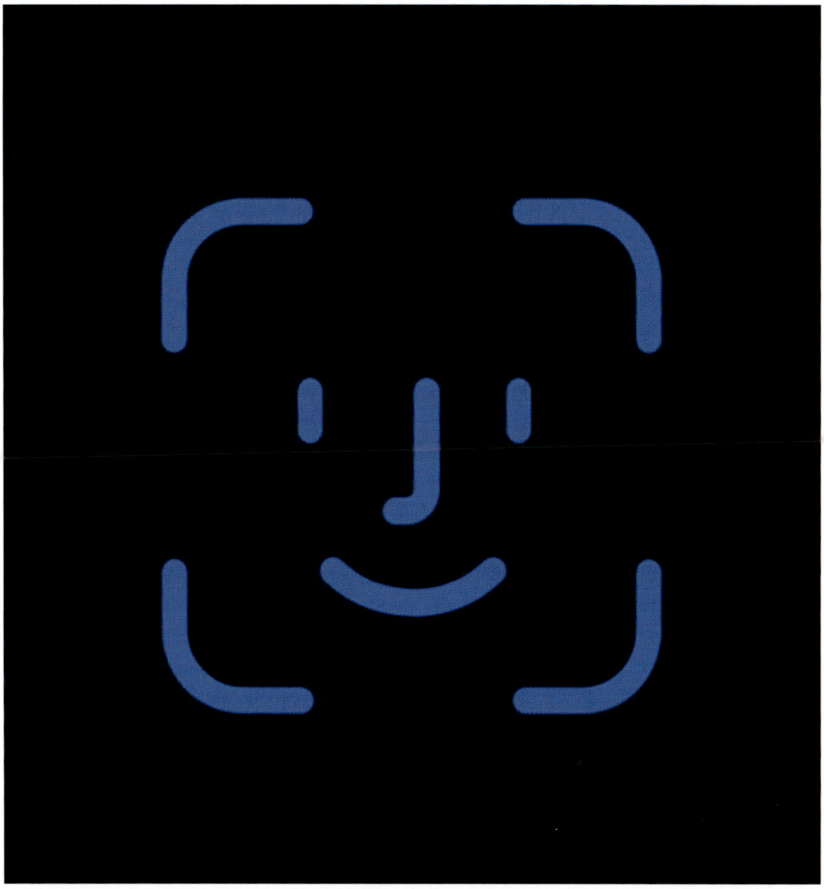

2.7. Apple Computer's Face ID icon, 2017

of the Macintosh computer's design, and as a parallel to the Selectric and the Apple II, the plastic sheath was not just a shell but a form that conveyed a certain feeling. Part of this feeling was communicated by scale. The Macintosh case was manageably sized because of its smallish, embedded nine-inch monitor. With a handle on the back, the Macintosh could be picked up by the scruff of its neck like a puppy. Also, the screen was cantilevered forward from the base, giving the impression of a welcoming face that gazed at the user expectantly. That screen also introduced the Macintosh's most famous feature, its GUI.

As Erik Sandberg-Diment noted in his contemporary review of the Macintosh for the *New York Times*, "The fundamental difference between the Mac and other personal computers is that the Macintosh is visually oriented rather than word oriented." Along these lines, much has been made over the years of the visit that Apple Computer engineers made to Xerox's PARC laboratories in 1979. This visit seems to provide the clearest conduit whereby elements originally derived at PARC ended up as part of the 1984 Macintosh interface. (Of course, a year before the Macintosh, the Apple Lisa, an overly expensive precursor, shared much of the same technical DNA but was quickly rendered obsolete by its successor.) The PARC mouse and GUI with a desktop metaphor were first successfully mass marketed through the $2,500 Apple Macintosh. At a time when IBM PCs and the like still used cumbersome text commands, the Macintosh was intuitive and approachable, with little sense that engagement with the machine would require advanced technical skills.

While the case was sleek, and interacting with the GUI was a satisfying experience, the overall suggestion of friendliness the machine engendered had the greatest impact on its users. A large part of this sensibility was communicated by the icons and typefaces that established the Macintosh's visual style. These now iconic glyphs—trash can, save and print buttons, Happy Macintosh, and so on—had been hand drawn by Susan Kare, an artist turned designer when she joined Apple in 1982 (figure 2.7). Kare sketched out what would become some of the most recognizable images of the digital age in an analog sketchbook, giving each of them a feeling of perky efficiency and desire to please. At the same time, Kare channeled the company's well-known penchant for simplicity. Because of these icons, the Macintosh was able to overcome the inherently staid, boring message of working (or playing) at a desktop. Kare's icons also communicated relatability through their skeuomorphic design. Under this paradigm, your virtual "trash" looks like a trash can, and your documents are put away in diagrams of "folders." Skeuomorphism is so effective because the glyph is an affordance, meaning its look communicates its function. Skeuomorphism was destined to become a staple of GUI design and still plays a large role today.

Along with the icons, Kare designed one of the earliest sets of what would later be termed screen fonts, lettering that was optimized for display through a bitmap of pixels. All the text in the Macintosh interface appeared in her new typeface Chicago, a sans serif with a curvilinear rhythm and contrasting stroke widths. These facets of the typeface represented a decisive turn away from the prevailing fashion for sturdier, more neutral-looking fonts, such as Helvetica and Akzidenz-Grotesk. Kare's new typeface was proportional, so that the different letters occupied horizontal space according to their natural width and were not forced into a standardized box. This avoided the stilted look that was characteristic of many screen fonts in the early eighties. Most importantly, nothing about Chicago conveyed technological sophistication, again reinforcing the approachability of the digital device. In addition to Kare's typefaces, the Macintosh word-processing program MacWrite offered a wealth of typefaces at a range of point sizes, allowing for creative flexibility with type that could not be found elsewhere.

While the GUI was the main attraction, other aspects of the Macintosh pushed potential customers to view it as a different sort of machine. Bill Atkinson, who was the chief designer of the GUI, also created the QuickDraw raster graphics library, which embedded drawing into the operating system. Additionally, Atkinson wrote the MacPaint program, software that helped further the idea that Apple products were for creative-minded people, not office drones performing mundane tasks. Rather than the program itself, it was the promise MacPaint offered that really mattered. Taken together, the case, the GUI, the icons and typefaces, the software—all of it suggested that artistic aspirations were in reach.

The tendency of creative types to gravitate toward the Macintosh was by no means the original intention at Apple Computer. The company had spent years developing a business plan for the product, and there is extensive documentation of the marketing strategy overseen by famed Silicon Valley consultant Regis McKenna. McKenna created what has become a significant case study for retail professionals, particularly how he calibrated the Macintosh campaign toward a new segment of the market he called "knowledge workers." According to the plan, "Knowledge workers are professionally trained individuals who are paid to process information and ideas into plans, reports, analyses, memos and budgets." Given that this group includes neither CEOs nor clerks, the term clearly refers to white-collar middle managers grinding away in the expanding service economy of the eighties. At this time, Apple was consumed with the IBM PC's dominance in the business market, and there was intense pressure to make the Macintosh garner a hold on the number two position as the clear alternative to the PC. There was no concern whatsoever for artists or designers because, of course, there was no digital design industry to cater to at this point.

The obvious advantages of the Macintosh GUI spurred Microsoft to develop its own visually oriented overlay for DOS, leading to the release of its Windows interface for IBM PCs and their clones in 1985. Windows used a desktop metaphor and a GUI replete with clickable navigation, much of which they had bartered for with Apple. A few years later, as new versions of Windows were released, Apple attempted to enforce a patent claim for the GUI and the desktop but was defeated in the courts, setting the stage for the continuing similarity of GUI design in the ensuing years.

The Macintosh marketing plan was mainly predicated on the idea of making the machine approachable and easy to use for office workers. As one print advertisement put it in 1984, “Wouldn’t it make sense to teach computers about people, instead of teaching people about computers?” This text was paired with a friendly computer that was inscribed by MacPaint with “hello.” But Apple did not just emphasize users of the product; it also showcased the designers of the Macintosh themselves. This aspect of the print campaign, which fed into the notion of Apple products as the foremost creative choice, involved how Apple marketed not just the product but also its employees. Many of the print advertisements featured an image of members of the Macintosh development team posed in a casual array. Mimicking the look of contemporary photos of rock bands (with one engineer casually holding a Macintosh in place of a guitar), these photos presented technology workers as hipster creative types, with computer engineering having more in common with art and entertainment than research laboratories.

Designing the Designer

How the self-image and public persona of the designer evolved during the early digital age is important to recognize. During the 1920s, in the formative year of modernist design at the Bauhaus and amid various constructivist groups, the notion of the creative worker as something of an analytical engineer came to the fore. This transition was clearly marked by photos of the designers themselves. For example, the tremendous contrast between the shaved head and flowing robes of the mystically inclined early Bauhaus master Johannes Itten and the neutral clothing of his successor, the Hungarian constructivist László Moholy-Nagy, could not be starker. In contrast to Itten’s monk robes, Moholy-Nagy appeared in photographs in uniform-like overalls, clothing that was suggestive of a workmanlike, practical approach. In the Russian milieu, El Lissitzky’s famed 1924 self-portrait known as *The Constructor* (figure 2.8) crystallized the role of the modern designer. A composite print made out of six different photographs, the image shows El Lissitzky’s eye piercing through his hand, the latter appendage holding a compass suspended above graphing paper. In this image, the designer melds the cerebral talents of the intellectual with the skilled hands of the worker to produce exacting designs; the designer is an engineer.

The 1920s vision of the designer as engineer continued well into the postwar era and was most famously adopted by the graphic designers at the Milan branch of the global firm Unimark. In a famous image from 1966, Unimark employees

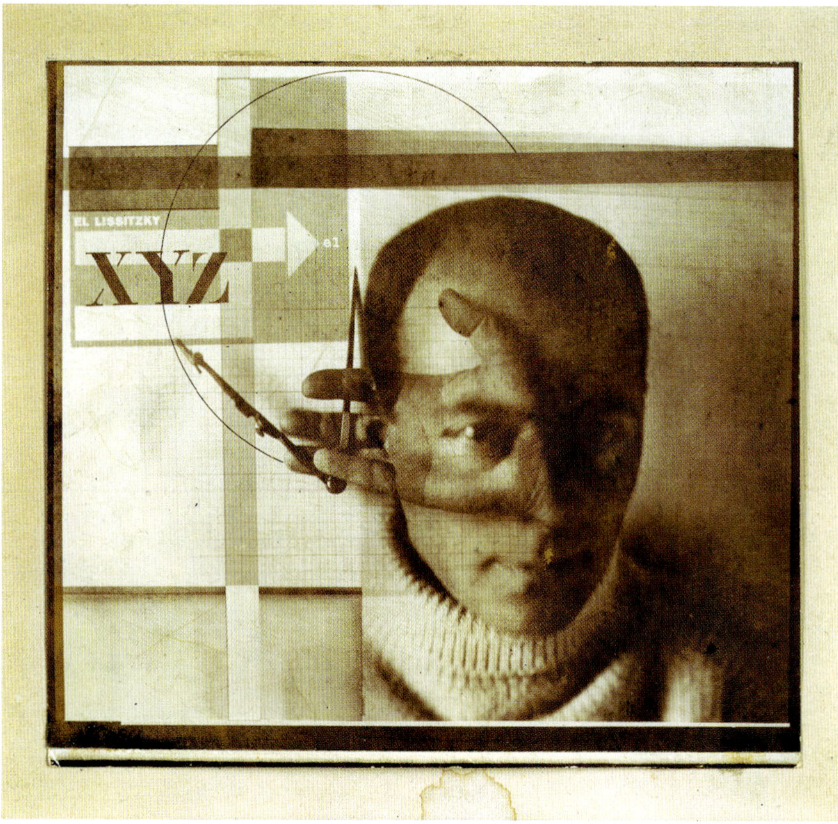

2.8. El Lissitzky, *The Constructor*, 1924

in white lab coats are grouped around a table displaying a spread-out portfolio of their works. This idea derived from Massimo Vignelli, who wanted the staff to convey a sense of professionalism and seriousness. Soon, Vignelli et al. were swimming upstream against the sixties counterculture, and many young designers started to emulate the more flamboyant, hippie-infused look so well modeled by rock stars. The strongest examples of counterculture designers in this new mold were the creators of music posters, such as Michael English and Nigel Waymouth, who called themselves Hapshash and the Coloured Coat, in Britain, and the "big five" psychedelic poster makers—including Wes Wilson and Victor Moscoso—of the San Francisco scene. Somewhere along the way, the role of the designer moved somewhat back toward the outlandish expressionism embodied by Itten at the early Bauhaus, eschewing the lab coats of the engineer.

At design-centric Apple, the company adopted an ethos influenced by the creative designers for whom they ideally built their machines, establishing a culture that blended technological sophistication with the human warmth of the Summer of Love. That is the message conveyed by the Macintosh advertisement shown in figure 2.9. The influence of the company was considerable, so the new converse theme—digital engineer as artist—had a broad effect outside the culture of just one company. Like Hans Namuth's famous photos of the abstract expressionist painter Jackson Pollock at work, which have proved to be more influential than his paintings, these images of Apple engineers may well have had a much greater long-term impact on the consumer perception of the industry than any other factor, including the famed Super Bowl commercial of January 1984.

The sixty-second Macintosh television commercial called "1984," a play on George Orwell's 1949 dystopian science-fiction novel, was developed by Steve Hayden and Lee Clow of the firm Chiat/Day. Its presentation to Apple executives met a mixed response, with many concerned that focus groups had rated it quite poorly; Apple even sold back to the network one of its two planned slots. The commercial features a dark scene of massed workers trudging to a video conference overseen by a Big Brother–like ideologue. The leader gives a kitschy faux-totalitarian speech—"We have created, for the first time in all history, a garden of pure ideology"—after which a young woman, dressed colorfully, throws a sledge hammer into the screen, smashing it and presumably fomenting a rebellion against fascist tyranny.

The commercial was an astounding hit and is credited with greatly accelerating sales of the Macintosh. While its importance to the

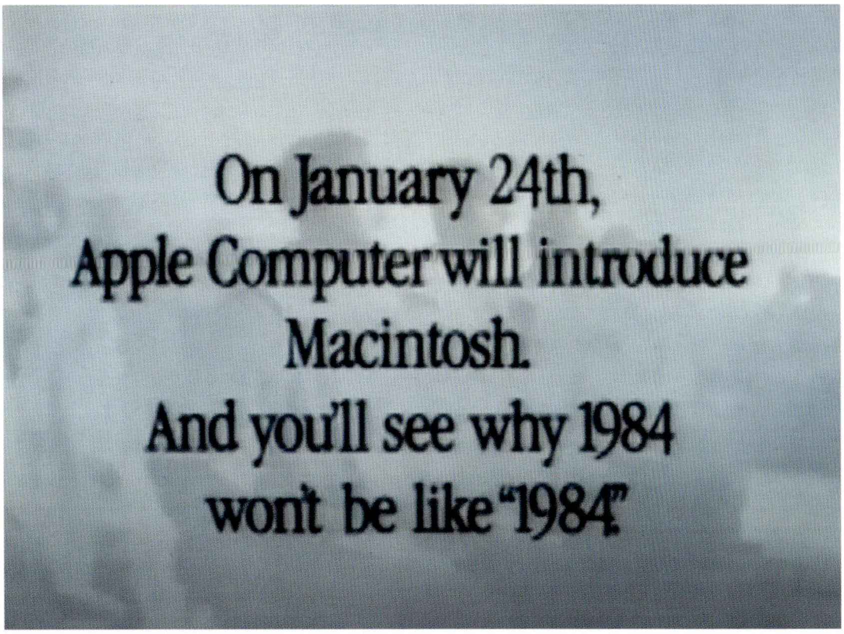

2.9. Macintosh computer advertisement, 1984

television advertising industry is undeniable—it created the era of the Super Bowl commercial as event—it has arguably been overvalued in terms of Apple's long-term success versus the "engineer as rock star" meme of the print campaign. This is reinforced by the failure of Apple's attempt to reconstitute its success with a second commercial that imitated the dystopian look and feel of the original; that "Lemmings" advertisement for the ill-fated Macintosh Office suite of products was a monstrous failure, and within months almost a quarter of the workforce—including Steve Jobs—had been laid off. In contrast, the creative theme was still thriving and would come to define the company; Apple was in fact on the cusp of a technological collaboration that would transform the graphic design world and set the stage for the Macintosh to become the preferred machine for the graphic fields.

Apple's famous 1984 commercial had been overseen by none other than Ridley Scott, the film director who two years previously had released the science-fiction noir film *Blade Runner*. While not an initial commercial success, *Blade Runner* gradually became part of a constellation of futuristic books and movies that defined a new genre of eighties fiction: cyberpunk. Cyberpunk refers to works that portray the future as some sort of mash-up of digital spectacle and urban misery. Perhaps the most influential work of this genre was the 1984 book *Neuromancer*, published in the summer following the release of the Macintosh. Written by William Gibson, *Neuromancer* vividly describes the life of a disaffected computer hacker named Henry Case, an unemployed nobody stuck on the streets of a futuristic, but grimy, megalopolis. This romantic protagonist feels most comfortable in "cyberspace," the term that Gibson coined in 1982 to name the virtual world that was a digital corollary to the physical space of the city. In a famous passage from *Neuromancer*, cyberspace is described as "a consensual hallucination experienced daily by billions of legitimate operators, in every nation, by children being taught mathematical concepts. . . . A graphic representation of data abstracted from banks of every computer in the human system. Unthinkable complexity. Lines of light ranged in the nonspace of the mind, clusters and constellations of data. Like city lights, receding."

Of course, in 1984 the internet—another Gibsonism was the term "the matrix"—was a decade away, and a contemporary Macintosh had no access to cyberspace. Still, the case can be made that Apple machines benefited most from this cultural tsunami, as the Macintosh seemed to offer the most promise of a cyber-future made richer by technology. Note the dystopian elements present in *Blade*

Runner, Neuromancer, and the "1984" commercial; in the formative years of personal computing, companies did not run away from the dark side of technology, perhaps because it offered a frisson of danger and excitement (in later decades, digital behemoths like Apple have dramatically changed their attitude toward dystopic renderings of their technology). The cyberpunk phenomenon also added another layer of technological burden to digital designers. In terms of the visionary discourse discussed above, works such as *Neuromancer* added another layer of popular expectations for what the digital world could become. Like *Wired* magazine in the nineties, cyberpunk books and movies promised a future that designers were tasked with delivering as soon as possible.

Design Software

Although Macintosh Office, the suite of products offered up in the ill-fated "Lemmings" commercial of 1985, was quickly sidelined, one element of it, the networked LaserWriter printer, would prove a runaway success. Laser printing was yet another technology invented at Xerox's PARC lab but never brought to market as a personal printer by the copier company, which saw its market as the sale of massive printers to large organizations. Hewlett-Packard had sold a low-cost laser printer as early as 1980, but Apple's machine had two built-in advantages. First, users were able to offset the high cost of the LaserWriter, $6,995, by connecting it to multiple computers via the AppleTalk system. The most important aspect of the Apple system, however, was that the company had licensed PostScript, a device-independent page description language that allowed the LaserWriter to print out integrated text and graphics with a high level of sophistication.

PostScript was an Adobe product devised by Charles Geschke and John Warnock, two more former PARC engineers who together had founded the company in 1982. One of the most important elements of PostScript was that it included font rendering subprograms that could originally communicate to the printer a set of four different typefaces (Courier, Helvetica, Times, and Symbol) in different styles and a multitude of text sizes. PostScript fonts, called Type 1 by Adobe, were outlined in 300 dpi using Bézier curves, with the one drawback being that users' screens could show the type only in a lower-resolution bitmapped format. Type 1 fonts quickly proliferated into the thousands and became the industry standard, allowing Adobe to enjoy several years of a lucrative monopoly on the digital type business. Printers and print software were so central to early digital graphic design because print was the end product. In the eighties and well into the nineties, designing for the virtual environment scarcely existed; digital design *was* print.

Another important advantage of the Macintosh came through the creation of type design software. In the early eighties, several programs emerged that allowed designers—like Susan Kare at Apple—to create and edit bitmap fonts, low-resolution type that could be printed on a dot-matrix printer. After the LaserWriter appeared, printing out bitmap fonts at high resolution was possible only by using large sizes and scaling them down. Then in January 1986 Altsys premiered its PostScript editing program, Fontgrapher, for Macintosh. Fontgrapher could inexpensively create outline fonts using Bézier curves, beginning the first great surge in the creation of digital type. The Macintosh also benefited from the release in 1986 of PageMaker, the original desktop publishing software sold by Aldus (a company named after the famed Renaissance type designer and printer Aldus Manutius). PageMaker combined with PostScript and its Type 1 fonts, running on a Macintosh networked to a LaserWriter, transformed graphic design. Printing was no longer the province of ten-or even hundred-thousand-dollar phototypesetters; it was available to a whole new class of creative professionals.

The reign of the Macintosh in graphic design did not end there. Soon Adobe released Illustrator, a vector drawing and type design program, for Macintosh in 1987, and then Photoshop, for editing digital images, for Macintosh in 1990. Soon thereafter, Premiere for editing video (1991) appeared, to be followed by After Effects for motion graphics in 1993. At the same time, Apple continued to expand and refine its GUI with each new operating system, including the new full-color System 7 from 1991. Note that all of these design programs were subsequently released for Windows, and the relationship between Apple and Adobe would be complex and fraught over the ensuing years. But to designers, the details did not matter, as the Macintosh had become entrenched in people's minds as the design-centric choice. Apple had established a culture that has now become a tradition, and the elite status of Apple products amid designers continues to today, despite the fact that Windows machines are and have been for years complete equals.

While paramount in graphic design, the notion that the Macintosh was superior has taken hold to a lesser extent in other design professions, despite there being little real technological basis for the preference. The first architectural drafting software, Radar CH, by the Hungarian company Graphisoft, was originally devised for the Lisa but was quickly reengineered for Macintosh. Radar CH later became ArchiCAD and was joined on the market by several other European programs, including the French product Architrion and, in 1990, the Italian parametric modeling software Domus.CAD. The general advantage of these programs again came down to the Apple GUI and the mouse, which allowed for a more intuitive design process than that of the command line and the tablet, typical for DOS software at the time. Still, the architectural profession was slow to adopt digital tools outside the realm of enhanced productivity. A sense of the tenuous state of the situation was evident in a 1988 how-to manual, *The Architect's Guide to Computer-Aided Design*. The author, Mark Crosley, clearly felt the need to take readers by the hand and bring them into the digital age using baby steps: "An initial encounter with a whirring, beeping, flashing, electronic beast can be unnerving. Drawing with such a tool, using a typewriter keyboard, or perhaps a plastic 'mouse,' is obviously not like drawing with a pencil."

Probably the weakest area of Macintosh software was the generalized CAD program used by industrial designers and engineers. Here the situation was reversed, and software companies tended to favor Microsoft operating systems. When AutoCAD for DOS appeared in 1982, so did CADapple; but the creator of the latter, T&W Systems, quickly jumped ship and by 1984 was focusing on VersaCAD for DOS. A Macintosh version of VersaCAD would not appear until late

1987. Today, architects and designers using CAD and its progeny represent one market, which Microsoft products dominate.

Without getting deeper into the technical weeds, it is clear that in the eighties Apple established a design-centric culture through graphic and UX design that bolstered the brand for decades. Importantly, it was in these areas that a critical mass of designers first readily embraced digital technology. If the age of digital design began with the computational curve devised in the fifties at automobile companies, it was consolidated in the eighties with the Bézier curve, which made possible digital graphics on personal computers.

In the nineties, the digital world changed again with the release of a new software program called Photoshop, one of the few software brand names to actually become a verb. It was developed by two brothers, Thomas and John Knoll. While Thomas Knoll was working on a PhD and tinkering with image processing on an early Macintosh in the late eighties, John was employed at Lucasfilm's special effects division, Industrial Light and Magic (ILM). At ILM, John Knoll gained some experience in custom digital image editing, particularly using the complex and expensive Pixar Image Computer, a machine that literally required the resources of a large corporation to own and operate. He was intrigued when the brothers discussed their work to discover that Thomas's DIY software had nearly the same functionality as a bespoke special effects workstation. Over the following few years, the Knoll brothers improved what was then called Display, eventually licensing the software to Adobe at the behest of an art director there, Russell Brown. Adobe released the first iteration of Photoshop for the Macintosh in 1990.

Photoshop, which soon displaced the artisanal craft of airbrushing photographs—particularly media images of celebrities—helped to make the digital realm a place of unattainable beauty. It provided one of the seminal tools, for better or for worse, that allows virtual spaces to appear outside the grasp of the dirty, degraded, or prosaic. By enabling visions of computer-mediated perfection, Photoshop added a new glamour to the digital. By chance, this facet of Photoshop appeared even in the demos orchestrated by John Knoll years before the software debuted. The first Photoshopped image was a personal one for John Knoll, a photo he had taken of his then-girlfriend Jennifer on the beach in Tahiti a few hours before he would propose marriage to her (figure 2.10). On a visit to Apple Computer some months later, Knoll took advantage of access to an early flatbed scanner to digitize the photo, and subsequently it became the mainstay of his image-processing demos. Nicknamed "Jennifer in Paradise," the photo has everything: stunning sun, sand and sky, sex appeal, and saturated color. One of the first personal images to digitally circulate, it is the ur-Photoshopped image, offering anyone the promise of perfection and well-being. Conceptually, it is Malibu.

In 2013, Dutch conceptual artist Constant Dullart brought new attention to *Jennifer in Paradise*, an image that had in some ways defined digital photography but had become completely unknown to the contemporary world. Calling himself a "digital archaeologist," Dullart mused on the worldwide impact of this very personal image, its circulation, and what it says about our

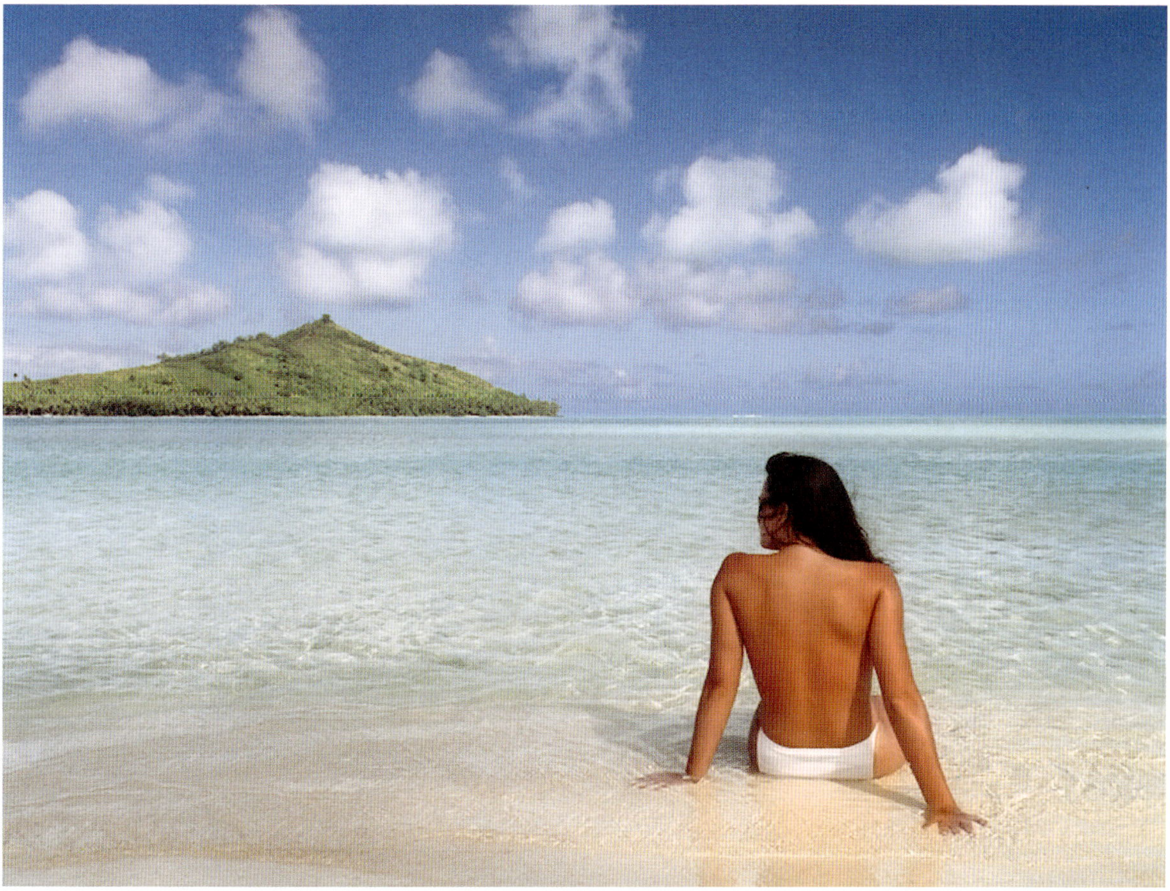

2.10. John Knoll, *Jennifer in Paradise*, 1989

burgeoning digital culture. As part of the project, Dullart wrote a poignant letter to Jennifer Knoll. “I still wonder if you felt the world change there on that beach. The fact that reality would be more moldable, that normal people could change their history, brighten up their past, and put twirl effects on their faces?... Sometimes, when I am anxious about the future of our surveilled, computer-mediated world.... I imagine myself traveling back in time... there on the beach in Bora Bora. And just sit there with you, watching the tide roll away.”

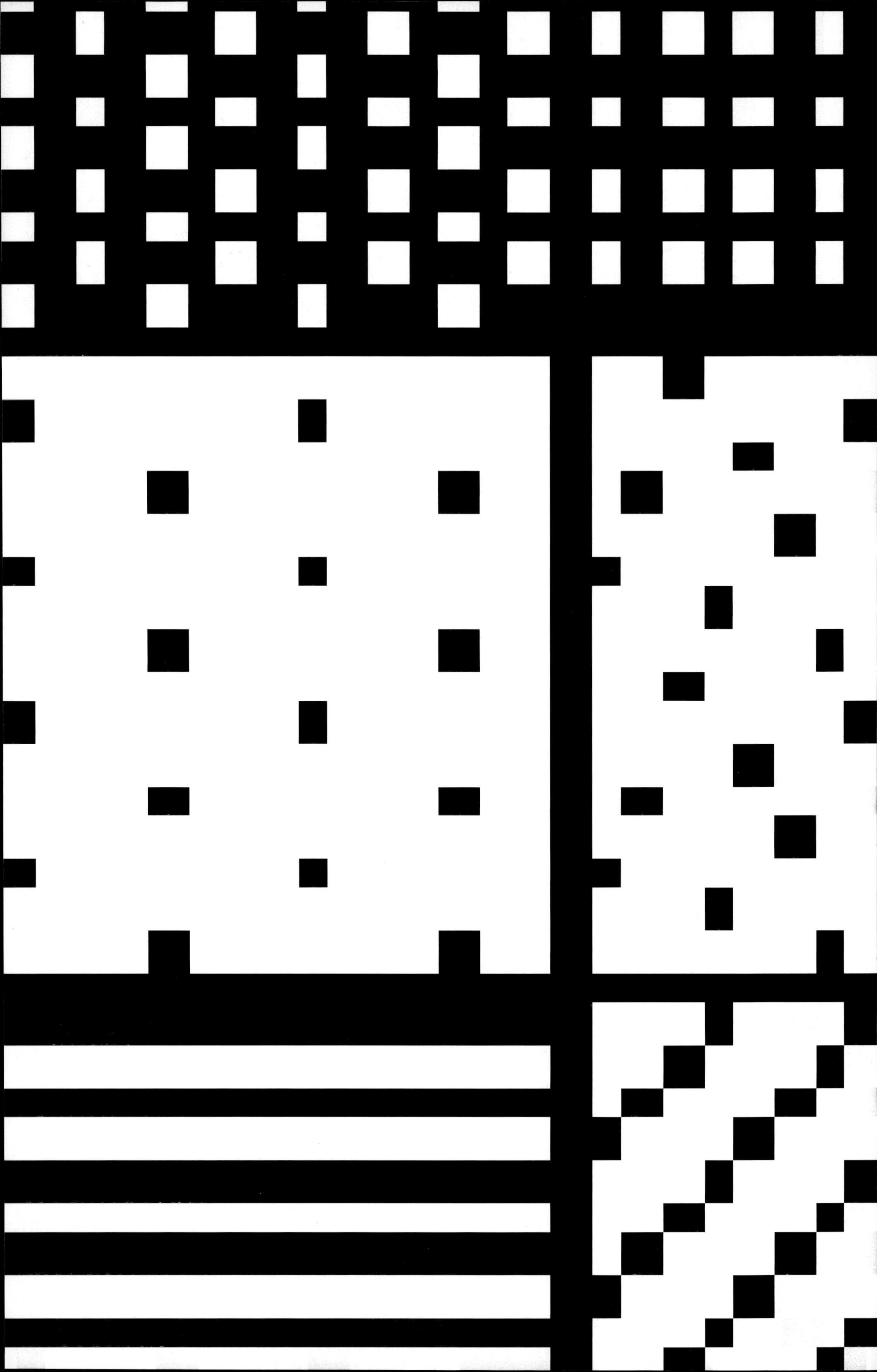

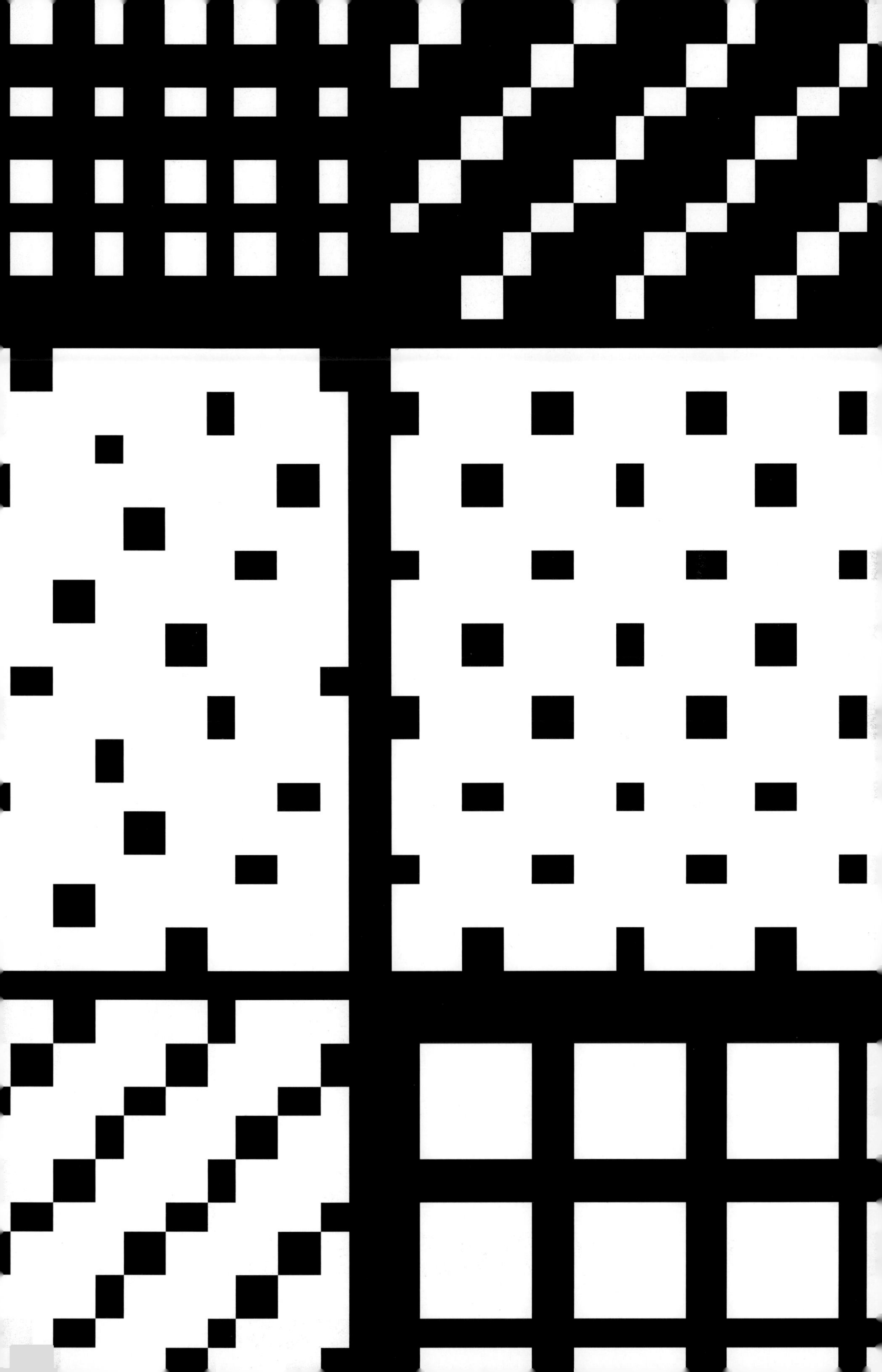

3.1. Zuzana Licko's Lo-Res typeface specimen, 1984

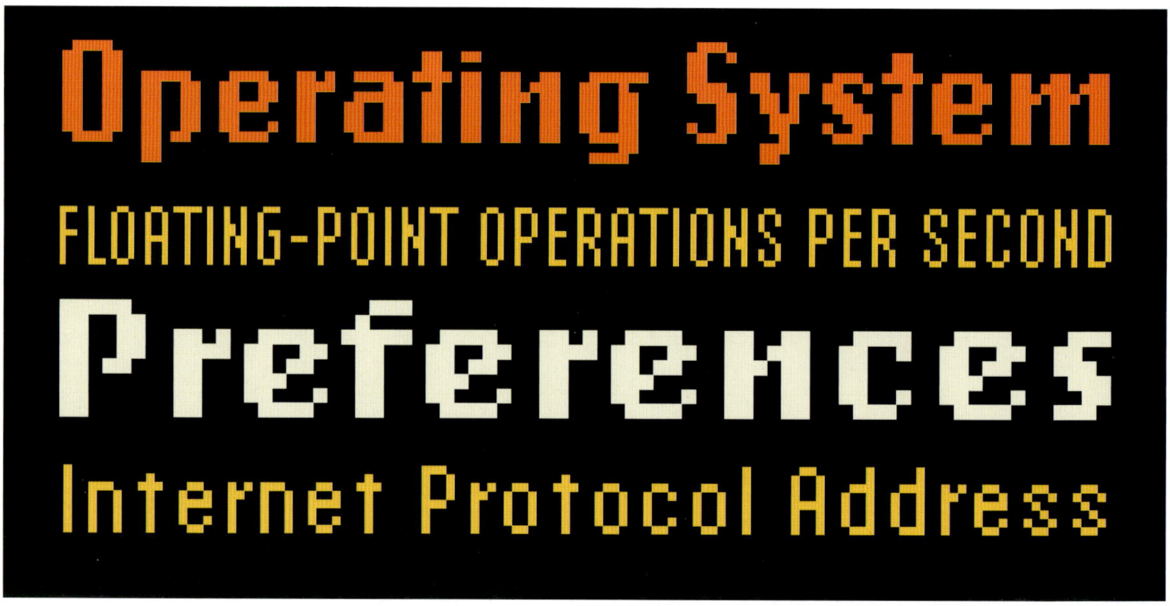

Three. Digital Type Design

Arguably no field has experienced as much transformative change catalyzed by digital technology as that of graphic design. While many design professions are still working within the framework of older conventions, the profession of graphic design has been completely rewritten, from a handmade artistic specialty to one that highlights technological skill. But the digital age did not just change the tool kit, it also changed the product: while architects still build buildings and industrial designers still make chairs, print has slowly but inexorably given way to the design of virtual media.

When the mechanical printing era began in the fifteenth century, it began with type. In the age of incunabula the core of the creative project was designing the letters, as layouts tended to be elegant yet nondescript. Type also had a central role to play at the onset of the digital era in the eighties; and type has maintained its preeminence in more recent decades, as every operating system graphical user interface (GUI), web-based human–computer interaction (HCI), or for that matter highway billboard of 2023 relies in one way or another on written text.

The years leading up to the digital era were complicated for the design and employment of type. A pair of older technologies using metal type—Linotype and Monotype machines—were still in widespread use in certain segments, while a multitude of phototypesetting, xerographic, and press display type systems, plus stat cameras for scaling, also served the industry. Importantly, design and printing were separate specialties with huge economic barriers, as a typesetting system could cost in the hundreds of thousands, and only a handful of large foundries had the resources to produce and market new typefaces.

The type design ecosystem began a new phase with the introduction of the Apple Macintosh in 1984 and its employment by forward-thinking type designers. Born in Bratislava of the current Slovakia, Zuzana Licko had immigrated to the United States as a child and subsequently studied architecture and graphic design at the University of California at Berkeley. Through an essentially organic process that speaks well to the benefits of a broad liberal arts education, Licko found a lifelong passion when she started experimenting with type design on a Macintosh. Through the Berkeley Macintosh Users Group, she came across a simple bitmap-based type-editing tool (pre-PostScript), along the lines of the software Susan Kare had used at Apple to create the first typefaces for the Macintosh GUI. Licko was enchanted by the strict parameters of letter design enforced by the coarse 72 dpi resolution of both monitor and dot-matrix printer, relishing the analytical puzzle of pushing against such a crude digital framework. Over the first year experimenting with the Macintosh, Licko designed four low-resolution typeface families—Emperor, Oakland, Universal, and Emigre—that were all based on building letterforms pixel by pixel (figure 3.1). This suite of typefaces varies mainly in stroke width and overall proportion.

While Licko had been inspired by the digital type discussion centered on the work of Chuck Bigelow (see below), significantly, she wanted to make type that was not just digital but that looked digital too. This issue would become a defining feature of the digital type world: Should the designer seek a solution that jostles the viewer with a computer-age aesthetic, or comfort them with a conventional form? Licko, of course, chose the former, stating, "It is impossible to transfer typefaces between technologies without alterations because each medium has its peculiar qualities and thus requires unique designs." Licko was very much attuned to these "peculiar qualities" and created one of the first digital aesthetics, making bitmaps that were generative of a new way of seeing.

Licko was not alone in her pursuits and quickly recognized that a growing community of like-minded designers was crystallizing around the Macintosh. When her typefaces appeared in the small independent magazine *Emigre*, founded by her husband, Rudy VanderLans, she quickly received inquiries from other emerging digital designers. Licko's digital typefaces soon became a foundation of the magazine's aesthetic, and the couple went on to establish the digital foundry of the same name, while *Emigre* became a graphic design publication that served as the house organ of the type business.

It is worthwhile to compare Licko's bitmapped experiments with type from the mechanical revolution some five hundred years previously, like that created by Nicolas Jenson around 1470. Both Jenson and Licko worked to create a new aesthetic based on preestablished revolutionary technologies they had not invented themselves. Jenson was one of the key figures in transitioning metal type from a heavy reliance on the look of calligraphic handwriting to an aesthetic more fitting for the "peculiar qualities" of metal type. He sought to balance multiple different threads and create letters that "are neither smaller, larger nor thicker than reason or pleasure demand." Licko likewise explored the parameters of a new technology and sought to design letters that made digital sense and were not simply older designs reproduced on a new machine.

For all the focus on technology, both Jenson and Licko pursued truly artisanal crafts. Whether

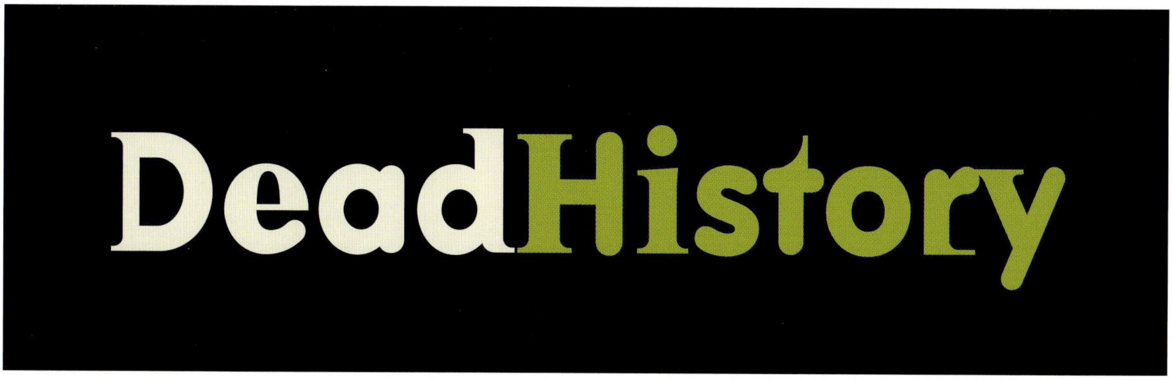

3.2. P. Scott Makela's Dead History typeface specimen, 1994

meticulously carving punches or placing pixels on a bitmap, both type designers had to conquer laborious processes. This recalls another facet of digital graphic design writ large: how it brought designers back into the world of production. As mentioned above, in the near predigital era, typesetting was an entirely separate world from graphic design, a separateness maintained by the expense of the associated equipment. With the Macintosh, Licko and VanderLans found that they could lay out and prepare print-ready galleys of *Emigre* magazine themselves. Soon, they were contributing typefaces, layouts, and illustrations to a succession of small magazines designed on the computer, many of them, like *MacWeek*, essentially fanzines dedicated to the Apple computer. Like Jenson before them, the design and typesetting of print was brought under one roof, and desktop publishing came to the fore once again.

Through an essentially organic process, Licko and VanderLans realized that the type business was the strongest part of their professional practice and reorganized the business as a digital foundry. Emigre Fonts quickly became the flagship provider of type to any designer with a counterculture edge, with many of their releases sharing Licko's same experimental, even revolutionary, belief in the need for new forms for the nascent digital age. Dead History (figure 3.2), first designed by P. Scott Makela while he was a student at the Cranbrook Academy of Art, showcased this aesthetic while also indicating that a critical mass of designers shared the same vision as Licko and VanderLans. The name, Dead History, says it all: Makela sought to create a type that would speak to a digitally transformed society, one where the moribund burden of type history would be eschewed in favor of new, provisional hybrid forms. Despite his rejection of historical fonts, Makela's new type was in fact a postmodern pastiche that had some engagement with history, mixing elements of Linotype's Centennial (a fairly conventional serifed type by Adrian Frutiger that Linotype had commissioned in 1986 to celebrate its one-hundred-year history) and Adobe's Volkswagen AG Rounded (known as VAG Rounded), a geometric sans serif that was the house type for the automobile conglomerate after 1979 and digitally released by Adobe ten years later. For this reason, Dead History features a mash-up of forms, some of which are characteristic of serifed fonts, others of the sans serif variety; for Makela, this history is dead.

While type design was definitively a manual project, Makela also experimented with an early version of parametric design, meaning that the author inputs certain parameters into a computer and then allows the machine to output a new digital creation. Parametric design at this point was largely aspirational, but the notion that humans could collaborate with machines hearkens back to the earliest experiments in creating digital environments. A major force in architecture beginning in the midnineties, parametric design today still represents in a sense the holy grail of digital practice, a world where computers are not tools but creators. In 1994, Emigre licensed Dead History, and Licko redrew the typeface, adding yet another layer of authorship.

Alongside Emigre, several new independent digital type foundries arose around 1990 that together challenged the hegemony of the age-old foundries such as Linotype. In Europe, Erik Spiekermann and Neville Brody started

FontFont, a purveyor of radical new digital designs. One of the first types released by FontFont was called Beowolf. It was an old-style serifed type designed by Erik van Blokland and Just van Rossum, who together had just cofounded the letter-design studio LettError in the Netherlands. Through Beowolf, Blokland and Rossum subverted Adobe's PostScript coding language, substituting a command that would randomize the outlines of the letters. In this way, Beowolf does not output in the exact same manner every time as standard fonts do, but instead produces an ever-shifting set of erratic, even ragged, letterforms. The result has a rough, raw texture, akin to a wall of weathered brick, where the individual building blocks are melded into a rich, worn surface. Insomuch as Blokland and Rossum sought to overturn the sameness of conventional typography, they reprised the iconoclastic rejection of authorial control initiated by members of the Dada movement in the early twentieth century; like Makela, they allowed the machine to partially author their work.

Zuzana Licko has noted her awareness in the late eighties of the parallel pioneering digital type designs created by Charles Bigelow and Kris Holmes. Bigelow and Holmes took a somewhat different trajectory than Licko, partly because they began their type design careers not with the Macintosh, but with the earlier generation of cathode ray typesetters. When Licko suggested that Bigelow's writings on digital type were not experimental enough for her taste, she was referring to some of his early essays, which dealt with the pre–desktop publishing era. For example, in 1983, Bigelow opined that digital type must go through an evolution, the first stage being "a period of imitation, in which the outstanding letterforms of the previous typographic generation serve as models for the new designs." This type of measured, conservative point of view was perhaps somewhat at odds with the revolution that Licko strove to foment at Emigre.

In September 1984, Bigelow and Holmes introduced a serifed typeface in three weights, Lucida, which was intended to represent what Bigelow considered to be the final stage in digital type's evolution, when "designs emerge that are not merely imitative but exploit the strengths and explore the limitations of the medium." Like many designs from this transitional moment, Lucida was a digital hybrid: it is actually a hand-drawn type that was then digitized using a seventies spline software called Ikarus, a pre-PostScript program that used computational curves to store the letterforms. Lucida was not aimed at the personal computer market but was designed for professional typesetters using commercial equipment, such as the laser printers marketed by Imagen, for whom the first specimen was created.

In 1985, Bigelow and Holmes added a sans typeface to the family (figure 3.3). Both Lucida and Lucida Sans were characterized by large x-heights and wide letterspacing, allowing them to maintain their legibility even at poor resolutions on computer screens. Bigelow, in line with his conservative outlook, was quite aware of Lucida's relationship to the fifteenth-century fonts of the Gutenberg age. He made consistent analogies to the mechanical revolution, noting that the spacing was akin to that of Jenson's roman type, and referencing Francesco Griffo, the punch cutter for Manutius who pushed

a quick brown fox jumps over the lazy dog
a quick brown fox jumps over the lazy dog
a quick brown fox jumps over the lazy dog
a quick brown fox jumps over the lazy dog
a quick brown fox jumps over the lazy dog
a quick brown fox jumps over the lazy dog
a quick brown fox jumps over the lazy dog
a quick brown fox jumps over the lazy dog
a quick brown fox jumps over the lazy dog
a quick brown fox jumps over the lazy dog
a quick brown fox jumps over the lazy dog
a quick brown fox jumps over the lazy dog
a quick brown fox jumps over the lazy dog
a quick brown fox jumps over the lazy dog
a quick brown fox jumps over the lazy dog
a quick brown fox jumps over the lazy dog

3.3. Charles Bigelow and Kris Holmes's Lucida Sans typeface, 1985

further away from handwritten models for the types he designed in the 1490s.

Bigelow and Holmes's Lucida and Licko's Lo-Res types represent two different strategies for dealing with the onset of the digital era. In one sense, Licko's bitmapped designs—sometimes referred to as a type of "new primitivism"—seem to be more daring in their embrace of a self-conscious break with prevailing norms. In this view, Lucida is uninspiring in its staid humanist proportions. From another vantage point, however, the Emigre types represented more of a stunt than a serious design, as the aliased (stepped-edge) forms of the bitmaps were not suitable for any sort of long-term or varied use. Of course, Licko was responding to the technology at hand and soon moved on to new designs as the PostScript revolution developed. In many ways, these two respective strategies would play out as defining trends in subsequent decades, as some typeface designers would embrace experimental forms made possible by new technology, while others would seek to negotiate the world of digital type by channeling the past.

The Reign of the Sans

As much as the digital age values its reputation for disrupting known practices and industries, the relatively understated aesthetic of Lucida Sans—type with a sophisticated pedigree that goes back a century at minimum—has come to define much of the technology industry itself. This is especially significant because, upon the development of the desktop-themed GUI, very little has changed in regard to the most common human computer interface, that of the screen, keyboard, and mouse. While refinements abound, and speculation is always rampant, most users' daily experience of computers has been refined, but not overturned, in their lifetime. One of the greatest signifiers of this continuity has been communicated through typefaces; arguably, type is the core interface of the digital age. While the colors, shading, or other details of the desktop metaphor may be refreshed periodically, type has had an oversized role in setting the tone for human–computer interaction.

The most ubiquitous digital types that dominate big technology today—sans serifs, including the house types Segoe UI (Microsoft), San Francisco (Apple), and Roboto (Google)—all have roots in the modern movement that crystallized in Europe during the second and third decades of the twentieth century. Before that time, sans serif type had existed for a century without claiming a central role in visual communication. While often used in large sizes as display types on ephemera such as handbills, posters, and the like, sans serif "grotesques," as they were known, were treated as just part of the vulgar background noise of everyday life in an urban world slathered with print advertisements. These typefaces featured rather regular proportions, little stroke contrast, and large x-heights so as to be visible as part of a hurried glimpse at the passing scene. Of course, the nickname "grotesque" referred to their perceived strangeness in a typographic world where serifed type was the unassailable standard for printing of any stature. Even examples of the genre that had been elegantly designed, such as Franklin Gothic (USA, 1902) and Akzidenz-Grotesk (Germany, 1896), just did not fit neatly into the prevailing visual culture.

Not until the second decade of the twentieth century, when an unlikely type designer, Edward Johnston, drew a new type for the London Underground, did the perception of the sans serif as a signifier of cutting-edge technology first emerge. Johnston came to this breakthrough role in type design by a circuitous route, having developed a youthful interest in the Victorian pastime of manuscript illumination. His skill at hand-drawn medieval calligraphy eventually led to a position at London's Central School of Arts and Crafts (now part of Saint Martins), where he taught all manner of letter drawing and authored the handbook *Writing & Illuminating & Lettering* (1906).

Johnston's brief to design a new sans typeface (figure 3.4) came about in 1913, after he came to the attention of Frank Pick, a railway executive with a keen interest in reforming the Underground's rather haphazard way-finding signage and overall visual identity. Johnston began drawing a set of letters that would gradually become the house type of the Underground. His new sans serif embodied two sometimes opposed qualities that together have become the basis for many digital type designs. First, Johnston Railway type—also called Johnston Sans at times—has a humanist structure underlying its letter shapes. A natural fit for a designer with a background in calligraphy, humanist typefaces have some of the rhythm and contrast of handwriting. While the term hearkens back to the scholar-printers of the Renaissance, it also registers the fact that this typeface form conveys a certain human warmth and individuality. Second, Johnston Sans also has strong geometric features, meaning that forms such as the O appear to be quite close to the shape of a perfect circle. This second quality gives it a fresh, technological feel and was one of the earliest manifestations of the machine aesthetic that would come to define much of 1920s modernism. Likewise, his nearly monoline strokes describe forms that lock together ever so tightly, showing a concern for molding the negative space between letters that makes the whole alphabet in use much greater than the sum of its parts.

For the London Underground, Johnston Sans was the interface. In seamlessly meshing the strengths of humanist and geometric styling, Johnston brought a new verve to the sans serif form. He gave it more than just a new style; Johnston created an aesthetic that repositioned the whole meaning of sans serif fonts. Johnston Sans established a new raison d'être, combining approachability, clarity, and contemporaneity in a tight package. And just as the Underground wanted to establish a functional yet friendly connection with its passengers, so today big

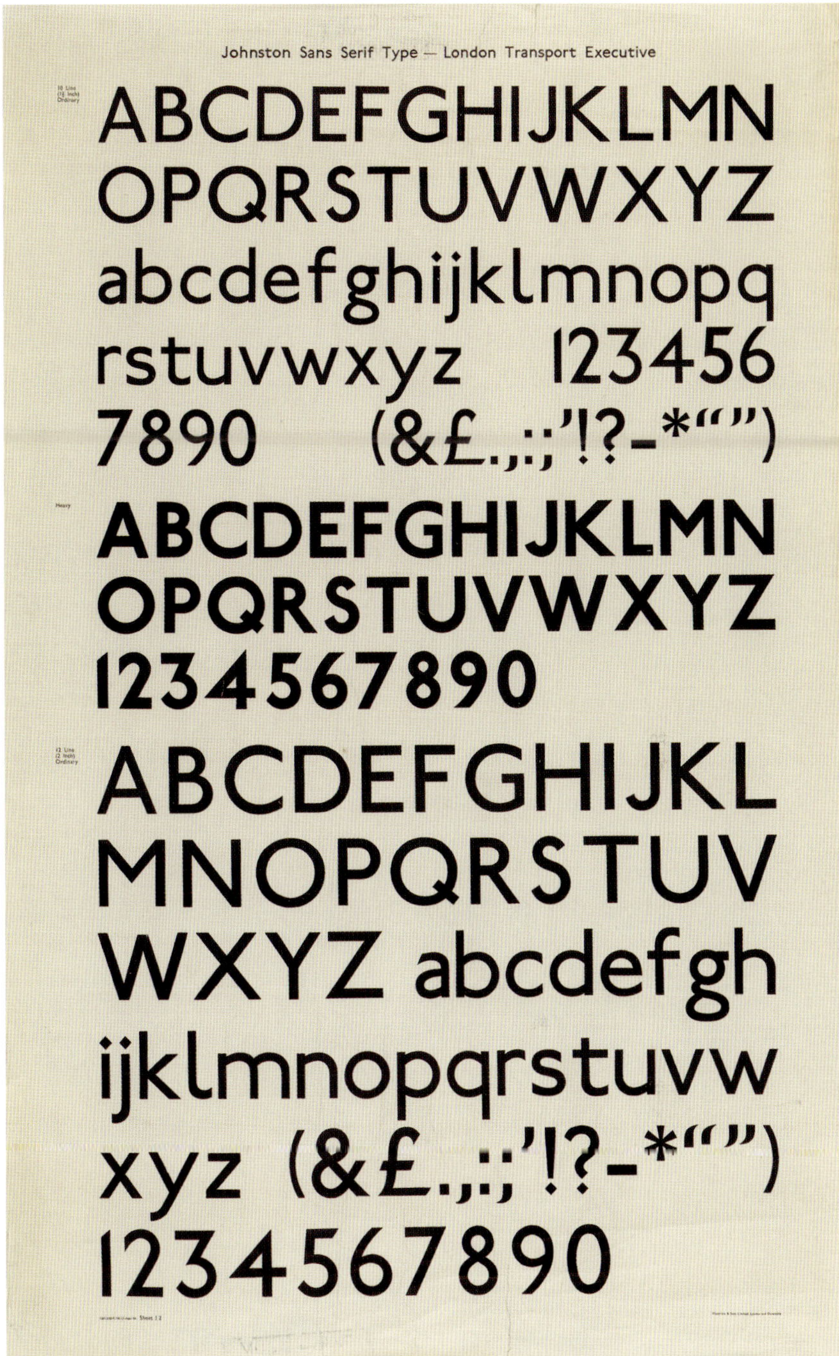

3.4. Edward Johnston's Railway typeface, 1913

technology companies seek to connect through the same combination of qualities.

Johnston Sans never quite made the leap into the digital era. Available in only a single weight, it was supplemented even at the Underground over the decades by its close descendants Gill Sans (1926) and Granby (1930) and never achieved the ubiquity of the former (Eric Gill had been a student of Johnston's). In 1979, Eiichi Kono developed a new version in multiple weights for phototypesetting machines, drawing each letter by hand. This version, New Johnston, was eventually digitized by Monotype, and was later joined by another digital version, P22's Johnston Underground. To contemporary eyes, these Johnston types have something of a retro art deco stylishness to them, which makes them an imperfect fit for the universal solutions sought by the technology industry. Though Johnston had got the ball rolling, subsequent developments in the 1920s would more fully establish the sans serif form as the type of the digital future.

Modernism in the Digital

The history of the German Bauhaus is well known to anyone with an interest in design, and it has if anything become even more high profile

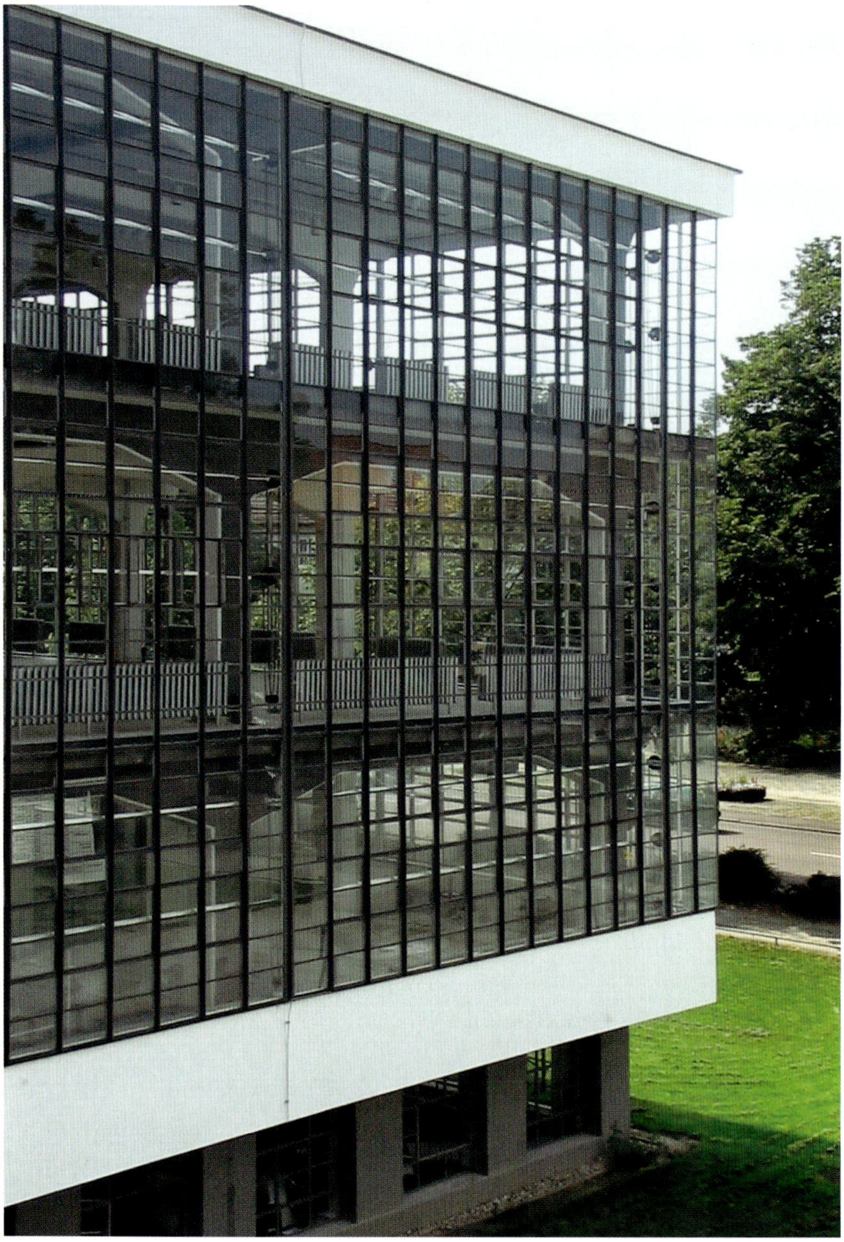

3.5. Dessau Bauhaus studio building, designed by Walter Gropius in 1926

in the digital age, as the sleek machine aesthetic promulgated there in the 1920s became a standard touchstone for digital designers. Founded in Weimar in 1919 amid the aftermath of World War I, this state-funded enterprise merged a design school and a fine art institution under a unified curriculum directed by architect Walter Gropius. Though over the first few years, the Bauhaus failed to establish a clear identity, with the hiring of the Hungarian émigré László Moholy-Nagy in 1923, the school adopted a focused constructivist mission. This new phase of the school was given a physical presence a few years later when the retrenched Bauhaus—the school was beset with political conflicts throughout its fourteen-year run—reopened in Dessau in a building designed by Gropius himself (figure 3.5). After its predictable closure by the National Socialist government in 1933, the impact of the Bauhaus actually accelerated, as its former students and professors fled Germany and resettled throughout the United States and Europe.

As members of one of the leading centers of experimental design thinking in the 1920s, several Bauhaus thinkers dedicated themselves to a consideration of type design and typography. As part of the emerging consensus of multiple like-minded designers, including El Lissitzky, Jan Tschichold, Theo van Doesburg, and Paul Renner, Moholy-Nagy advocated on behalf of sans serif type as a marker of modernity. Synthesized with photography into a new format he christened "typophoto," Moholy-Nagy adopted the Bauhaus view that the simple geometric forms of the sans serif best expressed an urbane, industrial zeitgeist. In Bauhaus

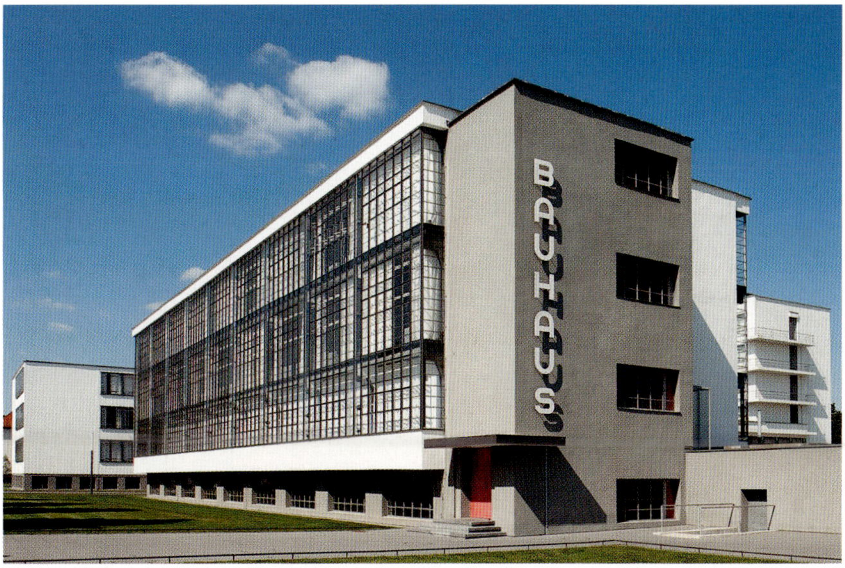

3.6. Herbert Bayer's Dessau Bauhaus signage, 1926

Book 8, *Painting, Photography, Film* (1925), he expounded on how the "flexibility and elasticity of these techniques bring with them a new reciprocity between economy and beauty."

Moholy-Nagy was a highly influential presence at the Bauhaus, and he found a ready collaborator in Herbert Bayer, a former Bauhaus graduate (1923) who became a jungmeister in 1925 and helped lead the advertising workshop that was formed when the school reopened in Dessau. In terms of type, Bayer devoted himself to a project he called "Research in Development of Universal Type," which resulted in several iterations of a decidedly geometric-looking lowercase alphabet (figure 3.6). With Universal, Bayer eschewed the approachable warmth of Johnston Sans, opting instead for a more futuristic version of the nascent machine aesthetic. Universal was always intended more as a statement than a mainstream typographic tool, and Bayer's eventual insistence on the elimination of "superfluous" uppercase lettering mixed utopianism with a leftist political edge because of majuscules' relative predominance in German orthography.

Outside the Bauhaus, two typographers with informal ties to the school—Jan Tschichold and Paul Renner—would prove essential to the spread of the reinvented sans serif of the 1920s. Tschichold was a tireless campaigner in favor of sans serif type and asymmetric typography during the late 1920s. While his name is most strongly credited with another catch-all term for this movement, the "new typography," that phrase had in fact also been coined by Moholy-Nagy. Tschichold published frequently, and his 1928 book *The New Typography* still stands as one of the best summaries of sans serif, typophoto design. Tschichold called for modern type that rejected anything outside its core geometric form, and so sans serif "must become the basis for all future work to create the typeface of our age." From the standpoint of 2023, it is striking to review 1920s type theory and witness how easily one could adopt these texts—perhaps substituting "digital" for "machine" in a few instances—and produce design theory for today's internet industry.

Futura, "Die Schrift Unserer Zeit," was officially released in November 1927 by the Bauer foundry of Frankfurt (figure 3.7). Its designer, Paul Renner, had worked in the publishing industry for over two decades and had been recently inspired to engage with constructivism after viewing an exhibition of Bauhaus work. He conceptualized the project in much the same way that Johnston had for his eponymous type a decade before; like Johnston, Renner had a background in traditional type and a love of the structured majuscules of ancient Rome. Renner also lectured in academic settings and for the Deutscher Werkbund, while serving as a typography and commercial art instructor at the Frankfurter Kunstschule at the time he was commissioned to draw Futura. Frankfurt at the time was known for the aggressively modern styling of its newest buildings, a visual environment that surely also influenced Renner's design.

In contrast to the stark geometry of Bayer's Universal, Futura blended geometric fashion with humanist structure. In taking the same middle road as Johnston before him, Renner created the first sans serif typeface that broke into the mainstream. Partly because of the marketing might of Bauer and its ongoing commitment to expanding the Futura family, Renner's

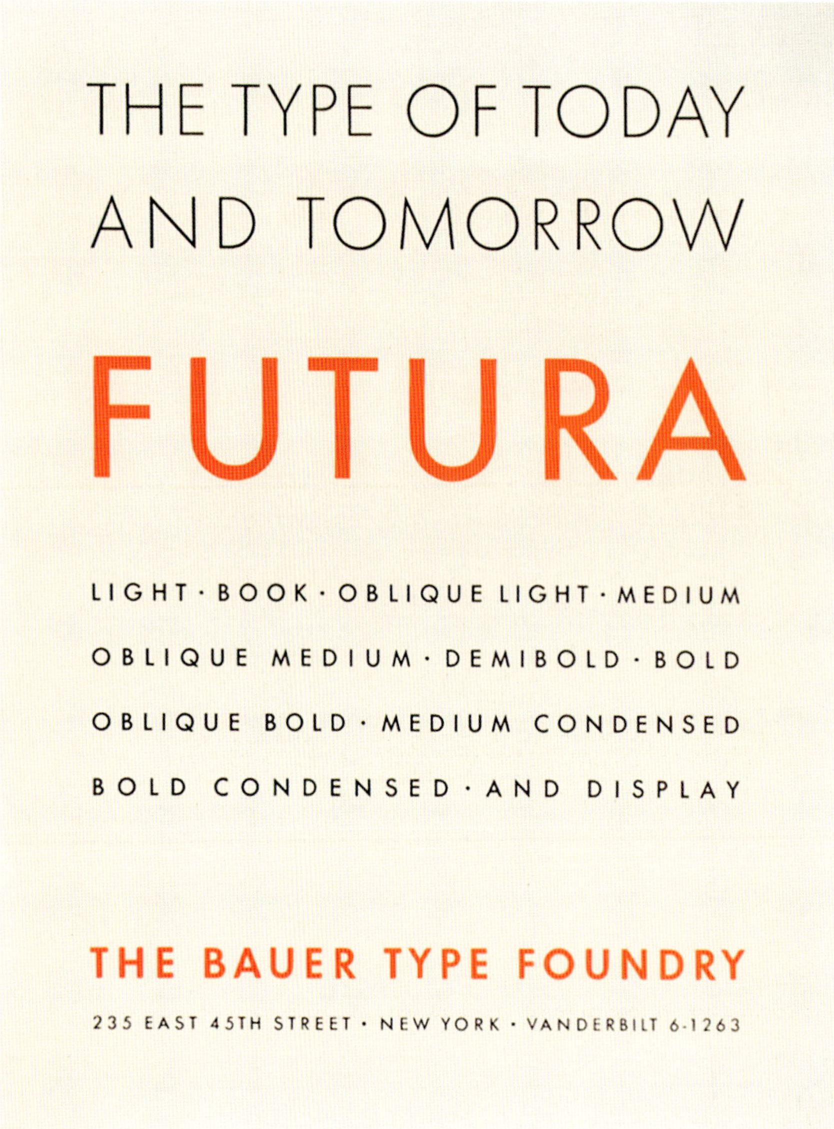

3.7. Paul Renner's Futura typeface, 1927

typeface quickly spread through international markets. While Johnston Sans languished as a house type that was not distributed effectively, Futura became the default type for typographers seeking a modern geometric look without the smell of radicalism.

Introduced in the United States in 1928, "The type of today and tomorrow" gradually built an American audience. As the scattered staff of the Bauhaus assembled themselves in new countries, Futura became associated in many people's minds with that institution. Bayer furthered this fusion in 1938, when he cocurated an exhibition on the closed design school at the Museum of Modern Art. To demonstrate how typography had been practiced at the Bauhaus, he designed a section of the exhibition catalog in lowercase Futura. Of course, Bayer's own Universal was not an actual typeface so was unavailable for the catalog. Still, this appropriation of Bauer's popular success was also exemplary of the depoliticized, business-friendly vision of the school that was promulgated by many European émigrés to the United States.

In the aftermath of World War II, sans serif type went mainstream for the first time. Beginning in Switzerland, and later spreading internationally, neutral-looking grotesques led by the decades-old German sans serif Akzidenz-Grotesk (marketed as Standard in the United States), became the preferred default for global capitalism. In the decades following the war, the sans serif was stripped of its 1920s association with revolutionary communism; in suppressing experimental modern styles in the thirties, Hitler and Stalin had inadvertently opened the door for a new interpretation of the form as signaling freedom and democracy. When foundries noticed the increasing adoption of Akzidenz-Grotesk, they responded in the 1950s by releasing new, similar-looking type-

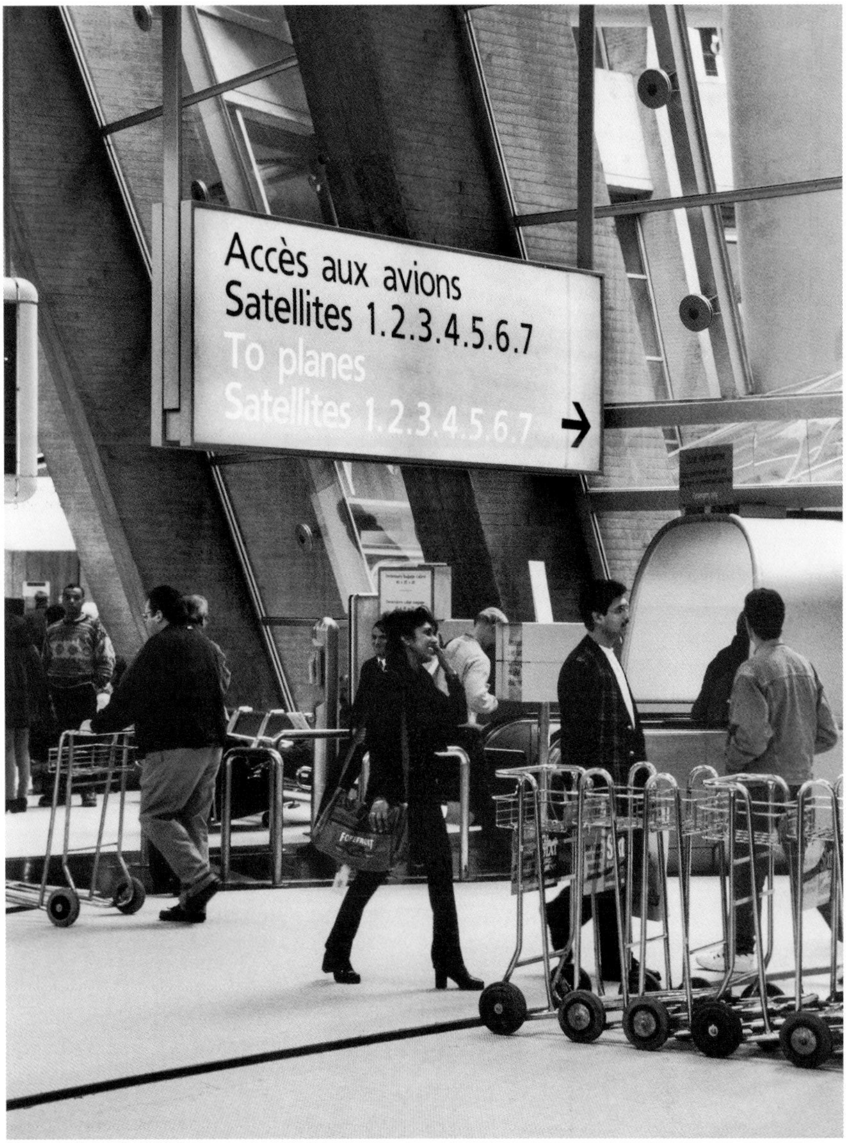

3.8. Frutiger typeface, first designed by Adrian Frutiger in 1968

faces punctuated by Deberny & Peignot's Univers (Adrian Frutiger, 1957) and Stempel's Helvetica (née Neue Haas Grotesk, 1956).

At this point in history, the sans serif's established meaning, as a marker of efficiency, clarity, and up-to-date technology, came to the fore. Additionally, the sans serif gained two new layers of signification that would serve it well in the digital age: banality and prosperity. First, the whole aesthetic of the renewed grotesques was one of dull understatement. Conjoined with a dollop of Swiss political neutrality, the form resonated, in a way, with nothing in particular but could serve as a blank slate for clear communication. As Microsoft related in 2018 regarding their choice of Segoe UI as the core textual element of their screen presence, the choice was for a typeface that had "no strong character or distracting quirkiness." Second, while much has been said about how postwar sans serifs contributed a feeling of stability and forward-thinking strategy to myriad corporate customers, few have considered the inverse: that decades of employment of the sans serif form by prosperous corporations that have strong, positive brand recognition helped the typefaces as much as it helped the clients. By the time digital type, cleansed of its radical history, became a major concern of big technology companies in the nineties, the form was perfectly situated to convey corporate success for a new generation of upstart companies.

While sans serif as a whole class has an outsize role in the digital age, the variant introduced by Johnston in 1916—a balance of humanist proportions and geometric styling—has come to dominate the field. In many ways the ur-type of the digital age is Frutiger (figure 3.8), an eponymous font released in 1976 by Stempel and Monotype. Like Johnston before him, Frutiger had originally created the typeface as a way-finding aid, and its nickname Roissy refers to the French airport for which it was first commissioned in 1968. It also proved a perfect match as the default type at the futuristic Charles de Gaulle airport, which supplanted Roissy in the midseventies. Like Johnston Sans, Frutiger née Roissy combines functional clarity, a contemporary feel, and warm approachability. Where Helvetica or Akzidenz-Grotesk might feel too boring, Frutiger found the perfect blend of desirable qualities while also benefiting from the overall strength of the sans serif brand. In 1988, Frutiger designed a second font of a similar character called Avenir. First released in Germany by Linotype, the name translates from the French as "future," which is both a nod toward its contemporary styling and an acknowledgment of its lineage through to Renner's influential font of the 1920s.

"Bauhaus" in the United States

All the vagaries of modernist type design over the decades have been collapsed into an abstraction that contemporary designers tend to call "Bauhaus." All the politics, the eccentric experiments, the half-truths and human foibles were elided as the modern movement was pushed through an alembic and came out clean and new. There are many players in this story, but one notable site for this transformation was at the Massachusetts Institute of Technology (MIT)

Importantly, MIT housed a critical mass of computer programmers, architects, and designers with an experimental, collaborative mindset. One of the key figures at MIT during this era of emerging technology was Muriel Cooper, a graphic designer and an educator who influenced digital design in myriad ways. Cooper first came to MIT in the fifties as an in-house designer for the university's Publications Department. Then, in 1962, the university moved to rebrand its technical publishing division into the newly established MIT Press, which broadened its scope to include less-technical works. Cooper soon became the design director at MIT Press, where she worked with the editorial staff to produce a design-centric list.

The design culture at MIT and MIT Press quickly coalesced around the increasingly fashionable theories that had first been promulgated in the 1920s at the Bauhaus. One key figure in this regard was the experimental artist Gyorgy Kepes—cofounder of the New Bauhaus in Chicago with his fellow Hungarian émigré László Moholy-Nagy in 1937—who joined MIT in 1945 as its first faculty artist. Over the next few decades, Kepes would help establish a Bauhaus-derived culture (although he had never attended the German school himself) whereby there was a fluid interaction between experimental artistic projects and more practical, technical research. Kepes's own hybrid photographic and film-based montages inspired a generation of designers at MIT, where his students included digital luminaries such as Nicholas Negroponte. The Hungarian artist eventually founded the new Center for Advanced Visual Studies at MIT in 1967, which was a vital site for collaborative research into art and technology. Also during this era, Bauhaus founder Walter Gropius was working right down the street as a professor of architecture at Harvard, while his firm, The Architects Collaborative, was highly active in Boston. Taken together, MIT now seemed destined to become one of the key conduits whereby Bauhaus DNA ended up embedded in the digital realm, which helps to elucidate how today's references to Bauhaus simplicity have perhaps

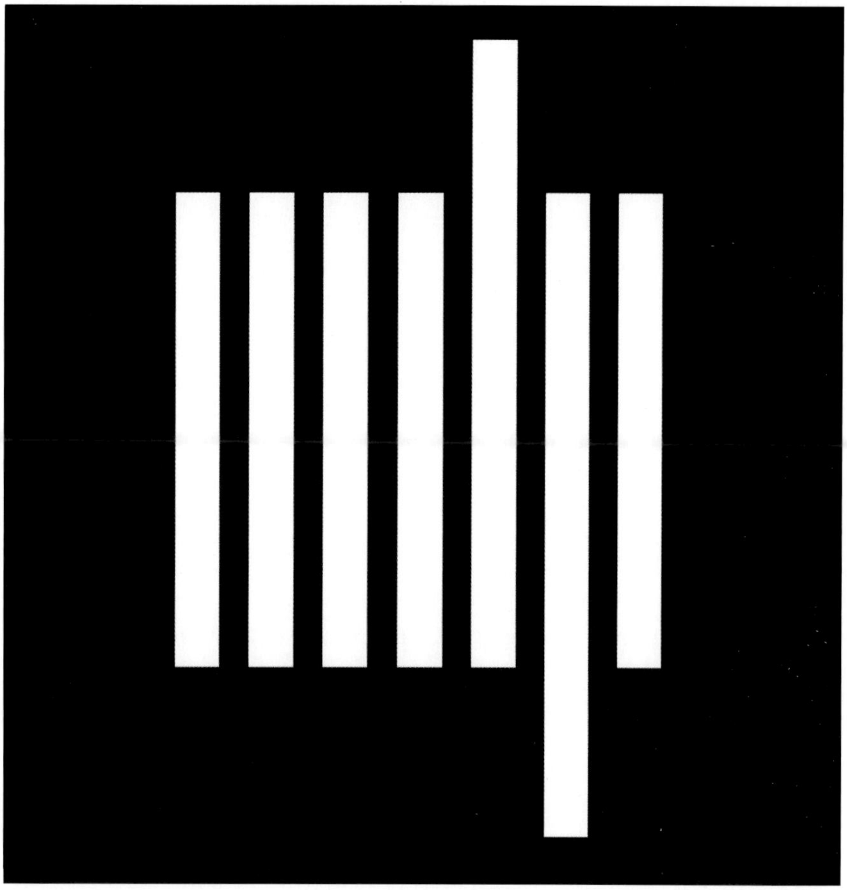

3.9. MIT Press colophon, designed by Muriel Cooper in 1964

become an overused trope of technology workers.

At MIT Press, Cooper had a significant role in nurturing this accelerating Bauhaus culture. In 1969, she oversaw the design of perhaps the most consequential book ever published on the school, *Bauhaus: Weimar, Dessau, Berlin, Chicago*, an epic tome by Hans Wingler, founder of the Bauhaus Archive, which has done so much to sustain the memory of the school. Wingler's book—a translation of the original German version of 1962—was copiously illustrated with a comprehensive array of period documents and photographs. Cooper designed the book using staunch modernist principles, and the layouts show her employment of core facets of the style including grids, dynamic asymmetry, and an understanding of the interaction of positive and negative space. Likewise, the book is set in Helvetica, and most pages feature only two weights, a hallmark of constructivist, and later Swiss, styling. *Bauhaus* was typeset using the Linofilm system, part of the predigital era during which phototypesetting had displaced metal type at the forefront of technology.

Cooper also demonstrated her skill at Bauhaus design thinking in her creation of the MIT Press colophon (figure 3.9). This elegant mark is still in use today, its seven bars arguably the most visible brand of the university. Most viewers do not realize that it is an abstract logotype, as Cooper expertly distilled the four letters "mitp" into seven vertical strokes with the only identifiers being the ascender of the letter t and the descender of the letter p. Of course, sans type would continue to anchor "Bauhaus" design as it was reformulated in the digital age.

Sans System Fonts

As the two dominant companies Apple and Microsoft continued to refine their interfaces in the nineties, neither developed a totally coherent strategy for type. As in the early years of the Bauhaus, what visual strategy would come to the fore was not entirely clear. (Of course, as noted above, Macintosh computers as a tool for designing and setting type were far superior to the Windows environment, a fact that affected users' perceptions of the companies' system fonts.) During the nineties, Apple continued to use versions of Susan Kare's original Chicago typeface as its default screen font, until 1997, when it shifted to another sans serif, called Charcoal. At the same time, in print and packaging applications, Apple was wedded to a serifed face called Apple Garamond, a narrower version of the classic roman type. As a comprehensive identity, Chicago, Charcoal, and Garamond made little sense together.

Microsoft meanwhile had its own problems, as the company became strongly identified in the nineties with the Helvetica clone Arial, which was the primary default typeface for its multiple software programs beginning with the release of Windows 3.1 in 1992. Arial had been designed by Monotype for IBM laser printers as a way of sidestepping royalties on Helvetica when printing with PostScript. Despite Apple's shortcomings, it profited—even in the lean years before Steve Jobs returned in 1997—from the resulting perception that its rival was design averse, a view that dated back to the uninspired design of the IBM PC and its DOS command-line operating system.

Not until the turn of the twenty-first century did the tech titans' system fonts seem to coalesce around the sans serif in a more orderly fashion. At that time Apple replaced the somewhat idiosyncratic Charcoal with Lucida Grande, a new variant of the pioneering font by Bigelow and Holmes. As the text basis of the MacOS GUI, Lucida Grande had been tweaked to perform well on screens even at small sizes. A couple of years later, Apple shifted to a complementary type style for its print and packaging, choosing a variant of Myriad (Carol Twombly and Robert Slimbach, 1992), a humanist sans serif that had been part of the Adobe Originals project. A close simulacrum of Frutiger, Myriad combines humanist proportions with a certain understated geometric flair. In 2014, Apple abruptly, perhaps inexplicably, shifted to Helvetica Neue Light (a 1983 update of Helvetica), then regular Helvetica Neue, despite designers' complaints that neither variant worked well on screens at small sizes because of confusable characters such as the lowercase i and l. Finally, in 2015, Apple announced a new house typeface called San Francisco, aka SF, the name a nod toward Kare's bitmapped fonts for the original Macintosh. San Francisco is a touch more legible than Helvetica, especially its compact version, which is displayed in very small sizes on its first interface, the Apple Watch (figure 3.10). More importantly, SF combines a blend of "friendliness," versatile functionality, and geometric stylishness. One aside: in a notorious breach of Apple's vaunted design-forward branding, in 2001 Steve Jobs appeared before a Silicon Valley audience to present the company's new iPod digital music player; behind him, a slideshow unrolled set in—gasp!—a clone of Comic Sans, the ubiquitous type that designers for decades have loved to hate.

Microsoft went through a similar disjointed trajectory in the employment of type only to end up at roughly the same place as Apple. In 2001, Microsoft adopted Mathew Carter's Tahoma, a close relative of his earlier Verdana, as the default screen font, mainly in a bid to banish Arial once and for all. Then, starting with Windows Vista in 2004, Microsoft started implementing Segoe and Segoe UI, two fonts designed by Steve Matteson of Monotype. Segoe is a branding typeface used mainly for print, while Segoe UI became the mainstay of the GUI. Microsoft designers have noted, "Segoe UI is an approachable, open, and friendly typeface, and as a result has better readability than Tahoma, Microsoft Sans Serif, and Arial." This statement confirms the trend, while adding an interesting twist to the normal sense of "readability," as it astutely posits that

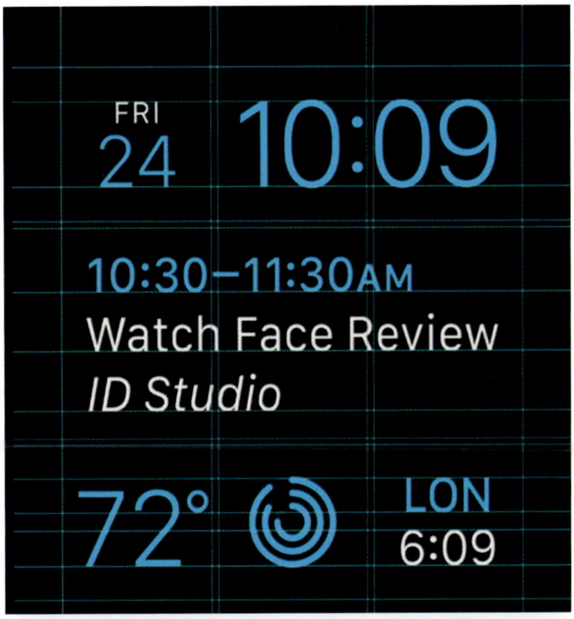

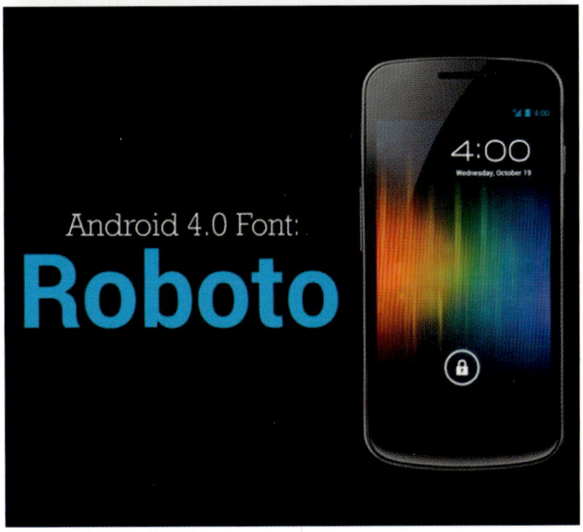

3.10. Apple Computer's San Francisco typeface, 2015
3.11. Christian Robertson's Roboto typeface, 2011

an emotional connection to the typeface may well facilitate its functionality.

Rounding out this set of the most influential screen presences, Google has also instituted a humanist sans serif as its main system font. Designed in-house by Christian Robertson and called Roboto (figure 3.11), in 2011 it was implemented across the platform. In line with the comments of Apple's and Microsoft's designers, Google's Matias Duarte has described this humanist sans serif as "modern, yet approachable" and "emotional." San Francisco, Segoe UI, and Roboto taken together attest to the continuity between the typographic forms developed a century ago and the mainstay fonts of the digital present. As of late, designers have taken to referring to this preponderance of neutral typefaces in the corporate realm as exemplary of so-called blanding. Like branding but without any personality, the carefully titrated blandness of "Bauhaus" type design has come to permeate the design fabric. Show me a digital design studio and I will show you a set of Barcelona chairs! One wonders if this homogeneity will ever be overturned, as great talent and wealth has been directed into nuanced variations that to most users must appear invisible or irrelevant.

In 2020, the eminent graphic designer Cheryl Miller shared a stunning insight about so-called Bauhaus design that identified it as anything but bland. Speaking at a 2020 conference hosted by the Illinois Institute of Technology (IIT) Institute of Design—a Chicago bastion of Bauhaus design whose faculty included at one time László Moholy-Nagy and Ludwig Mies van der Rohe—Miller argued that for her, the modernist style was an oppressive symbol. She recounted her words later for *Print* magazine: "'Take down the Paul Rand look,' I said. 'It's my confederate flag, my confederate statue.' The Helvetica, flush-left, rag-right grid bearing

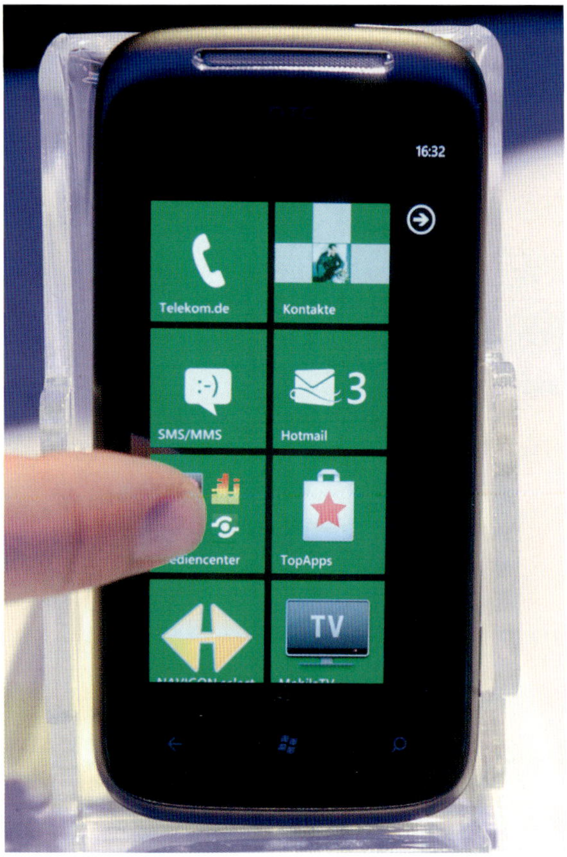

3.12. Microsoft's flat design shown on a Windows Phone, 2010

white space all around the page was the look of the oppressor. If you were a Black designer back in the day and you wanted to be employed by one of the established elite studios, well, good luck with that. The Swiss Grid system and Helvetica were the white male's design gospel. The look screamed in my memory bank, you don't belong here; even if you can design like us, we don't want you! Every time I see 'the look,' I feel the oppressor on my neck."

Miller was speaking at a virtual conference organized by IIT professor Chris Rudd called "The Future Must Be Different from the Past: Embracing an Anti-racist Agenda." Over the past few years tremendous attention and energy have been devoted to the cause of bringing more BIPOC designers into the field. In terms of big tech, much of the emphasis has been on funding; together, Google, Apple and Microsoft, and Netflix have pledged over a billion dollars in various streams designed to help diversify the industry. So far, these companies' self-assessments have not really broken through into the digital design realms they dominate. Despite Miller's protestations, the notion that the Bauhaus style is apolitical best practice has held on, bearing in mind that change can come abruptly in an industry that stakes much of its identity on disrupting norms.

Flat and Material Design

The evolution of the overall GUI designs has roughly traced that of the typefaces, as references to the Bauhaus and its progeny like the Swiss style of typography continue to abound in design-related press releases issued by big technology. Once the desktop and window metaphors had become pervasive, GUIs for the most part remained static outside refinements of the details. Clarity, functionality, and friendliness remain the goal. Also, type has come to play a larger role on the GUI, as realistic, skeuomorphic images have fallen out of favor because they diminish the sleek forms of the digital aesthetic.

The driver for UI in the last decade has often been mobile. As users shift to small portable screens, type legibility at tiny sizes and minimalist imagery have come to the fore. Despite Microsoft's long-established reputation as the "arbiter of uncool," it has at times led the way in this most recent phase of design innovation for GUIs. Microsoft started the trend around 2010 with the release of its smartphone operating system Windows Phone. Gone were not only the skeuomorphic icons, but many three-dimensional design elements such as shadows, gradients, and reflectivity. Microsoft called this new look Metro, but the name was later

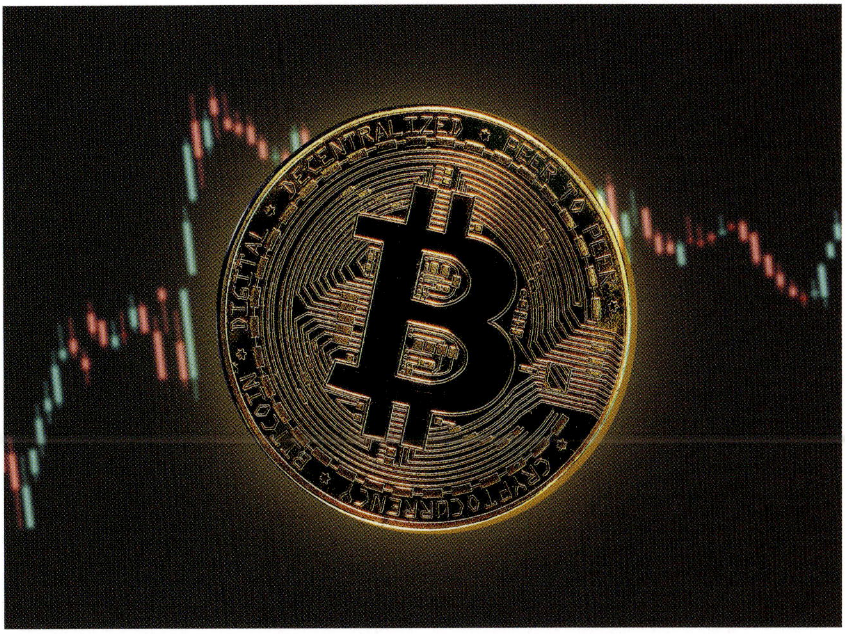

3.13. Bitcoin stock image, 2009

banished for a new term, "flat design" (figure 3.12). Apple has also embraced flat design, with the boldest implementation beginning with 2013's iOS 7 release.

The concept behind flat design is another modernist trope: the idea that a medium should be true to itself, so the digital should look organically digital at all times. Just as modernist painters of the late nineteenth century began disregarding linear perspective and emphasizing the two-dimensional qualities of a flat surface, so today's screen designers seek to remove "false" three-dimensionality and realistic icons. Skeuomorphism has not entirely disappeared from the digital interface, but it has been suppressed by flat design; at the same time, type has become more important, as tiles and icons become less recognizable, and the GUI user shifts to reading as opposed to looking. Take, for example, Instagram's 2016 reset of their original app icon, which had been introduced in the far-off age of 2010. That original glyph was pure skeuomorphism, showing a small camera that looked like a squarish relic of the seventies. A liberal use of gradients made it appear three-dimensional, as did complex reflections off the lens and flash. The 2016 replacement seemed intended as an abstraction of the first icon, but it truly bears no resemblance to a camera whatsoever; the lens is a circle, and the flash is a round dot not located anywhere near where an actual flash would appear. The flat background of a diffuse cloud of colors has no gradients. The lack of a monogram or reasonable facsimile of a camera makes the icon confusing amid the sea of like-minded flat designs on the average phone.

Legendary video game designer Chris Crawford recently felt compelled to address the functionality of complex abstract interfaces such as those used in flat design. Crawford opined that he had always relied on the intuitive nature of software designed for the Macintosh and felt discouraged by Apple's and other's current offerings. "Back in the twentieth century (oh, so long ago!), we used terms like 'user friendliness' and 'intuitive user interfaces.' Those concepts have been abandoned. The Mac reeks with a huge array of hidden verbs. A good rule of the Mac UI is, 'When in doubt, right-click on everything.' You'd be amazed at the discoveries you'll make." Crawford also cited the browser Firefox in a 2019 rant, frustrated that its user interface relied on small icons that lacked affordances. "Here's my interpretation, from left to right: ellipsis: must be something more / shielded chevron: something below? / star: who knows? / books on a bookshelf: a library? / thingamajig: who knows? / person: somebody / railroad tracks: who knows? / three bars: who knows?... Now, these sub-icons do not in any manner suggest their true meaning. They might as well be hieroglyphs." The point should also be made that abstract icons versus skeuomorphic ones can inadvertently worsen digital inequities, especially between younger and older users. The interaction with the machine becomes much less intuitive based on analog affordances.

In contrast to flat design and its brethren, one trend in the digital world that points to the continuing vigor of skeuomorphism is the representation of the cryptocurrency Bitcoin. The virtual blockchain currency first emerged in 2009

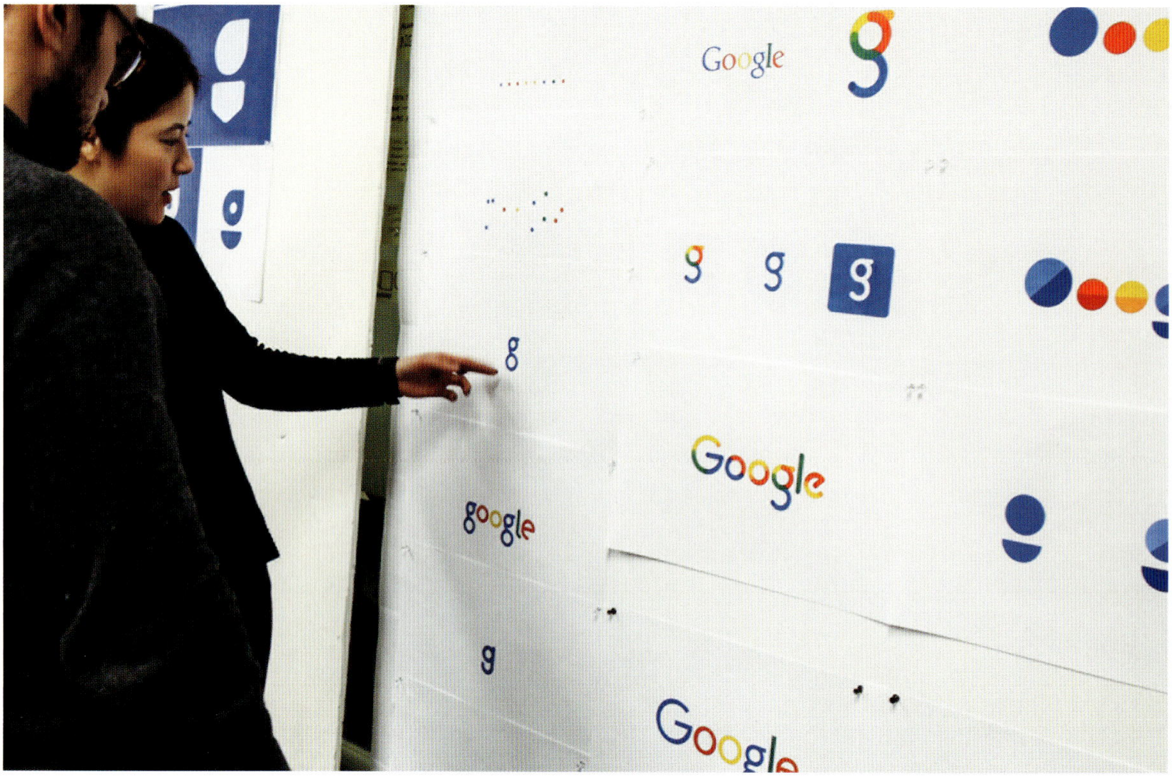

3.14. Google's corporate identity design, 2015

and over the last decade has become a worldwide phenomenon. Satoshi Nakamoto, one of the Bitcoin pioneers, is said to have created the currency's first symbol, a letter B with a pair of vertical bars top and bottom. Presumably, the bars were intended to provide a familiar reference, as they invoke the double crossbars of the Euro symbol. In recent years, this initial line drawing has been adapted by myriad sources into a slew of stock-photo variants in which the B is cast into a metal coin (figure 3.13). More elaborate versions of this phenomenon add what looks like an engraved microchip in the background. Going one step further, the coins in these pictures are always gold and weighty looking, as if one had grabbed a handful of gold doubloons.

There is clearly a hunger among people to think of Bitcoin as something tangible and relatable via skeuomorphism. While it might be okay to take one's photos with an abstract glyph, when it comes to people's finances, a natural insecurity seems to be at work. Conceptually, this imagery is reminiscent of the situation that arose with the architecture of banks during the height of the modernist 1950s. When Skidmore, Owings, and Merrill designed a new 5th Avenue showplace out of steel and glass—it looked immaterial, even ethereal, compared to classic stone designs—for Manufacturers Hanover in 1954, they put a massive steel bank vault right up against the first-floor windows. In this manner, consumers were reassured that their money was safe and secure despite the seemingly fragile architecture. Considering the huge sums of Bitcoin stolen in computer hacking attacks, it may take more than a picture of pirate treasure to convince most people that their virtual currency is real and safe.

In the last few years, Google has joined Apple, Adobe, and Microsoft as the preeminent trendsetter in digital navigation. With the creation of the open source type resource Google Fonts in 2010, the search giant became a major player in graphic design. This new alignment is clear after the 2016 joint announcement—by Adobe, Apple, Google, and Microsoft—of "variable fonts," a format through which a single font file will be extensible and customizable for any application.

Of the influential big technology companies, only Google has chosen to go somewhat against the flat design grain by emphasizing what it calls "material design." The latter is an aesthetic that, contrarily, draws its inspiration from ink on paper. Returning to the metaphor-based UI of the desktop age, material design emphasizes realistic visual cues while imagining the background of the UI as a sheet of paper, thus allowing for shadowing and the like. While ostensibly rejecting the flat aesthetic, most material design–era graphics share much of the same minimalist DNA.

In 2015, Google introduced a new comprehensive corporate identity complete with a typeface, logotype, monogram, and animated glyph (figure 3.14). In line with the other technological powerhouses, the company touted its "friendly, and approachable" style anchored by a sleek-looking geometric font. Keeping the multicolor palette that was one of its strongest brand visuals, the three facets of the new design work together seamlessly. The monogram G is a simple, clear app marker, while the longer logotype presides over the familiar search page. The four animated dots, however, are probably the most functionally elegant part of the design. Google had stated that they wanted to avoid animation for its own sake, and the solution here was to set the dots in motion only as an indicator of interaction; different patterns suggest working, listening, replying, and so forth. Channeling the perky responses of digital assistants through abstract animation, the four dots create an emotional connection with the user.

While Google's 2015 redesign had much to admire, the introduction of yet another custom geometric, humanist sans serif was not the high point. Indicative of the homogeneity that has beset the digital ecosystem, the typeface is as undistinguished as its name, Product Sans. Design writer Armin Vit has articulated the frustrations of many regarding this trend: "The new custom typeface is such a mash-up of every other sans serif out there that it's really hard to care that they made a new type family that looks like a dozen other typefaces. It's nice and everything but I think we have done every possible humanist-slash-geometric sans serif possible."

It is compelling to compare the virtual way finding of the Google brand interface with the physical one that appeared one hundred years earlier in the London Underground. While the most obvious connection exists in how Product Sans invokes the geometric/humanist balance pioneered by Edward Johnston, there are other corollaries as well. Under Frank Pick, the Underground glyph known as the roundel was modernized (also by Johnston) to look lighter and to coordinate visually with the new typeface. Taken together, the word Underground functioned as a logotype, while the roundel served as a monogram, much like the relationship between Google and the abbreviated G. Finally, you have the interactive dots; while the main interaction in the physical realm of the Underground was in taking the train, the cognitive equivalent was planning one's trip through a perusal of the famous 1931 station diagram. The final piece in the Underground puzzle, this geometrically styled route map was designed by an engineering draftsman named Harry Beck. Based on circuit diagrams, the Beck map made a bewilderingly complex system much easier to understand and navigate. In a foreshadowing of the dancing dots that indicate a solution to one's query is moments away, the Beck interface used a minimalist, material design to provide users with a friendly, approachable mediator.

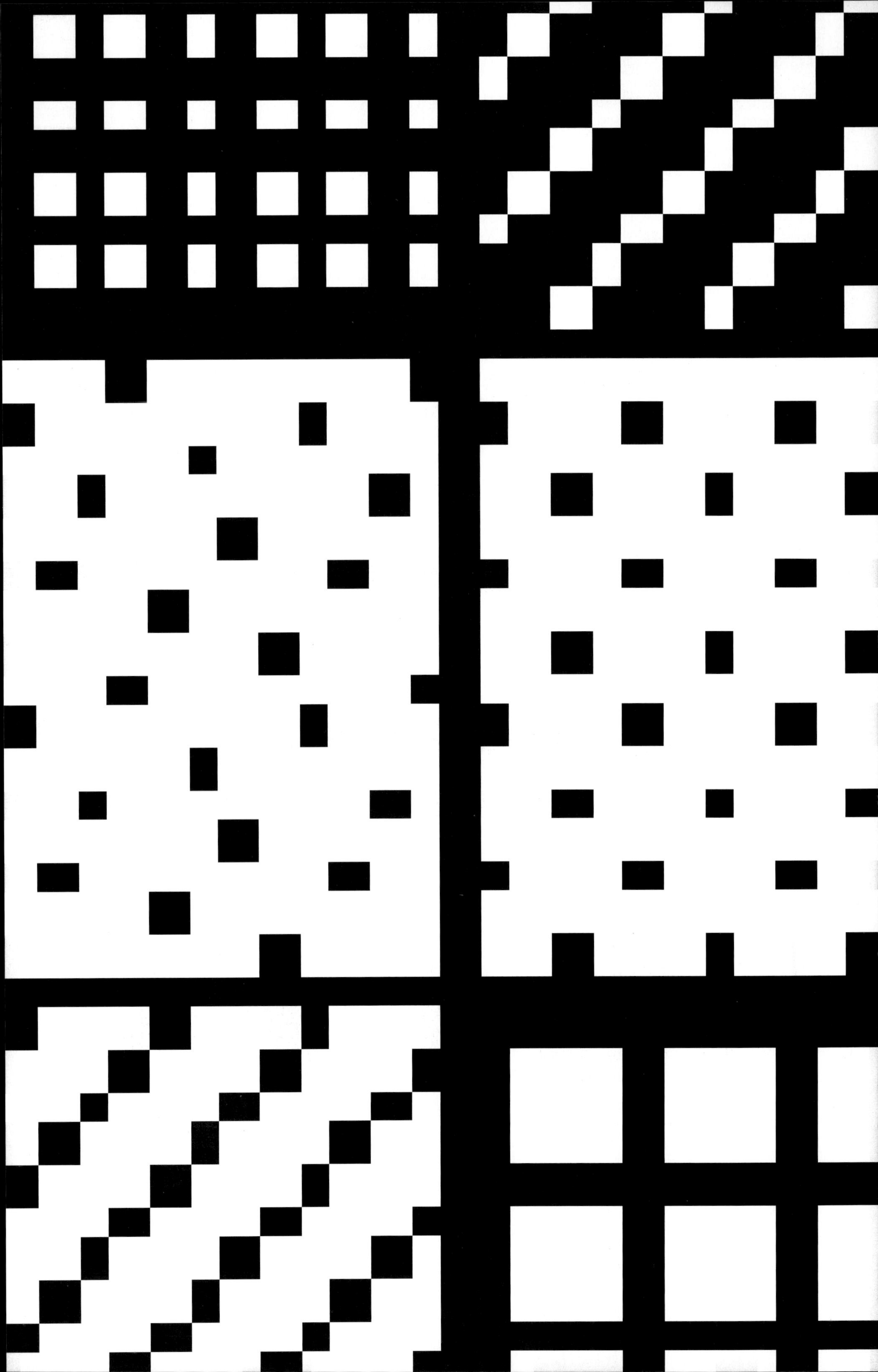

4.1. Muriel Cooper and Visible Language Workshop, *Digital Landscape*, 1985

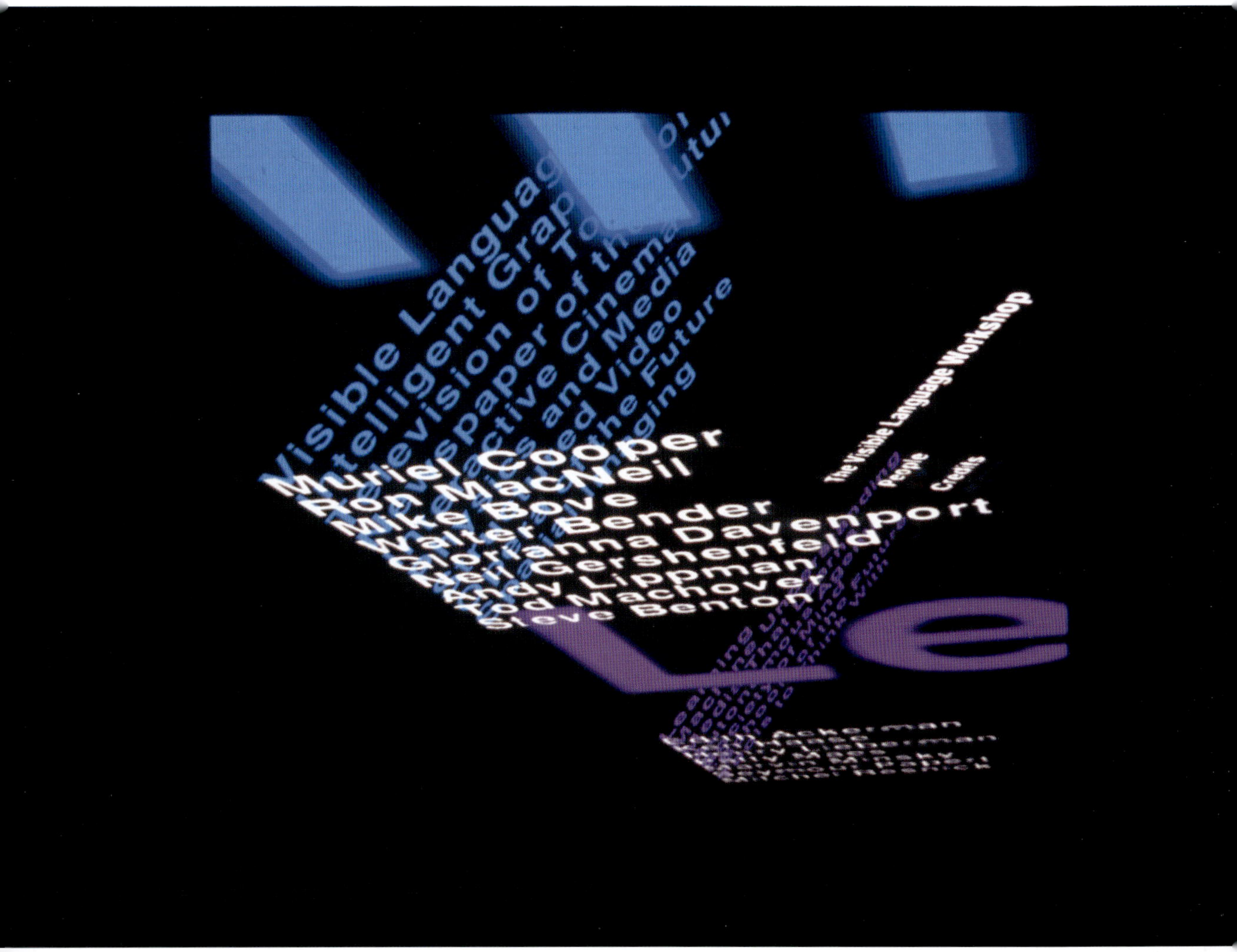

Four. Games and Experiments

While certain parts of digital design history display a crisp trajectory in hindsight—the development of the Apple Macintosh, for example—many significant developments emerged provisionally on the margins of digital culture. Experimental work that was never brought to market has also had a significant impact on the digital realm. Academic research, abstract film, even concert lighting have all contributed to digital culture and are worth examining; in contrast to these somewhat hidden topics, this chapter also considers video games, which have had an immense and acknowledged role in the center of human–computer interaction (HCI).

Muriel Cooper had been instrumental in promoting Bauhaus culture during her first tenure at MIT as a designer (see chapter 3). But during her second career there as a design instructor—she had left the school for a few years in the seventies—Cooper had another, greater impact on digital design. In 1975 she cofounded the Visible Language Workshop (VLW) at MIT and, as director, made it a center for courses and research in graphic design. At the VLW, Cooper espoused a blend of Bauhaus-derived design principles and an embrace of technological futurism. While there was a strong emphasis on technical skills, Cooper significantly recognized that graphic design was changing, and the "information age" was going to require new forms of graphical displays. Cooper had previously taken a computer science course taught by Nicholas Negroponte at the university, and she was one of the first designers to understand that a new type of interactive encounter with text and images was going to be made possible by digital environments. At the VLW, Cooper over fifty years ago established a model that still reigns in big technology today.

In 1985, the Visible Language Workshop was merged into the newly established consortium of research labs at MIT called the Media Lab. For the next decade, Cooper guided her students in an investigation of dynamic and interactive displays of data that have proved to be some of the most important building blocks of digital interfaces. She imagined a digital matrix whereby text could be presented on screens, not in the two-dimensional linear format whereby one reads word after word in sequence. Instead, Cooper sought to create digital "landscapes" in which data could be organized in a much richer three-dimensional format (figure 4.1). Zooming in and out, choosing new sorting methods, inverting text: all of these now commonplace functions in contemporary apps and websites were delved into at MIT under Cooper's direction.

Since its founding in 1985, the MIT Media Lab has in multivalent ways been on the leading edge of digital technology and culture. One of those important threads has been the development of motion graphics, including both type (exemplified by Cooper's work at the VLW) and image. Part of the success of the Media Lab's digital projects can be attributed to the Bauhaus model of seeking synergies between technologists and artists. In the 1920s at the German design school, numerous artists—most notably two expressionist-minded painters, the Russian Wassily Kandinsky and the Swiss Paul Klee—had interacted with designers in a way that influenced each other's work. Of course, the interconnections between fine and applied art practices had been the raison d'être at the Bauhaus from its beginning.

In the nineties, this Bauhaus model of open communication between artist and technologist has been furthered by designers such as John Maeda, who conflated both streams into his digital work. Maeda had first matriculated at MIT in the eighties, when he received his bachelor's and master's degrees in computer science. While pursuing those degrees, he developed an interest in graphic design driven by Cooper's work at the Media Lab. Maeda next decided to pursue more artistic education, and he moved to Japan, where he studied art and design at the University of Tsukuba. These two interests came together in the nineties when he returned to MIT and subsequently founded the Aesthetics + Computation Group (ACG) as a research unit under the umbrella of the Media Lab. At the ACG, Maeda focused on interactive motion graphics (he used the term "reactive" at the time) that could serve as an expressive conduit between people.

The ability to both design computer code and theorize like an artist led Maeda to a project called Reactive Books, a planned set of five digital artist's books that each explored a different type of interaction. Like many artistically inclined technologists, Maeda felt that the standard keyboard-mouse-desktop GUI was restrictive, even boring, and sought to explore new avenues of HCI. The first digital book was called the *Reactive Square* (figure 4.2), and it features an obvious visual reference to the bold geometric graphics of the Russian avant-garde, including Kazimir Malevich and El Lissitzky. This first volume explored sound as a medium of HCI: with a microphone as the interface, speech would cause a black square to squirm and morph in response. Subsequent "books" explored typographic and time-based interactions. Note how the conceptual model of an artist's book was both literal—as the works consisted of actual printed books as well as software—and a relatable, skeuomorphic device, demystifying technology with a tangible object: after all, one can curl up with a book.

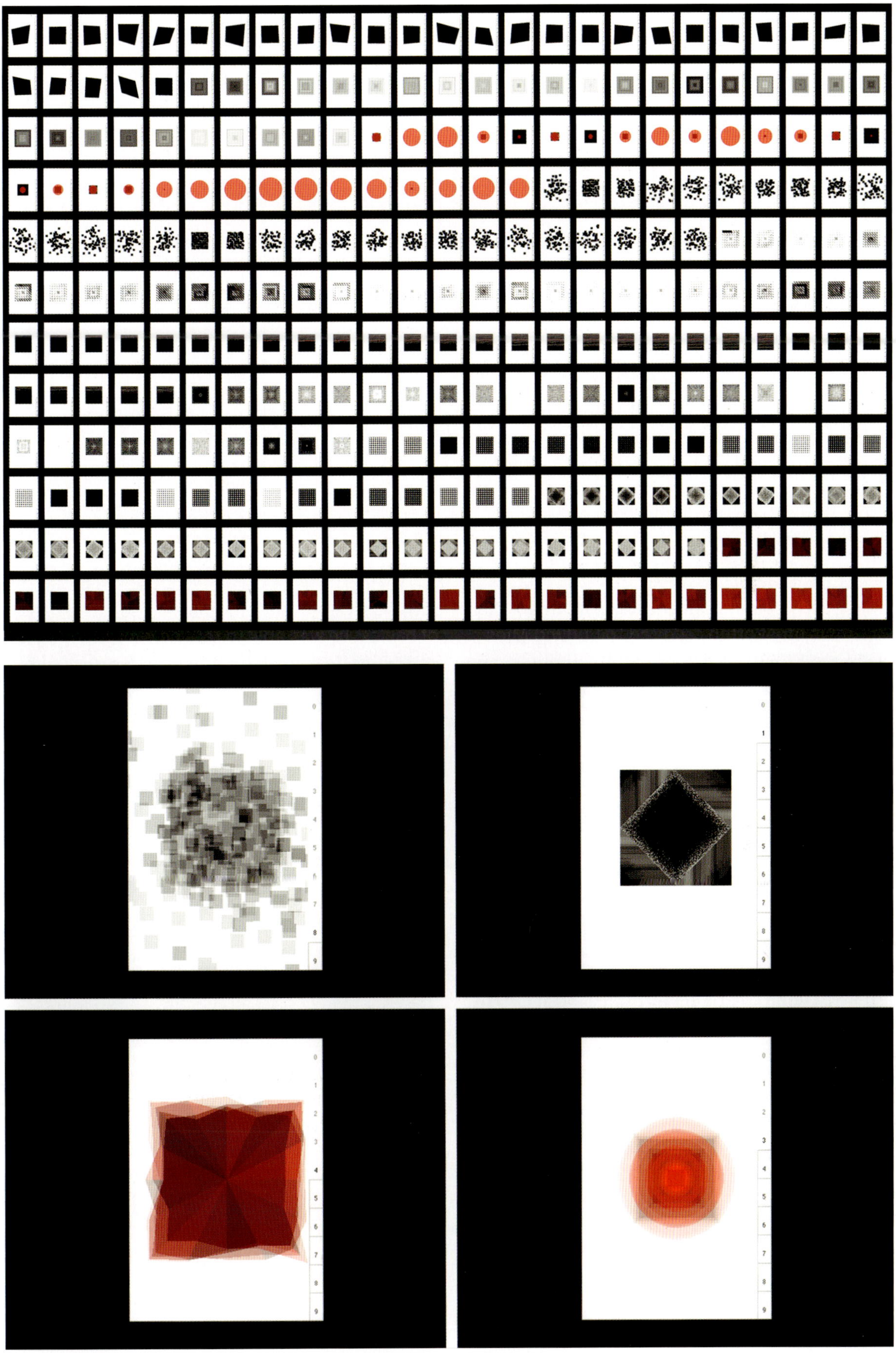

4.2. John Maeda, *Reactive Square*, 1994

At the MIT Media Lab, Maeda also became inculcated in the guiding ethos of the Bauhaus as it was reimagined in the American academy. Part of the American view of the Bauhaus was the notion that "less is more" was a guiding principle of modern design. This minimalist dictum is most often credited to Ludwig Mies van der Rohe, the last director of the Bauhaus, whose career blossomed exponentially in its postwar American incarnation. Note, however, that the historic Bauhaus of the 1920s by no means had adopted this sentiment with any finality. Of course, as part of the generalized rejection of ornamental styles, less was indeed more, but this belies the conceptual and practical complexity of so much of the 1920s experience there. Page through the photographic record in Hans Wingler's survey, and one is forced to reckon with a blizzard of hybrid projects, theatrical conceits, and conceptually obtuse experiments. Miesian purity represented just one of multiple avenues that had opened at the Bauhaus, but it was the one that his architectural practice embodied and that became communicated to American acolytes as the one true response to technology. Flowing through a Miesian alembic, the complexity of the Bauhaus was distilled in the academy, and thereafter, less is more became the canonical interpretation of the school—and of "modern"—carried forth by the technologists and financiers who would create contemporary digital culture.

Maeda's work has been an influential part of the construction of this thread; his 2006 bestseller, *The Laws of Simplicity* (MIT Press), espoused a process that has obvious roots in the American view of the Bauhaus. One telling anecdote: Maeda relates how he watched Wolfgang Weingart repeat the same introductory lecture to successive groups of students and that this diminished the typographer in Maeda's eyes. Next, however, Maeda had an epiphany: "I realized how although Weingart was saying the exact same thing, he was saying it simpler each time he said it. Through focusing on the basics of basics, he was able to reduce everything that he knew to the concentrated essence of what he wished to convey." Note that the process described here, whereby the interpretation of the Bauhaus was oversimplified, was an organic one; the next generation of technologists adopted minimalism not to emulate that process, but because the misconstruing of the Bauhaus was complete and invoking the name ties one's work to the singular avant-garde brand. In 2023, type "Bauhaus" and any technology brand into a search engine and the results will roll in. For Maeda, simplicity is a tool not an absolute, and the seventh law demonstrates how flexible the construct can be: "More emotions are better than less." In this fashion, Maeda anticipates what will become the dominant paradox of big technology: a desire to express both design purity and relatable human emotion.

Emerging Digital Graphics

Another experimental digital designer who combined a background in both art and computer science, Scott Snibbe, first developed his practice at Brown University, where he studied in the research lab led by Andy van Dam, the latter a noted pioneer in the realm of hypertext and computer graphics. An informal collaborator with denizens at the MIT Media Lab, Snibbe combined his coding skills with a commitment to the expressive power of abstract graphics. His invocation of analog precedents for digital culture—Snibbe has worked on his own

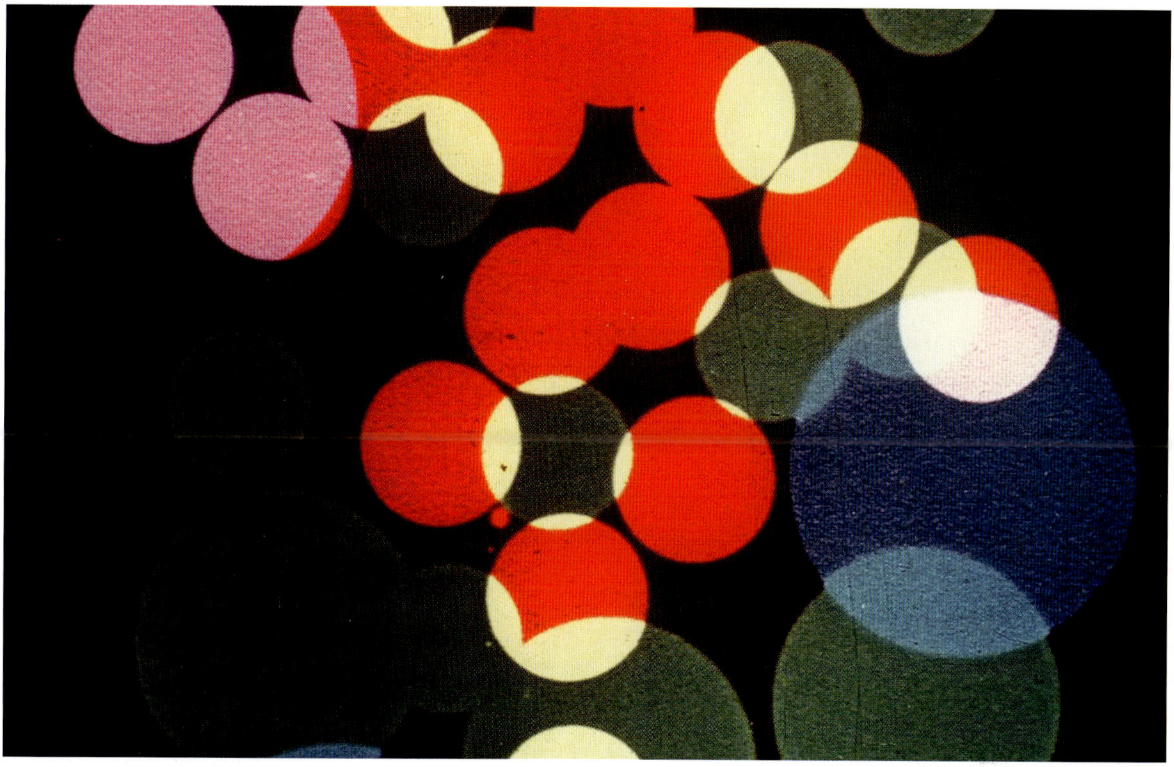

4.3. Oskar Fischinger, *Kreise*, 1933

experimental projects as well as Adobe's After Effects CGI software and Facebook's sound and music generators—raises the question of what the relationship is between predigital experiments in mobile color and the emergence of abstract HCI.

Over the course of the twentieth century, a substantial number of artists have sought to harness the emotional power of color and light through various techniques. Some artists, such as the Danish American Thomas Wilfred, built so-called color organs, which were essentially custom-made electro-mechanical machines that could manipulate colored light through lenses, filters, and light bulb filaments. While Wilfred achieved a certain renown in the 1920s, the restrictive, performative format of his concerts meant that the work was largely sidelined after the death of the artist. A more lasting format has proved to be abstract films, many of which have been conserved and collected so that excerpts are still screened in theaters and, of course, available on the internet.

Perhaps the most enduring precursors to digital color have been the animated films of Oskar Fischinger. Born in 1900, Fischinger had some early training in both music and mechanical engineering. In the 1920s, Fischinger turned to experimental animation and gradually built up his practice in Munich, producing abstract films that were screened across Europe and the United States. An acquaintance of Moholy-Nagy at the Bauhaus, Fischinger's aesthetic evolved in parallel to the constructivist embrace of geometry characteristic of that design university, with Kandinsky's paintings from that era providing perhaps the closest visual corollary. Fischinger continually adapted to new film technologies, first integrating sound after 1928, and next, color when it became available around 1933. In that year Fischinger gained access to the Gasparcolor system, a three-color process invented by Bela Gaspar, a Hungarian chemist.

As with many of today's digital designers, Fischinger's work bridged the artistic milieu and the strictly commercial one—for example, in his 1933 animated color short *Kreise* (Circles, figure 4.3). Per the title, *Kreise* features a kinetic array of pulsating dots and circles, which fly back and forth across the screen while occasionally plunging into space on the z-axis. The graphics are synchronized with a rousing orchestral score, which determines the velocity and rhythm of the dancing groups of circles. While *Kreise* at first appears to be strictly an artistic composition, in the final frames, a tagline appears: "Tolirag reaches all circles of society." Tolirag was an advertising agency that Fischinger collaborated with on a few projects, and *Kreise* is in fact a sophisticated example of the company's brand building. While of course there is no absolute binary contrast between art and commerce, it is refreshing to see such

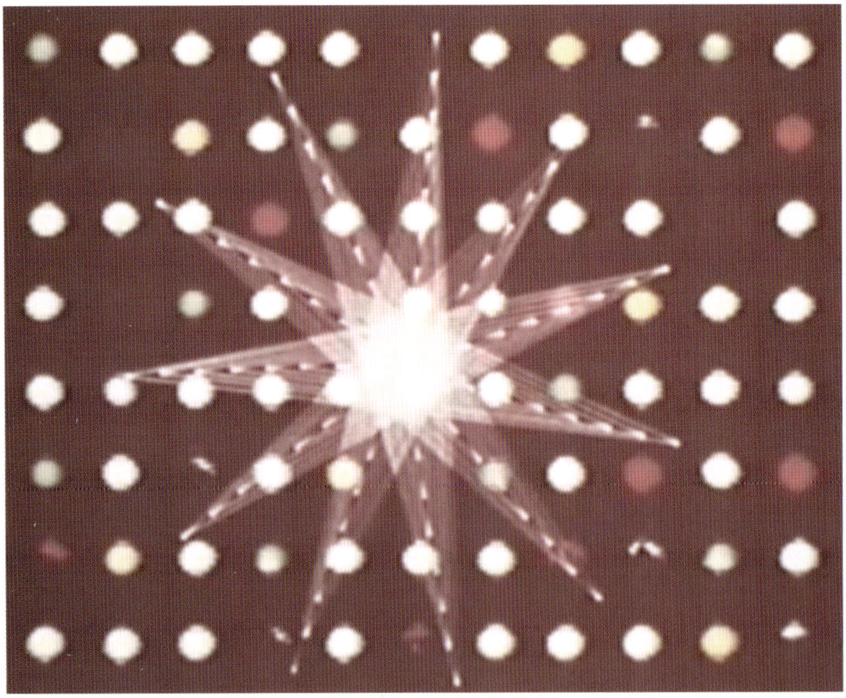

4.4. John Whitney, still from IBM S/360 film, 1966

integration in an era when most conventional abstract artists went to great lengths to separate their work from the vagaries of making a living in everyday life. Based on the success of a handful of like-minded works, Fischinger was enticed to move to Los Angeles in 1936 by the Paramount movie studio. For the rest of his career in the United States, Fischinger was never able to break through as either an artist or a designer despite a few small successes, including some work for Walt Disney. He continued to dabble in abstract color, constructing a color organ that he called the Lumigraph.

A second notable precursor to digital color came about because of the work of James and John Whitney, the latter also making the leap into the computer age. Born in California around 1920, the Whitney brothers developed a plethora of techniques with which to make abstract animated films. In the fifties they scavenged parts from vintage military hardware—an anti-aircraft system called the M5 Gun Director—to build an analog computer capable of producing psychedelic special effect and title sequences. This device was famously used to create the spiral animations designed by Saul Bass for Alfred Hitchcock's 1958 film *Vertigo*. That set of titles utilized Technicolor, the American rival to Gasparcolor until the US company purchased Gaspar's system.

Based on the success of his commercial work for the film industry, in 1960 John Whitney founded a computer animation company he called Motion Graphics Incorporated. After James Whitney left the business, John carried on his experiments in art and design: in 1966 IBM appointed him as their first artist-in-residence, giving him access to the S/360 mainframe on which Whitney made the first truly digital abstract film (figure 4.4). Until his death in 1995, John Whitney continued to produce abstract motion graphics, exploring an eclectic, even eccentric, range of psychedelic musical compositions. Like Fischinger before him, Whitney turned to the color organ model later in life, directing the design of a custom digital instrument in the eighties that brought this age-old dream of expressive color into the computer age. While neither Whitney nor Fischinger were ever integrated into the emerging computer graphic industry of the nineties, their work directly inspired a handful of subsequent strategies, while also diffusing into the digital atmosphere a reverence for abstract color.

Another facet of digital color came about through the music visualizers created by concert lighting designers over the past several decades. This field came of age amid the explosion of live rock music performances in the sixties. While dramatic stage lighting has a long history, the psychedelically inclined bands of a half century ago found that abstract color and light formed the perfect complement for their trippy, otherworldly sound. Bands such as Pink Floyd, the Grateful Dead, and Jefferson Airplane helped pioneer psychedelic stage lighting, whereby "liquid light" accompanied the music of the counterculture. A new generation of stage lighting experts arose to fill the demand, using labor-intensive analog technology, including hand-drawn transparencies, gels, and mechanical devices to produce varied effects.

Glenn McKay was one of the notable light designers of this era, using his skills as a painter to create a psychedelic atmosphere at the Fillmore, a legendary San Francisco music venue. McKay had been inspired by Tony Martin, one of the first artists to use splashed paints to create the hallucinatory liquid light that came to define the genre. Martin had also produced the light at the Trips Festival, a concert held at San Francisco's Longshoremen's Hall in January 1966 that is often thought of as a breakthrough moment for light shows. The Trips Festival also featured a dramatic poster by Wes Wilson, one of the group of designers who pioneered the psychedelic style in print. Overall, the music scene organically led to a novel visual culture, one in which the stage lighting created an immersive multimedia spectacle not unlike the one that today's virtual and augmented reality designers seek to provide.

With dramatic abstract stage lighting established as an expected part of the concert experience, digital technology first entered the scene more as a facilitator than as the generator of a new aesthetic. One of the designers who helped to transfer stage lighting into the digital age was Andi Watson. In the eighties, Watson, who was then studying electrical engineering and computer science at the University of Sussex, developed a sideline working as a lighting tech at small clubs. Watson was well acquainted with digital technology from his studies, which included building a microcomputer that used the legendary Motorola 68000 chip. (The 68k was a hybrid 16/32-bit semiconductor first released in 1980, which became famous because it was adopted for the Apple Macintosh in 1984. It then served for decades as a processing workhorse, laboring for decades behind the scenes in multiple computers, smart devices, and video game consoles.)

In the eighties, Watson's experience in both computers and lighting led him to a position with the Vari-Lite company, which had revolutionized concert lighting over the previous few years. Vari-Lite manufactured and managed the Vari-Lite system, the first computer-controlled concert lighting system. The founders of Vari-Lite, Rusty Brutsché and Jack Maxson, worked for years to automate and expand the illumination of live music performances. The breakthrough came in 1980, when they devised luminaires featuring dichroic filters, which enabled instantaneous color changes. Whereas spotlights had formerly required labor-intensive gel switches and refocusing by hand, these new lights could be controlled from afar. The addition of electric motors to move the lights in a synchronized dance added yet another dimension. Networked through computers, the Vari-Lite system debuted for a 1981 Genesis concert and soon became a staple of the touring business. Working as a Vari-Lite technician in the late eighties, Watson found that his skills diagnosing and fixing circuit boards were more important than any aesthetic ideas he had, as the system was built around several standard arrays and illuminated sequences.

After Watson left Vari-Lite to pursue his own projects, he eventually became the chief lighting designer for the British band Radiohead (figure 4.5). Reacting against the prevailing rock-star expectations, some of his early scenes for

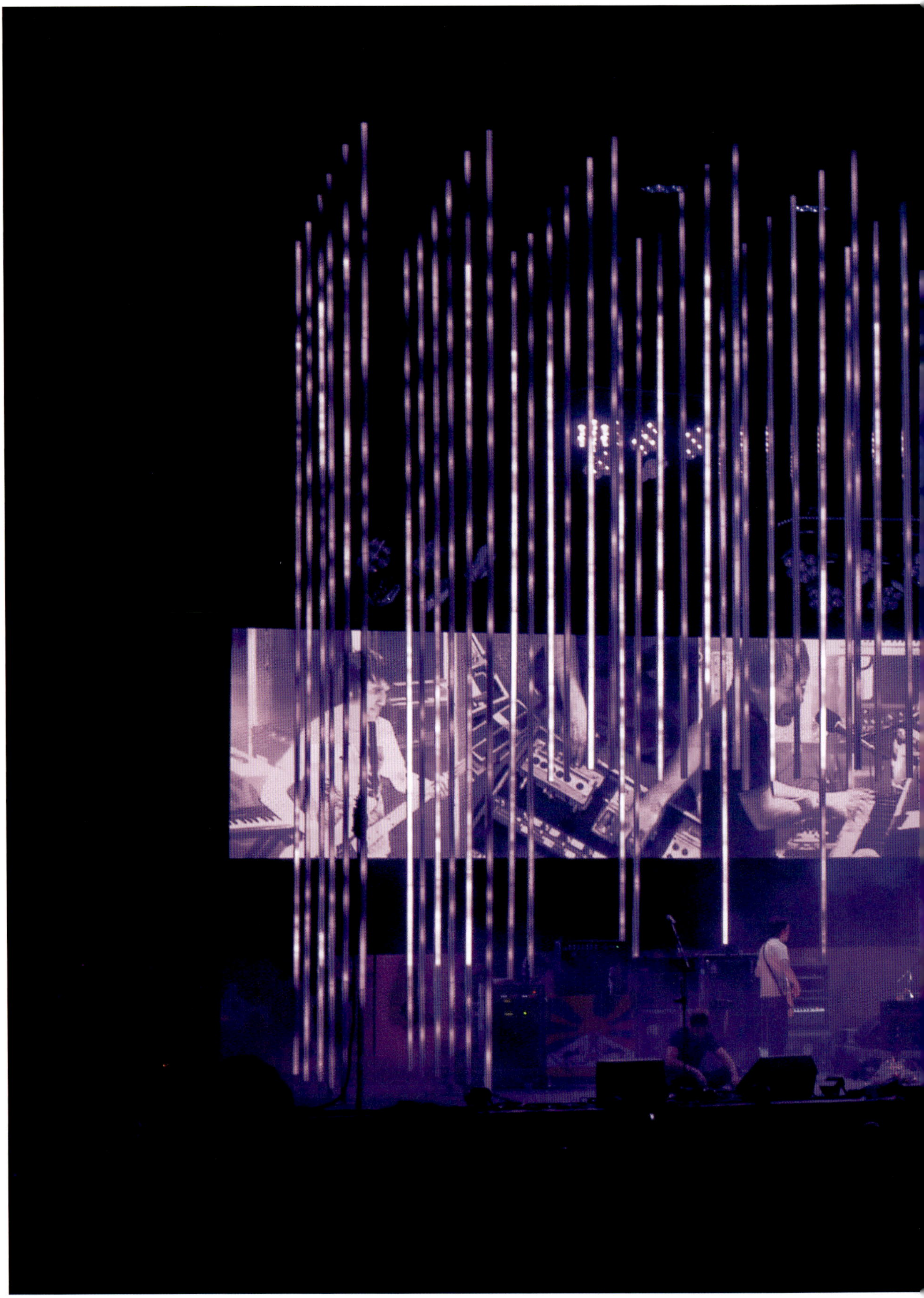

4.5. Andi Watson, lighting design for Radiohead's *A Moon Shaped Pool*, 2016

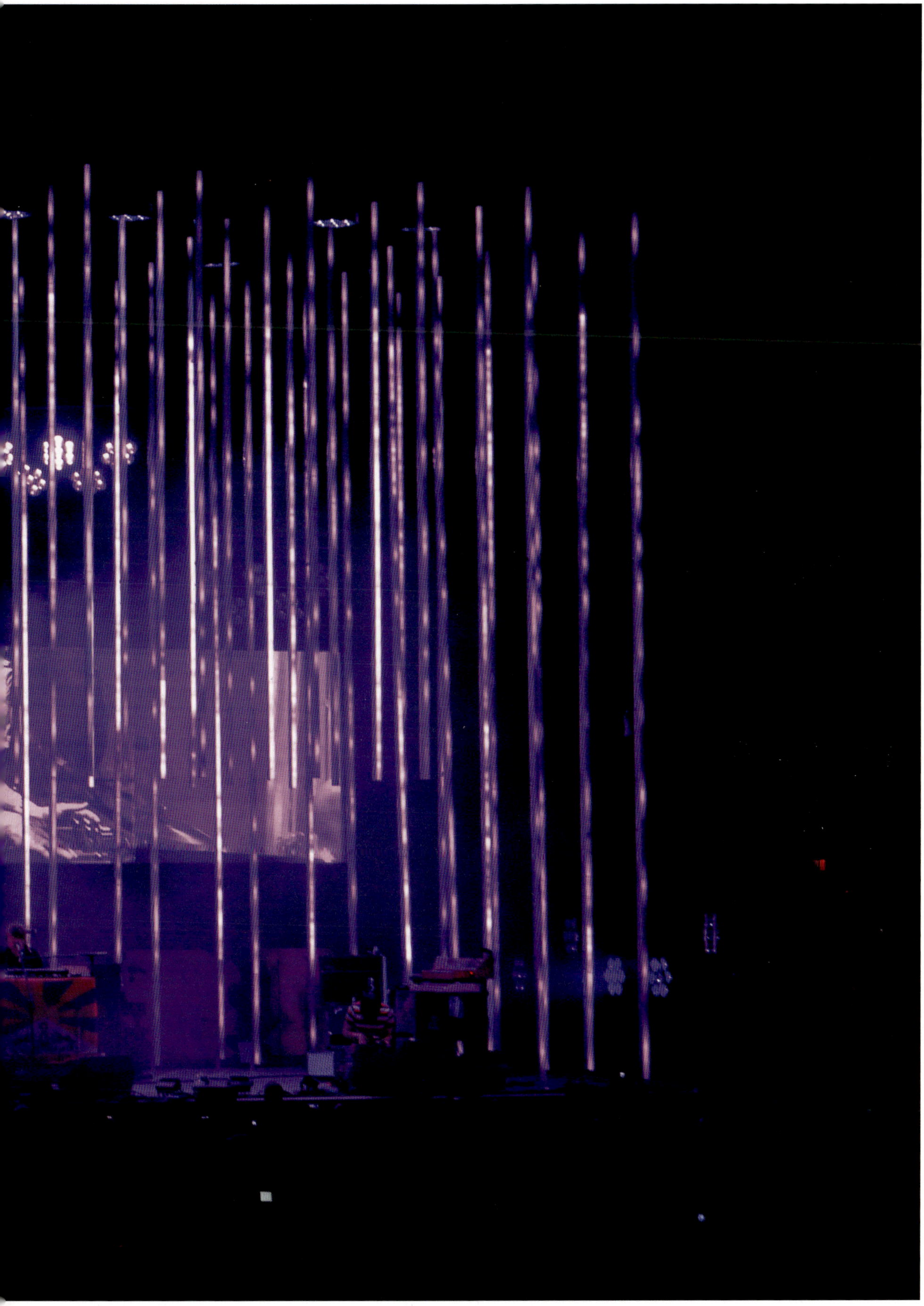

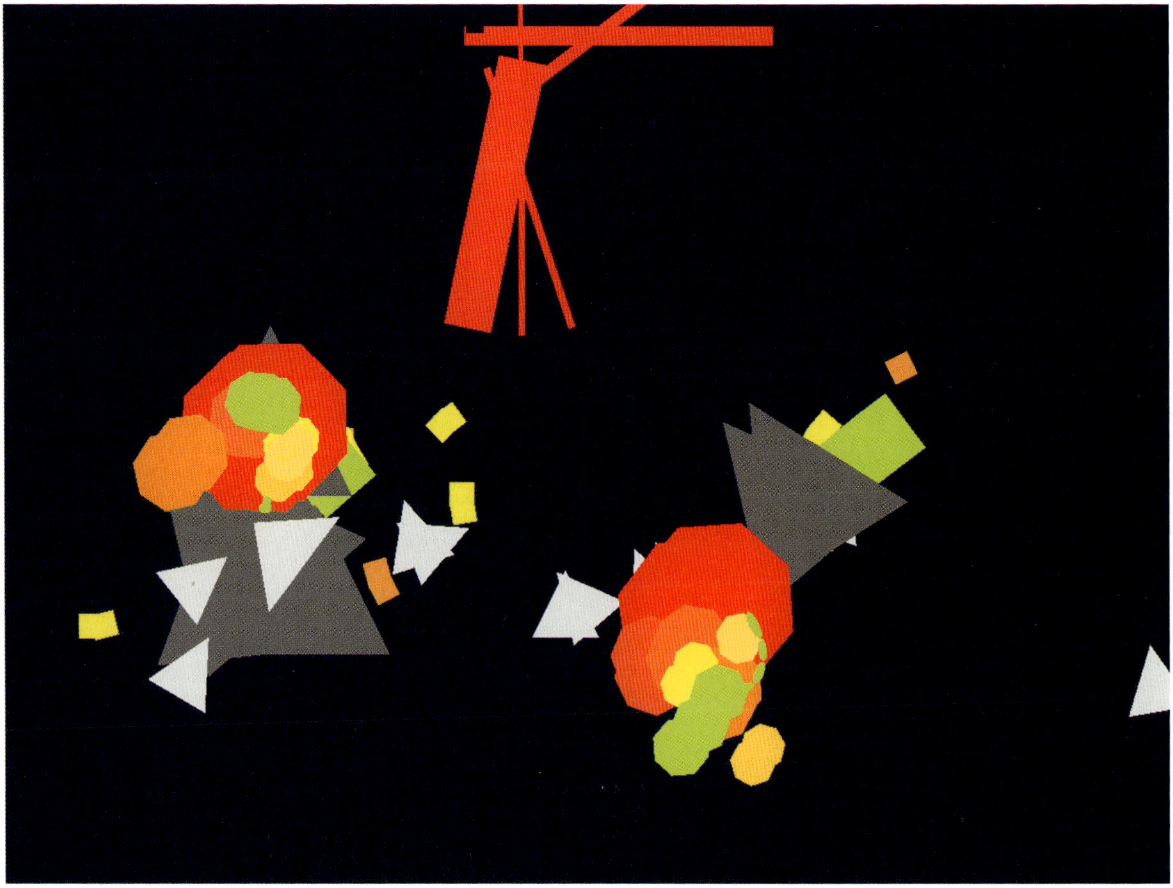

4.6. Scott Snibbe, *Motion Phone*, 1996

Radiohead eschewed moving lights and opted for an almost minimalist aesthetic. Over the subsequent two decades, Watson has become one of the first designers to create a digital aesthetic, not simply using computers as tools of automation. Watson's work has arguably shifted along with the band's music, as he began to delve into a more futuristic, digital style at the same time that Radiohead adopted some of the algorithmic effects of electronic drum machines, as with the album *Kid A* of 2000. As his style evolved, Watson has become known for his three-dimensional forests of LED tubes that hearken back to the work of the Czech lighting visionary Josef Svoboda (1920–2002). The latter was known for his experiments with analog illumination at the Czech National Theater, most famously the glowing pillar of light he first created in 1967. Svoboda always embraced forward-thinking technology, and that element and his use of closed-circuit video and experimental screens—including mirrors that distort the projected image—have all found their way into Watson's work. The advantages of digital technology, however, have allowed Watson to greatly expand on this repertoire in a way that is imbued with the digital atmosphere of the twenty-first century. Watson's digital aesthetic comes through most strongly in the layers of light and video displayed in recent Radiohead tours, for example, the series of concerts supporting the 2016 album *A Moon Shaped Pool*. This work featured a new degree of kineticism, as Svoboda's work appears static in comparison. Watson layers fragmented and curved screens at oblique angles, then plays a mix of prerecorded sequences and live video to create a matrix of sensory input. A viewer simultaneously sees the band members themselves and myriad layers of colored light and video; something of a synesthetic effect is achieved, as the lighting is not just a complementary spectacle but an immersive world from which the music appears. At times, Watson has experimented with direct synesthesia, generating wave forms through live audio. Digital technology has allowed Watson to perform at concerts in a manner analogous to that of Thomas Wilfred, who a century earlier had played color-light concerts on his Clavilux instrument. In Watson's case, much of the visual material is channeled through a Catalyst media server and software, which allows the crew to manipulate the projections for eighty to one hundred possible songs in real time.

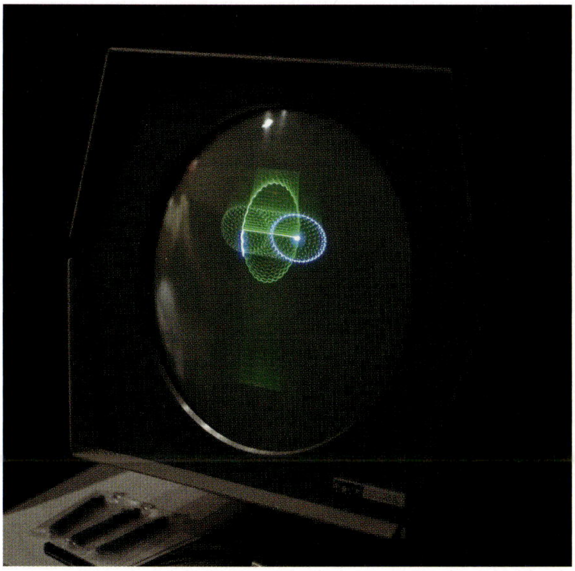

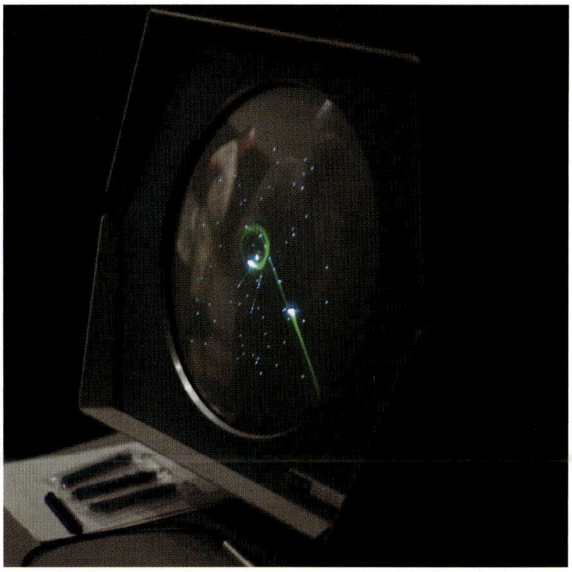

4.7. Steve Russell, *Spacewar*, 1961

The impact of analog mobile color is explicit in the nineties experimental digital projects Snibbe designed and engineered. For example, *Motion Phone* (figure 4.6, 1996), features forms that share a basic geometric vocabulary with *Kreise* and have the intent of channeling human emotion, but *Motion Phone* has the additional element of interaction. A viewer of a Fischinger film is passive, not involved in generating or inflecting the work. In contrast, *Motion Phone* was a digital communication system that relied on the direct input of the user through the gestural mouse. Snibbe wanted to create a work that involved actual touch, and he has cited the influence of another animator, Len Lye, as an inspiration because Lye physically scratched and painted colors directly on film. In Snibbe's work, the hand of the user reaches into the digital world. Two participants can communicate by each manipulating aspects of mobile color in a virtual world. *Motion Phone* is not a pure collaborative utopia, however, because the communication can express or lead to conflict as polychrome shapes dynamically interact.

One can draw a line from the spectral circles of Fischinger's *Kreise* to Maeda's *Reactive Books*, Watson's illumination, and Snibbe's *Motion Phone*, and then through to the abstract graphics of today's internet, though it is a meandering course. Google's identity system of 2015 stands as a perfect distillation of this thread in digital design. The four dots that, through animation, can morph into the logotype or monogram while also communicating a range of activities visually recall the dynamic forms of the animation pioneers. Likewise, they are activated by the user's hand, after which, their perky motions communicate; that communication is not strictly analytical but invokes a relatable, emotional response in the user. They make the interstitial moments in human–machine interaction—Google calls them "interactive, assistive and transitional"—feel like a true conversational pause.

Video Games

While academic projects have played a key role in digital culture without necessarily reaching the mainstream or being brought to market, video games represent almost the opposite situation, fueling digital commerce at every turn. Screen-based HCI is hard to imagine without video games. Aside from their myriad cultural impacts, video games have oftentimes driven technological advances in hardware and software.

Unsurprisingly, one of the first functioning games—a spaceship battle known simply as *Spacewar*—had its origins at MIT. *Spacewar* (figure 4.7) was designed in the Electrical Engineering Department, which was a hotbed of computer innovation at the time and in 1961 had just purchased a new, powerful minicomputer. With 9k RAM, Digital Equipment Corporation's PDP-1 had also shipped with a cathode ray screen. In an effort to deduce the machine's capabilities, a group of engineers, including Steve Russell, wrote a program that allowed for simple combat between two ships zooming around in space. Like many games, *Spacewar*'s addictive nature lay in a combination of initial simplicity matched with technical difficulty, as the ships were hard to maneuver and their firepower rather modest.

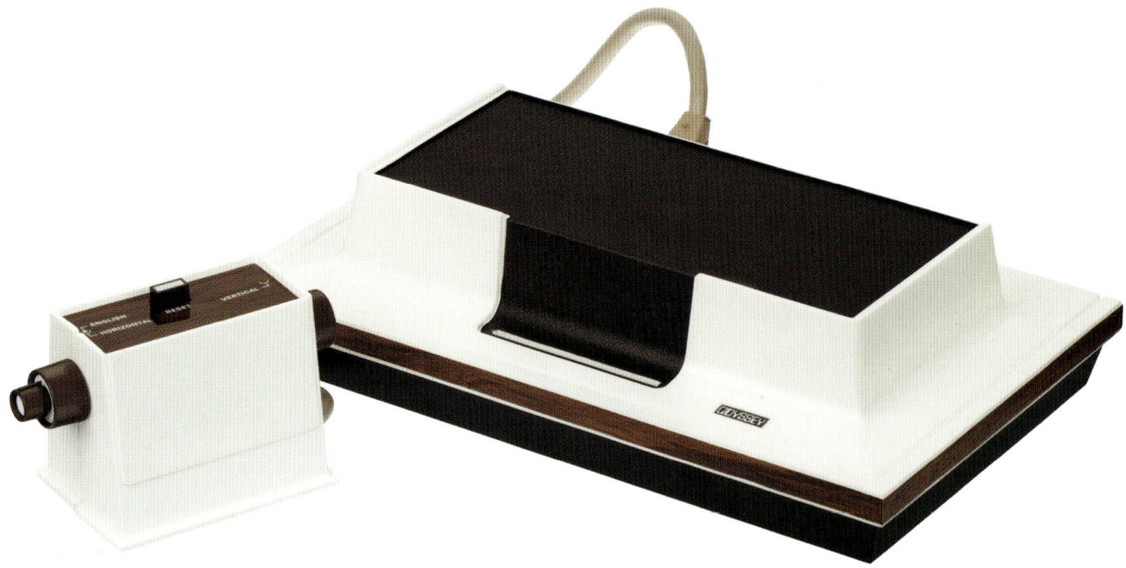

4.8. Magnavox Odyssey console, created by Ralph Baer in 1972

Shared freely with other researchers through a DEC user's group, *Spacewar* was the first computer game to allow people the immense emotional satisfaction of shooting things. The pure pleasure of gunfire, either real or virtual, was perhaps best expressed in another context by the French American artist Niki de Saint-Phalle, who in the early sixties was in the midst of creating her famous shot paintings. "I shot because it was fun and gave me a great feeling. I shot because I was fascinated to see the painting bleed and die. I shot for the sake of this magical moment. It was a moment of scorpion-like truth."

It would take about a decade after *Spacewar* was coded for the computer game to be launched into the mainstream. In the era before desktop computers, the first video games were run through either consoles harnessed to one's television or outside the home by arcade machines designed to relieve users of their quarters. In the early seventies, an engineer at the television manufacturer Magnavox, Ralph Baer, had recognized that a potential market existed for gameplay on the firm's sets and devised the console later marketed as the Magnavox Odyssey (figure 4.8). Magnavox released it in 1972, packaging the device with some analog gameplay elements, including a deck of cards. Like the desktop metaphor of the early GUIs, the cards were seemingly intended to draw an analogy between digital play and the comforting conventions of the past.

The design of the Odyssey's packaging was positively futuristic, dominated by lettering that exuded a technologically advanced aesthetic. The display typeface on the box appears to be a version of Computer, an all-capitals alphabet designed for optical character reading (OCR) by David Moore and released in 1968 by the Visual Graphics Corporation, a maker of phototypesetting equipment. Computer was one of a slew of OCR typefaces released in 1968; these fonts were designed to be readable by both humans and machines (when printed with magnetic ink) and were used mainly in the banking sector. The most successful of the genre, OCR-B, was drawn for Monotype by none other than Adrian Frutiger, who was responsible for several typefaces that have thrived in the digital age. As was the case with the Odyssey packaging, OCR types became favorite tools for designers wishing to give a product a gloss of technological sophistication.

The black-and-white screen graphics produced by the Odyssey were minimal, consisting mainly of a vertical white line in the center and various rectilinear shapes that could be manipulated by rotating nobs on a pair of controllers. Color and more varied background forms were provided in the guise of translucent plastic overlays that could be applied to the television screen. While consumers could purchase an accessory rifle for shooting at targets, the "killer app" for the Odyssey was a simple game called *Pong*. As it turned out, virtual paddle tennis provided the most compelling experience for users considering the Odyssey's rudimentary graphics, while also avoiding the fussiness engendered by the plastic overlays. Decades before networked gaming would enter the scene, *Pong* allowed for

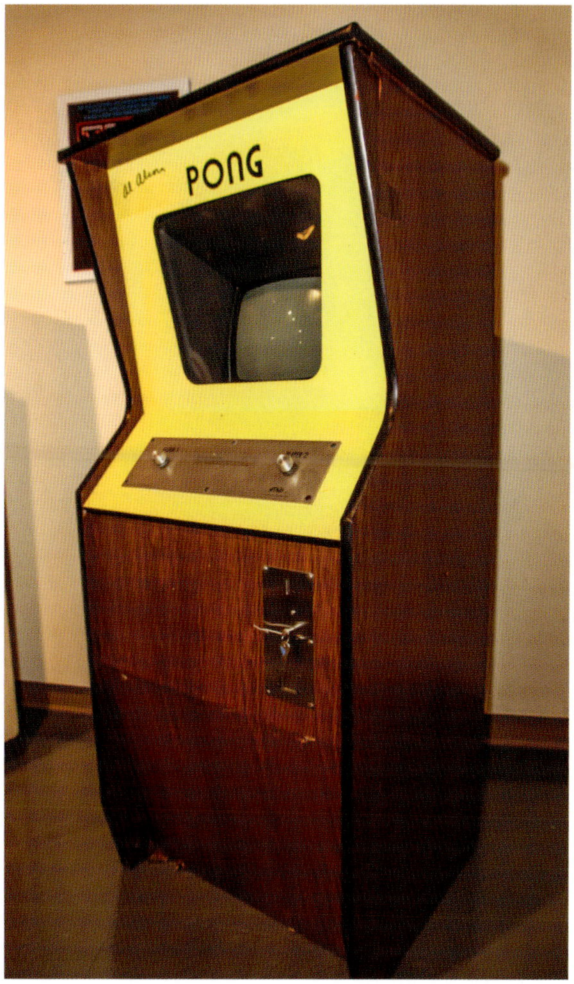

4.9. Atari's stand-alone *Pong*, created by Nolan Bushnell in 1972

a warm interaction mediated by machines, not determined by them.

While Baer's Odyssey console was not a huge success, it did launch *Pong*, which was soon pirated and then enhanced by Nolan Bushnell, a founder of the Atari Corporation. It was Bushnell who fought for his dream of making video games a staple of the arcade. In 1972, he started selling stand-alone *Pong* machines, which included two tweaks that enhanced gameplay: acceleration and sound (figure 4.9). First, Bushnell recognized that effective games had to continue to challenge the user, and Magnavox's original *Pong* could be played until boredom set in once the basic skill was mastered. In contrast, Atari's *Pong* featured a gradually accelerating ball, which ensured that the game would increase in difficulty until one player lost: more combat than pastime.

The second element added by Atari is one that has a signature place in computer graphics: sound. As staunchly visual a medium as video games may appear on the surface, the emotional power of abstract sound is not to be denied. Artists like Fischinger and Whitney had understood this fact decades earlier, devoting their lives to integrating mobile color with musical soundtracks. Silent *Pong* is empty and dead compared to the vitality of the Atari version, even though the sound was no more than a limited range of beeps. *Pong* was followed up by multiple similar arcade games, including in 1979 a science-fiction battle scenario, *Asteroids*, that would bring an enhanced version of MIT's *Spacewar* to millions of new users.

Amid the video game gold rush of the seventies, many companies vied for a piece of the business. Fairchild Semiconductor, a Silicon Valley pioneer founded in 1957, had found initial success through transistors. Switches that are one of the key building blocks of any microchip—today one might find billions of transistors in an advanced chip—transistors made Fairchild one of the most dynamic, if today lesser-known, digital businesses, spawning countless start-ups, including Intel. Fairchild's attempt to enter the video game console market never took off; its clumsily named Fairchild Channel F console sold fewer than 300,000 units. Nonetheless, the Channel F featured one quite significant element with a bright future: the video game

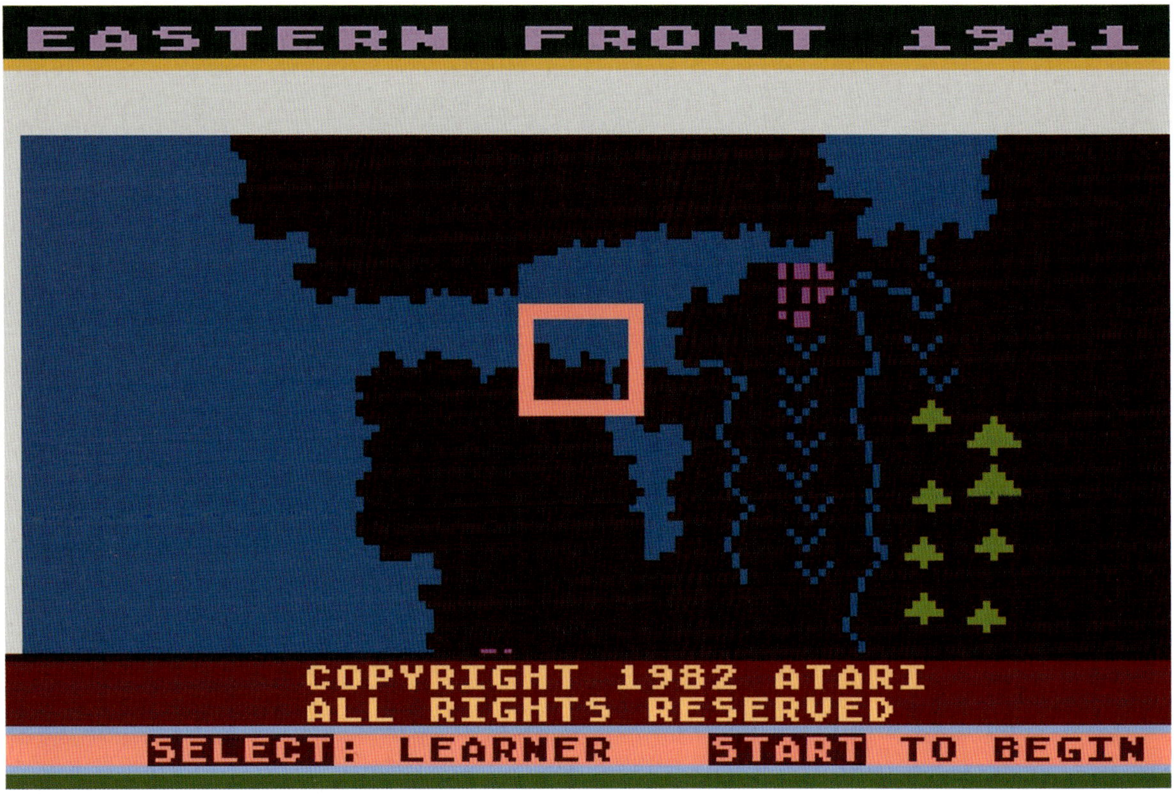

4.10. Chris Crawford's *Eastern Front (1941)*, 1981

cartridge. While Fairchild engineers led by Gerald Lawson had not invented the cartridge from scratch, they achieved the goal that would later make Apple Computer such a legend: bringing new technology to market. The Channel F allowed consumers to own a library of games, as opposed to the existing consoles, for which only preprogrammed content was available over the life of the machine.

Whereas Fairchild stumbled, Atari soared. Building on its success with arcade games, Atari soon entered the console business, introducing the Atari 2600 (née VCS) in 1977. The Atari console was initially a mixed success (Bushnell was pushed out and went on to found Chuck E. Cheese), until the idea arose in 1980 of licensing arcade hits for the 2600. Atari then ported *Space Invaders*, another late seventies arcade hit, originally designed by the Japanese company Taito, out of the arcade and into the home. During these halcyon years at Atari, former PARC denizen Alan Kay—a key part of the invention of the GUI—was hired as chief research scientist. As such, Kay took to mentoring one of the soon-to-be legends of video game history, Chris Crawford. Having first arrived at Atari in 1979 as a self-taught designer, Crawford two years later worked with Kay to publish his turn-based strategy game *Eastern Front (1941)*. *Eastern Front* (figure 4.10) soon became a killer app for Atari, as it was playable on the new Atari 400 computer, a $400 16k machine nicknamed Candy. The nickname says it all, as the 400 was not much of a serious computer but really a game console with a keyboard.

Eastern Front represents an important moment in the history of gaming, as it embodied the transition from analog military strategy board games to digital ones. Crawford addressed this shift in an article for *Computer Gaming World* (1981), "The Future of Computer Wargaming." In this essay, Crawford argued that there was a "universal misconception" among gamers that the new digital product "will be just like a good boardgame, with the computer somehow making it better." Crawford argued that, in fact, the change in format to digital was a radical one, and that designers needed to be aware that they were dealing with a paradigm shift, not incremental progress. *Eastern Front*, with its roots in hexgrid board games, also introduced two new digital features. First, different areas of the game map were manipulated through smooth scrolling, so that the player could view a portion of the map and then move elsewhere without necessitating a slow and disruptive reloading of the rest of the map. Second, *Eastern Front*'s CPU was programmed to use pondering, meaning it could perform calculations in the background that improved its gameplay.

Because of the sophistication of *Eastern Front*, which challenged the player intellectually and strategically at a much higher level than most computer games, Crawford soon became a sought-after authority in the field. His 1984 book, *The Art of Computer Game Design*, emphasized his evolving belief that games were best situated to maximize the potential of the computer; as computer graphic and sound capabilities continued to develop, Crawford foresaw a coming age of dramatically more meaningful HCI. Computers can "now communicate with human beings, not just in the cold and distant language of digits, but in the emotionally immediate and compelling language of images and sounds. With this ability came a new, previously undreamed-of possibility: the possibility of using the computer artistically as a medium for emotional communication. The computer game has emerged as the prime vehicle for this communication." Crawford advocated a game design that was more than just a frivolous time waster but broached serious topics in an emotionally rich digital environment. In 1985, working as a freelance designer after the near collapse of Atari, Crawford released *Balance of Power*, a Cold War geopolitical strategy game for the Macintosh. A critical and commercial success, *Balance of Power* reaffirmed his status as the doyen of game designers.

In 1988, Crawford founded the Computer Game Developers Conference. Now called simply the GDC, its first annual meeting took place in Crawford's living room. As the GDC grew in size and scope, Crawford continued to advocate for games that were intellectually substantial and emotionally satisfying, but they did not sell. The watershed for Crawford came in 1990, when his environmentally themed strategy game *Balance of the Planet* failed miserably. *Balance of the Planet* involved myriad complex policy decisions and, as critics quickly pointed out, was simply not much fun to play. The lack of interest in *Balance of the Planet* led Crawford to rethink his role as a game designer, a professional crisis that led to perhaps the most famous rhetorical outburst in digital design history: Crawford's Dragon Speech, which he gave at GDC in 1992. Worth a look on YouTube, in the Dragon Speech, Crawford enthusiastically recounts the events of his career up to that moment, whereupon he stunningly announces that he is leaving the computer game industry. Building on ideas that he had first expressed years earlier in *The Art of Computer Game Design*, Crawford used the metaphor of a dragon to represent the new challenge he must now face: using the computer as an interactive mode of artistic communication. At the end of the speech, Crawford brandished a sword and ran from the room to slay the metaphorical dragon, yelling, "For truth! For beauty! For Art! Charge!" Crawford was true to his word and has spent the subsequent decades chasing his dream of interactive entertainment. In a poignant aside, he wrote in early 2020, "I recently realized that I have been wasting my time on a dumb effort for the last 35 years."

In the soon-to-be well-worn manner of big technology companies, Atari and its competitors went through a series of boom-and-bust cycles, the most famous of which involved the legendary debacle of a game based on the hit movie *E.T. the Extra-Terrestrial*. In 1982 Atari paid $25 million to license the rights to the film, and then produced a game so bad that millions of unsold copies were surreptitiously buried in the Desert Southwest. In 2014, a faux-archaeological expedition excavated the dump in Alamogordo, New

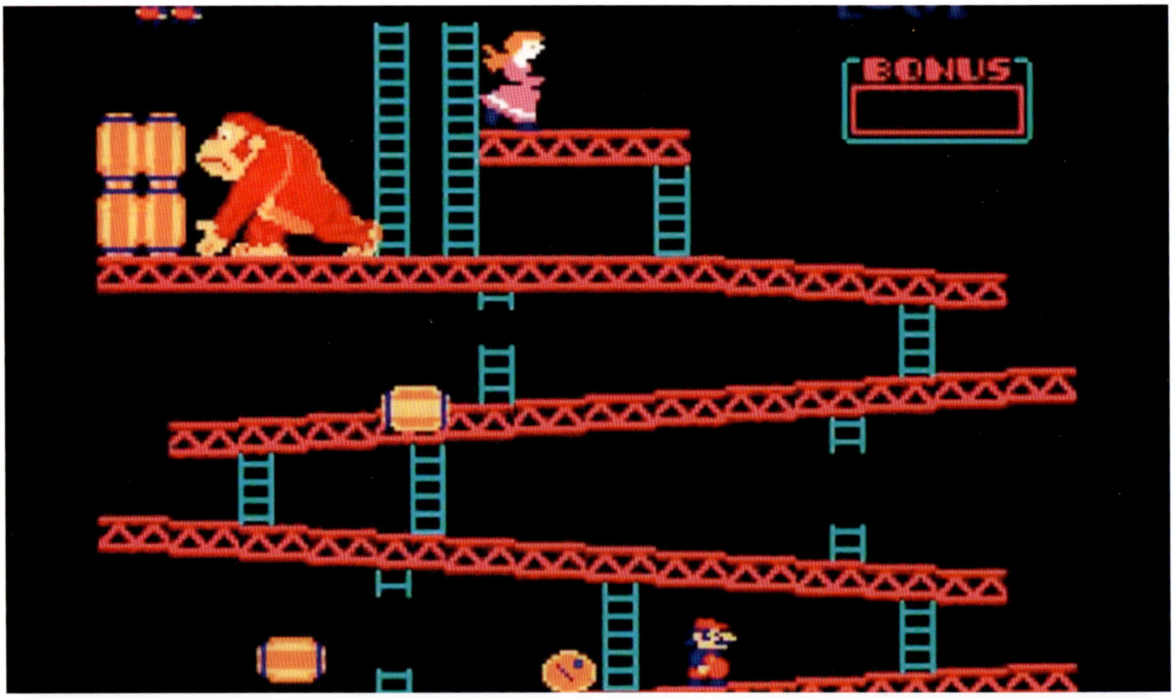

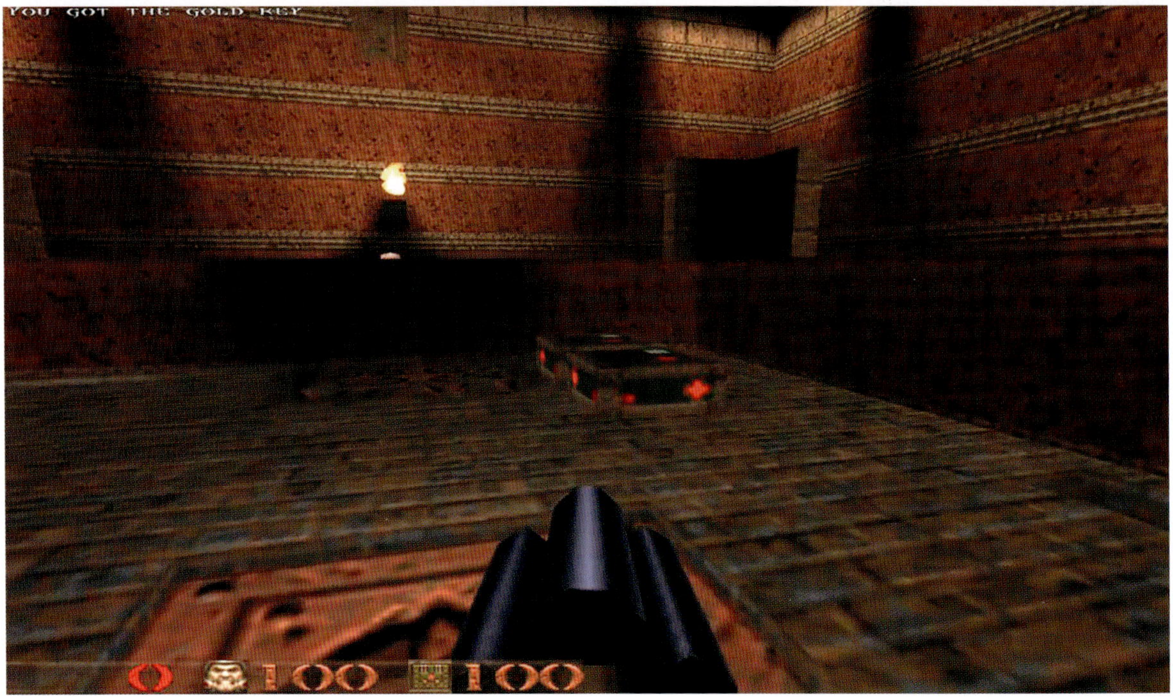

4.11. Nintendo, *Donkey Kong*, 1980
4.12. id Software, *Quake*, 1996

Mexico, unearthing definitive evidence of a rumored crime that had captivated video game aficionados for more than three decades.

Two subsequent developments in the video game industry enhanced the relatability of computers. First, in 1980 the Nintendo corporation started distributing *Donkey Kong* (figure 4.11), a platforming arcade game that featured accelerating difficulty melded to a storyline. Like many toy companies of the seventies, Nintendo—a Japanese company that dated back to the nineteenth-century gaming business through *hanafuda*, or flower cards—hoped to capitalize on the building momentum of the arcade. With *Donkey Kong* the company succeeded beyond any wild expectation. Designed by Shigeru Miyamoto, *Donkey Kong* introduced a new type of experiential gameplay. The narrative of *Donkey Kong* introduced Jumpman, a little red hero who seeks to save the princess from the titular character. Of course, Jumpman would soon morph into Mario, one of the most beloved characters of recent decades in any media.

With *Donkey Kong* and the empire that it initiated, Nintendo pioneered cuteness in computing: Trip Hawkins, founder of Electronic Arts, has called it "plush toy" gaming.

The second key innovation came to occupy the opposite end of the emotional spectrum: the first-person shooter. In the early nineties, id Software released a flurry of games that came to define the genre. *Wolfenstein 3D* of 1992, followed by multiple iterations of *Doom* (1993) and *Quake* (figure 4.12, 1996), displayed ever more fluid motion through 3D environments filled with Nazis and monsters, all of whom would bleed and die in the most satisfying way. These games also led to two dramatic new experiences: multiplayer gaming and mods. It was *Doom* that first allowed players to link two computers with a network cable, enabling them to face off against one another. As multiplayer capabilities expanded, this feature gradually allowed the creation of many communities of gamers, social networks in the virtual world. *Doom* also inaugurated the ability of users to create custom content, enriching the game with new maps, mods, and character skins.

On the technological side, the gaming industry has been critical to the development of computing power. Since the eighties, when video gameplay first migrated to the personal computer, game companies have thirsted for more memory and faster processing. Roberta Williams, a founder of Sierra On-Line and a key creator of the adventure game genre, famously demanded sound cards for desktop computers to enrich game play. Eight-bit color, video graphics display (VGA) cards, rendering engines, 3D graphics, networked play—all of these enhancements to the interface were fomented largely by and for video game companies. At a time when artist-researchers such as Maeda and Snibbe were delving into fairly simple graphical interactions, the purveyors of video games were offering immersive digital environments and gripping, emotional narratives.

As graphical interfaces advanced and gaming environments became ever more realistic, the sense that one could escape into a virtual world became manifest. By the late nineties, video games, many of them iterations of first-person shooters like *Wolfenstein* or *Quake*, had become something of a raison d'être for home computers, many of which served largely as game consoles. The glamour, feeling of control, and virtual bloodshed provided by the industry represented one of the major, reliable mainstream conduits of digital culture. For this reason, it is perhaps unsurprising that artists and designers have targeted games for subversion. Such was the case with perhaps the most influential net art iconoclasts of the nineties, JODI, a collaborative project formed in 1995 by Joan Heemskerk and Dirk Paesmans (JODI is a combination of the first two letters of their first names), who were recent émigrés to California (from the Netherlands and Belgium). Some insight into their work must come from the fact that Paesmans had previously studied in Europe with Korean American artist Nam June Paik. An influential member of the Dada-esque cooperative known as Fluxus in the sixties, Paik had famously brought an edgy, even destructive flavor to his performance work. For example, in *One for Violin Solo* (1962), he abruptly smashed the titular instrument after slowly raising it over his head. Later in his career, Paik sought to disrupt the dominant media technology of television.

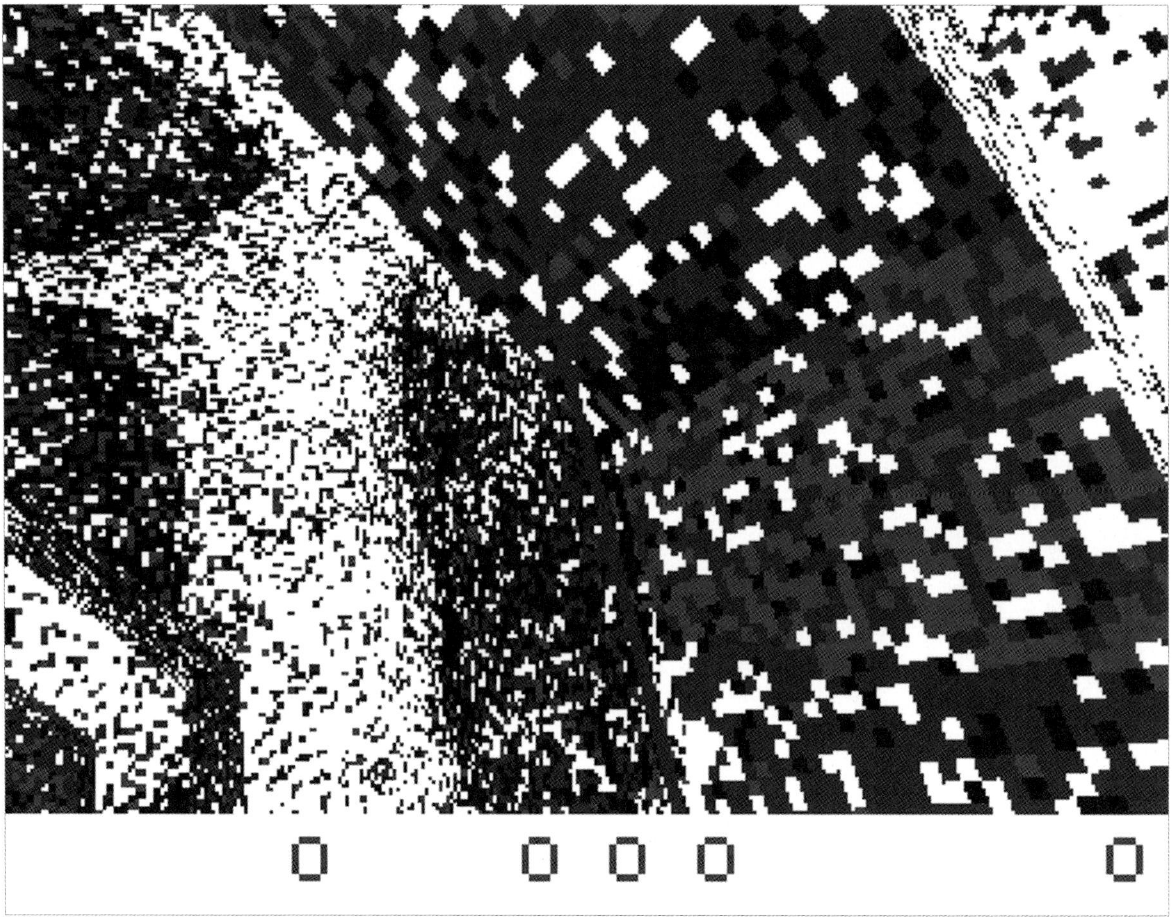

4.13. JODI, *Untitled Game*, 1996–2001

JODI was formed in San Jose, the heart of Silicon Valley, after Heemskerk and Paesmans moved there in 1995. Soon thereafter, they established the website jodi.org and began experimenting with HTML, creating browser-based works that reveled in complexity and purposeful errors. At the same time, JODI began interrogating the source code of first-person shooters, starting with id Software's *Quake* in 1996. Over the next five years, JODI created the work *Untitled Game* (figure 4.13), producing over a dozen mods for *Quake* and altering the graphics and gameplay in strange and wonderful ways. In one Fluxus-like mod called *Arena*, the entire game is erased as its graphics engine stalls on a white field. In a sense *Arena* is also reminiscent of Robert Rauschenberg's *Erased de Kooning Drawing* (1953), in which Rauschenberg symbolically hacks all the emotional sturm und drang and gestural line of the abstract expressionist's work. It is noteworthy that *Erased de Kooning Drawing* entered the collection of the San Francisco Museum of Modern Art in 1998, and perhaps Heemskerk or Paesmans had come across it in that museum. Part of the deconstructive effect of *Untitled Game* came from the disjunction between sound and image, as the game's cacophonous audio tracks and sound effects were left unmolested while the visual component was pared down. While JODI's modifications to the game were done with an iconoclastic spirit, of course the gaming industry soon came around to recognizing the value of mods to their product and have encouraged and facilitated the practice for many years. In this way, a formerly subversive strategy was recuperated into a form of enhanced commercial engagement.

Invariably, the sense of autonomy that video games offered came to intersect with the utopian urge in digital culture. Massive multiplayer adventure games networked on the internet further facilitated social interactions in a magical space. In the nineties, Philip Rosedale, an executive at a video-conferencing company, began planning the creation of a virtual world that, unlike most massive multiplayer sites, was not so much a game but an experience. Eventually christened *Second Life* (figure 4.14), it finally opened to the public in 2003. In *Second Life*, people live vicariously through their avatars, nurturing relationships and building a world through user-generated content. While establishing a new avenue through which people could interact with the digital world, Rosedale's

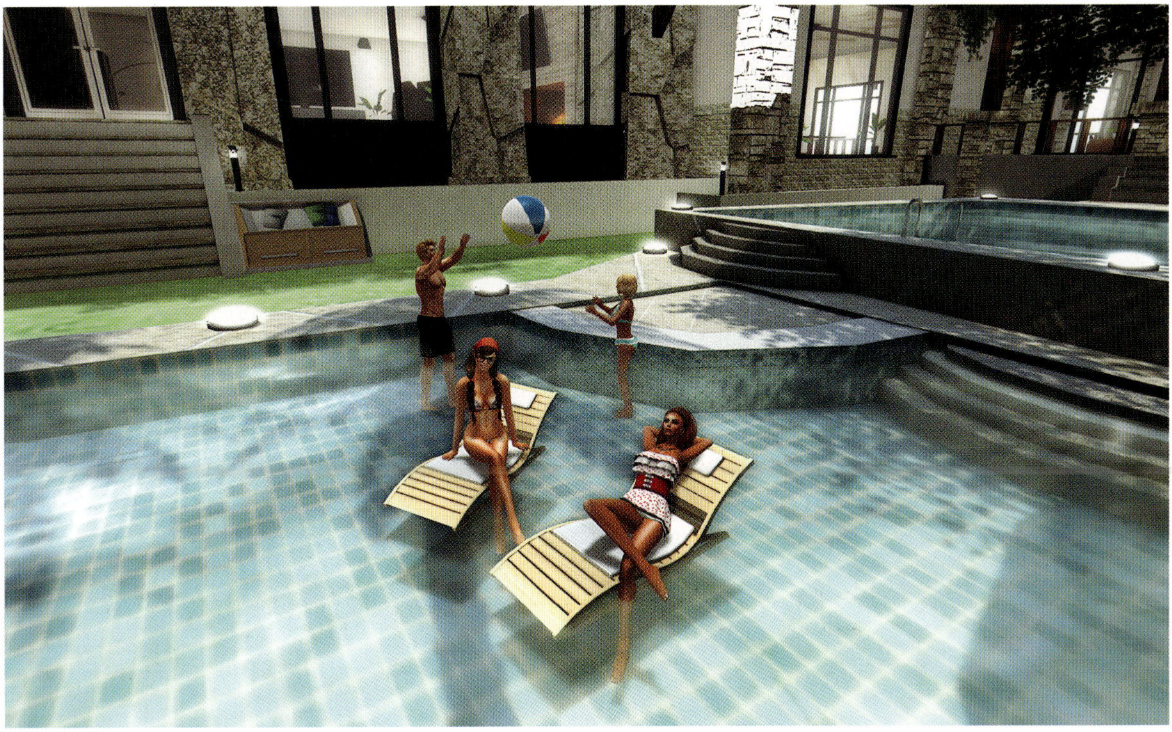

4.14. Philip Rosedale, *Second Life*, 2003

nineties dream of an unchained artistic utopia à la Burning Man has mainly crashed on the shoals of human nature. He told a writer for the *Atlantic* in 2017 that he "thought the landscape of Second Life would be hyper-fantastic, artistic, and insane, full of spaceships and bizarre topographies, but what ended up emerging looked more like Malibu. People were building mansions and Ferraris." The trajectory of *Second Life*—from dream to reality—has been repeated in many different realms of digital culture.

The artificial gloss and staged perfection of *Second Life* has also crept into the digital world writ large. Witness the so-called Instagram aesthetic, a quasi-virtual scene in which filters and color-correcting apps are the rule. The photo-sharing app Instagram was first released in 2010, and then launched into the digital stratosphere beginning in 2012, after Facebook acquired it. Today hosting well over a billion users, Instagram has become the global locus of "curated" sets of images through which people can present an idealized—*Second Life*—version of their most mundane moments. Another adventure in digital blanding, these visions of confident prosperity have a visceral appeal that cannot be denied. Notably, in a design-centered universe of social media like Instagram, the behemoth Facebook stands apart; Facebook is as ubiquitous and unspectacular as the IBM PC. Instagram in this analogy is of course the stylish Apple product. Although there is chatter amid the digerati of rejecting the Instagram aesthetic for more authentic-looking imagery, it would seem that the sleek video game aesthetic would be hard to dislodge permanently.

Because gaming has been a central locus of HCI, it has also been the site of some of the purest emotional connections, from euphoria to despair. In Eva and Franco Mattes's *My Generation* of 2010, the tangible effects of these strong feelings are made evident. The work consists of a PC smashed to smithereens on the floor, while an audio track plays the sounds of young people screaming in frustration at having failed in their gaming pursuits. The world may be polished and virtual, but the emotions are quite real.

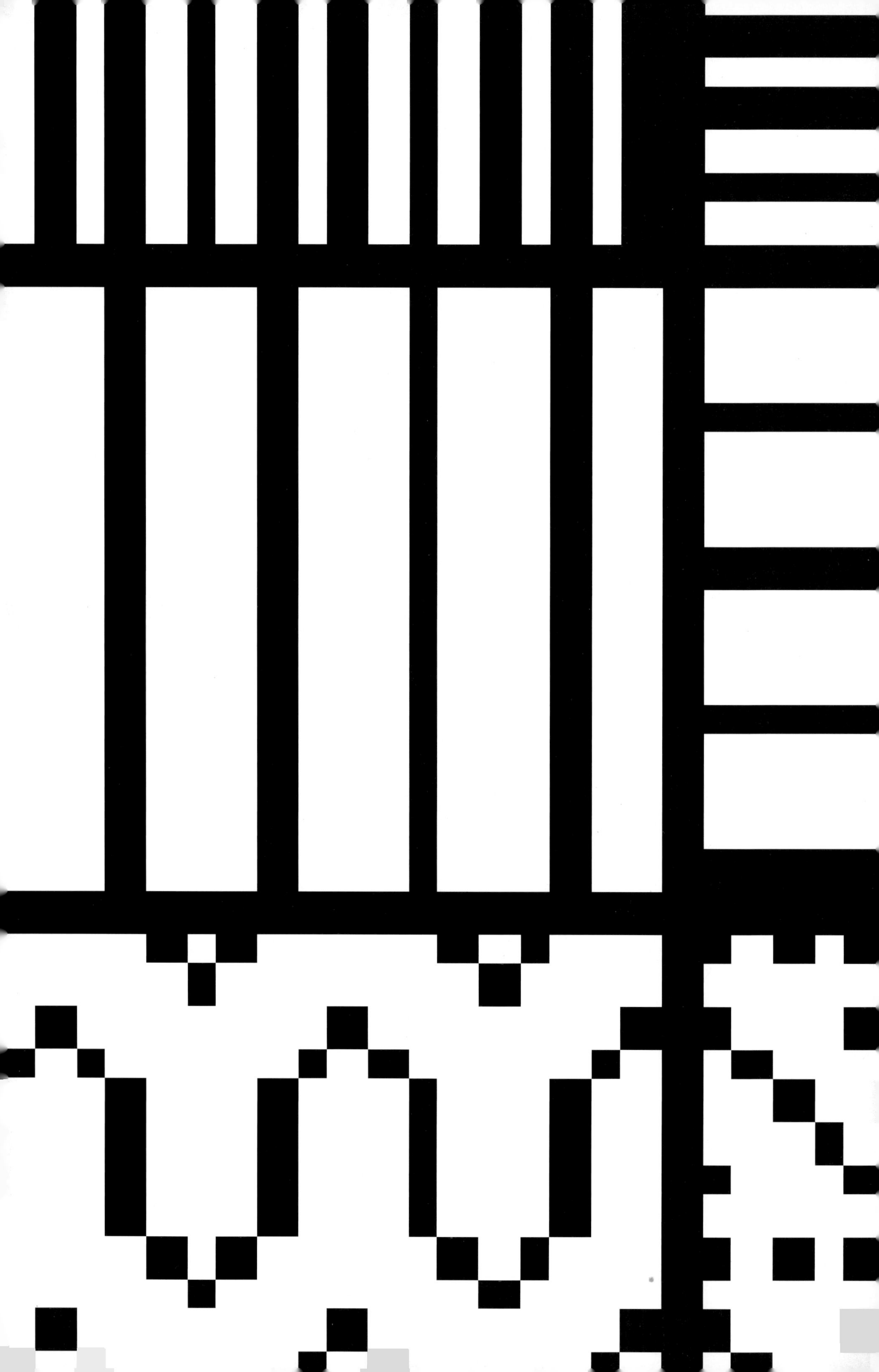

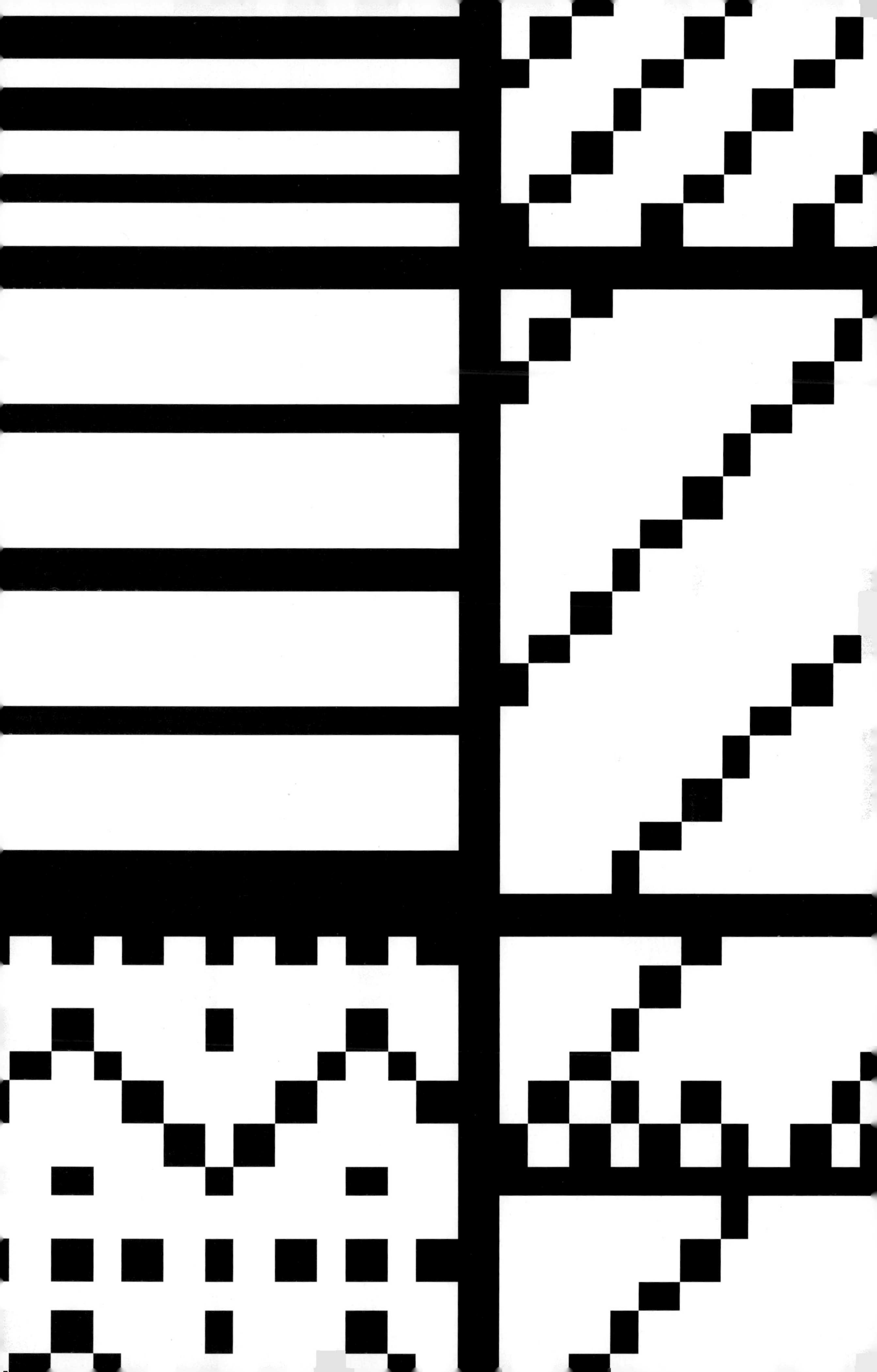

5.1. April Greiman, LAICA poster, 1986

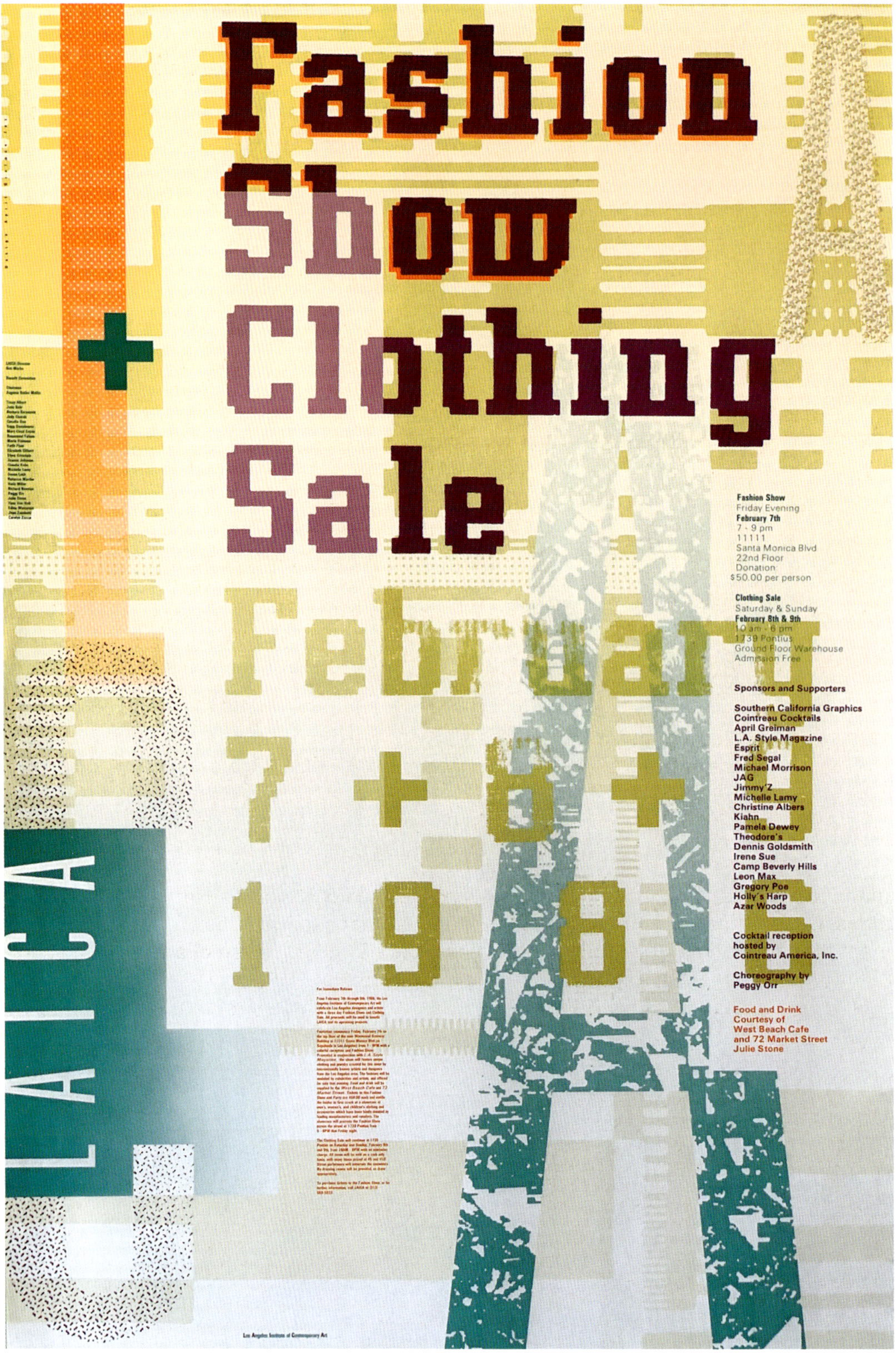

Five. Digital Print and Web 1.0

Paradoxically, the first digital innovation in graphic design outside the computer industry came through print. In the late eighties, as computers emerged as design tools, print *was* graphic design. Furthermore, the first digital graphics to break through into the mainstream were designed in a style that in fact had no digital roots. This situation comes up repeatedly throughout digital design history, in which many works that are celebrated as establishing a new digital aesthetic actually represent the digitalization of something older.

An excellent example of the complexities of the emerging digital years comes through the work of April Greiman. As a professor at CalArts in the early eighties, Greiman began using digital video equipment that allowed her to capture and edit still images. Like Rudy VanderLans at Emigre, Greiman bought a Macintosh in 1984 as she reentered private practice. Then, at a time when few other designers saw the creative potential of the technology, Greiman pioneered one of the earliest digital styles. Using bitmapped fonts and balky software, including MacDraw (a graphical program that she actually used for layouts), MacVision (a desktop version of the custom video interface software she had used at CalArts), and MacPaint, Greiman created collaged compositions of type and imagery that positively sizzle with energy. Greiman's 1986 poster for the Los Angeles Institute of Contemporary Art (LAICA) exemplifies this hybrid historical moment; the large display type is formed of bitmapped letters at a coarse resolution that explicitly declares its digital origins (figure 5.1). Yet, the smaller type that sets out the exhibition's details was traditionally set and has some of the tightness and clarity associated with the Swiss modern style. Greiman has noted how she quickly realized that the computer—and its ability to "undo"—freed her to be more creative, knowing she could instantly start over again and again. Overall, what really exudes a digital aesthetic in this poster is the layered composition; these textured riffs of type and image create a dizzying sense of virtual space. Collaged layers were destined to become the essential, most recognizable element of digital design for print. Spanning the rough decade from Greiman to *Wired*, layering is the most potent visual signifier of the matrix, cyberspace, or the net. Combined often with a prismatic palette of artificial-looking hues, layers went completely mainstream after 1994, when a new iteration of Adobe Photoshop (3.0) made them digitally more accessible. But herein lies the paradox, as the kinetic layered look had actually arrived over a decade before the Macintosh, and one must look at an earlier phase of Greiman's career to understand its origins.

After receiving her undergraduate degree from the Kansas City Art Institute in 1970, Greiman had almost immediately enrolled at the Basel School of Design, which many of her college professors had attended. Over the next two years, she studied under the legendary modernist Armin Hofmann and the younger instructor Wolfgang Weingart. The latter designer had enrolled in the Basel Kunstgewerbeschule in 1963, after having completed a typesetting apprenticeship; in 1968 he began teaching typography in Basel's new postgraduate design program. Inspired by the experiments in collage and photo montage of the various 1920s constructivist and Dadaist groups, Weingart used every material at his disposal to build up his compositions. Importantly, the invention of transparent films that could be printed on and then layered allowed for a new collaged aesthetic to emerge. Furthermore, contemporary repro cameras allowed him to improvisationally scale and edit films of type and image, creating a new look that subverted the dogmatic orderliness of the conventional Swiss style. There were no computers in the Basel studios. Rather, the layered look devised by Weingart and his erstwhile students such as Greiman would be carried forward into the digital age.

Soon after the postgraduate program was first instituted at Basel in 1968, Weingart's ideas began to be disseminated throughout the United States. There, they had a substantial impact, particularly on the more adventurous, scholarly-minded subset of the profession. One can witness the eighties alchemic melding of Weingart's "New Age" Swiss typography and the digital world through the pages of *Design Quarterly*, a journal published by the Walker Art Center of Minneapolis, Minnesota. *Design Quarterly* had begun its run back in 1946 as the *Everyday Art Quarterly*, a name that correlated with that of the newly established design galleries at the Walker. Beginning in 1969, the journal was edited by Mildred Friedman, who would work there for decades as an influential curator of architecture and design.

Issue 130 of *Design Quarterly* (1985) was guest authored by Armin Hofmann and Wolfgang Weingart, who Friedman pithily described as the "Apollonian theoretician" and the "Dionysian eccentric." While ostensibly devoted to Hofmann's long career, the issue related it through the lens of Weingart's subsequent reaction against the rigidity of the Swiss model. Weingart notes that his teaching method was devoted to creating a "backpack" of typographic tools that could prepare students to work in any technological context. While this retrospective issue has little digital work, Weingart does note that the Basel school had recently acquired an Apple computer, and that "the infinite graphic possibilities of computers are perhaps the language of a new world of typography."

The following year, 1986, Robert Jensen and Friedman commissioned Greiman to guest

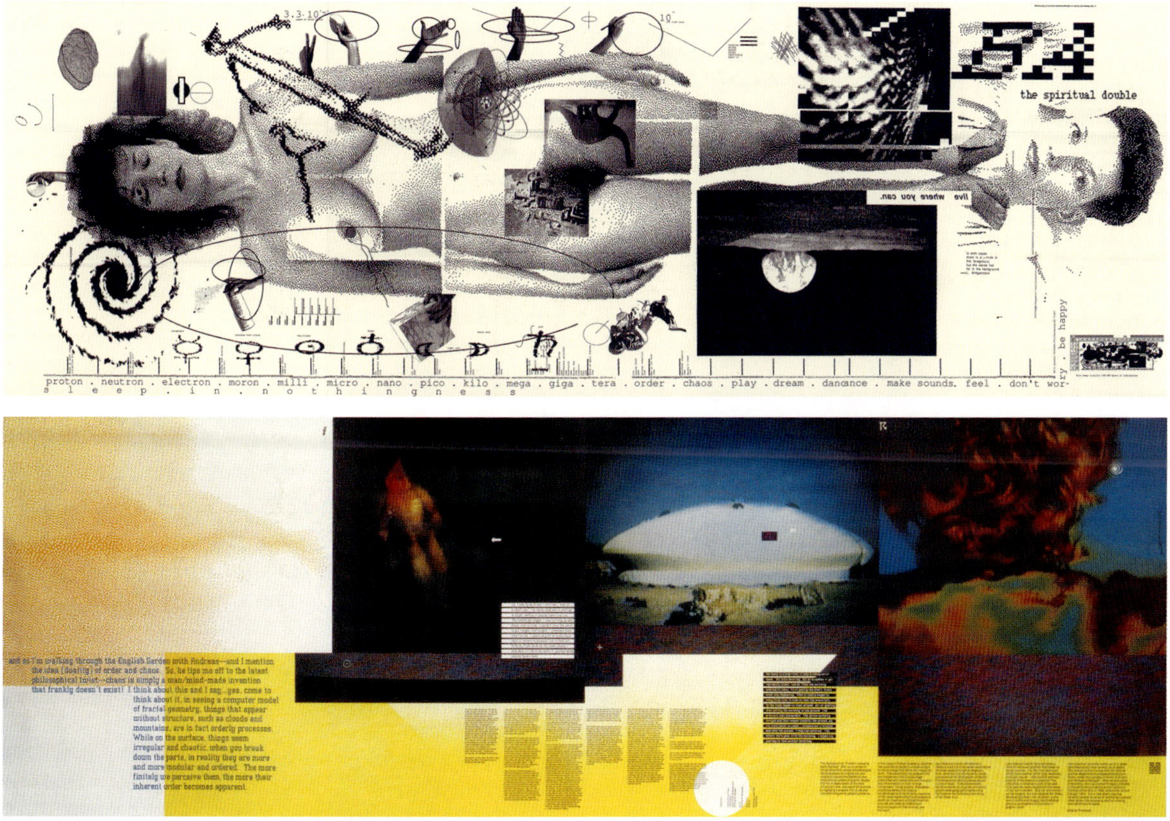

5.2. April Greiman, *Design Quarterly*, no. 133, 1986

author issue 133 of *Design Quarterly* and present a similar overview of her career (figure 5.2). This issue has rightfully attained legendary status in the canon of digital design, as Greiman artfully created an unconventional work that demonstrated some of the potential of the digital. Rather than produce a standard bound issue, Greiman instead dramatically eschewed the folio format in favor of a single-page poster measuring two feet by six feet. This double-sided page was anchored by one of the first all-digital collages, a life-sized portrait of the designer laid out amid a range of video captures, digital photos, bitmapped type, and illustrations. Using MacDraw as design software, she used all thirty-two pages of *Design Quarterly* to make up the total image. The lower right corner attests to this process, with a screenshot of the poster captioned on MacDraw with the notation, "This image contains 289,322 bytes of information."

The verso of issue 133 featured another collage (a hybrid of digital and conventional techniques) and text by Greiman detailing the conception and production of the work as well as sharing some inspirational thoughts. An additional brief essay by Friedman explained why the work was so revelatory, and this text represented a significant milestone in the critical understanding of digital graphic design. Friedman recognized that existing digital experiments had "yielded rather rigid, repetitive, formulaic results" and clarified how Greiman's work was different. "She not only stretches the imagery, but she expands the ideas, developing a fresh, rich pluralism, a mixture of words and images that challenge previous conceptions of the limits of graphic vision." Friedman presciently described the broader digital future, as seen, for example, in the realm of digital type described above, where entropic sameness and rousing originality coexist side by side.

The lasting legacy of issue 133 of *Design Quarterly* was how it sparked a reevaluation of digital graphics across the profession. At a time when computers were not yet a signifier of creativity—most designers saw them as a business tool or maybe productivity enhancer—Greiman's unorthodox format, daring nude self-portrait, and thoughtful writing brought a sense of warmth to the technology that had been otherwise lacking. She truly is the ur-digital designer, the first person who embodied a new, creative future. In the long history of *Design Quarterly*—it ceased publication in 1996—the creation of issue 133 rightly stands out as a transformative moment unlike no other.

One important facet of Greiman's work is that not only is it created using computers, but it

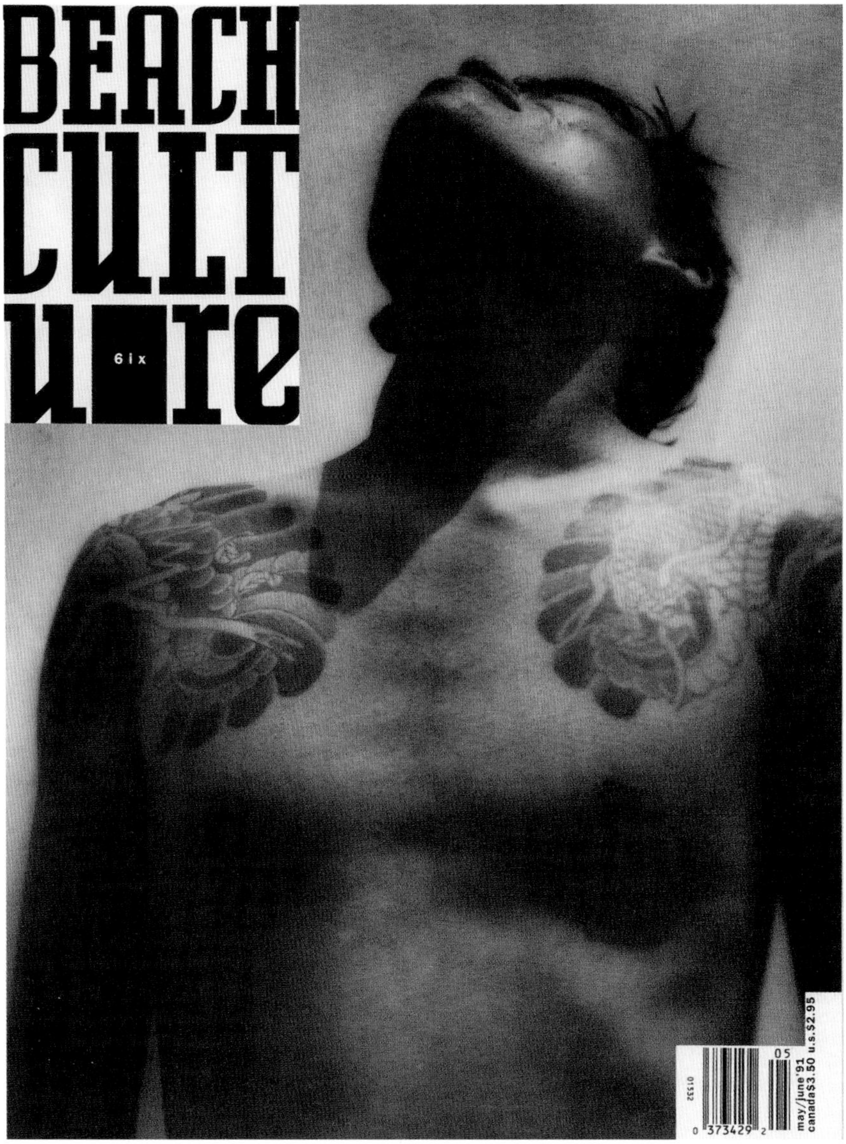

5.3. David Carson, cover of *Beach Culture*, May/June 1991

looks digital. There is something futuristic about both the bitmapped type and the floating layers, replete with artificial colors that commune with one another in a matrix-like universe. In stark contrast, for another legendary graphic designer of the late eighties, David Carson, the digital roots of his work are often completely overlooked. There are two threads working against the notion of Carson as a digital pioneer: his backstory and the style of the work itself. In terms of biography, Carson had gradually worked his way into the mainstream through tenures at a succession of small skater and surfing publications. A nigh professional surfer himself, biographies of the designer are much more likely to portray him as a rebellious creature of the beach than someone who had sought out typographic instruction at the University of Arizona and in Switzerland (where he had studied with Hans-Rudolf Lutz).

And then there is the work itself. Carson proved a master of "grunge" illegibility, mixing and matching, blurring and cropping, layering and obfuscating the text and photos in his layouts (figure 5.3). The whole atmosphere produced by grunge typography is one of handmade chaos, everything raw and ragged as if it had been torn and pasted in some basement studio. The exact opposite of Greiman's aesthetic, with Carson nothing seems to convey an immersion in the digital. Yet, Carson was in fact deeply devoted to digital tools, and they underlie much of his aesthetic. Part of this thread is evident through his attachment to Emigre typefaces, which he used extensively—so much, actually, that one issue of *Beach Culture* was jokingly subtitled the "Special No Emigre Font Issue." Additionally, Carson was a devotee of the new layout programs: first Aldus's PageMaker (Aldus merged with Adobe in 1994), but then, the program that came to rival and even surpass it in nineties

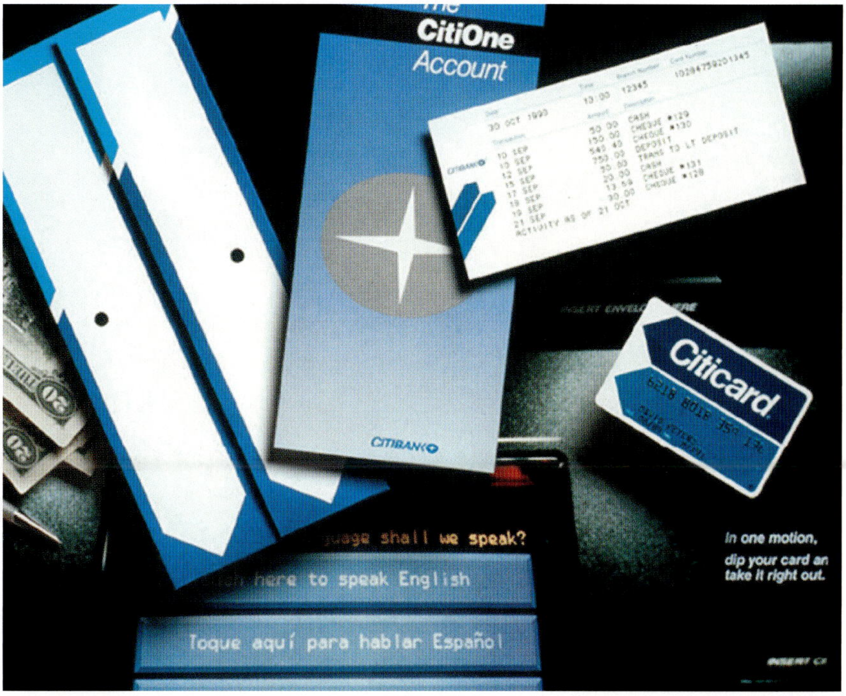

5.4. Sylvia Harris and Two Twelve Associates, Citibank corporate identity, 1989

graphic design, QuarkXPress. First released in 1987 for the Macintosh, QuarkXPress for a while offered a more powerful and intuitive GUI than PageMaker, and the two programs battled for market share throughout the decade via multiple upgrades on both Macintosh and Windows platforms.

Notwithstanding the work of the digital pioneers, it was really the high functionality and low cost of these two programs that pushed digital tools firmly into the mainstream of graphic design. At *Wired*, for example, QuarkXPress was the preferred choice, used to produce the magazine from the very first. The colophon of the premiere issue (1993) noted that “Wired is designed and produced digitally” and listed QuarkXPress along with Adobe Illustrator and Photoshop as its layout software. Perusing that premiere issue, one might be surprised that David Carson is featured, grunge and all, as part of a piece labeled “A New Breed of Designer.” Notably, this title and most of the headings in *Wired* were set in Myriad (1992), Adobe’s influential humanist sans serif, which later was an Apple system font for years and is as lacking in grunge as can possibly be. Observing that computers had not yet had much impact on the aesthetic of magazines, the anonymous writer saw the paradox in Carson’s digital grunge. “Carson’s work is testimony to the unexpected and surprising consequences of technology: that a neato, cute machine like the Macintosh could enable grit and grunge, sand and sin.”

In the late eighties, most people had little or no direct interaction with computers, which mostly functioned behind the scenes as they did in the print magazine realm. One of the only front-facing digital interactions woven into everyday life was with the ATM, or automated teller machine. ATMs had been introduced in the late sixties, and over the next fifteen years, became a standard way of completing minor financial transactions. While the machines became ubiquitous, the user interfaces remained quite rudimentary, without much more brand personality than a calculator. In 1989, however, Citibank unveiled a refreshed corporate identity that for the first time included its ATMs (figure 5.4). Led by Sylvia Harris, a founder of Two Twelve Associates, in collaboration with the bank’s in-house designers, this new branding for the first time focused on human–computer interaction (HCI). Through Harris, the ATMs became as friendly as a Macintosh; for the first time, a computer asked customers, “How may I help you?” and “What language shall we speak?” In reevaluating the potential of a seemingly dry conversation, Harris had found her calling, as she went on to have a storied career designing public information systems, including the US census forms.

Comes the Web

While print became digital, the digital screen would emerge and quickly become like print. In 1991, Tim Berners-Lee would set in motion the most ubiquitous computer interface of all time, the World Wide Web. Like Johannes Gutenberg more than five hundred years before

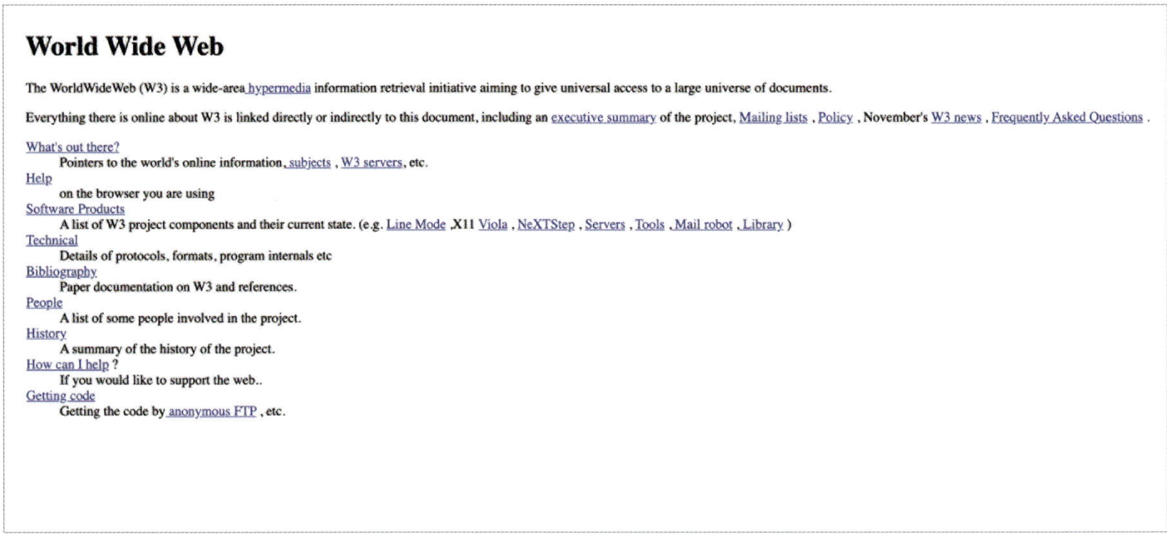

World Wide Web

The WorldWideWeb (W3) is a wide-area hypermedia information retrieval initiative aiming to give universal access to a large universe of documents.

Everything there is online about W3 is linked directly or indirectly to this document, including an executive summary of the project, Mailing lists , Policy , November's W3 news , Frequently Asked Questions .

What's out there?
  Pointers to the world's online information, subjects , W3 servers, etc.
Help
  on the browser you are using
Software Products
  A list of W3 project components and their current state. (e.g. Line Mode ,X11 Viola , NeXTStep , Servers , Tools ,Mail robot ,Library)
Technical
  Details of protocols, formats, program internals etc
Bibliography
  Paper documentation on W3 and references.
People
  A list of some people involved in the project.
History
  A summary of the history of the project.
How can I help ?
  If you would like to support the web..
Getting code
  Getting the code by anonymous FTP , etc.

5.5. Tim Berners-Lee, first public web page, 1991

him, Berners-Lee did not invent a new platform so much as combine existing technologies in a practical way. This first web page went live on August 6, 1991 (figure 5.5), solipsistically offering information about itself. Running on a NeXT computer at the Switzerland-based CERN research center, the first page was focused on the distribution of linked information. Billed as a "hypermedia information retrieval initiative aiming to give universal access to a large universe of documents," the first web page promised to provide information in a nonlinear, nonhierarchical format as a resource for researchers.

Although the term "hypermedia" aspired to a network that included images, the first web page was strictly text based. Berners-Lee sought universality of information, and the straightforward layout was instantly navigable. At this point, the web was an example of pure undesign, with Berners-Lee's browser showing black text on a gray neutral background, justified left and ragged right as it would appear on a piece of paper. Of course, the early web was modeled on print media in the same way that Gutenberg's bible had been modeled on the manuscript format. The only overtly digital element of the first web page was the bright blue color that indicated hyperlinks, fortuitously recalling the rubrication in red ink of the first printed books, through which scribes had likewise provided a point of emphasis amid a sea of text.

The birth years of the graphical internet were designed by technologists, not designers. As a source for sharing scientific information, the web was a visual medium only in the most literal sense. In 1993, the direction of the web started to change as CERN opened up the technology as a means of mass communication as opposed to a specialist network. That same year also saw the introduction of the first browser that could support inline images, Mosaic, by the National Center for Supercomputing Applications (NCSA). *Wired* magazine also started publishing in 1993, as the cultural transformation of the web advanced alongside the technical and, soon, mercantile realms. The code behind Mosaic led to the first commercial browser war starting in 1995, a quest for dominance between Marc Andreessen's Netscape Navigator—Andreessen had worked on Mosaic at the NCSA/University of Illinois—and Microsoft's Internet Explorer. Initially, Navigator dominated the web interface business, while its 1995 IPO initiated the dot-com gold rush, but over several years, Microsoft's built-in advantages pushed Netscape over the brink. Whereas Netscape needed the revenue from charging for commercial use of Navigator, Microsoft could afford to distribute Internet Explorer for free. With over 90 percent of the personal computer market of the early nineties wedded to Windows, Microsoft bundled its browser with its operating system, creating an incomparable advantage.

The invention of the browser interface opened up a new type of digital experience: browsing, or as it soon became known, "surfing" the internet. As new web pages proliferated, one could follow a rhizomatic path through the web, sometimes finding dead ends and dead links, other times fortuitously finding new facts or entertainment, or perhaps pornography. Surfing has remained a constant on the web over subsequent decades, with only the quantity and graphical sophistication ever changing. While digital experiences have often drawn analogy

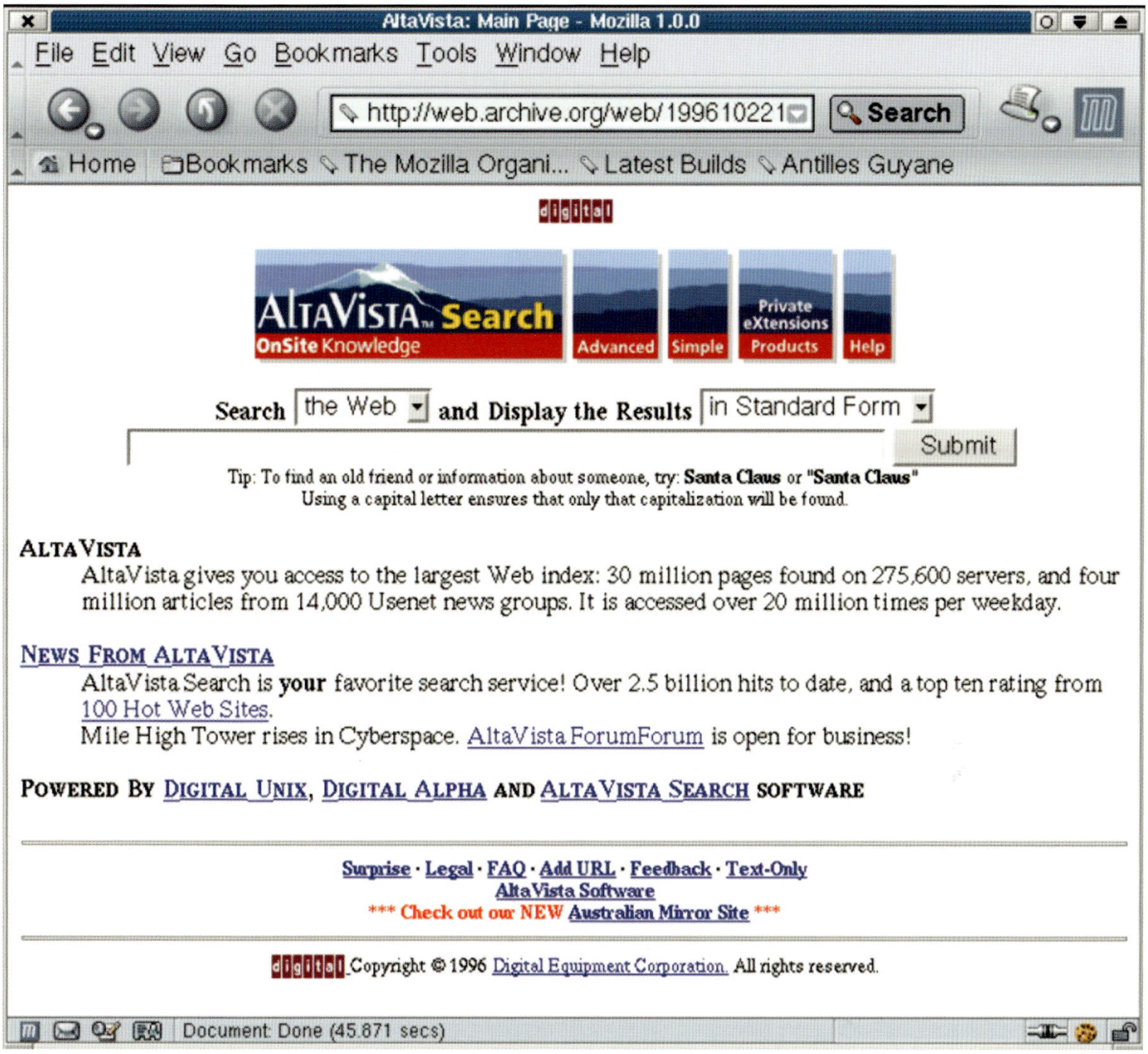

5.6. Digital Equipment Corporation's Alta Vista home page, 1996

to actual physical activities—surfing from wave to wave—the artist Ryan McNamara in 2013 attempted to invert that tendency. His dance-based performance piece, *MEEM: A Story Ballet About the Internet*, is one of the most evocative analog simulacra of a virtual experience ever produced. *MEEM* featured around a dozen dancers, some professional, others, including McNamara, not, riffing on a range of movements found surfing on YouTube. From hip-hop to ballet to uncategorizable, the piece presents a mélange of clashing styles and unexpected correspondences. To allow the theatergoer to actually feel the surf, the audience's seats were mounted on wheels, and viewers were abruptly shifted between different spaces with different dancers, simulating the kinetic experience of traversing the internet.

Web Design, Sorta

A web user of 1996 found HTML pages that were rigid and static: gray backgrounds, pixelated type, and garish colors inhabiting a low-resolution universe. To today's eyes, it is hard to imagine how such crude designs could have inspired such feverish futuristic speculation about the coming virtual existence. On the backend, new developments—the World Wide Web Consortium (W3C) standards, JavaScript, Cascading Style Sheets, search engines—were gradually emerging, but they had little immediate effect on the way the web looked. Consider the home page for DEC's Alta Vista search engine (figure 5.6), one of the original high-profile "super spiders" that scanned the roughly 30 million web pages of the early internet.

The only polished part of the Alta Vista page is barely visible at the top, and that is the DEC logotype. It had been designed in 1957 for print in a modernist vein by Elliot Hendrickson, and it showcased a then cutting-edge style, including all lowercase letters carved out of the negative space of a series of boxes. The hand lettering was custom designed, but in accordance with the fashion for geometric sans serif type, it appeared machine-like in its regularity. Over the years the original lettering had apparently been replaced at times by lowercase Helvetica, while the boxes had varied in size. In 1987, a DEC PostScript specialist named Ned Batchelder acquired photo scans of the old logo and imported them into Adobe Illustrator, bringing the logo into the digital age as a PostScript Type 3 font. Batchelder also regularized the width of the boxes and reshaped some of the letters. The result was an elegant example of the golden age of modernist corporate identity.

Outside the logo, the rest of the Alta Vista page is a hot mess by any design standard. At the top a centered, splintered banner meshes an abstract view of mountains—alta vista means "high view" in Spanish—with type of various weights and proportions. The Alta Vista logo itself features interspersed towering letters that are presumably meant to symbolically convey mountaintops. Nondescript pixelated type and conventional drop-down menus complete the composition, the layout of which shifts back and forth between centered and flush left. At the bottom of the page, the DEC logo reappears, reinforcing the contrast between digital design and simple functionality. The bar at the top of the page shows the Mozilla browser tool kit, featuring many of the same fundamental navigation options that still define browsing today.

The year 1996 was in fact pivotal in terms of the recognition that the HTML web lacked fundamental design principles. Web design at this point would experience a version of the process that had taken place over a century earlier in modern industrial design. At that time, a critical mass of design reformers arose organically to demand better designs of industrial objects. Before that cry rang out, industrial and graphic design had been left in the hands of the technologists, engineers who for the most part had little time or appreciation for aesthetic issues. Reformers succeeded by publicly calling attention to design deficiencies; a famous example came through the establishment of the Victoria & Albert Museum (V&A) in London in 1852. The founders of the V&A hoped to educate the public to join their cause and demand better industrial products. Over the ensuing decades, good design writ large gradually came to the fore; the modern design style emerged not so much because of some sort of artistic awakening, but because it became manifest to industrialists that good design was good business.

As the digital age supplanted the industrial, this same trajectory was repeated at a greatly accelerated pace. In 1996, the web was still largely planted in the technological milieu in which it had been invented. The thirst for change, however, was right under the surface, as proved by the success of one of the first web design guidebooks, David Siegel's *Creating Killer Web Sites* (figure 5.7). Siegel's book stormed to the top of the bestseller list at Amazon, then a one-year-old e-commerce bookseller. It was quickly translated into ten languages, and a revised edition appeared the next year. Siegel sought to "make the world more beautiful together," and in his second edition, he advised readers to peruse Jan Tschichold's *The Form of the Book: Essays on the Morality of Good Design*, which had been edited by Robert Bringhurst for an English edition released in 1991. Tschichold, a fervent promoter of the New Typography in the 1920s, who had turned apostate and embraced more classical styles after the war, had taken

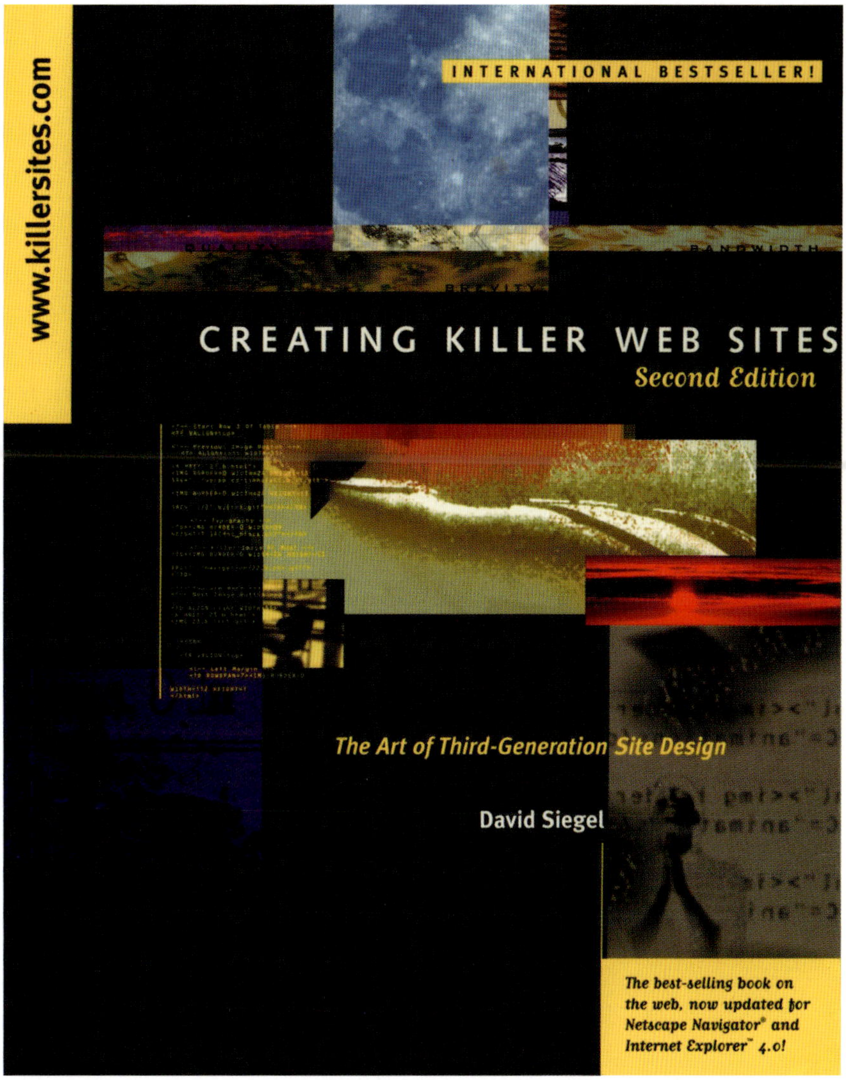

5.7. David Siegel, cover of *Creating Killer Web Sites*, first published in 1996

over the design brief at Penguin Books in the late forties. At Penguin, he established a culture that promulgated effective visual communication without ever becoming dogmatic about a single master style. Tschichold was a prolific author, and one of his shortest pieces, *Penguin Composition Rules*, which he compiled at the publishing house, had lasting influence, as it was one of the first ever corporate design standard manuals. Penguin's product, mass-market paperback books, was truly consonant with the early web. In the forties, paperbacks were exploding in popularity, but they were largely treated as consumables with little attention paid to the design.

Tschichold's *The Form of the Book*, which was a collection of general essays he had written over the two decades before his death in 1974, would find new life in the digital era thanks to Siegel's and other's recommendations, and it is still often cited by web designers as a formative text. While none of the suggestions in the book would prove earth shattering, Tschichold's moderate, pragmatic approach to books offered web designers of a later generation a set of flexible design fundamentals. Consider this: "Harmony between page size and the type area is achieved when both have the same proportions. If efforts are successful to combine page format and type area into an indissoluble unit, then the margin proportions become functions of page format and overall construction and thus are inseparable from either." Distributing this sort of sound advice in the web community was especially important, as many early practitioners had little design experience or education.

In *Creating Killer Web Sites*, Siegel argues, "Design drives the user's experience of the content," adding value in both an aesthetic and a commercial sense. "Who cares how great your content is if people aren't attracted to it or don't find it pleasurable to read?" He advocated for designers to take the web out of the hands of the technologists, or to at least strive for greater input. In today's terms, Siegel saw web engineers as a hindrance to both UI and UX, assert-

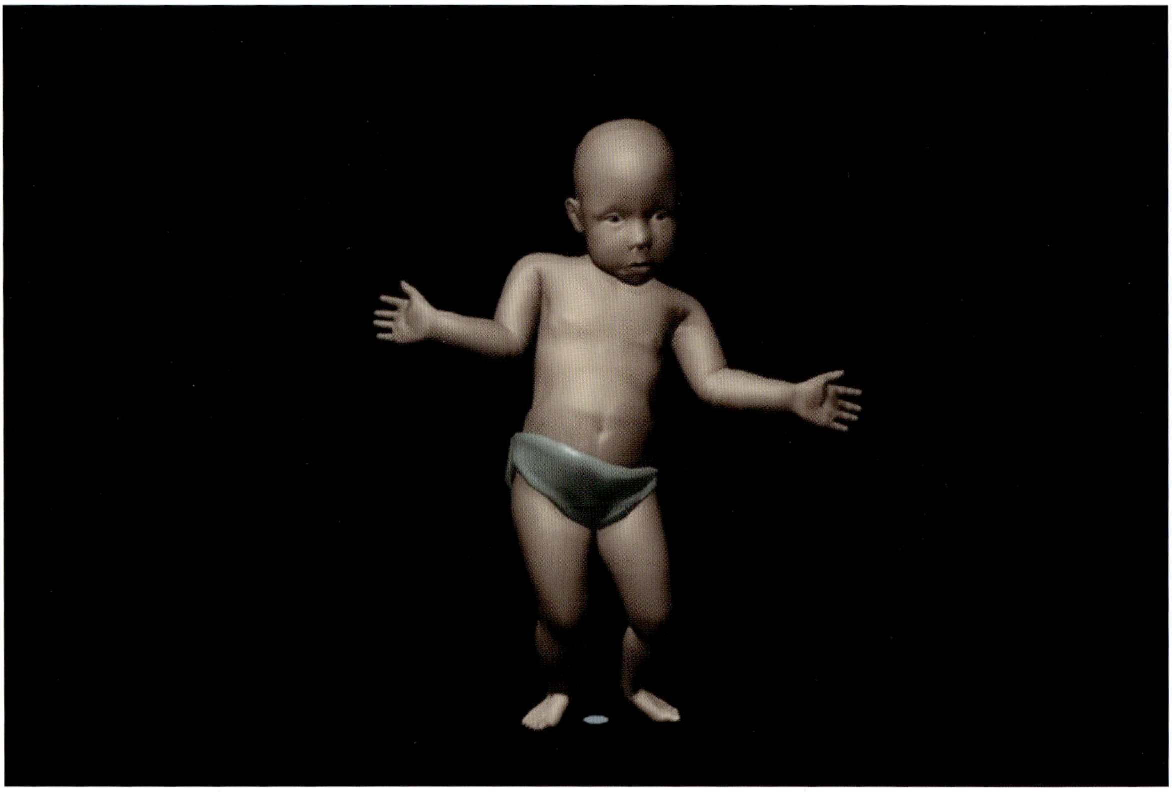

5.8. Michael Girard, Robert Lurye, and Ron Lussier's Dancing Baby GIF, c. 1995

ing that beauty and ease of use needed to be added to the graphical internet post haste. As another designer put it in late 1995, "Right now, the web looks like a collage of bad term papers."

Technologically speaking, Siegel was writing at a moment of constant flux, and his major strategy for adding design to the web was in fact a series of elaborate hacks, or workarounds, as he called them, that used inventive off-label strategies to improve typography and layout. The most famous of these he called the "Single-Pixel GIF Trick," which involved placing transparent, tiny GIFs amid the web page to lock in aspects of the layout. Siegel called it the "official duct tape of the web," and by his second edition he was encouraging designers and browser developers to find a way to make it unnecessary. Cognizant of the fact that his technical advice would soon be obsolete, Siegel hoped to make a lasting impact through his general call-to-arms and to spur a mass of designers to commit themselves to creating web pages that were as beautiful as a paperback book.

Siegel was not the only designer who experimented with GIFs, which at the time were one of the most important web technologies. GIF, short for "graphics interchange format," is a graphical file compression technique invented by Steve Wilhite at CompuServe in 1987. In that preweb age, CompuServe sold access to the internet for email, file sharing, and the like. Because modems were ever so slow and memory expensive, CompuServe engineers had sought an algorithmic strategy for compressing image files without losing the underlying data. Ingrid Daubechies was another pioneer of compression technology, known especially for her 1987 discovery of "wavelets," a mathematical strategy that allows compressed image files to maintain better resolutions (Daubechies is a baroness, and her coat of arms is inscribed "Divide ut comprimas," or, "Divide so you can compress"). GIFs were superior in some ways to the rival JPEG format, mainly because the latter's compression led to the loss of underlying data. While JPEGs tended to work well with photographs that have data to spare, the first photo published on the web was in fact a GIF.

With the launch in 1993 of the Mosaic web browser with its <img> tag, GIFs became an important way of adding static images to a website, often logos or other glyphs. But GIFs had another feature: they could be animated to produce short little moving vignettes. Like a flip book, the GIF would show a timed sequence of static images to produce the illusion of motion. This feature really came into its own in 1995 when Netscape Navigator 2.0 was released, the first iteration of the browser that supported animation. Readers of a certain age will surely

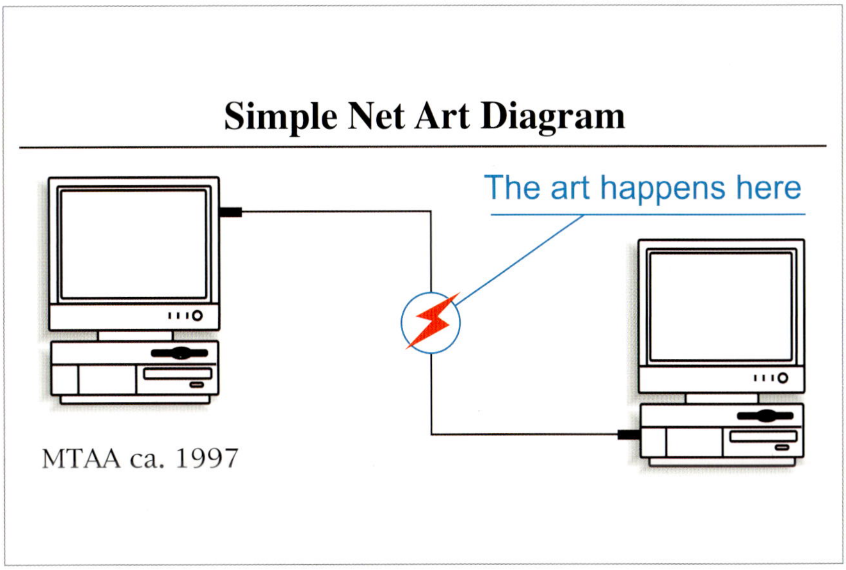

5.9. MTAA, *Simple Net Art Diagram*, 1997

remember the Dancing Baby of the midnineties (figure 5.8), an animated GIF that was created to demo some Autodesk character animation software but later circulated across the web as one of the first viral entertainments of the digital age.

The GIF also caught the attention of experimental digital artists who were just beginning to negotiate new web-based opportunities. The Brooklyn-based net art collective known as MTAA (an acronym formed by the founders' first initials plus "Art Associates") was formed in 1996 by Michael Sarff and Tim Whidden. Around 2000 they uploaded to the internet a simple, cheeky animated GIF called *Simple Net Art Diagram* (*SNAD*, figure 5.9). The flashing GIF acts like a roadside neon sign, with the interstitial lightning bolt blinking as a metaphor of creative magic. While *SNAD* became something of a minor art meme, the 2003 release of Abe Linkoln's new take, *The Complex Net Art Diagram*, solidified *SNAD*'s iconic stature. Linkoln's work expands the original diagram into the absurd, outlining a flow chart of byzantine complexity and surreal references. Along with April Greiman's version of a timeline, *Complex Net Art Diagram* subverts empirical knowledge keeping through fanciful digital pastiches.

On a grander scale, Moscow-born artist Olia Lialina in 1996 created her epic digital narrative *My Boyfriend Came Back from the War*. Lialina had previously worked in experimental film and trained as a film critic, and *My Boyfriend's* nonlinear storytelling and some of its visual strategies are recognizably cinematic. Yet, Lialina used HTML frames, hyperlinks, and GIFs—both static and animated—to invent a new kind of artistic communication on the web. The first line of simple text is quite powerful: "My boyfriend came back from the war. After dinner they left us alone." Per this setting, the work traverses the prickly terrain of a reunited couple, and clicking through the story advances the narrative but in a discontinuous, rather poetic format. New HTML frames keep opening on the same screen as you click, cluttering it visually and emotionally. *My Boyfriend* (like *Simple Net Art Diagram*) also opened the door to one of the most iconic qualities of digital media: the remix. Since its initial exhibition, other artists have re-created *My Boyfriend* dozens of times, adding new takes on the original material. These multiples—Abe Linkoln created a blog version in 2004—display the trajectory of digital technology, as new versions adapt the sentiment to new software. For example, Linkoln made his blog version at the height of personal blog mania. *My Boyfriend* has even been adapted into the social media realm, in a Twitter version (Anna Russett, 2014) as well as on Instagram (Kelsey Ford, 2017). The fluidity of *My Boyfriend* perhaps points to an important survival strategy of digital art insomuch as it defeats the accelerated technological obsolescence that has bedeviled many artists since the nineties.

While Lialina's work would colonize the future, some iconic nineties net artworks reclaimed concepts from the predigital era. Such was the case with Lynn Hershman Leeson's 1996 *CybeRoberta* (figure 5.10), which was a continuation of a project she had initiated in 1973. In that year Hershman Leeson had first introduced Roberta Breitmore, a fictive person who gradually gained the modern trappings of an identity. Breitmore got a driver's license and joined Weight Watchers in San Francisco, while also

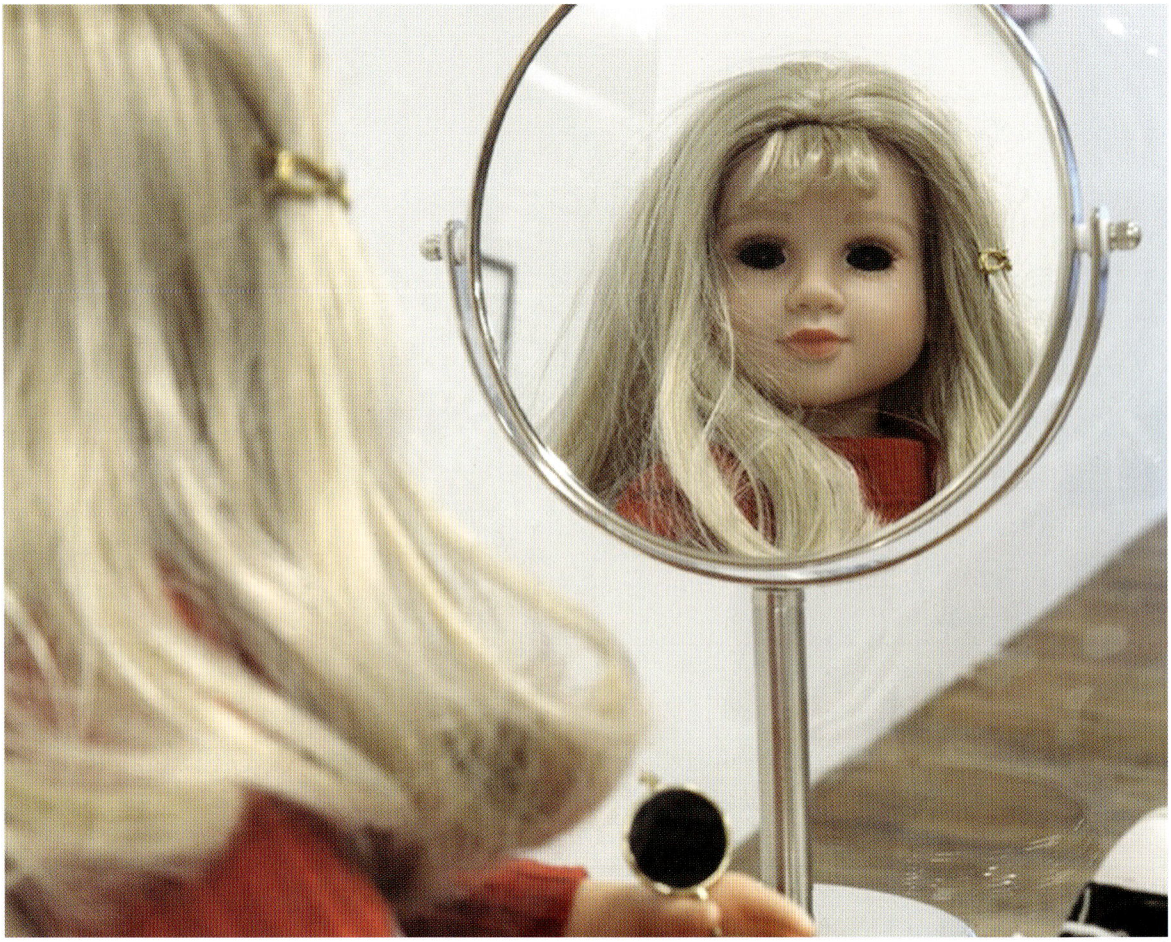

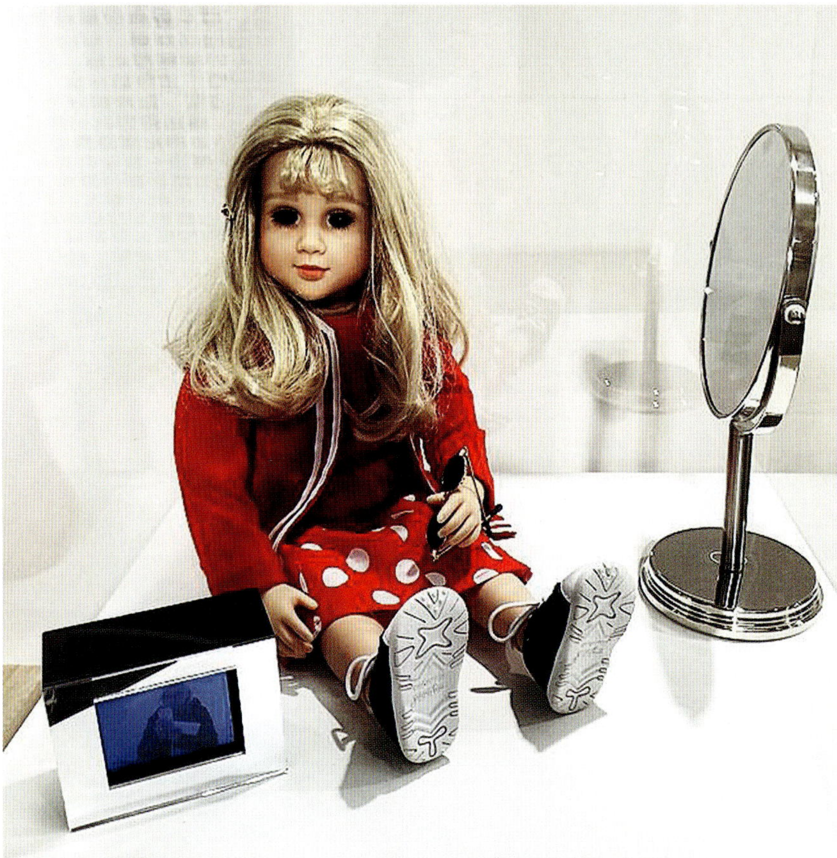

5.10. Lynn Hershman Leeson, *CybeRoberta*, 1996

developing her own sense of personal style. Breitmore was like a predigital avatar, interacting with real people in tangible situations. This meditation on identity ended in 1978. Eighteen years later Hershman Leeson revisited Breitmore as a form of net art newly christened *CybeRoberta*. This new iteration consisted of a robotic doll with video cameras for eyes. Users on the internet could watch the livestream from the doll and even turn its head back and forth to survey its surroundings. Clearly, artists such as Hershman Leeson were aware of the discourses around surveillance and cyborgs that are threaded throughout the digital world.

Web Design Studios

During the same years that Hershman Leeson created *CybeRoberta*, and Siegel was writing *Creating Killer Web Sites*, several entrepreneurial young designers, including Siegel himself, were establishing some of the first digital media studios. One designer, Maria Giudice, cofounded YO Design in San Francisco in 1992. The trajectory of Giudice's career offers insight into how the web design field emerged. Giudice had studied graphic design at Cooper Union in New York City during the eighties, and then gotten a job working for noted information designer Richard Saul Wurman (who went on to create TED in 1984) at the San Francisco design studio he christened The Understanding Business, or TUB. Wurman had developed a line of travel books called the Access Guides, which were notable for organizing information by neighborhood—for example, the Marais in Paris—as opposed to by subject matter: hotels, restaurants, major sites, and so on. Giudice worked on the Access Guides but in 1987 moved to San Francisco as part of the Wurman team that was designing new Pacific Bell telephone books.

Years later, when she cofounded YO along with Lynne Stiles, Giudice was still working strictly in print. One of her clients, Peachpit Press, was a nascent purveyor of computer books, especially oriented toward the Macintosh and digital design topics. One day, Peachpit came to Giudice and asked if she would design a website for them. As she later related in an American Institute of Graphic Arts (AIGA) interview, "I didn't know what a website was but I was sure I could do it. We applied the principles of information design to the Web and it worked perfectly." The resulting site had a playful feel to it, with bright colors and quirky little low-resolution illustrations setting apart a row of buttons set as a banner. Clearly based on static print models, the design was not too far from the original plain hyperlink-infused pages that had inaugurated the web only a few years before. Despite its design limitations, one could make the case that the eclectic assortment of links to various books—each with its own illustrated logo—conveyed the excitement and variety of Peachpit's offerings effectively.

The colophon to the Peachpit website showed how the internet was already changing commerce, as Peachpit in 1996 employed a ten-person web team. Still, the web had not yet become central to the work of design studios, as Giudice and Stiles's names linked only to their AOL email addresses, and YO did not have its own website. Almost overnight, YO had become a digital media studio, although print would remain the mainstay of the business until the closure of the firm in 1997. Clearly, the existing print design profession was determinant in establishing parameters—static, booklike pages—for early web design.

In 1997, Giudice and Stiles, along with technology writer Darcy Dinucci, authored *Elements of Web Design*, a combination showcase book and how-to guide. Published by their erstwhile client Peachpit Press, the book opened with a *Wired* magazine-esque boldface pronouncement: "The World Wide Web has fired a fuse under the internet, transforming it from a mysterious buzzword to one of the hottest topics in business and the media." *Elements of Web Design* stood right on the cusp of major changes in web design, as the static model held firm—the book is replete with analogies to print design techniques—but it also conveyed how animation and interaction were on the horizon. Also, in 1997, the Giudice and Stiles partnership faltered, and Giudice opened her next design venture, a firm christened HOT. She has recounted that her commissions did not transition to majority digital until the late nineties, after the point when all design tools—the book *Elements of Web Design* is typical as it had been produced using QuarkXPress, Illustrator, and Photoshop—had shifted to screens. Giudice has noted that the collaborative nature of web design won her over, as she preferred the camaraderie of a diverse team. "It was art and science combined. You had to work with people with different skills: engineers, coders, writers, and business people. It wasn't just about design anymore."

Another leading digital designer of the era, Loretta Staples, got her West Coast start at Wurman's TUB in 1988 after having graduated from the Rhode Island School of Design and Yale. Although Staples would go on to enjoy a fairly brief albeit top-flight career—she worked at both TUB and Apple before opening her own studio U dot I in 1992—she is perhaps best known for walking away from the practice of digital design. A little backstory: Perhaps because so many of the design professions were formed amid the counterculture of the sixties, it had become something of a trope for designers to question the social values of their line of work. As early as 1964, British graphic designer Ken Garland had published an essay called "First Things First," a manifesto asserting that designers needed to use their skills "for worthwhile purposes." This idea of design for social justice had gained further traction in the eighties as it became associated with the uber-influential designer Tibor Kalman; Kalman attempted to navigate a career based on selling products while feeling that he had maintained certain moral principles.

Near the end of the twentieth century, Garland's original manifesto was updated and republished as "First Things First 2000" by a new generation of socially conscious designers. This is where Staples entered the fray. In response to "First Things First 2000," she wrote a short essay that argued, essentially, that feeling conflicted like Kalman was not enough. While hedging a bit, Staples made the case that digital design was simply untenable as a profession. "Could it be that increasingly graphic design is less the solution and more the problem? This is the squeamish possibility professional graphic designers are loathe to confront, because in so doing, the profession risks undoing itself. This is the threat posed by any rigorous discursive critique. And graphic designers are as seduced as their clients and publics into believing design's mythological status (after all, we made the myth; it's called "self-promotion").... In closing, I call on the manifesto's signers (and all its adherents) to take a close hard look at the cultural location of your own practice. If you're serious about your claims, take apart everything you ever thought you knew about what you're doing. Set out in uncharted territory. But if you do, if you really do, something tells me you'll no longer recognize what you're doing as design. Because that will no longer be what it is." While she taught design for a time after finishing her corporate career, Staples eventually opted out of the profession, becoming a painter and then a therapist. In 2008 she wrote a brief memoir aptly titled *Leaving Design*. Of course, just as Staples removed herself from the world of UI, the profession itself was extending its reach.

While many digital designers set up shop in the Bay Area near Silicon Valley, in New York City, the stronghold of the nation's advertising business, a handful of firms formed in a location jokingly referred to as Silicon Alley. One of the first East Coast digital design firms, Razorfish, was founded in 1995 in an East Village (back when that meant impoverished) apartment by two childhood friends, Jeffrey Dachis and Craig Kanarick. The two had lost touch over the years but serendipitously ran into each other one day on the streets of New York City, instantly developing a rapport over the potential they both saw in the graphical web. While Kanarick had degrees in computer science and visual communication (the latter from MIT), Dachis entered the field of digital design from a place of bricolage, having spent his twenties in various pursuits. Another significant line of influence was video games, as Dachis and Kanarick were part of the first generation to have spent their childhoods interacting with a screen. Intoxicated by the dawn of the digital age of commerce, Dachis and Kanarick set up shop as web designers without capital or even much of a business plan.

Perhaps because of their history playing video games, the founders of Razorfish were committed to the idea that animation was the key element of the web. When Navigator 2.0 was released in 1995, Kanarick immediately began experimenting with server-push technology and animated GIFs. The resulting website he christened The Blue Dot, a reference to the earth when viewed from outer space. The Blue Dot was an online art gallery, but what caught the imagination of legions of web designers was the eponymous dot, which bounced around the screen like nothing else on the web. The Blue Dot website proved to be key to Razorfish's success as a commercial business, as it became the promotional basis for their efforts to woo clients.

Within months of the Blue Dot site going live, Razorfish had won lucrative contracts with large corporations, including Sony and Bankers Trust. Dachis pointed to the technical acumen at Razorfish as the key to their success in 1995, when he told the *New York Times*, "We understand the technology, we eat and breathe it. With technology changing every six weeks, I'm not sure the big companies or the ad agencies can compete at that pace." For years Razorfish maintained the Blue Dot for its halo effect, assuring clients that the studio's creative energy was not strictly mercantile. In 1998, the Razorfish Subnetwork, a compendium of the firm's online art projects, was brought into the permanent collection of the

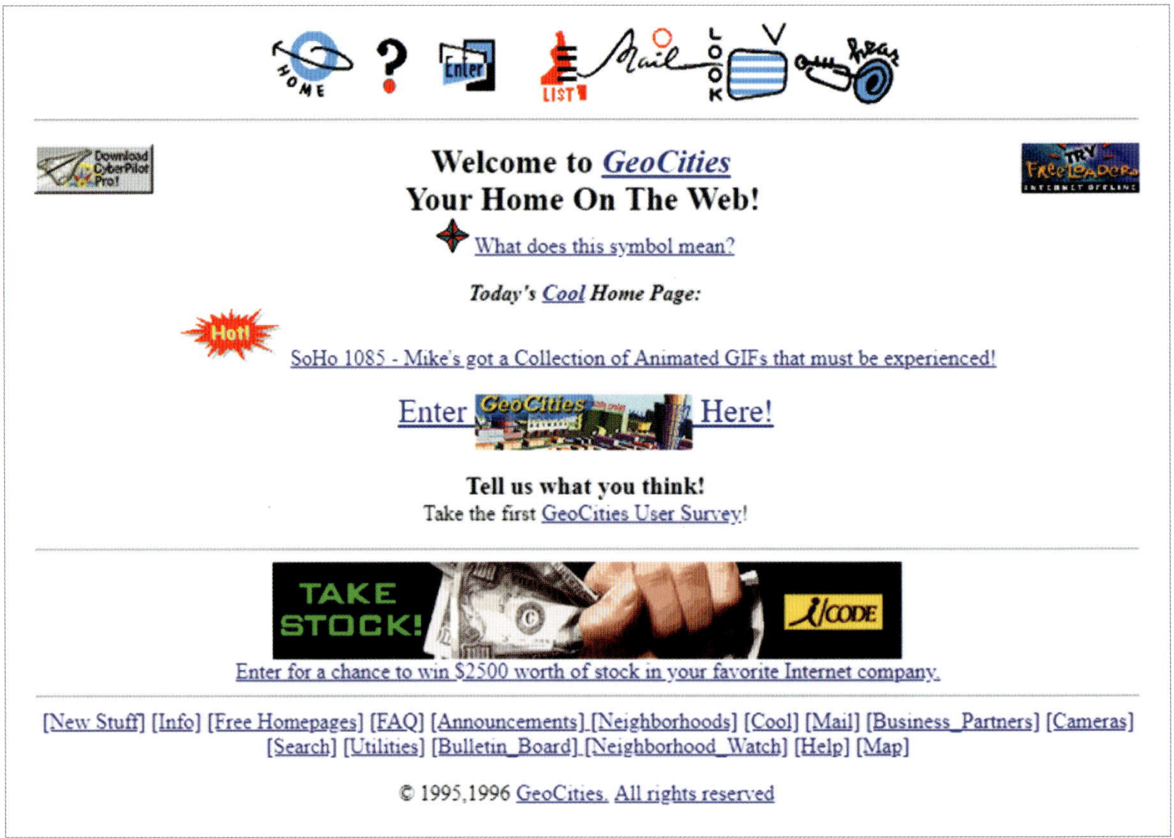

5.11. GeoCities, created by David Bohnett and John Rezner in 1995

San Francisco Museum of Modern Art, in one of the first instances of a museum recognizing and collecting digital design.

Home Pages

On the emerging web, professionally designed, artful sites were often lost amid the clutter of DIY home pages. A decade before social media colonized the personalized web, individual home pages represented many people's entrée into the virtual world, either as a creator or as a surfer looking for facts on a hobby, history, band, or the like. The center of this amateur universe in the early web was called GeoCities (figure 5.11), which was a free hosting service founded in 1995 by David Bohnett and John Rezner. GeoCities quickly found a ready audience, and by the late nineties, it would become one of the top three most-visited web fiefdoms, while its 1997 IPO reaped yet another dot-com fortune.

Users of GeoCities were called "Homesteaders," and the city, neighborhood, street theme was used as an organizing principle in the web directory. In practice, however, GeoCities functioned more like an undifferentiated sea of flotsam and jetsam, as some pages represented the fruits of a great deal of research and thought, while many were of only cursory interest and any information therein of questionable provenance. From a design standpoint, GeoCities would become notorious in later years for the unrestrained awfulness of many of its pages; today there is even a snarky website that features a "GeoCities-izer" that will transform any page into a GeoCities template so that viewers can look back and chortle about the nineties web. GeoCities pages typically offered clashing colors, blinking banners, distracting backgrounds, and ill-chosen display typefaces, all of this usually centered down the page with odd gaps. As the business model developed, GeoCities monetized the sites by placing banner ads on them that added yet another strained voice to the design cacophony. While GeoCities may not have helped average people learn web design skills, it did normalize the internet for many users.

Bought at the dot-com peak by Yahoo for almost $4 billion in stock in 1999, GeoCities represented yet another example of how web design had gained little traction overall before the turn of the millennium. GeoCities was finally shuttered in 2009, when it was already a relic of a past age. Most headlines failed to mourn its demise, with *TechRadar* summing up the common sentiment: "GeoCities Closes: Fond

Memories of Free Sites and Terrible Web Design." At the time of its end of life, almost forty million pages had been created for the site, and many decried the fact that Yahoo chose to erase this substantial record of the development of the personal web. In the end, fewer than a million pages were successfully archived for posterity.

Both midnineties web design books mentioned above—Giudice's *Elements of Web Design* and Siegel's *Creating Killer Web Sites*—made brief note of the evolving software that was enabling more sophisticated web animation. Giudice, for example, offered a few pages on Macromedia's Shockwave Player, which the company released in 1995 as a complement to its Director multimedia-authoring software. Digital as print was thriving, but interactivity and animation appeared on the horizon.

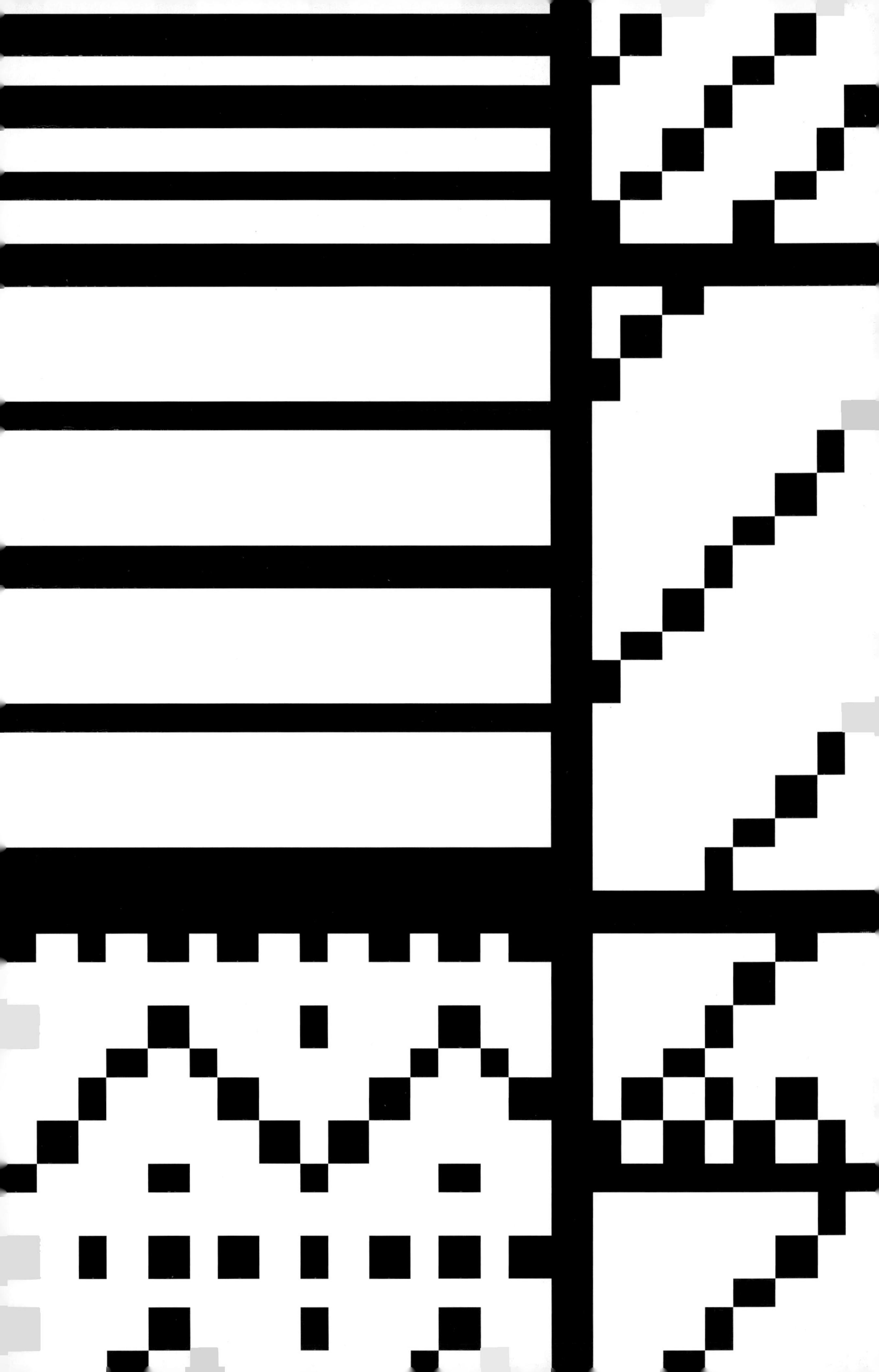

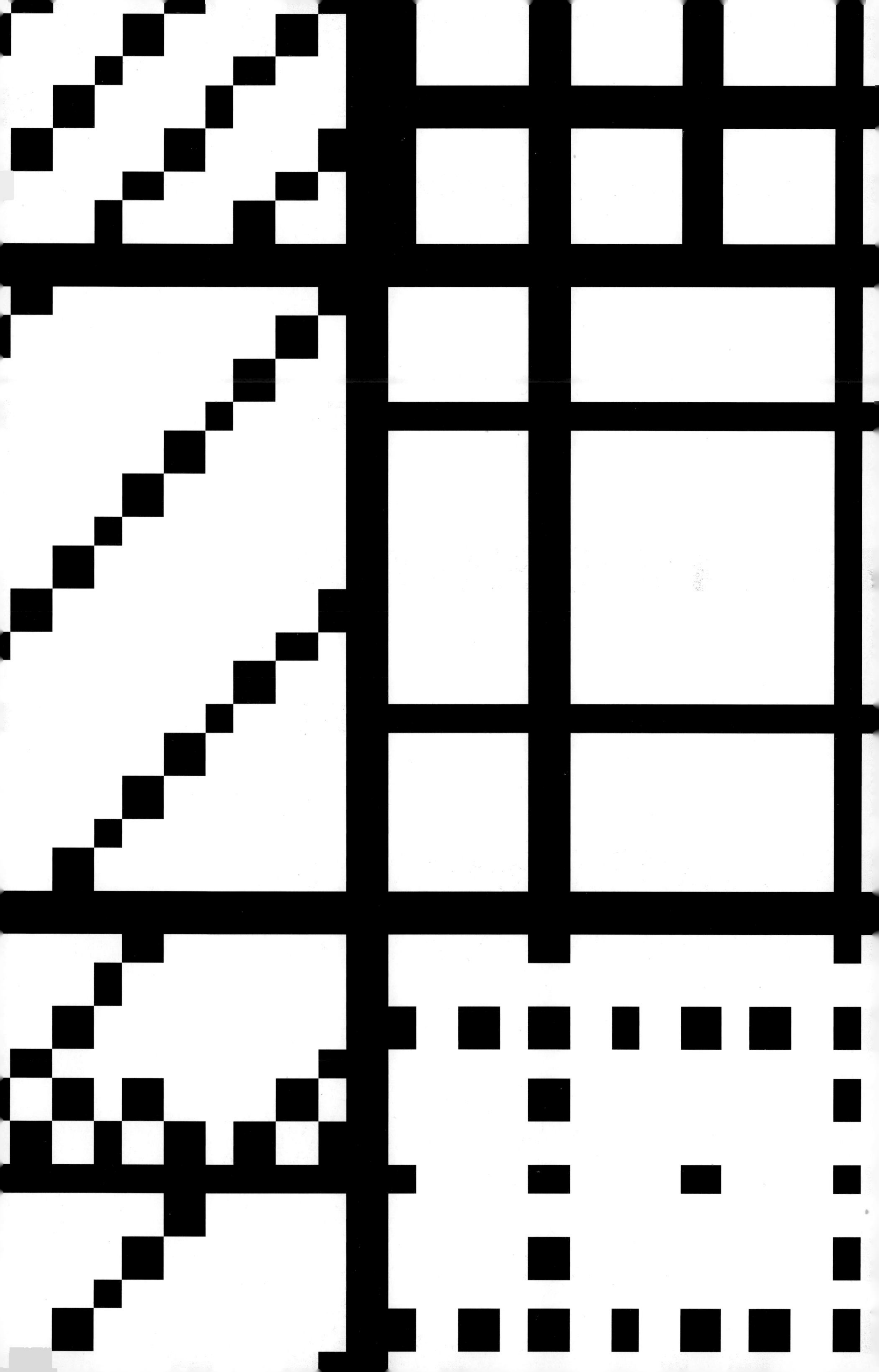

6.1. Jørn Utzon, Sydney Opera House, 1973

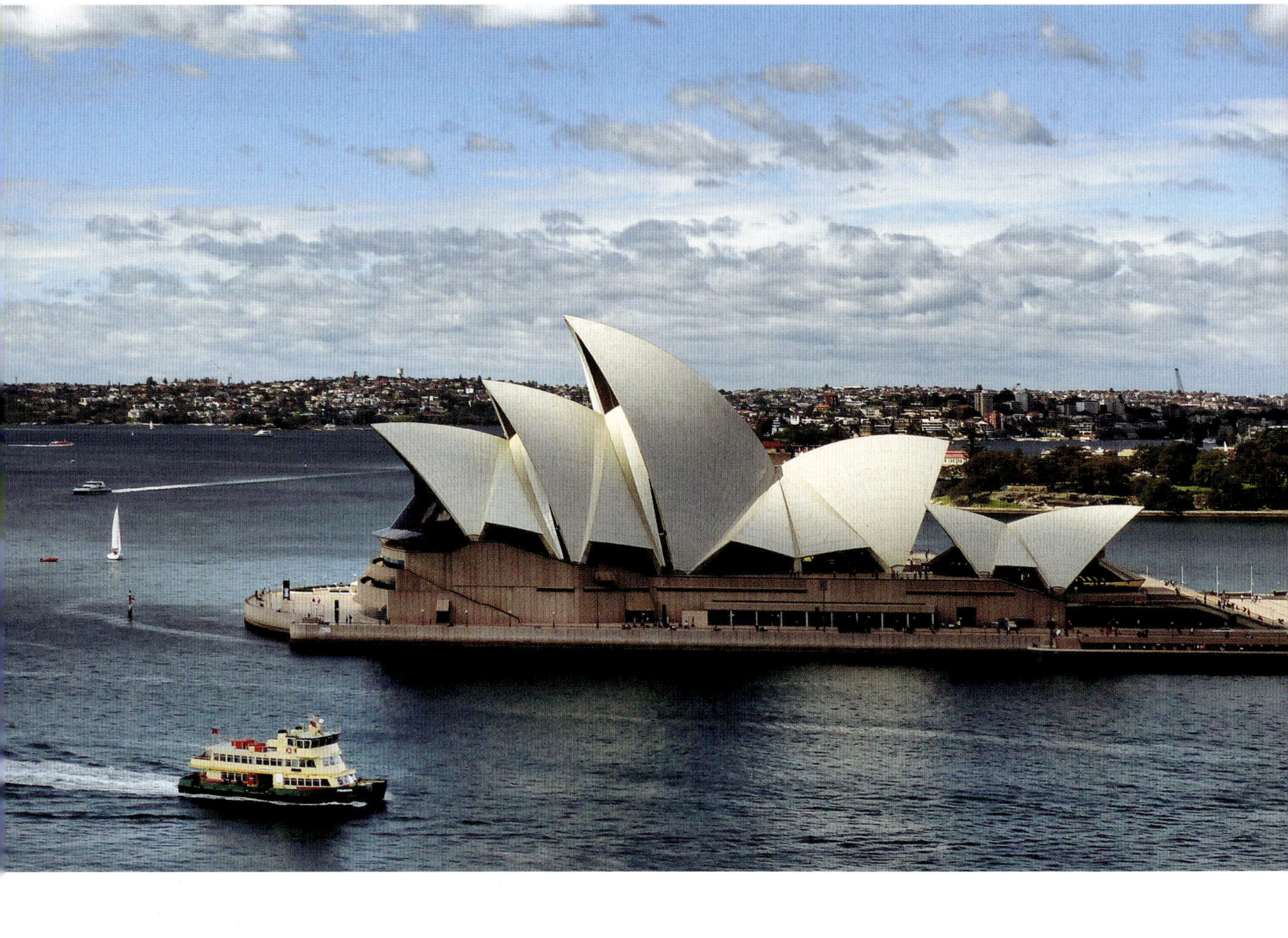

Six. Digital Architecture I: *Origins*

"The appearance of permanence (buildings are solid; they are made of steel, concrete, bricks, etc.) is increasingly challenged by the immaterial representation of abstract systems (television and electronic images)." It has now been over thirty years since Bernard Tschumi wrote these McLuhanesque words in the context of his *Glass Video Gallery* (Groningen, 1990). Since then, numerous physical and virtual projects have responded to the idea that the digital world has materially, perceptually, and ideologically fractured the conventional norms of architectural practice. While today computers are mundane, and all contemporary architecture is digitally designed, only a small fraction of buildings announces those circumstances declaratively: most contemporary structures are indistinguishable from their analog predecessors.

In December 1964 the Boston Architectural Center—a collaborative effort largely sponsored by Harvard University and the Massachusetts Institute of Technology—hosted a pathbreaking one-day conference entitled "Architecture and the Computer." The participants included a cross section of the field, including various engineers, design architects, and historians. The proceedings ran the gamut; many of the sessions dealt with technical issues, as when MIT engineer Steven Coons showcased Ivan Sutherland's Sketchpad (1963) for computer-aided design.

The evening session featured design luminaries, with the panel opened by the reading of a short paper penned by the octogenarian Walter Gropius. As could be expected, Gropius offered platitudinous advice urging acceptance of computers as facilitators that "might help us to free our creative power." It is notable to witness how Gropius was still navigating the treacherous waters of "mechanization," as he and Siegfried Giedion had referred to the impact of industrial machines on design in an earlier era. In 1923 Gropius had proffered choice words on the subject, asserting as director of the Weimar Bauhaus, "Mechanized work is lifeless, proper only to the lifeless machine." In 1964 his thinking had been inverted, and he wrote of computers, "Some people scorn violently the idea that lifeless machines could be of any advantage to inventive thinking." Clearly, over the decades Gropius had adopted Giedion's view that machines were like fire, a volatile tool that creative people must harness to their will.

In any event, Gropius provided both star power to the conference and an actual living link to the Bauhaus, which has served as a digital touchstone. His emphasis on computers as helpmates represented one of the clearest threads in the conference, especially insomuch as MIT's Sketchpad was repeatedly invoked as opening the field to digital draftsmanship. Also, the conference featured a demonstration of STRESS (Structural Engineering Systems Solver), a parametric program and precursor to building information modeling (BIM) software, which could calculate structural loads when run on MIT's IBM 7094. The 7094 mainframe is a legendary machine that was at the cutting edge of early sixties technology, and although there was much talk of computer time shares, clearly few if any architects would have realistic access to either Sketchpad or STRESS.

The other major thread at the conference was a more theoretical consideration of what digital technology would mean for the design of buildings. There were no answers given, but the most thoughtful remarks came from Christopher Alexander, the architect and design theorist famous for his insights into human-centered design and pattern languages. Alexander argued that contemporary computers at best represented access to an "army of a thousand clerks," who were "all stupid and entirely without initiative." Alexander insisted that architecture as it was currently practiced was altogether not that complicated, and there was no need to employ this army of clerks because they were essentially superfluous. While he saw no "unanswerable complexities" that necessitated computational power, Alexander warned that the growing enthusiasm for digital tools would lead architects astray. He stated, "The effort to state a problem in such a way that a computer can be used to solve it, will distort your view of the problem." As an example, Alexander recounted the story of a hospital design in which the architects used computers to precisely project foot traffic in the hallways, mainly because that was what the computer could accomplish. The resulting building was functionally unsuitable because it had been designed around a parameter that did not produce a holistic success, just a bad building with precisely measured foot traffic. Alexander's future espousing human-centered software design was evident even at this early stage of his career.

As could be expected from such a forward-looking conference, the Architectural Center's proceedings feature more questions and speculative assessments than answers. That being said, the unbridled fascination with early iterations of CAD and BIM—as mundane as they might be from a theoretical perspective—proved more than prescient in the decades to come. By far the most defining thread in the development of digital architecture has been the development of software for both design and engineering tasks. Of course, drawings and models have a long predigital history. None other than Leon Battista Alberti codified his views on the subject in the middle of the fifteenth century. In the book *De re aedificatoria* (*Ten Books on Architecture*, 1452), Alberti set several precedents in the use of architectural drawings and models. In book two of the tome, he made the case for building three-dimensional models, as they "allow one to increase or decrease the size of those elements freely, to exchange them, and to make new proposals and alterations until everything fits together well and meets with approval. Furthermore, it will provide a surer indication of the likely costs—which is not unimportant—by allowing one to calculate the width and the height of individual elements, their thickness, number, extent, form, appearance, and quality, according to their importance and the workmanship they require." This passage sounds like a contemporary pitch for a full suite of digital design tools!

Alberti also devised 2D standards and was essentially the first architect to devise a computational strategy for producing drawings. Using an algorithmic process, Alberti developed a system for indicating precise scale on these "blueprints." As noted in the introduction, Alberti used drawings to shift the practice of the architect from an artisanal one to a theoretical one. The architect no longer needed to be present at the building site.

The trajectory of developing today's architectural software appears fairly straightforward in hindsight. It began with the development of computer-aided design programs such as AutoCAD (Autodesk, 1982) and ArchiCAD (Graphisoft, 1987), both of which sought to offer a suite of digital tools for architecture based on CAD programs used for industrial design. Before these consumer products came out, only large firms with the resources to purchase bespoke systems had had any access to the digital. These first programs really only allowed for two-dimensional drafting to move from paper to screen and represented more of a productivity enhancer than a digital turn.

The next wave of software came to market in the late nineties and enabled a shift from 2D drafting to fully three-dimensional modeling of prospective buildings. At this point virtual-minded architects gained the same tools as Alberti. McNeel Rhinoceros, known as Rhino, first appeared in 1998, followed quickly by Revit in 2000 (the rather awkward name is a contraction of "Revise-Instantly": Revit was bought by Autodesk in 2002). SketchUp, a 3D modeling program, appeared in 2000 and was bought by Google in 2006, thus becoming freeware that helped to popularize the genre. Finally, another 3D CAD package, Digital Projects—a collaboration between the Frank Gehry studio and Dassault Systèmes, the latter a longtime maker of CATIA (computer-aided three-dimensional interactive application) for industrial design—joined the competition in 2002 (Digital Project and SketchUp are now owned by Trimble). It should be noted that architects often used CAD software that was not developed for their profession. In the years before architecturally specific software came to dominate the market, many architects used drawing, animation, and modeling programs such as Photoshop or Maya for their work.

From an aesthetic standpoint, one of the greatest challenges of the digital age may be combating the homogeneity that can creep into the designs made by architects using the same computer programs. While software programs may seem to represent a type of open-ended creative medium—a sandbox if you will—in practice they tend to lead architects and designers down a certain path because of the programs' UX and UI. Anyone experienced with design software knows that certain tasks or a given sequence of clicks work more smoothly than others on an intuitive level; inadvertently, a group of designers will be channeled into a narrower range of solutions than they might admit. This was equally true twenty years ago as digital design came of age in architecture; for example, Charles Stilworth told the *New York Times* in 2000, "Sometimes I see a finished building and say, 'oh, yeah, that was made using Form Z [a 3D modeling program by AutoDesSys first released in 1991].' " Stilworth also noted that Maya promulgated wavelike forms while AutoCAD "favors extrusions." Of course, banal regularity is not an issue just in digital architecture but has been notable across the spectrum of contemporary design arts.

Rhino, Revit, and the others have continued over the last two decades to successfully add features such as parametric modeling and generative applications, which have made them an essential, even defining, feature of architectural practice. As the major platforms have grown, they have gradually absorbed more specialized tools; for example, the environmental planning software Ecotect became Revit: Solar Analysis in 2015. Finally, these design programs have gradually become integrated with specialized construction and engineering software, as a whole other run of programs from the early 2000s have enabled the integration of design with BIM programs, such as Tekla Structures. With BIM software, all stakeholders in a given building—architects, engineers, and construction managers—can work together on a single cloud-based virtual model that warehouses all technical and aesthetic details.

The design and construction of two iconic structures—the Sydney Opera House (figure 6.1, 1973) and Guggenheim Museum Bilbao (figure 6.2, 1997)—amply demonstrate how software first entered the architectural profession. While many people may associate Frank Gehry's museum with the onset of the digital age, few recognize how central digital technology was to the creation of Jørn Utzon's design almost five decades earlier. In 1957, unknown Danish architect Utzon won a worldwide competition with his dynamic, decidedly analog, hand-drawn sketches. Enthusiastically synthesizing references to sailing ships and Mesoamerican temples, the northern European architect designed a striking building for an Australian city he had never visited.

Importantly, Utzon had little engineering background and had not entered the competition expecting the need to make good on his ambitious design. Fortunately, the legendary British

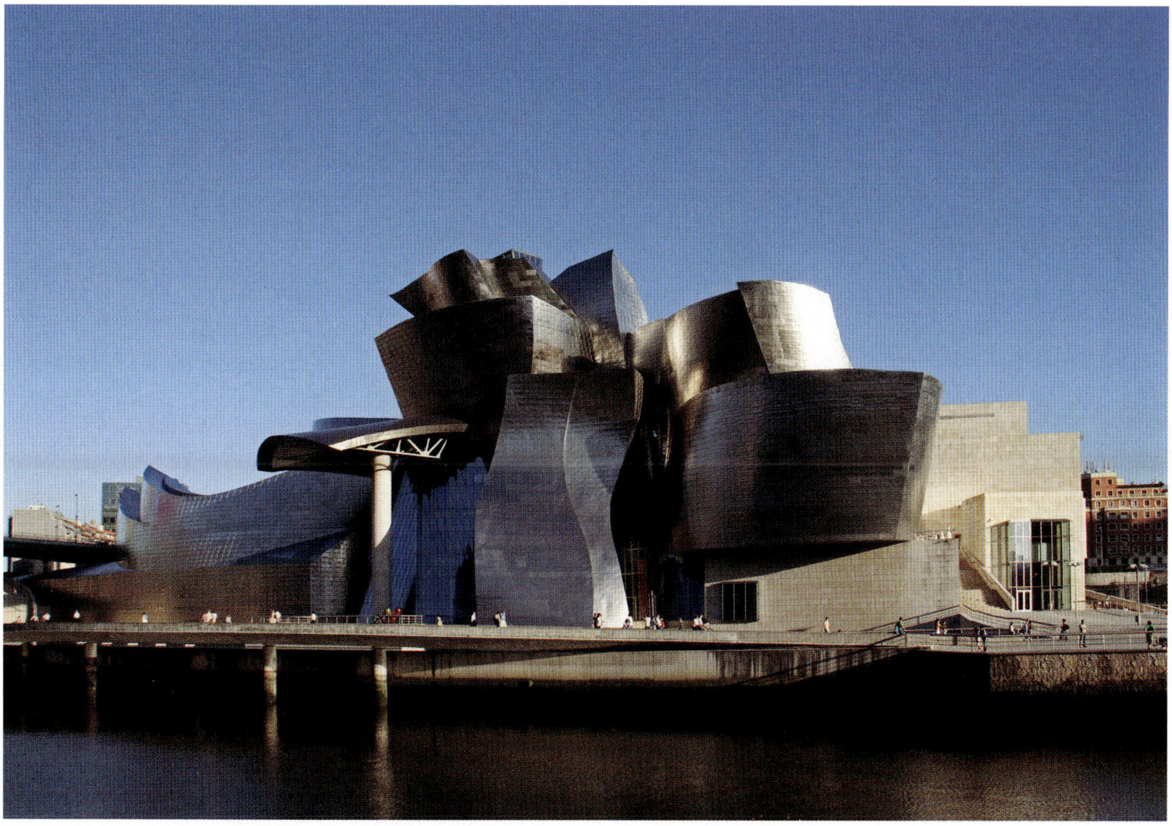

6.2. Frank Gehry, Guggenheim Museum Bilbao, 1997

engineer Ove Arup heard of the project and reached out to Utzon to offer his firm's expertise. Over the next half decade, Utzon and Arup worked to make his sketches into a buildable structure. Much of this labor was accomplished through conventional means, especially the production of acrylic models in varying shapes that could be subjected to stress tests. Arup pioneered the use of computational analysis, however, using a Ferranti Pegasus Mark 1 computer and custom software to further investigate a structurally sound design for the building's curving, sweeping roofs. This engineering work resulted in a major change to the design, as the proportions of the actual building were changed in response to the calculations (it is narrower and a bit taller than the original plan). Insomuch as the opera house's design was modified because of the results of a pathbreaking use of a computer program, more attention should be paid to the historical fact that it is arguably the very first digital monument.

Almost four decades after Utzon entered the Sydney Opera House competition, American architect Frank Gehry won the commission for a branch of the Guggenheim Museum to be sited on the banks of the River Nervión in Bilbao, Spain. At that time, Bilbao had become inextricably linked with the words "fading industrial city" and was looking for a cultural landmark that could rebrand it for the world. Gehry has recounted the pressure he felt: "They said: 'Mr. Gehry, we need the Sydney Opera House. Our town is dying.'" The subsequent design of sweeping asymmetric curves glittering in titanium is one of the iconic structures of the contemporary digital. But of course, its design—part fish, part boat, part Corbusian curves—was strictly analog. Gehry was in his sixties at the time and had spent his entire career using a traditional sketching and model-making process, one he was not looking to abruptly discard. Where the building became digital was through its fabrication. Gehry's staff transferred his design to what was essentially CAE (computer-aided engineering) as opposed to CAD software. The program was Dassault Systèmes's CATIA, a 3D modeler from the seventies that had been developed for engineering aircraft. What the software allowed for was the construction of a complex assortment of bespoke titanium panels that came together like a puzzle to create the overall form. Presumably, the Guggenheim could have been constructed in an artisanal, predigital fashion, but of course the expense would have been astronomical. The Sydney Opera House and Guggenheim Bilbao are alike in terms of both design and stature. What is notable is how their roles are actually the reverse of their reputations; the opera house in fact pioneered digital design in a way the museum did not. The latter, however, led the way in opening architects' eyes to the design freedom that could be facilitated by digital fabrication.

While Frank Gehry at times in his career has been grouped with the deconstructivists—he was included in Philip Johnson's exhibition of that name at the MoMA in 1988—he had never gravitated toward the more radically theoretical side of architecture favored by many of that cohort. In many ways, Gehry's adoption of the digital was practical and straightforward. In contrast, during the same years in which he labored on the Guggenheim commission, a group of architects centered around Peter Eisenman worked to envision a digital age marked by byzantine theoretical complexity.

Digital Theory Colonizes Architecture

A correlative relationship—or was it causal?—was espoused beginning in 1992 by a circle of contributors to *Architectural Digest* (*AD*) magazine that associated digital architecture with aspects of poststructuralist theory, especially that of Gilles Deleuze. This episode, whereby the most complex, at times impenetrable, poststructuralist theory was wedded to digital design, represents a singular happening in the field of technology. While thinkers such as Walter Benjamin had famously sought to investigate changes in subjectivity of the recent past—the experience of the bourgeois-dominated urban environment, for example—never before had practitioners adopted such a forward-looking stance concerning the future.

In architectural shorthand, Eisenman and Greg Lynn are known for having promulgated the idea of the digital fold, an extrapolation of the theoretical preoccupations of the French philosopher Gilles Deleuze. Allow for a brief segue into the theoretical weeds: it is important to sketch out a bit of the context of the Deleuzian fold, as it forms a thread that runs through much of the philosopher's prolific oeuvre. In the eighties, Deleuze, along with his collaborator and coauthor the psychoanalyst Felix Guattari, mounted a reconsideration of what they saw as the static hierarchies of modern thought. Focusing less on the exercise of state-sponsored macropower as in fascist regimes, Deleuze and Guattari sought to explore a micropolitics of desire, an overturning of conventional subjectivity. Elaborating a new type of deconstructive semiotics, the authors celebrated a heterogeneous bricolage that valued difference and pluralism. This project existed in words as well as in writing structure, as the 1980 book *A Thousand Plateaus: Capitalism and Schizophrenia* (English translation 1987) is a discontinuous, fragmented conglomeration of short sections (hence the title).

Probably the key metaphor in *A Thousand Plateaus* and other works of this era is the rhizome. According to Deleuze, knowledge in society has been conventionally structured in an arborescent fashion: like a tree. Trees have roots, trunks, and branches that create a clear linear separation of functions vertically organized. It is a strongly hierarchical scheme. Deleuze, in contrast, sought to celebrate what he called rhizomatic subjectivity. A rhizome is a plant structure of open-ended possibility, as it can morph in and out of various forms and functions: a rhizome flows horizontally and can become root, stem, or other. Also, a rhizome can develop many lateral branches or none at all: difference and multiplicity made manifest.

In 1988 Deleuze published *The Fold: Leibniz and the Baroque*, which detailed a similar rhizomatic metaphor: the fold. Spatially, the fold is like a rhizome, elastic and continuous as it meanders through infinity. The fold disrupts hierarchies, as it breaks down any type of Cartesian dualism (interior/exterior, mind/body) that restricts and hierarchically structures subjectivity. While the fold is in some ways an organic formation, Deleuze also used an architectural analogy—the baroque house—to explicate it. The orthogonal structure of the house actually hides a complex series of folds that unites all matter. The fold is therefore both disruptive and comforting, as it encompasses all aspects of human experience. Deleuze's invocation of the baroque also provides a visual semblance of the fold, as the seventeenth-century style is known for its intense curvilinear formal qualities.

The poststructuralist fold made its debut in architecture through the essay that Eisenman published in 1992, "Visions Unfolding: Architecture in the Age of Electronic Media." Eisenman argued that Deleuze had opened the path to a dramatic new type of curvilinear architecture that would collapse the confining scopic regime of the Cartesian subject. "Suppose for a moment that architecture could be conceptualized as a Moebius strip, with an unbroken continuity between interior and exterior? What would this mean for vision? Gilles Deleuze has proposed just such a possible continuity with his idea of the fold. . . . The fold produces a dislocation of the dialectical distinction between figure and ground; in the process it animates what Gilles Deleuze calls a smooth space." In this first article Eisenman did not directly identify the fold with the digital, and his use of computers was minimal at the time, but it quickly became obvious to the ring of architects associated with *AD* that the new machines presented the best opportunity to visualize the labyrinthine folds of their imaginations.

Deconstructivism, displacement, and dislocation: Eisenman's theoretical musings resonated amid the history of disruptive architectural visionaries of the modern age. First, the propulsive enthusiasm of his text is reminiscent of the utopian aspirations of expressionists such as Paul Scheerbart and Bruno Taut, who likewise envisioned a new architectural age of novel buildings that unified humanity. Second, many critics have noted how the fold seems to resonate with the elastic, "endless" architecture formulated by Frederick Kiesler. The latter's continually evolving *Endless House* (figure 6.3, built only as a model in the 1950s) sought to demonstrate an organic, curvilinear succession of flexible spaces that flowed one into another, walls into floors, and had a similar goal of reenvisioning architecture as well as human experience writ large.

While Eisenman initiated the discourse, his erstwhile acolyte Greg Lynn played the largest role in connecting the theoretical Deleuzian fold to the world of building. Lynn provided the core essay for *AD*'s thematically centered 1993 issue, "Folding in Architecture." Lynn's contribution was titled "Architectural Curvilinearity: The Folded, the Pliant and the Supple." While Eisenman had invoked the Moebius strip and

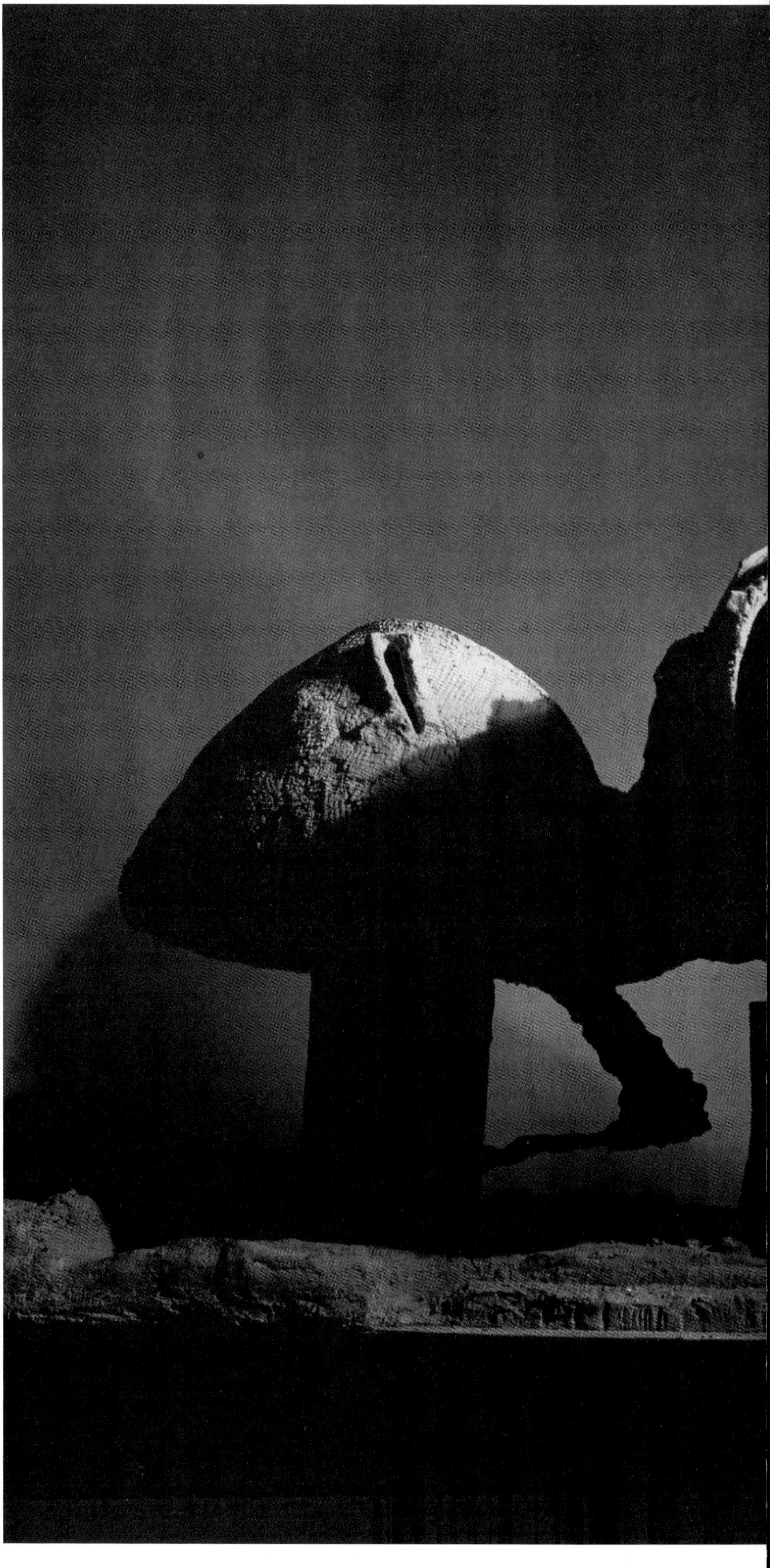

6.3. Frederick Kiesler, *Endless House*, 1950s

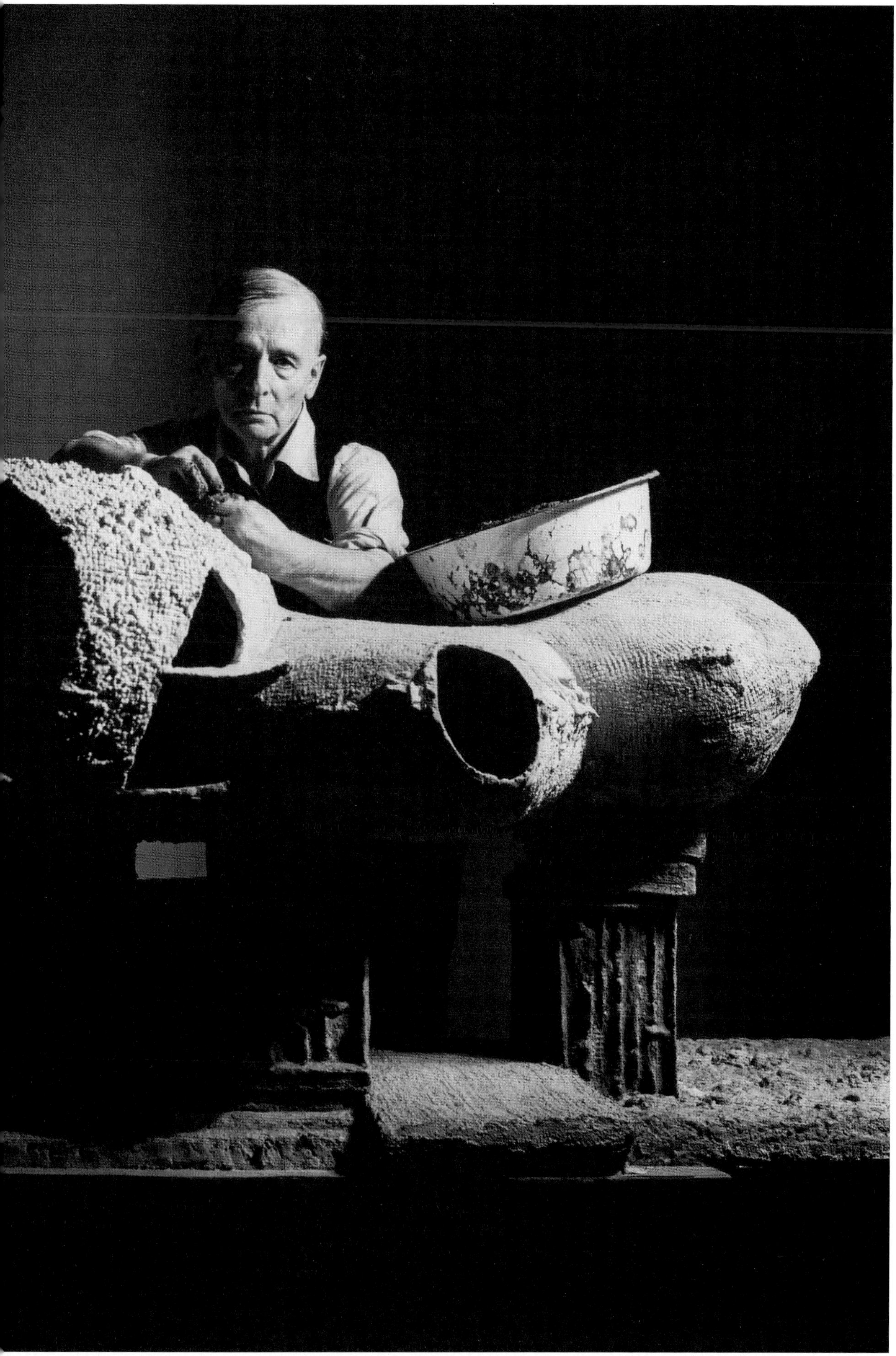

the baroque, it was Lynn who asserted that the fold could be best visualized through digital special effects. He recounted the breakthrough example of the movie *Terminator 2* (1991), in which the central villain was made to fluidly morph into different material states through CGI. "Computer technology is capable of constructing intermediate images between any two fixed points resulting in a smooth transformation." Lynn sought an architecture that would have the same type of smooth, continuous transitions; he compared CGI morphing to the "supple geometry" of Gehry's contemporary Lewis House: "Forms of bending, twisting, or folding are not superfluous but result from an intensive curvilinear logic which seeks to internalize cultural and contextual forces within form." Perhaps the most paradoxical element of this architectural moment was how Lynn and Gehry had arrived at a like-minded place through completely different avenues. Where Eisenman and Lynn valued theory, architectural critic Herbert Muschamp noted in 1997 that in some ways Gehry "distrusts words. . . . He lives on the opposite side of the world from architects like Peter Eisenman."

As Mario Carpo has pointed out, folding writ large described a theoretical process, not a pragmatic approach to actual building; also, Eisenman et al. had been contemplating a generalized electronic age, not the specifics of a digital product. A rather fortuitous correspondence with mathematics, however, would lead the group of architects interested in folding to connect it with the building of digital architecture. Deleuze and his architectural expounders tied the fold to differential calculus, which offered a mathematical basis for contemplating the continuous change and flexibility embodied in the fold. This philosophical analogy found its material form in the evolving computer-aided design software of the nineties. As related in chapter 1, CAD software had developed in pursuit of the computational curve, a spline that could connect a series of points into a curved surface. Dassault's CATIA, for example—used for modeling the curved skin of aircraft and later to produce the sheets of titanium on the Guggenheim—was designed around the mathematic representation called NURBS (non-uniform rational basis splines). A joint accomplishment credited mainly to researchers at Syracuse University and Boeing, NURBS was an advance over the Bézier curves of a previous generation of computational software. In 1989, Silicon Graphics brought to market the first NURBS software, which had to be used on their workstations. But in the nineties, all the major CAD programs adopted NURBS as the mathematics behind the ability to flexibly design and alter curves and curved surfaces in a virtual environment. Those files could be exported to a CAE program such as CATIA, and, voilà, architects had the potential to economically produce whatever type of curvilinear forms rocked their imagination.

By definition, a NURBS-derived curve or surface is infinitely continuous and flexible, meaning it resonated with the Deleuzian musings of the Eisenman group. In the nineties, folds and NURBS came together in such a way that architects could start planning digital buildings that would be buildable while also signaling the architect's embrace of the most au courant intellectual concerns. The opaque process became a catalyst for a new type of digital architectural product. These new curvilinear buildings—which Lynn christened "Blobs" in a 1996 article—would not just serve as experiments aimed at other architects and esoteric museum exhibitions, but would enter the built environment.

Of course, the first and most memorable NURBS-assisted building—Gehry's Guggenheim Bilbao—had nothing whatsoever to do with the Deleuzian blobs favored by Lynn et al. In 1997, when the building opened, Lynn was initiating an experimental blob-based project he called Embryological House. This project sought to explore the potential for digital architecture at a time when it was still emerging, hence the name. In contrast to Gehry's one-of-a-kind monument, Lynn imagined these houses as a series of suburban dwellings, creating an almost endless range of variations on the banal domestic habitat. Lynn recognized how NURBS opened the door to parametric design, whereby the computer could be given a set of guidelines and then tasked with producing a sea of alternatives. The houses would not be orthogonal and rectilinear in any way, but rather wall would morph into floor or ceiling through the continuous curves of the Deleuzian fold. Lynn used twelve points to set the basic parameters for the Embryological House (he settled on a number that would be flexible yet manipulatable), using CAD software, then imported the files into Maya because it was best able to render the smooth flowing 3D surfaces of the buildings.

While Lynn's work highlighted the conceptual and aesthetic dimension of digital architecture, he was also attuned to the economics of the digital. Because most architecture made use of standardized parts, structures were often overbuilt from an engineering standpoint because of standardized beam sizes and the like. The digital would allow for mass customization of bespoke buildings, but they would also be more sustainable because the parts would be individually fabricated by CNC machines to custom specifications.

While the Embryological House might seem to have had little immediate practical application in the late nineties, it was an effective conduit for publicizing digital architecture. Then, in 1999, in the midst of the project, Lynn published a book and finished a building that would popularize and showcase his ideas to an even broader public. The book was called *Animate Form*, and it offered the term "animation" as a more accessible entrée into the realm of the fold (Lynn meant "animation" in the sense of enliven not as a corollary to actually moving images). This rebranding of Deleuzian blobs stressed the same qualities in architecture: elasticity, mutability, and vitality. Lynn argued that modern architecture had become inert and static, and digital forms could release its animalistic, visceral power to a new generation. Lynn wanted architecture to embrace instances of movement and time, as "animate design is defined by the co-presence of motion and force at the moment of formal conception." He compared animate buildings to a sailboat hull, which does not change form itself but is reactive to differing flows of water. Lynn also explained the basis of parametric design and the topological characteristics of the isomorphic polysurface, or blob. At times *Animate Form* is demanding and opaque, showing its roots in poststructuralist theory. Leibniz, Bergson, Foucault, and Deleuze all frequently appear, and thinkers from far afield, such as the eminent biologist Lynn Margulis, are invoked and reframed: "A body, Margulis suggests, is the fused assemblage of an ecosystem operating with a high degree of continuity and stability. . . . It is a logic of differentiation, exchange and assemblage within an environment of gradient influences." In the end, amid all the intellectual posturing, Lynn succeeded in conveying his main point—that digital buildings should be animated not static—while more than anything else displaying a fiery passion for the computer age of architecture. *Animate Form* also included a CD-ROM that supplemented the illustrations in the book, and one can easily imagine how a generation of young architects was animated by the futuristic images and unbridled enthusiasm of the author. The fold had come into the mainstream.

In 1999, Lynn, in concert with Doug Garofalo and Michael McInturf (the latter had worked for Eisenman), unveiled the New York Presbyterian Church (figure 6.4) in Queens, New York. While architects have worked together across countries and oceans for many years, digital files, and later cloud-based practices, have facilitated this type of collaboration. The Presbyterian Church was partly a renovation, as it was formed around an extant thirties industrial building that had housed a laundry works. The new building was based around a curvilinear form the architects deemed Nestor, a mutable blob of space that could nestle within itself. The most striking element of the exterior is a series of undulating shells that shelter the main stairway, which leads up to the main sanctuary on the upper floor. The overall roof also tips and swerves in a manner suggestive of a surface modeled through NURBS. All of the structure is designed to flow together erratically, suggesting animation and continuity in contrast to the modernist box that had dominated architecture for so many decades. In one of his most vivid analogies, Lynn has compared his architectural forms to a handkerchief, noting how it has a fluid form that does not enclose space in a rigid, hierarchical fashion.

It is important not to overlook the evident jouissance enjoyed through experimenting with new digital design software; in one sense this represents the greatest impact that video games have had on digital design. How many architects and designers have shifted between designing, coding, and playing in the same sitting on the same screen? Whether the game is an urban simulation or a shooter, there is a correspondence between working through a game and working through a set of digital tools. This playful, experiential mindset comes through in the building of the aptly named Villa Nurbs (figure 6.5) by the Spanish architect Enric Ruiz-Geli. Head of the studio Cloud 9, Ruiz-Geli began work in 2003 on this organic blob of a summer house on the Costa Brava not too far from Barcelona, designing and redesigning it over the ensuing eight years. Looking somewhat like a bug, the Villa Nurbs is founded on a concrete base with a swimming pool at the center. The experimental play at work in the design also extends to the use of futuristic materials, including various ceramic parts and a roof largely composed of ethylene tetrafluoroethylene (ETFE) plastic.

The Villa Nurbs truly served as a digital design laboratory, as Ruiz-Geli added several features that he later patented (a key source of revenue for Cloud 9). While the ideal in the early 2000s for digital architecture may have been mass customization at the price of mass

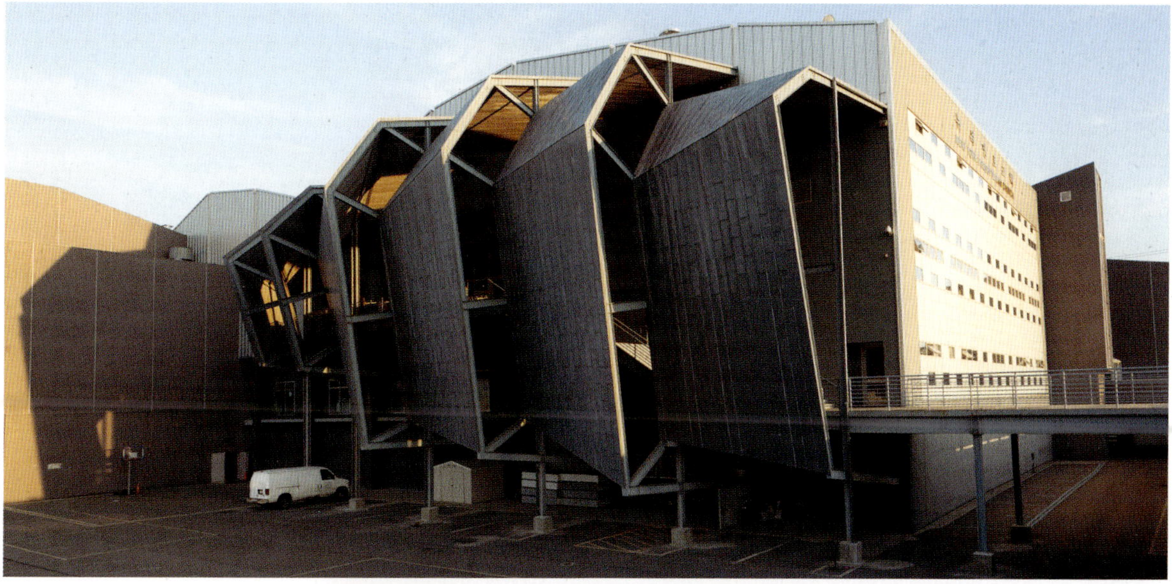

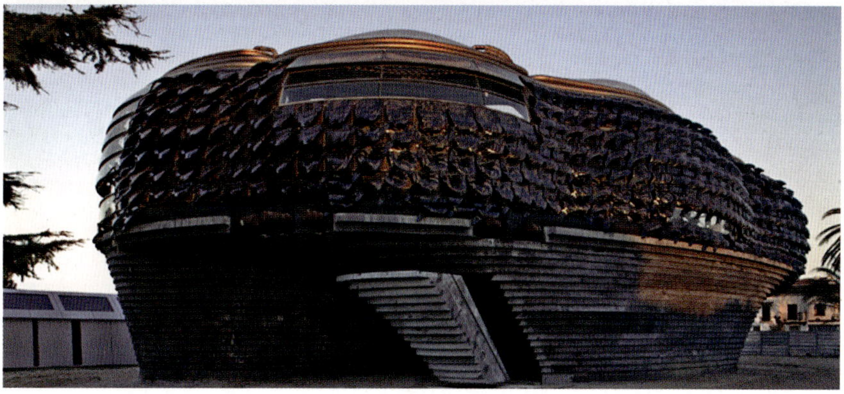

6.4. Greg Lynn, New York Presbyterian Church, 1999
6.5. Enric Ruiz-Geli, Villa Nurbs, 2011

standardization, the Villa Nurbs is more like the Villa Savoy in that it represents a bespoke lifestyle. The house cost more than three million Euros by the time of completion, after numerous delays and cost overruns due to the complexity of fabricating such unique forms. The Villa Nurbs was more one of a kind than mass customized in the end.

As NURBS software and Lynn's notions of a hybrid, mutable, and animated digital architecture came to the fore, experimentally minded architects created some stunning new structures. What is perhaps the quintessential blob building, the Kunsthaus in Graz, Austria (figure 6.6), was completed in 2003. Peter Cook, one of the founders of Archigram, and Colin Fournier received the commission after winning an international juried competition. The body of the Kunsthaus is a plump, flowing pillow of a form festooned with tubular skylights. Fournier memorably referred to the structure as a "friendly alien." Like Gehry's work, the Kunsthaus had analog roots, as the first sketches and models were made by hand before working out the details of the structure through software. At this point, however, it would seem that analog drawing had been hijacked by software even when the digital tool was not at hand, because the form of the building resonates with the curves that defined the digital. Also, the range of visual references that the architects cited in describing the building—from a chocolate cake to a dragon—is telling both of their own sensibilities of how digital culture embraces eclectic paradigms.

Colin Fournier wrote, "One of the key formative ideas we were most fond of pursuing was that the outer envelope of our building would, like the skin of the chameleon, be able to mutate, change colour, transparency, reflectivity, etc. In line with Bernard Tschumi's vision of architecture as screen, Cook and Fournier sought to use digital technology to make the double skin of the Kunsthaus a display surface; while many of their ideas were dropped because of cost, in the end realities:united, the Berlin-based new

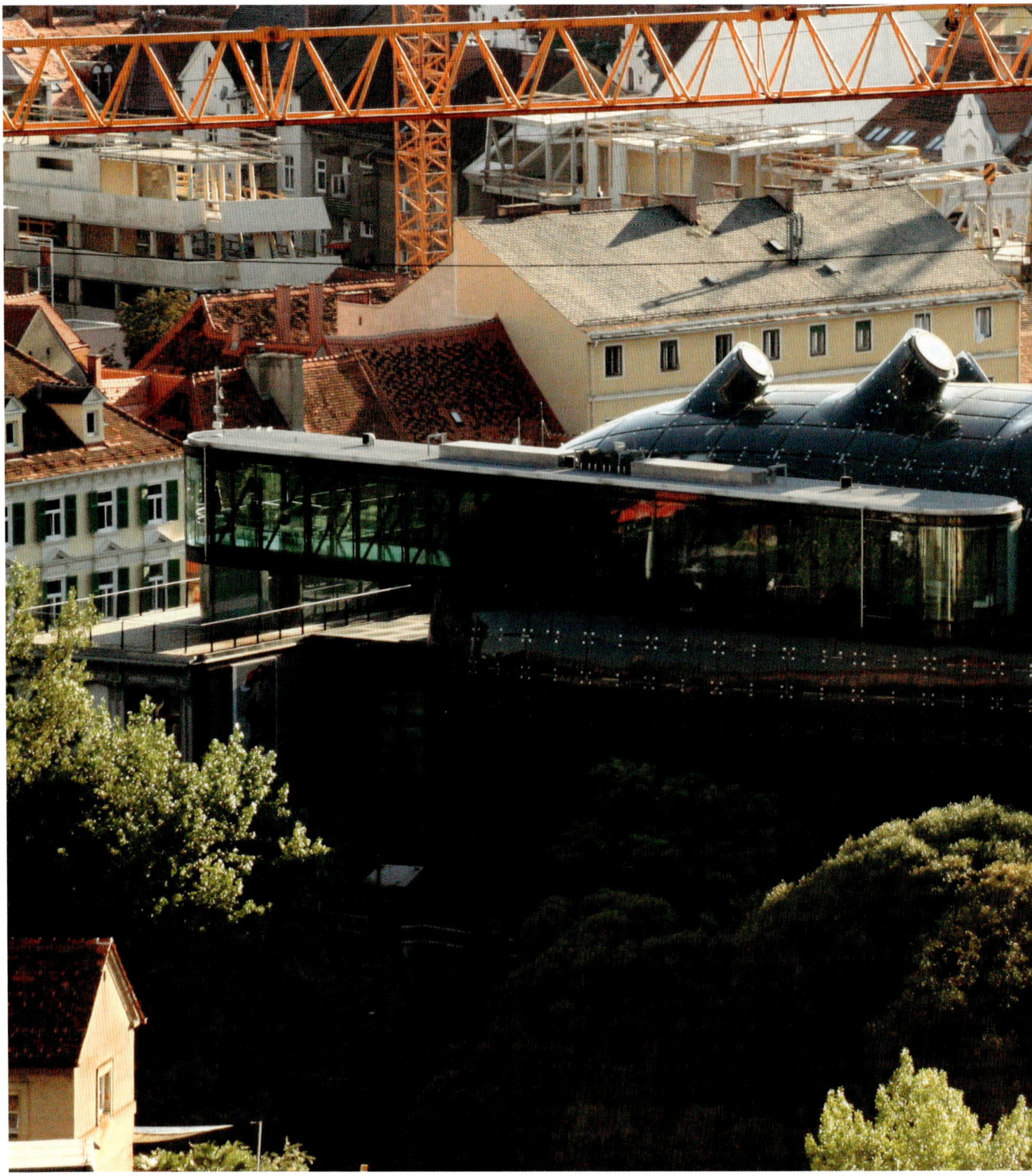

6.6. Peter Cook and Colin Fournier, 2003

media studio, created a light installation called the BIX. Covering almost 900 square meters of one façade, the BIX—a contraction of "big pixels"—consists of hundreds of fluorescent tube lights, one hidden behind each acrylic panel of the eastern facade. As each bulb corresponds with one pixel, the BIX can act as a low-resolution digital projector so that images appear seamlessly on the display skin.

Cook and Fournier's conception of the Kunsthaus also resonated with the emerging theme of the biological digital. The biological metaphor had always existed in the background of the fold, which was a rhizomatic process of searching and becoming that speaks of organic existence. Likewise, in discussing their building, Cook and Fournier offered up a veritable menagerie culled from the animal kingdom: the Kunsthaus was a stray dog, a sea slug, a whale, a porcupine, or, of course, an alien creature. Fournier explained later that the building was not simply a metaphorical creature, but rather he hoped for "an

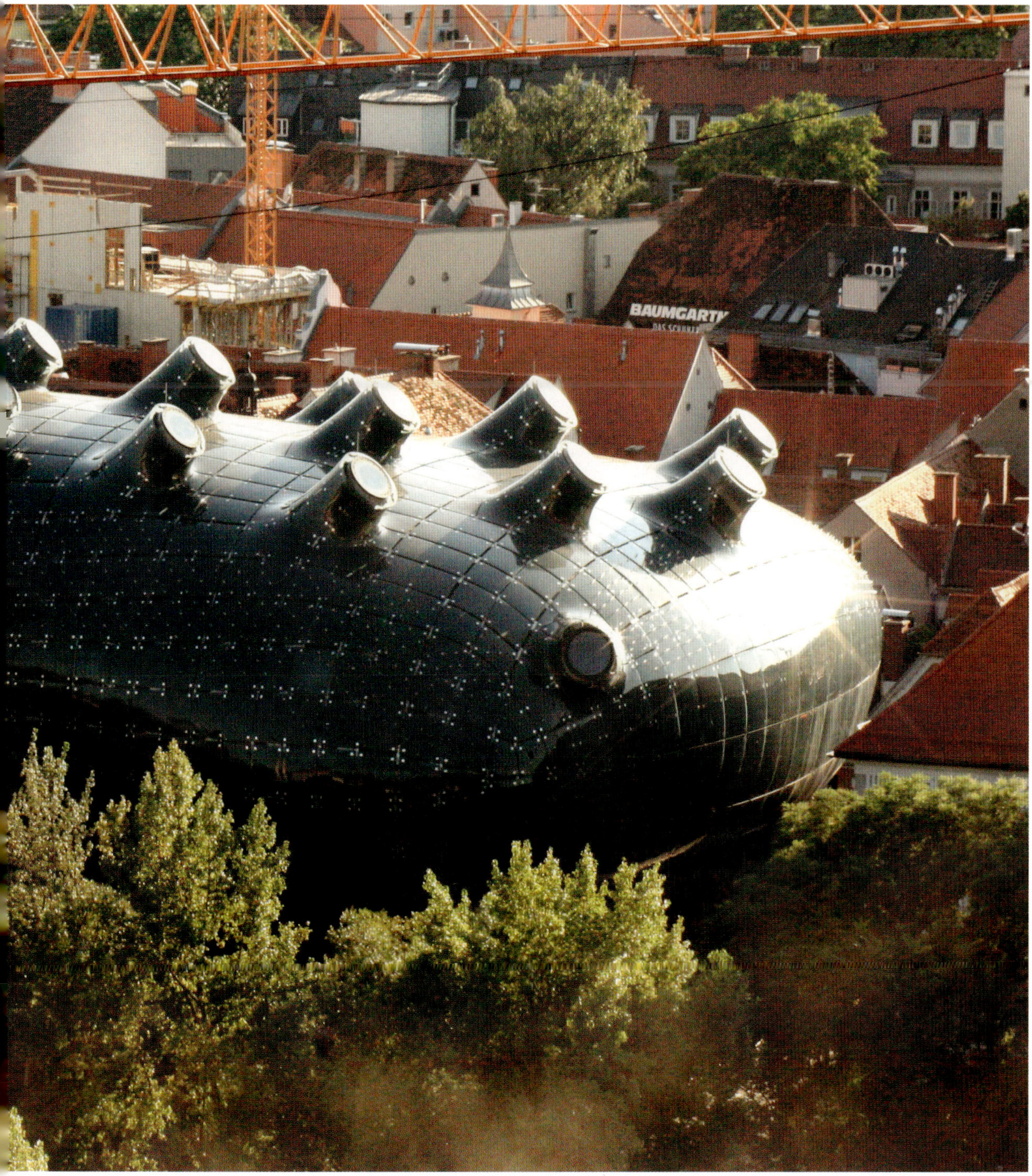

architecture that, with the aid of robotics and artificial intelligence, might one day become truly alive and responsive to environmental forces and human needs as well as desires." All aspects of the building work together to communicate this message: the biologic morphology and mutating skin animate the building in dramatic fashion.

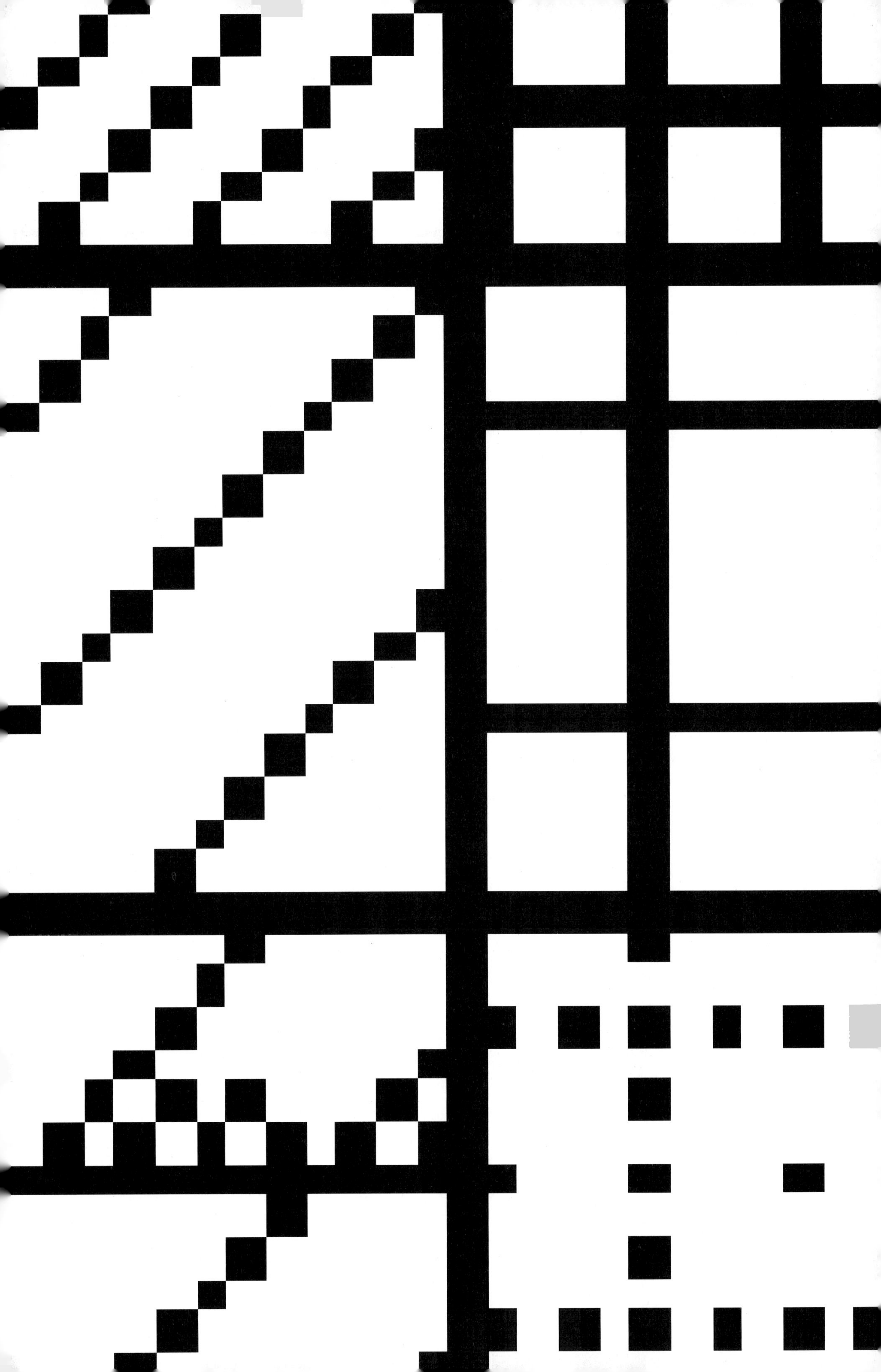

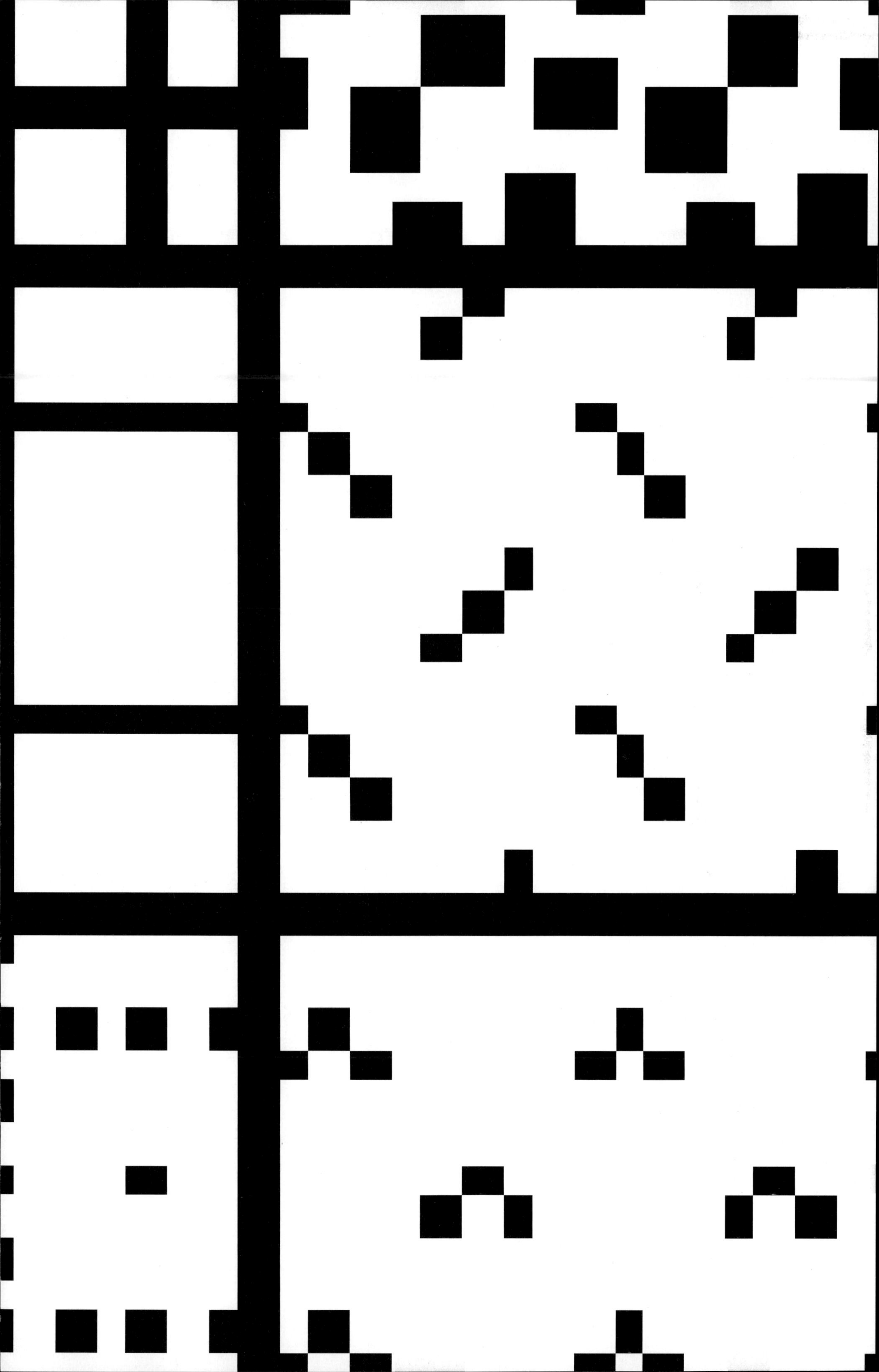

Seven. Digital Web 2.0

In the midnineties, Macromedia's Shockwave software began to change the internet. It allowed for a dynamic new level of interactivity and animation, and its file compression offered the ability to display Director-created movies on the internet. For example, Shockwave was the software behind one of the very first interactive web pages, Intel's 1996 celebration of the twenty-fifth anniversary of the microprocessor. Intel, founded in 1968 and the dominant semiconductor company of the nineties, in 1971 had released the fabled 4004 chip that would eventually lead to the creation of the desktop computer. Intel's 1996 "interactive celebration" offered the viewer the opportunity to "launch a start-up called Intel and create the microprocessor in *Interact with History*." While this type of blatant commercialism is representative of the early years of the internet, when home users were less jaded—the first banner ads had an over 80 percent click-through rate!—the use of soft marketing through gameplay and experiential history was far ahead of its time. Note that the website offered users the alternative of using a basic

HTML version of the site, because the Shockwave plug-in was by no means universally installed on web surfers' computers. In fact, while Shockwave would remain on the market for more than a decade, its overly complex architecture and the fact that it was tied to Director would forestall it ever becoming a market leader.

Elements of Web Design paid less heed to another product that had just been released in 1995, FutureWave's FutureSplash plug-in. Once installed on a browser, the FutureSplash player could display interactive animations through compressed vector-based graphics. The example illustrated in Giudice's book is quite modest, simply a rollover animation for a pizza parlor website (the pizzas would jump when the cursor floated above them). FutureSplash originally combined two capabilities, as the animation player was paired with a simple drawing program called SmartSketch. The FutureSplash player was cross platform, at the time meaning simply that it could run on both Netscape Navigator and Internet Explorer. Because of the vector-based graphics, file sizes were small and ran smoothly. In 1996, FutureSplash started to gain traction, as Navigator added it as an extension, and then Microsoft chose it as the featured player for its MSN.com web portal. In true Silicon Valley fashion, by the end of 1996, Macromedia had bought its rival FutureWave and began marketing the FutureSplash player as an alternative to its own Shockwave plug-in. Macromedia made one key branding decision, shortening the rather ungainly FutureSplash into the much tighter-sounding Flash. For a time, Macromedia called the product Shockwave Flash, which led to the standard file extension .swf.

In Siegel's *Creating Killer Web Sites*, he made note of one of the most thorough implementations of Flash in 1997: Microsoft's *Mungo Park* online adventure magazine. In a branding effort that would be unimaginable today, Microsoft named the site after an eighteenth-century Scottish explorer famous for his sojourn into west-central Africa up the Niger River, later recounted in *Travels in the Interior Districts of Africa* (1797). Park had been saved by a slave trader on this first excursion, although a subsequent expedition (1806) ended in his demise. Microsoft promised that its site would offer stimulating virtual experiences: "Mungo Park delivers multimedia, interactive adventure travel reportage and high caliber writing to the Internet's World Wide Web, providing exciting, provocative and timely stories, as well as potent sound, video and graphics of great expeditions and adventures around the globe." As Siegel recounted, the Flash-based site offered smooth rollover animations and animated maps. In an incremental sense one could see general design values improving, as the palette, layouts (some horizontal), and text (much of it text as image) were more advanced than was typical at the time. The design was indicative of how in a broader sense, the web was gradually becoming more visual and less text based.

While early iterations of Flash continued to garner users in the late nineties, the rollout of Flash 4 in 1999 and, especially, Flash 5 in August 2000 truly saw the software emerge as the defining technology of the web. Flash 4 and 5 were the first to employ ActionScript, an object-oriented programming language that enabled Flash websites to exponentially increase their animation capabilities and interactive features. Sometime in 2000 one gets the feeling with hindsight that design was finally insinuating itself as a defining characteristic of websites, and it was mainly through Flash that this evolution occurred.

A book that captured this moment more than any other was the collaborative tome titled *New Masters of Flash*. Conceived of and then rapidly published in 2000, *New Masters of Flash* surveyed the work—both conceptual and technical—of nineteen successful designers, most of whom had been working with Flash for only a couple of years. The five Flash designers discussed below—Brendan Dawes, Luke Turner, Irene Chan, Yugo Nakamura, and Joshua Davis—each produced work that highlights an important facet of the new "designed web." Web design really came of age in the Flash era, as only a few years earlier a cohort of artistically minded web designers did not really exist. Flash is the formative moment when designers came to rule the web.

For Brendan Dawes, along with a whole generation of designers, Flash provided entrée into the design of motion graphics. Previously the province of film and animation studios based in Hollywood, Flash allowed graphic designers to expand their practice out of static print-based work and into a new realm of movement, color, and light. As he related in *New Masters of Flash*, viewing a videotape of the then over three-decades-old movie *Charade* (1963), starring Cary Grant and Audrey Hepburn, completely transformed Dawes's outlook on design. The titles for *Charade* had been designed by Maurice Binder and feature an animated sequence that shows the strong influence of Oskar Fischinger. Abstract colored shapes sweep back and forth across the screen in sync with a musical score by Henry Mancini. In awe of the visual and emotional power of these titles, Dawes soon discovered the stunning work of Saul Bass, who is largely credited with having made the first movie titles intended to be viewed by the audience. In 1952–55 Bass was working with film director Otto Preminger on some illustrated graphics for the new movie *The Man with the Golden Arm*. At some point in the process, Bass and Preminger hit on the idea of animating the print graphics and turning them into something that could set the stage for the film itself. *The Man with the Golden Arm* was a film about heroin addiction starring Frank Sinatra, and Bass's flat drawing of a jagged arm, a reference to the physical act of injecting drugs while also alluding to a Pietà-like suffering and martyrdom, became emblematic of the film. Bass had managed to distill the essence of the story in a way that caught the attention of Hollywood and launched his new career as a title designer, whereby he famously produced work for Alfred Hitchcock, Stanley Kubrick, and Martin Scorsese.

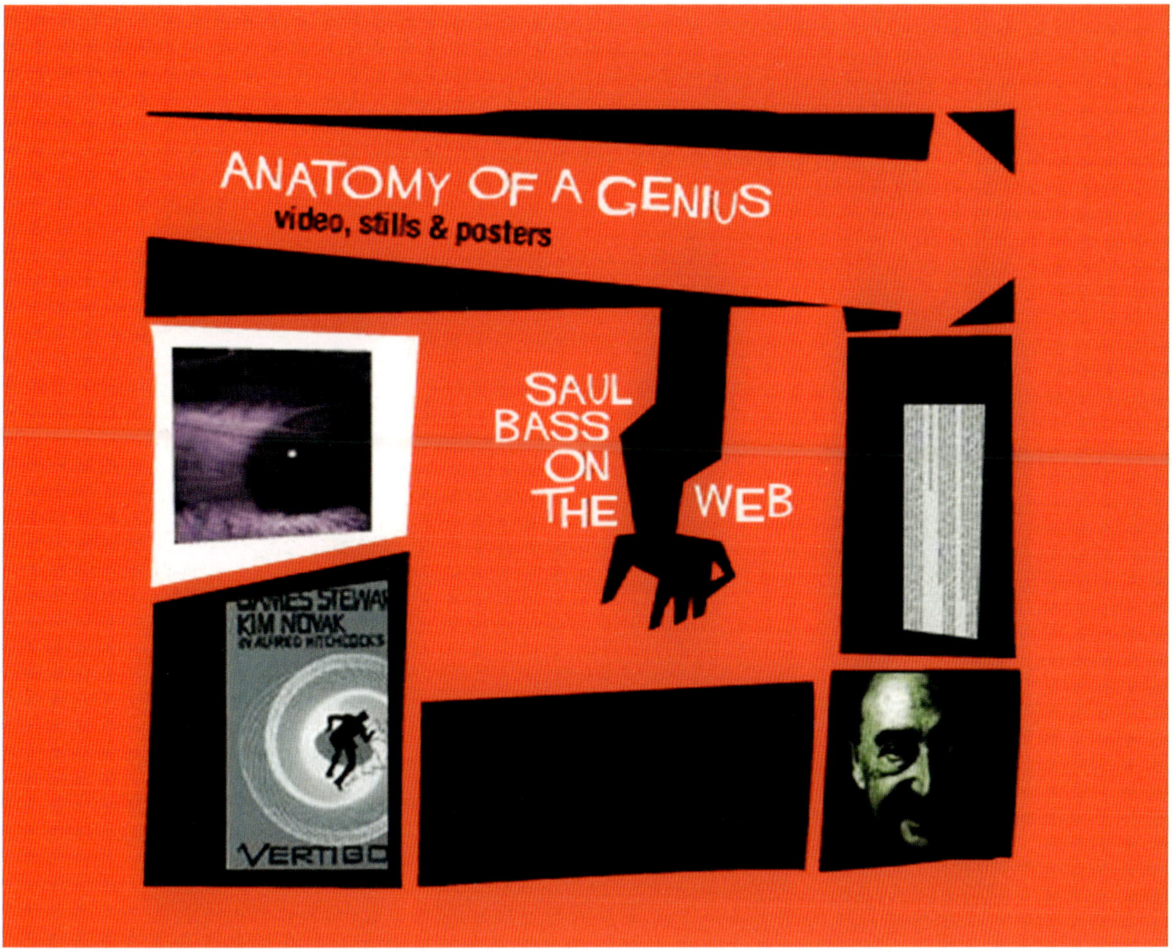

7.1. Brendan Dawes, Saul Bass website, 1998

"Were Saul alive today, I feel sure he would be using Flash as his creative medium." In a curious twist of fate, Dawes ended up building his own career as a prominent digital designer because of his high regard for Bass. In 1998, Dawes built a website dedicated to Bass (figure 7.1), who had died in 1996. Dawes's fan site was a compelling homage, as he used Bass's various title designs as the basis for different pages. Importantly, Dawes sought to minimize the visual bells and whistles, seeking a toned-down aesthetic akin to that of Bass, who had worked partly under the influence of the Swiss typographic style. Essentially, Dawes was channeling through Bass the modern "Bauhaus" style that is such a significant part of internet design. Dawes also adroitly recognized that he could use Flash load times as an element of the design—not a pause—and so he chose to "treat the loading progress typographically, as if it's part of a title sequence." Dawes understood that watching film titles was a passive experience, and he hoped that designers would not overlook the interactive capabilities of Flash. "Now Flash and the web allow us to explore new heights, coupling that same motion graphic design with interactivity." He cites, for example, the Flash-enabled ability to create fluid rollovers, and how that can allow users to play audio clips, giving them a semblance of control over the experience.

Like Brendan Dawes, Luke Turner, who in 2000 ran a UK-based studio called thevoid, aimed for a stripped-down functional aesthetic with roots—whether acknowledged or not—in the modern movement. Turner called his philosophy "content without clutter." Turner's section in *New Masters of Flash* is mainly devoted to a technical explanation of one of his preferred stylistic gambits, the ripple effect. Discoveries like this are what made the Flash era so exciting to digital designers, as they could explore and experiment with ActionScript to open new stylistic avenues. There was also a spirit of openness in the community, as designers such as Turner were willing to share their innovations. Turner's ripple effect (figure 7.2) is something familiar to any web user today; a block of animated text moves as if a wave is traversing it, and the letters fluidly push forward and then fade back into the virtual space. As the letters flow, their scale and transparency changes to enhance the effect. Turner gave the reader a

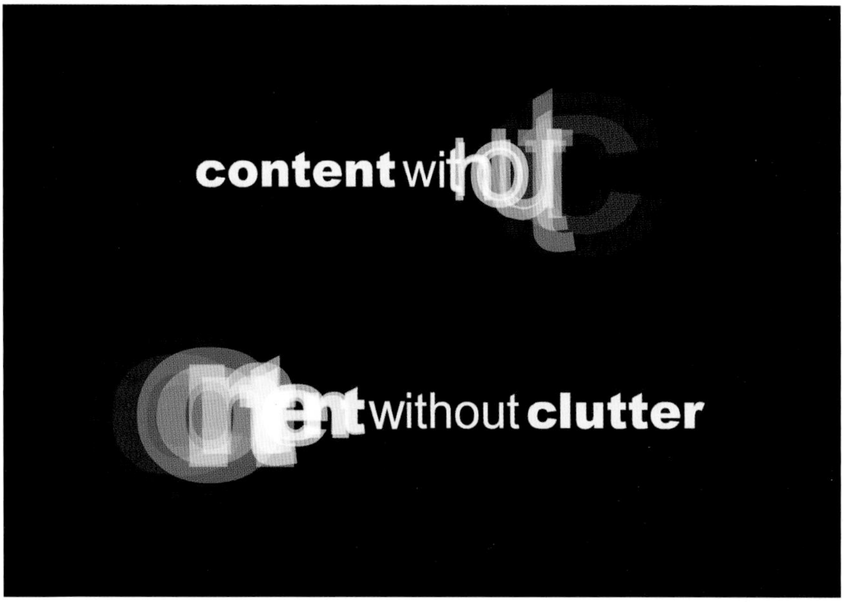

7.2. Luke Turner, ripple effect described in *New Masters of Flash*, 2000

step-by-step guide to the basic effect, explaining keyframes, layers, blurring, and the like. One of the major advances of Flash was its ability to enable fluid transitions that appeared as seamless as those in conventional film titles. Realize also how attention to file size and loading time was necessary for Flash designers in the year 2000. As Turner noted, "Every last kilobyte makes a difference." He suggested that a file size greater than 50k would likely try the viewer's patience, as the load time would stretch past ten seconds at that point.

Irene Chan was the only woman of the nineteen artists featured in *New Masters of Flash*. This fact is probably less indicative of gender bias than exemplary of how web design was trending at the time. Exposure and opportunity had undoubtedly played a large role in this situation. The first generation of Flash designers tended to have a natural affinity toward working with computers—partly because of the entrée provided by childhood gaming (as was explicit with the founders of Razorfish)—and that type of play and engineering had long been the province of sexist attitudes.

What made Chan unique among the *New Masters of Flash* contributors was not her gender but her forward-thinking view of digital design. In discussing her personal website (www.eneri.net, which is Irene spelled backwards), Chan stated, "I wanted my site to have an emotional impact on its visitors, not just entertain them with interactive craziness and experimental graphics." In the year 2000 such a sophisticated view of the web was very rare amid digital designers, as the whole notion of designing digital experiences and telling emotional stories, which is part of the bedrock of digital design today, had not nearly pushed into the mainstream. Chan cites Barbara Kruger as an inspiration for her work, especially Kruger's bold pairings of text and image. Kruger actually represents another interesting precursor to web design, as her adoption of a declarative style based on advertising is exemplary of analog works that look digital. Chan was also technically adroit as a designer and offered a how-to section, as Turner did, that explains the creation of a "bright glow/explosion" animated effect.

Flash brought to the web a degree of visual pleasure that it had previously lacked, as many websites became just plain beautiful. Whether artistic or commercial, the work of Yugo Nakamura was exemplary of the new "eye candy" element in the digital world, a trend that accelerated after 2000. Nakamura first broke through organically into the ranks of elite designers because of his personal website, MONO*crafts 2.0, which beginning in 1998 showcased his experiments with Flash (this in the age before even Flash 4's ActionScript). MONO*crafts 2.0 led to a great deal of commercial work, and Nakamura eventually founded his Tokyo-based studio tha ltd. A fine example of how Nakamura's skills evolved along with the development of Flash can be seen in a prizewinning site he created in 2003 for the NEC Corporation. This trajectory—an artist blossoming alongside their software of choice—is a distinguishing element of digital design, be it Flash, type design, or motion graphics. Although there are parallels with earlier ages in design—Jules Cheret and the chromolithograph or Alexander Rodchenko and abstract film come

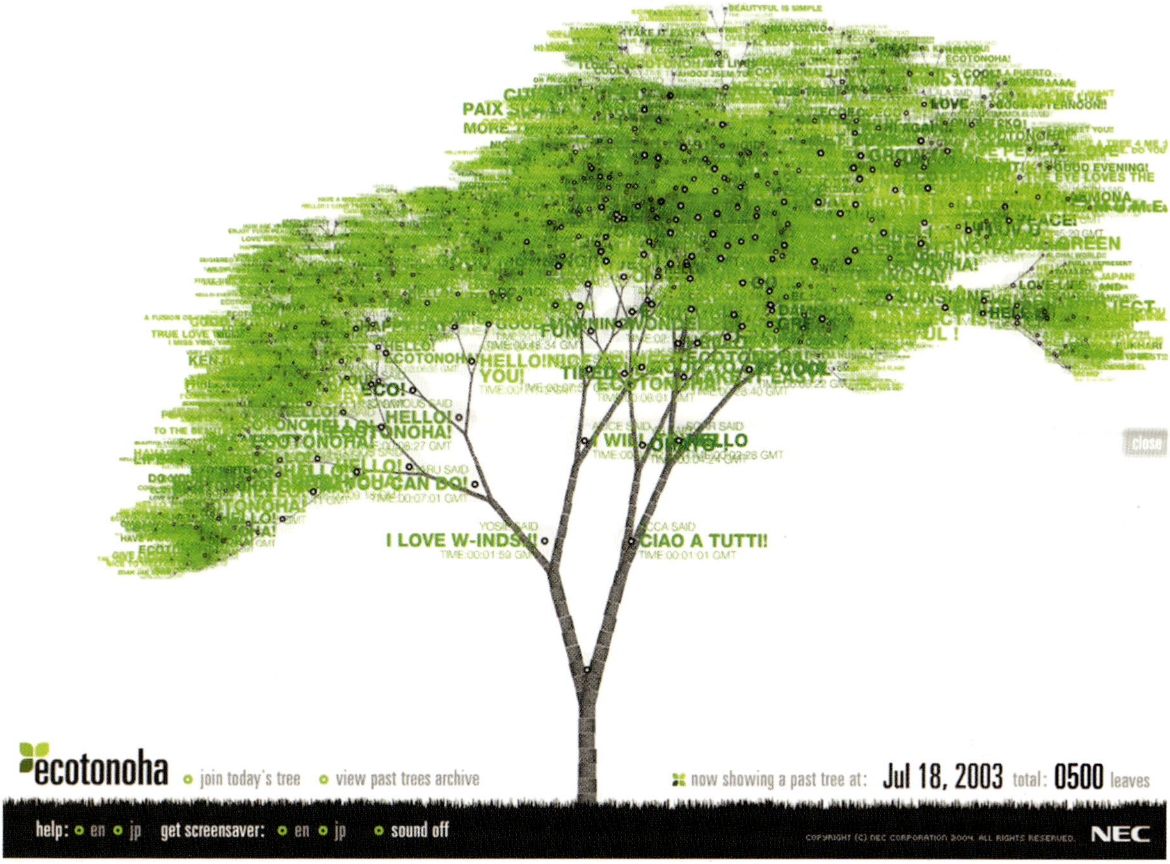

7.3. Yugo Nakamura, Ecotonoha website, 2003

to mind—never before was a group of artists trying to master a technology that kept changing month to month and always with new, added levels of complexity. Yes, Cheret improved on lithograph production, but once he accomplished that, he essentially worked in the same vein for decades. But to look at a page from MONO*crafts 2.0 circa 1999 versus Nakamura's NEC work four years later is in some ways to view two completely different eras.

The NEC project was called Ecotonoha (figure 7.3), a neologism based on the English word "ecology" and "kotonoha," a transliteration of the Japanese term that means "word." For this site, NEC was contributing to the reforestation of Kangaroo Island in Australia, part of a habitat restoration project that featured an annual tree-planting festival. Nakamura created a Flash site that showed a single tree against a minimal white background, its shimmering leaves displaying a rich range of greens. The point of the site was not just visual pleasure but also interactivity. In what was essentially a soft-marketing strategy, users who clicked on the site created a leaf on which they could compose a brief message (hence the name Ecotonoha: ecology and words). In this way they would help to build a virtual tree that would be matched by the planting of actual trees on Kangaroo Island. The participatory web at its best, commerce and philanthropy united for the common good.

In the first decade of the twenty-first century, this type of conceptually and visually rich site became a must have for major corporations, resulting in a gorgeous new interactive virtual world created in Flash. In 2006, the Brooklyn design firm Big Spaceship created just such a Flash site for Nike's newest iteration of its Air brand basketball and running shoes (figure 7.4). Using a red palette for basketball and a blue one for running, the website offered visitors an initial choice and then engaged them with a range of animations, clickable customizers, and sounds. This site was one of the first examples of a brand creating an immersive digital experience, hoping to imprint the user's emotions in a manner that would linger. Brands have always been about feelings, and here Flash allowed Nike to push its customers into engaging with the idealized adrenaline and effort of sport.

Joshua Davis was arguably both the most influential "master of Flash" as well as a strong driver of the web-design-as-art thread that emerged in this era. Around 2000, Davis worked for the design studio Kioken, which had been

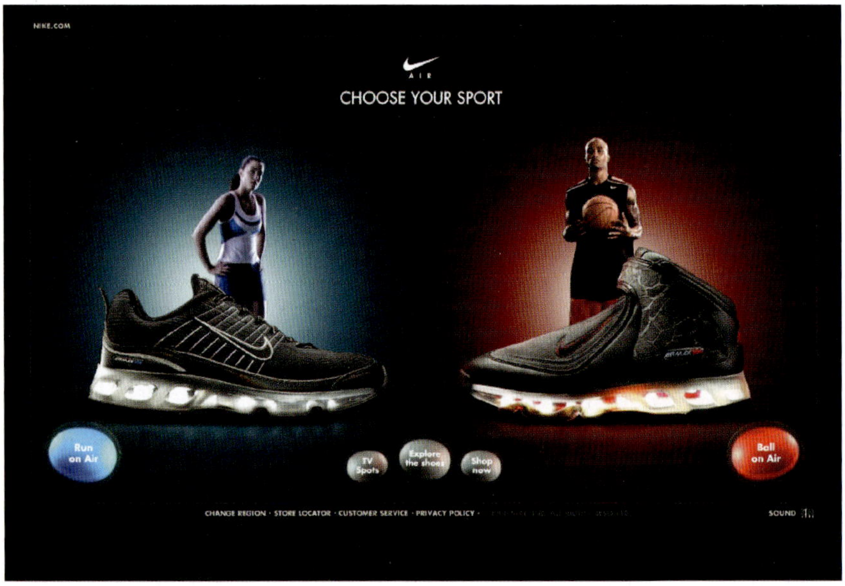

7.4. Big Spaceship, Nike Air website, 2006

founded by Gene Na and Peter Kang. At Kioken, Davis of course produced a lot of commercial work, including a Flash site for Barney's he co-designed with Erik Wysocan. His Kioken work paid the bills, but Davis's personal, experimental website, Praystation, made him into an iconic designer's designer, so to speak. Like Nakamura, Davis sought to expand and explore Flash as it developed. In his 2002 book *Flash to the Core*, Davis explained his approach to the software: "No offense to Macromedia, but I have really tried to bring Flash to its knees. Really break it. Slam it. Crashed my computer. It's only in breaking things—in the anomalies—that I find the accidents that in the end become techniques." Davis went on to point out that the resulting work is often ambiguous and uncertain, which is just the quality that corporate clients are looking for: a site that will prove sticky for users.

While commercially savvy, Davis also brought some of the participatory, even utopian flavor that characterized many tech visionaries. He always sought to give advice to other designers, and often made his proprietary files available for anyone to learn from and use. In fact, the entire Flash community for a time shared this collaborative spirit. Looking back in 2013, Luke Turner noted, "The community of Flash developers was very small back then, and there was a definite spirit of camaraderie, with each of us posting new innovations on a daily basis and challenging each other to better ourselves." Davis, after building his career through successive iterations of Flash, in 2009 decried the fact that the language had become too complicated for most designers (Adobe at that point had released Flash CS4, which was the tenth major revision). In that year he cofounded the HYPE Project, which was designed to provide a Flash sandbox for new designers, who could learn through play the way Davis had less than a decade earlier. Davis has also been supportive of the Processing Foundation (see below), which is dedicated to making free open source coding available to artists and other nontechnologists.

Although they are known more as masters of pixels than masters of Flash, eBoy designers' breakthrough commission was in fact a Flash game for MTV in 1999 (figure 7.5). The design studio eBoy features a core of three founders, Steffen Sauerteig and Svend Smital, who grew up in East Germany, and Kai Vermehr, who is also of German ancestry but has mainly lived and worked in Latin America and Canada. Together since the midnineties, eBoy is most known for digital nostalgia, 8-bit pixel graphics that have a joyful, cartoonish quality. In an era marked by ever-increasing resolutions and textures, the designers at eBoy reveled in the video game aesthetic of the recent past. It is tempting to relate their playful polychrome style to the lack of color Sauerteig and Smital experienced growing up in East Germany; they have each spoken of the revelation they experienced in joining the West after 1989 and being confronted with a sea of brilliant hues on consumer packages. The MTV online game represented a clash of technological worlds: it was designed in a retro pixel art style but then programmed in cutting-edge Flash to serve as interactive multimedia entertainment. The game—called simply *The Thing*—is an ironic parody of vintage *Pac-Man*, with players steering an MTV host around a maze with instructions to "fear the sailors" and "devour the kids."

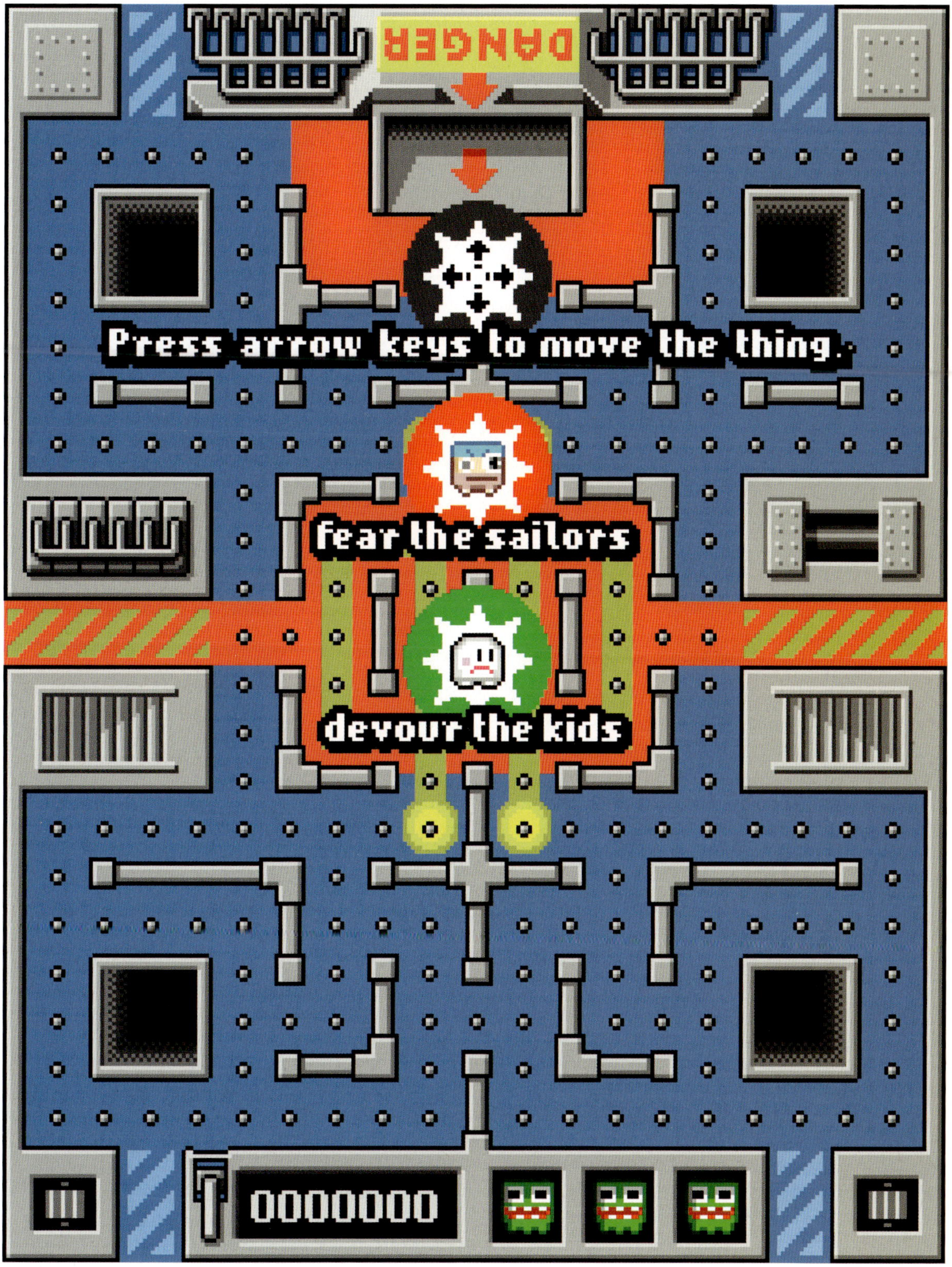

7.5. eBoy, MTV Flash game *The Thing*, 1999

Flash Art

Beginning in the late nineties, Flash became the preferred medium for a generation of web artists, as its widespread availability and multimedia flexibility allowed for almost universal distribution via browsers. By 2013, the digital art organization Rhizome estimated that about a third of the works archived in its ArtBase consisted of SWF files. Although artists had been working with computers for decades, Flash happened to be the dominant technology when new media and net art accelerated into the public's consciousness. In 2001, both the San Francisco Museum of Modern Art and the Whitney Museum of American Art (figure 7.6)

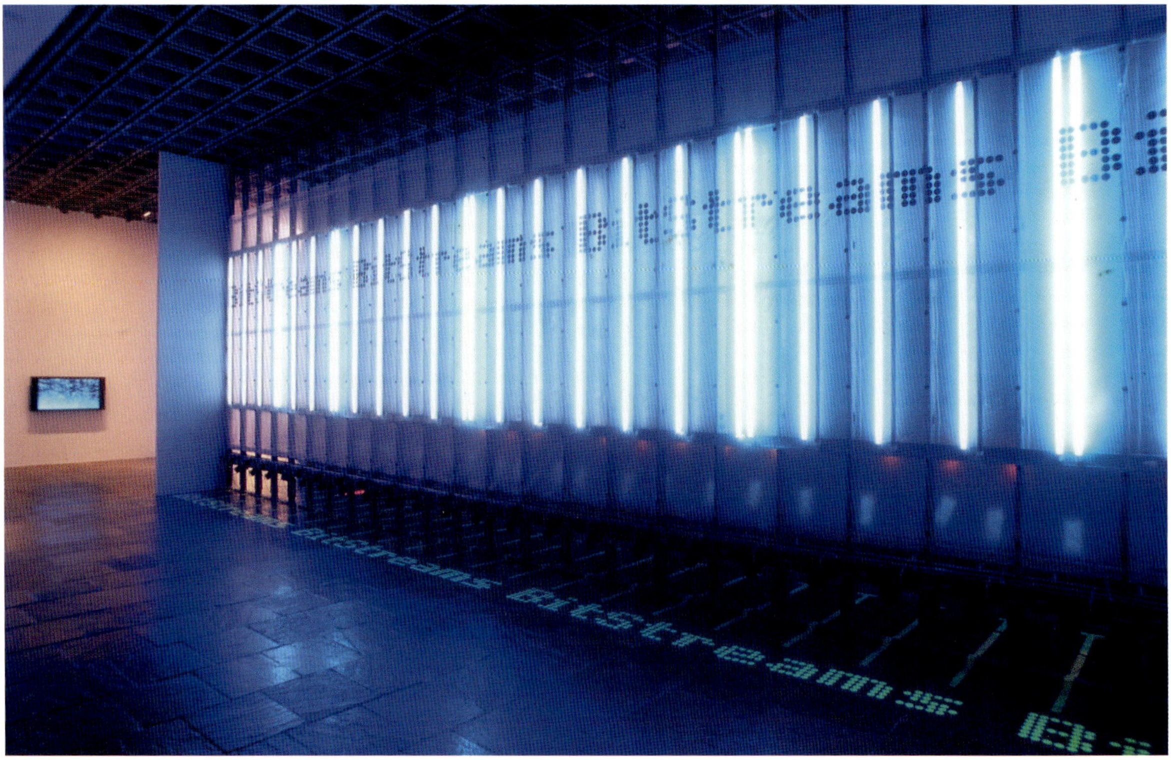

7.6. Installation view of *Bitstreams* (Whitney Museum of American Art, New York, March 22–June 10, 2001)

hosted major exhibitions of digital art. Also, Steve Dietz, director of new media initiatives at the Walker Art Center (Minneapolis), curated *Telematic Connections: The Virtual Embrace*, which opened in San Francisco in 2001. Dietz had been hired at the Walker in 1996, becoming one of the first major museum curators to focus on digital art and design. In a symposium at the Walker held to supplement the exhibitions, Dietz pointed out that a critical mass of digital artists and designers had organically gravitated toward new media projects. "While the press likes to frame, say, the inclusion of net art in the 2000 Whitney Biennial as a 'seal-of-approval' event, I would argue that it's fundamentally an artistic choice, not a museological or curatorial one." Notably, very few crossover artists appeared in more than one of the exhibitions, perhaps a signal that little in the way of canon formation had yet occurred in the digital realm.

Of course, all three exhibitions featured extensive multimedia websites, *Telematic Connections* in Shockwave, the other two in Flash. The site for the Whitney's *Bitstreams* was designed by the New York studio Nettmedia, which had been born out of the music industry. Nettmedia was originally the Vancouver-based in-house Web Design Department of indie label Nettwerk Records, among the first companies to offer multimedia content on their CD releases (this at a time when cassette tapes were still a relevant product). The *Bitstreams* site's most dramatic flourish was simple and elegant, as the exhibition's title sweeps in as a cloud of dots that momentarily form the name "Bitstreams," then sweep away again like a cloud of dust. This animated effect captures the fluidity and impermanence of the digital. The exhibition website also provided a new digital setting for the Whitney's then year-old logotype, which had been designed by Abbot Miller of Pentagram. While the logo's staunch orthogonal design might look like a nod to the constructivist avant-garde in one context, on the *Bitstreams* web page, it takes on a futuristic flavor. There, its regularity looks like a machine-made design, type as one might imagine created by an artificial intelligence.

Many of the works exhibited in *Bitstreams* displayed the closeness between multimedia digital art and design. One of the stars of the show was Jeremy Blake, whose colorful abstract animations mesmerized visitors. Blake's *Station to Station* consisted of five animated "paintings" that combined polychrome visual textures with architectural motifs. This success led to a pair of high-profile design projects, as the next year Blake was commissioned to create work for Paul Thomas Anderson's film *Punch-Drunk Love* and the musician Beck's newest album, *Sea Change*. In a parallel to Oskar Fischinger's work on Walt Disney's *Fantasia* (1940), Blake devised an abstract, hallucinogenic sequence for *Punch-Drunk Love* synchronized to music by Jon Brion. The set piece aimed to convey the emotional intensity of falling madly in love per the title. While abstract animation of course has a lot of precedent, Blake's forms and palette overall appeared "digital" in an original manner that captured the visual zeitgeist. Tragically, Blake and noted artist and game designer Theresa Duncan, who together formed a glamourous digital art world couple in the early 2000s, both committed suicide in 2007.

In terms of the connection between digital art and design, a number of the early Flash artists have since changed paths and started pursuing gallery art careers. Luke Turner, the self-taught wunderkind who had created thevoid at age seventeen, enjoyed a few years of pleasing high-profile clients with his Flash skills, only to abandon the field in 2003 at age twenty. After pursuing music for a bit, he enrolled in London's Central Saint Martins art school and found a new profession in fine art. In recent years he has worked as a proponent of the metamodernist movement, which seeks to reconcile the respective characters of modernism and postmodernism. Turner authored the group's manifesto, in which the first declarative statement reads, "We recognise oscillation to be the natural order of the world." Since 2014, Turner has also formed part of the collaborative performance trio known as LaBeouf, Rönkkö & Turner, formed with Finnish artist Nastja Säde Rönkkö and American actor Shia LaBeouf. Turner has noted that his formative experience as part of the Flash community still resonates with his artwork and his desire to make art that builds community. He still values the noncommercial ethos of those early experimental years before the Flash gold rush began. Like so many digital designers and artists, Turner seeks to imbue the virtual with emotion.

Preserving these works presents real challenges, as Rhizome Digital Preservation Fellow Alexander Duryee has noted. "As a binary format, it cannot be immediately parsed by text-friendly tools (such as web crawlers and text editors), and is thus machine- and human-unreadable. . . . Flash can link out of itself—and with no easy method to parse out URLs, these links are functionally invisible. Worse, the power of Flash allows for the creation of URLs on the fly: ActionScript can be used to generate an arbitrary string, which can then be passed to a resource call. Thus, even an exhaustive search for external links in a SWF object can miss potentially tens of thousands of necessary files." With Flash's imminent end of life, the future of these works is quite uncertain, as software that came into artistic use largely because of its omnipresence becomes the province only of specialized archives. Digital artworks that are of relatively recent vintage are disappearing from users' computers, as few people today pass through the increasingly obsolete link "Click to enable Adobe Flash Player."

Flash Gaming

As had been the case with the internet in general, gaming also played a large role in the emergence of Flash. Microsoft, one of the earliest adopters of Flash, had joined the online game industry as early as 1996, when they opened a website called the Internet Gaming Zone. The Zone went through a series of name changes, while offering a plethora of simple Flash-based animated games. Along with

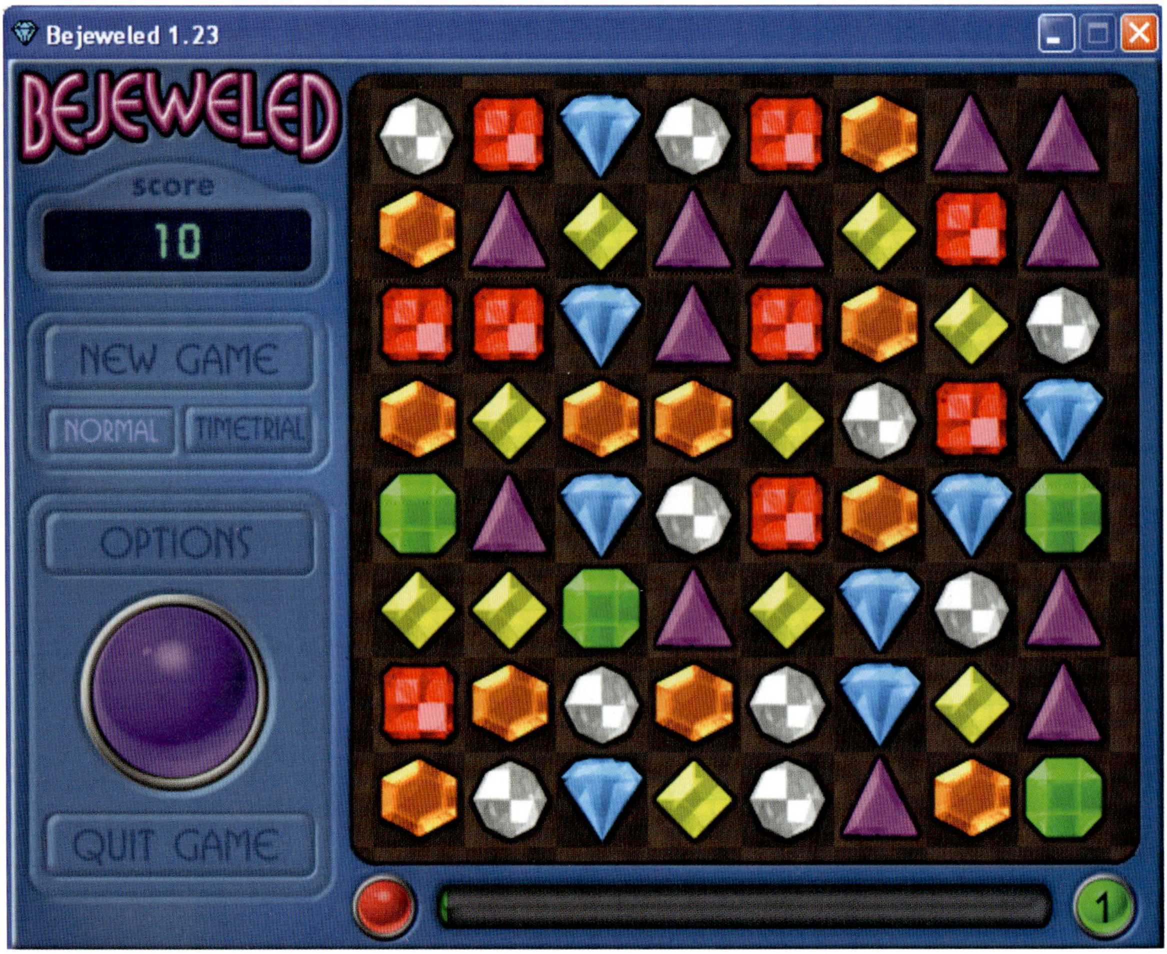

7.7. Microsoft's Internet Gaming Zone, *Bejeweled*, 2001

competitors such as Yahoo and AOL, Microsoft deployed "browser games" as a way of drawing people into its overarching virtual ecosystem. The Zone hosted one of the most successful browser games of all time, a dynamic puzzle solving diversion called *Bejeweled* (figure 7.7). Released in 2001, *Bejeweled* was a Flash reboot of *Diamond Mines*, which had first appeared as a Shockwave product a few years before. Games such as *Bejeweled*—many readers will recognize its contemporary progeny *Candy Crush*—helped to establish the idea that the internet was a place filled with animated interactivity.

Flash as a game platform actually peaked around 2010, at a time when the software had become so ubiquitous on desktop computers as to become an invisible part of the web's architecture. Amateur designers at that point became hard to separate from the professionals, as Newgrounds hosted games such as *Super Mario 63* (figure 7.8), a 2009 fan-built homage to the venerable platforming plumber. These amateur games carried the idea of active participation to a whole new generation of computer users, as they were the first to allow ordinary users to build their own levels and create modifications for a custom experience: in true DIY spirit, everyone could be a part of the game design. That same year also saw the onset of the *Farmville* phenomena, when that Flash-based social networking game released on Facebook. A "freemium" product that combined easy entry with gameplay that motivates the user to accelerate their progress by buying upgrades, *Farmville* for a time captured the attention of tens of millions of daily users. Flash games represented yet another instance of game design evolving into an independent design field.

Another important part of the rise of Flash was the creation of online communities—many focused on gaming—that acted as a clearinghouse for new tools and strategies. Newgrounds, which was formed in 1995 by Tom Fulp, hosted user-generated content based on uploads of all sorts of digital games and other experimental works. In the late nineties, Flash became the dominant technology on Newgrounds, and its users worked and reworked their creations as the software became more powerful. Likewise, Flash Kit, a developmental community founded

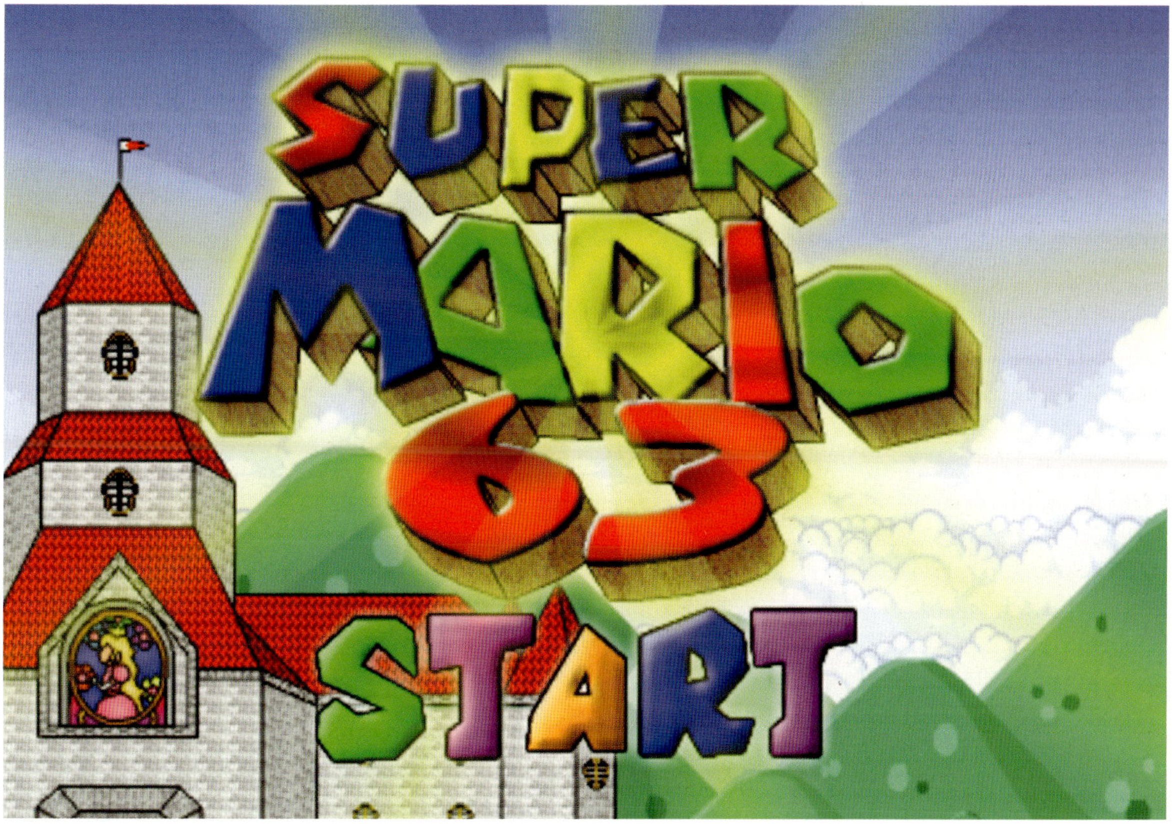

7.8. Newgrounds, *Super Mario 63*, 2009

by Mark Fennell in 1999, also spread knowledge and tools among the software's enthusiasts. Virtual communities like these are what made Flash different from any other programming software up to that time, as amateur computer users could learn Flash on the internet alone. In this way, Flash moved out of the exclusive domain of professional programmers and designers, becoming one of the first true participatory aspects of the web. Early 2000s-era Flash witnessed a halo moment, as it was powerful enough to design cutting-edge websites yet still simple enough to be accessible to anyone with a determined will to program.

As an aside, the participatory element of Flash and the ease with which some of its showier effects could be implemented led to a parallel Flash web filled with clichéd animations. Overzealous amateurs and lazy professionals alike produced millions of sites and, of course, Flash-based banner ads that blinked in a strobe-like palette of garish colors. The tendency toward overdecorating Flash sites is probably partly responsible for the purposeful minimalism that becomes characteristic of "serious" designers. Today, the parody website Zombo deftly satirizes the excesses of a not-so-distant age.

Peak Flash, and Then the Fall

The year 2005 would be a logical choice to cite as the moment when computer users began to experience peak Flash. After ten years, the platform had been continually updated, while creating and meeting new expectations for multimedia and animated content. Then, in 2005, Flash became the default technology for a new company called YouTube (figure 7.9). Founded by three PayPal employees, Chad Hurley, Steve Chen, and Jawed Karim, the video-sharing site soon accelerated into a cultural phenomenon. Bought by Google in 2006, by its fifth anniversary, YouTube hosted more than two billion views per day. It was through YouTube that Flash seemingly became an indispensable part of the architecture of the web, so important that it was invisible; in a way, it was the web. With YouTube, Flash became more of a utility than a creative tool, as the content came to drive the user experience.

The year 2005 also saw the publication of a revision of Lev Manovich's three-year-old essay "Generation Flash," in which the computer scientist argued that Flash had led to a profound cultural shift. "More than just a result of a particular software / hardware situation (low bandwidth leading to the use of vector graphics), Flash aesthetics exemplifies cultural sensibility

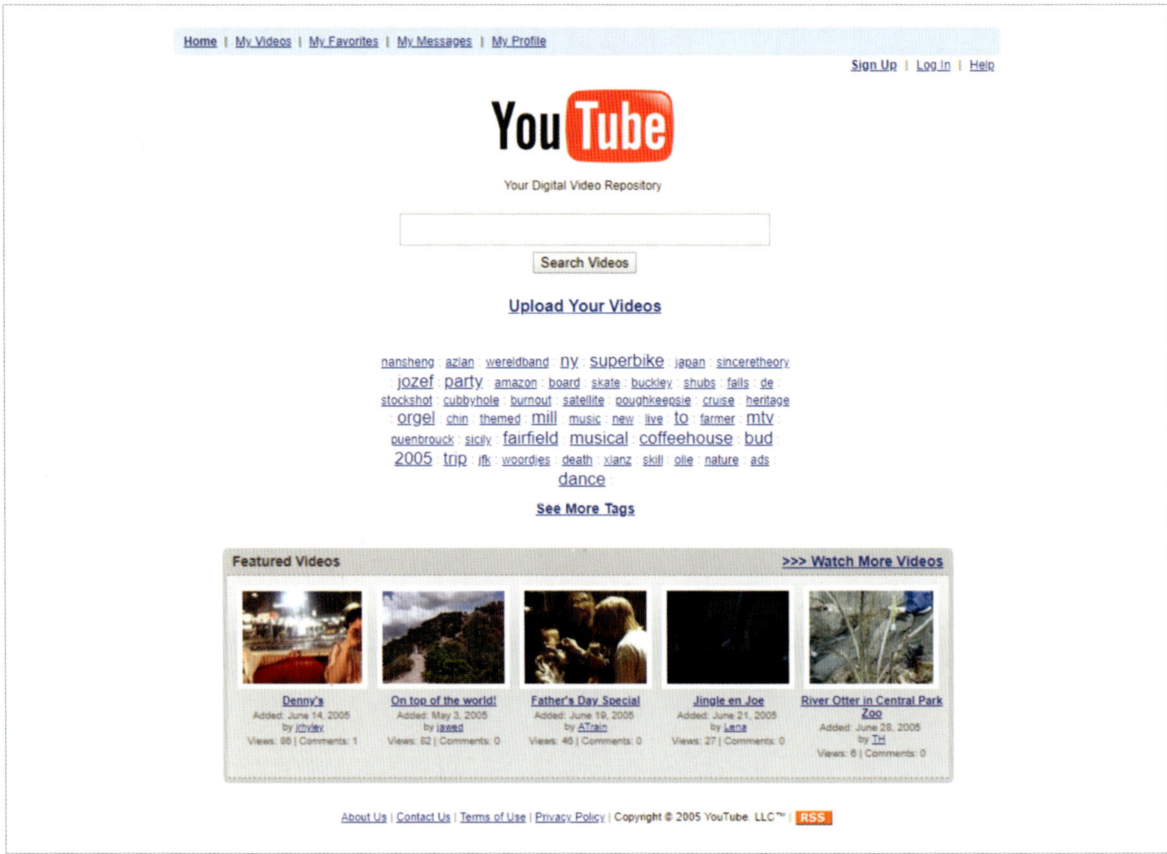

7.9. Screenshot of YouTube, created by Chad Hurley, Steve Chen, and Jawed Karim in 2005

of a new generation. This generation does not care if their work is called art or design." Curiously, Manovich saw 2005 as the youth-driven crest of a new wave of participatory design via Flash, but he also hearkened back to the modernists that have been such a touchstone for digital technologists. Manovich asserted that Flash allowed for a midcentury sensibility to be revived: "The result is the new modernism of data visualizations, vector nets, pixel-thin grids and arrows: Bauhaus design in the service of information design."

In Manovich's essay, one can see a reassertion of the visionary thread that has emerged and reemerged in digital culture. Not surprisingly, some scholars have tied Flash to the hoary old chestnuts of Marshall McLuhan (discussed in chapter 1). For example, Anastasia Salter and John Murray, in their 2014 book *Flash Building the Interactive Web*, tie together Manovich and McLuhan under the rubric "the medium is the message." Salter and Murray argue that Flash had not just reconfigured the web interface, but had rescaled the ability of people to reach out to one another. Following McLuhan's notion of technological extension, they wrote, "Generation Flash is a prime representation of this consequence of extension. The scale of self-amplification and creation that Flash enables likewise amplified the web." This utopian interpretation of the platform of course has a certain poignancy, as by 2014, when the book was published, Flash's total collapse was imminent.

The downfall of Flash is a complicated story involving corporate rivalries as much as technological advances. At its simplest core, the iPhone killed Flash. After over two years of rumors and a sophisticated marketing buildup, in the summer of 2007 the first iPhone went on sale. A cell phone with a touchscreen that could conveniently access music, photos, and the web, the iPhone set the stage for a new era of mobile computing. Of course, neither the iPhone nor the newer iPods or iPads (2010), used Flash. For the first few years of the iPhone, this rejection of Flash was viewed as a needless heresy, as it was opined that Steve Jobs's controlling nature had led him to a losing battle with the dominant Adobe platform. In 2008, *Wired* magazine reported that the British Advertising Standards agency had rejected an Apple advertisement with the tag line, "All the parts of the internet are on the iPhone," because Flash was the internet. While Apple quickly devised an app that allowed iOS users to watch YouTube,

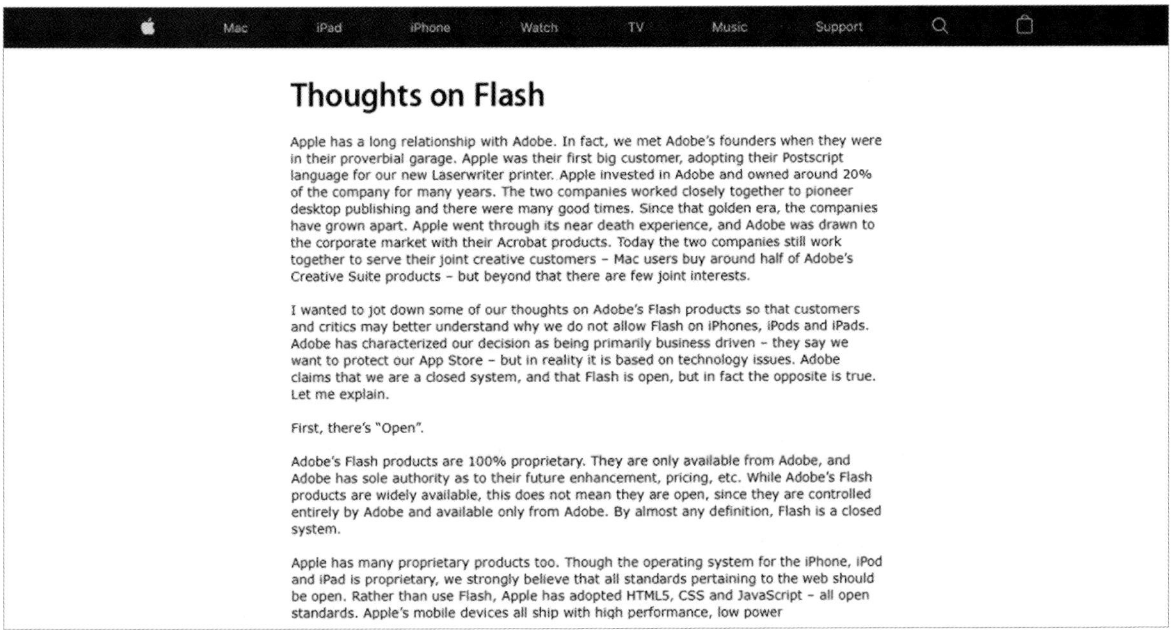

Mac iPad iPhone Watch TV Music Support

Thoughts on Flash

Apple has a long relationship with Adobe. In fact, we met Adobe's founders when they were in their proverbial garage. Apple was their first big customer, adopting their Postscript language for our new Laserwriter printer. Apple invested in Adobe and owned around 20% of the company for many years. The two companies worked closely together to pioneer desktop publishing and there were many good times. Since that golden era, the companies have grown apart. Apple went through its near death experience, and Adobe was drawn to the corporate market with their Acrobat products. Today the two companies still work together to serve their joint creative customers – Mac users buy around half of Adobe's Creative Suite products – but beyond that there are few joint interests.

I wanted to jot down some of our thoughts on Adobe's Flash products so that customers and critics may better understand why we do not allow Flash on iPhones, iPods and iPads. Adobe has characterized our decision as being primarily business driven – they say we want to protect our App Store – but in reality it is based on technology issues. Adobe claims that we are a closed system, and that Flash is open, but in fact the opposite is true. Let me explain.

First, there's "Open".

Adobe's Flash products are 100% proprietary. They are only available from Adobe, and Adobe has sole authority as to their future enhancement, pricing, etc. While Adobe's Flash products are widely available, this does not mean they are open, since they are controlled entirely by Adobe and available only from Adobe. By almost any definition, Flash is a closed system.

Apple has many proprietary products too. Though the operating system for the iPhone, iPod and iPad is proprietary, we strongly believe that all standards pertaining to the web should be open. Rather than use Flash, Apple has adopted HTML5, CSS and JavaScript – all open standards. Apple's mobile devices all ship with high performance, low power

7.10. Steve Jobs, "Thoughts on Flash," 2010

many were still forced to turn to balky Flash emulators to watch web content.

In 2010, Steve Jobs was forced to address the controversy, which he did in a press release, "Thoughts on Flash." In an understated, personal tone that should remind readers of his vaunted skill at corporate communications, Jobs set out to defend Apple's rejection of the platform, citing a litany of problems (figure 7.10). Jobs questioned Flash's "reliability, security and performance," asserting that it destroyed battery life and created opportunities for hackers. Jobs also argued that it just did not work. "In addition, Flash has not performed well on mobile devices. We have routinely asked Adobe to show us Flash performing well on a mobile device, any mobile device, for a few years now. We have never seen it." Also, with mobile hardware interfacing via touchscreens, the famed Flash rollover no longer functioned. The Apple leader also argued that it was not in Apple's interest to allow a third-party proprietary software platform to have a modicum of control over its iOS. Advocating the open architecture of HTML5, JavaScript, and Cascading Style Sheets (CSS) as an alternative, Jobs seemed to be swimming upstream at a time when Flash completely dominated the personal computing environment.

From 2010 to 2015, the problems for Flash continued to multiply. By 2011, Adobe admitted that it was not going to succeed on any mobile device. YouTube had started experimenting with HTML5 as early as 2010, and in 2015 it shifted to that markup language as its default standard. Finally, in 2017, amid the ten-year anniversary of the iPhone, Adobe officially relented, announcing that they would end-of-life (a favorite tech euphemism) Flash in 2020. The end of Flash had a wide-ranging impact, even poignantly causing millions of Neopets to be put down. Today, about 80 percent of websites run on HTML5, while the rest use the older XML standard. In both cases, JavaScript enables interactivity, and Cascading Style Sheets complete the picture. The end of the Flash era represented a maturing of web design, as it would gradually shift away from the visual pyrotechnics of the early 2000s.

From a design standpoint, CSS has become the key to web page development, because it allows the design of the web page to be separated from the HTML5 architecture. In an age with no default environment—like the desktop in the nineties—but rather a diverse mix of often mobile devices with various screen sizes and capabilities, CSS allows the web page to adapt to the available interface. The key to web style in the post-Flash era has become flexibility, as fluid grids and scalable elements have become paramount. As transience and mutability have come to define the web, sophisticated designers have turned toward storytelling and experience design, emphasizing the cultural more than the visual. Although eye candy is still desirable to catch the user's attention, deeper engagement and effective UX have displaced style as an end in itself. One part of this shift has been caused by prototyping software such as InVision, which allows the designer to make evidence-based decisions based on UX analytics.

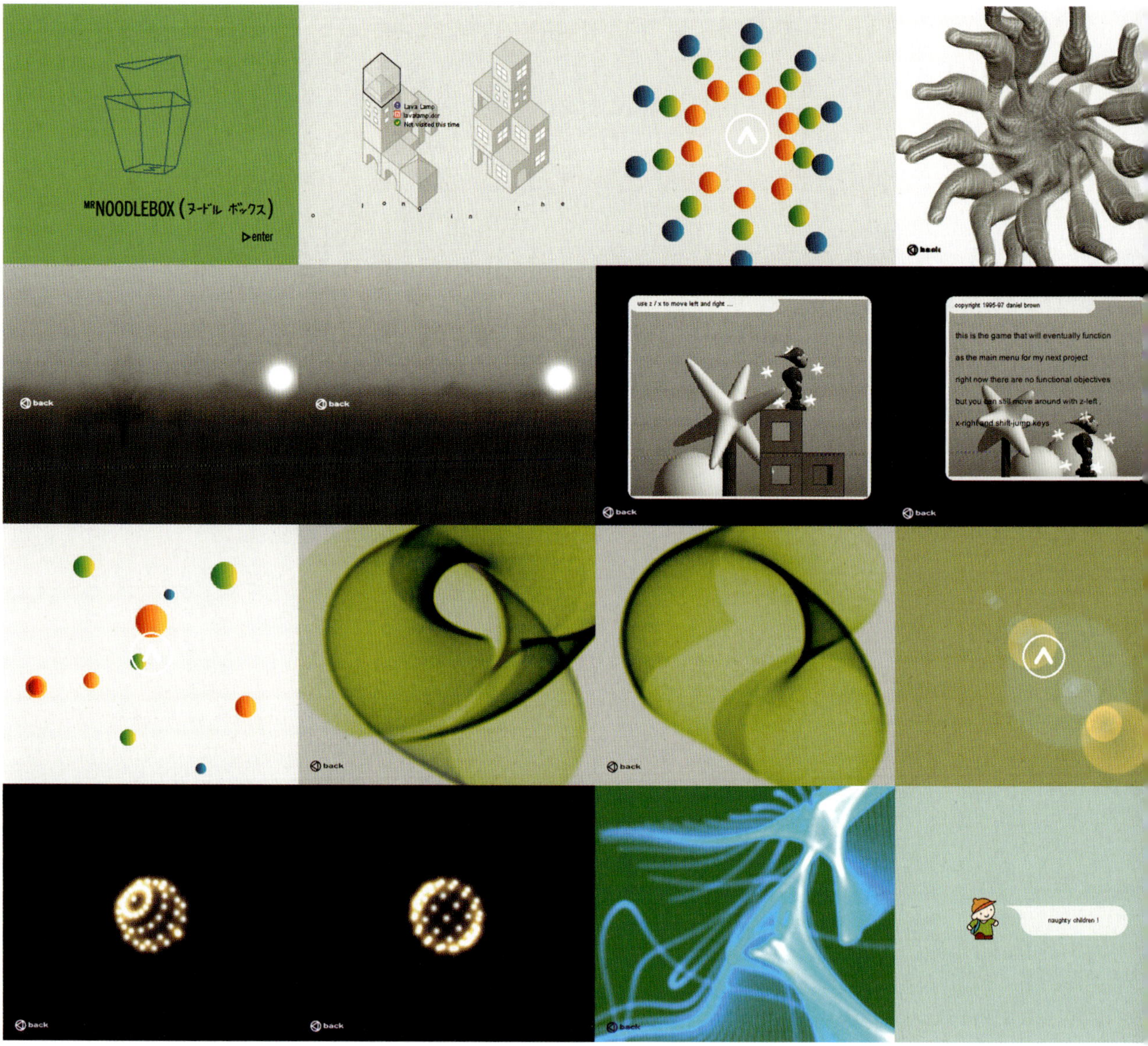

7.11. Daniel Brown, Noodlebox website, 1999

Web Design: A Case Study

Digital design studios have come and gone repeatedly since the nineties; a good sense of the overall trajectory of web design emerges from a case study of one of the longest thriving studios, Amaze, which was founded in London in 1995 and is now part of Kin + Carta. One of the founders, Roy Stringer, was a self-taught designer and web visionary who had been originally hired as creative director for a digitization project for the Henry Moore Trust in 1990. The project, called Sculpture Interactive, was based at Liverpool Polytechnic (renamed John Moores University [JMU] after 1992) and involved organizing thousands of images cross-referenced with audio and video clips. Stringer called it "hypermedia," as hyperlinks facilitated navigation through the laserdisc. Stringer had become a cutting-edge multimedia designer before there even was a web.

After pursuing several collaborative university-based projects, in 1995 Stringer cofounded Amaze while still maintaining a connection to JMU, from which many of the studio's first employees were recruited. Amaze would be a way of facilitating commercial work outside the aegis of the academy. From the beginning, Amaze benefited from the work of Daniel Brown, a teenage designer comfortable with writing his own code. Like other artists from this era, Brown established a personal website where he could pursue experimental projects. Called Noodlebox (figure 7.11), Brown's site was one of the first devoted entirely to interactive projects; in a precursor to today's web, Brown used Shockwave to make the entire site showcase dynamic multimedia, as opposed to just adding a few bells and whistles to a static page. Noodlebox gained a measure of mainstream attention; for example, it was prominently featured on the Netscape home page—a typical static HTML buffet of

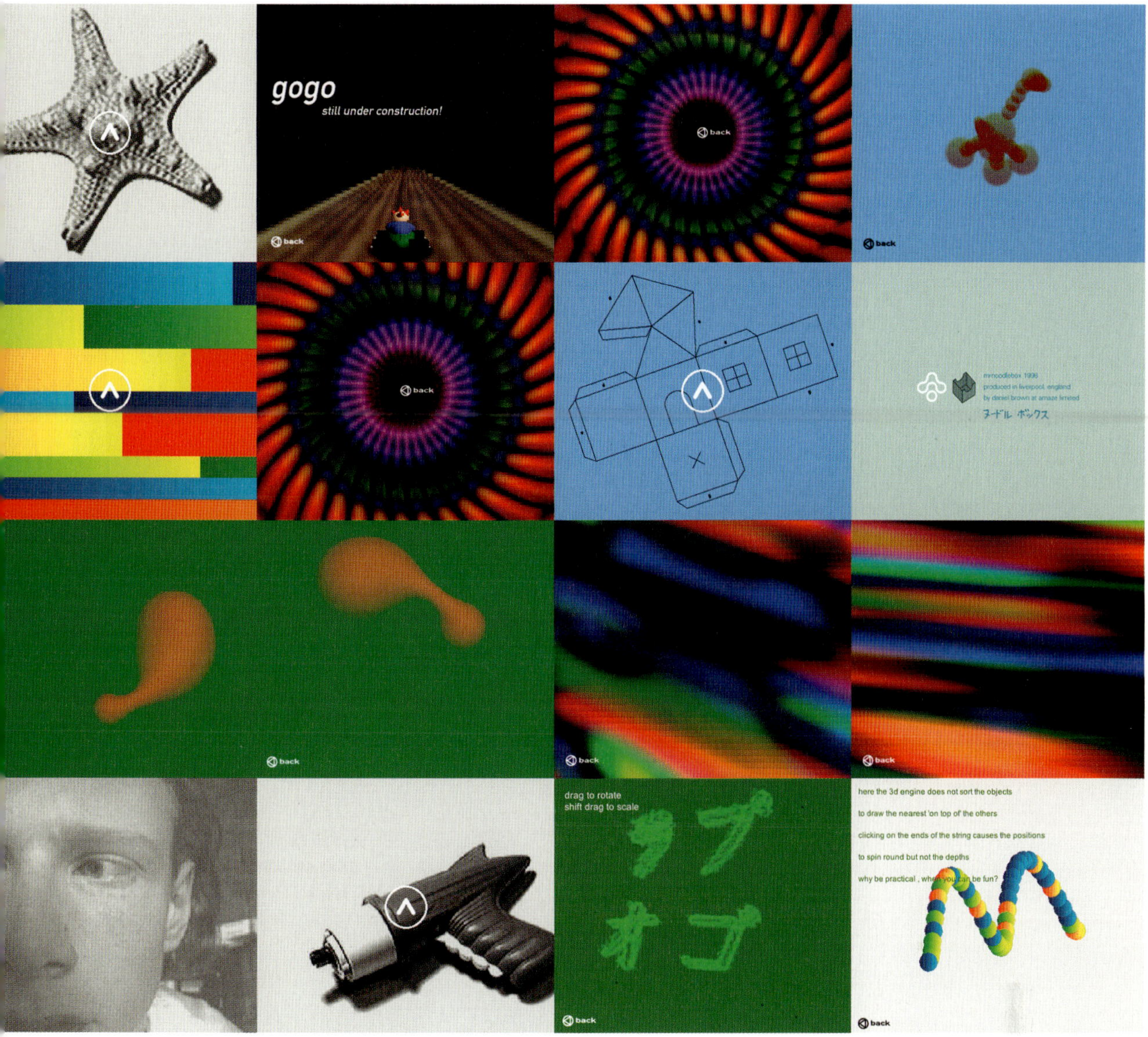

links—as an example of the "Rage of the Day" in May 1999. "Danny Brown's Mr. Noodlebox mixes the glean of Metropolis, the disturbing innocence of Japanese anime, and the dry wit of Brittania to form an interactive graphical landscape that'll seep into your dreams at night." The author here captures in words something of the diverse mélange of flavors that Brown worked into the web.

Brown represented a very rare type of designer at the dawn of the web age: one who was equally comfortable with computer code and artistic choices. Two decades later the ability to navigate both worlds, classic design plus what John Maeda has called computational design, has become somewhat more common. At the very least, many of the older firewalls separating the technological and artistic realms have now broken down. A company like Facebook, for example, needs to take a holistic approach to designing digital products—filters and the like—that requires different types of designers to be able to effectively interact and understand each other's approaches and challenges. As the lines continue to blur, it would seem that the design fields are becoming ever more fluid in their identity and workflow.

The key to Noodlebox was its combination of a playful outlook and visuals that collapsed the arboreal hierarchy of the web, whereby information was still grounded in a fixed structure derived from past centuries of print. This interest in breaking hierarchies had been initiated by the work of Amaze's other design thinker, Stringer, who had for some years focused his attention on the Navihedron, an intuitive interface based on a dynamic icosahedron, a polyhedron with twenty faces. With Noodlebox, Brown made the Navihedron the basis of a gamelike experience, whereby users would move blocks into new combinations, opening them to find an eclectic range of content. Pure serendipity.

Amaze benefited by having two technically savvy creatives, Stringer and Brown, which perfectly situated it to push web design forward as the multimedia, Flash age took hold. Stringer was endlessly frustrated by the static web and vented to an interviewer in 1999, "It took us seven years to go from a command line... to the first graphical user interface. We've had graphical user interfaces for 15 years now and they still haven't changed." Stringer makes a strong general point here; while the conventional wisdom mandates that the internet is powerfully fluid, making and remaking itself week to week, the opposite case can also be made. The desktop, skeuomorphic icons, files folders: all of these dominated around the year 2000 and still resonate today. Furthermore, the Flash age that would see the establishment of multimedia interactivity as the core of the web experience happened two decades ago, and arguably much of what has occurred since involves adaptation and refinement, not transformation.

One difficulty faced by the designers at Amaze was the fact that in a prebroadband era, rich multimedia content just could not be delivered to the mainstream over the internet. Still, in 1999, the commercial promise of the Navihedron and Noodlebox garnered the attention of Volkswagen, a client that vaulted the studio to the forefront of digital design. For Volkswagen, Amaze built a website that was aimed at building the brand amid a youthful demographic. Volkswagen Zoon used the Navihedron for some of the navigation, but also worked to create one of the first commercial internet communities. Volkswagen was one of the first companies to attempt to channel the anarchic energy of young internet users into building a branded community. During its two-year run, Zoon also featured a live, offline studio component, and Volkswagen hired Stefan Ernsting as editor-in-chief of the web pages, making him one of the pioneers of the web content and social media consulting profession.

The Zoon youth-community campaign was a forerunner to a great deal of research by the industry into the digital molding of young consumers. At Amaze, this led to a project they called the Amaze Generation, a five-year (2011–2015) study of the digital behavior of a group of ten- to fifteen-year-olds. "We joined them as they explored the digital world. We watched as they took their first steps in the world of social media. And we discovered how technology and the internet are shaping their behaviors and attitudes, and how they, in turn, are changing society." Amaze and their clients hope that studying these digital natives—many of the conclusions are fairly nondescript, tracking the rise of mobile, for example—will lead to more effective marketing. Of course, as some consumers have become alarmed in recent years over the data collection practices of the industry, designers are facing new challenges in not appearing to facilitate intrusive surveillance.

Roy Stringer died suddenly in 2001, but the Volkswagen contract had put Amaze in a strong position to prosper going forward. In 2002 they won a contract with Toyota, and then in 2004 became the European digital content manager for Lexus. For Lexus, Amaze ran websites in more than thirty markets and dozens of languages. Aside from the day-to-day web support of this operation, some novel aspects of the

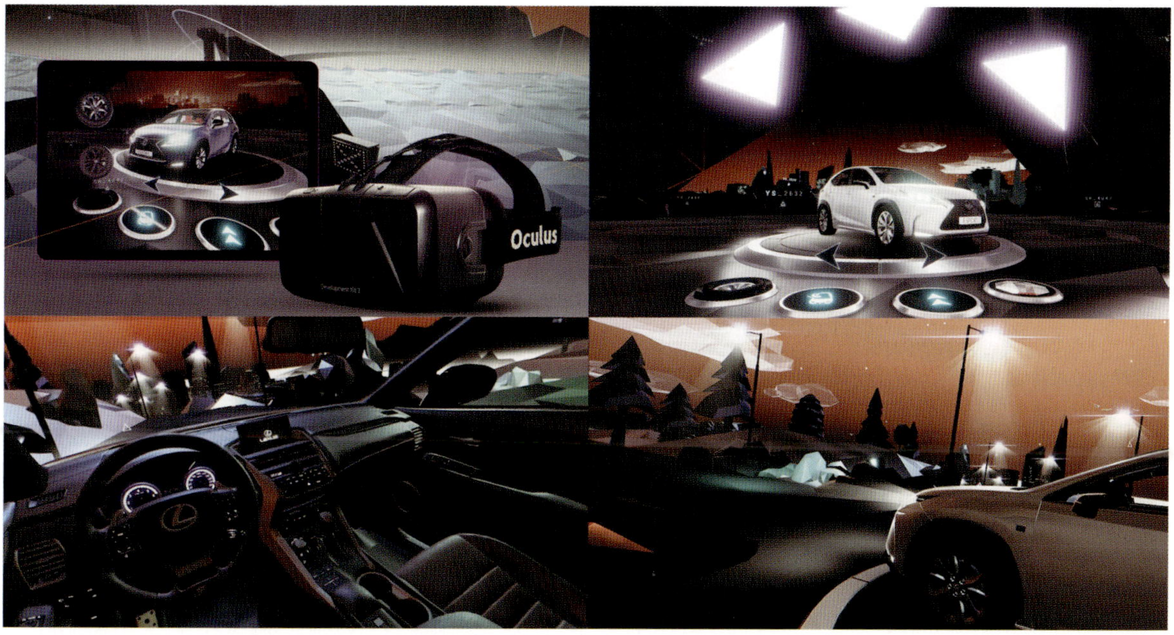

7.12. Amaze, Lexus NX virtual reality project, 2014

Lexus work recall the forward-thinking experiments of Amaze's founders, while also outlining the increasing complexity of digital design as it moves beyond the desktop computer. Each new model of car gets its own website and some mobile apps, of course, but these basic elements are also expected to be complemented by some sort of strikingly new interactive content. In the last few years, nascent virtual reality technology has provided the cutting-edge buzz sought by design studios and their clients. For example, in 2014, to fuel the run-up to the release of a new crossover SUV called the Lexus NX, Amaze designed a digital marketing tool focused on the Oculus Rift virtual reality headset (figure 7.12). One part of this campaign allowed users to customize the interior of a car and view the result using head-turning movements. More elaborately, using the Unreal gaming engine, the studio designed a driving experience over several miles of virtual roads. With a suggestion of cinematic narrative, the virtual reality drive again showed how the emotional rush of video games continues to penetrate the marketing realm.

As web design has shifted its focus from creating artifacts to developing immersive experiences—read the copy on the splash page of any design studio and the focus on narrative and emotional journeys is self-evident—virtual reality, which is discussed further in chapter 12, continues to position itself as the logical next step. Despite the expense and sometimes disorienting feeling of head-mounted displays, enough clients have come forward that some digital design studios have established virtual reality as a specialty; for example, the UK studio Rewind developed a VR campaign called the Hacker Hostel for HBO's comedy about the technology industry, *Silicon Valley*. The Hacker Hostel consisted of a virtual mock-up of the show's main set that allowed users to explore hundreds of objects while moving around and interacting with the actors through scripted set pieces. The basic premise of even the most advanced VR has been around for decades, back to the eighties when command-line programs allowed users to walk around and interact via text and their imagination. It is the production values that have truly changed.

In 2015, Amaze updated its logo, producing what it called a "living brand mark" (figure 7.13). In the history of corporate identity over the last fifty years, the logo has been the central design challenge. Esteemed modernist designers like Paul Rand and Otl Aicher made their reputations on the basis of logo designs. While branding eventually encompassed all aspects of a given client's visual communication, the logo was always at the heart of the enterprise. Somewhat displaced today by multimedia interactivity, Amaze's new logo artfully combined the simple power of a modernist glyph with the latest web technology. The logo consists of a three-dimensional red ribbonlike form with the name of the studio overlaid on top. The type part of the logo is contemporary tech modernism; the name is written in an all lowercase sans serif alphabet that recalls the typographic ideals of the Bauhaus. Perhaps intentionally, it in fact bears a strong resemblance to the Amazon logotype with which it shares its four initial

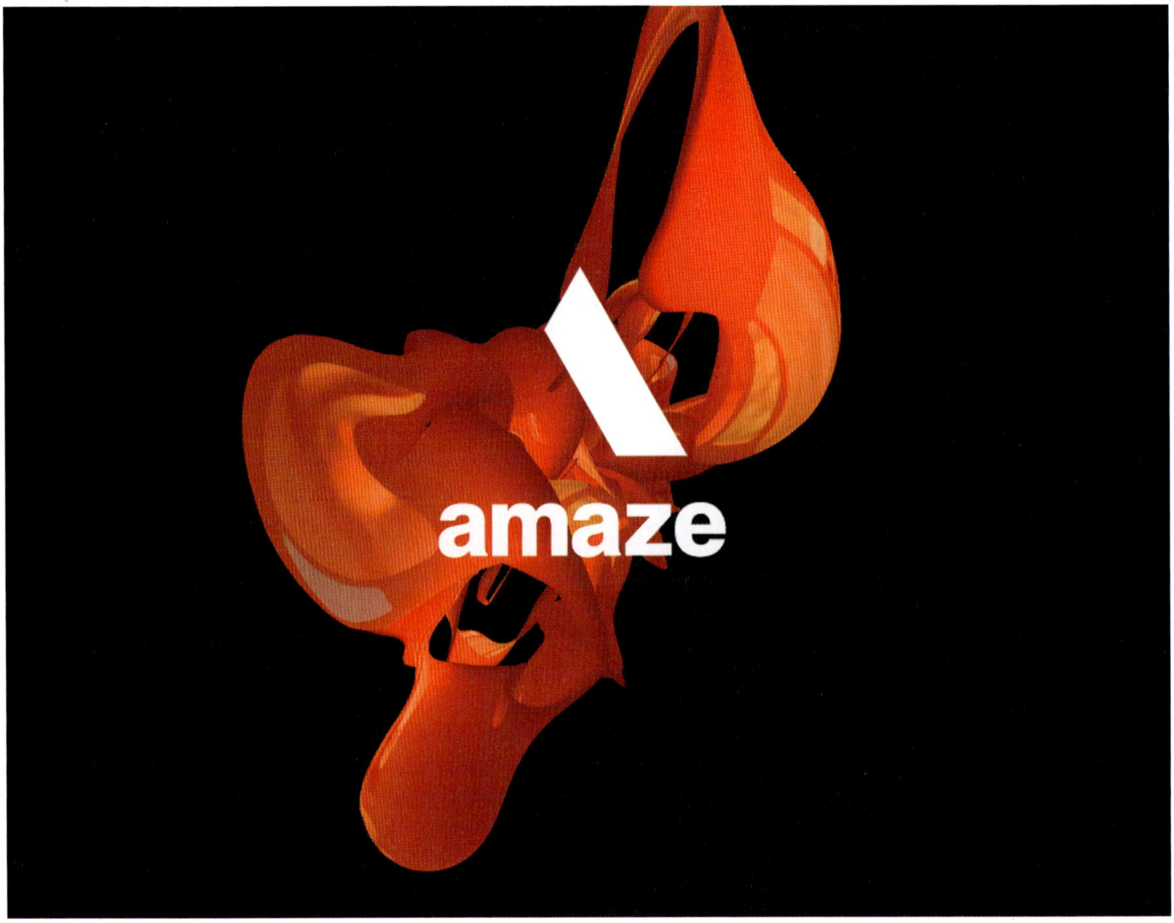

7.13. Amaze, updated logo, "living brand mark," 2015

letters. Above the name is a single stroke connoting a letter A, its elegant use of positive and negative space recalling Alan Fletcher's estimable 1989 logotype for the Victoria and Albert Museum. Together, the name and the A form a triangle.

Behind this static white lettering, the red ribbon provides a complementary burst of color and organic shape. But after a second's glance, one realizes that the background is in fact alive with sinuous motion. Designed by Paul Musgrave with the assistance of Daniel Brown, the animated ribbon twists and turns like some sort of sentient sea creature, branching outward asymmetrically from the stable triangular core formed by type. A key part of the effect is produced by using Web Graphics Library (WebGL), a JavaScript protocol first introduced by the Mozilla Foundation in 2011. WebGL allows for animation and interactivity in a post-Flash world, where browser plug-ins are unwanted and unwieldy. Through the use of WebGL, fluid animation can appear on just about any browser on any device.

Yet another dimension to the logo is that the ribbon is in fact an abstraction of the human and digital projects taking place at the studio. The logo is connected to various data streams, some audio and some visual, so that the shape and pace of animation will change in response to its environment. Like the experimental projects of John Maeda and Scott Snibbe, the abstract form communicates emotion, representing yet another example of the digital yearning for human connections, for warmth amid the technology. Increasingly, digital design has been driven by collaboration of the type represented by the ribbon logo. Flexible cloud-based software has enabled teams of designers and engineers to connect with one another in real time: Miro, Figma, Slack, Discord, and the list goes on. Because so many larger digital design projects require varied expertise, the industry has shifted rather abruptly away from the lone designer or boutique studio model. There is something of a chicken-egg situation here, as collaboration software facilitates complexity just as new strategies demand a greater range of professional skills.

Insomuch as digital design has succeeded in communicating warmth and human emotion, it has done so in a way that has often excluded many people. Activists have addressed this lack of diversity for decades; for example, in 1970 Dorothy Hayes arranged an exhibition of forty-nine Black graphic designers, and in 1987 Cheryl Miller (see chapter 3) wrote the essay "Black Designers Missing in Action." This latter article began by describing a photo of a recent design competition jury that was, predictably, made up of seven white men. While execrable in 1987, perhaps the more troubling fact is how this situation has not changed enough over the ensuing decades. As recently as 2017, AIGA reported that less than 4 percent of American designers are Black, and the same situation prevails for the broader BIPOC community.

Still, there are many reasons not to despair, as an incredible range of equity engines have come to the fore over the last few years. Today, TED talks, conferences, essays, and podcasts on diverse areas of digital design are widely distributed. Recent years have also seen new networking sites arise, such as Blacks Who Design, a resource founded by Wes O'Haire. Aside from directed DEI (diversity, equity, inclusion) sites, broader portfolio networking spaces—Behance, Slack, Tumblr, DeviantArt, and social media writ large—have served increasingly as virtual spaces that one hopes will continue to transform the digital design professions. There is a lot of challenging yet exhilarating work to accomplish here. As designer Rafael Smith put it, "The thing I wake up most excited about is figuring out how design and technology can contribute to diversity and inclusion and the larger movements around racial, gender, and (insert other identity) justice."

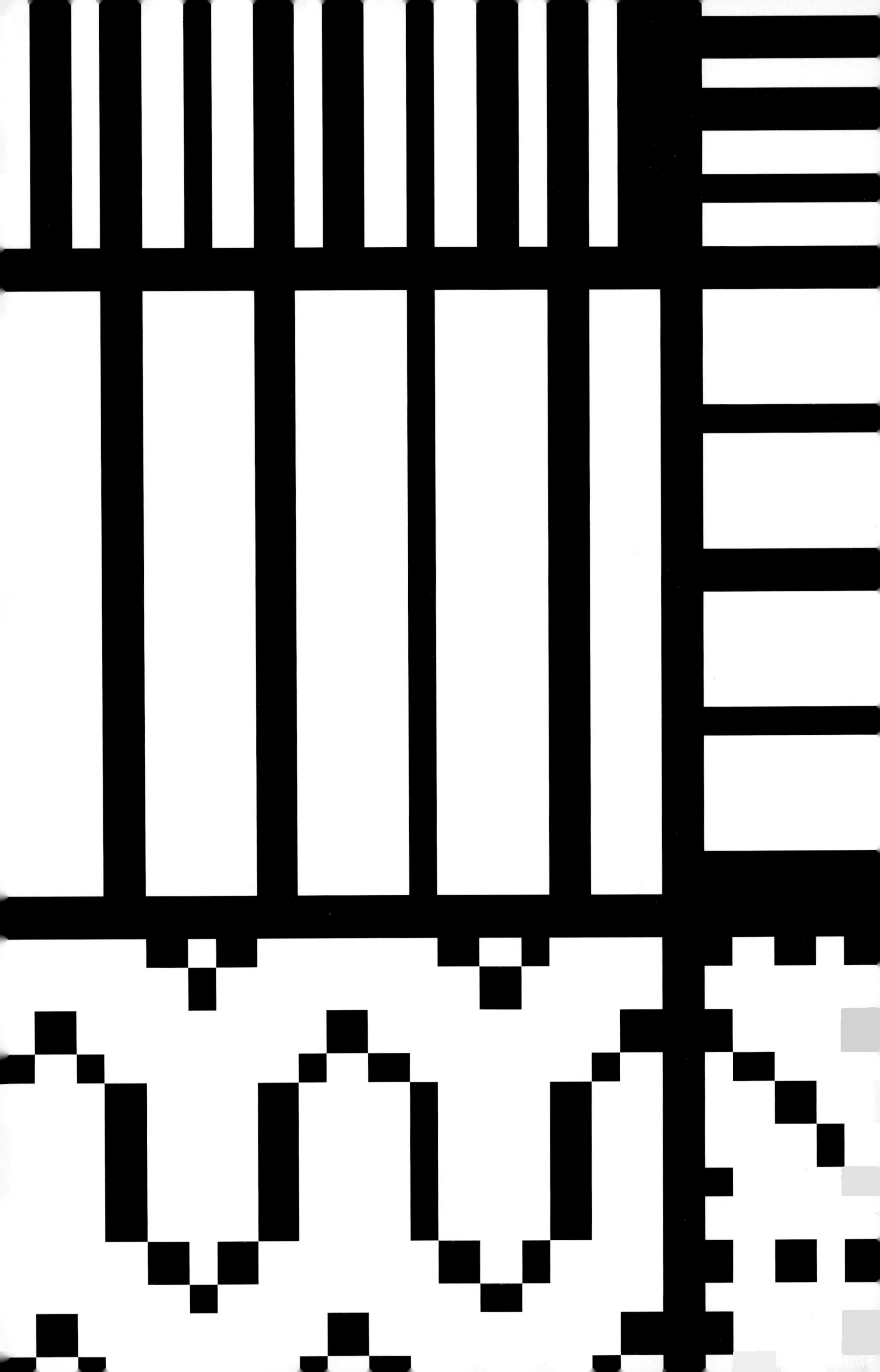

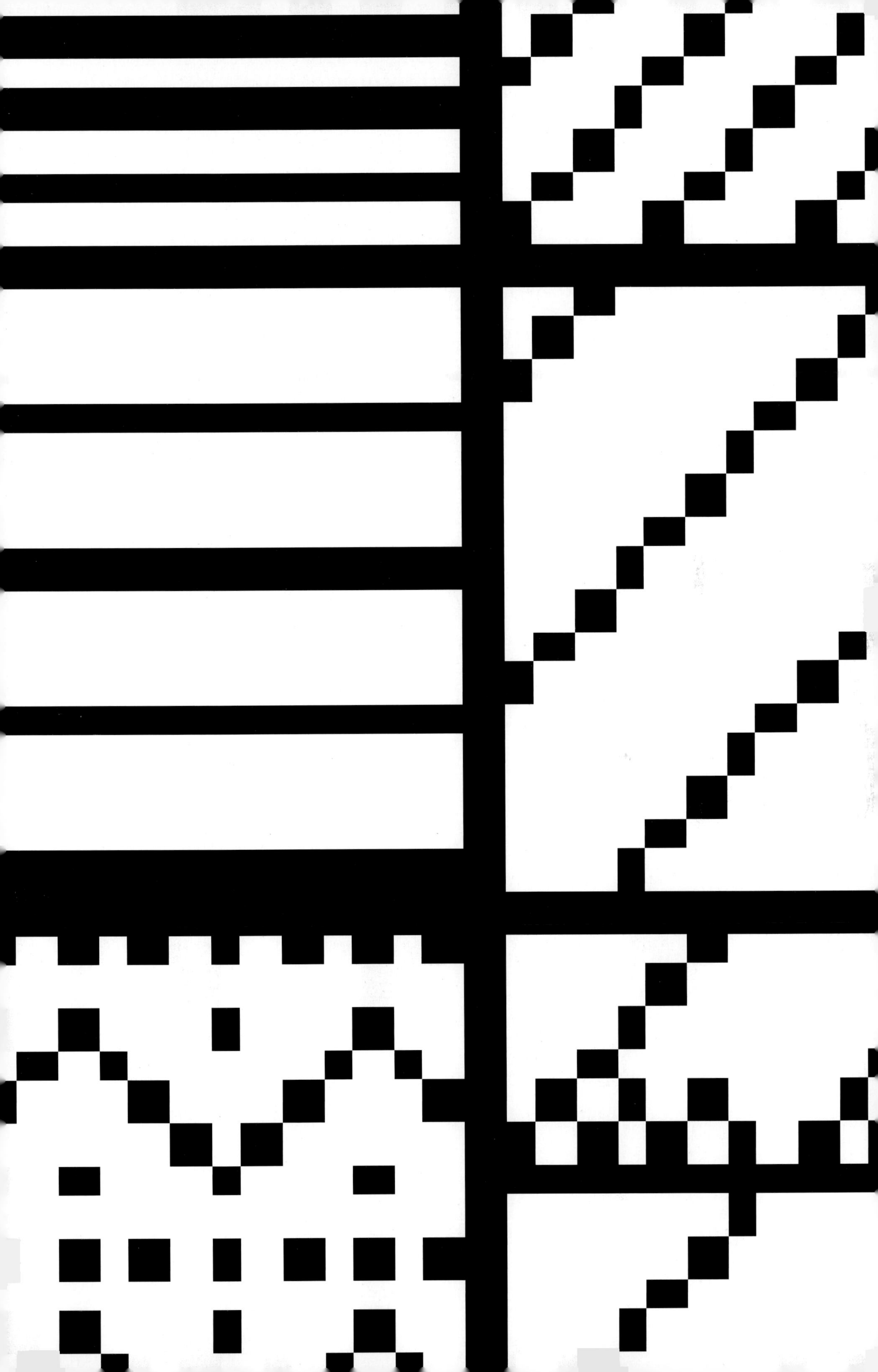

8.1. ZHA, Galaxy Soho, Beijing, China, 2013

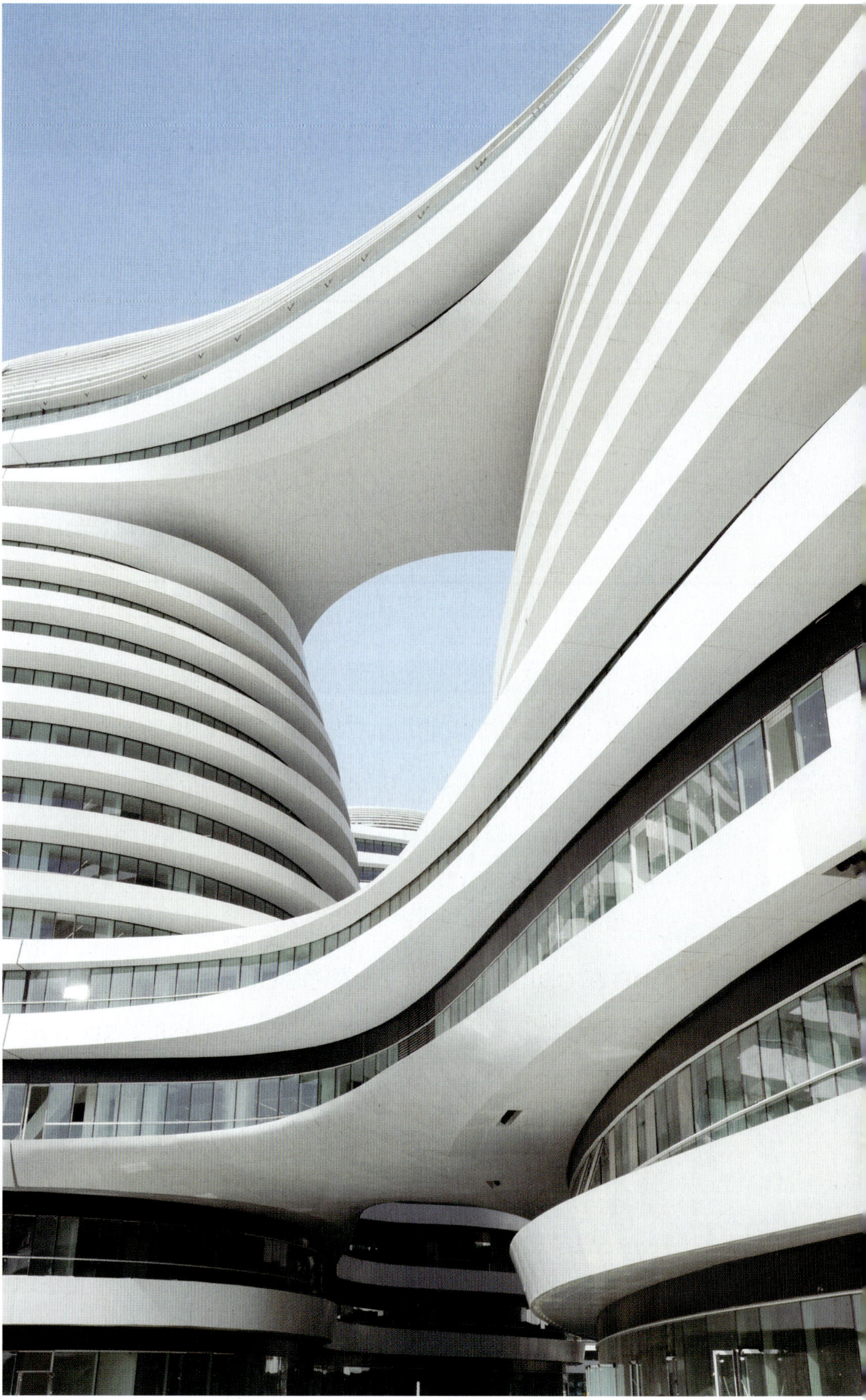

Eight. Digital Architecture II: *Parametrics and 3D Printing*

Though parametric blob architecture (see chapter 6) did not suddenly transform the urban landscape—a Kunsthaus Graz on every corner—it did have a diffuse impact even where not as explicitly evident. Fueled by the adoption of software, the stunning success of Gehry's Guggenheim Bilbao, and the intellectual gravitas of the Peter Eisenman / Greg Lynn circle, it is notable how many works from the early twenty-first century show a heightened curvilinear awareness. This partial blobism is visible, for example, through the architectural studios of Norman Foster and Renzo Piano, both of which were previously known for a more orthogonal and rectilinear vocabulary. And at one point, a curving Gehry structure, while perhaps more fish than blob, did seem to be around every urban corner.

Without question, Zaha Hadid did more than any other architect to festoon the globe with the computational curve. Hadid had a stellar intellectual resume—studied with Peter Cook and Rem Koolhaas, partner at Office for Metropolitan Architecture (OMA), designed avant-garde experimental paintings for MoMA's Deconstructivist Architecture exhibition—that pales in comparison to how her buildings have caught the public's imagination. Working in tandem with Patrik Schumacher, Hadid devised a beautiful visual language of sweeping white curves that morph one into another like so much sculptural taffy. In contrast to the blob

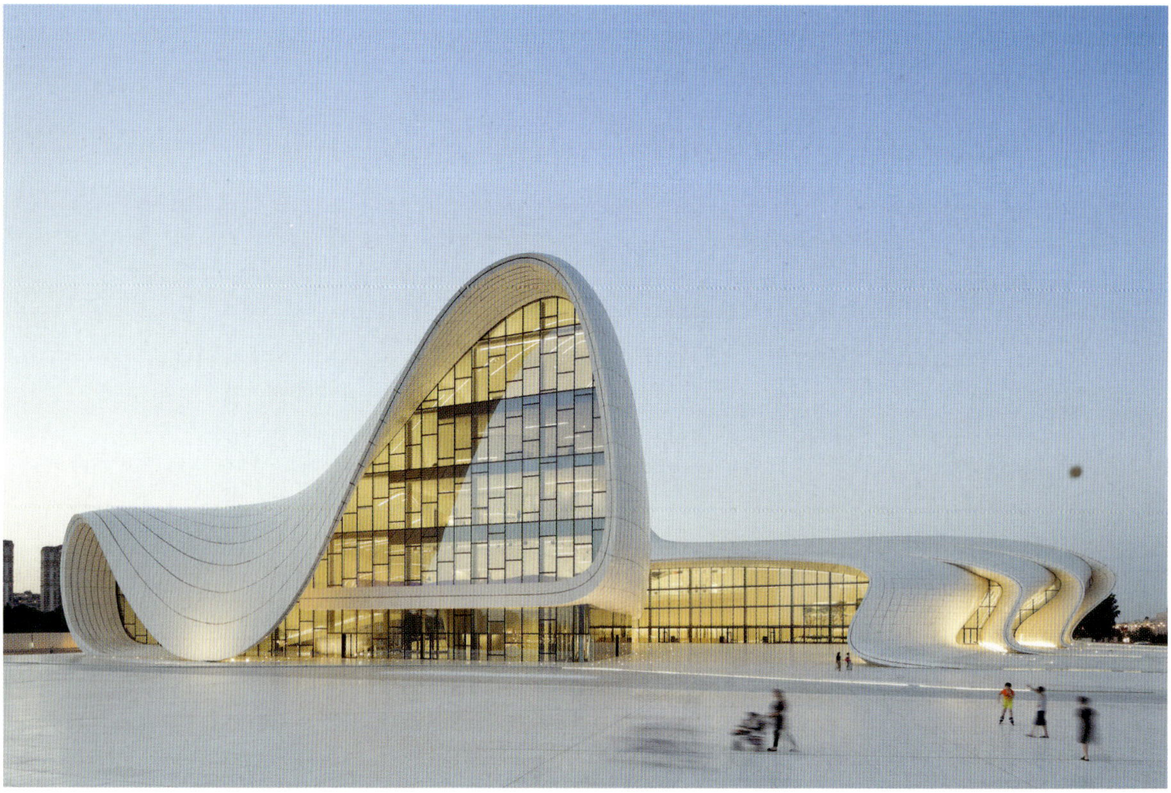

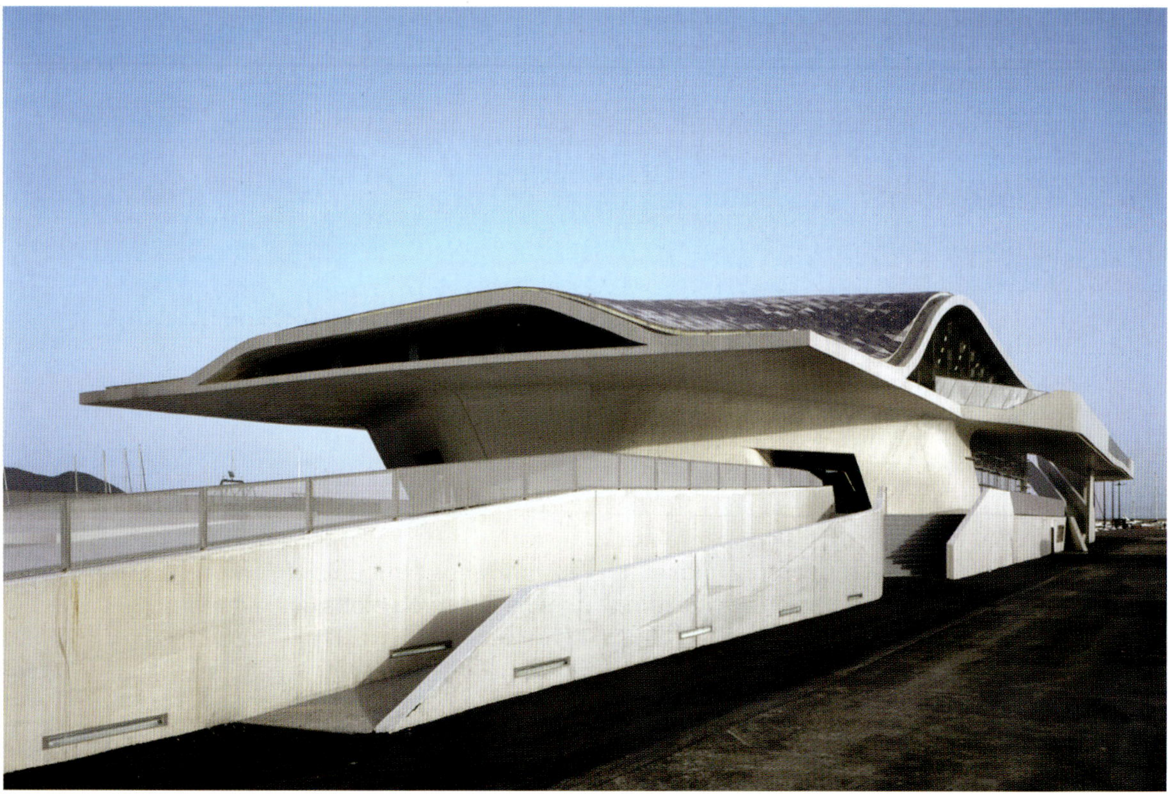

8.2. ZHA, Heydar Aliev Center, Baku, Azerbaijan, 2013
8.3. ZHA, Salerno Ferry Terminal, Italy, 2016

oddities of Lynn or Fournier/Cook, Hadid created a futuristic vibe whereby ceilings dissolve into walls, and various pavilions reach out to one another with elastic arms. Her work is really only comparable to Gehry's in terms of its ability to make eccentric digital forms into a spatially complex wonderland.

Two buildings Hadid's firm ZHA completed in 2013 perfectly embody the style whereby blobs flow together smoothly. Galaxy Soho in Beijing (figure 8.1) features four Lynn-esque egg-shaped forms, these main structures connected by fluid skybridges to one another. Dominated visually by horizontal elements, the buildings flow one into another, while pathways and landscaping repeat the formal elements at their base. Like a futuristic art nouveau, the structures organically relate to one another. The other Hadid building that was completed in 2013, the Heydar Aliev Center in Baku, Azerbaijan (figure 8.2), seems to resonate with Lynn's notion of digital architecture modeled on a handkerchief, as a single flowing surface repeatedly folds upon itself, forming walls, roof, and even sliding under the structure as its floor. Some critics have objected to what they see as the homogenizing, decontextualizing impact of CAD, as curving splines populate the landscape without relating to it in a substantive manner.

Hadid's relationship with the computational curve resonates with the nuanced connection between thirties art deco designers and streamlining. As a strategy aimed at reducing the wind resistance of a moving object like a train, functional streamlining served a technical purpose. Around 1930, however, architects and designers "borrowed" streamlining, in the parlance of Harold Van Doren, and used it as a styling device for immobile objects. Van Doren, an industrial designer who celebrated borrowed streamlining, noted that some of this utilization was rooted in manufacturing technology. He recounted the situation whereby a curved refrigerator sheath was in fact much more economical to stamp and assemble than a similar flat part. In a like manner, the curvilinear forms of contemporary architecture are responding to the CAD and CAM software that enables, even encourages, the computational curve.

Van Doren recognized that during the thirties, the curve had become a mannered device that signaled forward-thinking technology. "The manufacturer who wants his laundry tubs, his typewriters, or his furnaces streamlined is in reality asking you to modernize them, to find the means for substituting curvilinear forms for rectilinear forms." Hadid's sweeping curves perform a similar function, assuring the client of the work's contemporaneity while animating a static structure with implied movement. The skybridges of the Galaxy Soho, for example, connect curved blobs in a manner that resembles the forms of a streamlined bowling alley installation designed by Donald Deskey in the early forties. Likewise, Hadid's Salerno Ferry Terminal (figure 8.3, 2016) seems to sleekly duck under the wind. While much has been made of the view that curvilinear or blob forms can at times be unpractical, wasting space by creating eccentric interior voids, for example, such architecture today would find its defender in Van Doren; the designer argued that streamlining was eminently practical insomuch as it was appealing to clients and the public.

Hadid and Schumacher are also closely identified with the variant of digital design known as

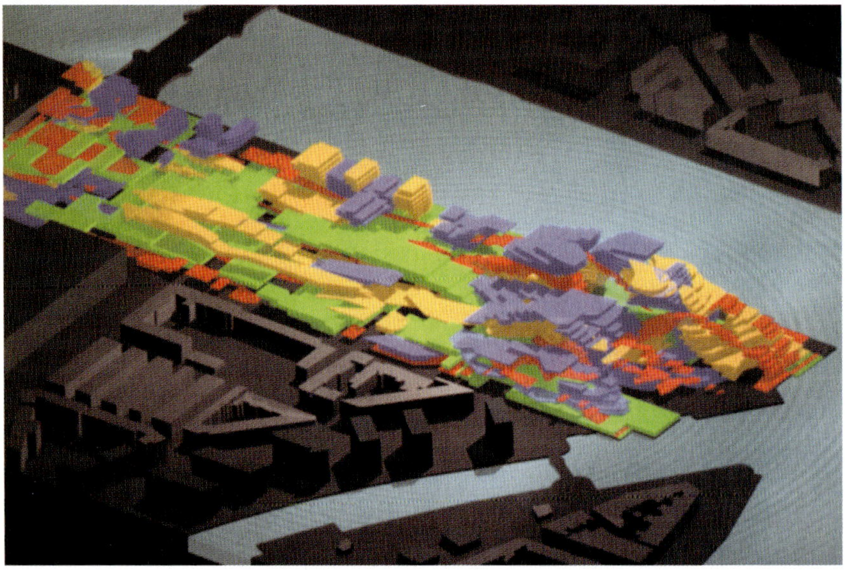

8.4. UNStudio, Rubber-Mat Project for Rotterdam 2045, Netherlands, 1995

parametric architecture, or sometimes, parametricism. Over the past two decades, the term has become increasingly elastic and can be tightly identified only in the context of its use. At its most basic, parametrics refers to the use of design software to work within parameters set down by the architect; for instance, a series of points can be fashioned into various splines by software. Parametric software in this way often functions as a utility, for example, by allowing revisions in one area—perhaps an increase in the weight of a roof—to automatically be reflected elsewhere, in this example by revising the load-bearing elements in response to the heavier structure. In the nineties, the Eisenman/Lynn cohort explored parametric design, which became embedded in their favored poststructuralist musings.

In 1995, Caroline Bos and Ben van Berkel of UNStudio introduced their Rubber-Mat Project for Rotterdam 2045, which applied the concept of parametrics to large-scale urban infrastructure (figure 8.4). Subsequently, the pair expanded on their ideas with the Move projects, which offered both theoretical and practical guidance in integrating computational parameters into digital architecture. An example of their thinking can be seen in the Burnham Pavilion (figure 8.5), which they designed for Chicago's celebration of the centennial of Daniel Burnham's Plan of Chicago. The architectural sculpture they designed used parameters from Burnham's original scheme, with squares to represent a grid and diagonal beams that resonate with Burnham's dramatic avenues. These beams were in fact concealed by the pavilion's skin. Folded skylights in the structure bent and twisted the underlying geometry, as parallelograms inputted into Grasshopper formed the basis for the parametric design.

Over the last decade and a half, Hadid and Schumacher (in particular) became invested in parametricism and succeeded in repositioning it somewhat away from the most arcane theory and more in the realm of the popular and buildable. In 2008 at a panel organized alongside the Venice Biennale, Schumacher presented his influential "Parametricist Manifesto." This polemical essay asserted that parametricism should henceforth be considered a mature style, one that was taking its rightful place atop contemporary avant-garde architecture. To support this view, Schumacher argued that parametricism had followed naturally after modernism, postmodernism, and deconstructivism, the latter two of which he deemed "transitional episodes" between the paramount practices. Schumacher argued that Lynn's concept of "continuous differentiation" lay at the heart of parametrics, which was the only style capable of expressing the complexity of contemporary society. On a visual level, Schumacher's invocation of "liquids in motion" connects to building projects such as Hadid's Heydar Center. In a follow-up 2010 essay, Schumacher demanded that architects "avoid clear-cut zones/territories, avoid repetition, avoid straight lines, avoid right angles, avoid corners," while creating buildings that "hybridize, morph, deterritorialize, deform, iterate, use splines, nurbs, generative components, script rather than model,. . . consider all forms to be parametrically malleable."

There is an interesting tension that developed via ZHA between the notion of parametrics as fomenting a type of digital "death of the author"

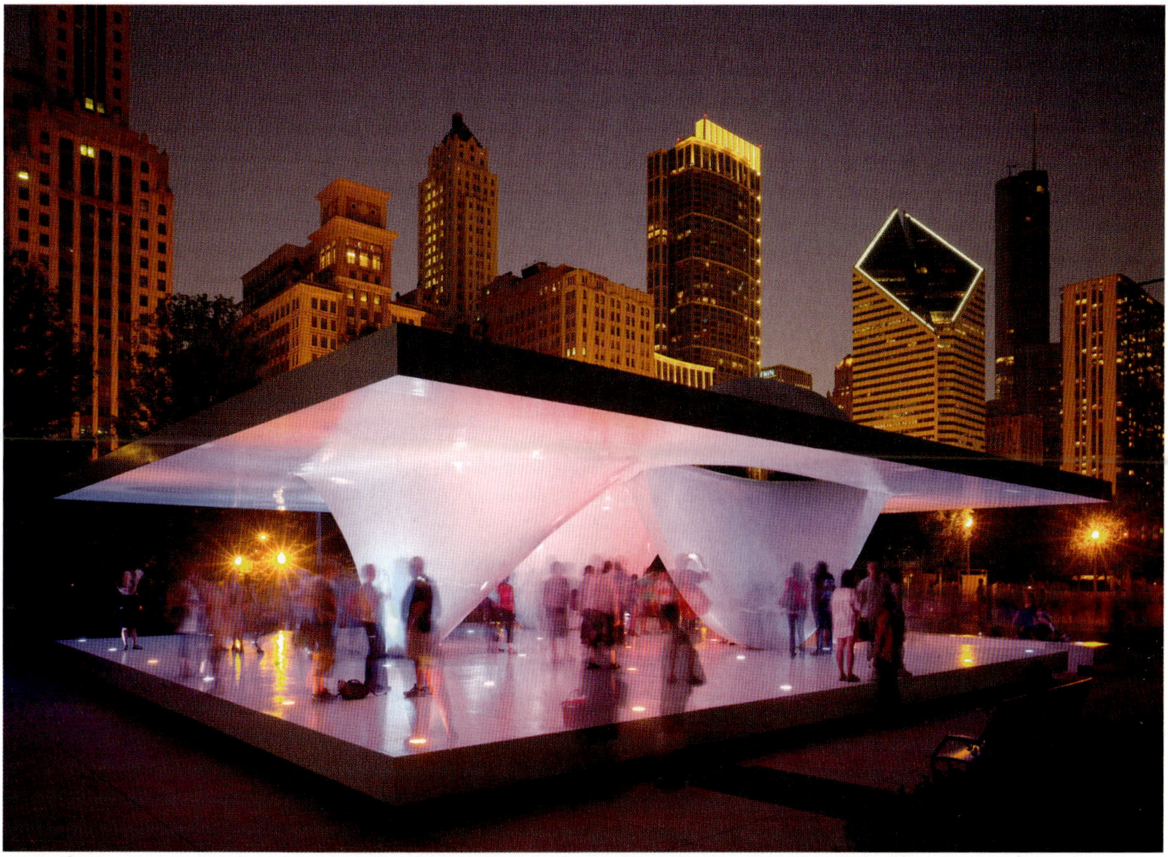

8.5. UNStudio, Burnham Pavilion, Chicago, Illinois, 2009

and the exploding celebrity and autographic style of Hadid herself. In Roland Barthes's 1967 essay "The Death of the Author," the author must relinquish their central role in cultural production, and a text (read building) will be recognized as "a multi-dimensional space in which a variety of writings, none of them original, blend and clash." The author's "passions, humours, feelings [and] impressions" are decentered, and the result is an open-ended design; the interpretation of it is pluralistic and situated with the viewer who receives the text. Parametrics would appear to be the ideal technology with which to implement this framework: as the architect relies on software to create variations and implement a design that has only been broadly sketched out, their individual vision is subsumed within a larger cultural realm. On the other hand, Hadid won both the Pritzker Prize (2004) and the Royal Institute of British Architects (RIBA) 2016 Royal Gold Medal, upon which the president of RIBA acclaimed, "Zaha Hadid is a formidable and globally influential force in architecture." This sort of praise must have at some point become almost mundane to Hadid, who was a worldwide celebrity at the time of her death in 2016.

Paradoxically, parametric CAD has in some ways reestablished a craft element in architecture that was lost in the modern era of standardized parts, mass-produced façade systems, and curtain walls. Anyone who has communed with contemporary software can recognize how the open-ended complexity of the programs requires an exacting understanding of materials and engineering processes. Mythically, contemporary architects loosely define the points on a curve and then export the file to a CNC machine or 3D printer with the click of a mouse. In fact, today's idiosyncratic digital architecture is quite the opposite, and the screen-based work demands a hands-on, often specialized understanding of building technology and close collaboration with engineers. This is especially true because of the bespoke nature of many digitally designed buildings, whereby no previous model exists, and unknown issues may crop up unexpectedly.

The digital craft element was strong in the design of the Louisiana State Museum and Sports Hall of Fame (figure 8.6, 2013). The design architect, Trey Trahan, wanted the interior of the building to respond to the Cane River, which flowed outside the museum. Just as the river had carved out the surrounding topography, Trahan wanted the sculptural interior to look as if it were formed by a flow of water over many centuries. Using Grasshopper software,

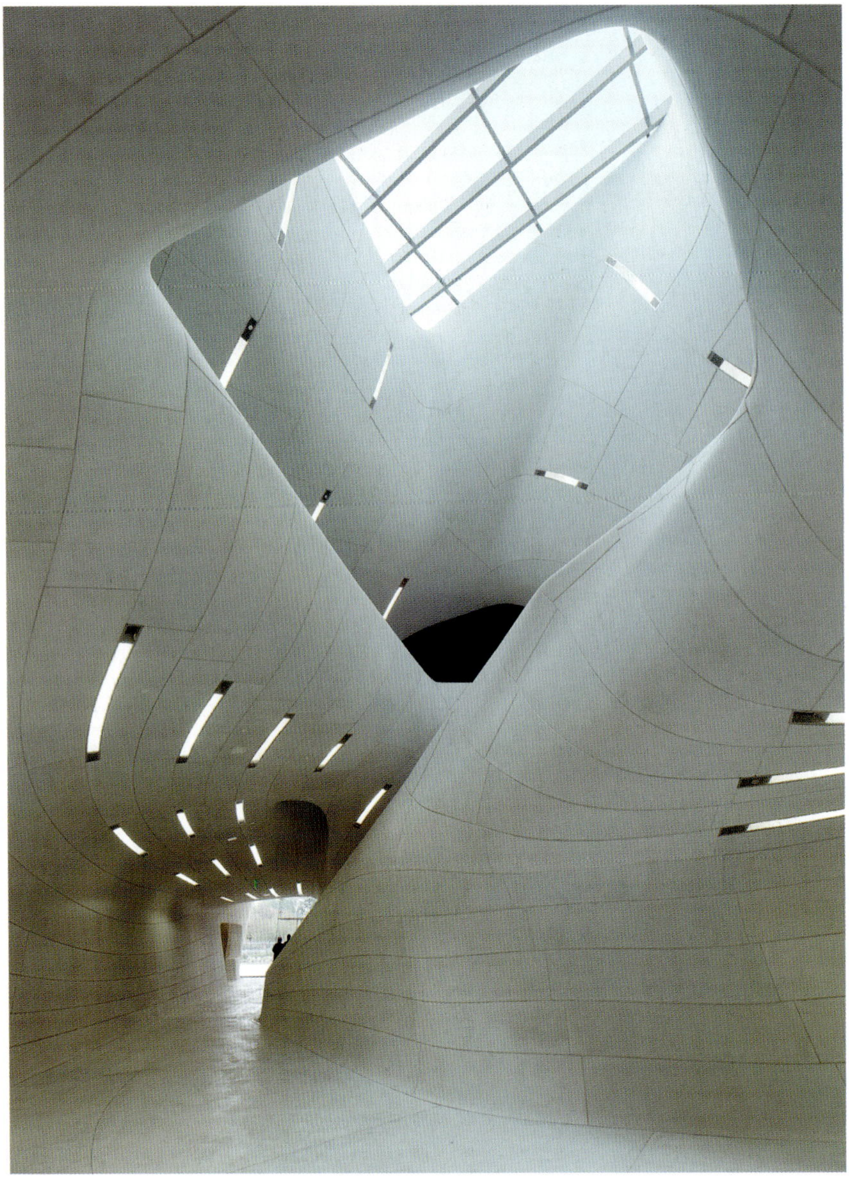

8.6. Trey Trahan, Louisiana State Museum and Sports Hall of Fame, Natchitoches, 2013

the studio mapped out more than one thousand custom-shaped cast stone panels that fit together to form a sinuous interior grotto. Digital technology was then at the heart of solving the engineering quandary of how these panels could be affixed to one another and the underlying structure; each flowing panel needed its own custom fittings. Using the CAE program Karamba3D in Rhino, the stone consultant David Kufferman could design individual hardware for each element. All these data could next be imported into an openBIM program like Geometry Gym, through which all the construction details could be consolidated.

While it is fairly simple today to solve an engineering problem such as this one or to create a design space catalog—whereby the software provides an assortment of options based on general plans—it has proved much harder for architects to use parametrics for more complex problem solving. In many other fields, algorithmic processing has been combined with big data to manage ever more complex analyses. At the MIT Digital Structures lab, however, Nathan Brown and Caitlin Mueller have published research that explains how data-driven architecture suffers, in a sense, from too much data and parameters that are too slippery. They point out the intrinsic advantages of data-driven chess, for example, which has been a huge success because it is knowable and its parameters completely programmable. "Based on computers that simulate millions of possibilities in great detail, chess players can see breakdowns of their mistakes, train with customized game scenarios that focus on their weaknesses, and if allowed, view real-time information about how each potential move increases or decreases win probability." In contrast, architectural design features both a range of nonquantifiable variables and no clearly

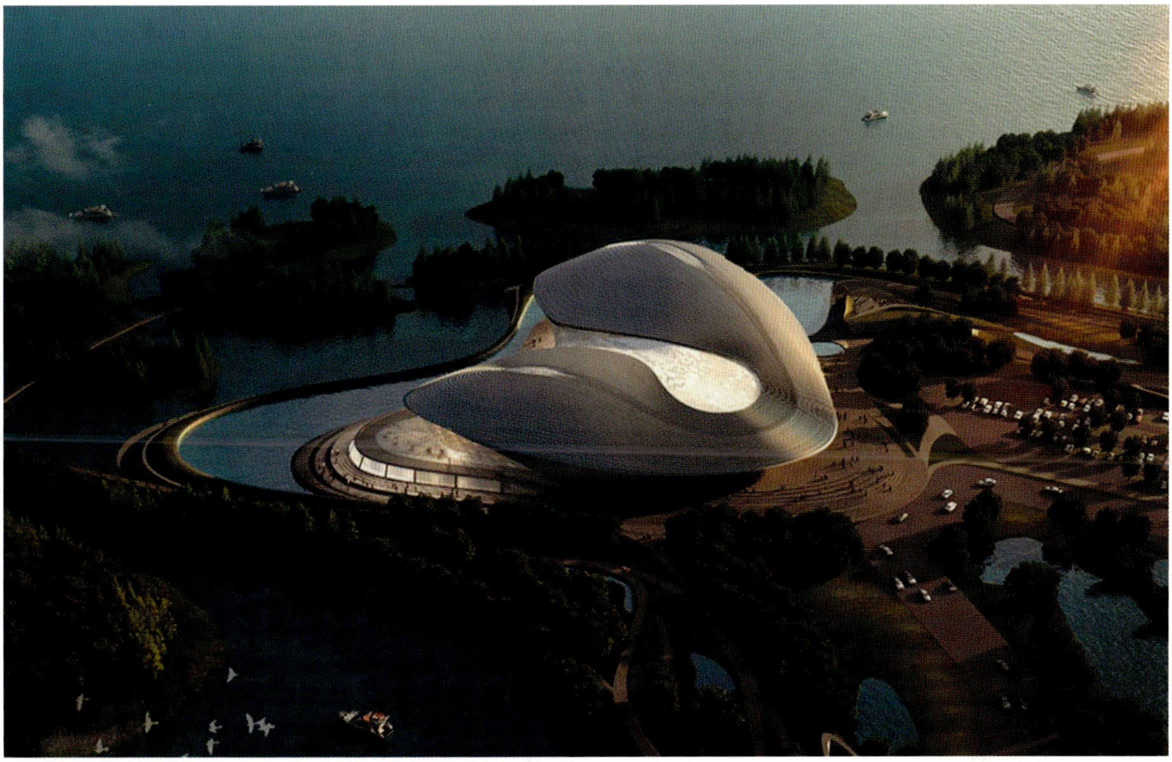

8.7. Luis Quinones, design for Bengbu Opera House and Music Hall, 2012

defined stakes (such as checkmate). While data and parametrics might help architects predict certain technical dimensions of a building—solar gain, for example—the software has not really done much to actually aid in the design itself. Buildings by Gehry or Hadid are digitally enabled, not digitally designed in the broad sense. Brown and Mueller speculate that advances could be made by better facilitating human–computer interaction (HCI); one path they advocate is more real-time HCI, whereby the architect receives feedback incrementally during all stages of the design process, as opposed to establishing every known parameter at the outset and then performing a single digital assessment.

For digital visionaries, the future for parametric design lies in the realm of the generative. Moving past quantifiable problem solving, it is hoped that artificial intelligence will be able to offer design solutions that are subtler and more complex than computers have until now produced. In this imagined world, the architect will not just offload the engineering details to the machine but will cede some design authority to the superior computational skill of the computer. True generative design is still more potential than reality, but some recent aspirational projects have given a sense of its promise. Still, successful examples of generative algorithmic projects have generally been first narrowed in scope by a human designer. Take, for example, Luis Quinones's plan for the outer shell of the planned Bengbu Opera House and Music Hall (figure 8.7), which was created as part of an international competition in 2012. Quinones is not an architect but a Los Angeles–based computational designer who was brought into the project as an algorithmic specialist. Quinones's design for the shell unites the barrier and its substructure through a metaphor of dripping water. The pathways generated by this motif are then used to plan the substructure of the overall skin.

Probably the most visually stunning examples of computational architecture have come from the studios of Benjamin Dillenburger and Michael Hansmeyer, who have collaborated on several projects. In 2015 they created the *Arabesque Wall* (figure 8.8) for a design exhibition in Toronto. Ten feet high and comprising 20 billion voxels, the *Arabesque Wall* features more than 200 million individual surfaces. A 3D printer took four days to fabricate the work out of silicate. The design was computationally generated; Dillenburger's studio explained the parametric process thus: "An algorithm folds a single surface over and over again until a structure composed of millions of individual surfaces emerge. Shifting the design process to this abstract level has a dramatic impact, creating a complexity and richness of detail that would

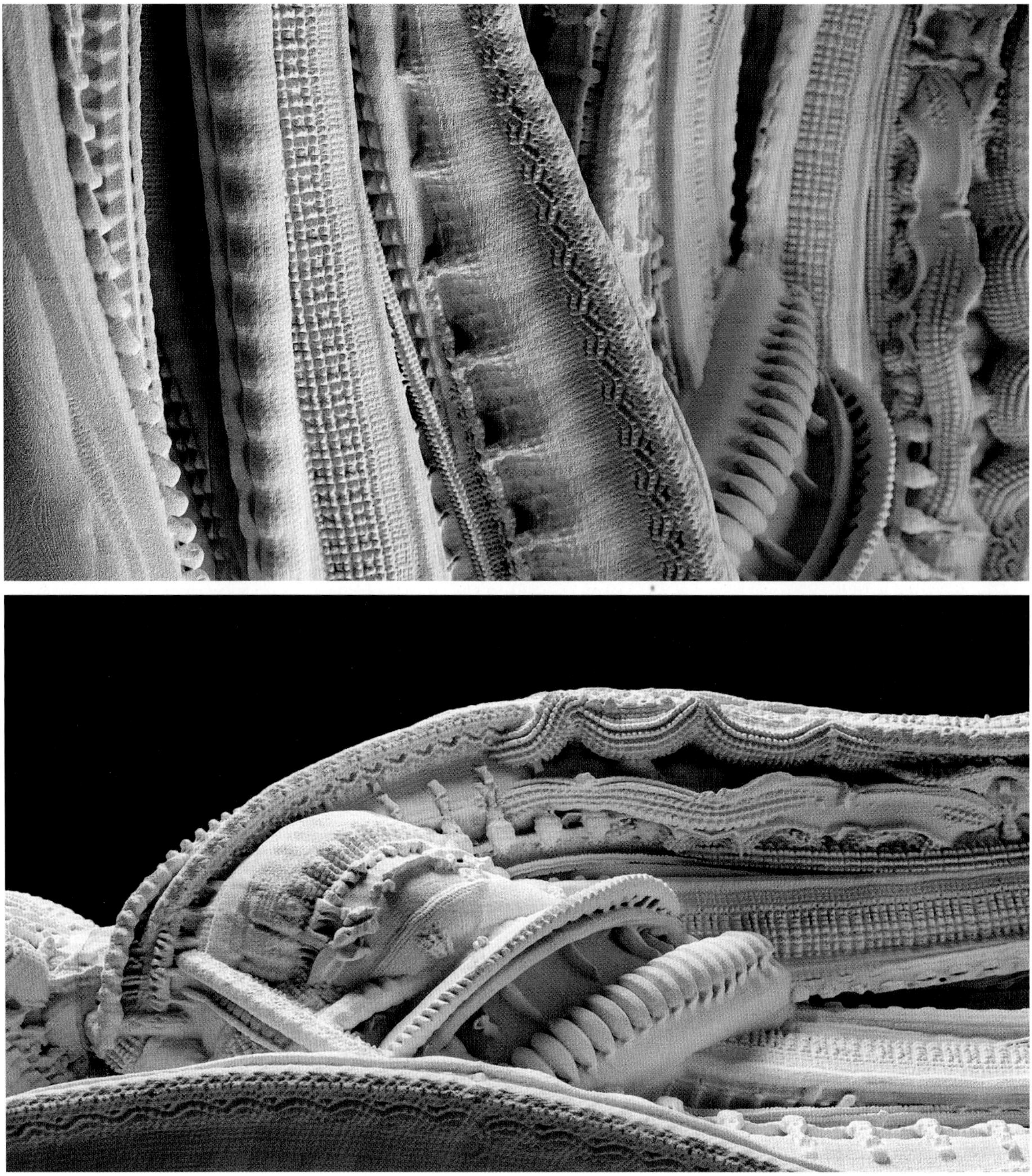

8.8. Benjamin Dillenburger and Michael Hansmeyer, *Arabesque Wall*, 2015

otherwise be almost impossible for a designer to specify or conceive of." This is true HCI, as the architect set the process in motion, but the computer not only executes the design but generates patterns itself. The concept behind *Arabesque Wall* therefore goes well beyond simply drawing a building on a CAD program or producing a design space catalog.

One fascinating dimension of *Arabesque Wall* is the architects' embrace of complex ornament, which stands in stark contrast to the minimalist strategy that pervades much of digital design. They are taking advantage of the fact that 3D printing allows for a millimeter-level of detail that would require tremendous skill and expertise to fabricate by hand. In fact, the artists capable of executing this work by hand probably would be nearly impossible to locate. In an age when 3D printing is often employed without taking advantage of this aspect of the technology, there is something refreshing about Dillenburger and Hansmeyer's willingness to see a future festooned with high-resolution ornament. With postmodernism in design a distant memory, these digital architects employ decoration without any irony or knowing skepticism. In a sense, *Arabesque Wall* displays the continuing relevance of the analog, as it uses contemporary technology to reprise a style of design associated with the artisanal work of the past. They have seen the future, and it is decorated.

Another set of issues that arise through *Arabesque Wall* results from the strategy of embracing a historical style with a complex cultural context. Whereas digital design has at times been criticized for its generic, ahistoric futurism, Dillenburger and Hansmeyer have connected their work to a dense thicket of history. An "arabesque" is of course a decorative pattern that originated in Arab and Moorish cultures and was widely appropriated by European designers in the nineteenth century. In short, it has a bloody history, and *Arabesque Wall*—designed by Westerners—is inevitably freighted with some of the baggage of European colonialism and orientalism. The question arises as to whether it is possible to dispassionately invoke such a fraught topic and whether the globalized digital age will somehow transcend the tribalisms of the past.

A mélange of styles is actually at work here, as *Arabesque Wall* combines that dominant design motif with a surface that appears to be made of ivory or polished stone. The whitish color here does not equate with the futuristic shimmer of Hadid's buildings, but rather seems also to come from the past. The piece resonates with nostalgia, as it could be a salvaged piece of decorative stonework from a bygone era. With an ornamental approach, one expects color; part of this issue comes down to technology. While 3D printers using PLA filaments can reproduce a broad chromatic spectrum, as yet the millimeter-fine threads of *Arabesque Wall* would represent a challenging endeavor.

For Dillenburger and Hansmeyer, the generative, computational approach is not locked to history but open ended and futuristic, allowing for a degree of artistic freedom that withered under the standardized strictures of modern mass production. There is something inherently theatrical about their ornamental work, which made Hansmeyer's design of sets for a production of Mozart's *Die Zauberflöte* (figure 8.9, 2018) a perfect embodiment of the style.

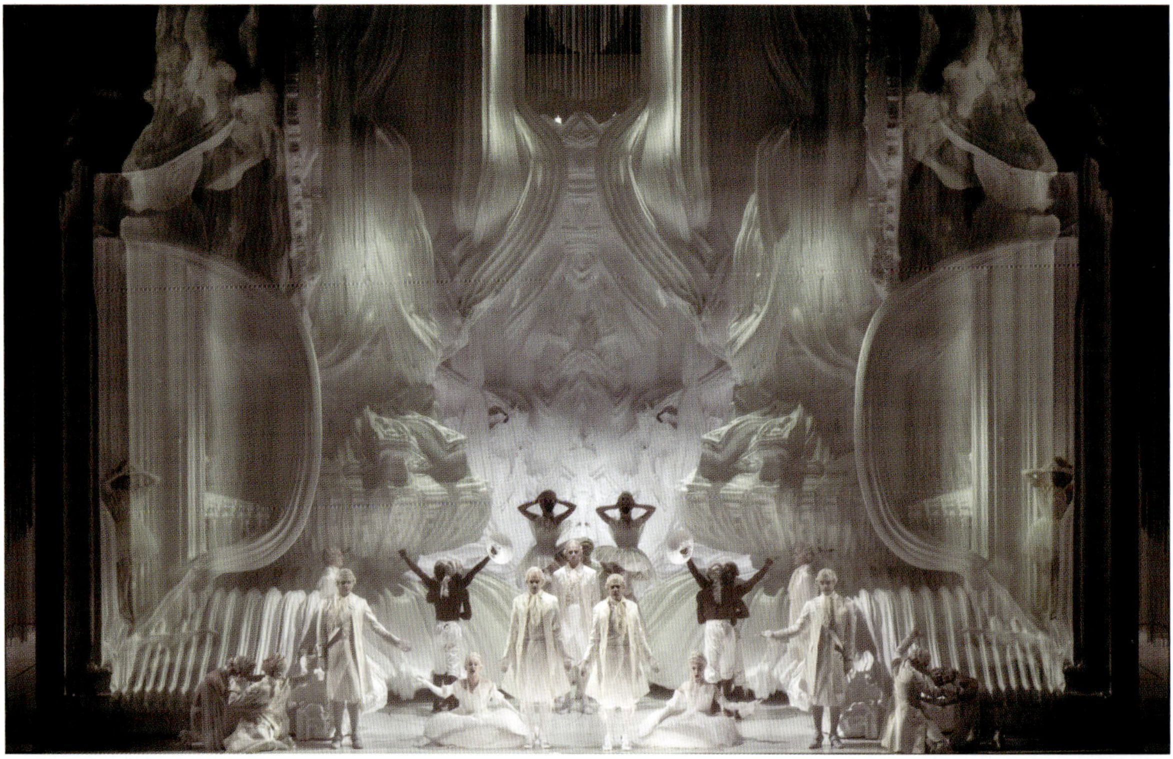

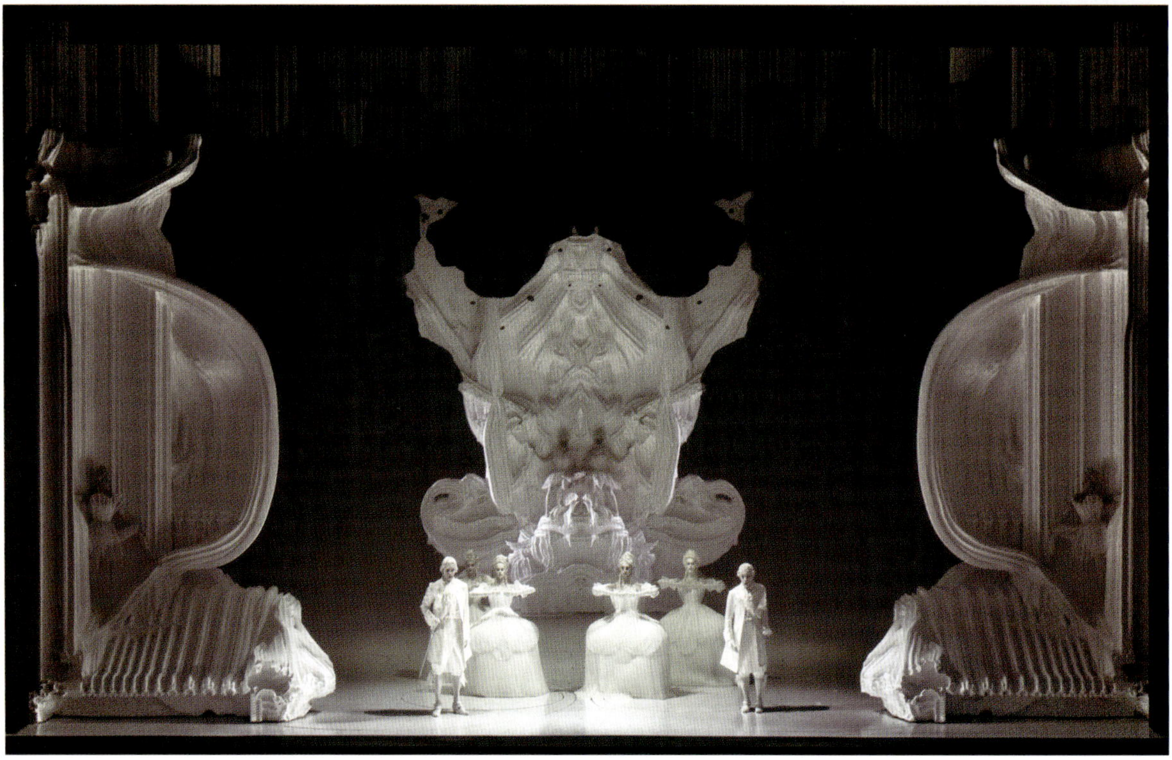

8.9. Michael Hansmeyer, sets for *Die Zauberflöte*, 2018

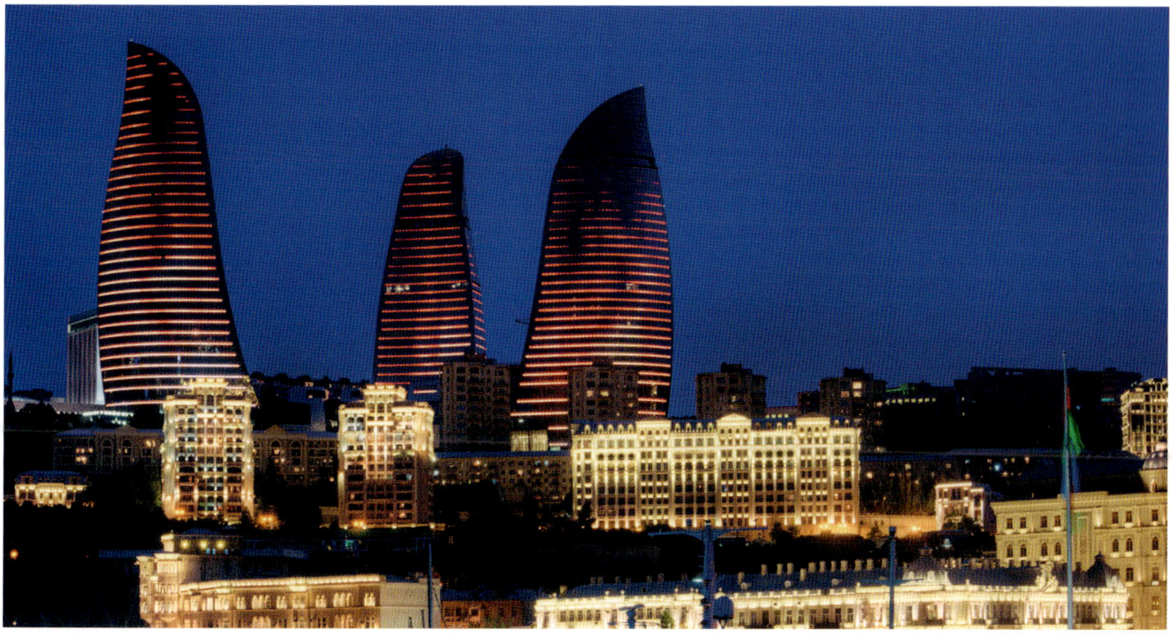

8.10. HOK, Flame Towers, Baku, Azerbaijan, 2012

While the sets were designed using an algorithmic process akin to that of *Arabesque Wall*, for *Die Zauberflöte*, the fabrication came through a subtractive CNC process. They were made of expanded polystyrene, a lightweight material that allowed for the fifty-foot-wide grotto structure—which gradually emerges during the opera—to be easily managed by stagehands. Hansmeyer sought to create a structure that was "at once synthetic and organic," invoking the contemporary theme that sees the digital as a relatable part of the natural world. It was important to the designer that computers be used not in a preprogrammed fashion, but rather "strike a balance between the expected and unexpected, . . . While the processes are deterministic, the results are not necessarily entirely foreseeable. The computer acquires the power to surprise us." This inspiring sentiment offers a path forward for human–machine collaboration that may one day transform our relationship with technology. Or, alternatively, Skynet becomes self-aware.

From Gehry to Gang, many digital projects showcase curvilinear forms, often in response to a site near a body of water. This enduring motif of parametric architecture is an organic response to the possibilities inherent in the software as well as architects' desire to make unusual buildings relatable to the larger public. Many buildings that present challenging floor plans and perplexing shapes are domesticated in a sense by this invocation of the natural world. Just as Vladimir Tatlin's Monument to the Third International (1920) aligned itself with the abstract heavens through its rotating spaces and spiral form, many of today's futuristic structures look to the oceans and rivers as a comforting analog of digital form.

One of the great opportunities presented by the parametric age in architecture has been the ability to model buildings on natural forms without incurring excessive cost. While water is the most common motif, fire is another organic analog that has worked well for parametric architects. One of the most compelling fire-inspired designs was completed by HOK in 2012 for a site in Baku, Azerbaijan (figure 8.10). The flame analogy is not just universal, as "Azerbaijan" loosely translates as "land of fire" and references the Persian religion Zoroastrianism, itself named after the ancient Iranian prophet Zoraster. Before Islam came to this region, the worship of fire was one of the central religious practices of Zoroastrianism. In Baku, flames can also refer to natural gas, which is one of the anchors of its contemporary economy. Commissioned to design a set of three mixed-use towers approaching 800 feet in height, HOK used parametric software to design flame-shaped buildings with unique, soaring curvature.

The shape of the Flame Towers was a partial success, although because most viewpoints in Baku feature only two of them, locals have come to refer to them as the "bunny ears." The flames really only come alive at dusk, as the buildings feature an extensive digital illumination system. Designed by Francis Krahe & Associates using fixtures and controls by Traxon Technologies, the Flame Towers' programmable LED system features more than

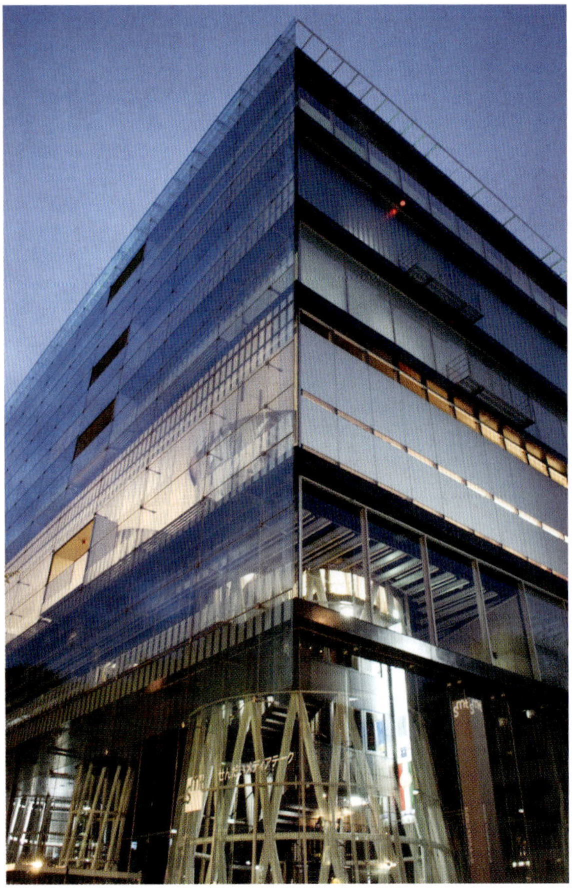

8.11. Toyo Ito, Sendai Mediatheque, Japan, 2001

ten thousand individual units. Located inside the building's glass curtain wall, these miniaturized fixtures on most evenings create the illusion of flames flickering over the tower's skin. The animated graphics are controlled by a custom lighting control engine that can display a flexible range of digital files aside from the basic fire effect. The Flame Towers are truly architecture of the night, displaying an animated spectacle akin to that produced at contemporary concerts (discussed in the next chapter). It is unusual to see such a strong synthesis of shape and illumination, buildings that do not really fulfill their symbolic mission by daylight.

To date, probably the most successful visualization of digital culture through architecture came in the form of Toyo Ito's Sendai Mediatheque (figure 8.11). A hybrid cultural center that combines a library, gallery, and media services, the building was designed beginning in 1995 and opened in 2001 at a time when digital architecture was still emerging. The eight-story building has a minimalist, cubic exterior, with a Domino House feeling produced by open floors sheathed in a double-walled glass skin. The most striking part of the design is the thirteen latticed tubes that connect the floors internally. As is the case with so many examples of digital architecture, the Mediatheque's tubes function as an organic analogy, similar to capillaries in a plant or animal. This natural, biomorphic symbolism is layered with another meaning, however, as the tubes also invoke the streams of digital information that flow through the virtual world. Furthermore, the tubes have a practical element, as conduit for both wired infrastructure and sunlight, which is channeled through these light wells from reflective lenses on the roof.

Altogether, the Mediatheque seamlessly unites multiple themes in a space whose overall openness, while derived from modernist tradition, also serves as a metaphor for the hybrid, open-ended experience of being digital. Ito has referred to the way in which the Mediatheque responds to what he calls an "electronic biomorphic" body, one linked to networks and nature alike. In the essay "Image of Architecture in the Electronic Age" (1998), he wrote, "People today are equipped with an electronic body in which information circulates, and are thus linked to the world through networks of information by means of this other body. The virtual body of electron flow is drastically changing the mode of communication in family and community, while the primitive body in which water and air flow still craves for beautiful light and

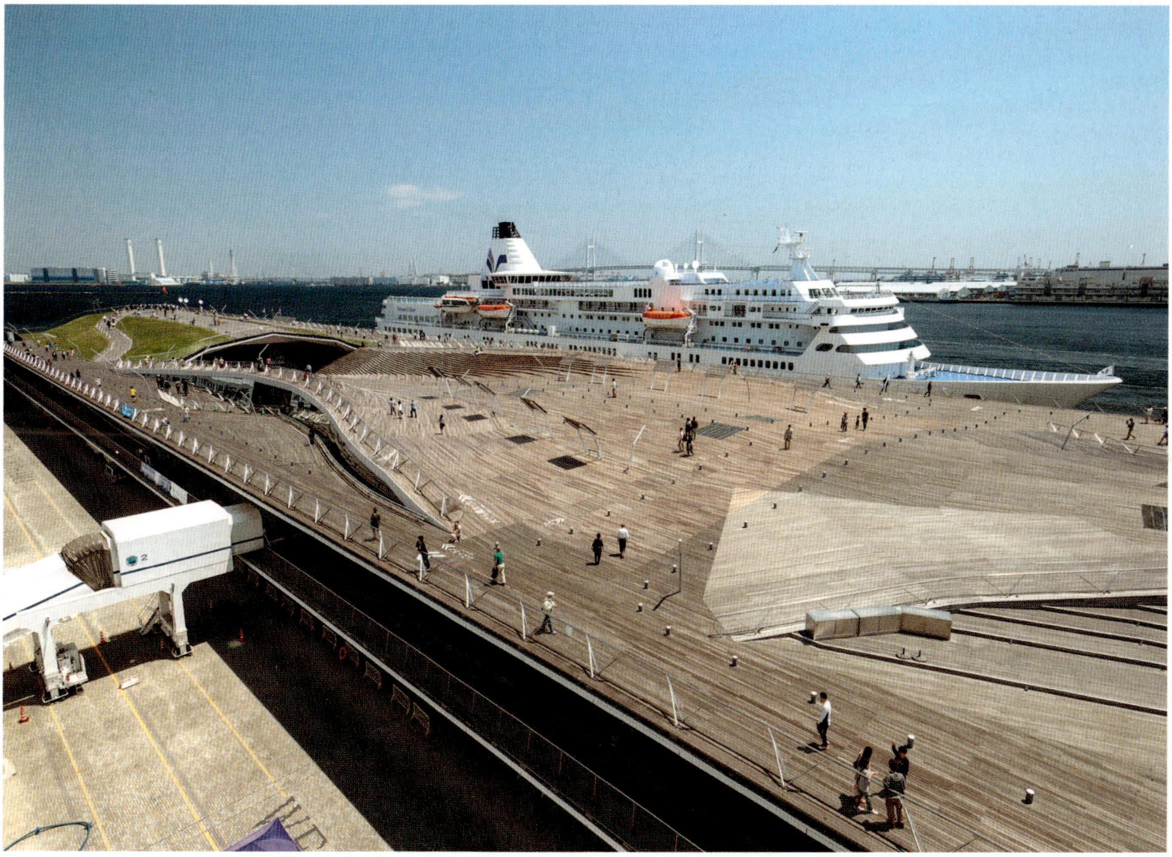

8.12. Foreign Office Architects, Yokohama International Passenger Terminal, Japan, 2002

wind." The Sendai Mediatheque succeeded where many other buildings did not, its form and layered concept executed to produce a brilliant result.

The platonic ideal of parametrics—as configuring an elastic, fluid space—is a design strategy but has also become something of a workable metaphor for socially conscious architects. Foreign Office Architects (FOA) staked a claim to this type of digital utopia with the firm's first major project, the futuristic Yokohama International Passenger Terminal (figure 8.12), which juts into Tokyo Bay. The firm was led by then couple Farshid Moussavi and Alejandro Zaera-Polo, who won an international competition in 1995. When it opened in 2002, the terminal showed the unmistakable imprint of CAD software, with its flowing curvilinear forms lapping one upon another. The obvious complexity of fabricating and assembling such a variety of bespoke undulating surfaces is typical of the parametric design genre insomuch as no two buildings or parts of buildings are exactly alike.

The most influential idea behind the Yokohama project was not its formal qualities, but the way in which FOA foregrounded human parameters. Their data points were not points on a spline but the circulation of people in and out and through the structure. Of course, this attention to *marché* has a storied history, but FOA reframed it in a new, digital context. In using parametric schemes to plot the flow of people, FOA rejected functionalism for a more whimsical approach that resounds with digital futurism. Moussavi has explained, "Instead of providing the specialized and isolated routes that are normally found in terminals, which prioritize passenger way-finding and discourage or eliminate other choices, the circulation system consists of a series of interlocking paths, designed to increase opportunities for exchanges between individuals and present them with choices." Integrated into the urban fabric that it abuts, the building seeks to build a shared space that enables fortuitous dialogue, a computer-designed path that fosters community IRL.

A similar attention to social parametrics helped guide Jeanne Gang in designing the Aqua Tower in Chicago (figure 8.13, 2009). The building's most striking element are the balconies that appear to ebb and flow over a rolling topography. The balconies were designed using both analog and digital technologies, with the paramount concern an attention to providing views to the occupants of the lower stories, as the tower is surrounded by skyscrapers. This visual consideration intersected with Gang's

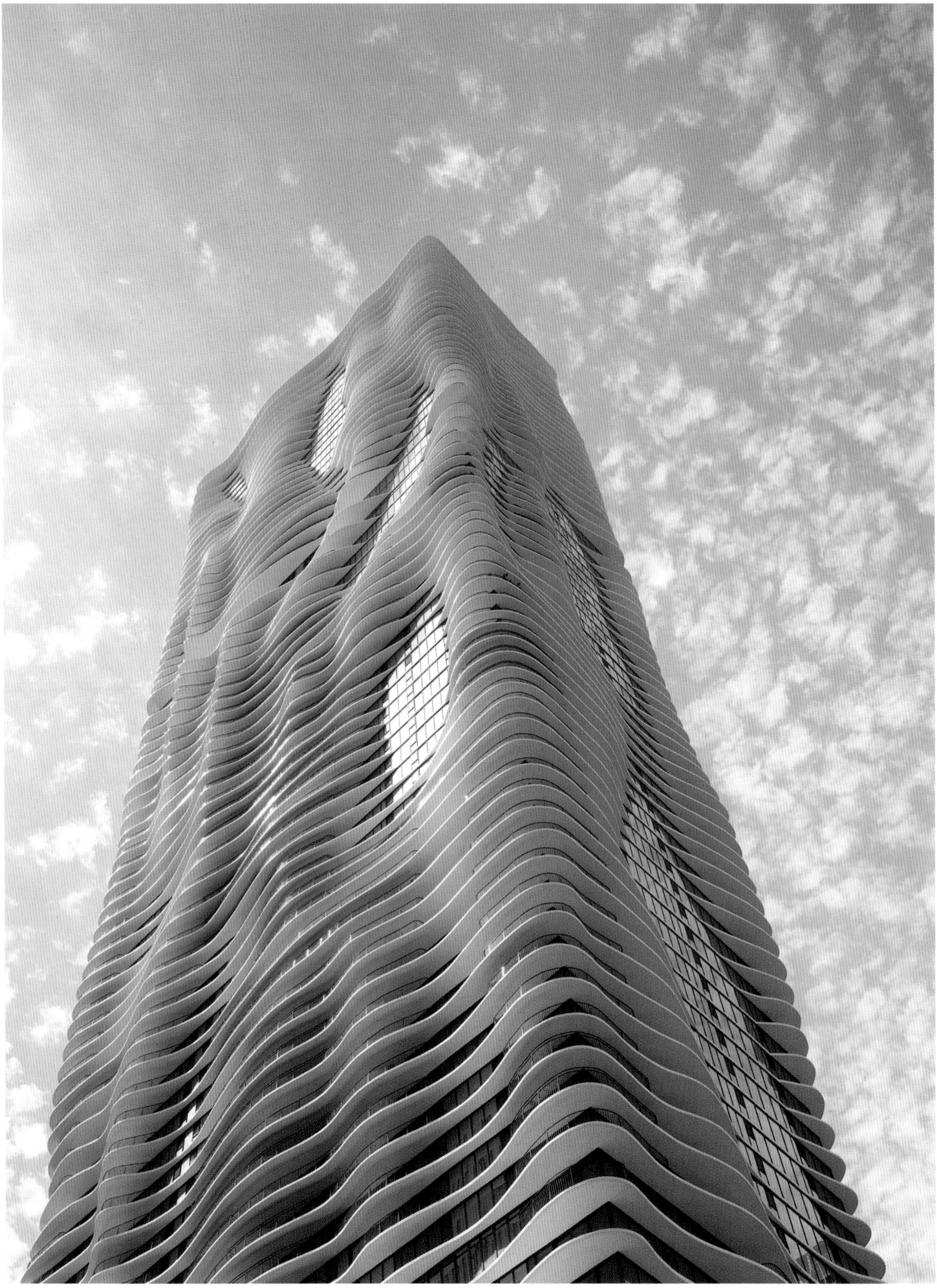

8.13. Studio Gang, Aqua Tower, Chicago, Illinois, 2009

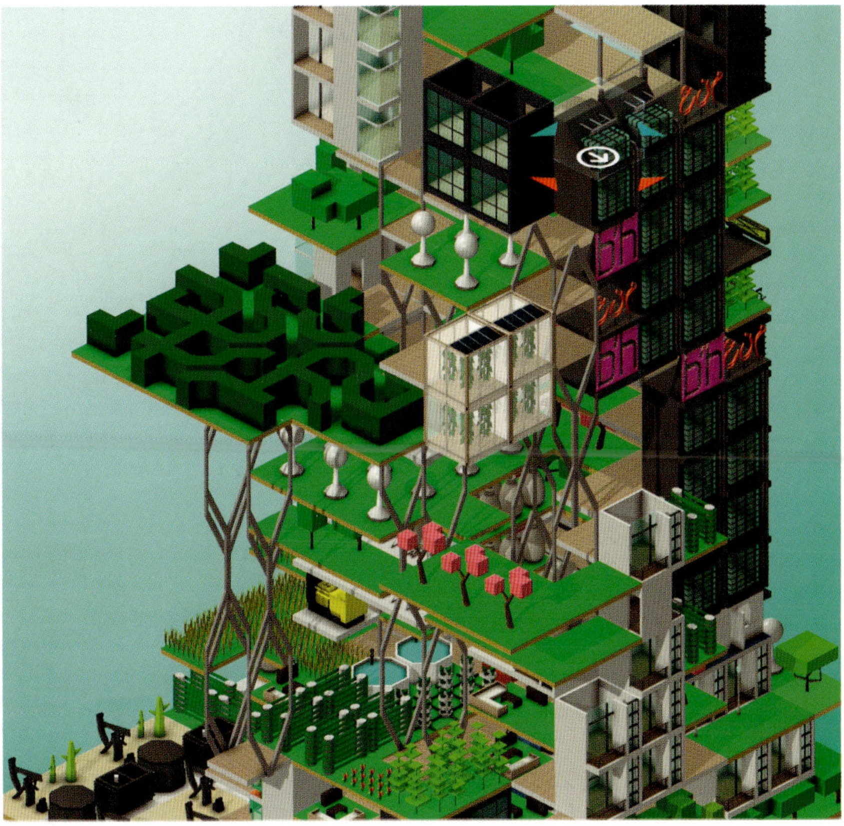

8.14. Jose Sanchez, *Block'hood*, 2016

desire to confront the atomizing impact of residential buildings, in which neighbors often remain isolated from one another in shared anonymity. Aqua's overlapping balconies caused people to serendipitously come into contact as the projecting shapes put them close to one another in the same manner as the pathways of the Yokohama terminal. In an interview, Gang noted, "You could say it was done as a parametric model, but with social and environmental purpose rather than iteration for form's sake."

Parametric design has in recent years become embroiled in contemporary politics. Specifically, the outspoken openness of ZHA principal and parametric guru Patrik Schumacher, particularly his expressed disdain for social housing, has roiled the field of digital architecture. Schumacher has also advocated for the privatization of most public spaces, a stance that puts him at odds with the historical precedent of avant-garde architects embracing public solutions and shared common spaces for better or for worse.

One critic of Schumacher's market-driven absolutism is Jose Sanchez, an architect and professor based in Los Angeles. Sanchez has connected Schumacher's political stances with parametric architecture, which he sees as a marker of the colonizing of communal space. He wrote, "Architectures for the Commons is an ideology that emerges as a form of resistance to a parametric agenda and the socio-economical implications it entails. Central to the argument is a criticism of the competition model in architectural design, which has conquered the decision-making process of public architecture, parametrizing the free labor of young architects and design firms and devaluing the practice of the discipline. By rediscovering the commons in an age of social connectivity, it is possible to make an argument for the production of design and value in distributed non-exploitative networks." Sanchez has also devised a digital simulation aimed at teaching urban planning, a *Minecraft*-like game that encourages players to create a virtual world. The game is called *Block'hood* (figure 8.14), and the gameplay is designed to encourage a type of collectivist balance that resonates with Sanchez's social ideals: "It is [in] the hands of the player to provide a positive environment for inhabitants to prosper."

Digital architecture has also facilitated a perhaps dystopian type of social parametrics, enabling a surveillance culture to populate the workplace. The goal of this management strategy is an age-old modernist one: productivity. It hearkens back to the pioneering studies of Frederick Taylor, a mechanical engineer who came to call the consulting field he invented

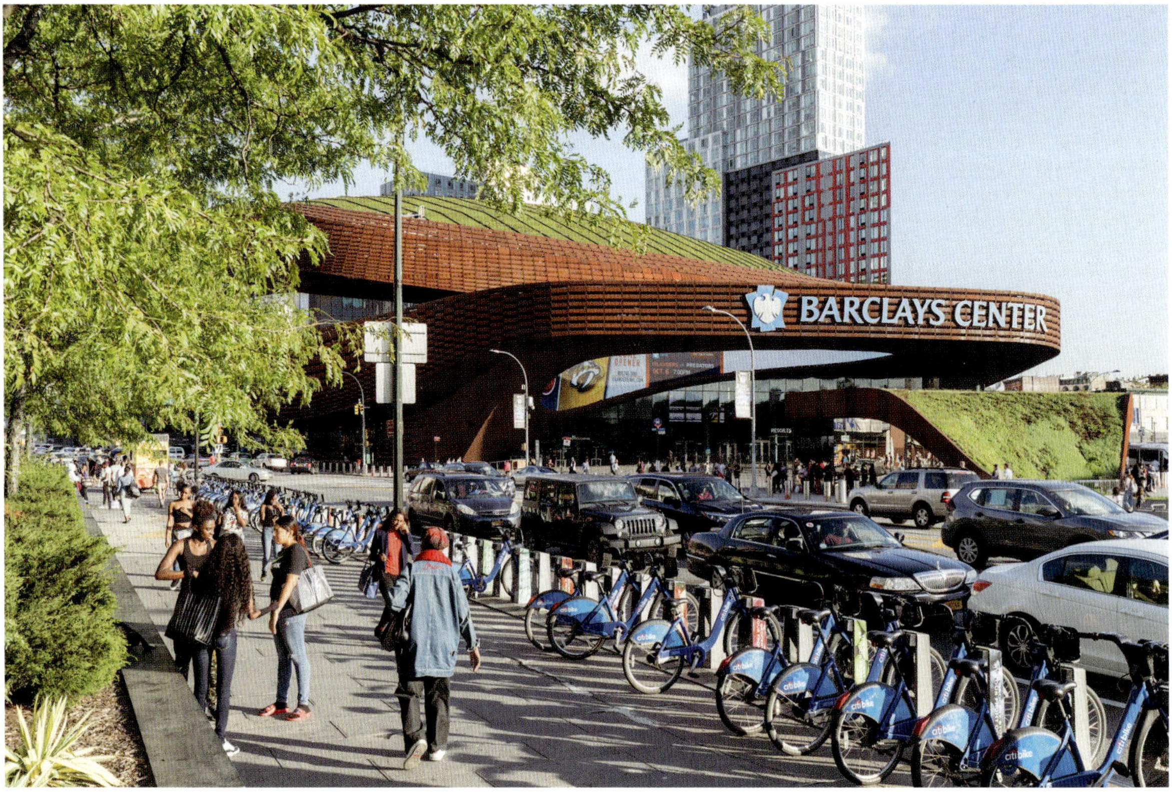

8.15. SHoP, Barclays Center, Brooklyn, New York, 2012

scientific management. In the early twentieth century, Taylor studied industrial workers' physical movements, especially their interactions with machines, in an effort to improve the efficiency of factory work. Today, Uli Blum, one of the founders of the Analytics and Insight Department at ZHA, is representative of a new Taylorist subspecialty in architecture, one that uses multiple sensors to acquire big data that can then be analyzed to make decisions about interior space. ZHA made a study of its own offices, using sensor data to better understand what environmental conditions facilitated more productive office work. The principles they gleaned have been implemented in their practice at buildings including the Galaxy Soho in Beijing.

In a parallel move, Gensler has proposed linking smart sensors—the kind embedded in devices, such as thermostats and fire detectors, that make up the Internet of Things—with BIM software. By collecting data from a building post-construction, it would be possible to create a living, virtual mirror world of the building in BIM that could then be used to study workers' habits and enhance their productivity. "By merging IofT data with the spatial framework of the digital twin, we can monitor the post-occupancy of our designs and recalibrate the designed space with an unprecedented frequency." Gensler promises to coordinate the design with the "ever-evolving human experience," which in this case comes in the form of dystopian surveillance.

Digital technology has also had an immense influence on construction. Of course, the most high-profile impact has come through the widespread use of CAE and BIM software. How a complex project like the Barclays Center (figure 8.15, 2012) in Brooklyn—designed by SHoP Architects and completed in 2012—benefited through the use of a universal set of construction documents is easy to understand. SHoP has trumpeted the advance: "Barclays stands as a pioneering achievement in construction technology—a digital landmark as well as a civic one." The bands of steel and glass that cover the façade, for example, may have started as a parametric model, but even more important was the ability of architects and engineers using software to coordinate the assembly of the fittings and panels. John David Cerone was the BIM manager for SHoP on the project, which required coordination with multiple contractors, including the lead structural engineers Thornton Tomasetti. The latter firm imported its CAE work into a BIM 3D virtual model, while SHoP construction designed the twelve thousand steel panels using CATIA, creating files that were then imported into SigmaNEST, which facilitated cost-efficient steel cutting. Revit, Rhino, Tekla Structures all also came into play during construction. The build-out of the Barclays façade represented the dawning of a new era, a monumental advance in digital construction technology more than fifty years since Arup first used computers to measure roof loads at the Sydney Opera House.

While digital technology has already had a profound impact on the virtual, software side of design, it also promises to transform the more tangible processes involved in building fabrication. Of course, technology has long fueled the modernist dream; it has been at least a century since architects first promised that it would solve the problems associated with sheltering millions of urban dwellers in clean, safe, and cost-efficient housing. "A house is a machine for living in," as Le Corbusier expressed the sentiment in *Vers une Architecture*, his influential 1923 compilation of thoughts and musings on building from the pages of *L'Esprit Nouveau*. He wrote that aphorism in a section celebrating airplanes, and his writings are also replete with references to ships and automobiles; the most notable example of this tendency came in the form of the Maison Citröhan, urban housing introduced in 1920 and named after the car manufacturer. The concept of house machine also signaled a respect for efficient, assembly-line fabrication, using the high-tech materials of the day in a standardized process.

Today's demonstrations of 3D-printed houses find a historical parallel in the 1927 Deutscher Werkbund–sponsored Weissenhofsiedlung, a block of modernist homes overseen by Ludwig Mies van der Rohe. The Weissenhofsiedlung was designed to demonstrate the aesthetic and technological advantages of architecture that at the time appeared outside the mainstream. In a striking parallel to Le Corbusier's invocation of the car-building analogy, the housing exhibition in Stuttgart featured a synergistic combination of modern housing and automobiles (figure 8.16) akin to those in *Vers une Architecture*. In that case, however, the roles were reversed, as the photographs of fashionable cars juxtaposed against modern architecture were in fact the work of Daimler-Benz, which had a large operation in the city. The new company was the result of a merger completed in 1926, and at the time of the Weissenhofsiedlung, it was promoting a new line of vehicles. In the famous photo of a Mercedes-Benz 8/38 hp Roadster in front of one of Le Corbusier's buildings, there is also an element of gender politics. The model—a local woman named Elsbeth Böklen, who had perhaps happened on the shoot while playing tennis at the development—was portrayed as a driver, adding a frisson of edgy sex appeal.

In the digital era, 3D printing has captured the imagination of architects seeking to promote cost efficiency and technological sophistication. So-called additive construction has roots in the twentieth-century strategy of prefabrication, which was used recently to assemble groups of façade panels at the Barclays Center. Prefabrication arose over a century ago as one the key strategies in constructing modern buildings. Like 3D printing today, some of the most successful prefabrication projects focused on smaller structures, especially single-family homes. During the first several decades of the twentieth century, for example, Sears, Roebuck and Company devised the Modern Homes mail-order program, which shipped out more than seventy thousand individual construction kits before midcentury. Sears developed three major lines at different price points,

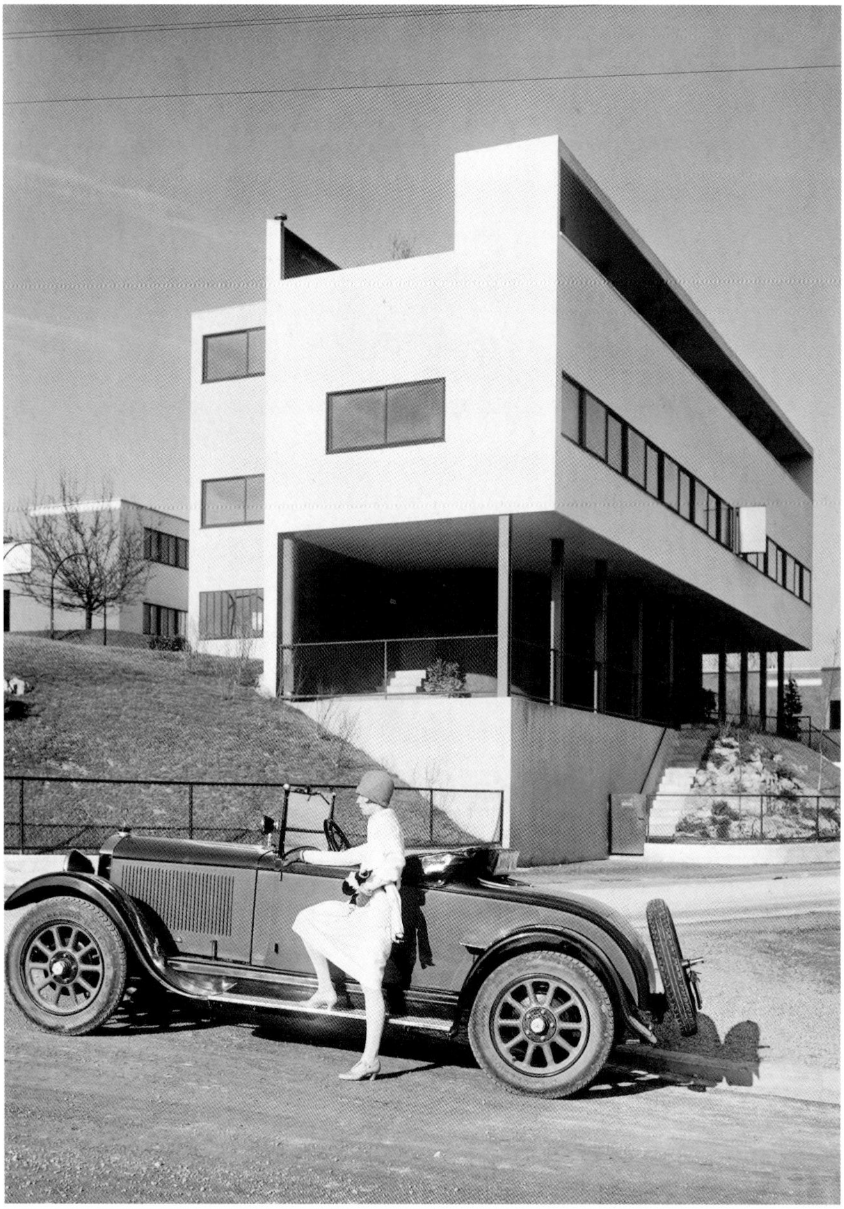

8.16. Daimler-Benz roadster and Le Corbusier building, Weissenhofsiedlung, Stuttgart, 1927

keeping costs low by mass producing precut lumber and fittings. The generally modest homes featured simple balloon frame construction, so they could be quickly assembled on site without requiring extensive carpentry skills. New materials that facilitated the system included drywall, a mass-produced, standardized material that eliminated the need for plaster and lathe craftsmen. In contrast to Le Corbusier, Sears did not attempt to glamourize the homes through technology, but instead downplayed factory-made materials in favor of emphasizing domestic simplicity and archaic-looking features such as cobblestone chimneys.

Another clear antecedent to the contemporary embrace of 3D-printed homes came after the Second World War, when *Arts & Architecture* magazine famously sponsored the design and construction of the Case Study Houses. In an intermittent process beginning in 1945 and spanning two decades, the magazine commissioned thirty-six designs, of which about two dozen were eventually constructed, most in the Los Angeles area. The project was the brainchild of editor and publisher John Entenza, who recognized that the demobilization of millions of soldiers would lead to yet another housing shortage in the United States. Entenza wanted to influence the coming building effort, especially toward new architectural styles that would take advantage of emerging technologies. The magazine later reported, "New plastics made the translucent house a possibility; arc welding gave to steel joints a fineness that was to gain the material admission inside the house; synthetic resins, stronger than natural ones, could weatherproof lightweight building panels; new aircraft glues made a variety of laminates a reality."

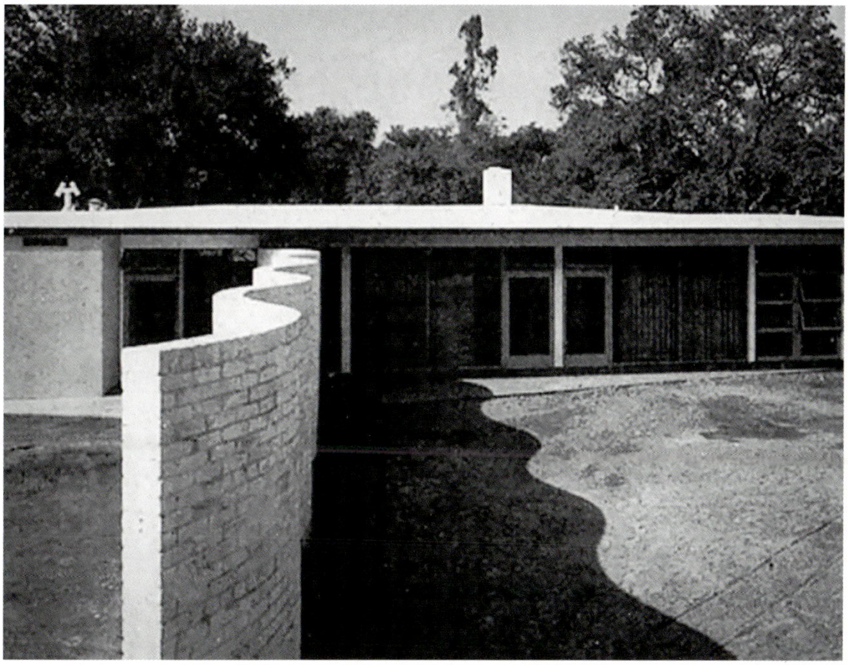

8.17. Sumner Spaulding and John Rex, Case Study House 2, Pasadena, California, 1947

The Case Study Houses diplomatically blended elements of modernism with traditional touches. While the glass walls, open floor plans, and flat roofs all featured the sort of forward-looking style that would be favored by a Corbusier, Entenza also wanted the homes to be approachable to the nonarchitect, as the stated goal was to design cost-efficient housing that could be mass produced, not to explore idiosyncratic visions. In fact, several homes that were deemed too eccentric were never built. A good example of one of the more successful designs was completed in 1947 (figure 8.17). It was designed by architects Sumner Spaulding and John Rex, who sought to base the design on a modular system, with the basic unit measuring fifteen feet square and ten feet high. The home also made ample use of plywood, a prefabricated industrial product that had been introduced into the building trades on a large scale in the decades before the war.

Le Corbusier, Sears, and the Case Study Houses all focused on fabrication costs one way or another and sought to industrialize the building of domestic structures. Standardized, prefabricated parts lessened the need for practitioners of trades, especially carpenters and masons. In the present day, echoes of this strategy exist in the push for digitally controlled robots to replace skilled humans. Fabio Gramazio and Matthias Kohler, founders of their eponymous firm, have focused their research on the potential for digital fabrication. Working with students at ETH Zurich, Gramazio and Kohler began exploring how robots could be integrated into one of the oldest of building crafts, bricklaying (figure 8.18). Their 2006 project "The Programmed Wall" involved the creation of algorithmic processes that instructed a robot to build a brick wall. A decade later, Gramazio and Kohler expanded their research practice, leading a group of students in the Robotic Fabrication Laboratory to explore more complex bricklaying techniques. There, they employed four robots to fabricate a labyrinth constructed of more than ten thousand bricks secured by gravity alone without mortar. While this work is experimental and university based, bricklaying robots have started to break out of the academy, as is the case with the SAM 100 (semi-automated mason), a product of Construction Robotics. In 2018 the SAM 100 demonstrated that it could lay up to four hundred bricks per hour, quadrupling the speed of a skilled human bricklayer. Robot bricklaying is still beset by limitations, however, as the machines need tending and are unable to build "leads," the corners of a wall that are crucial to establishing the overall layout.

Almost ninety years after the Weissenhofsiedlung, Branch Technology, a member of the 3D architectural printing industry, sponsored the Freeform Home Design Challenge. In an effort to publicize their C-FAB cellular-lattice printing technology, Branch sought out architects who would design inspiring works like those of the experimental avant-garde phase in the 1920s. Part of the intention is clearly to provide aesthetic glamour to the 3D printing industry, which up until recently has generally focused on cost-efficient conventional forms:

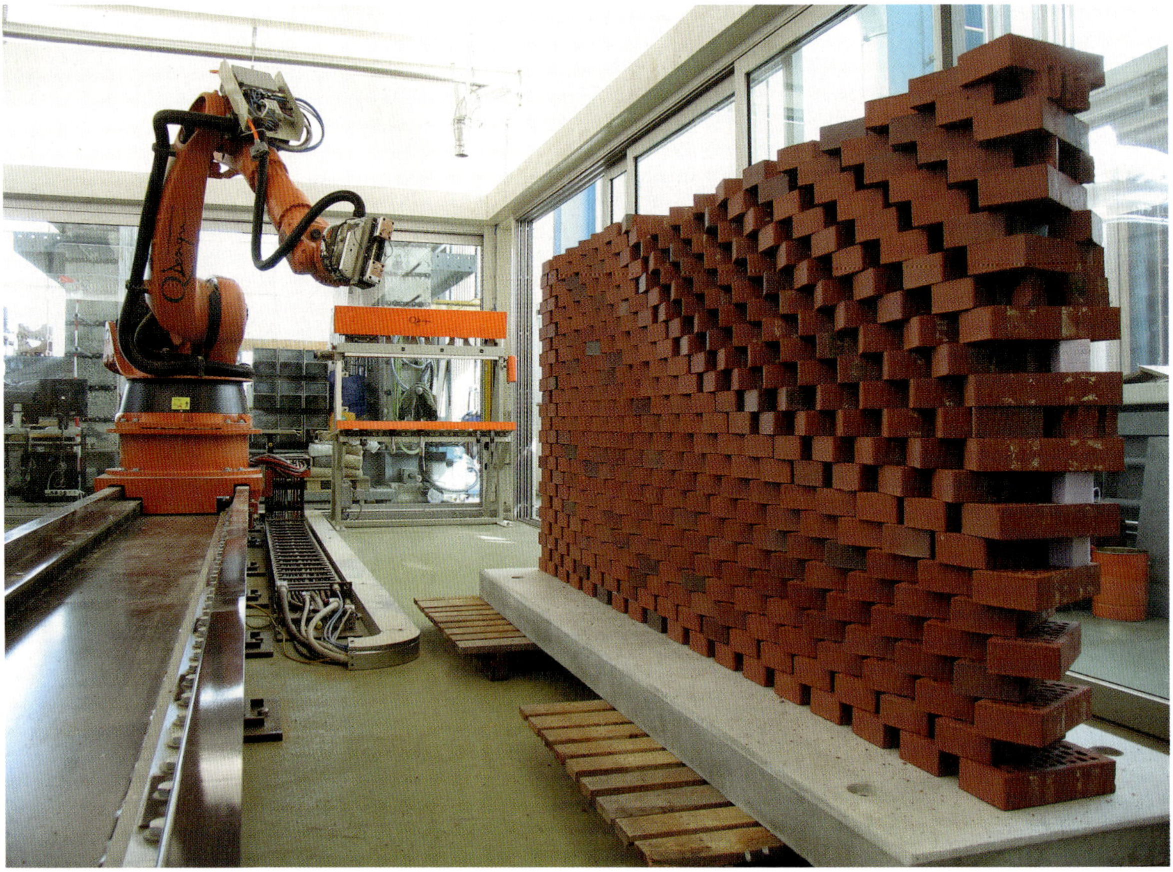

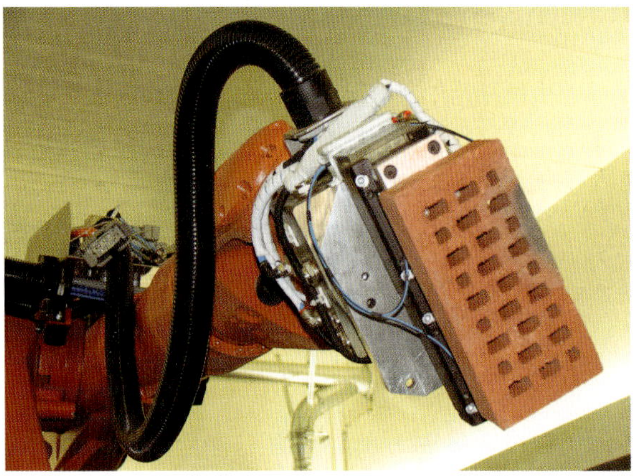

8.18. Fabio Gramazio and Matthias Kohler, The Programmed Wall, 2006

Branch is looking to do for 3D architectural printing what Tesla did for electric vehicles.

The winner of Branch Technology's Freeform Home Design Challenge, global multidisciplinary firm WATG Urban Architecture Studio, designed a house christened Curve Appeal (figure 8.19). It brings the curvalicious splendor of a ZHA creation to the humbler world of domestic architecture. Designed to enclose almost one thousand square feet of flexible interior space, Curve Appeal combines futuristic styling with sustainability features such as a photovoltaic paneled roof. The home is intended to be file to factory, with WATG providing BIM files to Branch Technology, which would prefabricate much of the building offsite using polyarticulated robots capped with various extruders. Branch Technology specializes in a printing matrix that has a strong cellular structure, enabling them to produce dramatic forms inexpensively. The digital renderings of Curve Appeal show that it invokes yet another modernist icon, Le Corbusier's Villa Savoy (1929), in that the structure seems customized to allow an automobile to nestle into the space. These same renderings connect car and building yet again, as the main view of the façade shows a sleek roadster parked out front.

Just as avant-garde architects often followed two threads—building bespoke homes for the wealthy as well as mass housing for the rest—so have the designers of 3D-printed structures

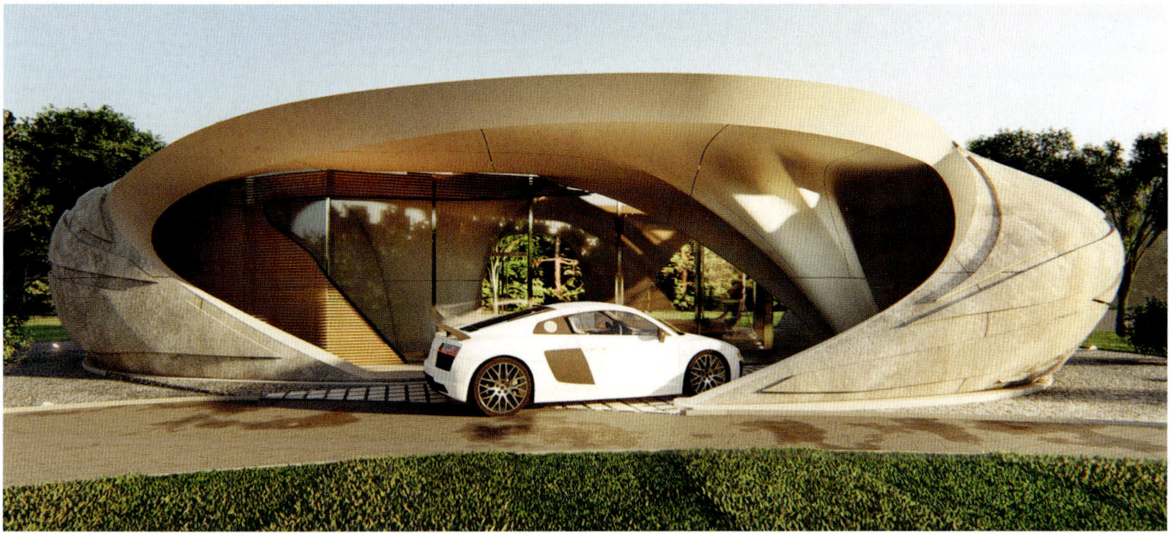

8.19. WATG Urban Architecture Studio, Curve Appeal, 2016

showcased a love of glamourous buildings such as Curve Appeal alongside a commitment to social housing. To a certain degree the modernist dream of the 1920s has been renewed by the promise of additive manufacturing, as architects aspire to offer low-cost housing that is clean and new. Notwithstanding the well-established fact that modernist housing failed to ameliorate the societal ills of urban poverty—and at times perhaps exacerbated them—the quasi-utopian dream of architectural salvation lives on.

In 2018, the Yhnova project, a collaborative work of the University of Nantes (France) and the local housing authority, resulted in the printing of a four bedroom one-thousand-square-foot house suitable for a family of five. Using an additive technology called BatiPrint3D, the new home was constructed on site by a digitally guided robot in less than sixty hours; the walls consist of polyurethane foam that, after drying, serves as a sandwich on either side of a layer of concrete. The Yhnova building is truly file to factory, as a digital model is the direct blueprint for the robot fabricator. At this point, it still took several months to fit out the structure with roof, windows, plumbing, and so forth, but the hope is that as the technology matures, this production time can be significantly shortened. Furthermore, the savings over conventional buildings stand at this point around 20 percent—significant, yet it is hoped this can be improved on. One of the key questions for 3D-printed architecture relates to prefabrication, as some companies—China's Winsun, for example—print out walls for later assemblage, while others, as in Nantes, transport the actual production robots to the building's final location.

While a social housing work such as Yhnova is focused on cost saving not aesthetic sizzle (as was the case with Curve Appeal), there is still room for the customization that additive manufacturing can facilitate. At Nantes, for example, the digital designer and fabrication robots built around a century-old tree without incurring significant additional cost. Overall, 3D printing is still in an embryonic state. As Francky Trichet, one of the Yhnova planners, noted, "We're at the start of the story. We've just written, 'Once upon a time.'"

As is often the case with emerging technologies, most heretofore printed buildings rely on a conventional strategy of building up walls in much the same way that a human contractor would frame out a house. Digital visionaries, in contrast, hope that 3D printing could open up building to radically innovative materials and design strategies. Probably the most cutting-edge 3D-printed construction material is graphene aerogel, synthesized from carbon atoms arranged hexagonally. Seven times lighter than air, graphene aerogel was first successfully printed at Kansas State University in 2017 and has the potential to serve as an insulating material.

Advances in 3D printing have also shown promise in replicating the internal structure of perhaps the least futuristic building material, timber. Wood has an anisotropic structure, meaning that its characteristics are directionally diverse, depending on its grain. While most 3D printing has up to now used only monomaterials, mainly resins, the ability to print anisotropic substances would greatly increase the technological potential of additive construction. For this project, a block of wood was cut with a

CNC machine controlled by a dithering algorithm. The resulting data were imported into a voxel-capable 3D printer, which was then able to print out a digital copy of the wood block complete with an identical internal structure.

Neri Oxman at the MIT Media Lab, for example, hopes to use 3D printing as the basis for what she calls "Material Ecology," an exploration of hybrid organic and digital technologies. In 2013, members of her Mediated Matter research group created the Silk Pavilion, composed of silk thread woven around a metal framework. In preparation, the researchers had studied the behavior of silkworms using motion tracking and then parametrically programmed a robot arm to weave the initial structure. Next, thousands of actual silkworms were placed on the structure, where they continued to produce silk and supplement the robot's work. The resulting elegant dome represents the fruits of a collaboration between nature and computation, creating a connection that is warm and relatable.

The Silk Pavilion was designed not only as a biomimic end in itself, but as a means of showcasing how digital design can completely reframe the architectural conversation. Like-minded researchers come together for the annual ACADIA (Association for Computer-Aided Design in Architecture) conference, where relationships between actual and virtual matter are explored in depth. The 2015 iteration, "Computational Ecologies: Design in the Anthropocene," included workshops that used Processing, a design-centric programming language, and software, including Maya and Rhino, to introduce students to "architectural and structural properties of biological behaviours, with the use of agent based algorithms, inspired by natural processes of growth and formation." The hope is to reach a critical mass of practitioners and move from the experimental-research phase into the mainstream of building.

The organic analogy did not begin with Oxman or ACADIA; really from the very beginning of the digital age, architects have invoked biological metaphors, processes, and forms. Back in 1948, pioneering mathematician Norbert Wiener published his book *Cybernetics: Or, Control and Communication in the Animal and Machine,* which had explicitly linked electronic control systems with the physiology of the organic body. Wiener coined the term "cybernetics," which he described succinctly: "Cybernetics attempts to find the common elements in the functioning of automatic machines and of the human nervous system, and to develop a theory which will cover the entire field." Despite its decidedly specialized nature and roots in abstract mathematical concepts, "cybernetics" became something of a cultural meme, and Wiener an almost McLuhan-like guru to the nascent digital community. The term gradually faded from view in the seventies, however, although it has been revived and repurposed at times by digital thinkers. For example, cybernetics has been invoked in the virtual reality community as a way of defining the relationship between information flowing in the body and through the computer. Contemporary mathematician William Fulton has explained, "When a person wearing a VR glove moves their hand and sees their virtual hand move accordingly, the implication is that a flow of information lies within the material substrate of their body, which can be translated seamlessly into a computer simulation. At the heart of virtuality is this

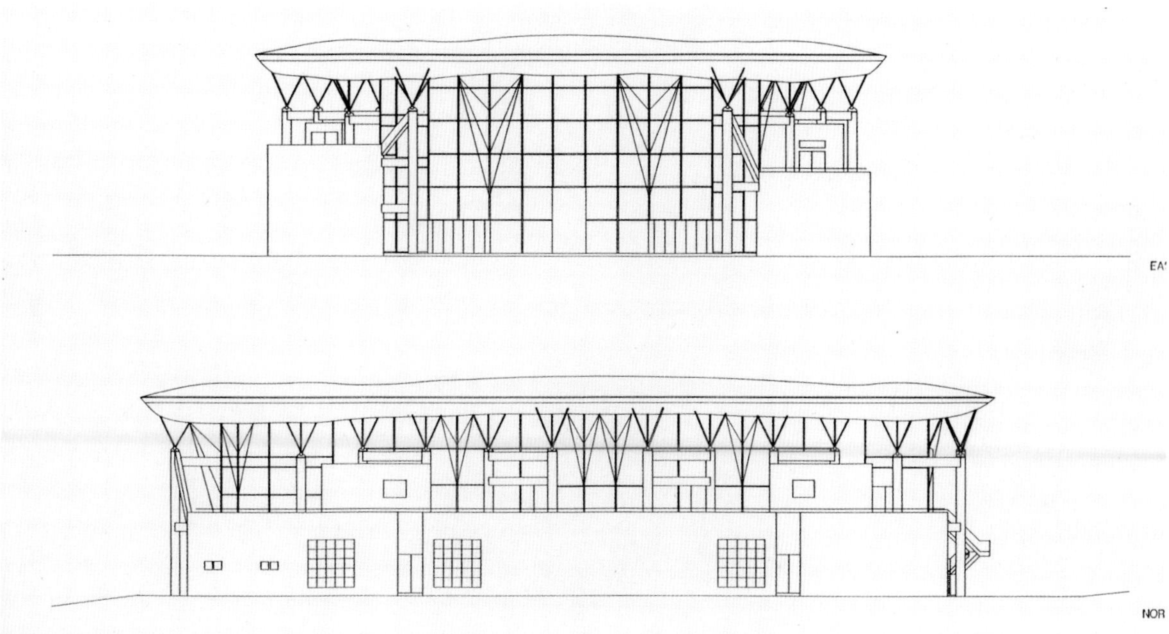

8.20. Shoei Yoh, plans for the Galaxy Toyama Gymnasium, Japan, 1992

duality between materiality and disembodiment." This broad foundational idea of cybernetics—the close relationship between organic and electronic systems—has also diffused into the broader culture of digital design.

Japanese architect Shoei Yoh is a paramount example of this theme as it arose in digital architecture. In the early nineties, Yoh designed a pavilion for the 1st Japan Expo, held in Toyama in 1992 (figure 8.20). The resulting Galaxy Toyama Gymnasium was one of the earliest structures partially designed using CAD software. Yoh invoked several natural forms for the structure, from a forest of concrete columns to a fluid, flowing roof that reminded the viewer of either water or floating clouds. The roof had an organic, variable form that was both beautiful and structurally determined, as the undulating form was largely a consequence of the need to respond to changing wind and snow loads. Working with the engineering firm Taiyo Kogyo, Yoh calculated the loads of his "3D topology" using computational techniques that echo with the process of constructing the Sydney Opera House.

Of course, architectural forms derived from the natural world have a long history, stretching from the Romanesque through the baroque at the very least. One historical style, however—art nouveau—represents a close, informative parallel to the digital age. Art nouveau architects had sought to find a new formal language for their work in response to a radically changed society; industrialization had become a dominant reality in the late nineteenth century, and designers attempted to reimagine urban buildings based on natural forms, which they felt had more integrity than the applied classicizing ornament that prevailed at the time. Organic forms also served as a conceptual model: art nouveau architects admired how beauty and structure were subsumed within one another in plants and flowers. Likewise, it could be argued today that digital designers continually invoke biological forms and processes partly in an attempt to seek a stable model for their experimental work; computational designs can be daunting, and there is something reassuring about tying them back to age-old natural processes. This strategy makes complex technology and abstract math relatable to the broader public.

There is another noteworthy parallel between the organic art nouveau and the organic digital: escape. It has long been recognized that the art nouveau style proffered something of a magical dream world to urban denizens. Aligned with French symbolist poetry and its invocation of the spectral and supernatural, a Hector Guimard–designed Metro canopy in Paris could take the riders' minds into a flight of fancy that obscured the at times dreary reality of working people's street life. At times the biological analogy may function the same way for digital designs ranging from the Kunsthaus Graz to the Silk Pavilion, providing a sense of escapism,

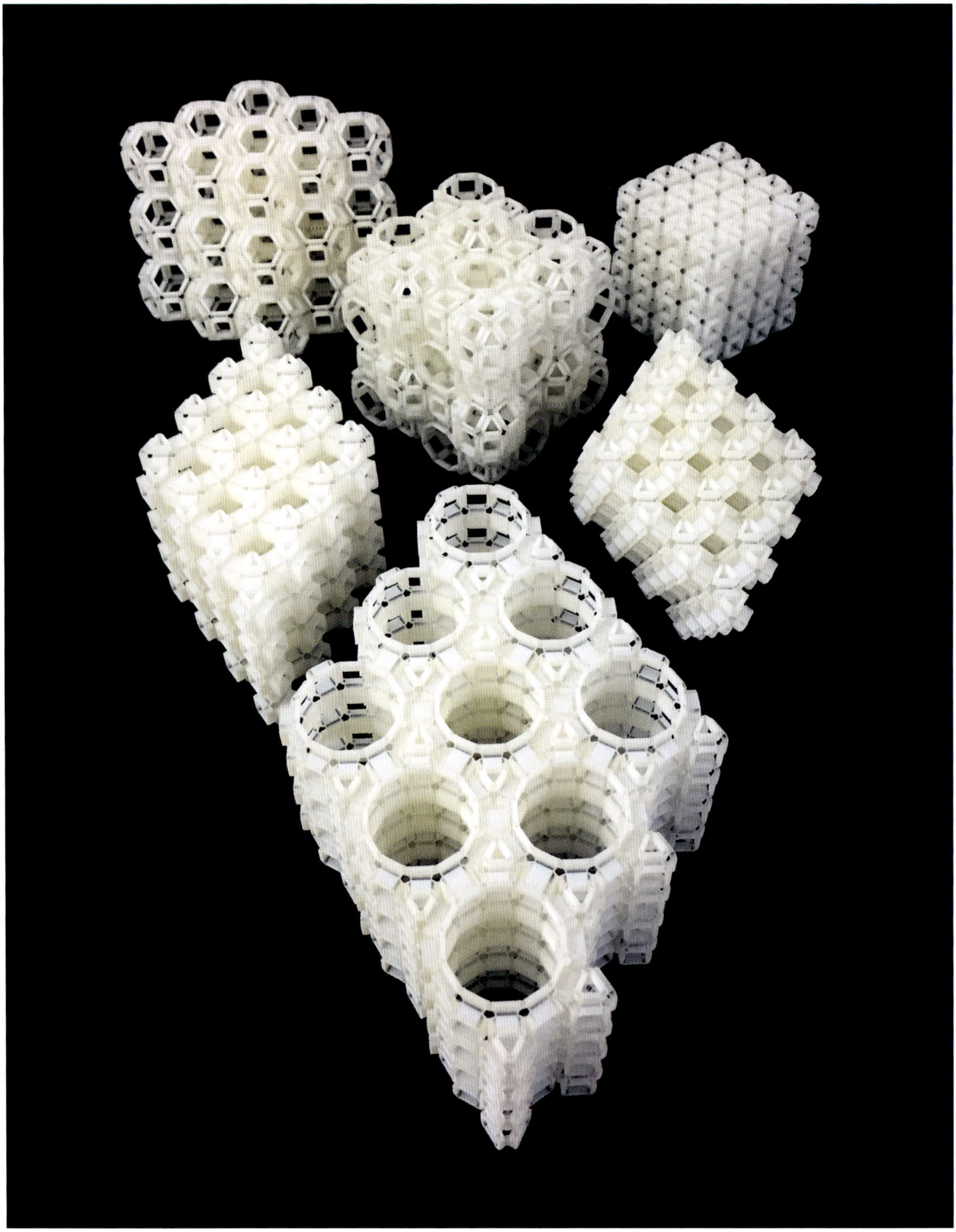

8.21. Chuck Hoberman and Katia Bertholdi, metamaterials, 2017

offering the virtual as a natural yet mystical realm that transcends mundane reality.

The organic analogy has also lent itself to the design of building materials. For example, one materials science project, Dana Cupkova's "Sentient Concrete," investigated thermally reactive concrete panels that were designed with embedded systems. Echoing themes that first arose amid the cybernetics movement of the sixties, Cupkova's research encompasses organic and inorganic structures. She has suggested that new materials may even function along emotional pathways, "shaping physical and human matter and their mutually perceptive capacities."

While most contemporary construction uses an admixture of the established materials of concrete, steel, and glass, it is hoped that computational design will help lead to a new age of technologically enhanced materials. For example, Chuck Hoberman and Katia Bertholdi led a team that in 2017 showcased its research work in the area of metamaterials (figure 8.21). The dream of metamaterials is a substance that can remake its characteristics in response to changing conditions; for example, imagine a hard material that softened and absorbed energy in response to an earthquake. Based somewhat on Hoberman's earlier work with kinetic façades, the team's metamaterials would be able to actuate different qualities by folding themselves in elaborate ways. The materials' forms are based on natural prismatic patterns that have been arrived at through a parametric analysis of a large dataset.

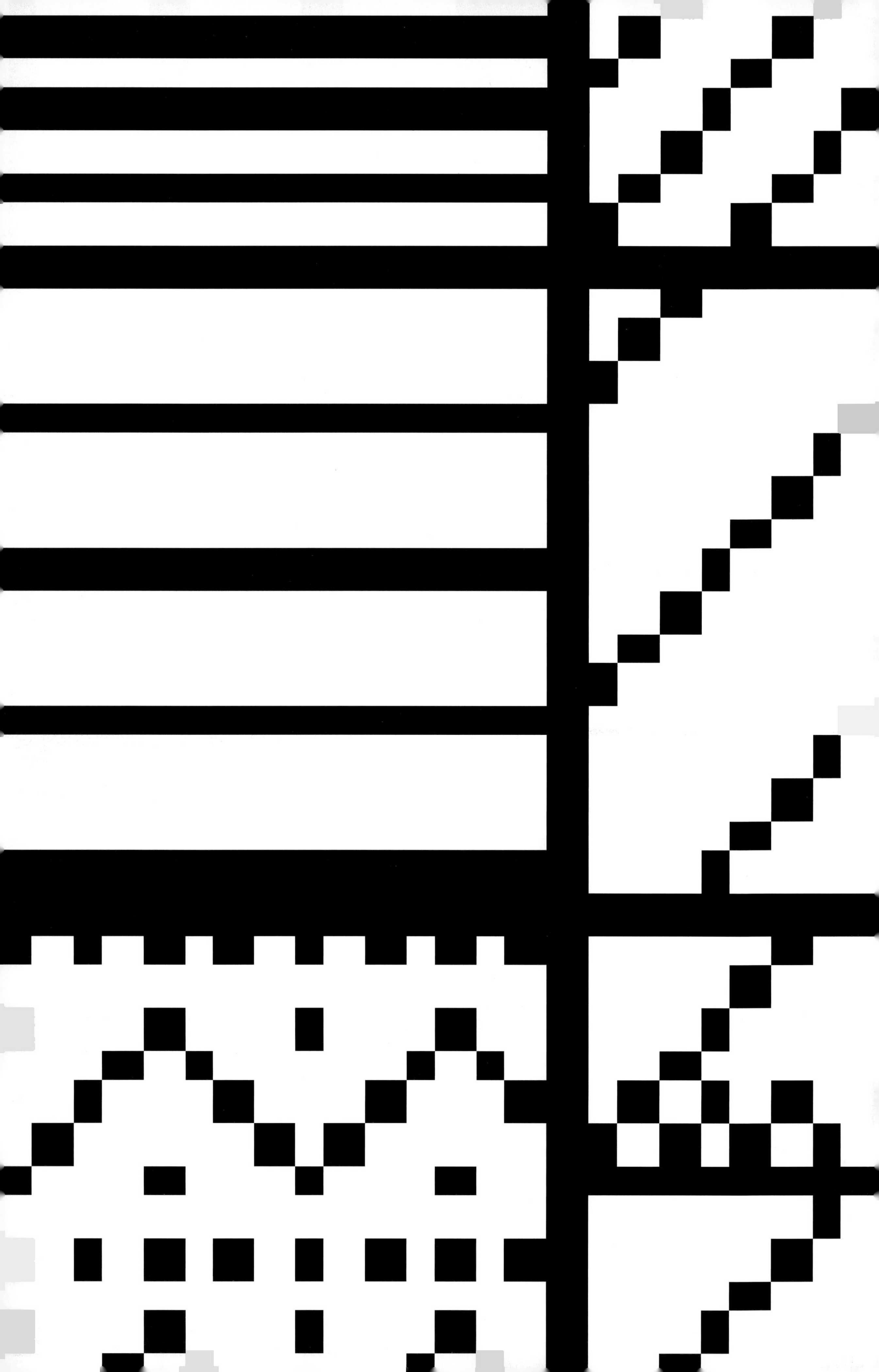

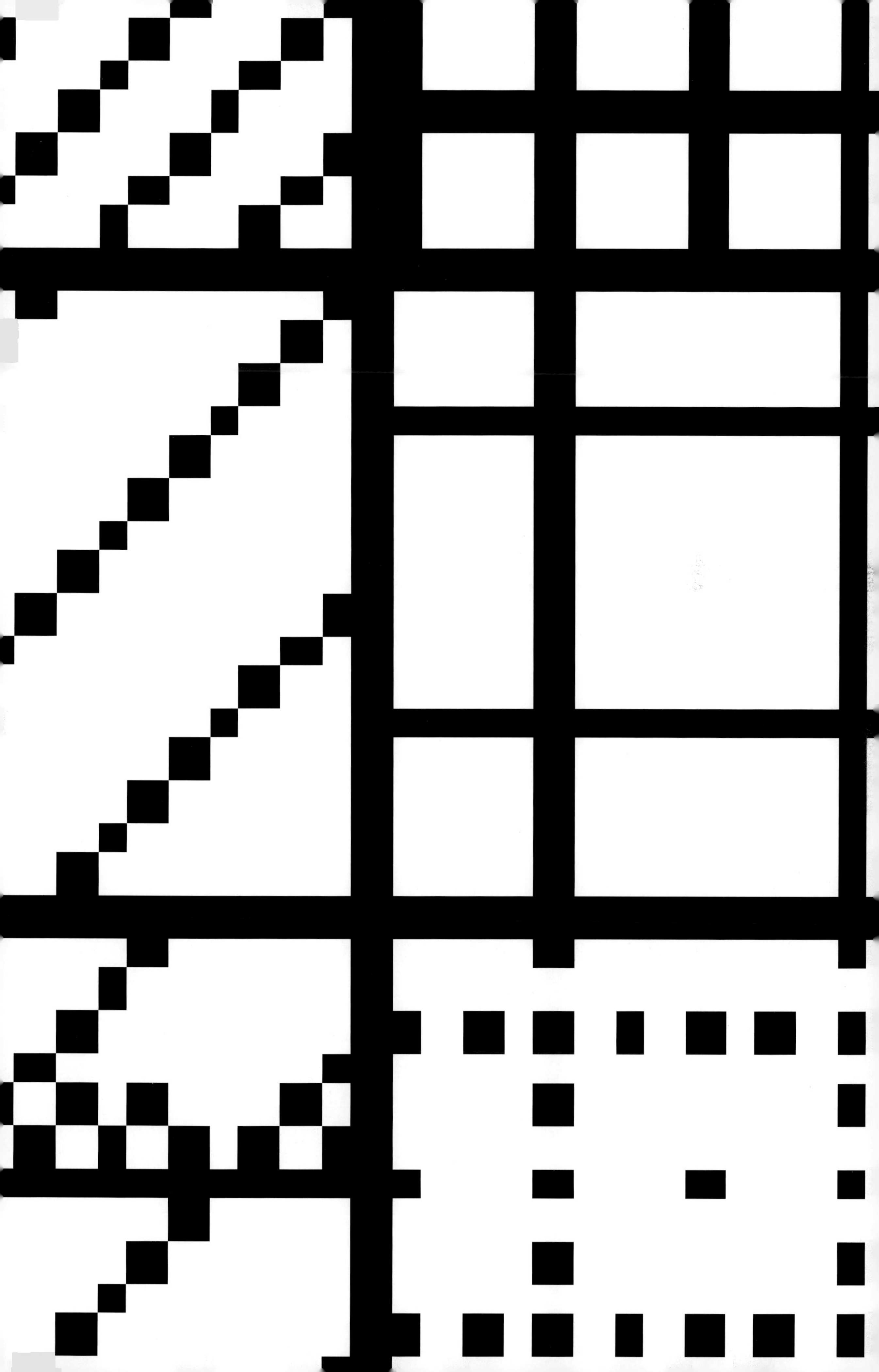

9.1. Dieter Rams, PS 2 stereo turntable, 1963

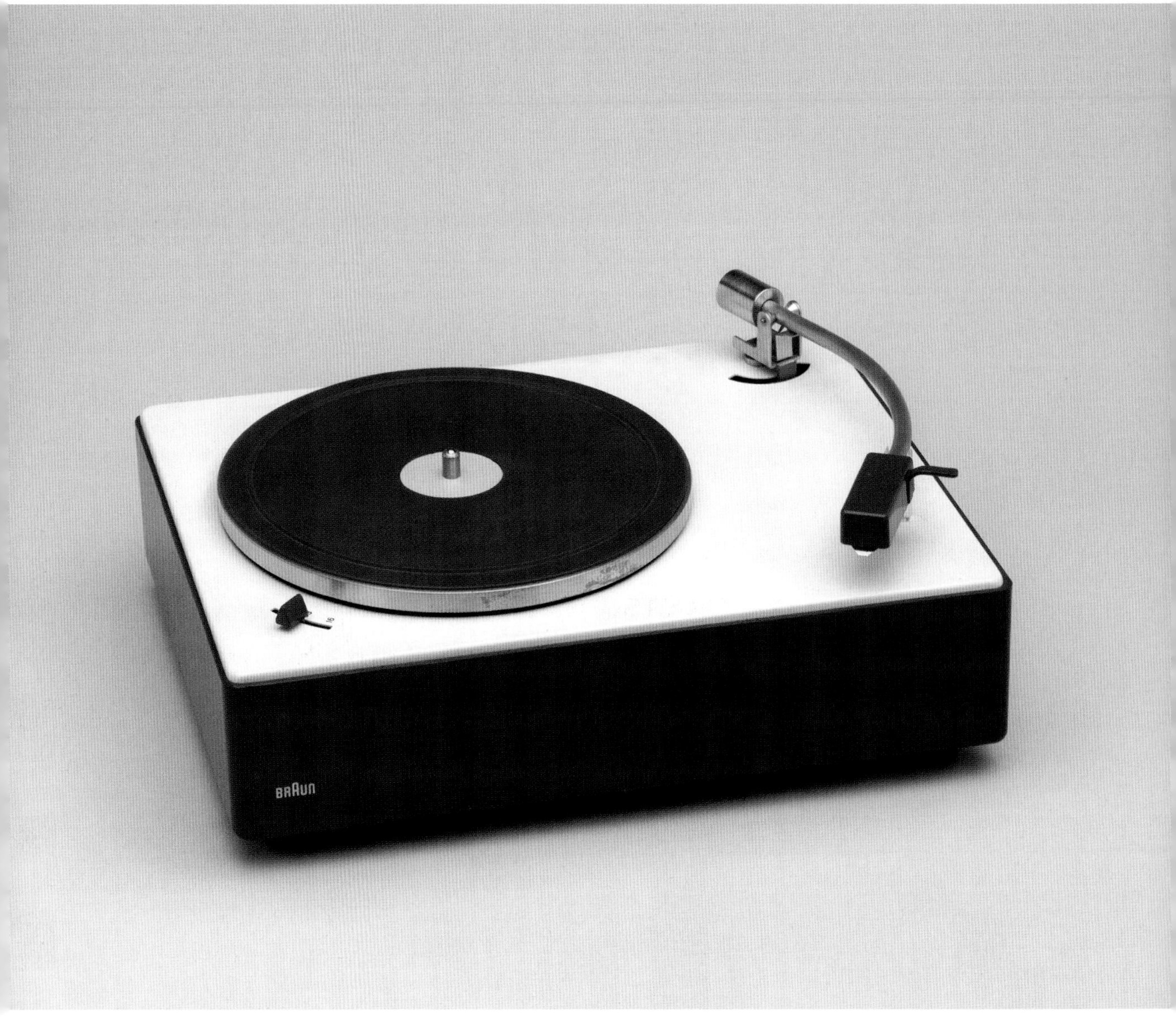

Nine. Digital Product Design: *Sexy Plastic*

In an age of virtual reality and screen-based lives, it is perhaps paradoxical how much conventional industrial design—molding metal and plastic into eye candy—continues to fuel digital desire. While chapter 2 surveys the design characteristics of the first personal computers in the United States, it is also important to recognize how much digital-age industrial design has been molded by a generation of postwar Germans. The ethnic inheritors of the Bauhaus, German designers in Europe and the United States played an outsize role in formulating the legend of that design school, a legend that defines the digital today. The actual 1919–33 Bauhaus had been a messy endeavor, replete with conflicting personalities, ideologies, and even metaphysics. After the shock of the Nazi era, the postwar Bauhaus was reimagined clean and new, a place of focused attention to solving design problems.

Of course, many former Bauhauslers, including Walter Gropius, Marcel Breuer, László Moholy-Nagy, Josef and Anni Albers, and Ludwig Mies van der Rohe, became expatriates and settled in the United States in the thirties. Once there, at various American universities and design schools, they promulgated the sanitized memory of the Bauhaus as an incubator of a clean new world where "less is more." Their design leadership, particularly the outsize reputation of Mies as the centerpiece of the International Style in architecture, laid the basis for the American embrace of minimalist aesthetics. None of the American expats, however, established much of a reputation in industrial design, which at the time remained besotted with midcentury stylishness coated with a sugary palette.

In contrast to the United States, in postwar Germany a fortuitous grouping of a designer, a design school, and a company established a vision for technology that continues to resonate. The designer was Dieter Rams, an erstwhile carpenter and architect who landed a job in 1955 designing exhibition spaces for a large consumer goods corporation. The company was called Braun, an eponymous name originally bestowed on it by its founder, Max Braun, in 1921. Braun made many products, from electric shavers to audio equipment, and was well situated to profit from postwar rebuilding in Germany. The design school was the Hochschule für Gestaltung Ulm, founded in 1953 by Inge Scholl, Otl Aicher, and Max Bill. The latter had himself been a student at the Dessau Bauhaus, while Scholl came from an illustrious family of anti-Nazi activists. Her husband, Aicher, had the slimmest résumé of the trio but would go on to establish himself as one of the pioneers of Swiss-style corporate identity.

In the 1950s at Braun, Rams allied himself with Aicher and another Ulm instructor, Hans Gugelot. Together they formulated a sleek style that exposed passages of industrial materials such as steel and plastic; the Braun style represented a dramatic turn away from the prewar tendency to embed technology in wooden cabinetry. As the age of the vacuum tube gave way to that of the miniaturized transistor, Rams came to design a veritable cornucopia of modern electronic products. Appointed design director in 1962, Rams designed the PS 2 stereo turntable (figure 9.1) the following year, a fine example of his precise vision for industrial design. The PS 2 embodies the new Bauhaus brand as expounded on by Rams at Braun. The designer would come to be defined by his aphorism "less, but better," and the PS 2 succinctly showcases these words: nothing superfluous, no decorative flourishes, just the requisite controls and the logo. (The Braun logo had been updated in 1952 by Wolfgang Schmittel, while the company favored Akzidenz-Grotesk for its publicity materials.) Note the subtly rounded corners of the turntable, and the exactness with which the white top has been implanted on top of the rectangular body, so that it seems to slightly float above it. "God is in the details," as Mies once said. More than any other company, Braun came to define the modern metal and plastic style as the archetype of a clean new world. Likewise, Rams became a legend, and his rather mundane principles of design have been prized and reprised through to the present day. Rams' ten principles called for designs that are what you would expect from looking at the PS 2: innovative, honest, unobtrusive, and consequent to the last detail (like any list of ten, there are redundancies guaranteed when one insists on reaching such an iconic number of commandments). While Rams never designed a computer—he also never adapted to them as design tools—in the metal and plastic that encloses the digital, his legacy would become most evident.

In terms of digital industrial design, the physical forms of the machines themselves—desktops, laptops, tablets, and smartphones—have become the icons of the age. While one would expect the virtual realm of the UI to be paramount, even today the major hardware brands

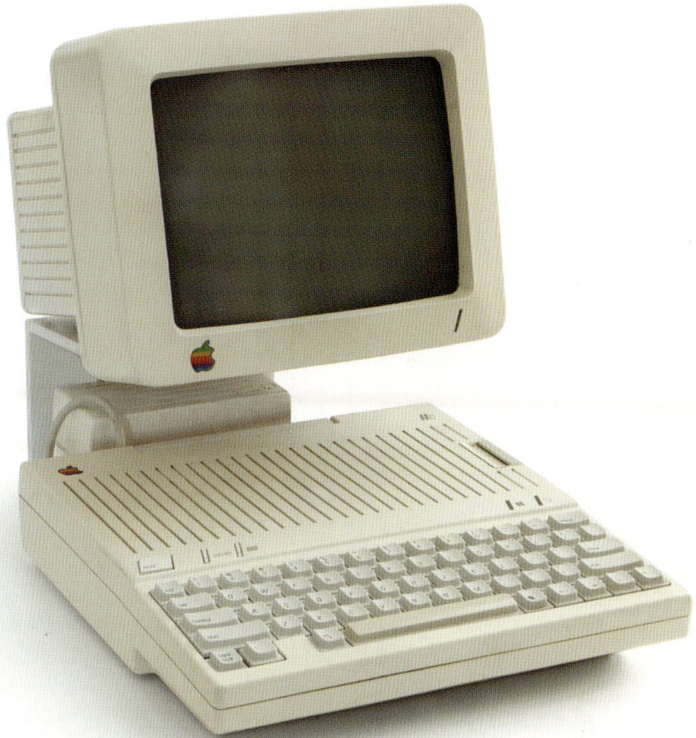

9.2. Apple IIc computer, designed by Harmut Esslinger in 1984

continue to put enormous emphasis on the sexy plastic and metal casings: those are the tangible objects you hold in your hands. If the automobile symbolically ruled an earlier age, today it is the computer and the smartphone.

Chapter 2 shows how the Apple Macintosh, in contrast to the IBM PC, facilitated the growing reputation of Apple as a design-centric corporation. As both an object and a tool the Macintosh transformed personal computing, but its physical design actually had little future. Rather, the company's other major desktop release of 1984, the Apple IIc (figure 9.2), established a visual language for the brand. The Apple IIc, like the Macintosh, featured an outsourced design by Frog, the studio led by Harmut Esslinger. Frog was a German company that had done work for Sony electronics, and the name Frog was a sly acronym for Federal Republic of Germany. Esslinger has recounted that he leveraged his German ancestry to win the Apple account, playing on Steve Jobs's love of German automobiles, which in the eighties dominated the high-end American market with brands like Porsche, BMW, and Mercedes-Benz. Esslinger has also claimed that he was responsible for the elevation of industrial design to the forefront at Apple, explaining to Jobs that American designers were crippled by their low status in most corporate hierarchies.

Like Dieter Rams, Esslinger was a devotee of elegant simplicity matched with an eye for detail, the style casually called "Bauhaus." For the Apple IIc, Frog developed the look they called "Snow White," which was notable for the parallel channels that visually lessened the bulk of the components. The channels also tied together the monitor and external floppy drive with the base, which held the CPU, while also masking cooling vents. Snow White featured the off-white color the company artfully called "fog," but which, in a more mundane terminology, is a cream or beige. The beige color of the plastic is today the most dated part of the Snow White design language, but at the time, it was viewed as a way of masking fingerprints while also increasing the machine's projection of warmth. It was eventually superseded by a neutral gray, which the company termed "platinum."

Around 1990, Apple started to phase out Frog and the Snow White style, although residual elements of the look remained, for example, in the channeling and gray color of some of the PowerBook line of laptops first released starting in 1991. At this point Apple was starting to move most of its design work in-house under the direction of Robert Brunner. Some of the PowerBook designs, however, had been outsourced to a small London firm called Tangerine,

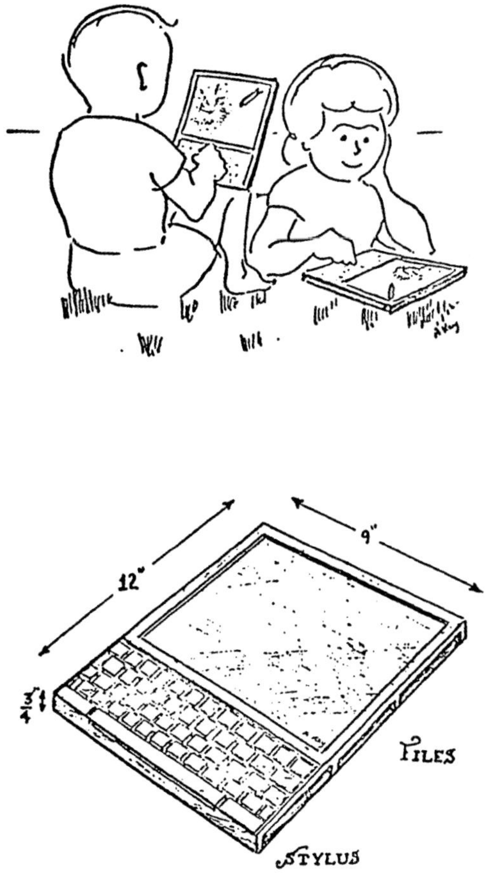

9.3. Alan Kay, Dynabook illustrations, 1972

where Jonathan Ive was a new employee. Ive had studied industrial design at Newcastle Polytechnic (since 1992 known as Northumbria University), a school with a decisively hands-on, "Bauhaus" approach. In 1992 Ive joined Apple, where, as a partisan of the Ulm-Rams-Esslinger framework, he found a corporation that matched his design outlook.

Ive's first work for Apple at Tangerine had focused on laptops, portable computers that had been around for a decade but were only just beginning to break into the mass market. The potential for portable computing went further back, to the 1972 essay that Alan Kay wrote while working at Xerox's Palo Alto Research Center. (In a sense writing on behalf of a generation of digital pioneers, Kay thanked "Xerox for providing a nice place to think about things like this.") Known as the Dynabook essay, Kay's paper outlined some speculative ideas—he called them "science fiction"—about the potential for building portable computers that could enhance children's learning and creativity (figure 9.3). Kay envisioned a device weighing under four pounds and about the size of a paper notebook, a "carry anywhere" machine that would have global connectivity to "bring the libraries and schools (not to mention stores and billboards) of the world to the home." It would have a flat panel display featuring a GUI, a keyboard interface, and perhaps also a spoken word UI. Obviously, Kay was as prescient about laptops (especially the XO laptop promoted by One Laptop Per Child; see below) and smartphones as one could imagine. Also, at a time when tech-based dreams were often far-fetched, Kay was one of the only people who predicted a reasonable device while recognizing possible pitfalls. He had followed up his aside about "stores and billboards" invading the Dynabook's learning mission with this: "One can imagine one of the first programs an owner will write is a filter to eliminate advertising!" As if.

The speculative Dynabook essay was written in 1972, at a time when the first "portable"—in the way a large suitcase is portable—machines started to appear in university research centers. But tech moves quickly, and less than a decade later, industrial designer Bill Moggridge was commissioned to mold the plastic of the first modern laptop. In 1982, GRiD Systems released model 1101 Compass (figure 9.4), securing Moggridge's fame as the designer of the first truly portable laptop brought to market. Successfully bringing new technology to market is, in many ways, the most important metric in digital

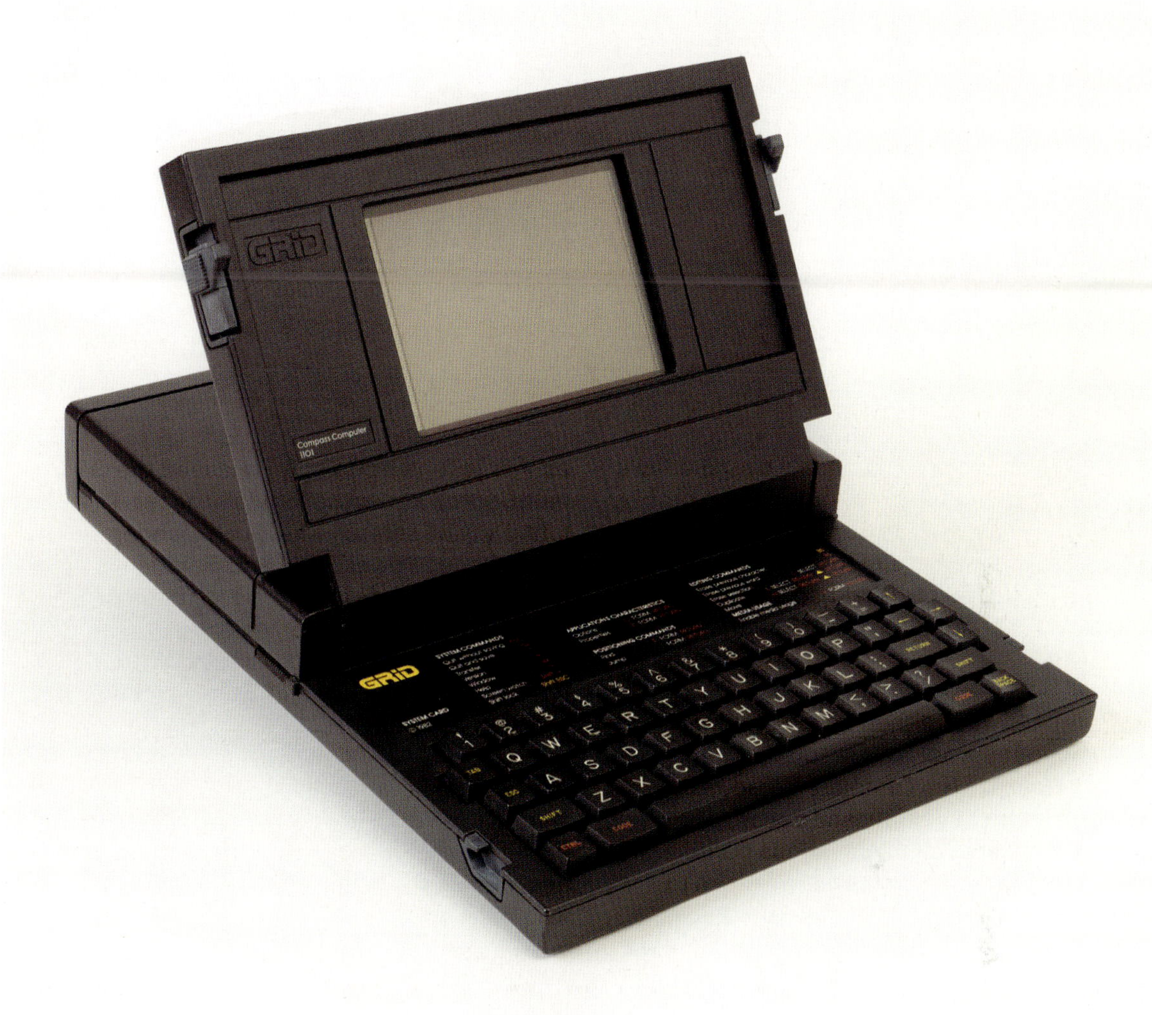

9.4. GRiD 1101 Compass computer, designed by Bill Moggridge in 1982

design, one that often reasonably overshadows inventors and unsuccessful products. Notably, Steve Jobs preferred this standard, as Apple has for decades laid claim to machines—the mouse, the tablet—that had already been invented or marketed elsewhere at an earlier date.

The Compass was neither light, weighing in at eleven pounds, nor a mass-market item like the Dynabook, as the complete Compass system cost close to ten thousand dollars. A port allowed the user to connect various peripherals such as floppy drives. Moggridge's claim to fame in terms of design was the partial clamshell, whereby the front half of the cover folded over the keyboard in a way that protected the display. While that element is deservedly celebrated as a key breakthrough, one needs to view it in the context of ubiquitous portable typewriters of the era, many of which featured clamshell cases long before the Compass came along. The Compass was a great example of a transitional machine, one that artfully blended familiarity and futurism. Moggridge's work on the Compass launched his stellar design career, and he would go on to cofound IDEO in 1991.

Probably the most curious factor in surveying the trajectory of laptop design through to the present is how mundane and incremental it appears in hindsight. Basically, Moggridge's hinged half-clamshell is extended to cover the whole machine; the keyboard moves closer to the screen to make room for a trackball or touchpad; and, of course, the screen gets bigger while the rest keeps getting lighter and thinner: from eleven pounds down to less than two today. The year 2001 witnessed perhaps the one recognizable pivot point in laptop design, as Apple (unsurprisingly) released the G4 titanium laptop known colloquially as the TiMac. It had a wide screen, was much slenderer than the previous PowerBook, and weighed in around six pounds. The G4 PowerBook (figure 9.5) is sleek, shiny, and silver, and would seamlessly fit into a crowd of laptops at any coffee shop today: maybe it is just a little portly compared to its newer brethren.

It is notable how invisibly the design of hardware shifted from an artisanal, analog approach to a digital one. For example, at Apple in the nineties, designers on computers and designers who drew by hand and then sculpted products out of foam and clay worked side by side. Exactly what percentage of any given piece of hardware was digitally designed versus handcrafted is unknowable via the naked eye. At Apple and elsewhere, designers gradually adopted software tools. Apple employees first worked on specialized Silicon Graphics workstations until the company's own computers were powerful enough for the job. Apple was one of the early adopters of Alias software—the precursor to Autodesk Studio and the modeling and animation program Maya—that was one of the first computer-aided industrial design (CAID) programs (in theory, CAID software has more aesthetic capabilities versus a straight CAD package). Also, like architects of the era, Apple designers in the eighties and nineties experimented with aerospace industry software such as Unigraphics, which could also be used for 3D modeling. Yet, many important, even legendary, product features, such as the dial UI of the iPod (2001), had strictly analog origins.

The plastic anatomy of the desktop computer has also undergone continual refinements since

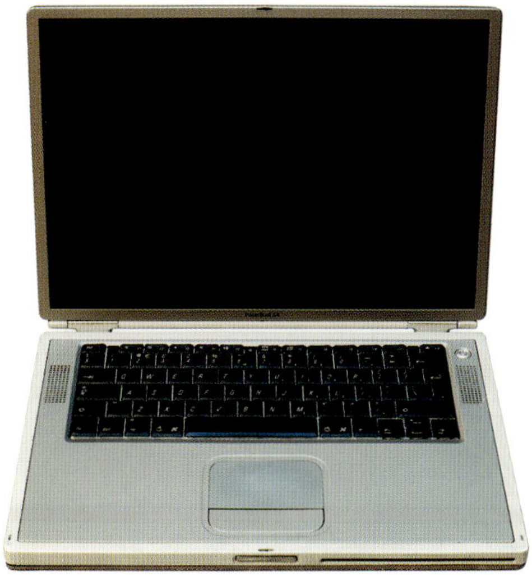

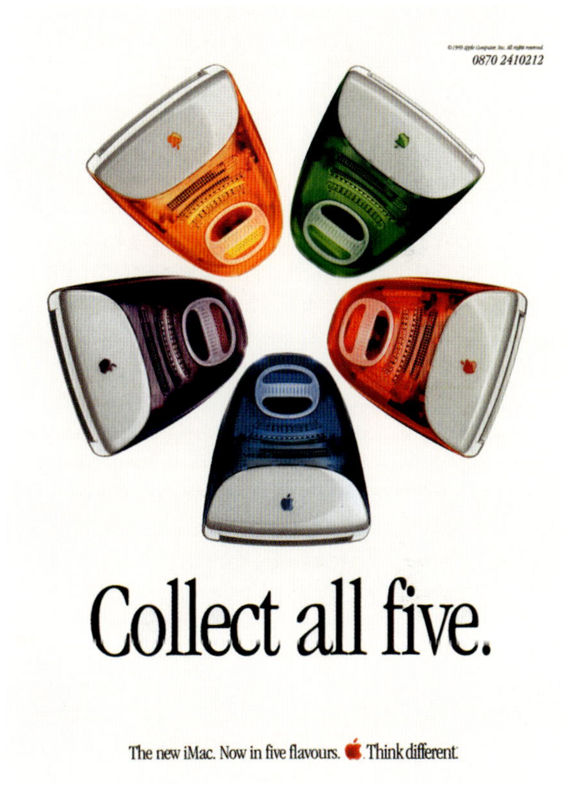

9.5. Apple Computer's G4 PowerBook computer, 2001

9.6. Ad for the iMac Computer, first released by Apple in 1998

the basic form was established in the eighties. Insomuch as Apple has maintained its lead in product design, its desktops have had a higher profile than most, especially after designer Jony Ive started collaborating with Jobs after the latter's return to the company in 1997. The first signature desktop product of Jobs 2.0 was the iMac (figure 9.6), a reboot of the iconic machine that had initially fueled the company's ascent. The revised all-in-one iMac was designed, like its namesake, as a mainstream consumer, as opposed to business, machine, and the "i" in the name indicated a focus on internet connectivity. The iMac was big and bulky because it needed to house a cathode ray tube, as the flat screen was still a few years in the future.

The most unusual feature of the iMac was its color; it was released in a turquoise hue Apple artfully called Bondi blue (after a beach in Australia), and later iterations featured an expanded rainbow palette. Cheery chromatics were a stark contrast with the prevailing minimalist aesthetic, perhaps indicating an attempt at garnering the adulation many in the design world felt for the famed 1968 Olivetti Valentine portable typewriter (figure 9.7). The bright red Valentine had been designed by Ettore Sottsass, aided by Perry King, and aimed at the same casual consumer market that the iMac intended to reach. Sottsass is generally credited with being one of the first designers outside the automobile realm to recognize that an industrial product could be sexy and desirable, with the Valentine using color to inspire consumers. Jobs may well have had the Valentine on his mind in the late nineties, as he reportedly considered hiring Sottsass as a design consultant.

Since the introduction of the iMac, bright color has occasionally resurfaced amid the dominant Bauhaus-esque style favored in the hardware industry. Like the sensual flash of colorist rococo painting that staked a claim counter to the eighteenth-century commitment to classicism, colorful palettes have popped up on various iterations of the iPod and iPhone. To a certain degree, Apple has used color as a signifier of casual fun, but also relatively lower cost. Just as the iMac was less expensive than the company's line of Power Mac business computers, so color has often been employed to jazz up the design of other inexpensive Apple i devices. The 1998 iMac differentiated itself from the Valentine typewriter of three decades earlier in another important way: the computer was a financial success. While the Valentine is beloved by creative types trafficking in nostalgia, it did not actually sell and did not have much of an impact on design culture overall. In contrast, the colorful iMac was a triple success. First, it was popular and profitable; second, it served as a halo product conveying the message that Apple was relevant again; and, third, that relevancy sparked a few years of colored plastic copyists, as numerous products were released with translucent colored plastic.

It is important to recognize how compartmentalized the industrial design of computers has been from the software interface it supports. Even at Apple, the first true design czar was Jony Ive in 2012, when he added interface design to his portfolio after the death of Jobs (the latter had of course served as an informal design overseer). The sometimes fraught relationship between hardware and software has a substantial history that is partially considered in earlier chapters; one of the tropes of both realms is the notion of a user experience that is human centered. Of course, this focus—that the designer should focus on larger issues of functionality, not as a decorator—has been perennially rediscovered during the modern age. The decidedly analog American industrial designer Henry Dreyfuss, for example, stressed the topic in his 1950s bestseller *Designing for People* (note the title). While by no means the first designer concerned with user experience, Dreyfuss wrote eloquently on the topic. "We bear in mind that the object being worked on is going to be ridden in, sat upon, looked at, talked into, activated, operated, or in some other way used by people individually or en masse. When the point of contact between the product and the people becomes a point of friction, then the industrial designer has failed."

Today, a slew of overlapping terms—interaction design, human-centered design, user interaction, user experience—refer to the process of lubricating digital points of friction. Bill Moggridge, cofounder of IDEO, became a legend for recognizing in the late seventies that the design of the virtual space superseded that of the plastic shell of the hardware. While working on the GRiD laptop, Moggridge had an epiphany: "I soon forgot all about the physical part of the design and found myself sucked down into the virtual world on the other side of the screen." He eventually settled on the term "interaction design" to describe this field.

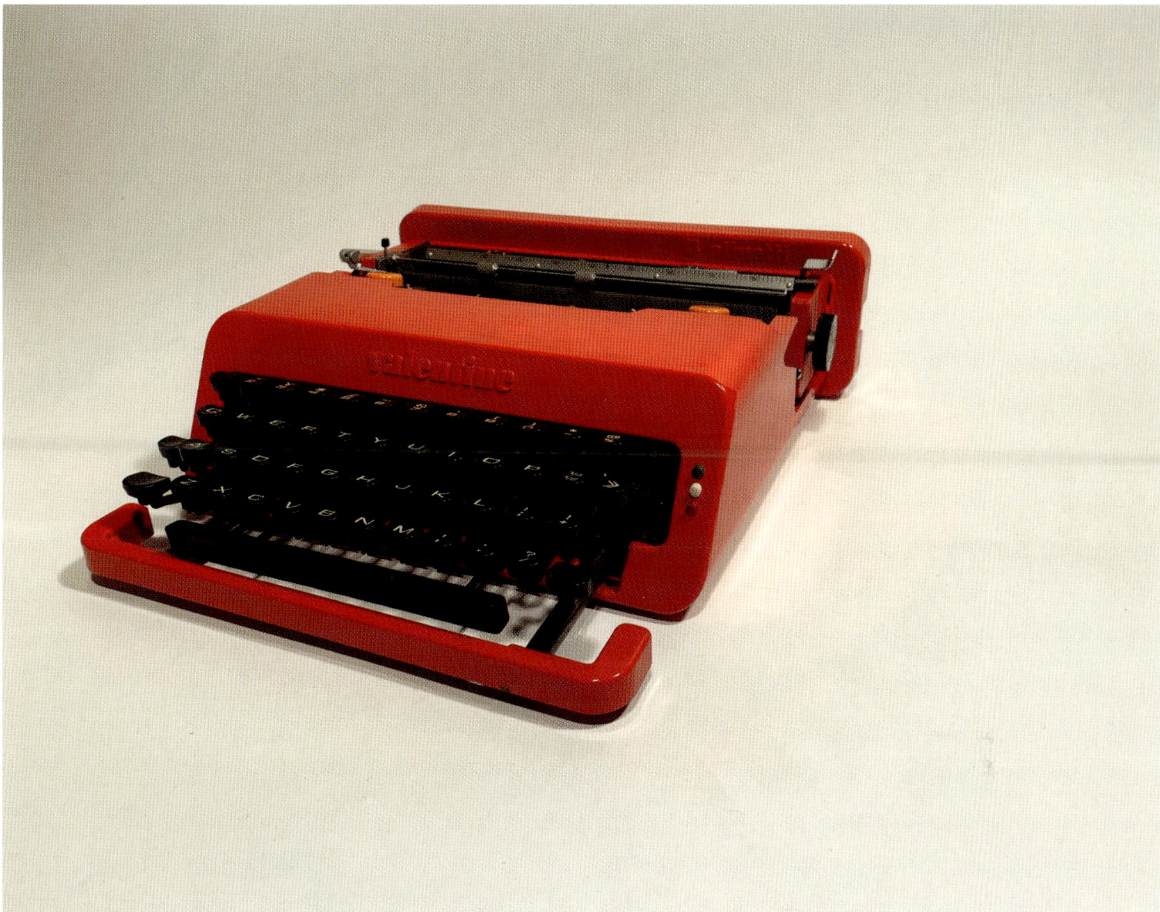

9.7. Olivetti Valentine portable typewriter, designed by Ettore Sottsass and Perry King in 1968

Perhaps because of the digital designer's tendency to inhabit a perpetual present and future, accolades have been showered on designers such as Donald Norman, a professor of cognitive science who transitioned into big tech, starting with a term as an Apple fellow in the nineties. Through the efforts of Jobs and Bruce Tognazzini—who wrote the earliest editions of Apple's "Human Interface Guidelines"—the importance of human–computer interaction was of course already a mainstay of the corporate culture. At Apple, Norman has been credited with popularizing the term "user experience," a not-so-new concept that was nonetheless often neglected by the engineers who had precipitated the digital revolution (outside Apple). Norman is also celebrated in the digital world for his coining of the term "perceived affordances," used to describe a thing whose function is manifest by its design (e.g., a button looks like you should push it). Notably, the word "affordance" is not a good literary example of a perceived affordance. In recent years, Norman and Tognazzini have taken issue with Apple's current interfaces, which they argue stress an extreme minimalist style with the *look* of clarity at the expense of effective human–computer interactions.

The importance of seamlessly connected physical and interface design is most apparent in the mobile age, when phones have become tasked with universal expectations. In this arena, the June 2007 release of the Apple iPhone still stands as the most significant introduction of an industrial product in the digital era (figure 9.8). The so-called Jesus phone fomented and then delivered on a mountain of marketing hype. Combining at baseline a cell phone, music player, camera, and web browser, the iPhone was designed around a multitouch UI. People could scroll through internet pages and zoom in on photos with their fingers, allowing for a more intuitive form of interaction than that of a complex set of buttons. Of course, Apple also needed to devise a new mobile operating system for the phone, eventually naming it iOS. The multitouch iPhone is all about affordances: icons on a touchscreen, tapping with your finger to open; the iOS user interface is simple enough to be invisible. The physical revolution was quite simple: more screen, less keyboard, combined with a smooth user experience made the iPhone

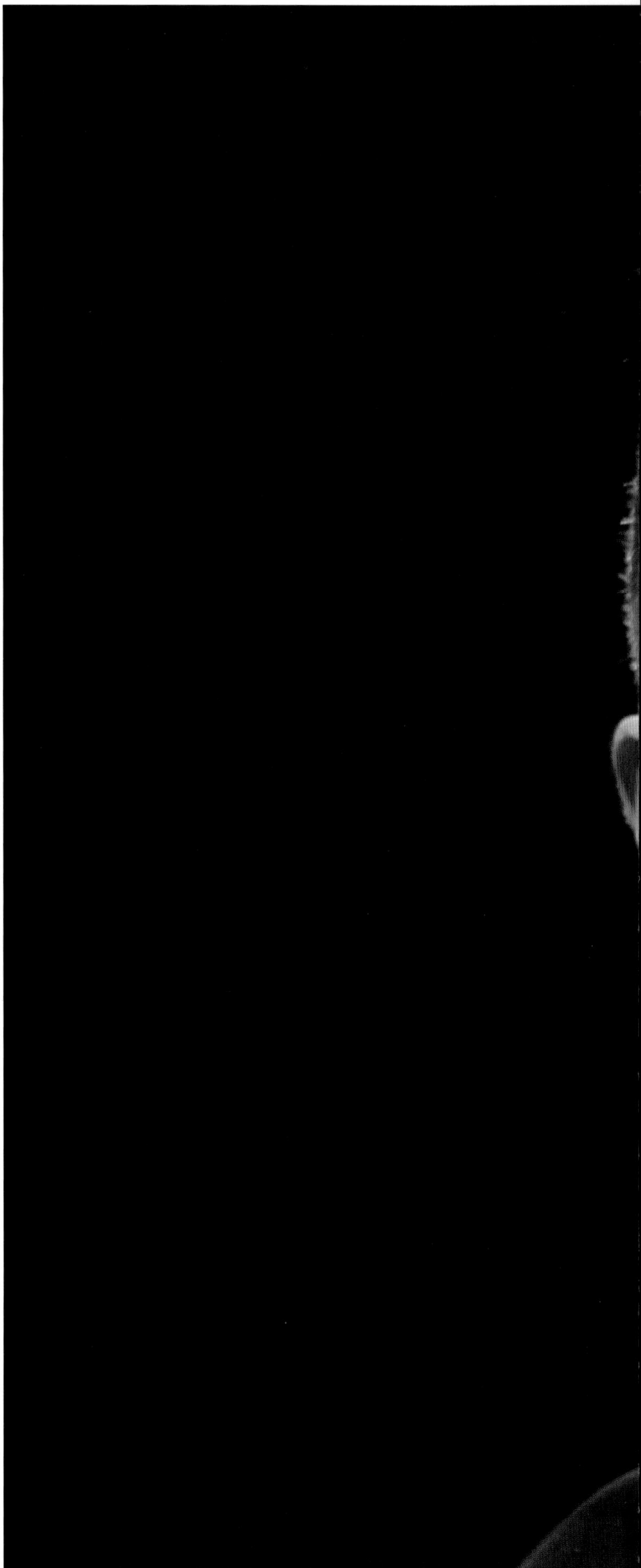

9.8. Steve Jobs holding Apple Computer's iPhone, first released in 2007

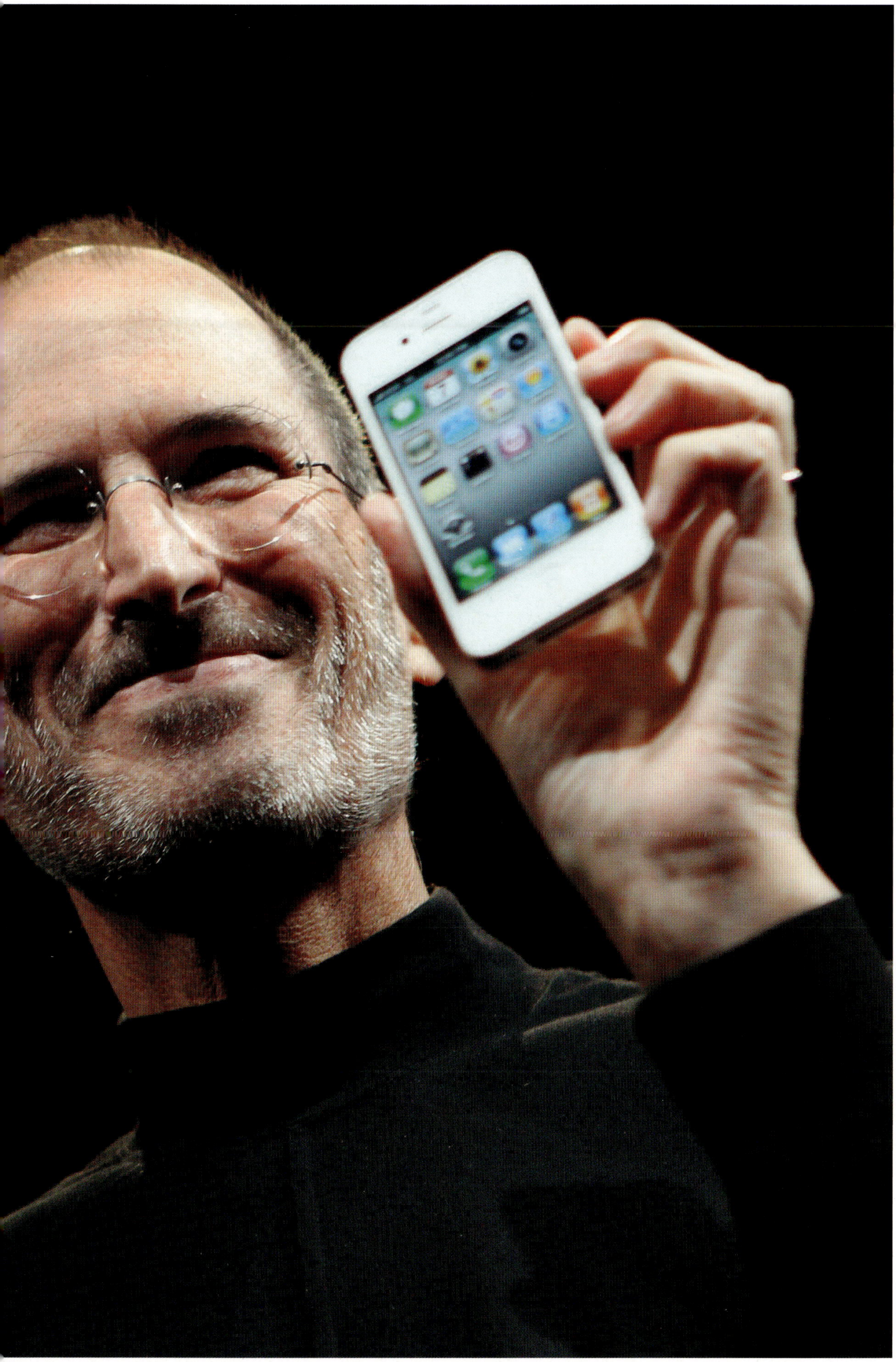

essentially a portable computer. Versus the keyboard-centric competition in 2007, especially Blackberry, the Apple formula allowed users to migrate from laptop to phone, as the iPhone's web capabilities in particular greatly exceeded that of its competitors.

Considering the importance of the user interface and the functionality created by an expanding app ecosystem, it may seem paradoxical that the tangible hardware itself continues to draw so much attention. While many people know of Jony Ive, who oversaw the industrial design, few outside the industry have heard of Scott Forstall, who ran the team that engineered the first iPhone OS. Although the iPhone looked a lot like an iPod music player sans wheel, the device was celebrated for its minimal design as if some sort of industrial design revolution were at hand. Of course, nothing about the physical design was new or unusual; sleek iterations of metal and glass and plastic had decades of prominence behind them in 2007. The iPhone was in a sense the perfect object, however, for the now unremarkable Bauhaus design aesthetic: it is a phone intended to be pocketed, and Apple needed it to be a tight, minimal package. If ever a device matched the call for "Less is more" or "Less but better," or any other modernist aphorism, the iPhone was it. Its screen-centric focus provides an entrée into everything digital, while the phone itself should efface its physicality. But it does not actually disappear, and that, in a sense, is the point. In a situation that is arguably the greatest example of the revenge, or resilience, of the analog, gripping an iPhone in your hand is what people remember. While Moggridge delighted in losing sight of his GRiD hardware when immersed in a screen, today users are still just as likely to be caught up in the heft of sexy metal and plastic.

Smartphones like the iPhone have also been tasked with solving one of the most irksome interactions of the industrial world, the quest to find and identify small missing parts. Jewel Burks Solomon addressed this issue several years ago with her start-up Partpic (figure 9.9). Using a smartphone camera, Partpic's virtual algorithms identify and facilitate the ordering of small hard-to-find pieces of the tangible world. Anticipating the promise of augmented reality, Amazon acquired Partpic in 2016. Solomon is now the head of Google for Startups and a partner at Collab Capital, through which she works to increase equity in the technology industry.

Since the late nineties, Hiroshi Ishii of MIT has pursued a thought-provoking area of research that likewise seeks to unite the virtual and the actual. In a 1997 paper, Ishii proposed the idea of "tangible bits," seeking to find a way to import digital information into the world of touch. Ishii refers to the pixels of a GUI as "painted bits," which he argues do not make a strong human–computer interface. Tangible bits would bring the shape and mass of actual objects into the HCI equation. In 2012, he rebranded his research as "radical atoms" (figure 9.10), with the goal of creating "a hypothetical generation of materials that can change form and properties dynamically and computationally, becoming as reconfigurable as pixels on a GUI screen." Ishii argues that giving digital information a physical presence will allow for a more visceral, direct interface.

While Ishii's research is still provisional and aspirational, the implementation of haptic responses—

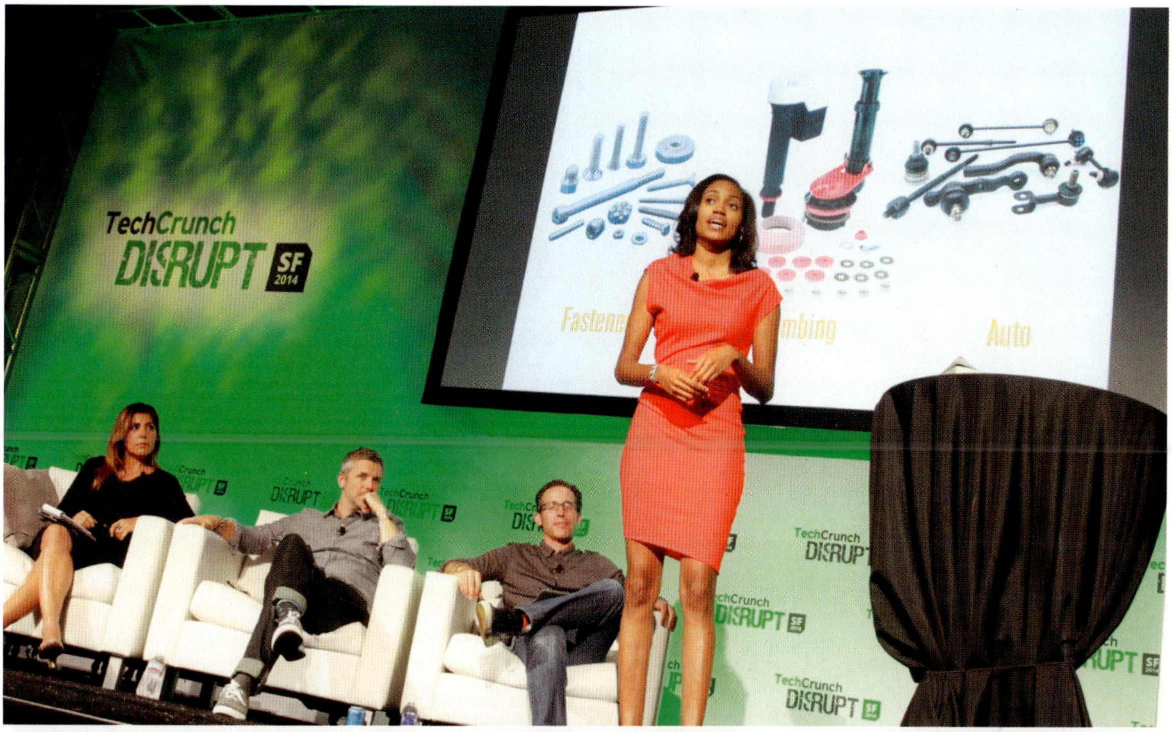

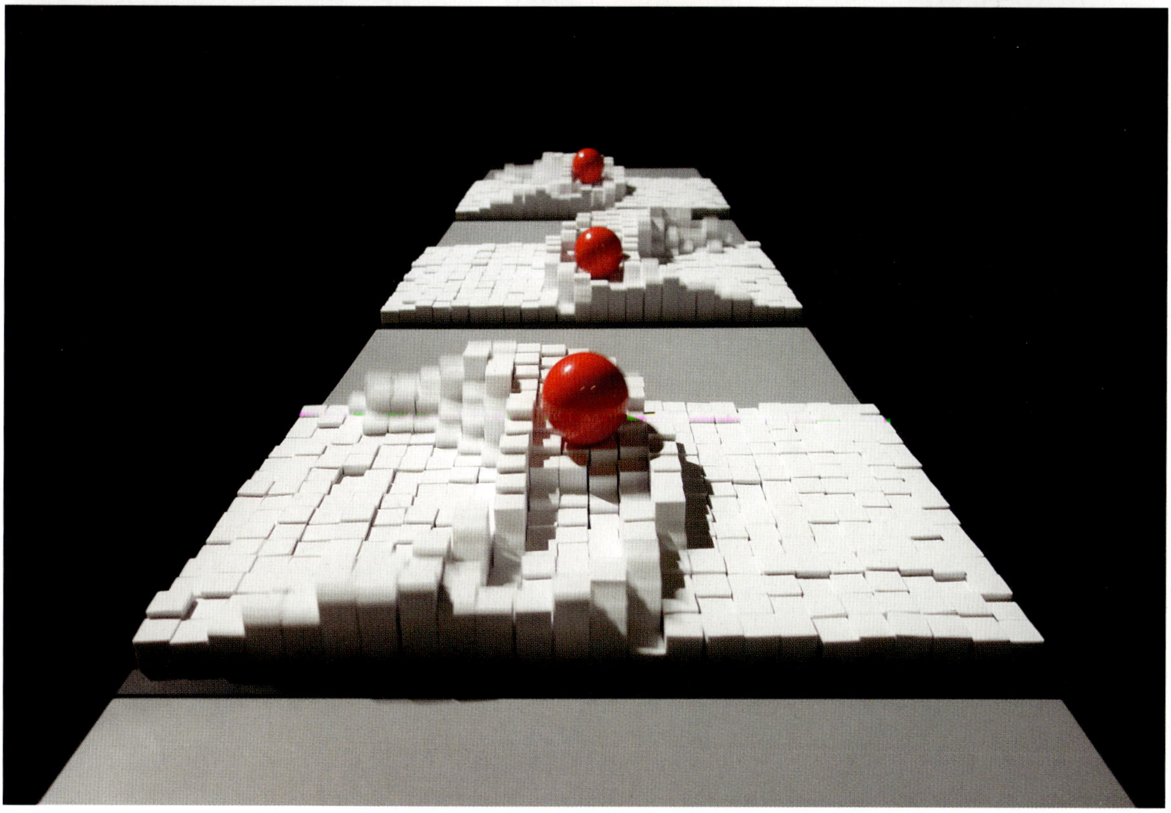

9.9. Jewel Burks Solomon, cofounder of Partpic, speaking at TechCrunch, 2014
9.10. Hiroshi Ishii, radical atoms, 2012

whereby the digital generates a physical sense of touch and pressure—points in the same direction. Though haptic feedback has been a part of arcade video games since the eighties, it was not used in that media as a simulation of the digital. The most common haptic effect in gaming was vibration, for example, used to evoke driving on a rough surface. Haptics really reached the mainstream when the iPhone 7 was released in 2016. The iPhone 7 featured a shift from an actual to a virtual Home button, so the device needed to create the illusion of a pushing sensation. Today, haptics are starting to play a major role in virtual reality, as the sensitivity of touch experiences are refined and expanded. In both the iPhone and virtual reality gear, the haptic sensations are still imperfect, signaling pressure and pushing rather than actually emulating it. Virtual sensations still pale in the face of the actual, which is what gives industrial design such a continuing central role amid the expansion of the virtual.

Yves Béhar is another iconic figure in the design of the tangible digital. Swiss born, he moved to Silicon Valley in the early nineties, where he worked at two well-known firms associated with Apple, Brunner's Lunar, and Esslinger's Frog Design. In 1999, he set up his own studio in San Francisco, Fuseproject. Béhar and Fuseproject enjoyed a breakthrough moment in 2006, when they introduced the green and white design of the XO laptop (figure 9.11). The XO was the original product of Nicholas Negroponte's One Laptop Per Child (OLPC) endeavor. Negroponte, a tech visionary and one of the founders of the MIT Media Lab, hoped to offer low-priced laptops to improve education in the developing world. In 2006 laptops were still something of an expensive device, and the XO represented a breakthrough insomuch as it showed that simplified yet robust machines could be produced economically. Béhar's design for the XO was a break from the sleek style customary for laptops, as he sought to create a device that, through color and shape, felt kid friendly; in particular, the little rabbit ears that popped up on either side of the case gave the open XO a warm, approachable look.

While Béhar has had tremendous success as a designer, his career has also showcased the excesses of Silicon Valley, where everyone has an idea for a start-up that will "disrupt" this, that, or the other thing. Béhar famously, or notoriously, designed one such ill-gotten digital solution in search of a problem, Mark One's Vessyl digital cup. The marketing of this smart device ramped up in 2014, as the cup promised to recognize whatever beverage was poured into it, and then calculate and display the calories and nutritional qualities of its contents. Additionally, the Vessyl would track hydration through a complementary app that relied on a proprietary algorithm called Pryme. As it happened, the two-hundred-dollar cup was doomed by a comedy bit on the Stephen Colbert show that ruthlessly mocked the device and its marketing materials. Colbert opined that Vessyl offered the "recommended daily allowance of Silicon Valley buzzwords." While Mark One eventually launched the product as the Pryme Vessyl personal hydration tracker, the company folded in early 2018. Of course, Béhar's sleek design played only a tangential role in this drama. Nonetheless, just as Fuseproject had profited from the goodwill generated through its connection to the nonprofit OLPC, so it also saw its brand diminished by its connection to

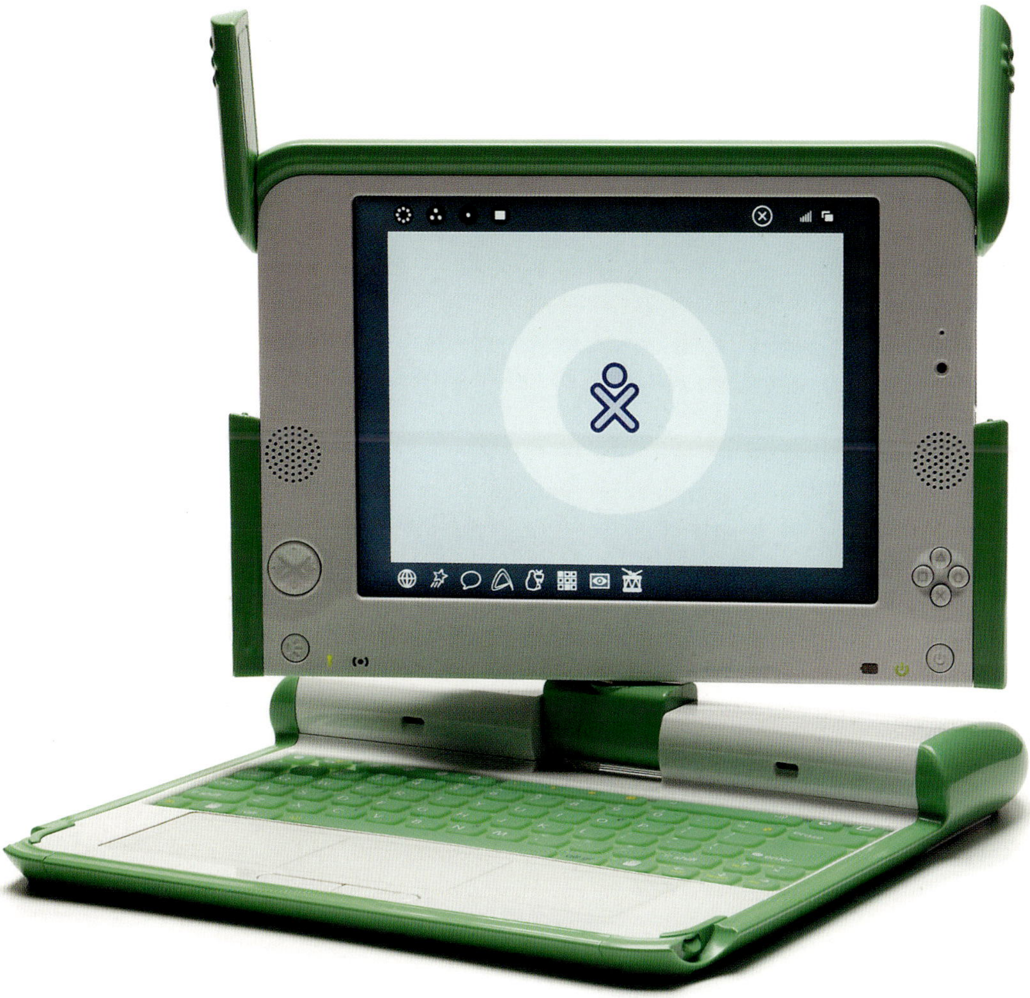

9.11. Fuseproject, XO laptop computer, 2006

a seemingly frivolous device aimed at affluent Americans.

One of the most striking trends of the last decade in digital design has been the impulse to advance the aesthetics of just about every manufactured object on earth. Take the example of the ultrafast laser, a device utilized in scientific research because of its ability to pulse in short bursts measured in femtoseconds (a quadrillionth of a second). Only a couple of decades ago, scientists needing one of these instruments would most likely build it themselves from a kit. Gradually, industrial suppliers began offering off-the-shelf iterations of the item encased in unremarkable plastic boxes. In more recent years, however, ultrafast lasers and other scientific instruments have come to be designer goods, encased in sleek curvilinear sheaths.

In 2015, Fuseproject designed a splendid case for a biotech firm, Fluidigm, whose device is used for genomics testing on low-concentration DNA samples. Fuseproject asked rhetorically, "Design touches everything. So why has it remained largely absent in the biotech and life science industry?" This trend appears to be part of the halo created by consumer technology, an "iPhone effect," whereby anything and everything digital needs to visually declare itself as part of the virtual imagination. In the biotech market, however, another messier, ethical question has arisen in regard to design. In 2015 Fuseproject designed the case for the Edison (figure 9.12), a blood-testing instrument devised by a company called Theranos. At its peak in 2015, Theranos was a company valued at over $9 billion on the basis of its promise to disrupt the blood-testing industry; its CEO Elizabeth Holmes had an estimated personal fortune of $4.5 billion, making her one of the richest people on earth. Of course, in 2016 Theranos collapsed as it gradually became apparent that the Edison did not work, and the company had evolved into a massive fraud. The design question here is, does Fuseproject—or any other studio for that matter—bear any responsibility for helping to market the Vessyl or the Edison? Or are designers no more implicated than a

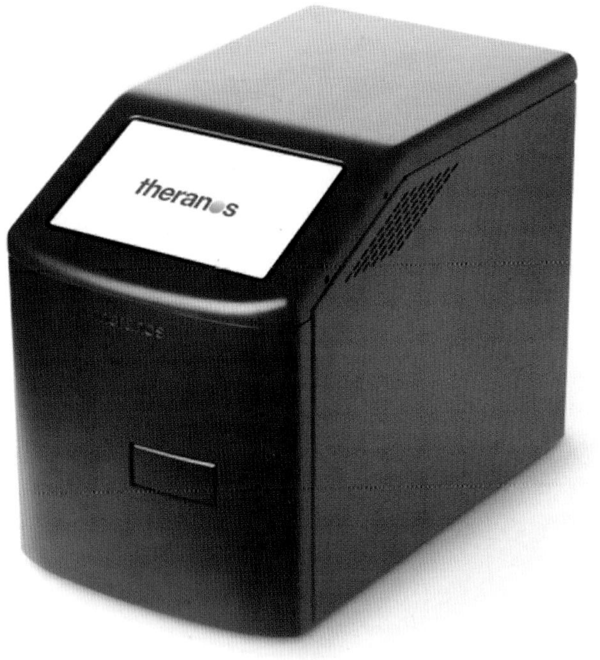

9.12. Theranos's Edison, with case design by Fuseproject, 2015

caterer or utility? Does driving desire create an added obligation?

The design of computers extends much further than it once did, when there were only desktops and laptops, as more and more of our daily interactions today involve interacting with a plethora of smart, or computerized, machines. From a design standpoint, contemporary smart devices hearken back to Moggridge's realization that digital design involves the formulation of both physical and virtual interactions. But these computer-controlled, internet-connected appliances, especially those that reside in people's most intimate environments—their homes—also often feature a third interface: voice. This last element, combined with their presence in a private domestic space, opens up a whole new landscape, as the silicon-powered device now takes on a simulation of personhood that triggers emotion in the user.

Computer-controlled manufacturing using embedded systems has a history, like many things digital, that stretches back into the automobile and aerospace industries of the fifties, before making the jump into the consumer market in the nineties. With that transition came the need to start thinking seriously about design; in an influential paper given at the 1992 Embedded Systems Conference, software engineer Larry Constantine called attention to the dreadful interface design typical of the time. He opened his speech, "User Interface Design for Embedded Systems," with an anecdotal reference to the joking response often elicited when one asked the time in a nineties home: "It's 88:88." Constantine was referencing the ubiquitous microwave and video-recorder clocks—some of the first embedded digital systems to enter the home—that were perennially unset because of the difficulty of navigating what should be a simple menu.

As engineers and designers worked to improve user interfaces, internet connectivity opened up the field to a new dynamic phase. *Wired* magazine predictably covered the topic ahead of its actual implementation, and by 1996 was touting how networked everyday products would transform the home. A reader responded to the article by chastising the magazine for its unbridled futurism, noting that machines of the nineties did not yet speak the same code and therefore could not be networked meaningfully. Still, he wrote facetiously, "I hope my new internet-ready toaster is more crash resistant than my PC." The networked toaster would of course appear some twenty years later, and the breed allows users to keep track of their seared carbohydrates through an app on their phone. While internet toasters perhaps represent the sort of digital design overreach made famous by the Vessyl—complicating rather than minimizing a given experience—there is currently a continuing gold rush as hordes of technology entrepreneurs are clearly hooked on digitizing the mundane.

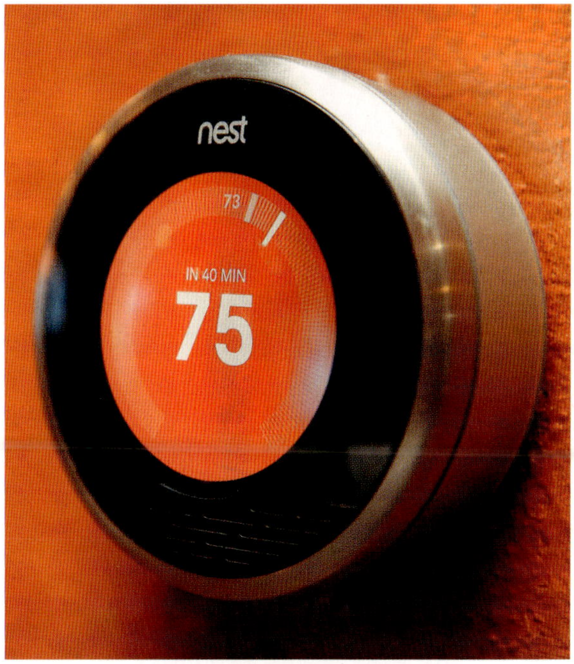

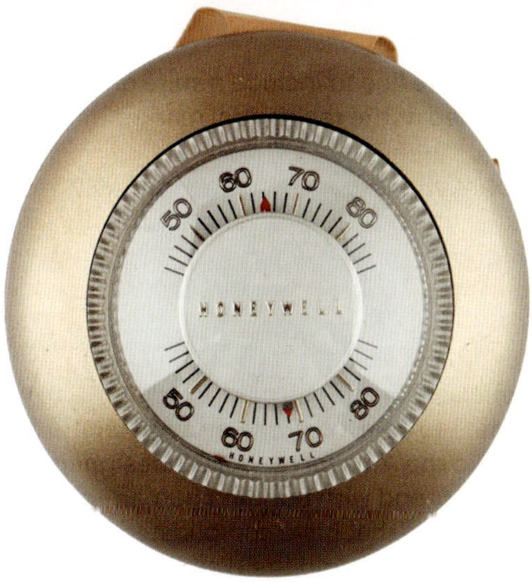

9.13. Nest smart thermostat, 2011

9.14. Henry Dreyfuss, T86 thermostat, 195

Today there is an Internet of Things, smart devices that have proliferated into most aspects of everyday life. The Nest smart thermostat (figure 9.13), released in 2011, became the breakthrough smart gadget that corralled the public's imagination regarding embedded systems. Nest was founded by Tony Fadell and Matt Rogers, two veterans of Apple who had worked on the design teams that devised the iPhone and iPad. The Nest thermostat was engineered to further energy savings, as it learns a household's habits through motion detection and a programming app. From a design standpoint, the Nest is predictable, as it exudes an obvious Apple pedigree. Fadell was quoted in the initial press release, stating that the thermostat demonstrates the "thoughtful design elements the iPhone generation has come to expect." The Nest design appears to represent a May–December union between an iPhone and Henry Dreyfuss's 1953 round thermostat (figure 9.14). Dreyfuss's T86 is famous for its round shape and intuitive interface, so that it looks clean on the wall—never askew like an accidentally tilted square or rectangle—and the temperature can be adjusted with a simple twist of the wrist. Likewise, the Nest's digital readout is intuitive and its case smooth and shiny; however, the Nest has the added element of conspicuous consumption as it projects sophistication and technological savvy to one's guests. In 2014, Nest was acquired by Google and has expanded

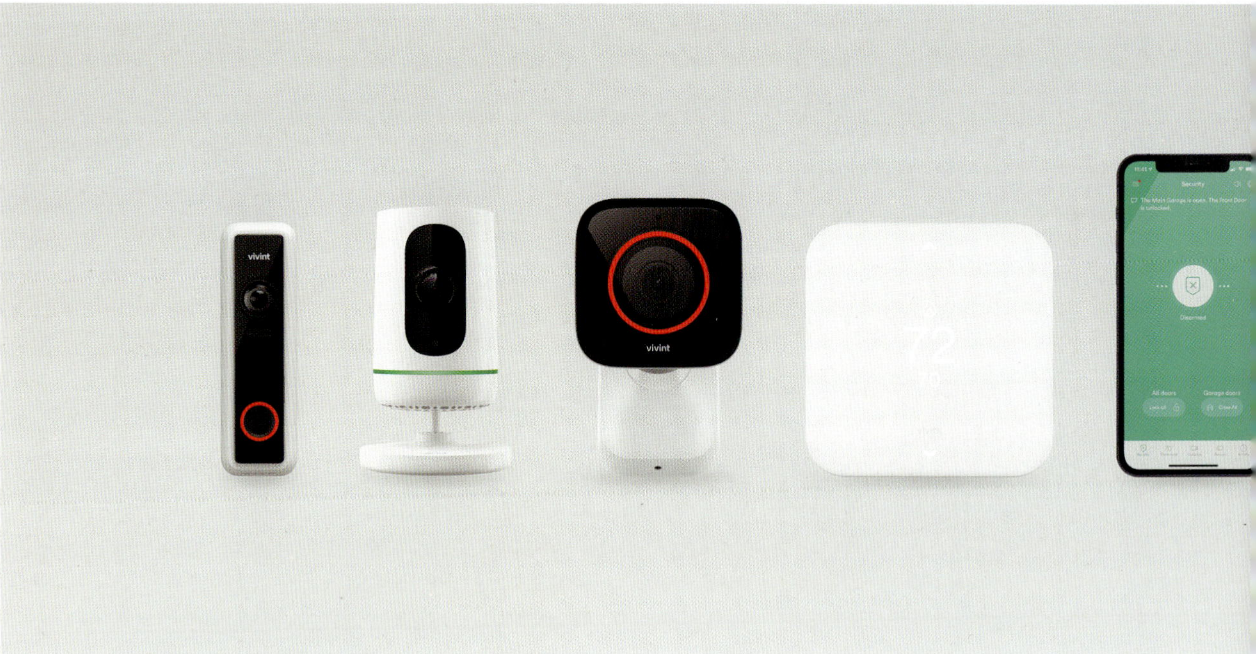

9.15. Vivint, smart home products, 2021

its hardware line to include a suite of smart gadgets aimed at the residential market.

As noted above, vocal interfaces add an element of nuanced emotion that far outstrips the cheery "Hello" opener on the screen of an early Apple Macintosh, let alone the cold efficiency of an iPhone. There are many pitfalls in this area, and the design of GE's Geneva line of talking networked appliances is a case in point. As voice became the core interface through digital assistants like the Amazon Echo, GE designers have had to contend with budding human–machine relationships that have complicated the interaction. Bill Gardner told the *Wall Street Journal* in 2017 that the appliance maker has struggled with the fact that people gradually added pleasantries when talking to their oven or refrigerator, confusing the machine. Miscommunication can lead to frustration, and so Geneva is programmed to exit the conversation if it becomes repetitive. The GE executive pointed out, "We don't want to get into this confrontational cycle where we make you mad." Voice recognition has also added a new dimension to the field of industrial design, as an ability to navigate this area is becoming a key skill set for professionals. For example, Lauren Platts, lead industrial designer at GE Appliances, has dual degrees in industrial design and English literature, with minors in linguistics and art. While trafficking in stereotypes, the notion that women are more emotionally intuitive and verbally skilled than men has created new professional opportunities for women industrial designers. GE designers such as Platts and user experience appliance designer Amy Goforth are typical of this refreshing trend.

The Vivint smart home line of products represent a perfect distillation of industrial design in the digital age (figure 9.15). Vivint was founded as a residential alarm company, but in recent years it has expanded tremendously based on its networked smart devices, including thermostats, cameras, doorbells, lighting, and the like. All of these products can be controlled by digital assistants or phones. Designwise, the various Vivint gadgets all share the same sleek, "Bauhaus"-inspired look favored in the digital age. The look is, frankly, bland and omnipresent; the digital design of the tangible today has seemingly reached a point of stasis, as the aesthetic has spread so much as to become mundane. Perhaps another flash of color and texture—a Sottsass Valentine or an Apple iMac—may come and go, but the dominant theme seems destined to continue to assert itself. One might speculate that the tangible digital will simply become a thing of the past, that physical objects will gradually be effaced as projected or even body-embedded screens come to the fore. It would seem, however, that the virtual world is unlikely to promote original design strategies, because today's virtual interfaces stress the same sleek homogeneity as the hardware that enables them. Whether physical or virtual, the smart spaces of the future may well be much more ordinary than has been foretold.

It is impossible to ponder the smart home without feeling the ghost of Ray Bradbury's 1950

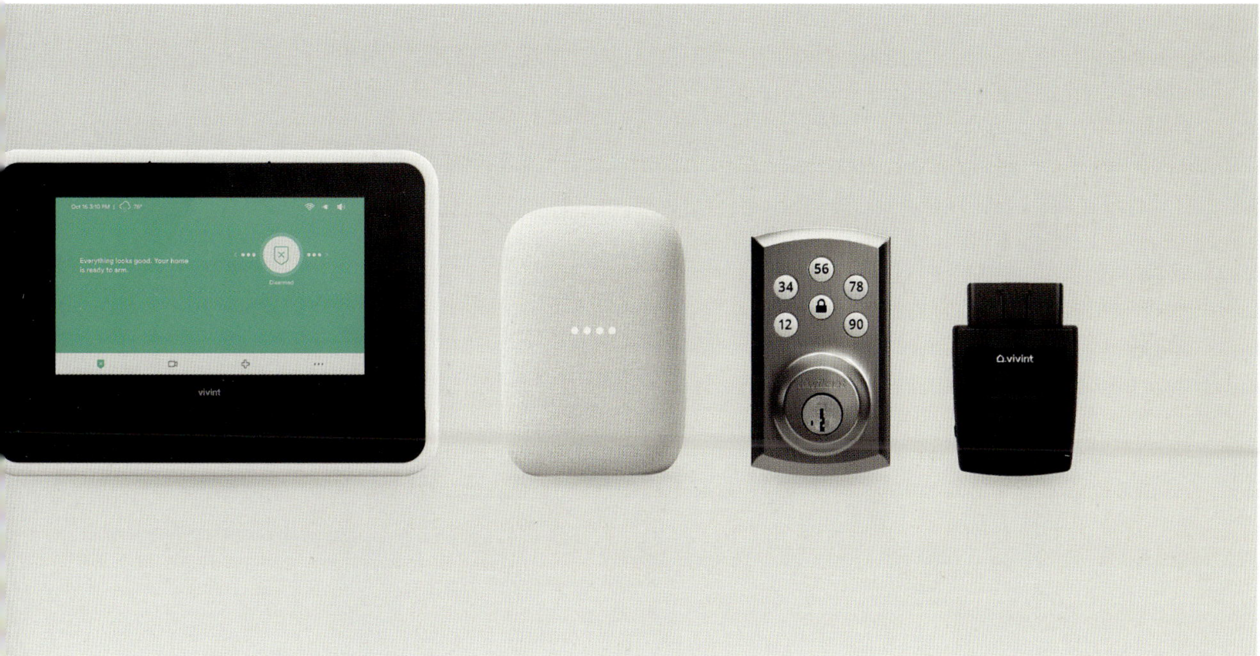

essay "There Will Come Soft Rains." In this evocative postapocalyptic short story, an empty home in a depopulated world continues its daily routines as if it were still inhabited. In the story, the human–machine interaction has broken down because the humans are gone for good, and the emptiness of smart machines relating to nobody is all that remains. "In the kitchen the breakfast stove gave a hissing sigh and ejected from its warm interior eight pieces of perfectly browned toast, eight eggs sunny side up, sixteen slices of bacon, two coffees, and two cool glasses of milk. 'Today is August 4, 2026,' said a second voice from the kitchen ceiling, 'in the city of Allendale, California.' It repeated the date three times for memory's sake."

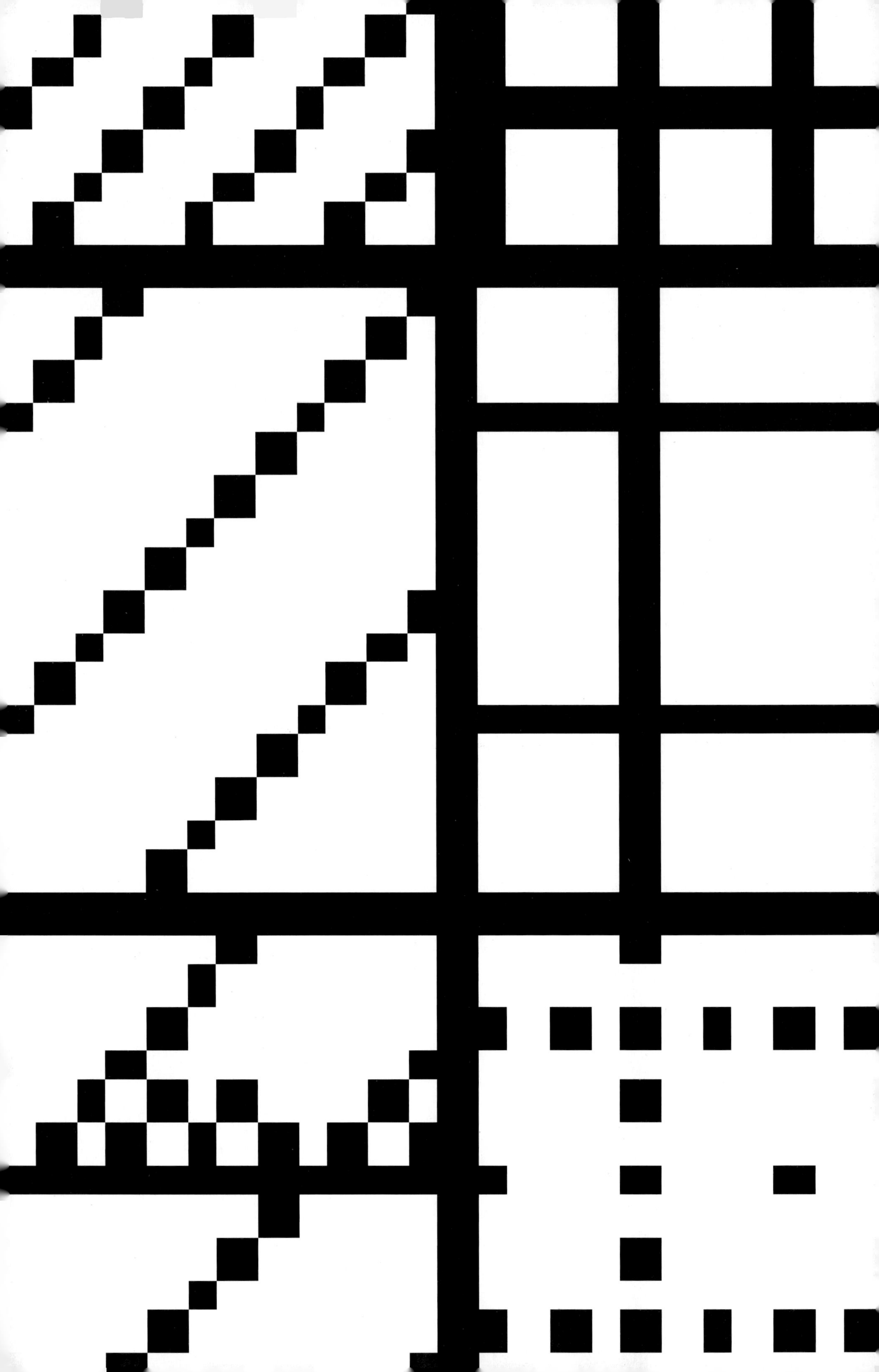

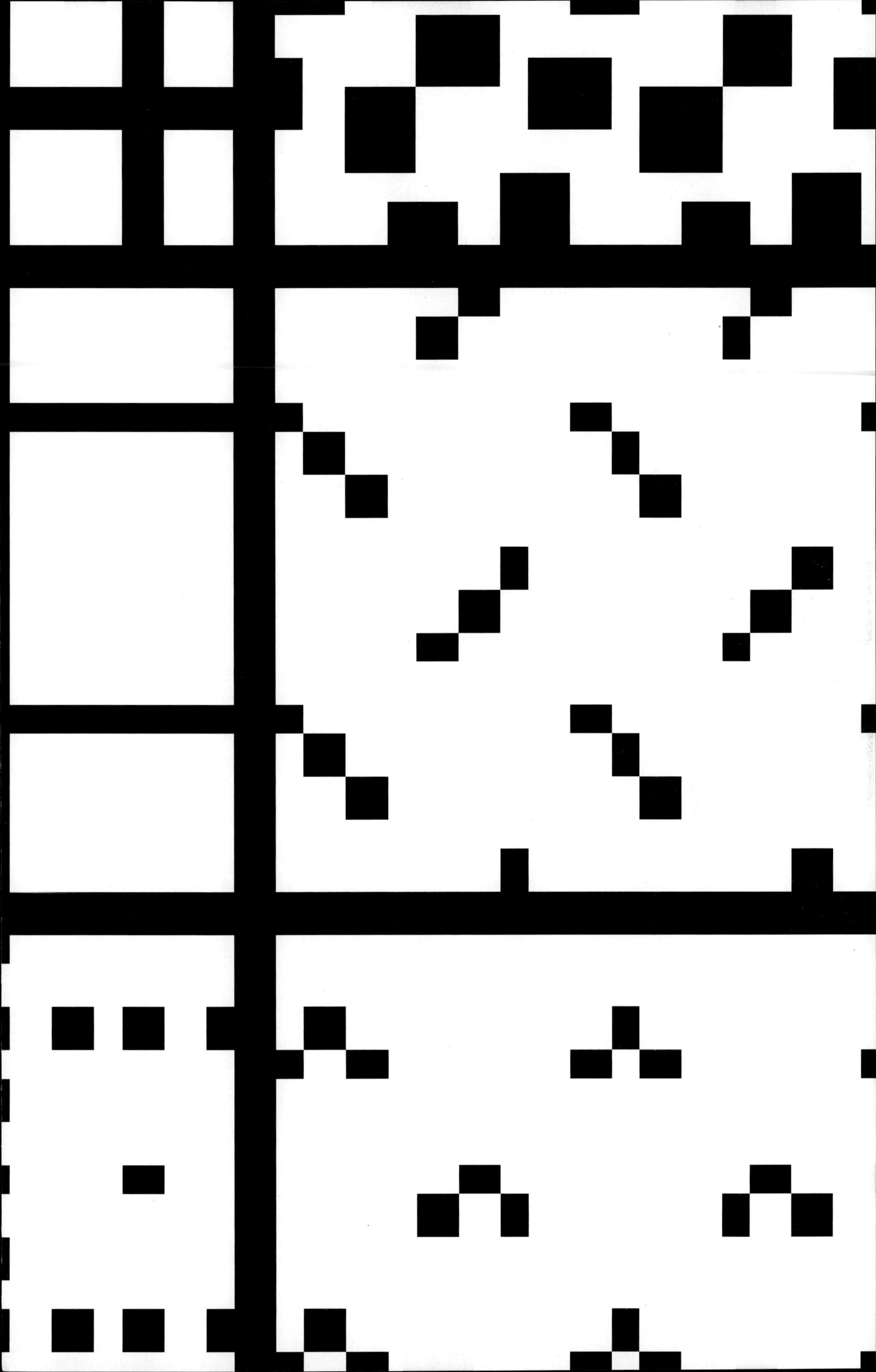

Ten. Algorithms and Artificial Intelligence

Artificial intelligence (AI) has long been more of an aspirational goal than an absolute when it comes to digital design and culture. This situation has made the term a murky one, as there are gaps between what different groups mean when they proclaim something as an example of AI. The digital iterations of artificial intelligence can generally be traced back to the legendary computer scientist Alan Turing, who published a paper in 1950 called "Computing Machinery and Intelligence." In this essay, Turing proposed a test, the aptly named Turing Test, that could be used to evaluate the success of a given AI. The Turing Test was based on a machine's ability to understand and provide conversation in so-called natural language. A true AI would converse in a way that was indistinguishable from human conversation. Turing's article marked the onset of a great deal of experimental research into the field, including at the 1956 conference, "Dartmouth Summer Research Project on Artificial Intelligence," organized by John McCarthy, where the term "artificial intelligence" became the consensus name for the field. Subsequent decades leading up to the twenty-first century saw much experimental work and incremental progress, but no real breakthroughs.

Not only scientists have contributed to the AI discussion, but multivalent purveyors of popular culture and science fiction have also had their say. The popular culture definition of artificial intelligence has helped to create one model of AI along the lines of Turing's hypothesis: a sentient being that can communicate and problem solve at or above the level of a person. Arthur C. Clarke's HAL 9000 is a perfect embodiment of this genre of AI. According to Clarke's book *2001: A Space Odyssey*, HAL was "born" (or activated) on January 12, 1997 (the film moved the birthday up five years). HAL is sentient and has a perfect grasp of natural language yet at the same time has superior processing power than a human. HAL also exemplifies another key component of AI theory, "machine learning." This term, also coined back in the fifties, refers to a computer that can gradually improve its problem-solving ability and general intelligence, not by being reprogrammed by a human, but through understanding its past experiences. While HAL is networked throughout the environment, like humans, he is made manifest through his eyes, glowing red orbs set into a console (looking suspiciously like today's digital doorbells, hmmm). Finally, HAL's cognitive abilities are wedded to very human flaws, as his emotional life at times impedes his workflow. Sentient AIs such as HAL abound in popular culture, where, like the people they emulate, they can appear as heroes, villains, love interests, conflicted protagonists, and the like.

Perhaps the closest real-life example of a sentient AI in popular culture came in the form of Watson (figure 10.1), a 2011 IBM supercomputer that appeared on the game show *Jeopardy!*. In this contest against two human former champions, Watson showcased an ability to understand and speak natural language, while accessing data that allowed it to answer general questions quickly and reliably. Watson also benefited from machine learning and eventually won the game despite some glaring errors caused by misunderstanding a given question's context. The "face" of Watson had been designed by Joshua Davis as an animated version of IBM's 2008 Smarter Planet logo (the original logo was designed by Philippe Intraligi). Strikingly, the

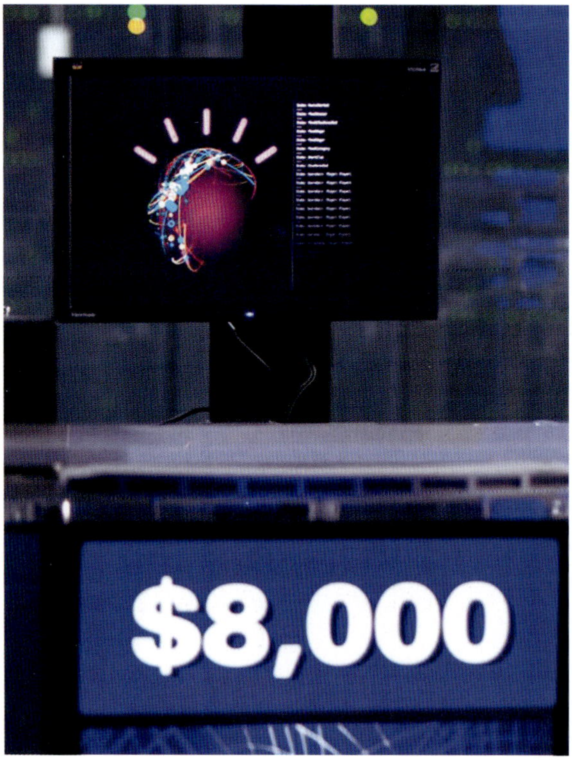

10.1. Joshua Davis's "face" design on the IBM Watson computer on *Jeopardy!*, 2011

logo was designed not to be expressionless, but to select from twenty-seven variations of color and form that appear in relation to Watson's predicted "confidence" in its answer.

Just as HAL embodied the dream of the sentient AI, Watson highlighted the reality of artificial intelligence: algorithms. Watson and other AIs are not sentient; they are in fact running problem-solving programs that depend on quickly sorting vast amounts of data to arrive at a result. A note on algorithms: although algorithms have been a part of mathematics for time immemorial, the term first appeared in the modern sense—a predefined set of computations that form a sorting mechanism—in the twelfth century. At that time in Europe, works by the ninth-century Persian mathematician Muḥammad ibn Mūsā al-Khwārizmī were first translated into Latin. In particular, the book *Algoritmi de Numero Indorum* (roughly "al-Khwārizmī on the Hindu Art of Reckoning") led to the European understanding of Hindu-Arabic numerals, decimals, and a great deal of algebra. The translator of this book used a transliterated spelling of al-Khwārizmī's name as Algoritmi, which eventually led to the coining of the new words "algorithm" and "algebra."

Algorithms really came into their own with the arrival of the digital age. The basis of all things digital from search engines to Snapchat, the history of algorithms also played a role in the establishment of computer science as an academic discipline. Maarten Bullynck has noted how the early works of computer scientists, such as Donald Knuth's *The Art of Computer Programming* (1973), sought to embed their new profession into the history of mathematics. Knuth wrote, "One of the ways to help make computer science respectable is to show that it is deeply rooted in history."

While functioning more like calculators than people, computers such as Watson have become capable of almost instantaneously implementing myriad algorithms on a vast trove of data, and they have therefore become able to simulate the intelligence and general knowledge of a sentient machine. At the same time, multiple researchers are trying to build AI systems that are human centered and project sensitive rather than dominating. Fei-Fei Li, a professor of computer science at Stanford who specializes in AI, has stated, "If everybody thinks we're building Terminators, of course we're going to miss many people." Li worries that this aggressive image has led fewer women to work in AI, which has reinforced the notion that the field consists of men making dangerous machines. Li has sought to collaborate with scholars in other fields, such as psychology, to find ways to design algorithms that are more human centered.

The fear of sentient machines has been a consistent trope throughout industrial history. In 1935, for example, the famed American poet

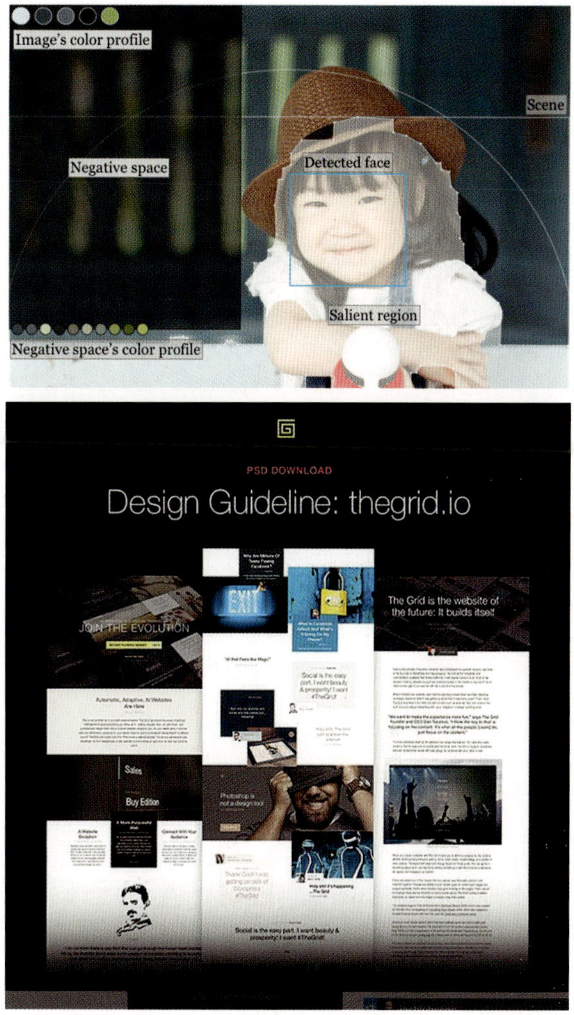

10.2. The Grid website, 2014

Stephen Vincent Benet published "Nightmare Number 3" in the *New Yorker* magazine. Also known as the "Revolt of the Machines," this poem offered a tragicomic vision of artificial intelligence run amok: "It was only the best machines, of course, the superhuman machines / The ones we'd built to be better than flesh and bone, but the cars were in it, of course. . . . And it's fair enough, I suppose. You see, we built them / We taught them to think for themselves. / It was bound to come. You can see it was bound to come." Benet's dark vision of technological progress is usually interpreted as a reaction to the economic struggles and rise of fascism of the thirties. While correlation is rarely causation, it is interesting to note how few dystopic visions react to contemporary digital culture. Perhaps because the digital world—despite two financial crises affecting the industry (2000 and 2008)—has merrily thrived in a historically strong economic and societal situation across the developed world, there has been little consternation among the digerati. The generalized "gee whiz" lust for riches and new wizardry remains unchecked; from the nineties printed pages of *Wired* to the latest social media filter, a consistent sense that "in five years" a given technology will transform life for the better or, at the very least, become a $100 billion industry, remains the word on the street.

Many design projects today that are branded as using artificial intelligence are more aptly described as examples of algorithmic culture. For example, the web design company the Grid launched to much fanfare in 2014 as a purveyor of websites that would be designed by thinking machines (figure 10.2). "The Grid harnesses the power of artificial intelligence to take everything you throw at it—videos, images, texts, urls and more—and automatically shape them into a custom website unique to you. . . . What's possible when an AI does all the hard work for you." To make the process more relatable while also suggesting that one is working with a higher intelligence, the Grid's interface features Molly, the skilled AI designer who is at work on your website. The idea behind the Grid is a powerful one in comparison to a standard template DIY shop. Molly will analyze the palette and composition of your uploaded images and avoid startlingly poor design choices that the average

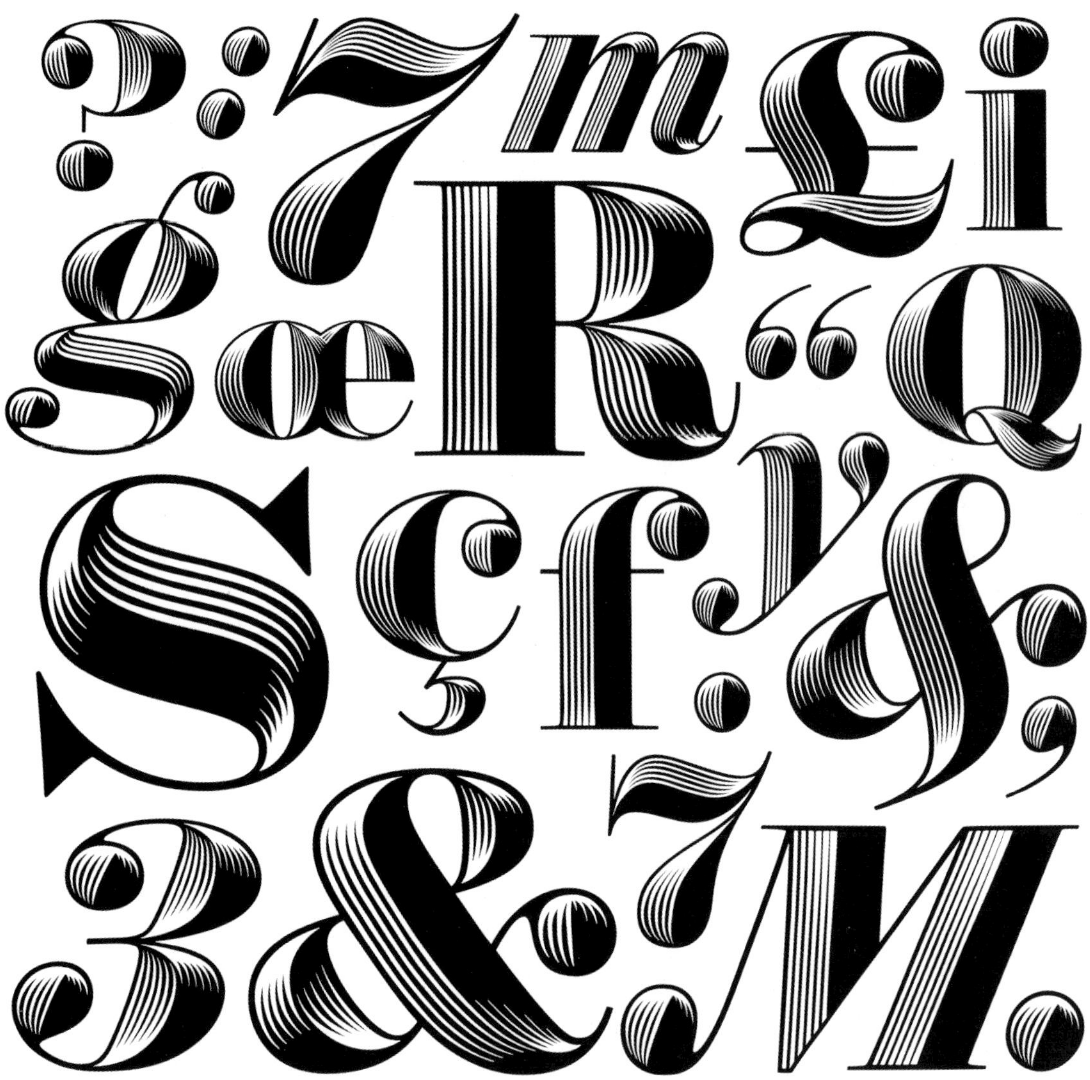

10.3. Adelia Lim, *Machine-Made, Human Assembled* Float typeface, 2018

small business owner (the target customer) might make on their own initiative. As with many products that are branded as artificial intelligence, however, there is a gap between what the term conveys to most people—think Molly as HAL—and the reality of a system where your content is being processed by algorithms, not curated by an omniscient digital machine.

Artificial intelligence has also shown promise as a facilitator of hybrid projects, whereby a machine and its human colleague work together. Often the designer's role is to create the algorithm—to set things in motion—while the resulting work is devised by a machine. Such was the case with Adelia Lim's experimental typography project *Machine-Made, Human Assembled* (figure 10.3, 2018). A recent graduate of the Glasgow School of Art/Singapore Institute of Technology, as global a program as one can find, Lim used Ben Fry and Casey Reas's open source Processing language to devise her project. Machine-Made is a group of typefaces created as a result of Lim's collaboration with a machine. One of the typefaces, Float, is a motion-tracking project whereby the AI uses its camera to follow a specific color and place white dots on the path created by the movement of a gesture. Lim has written, "The project aims to challenge and redefine the role of the designer—from one that is directly involved in formal aesthetic choices to one that simply indicates the ingredients and margins and allows a somewhat autonomous system to work out the consequences of those possible decisions."

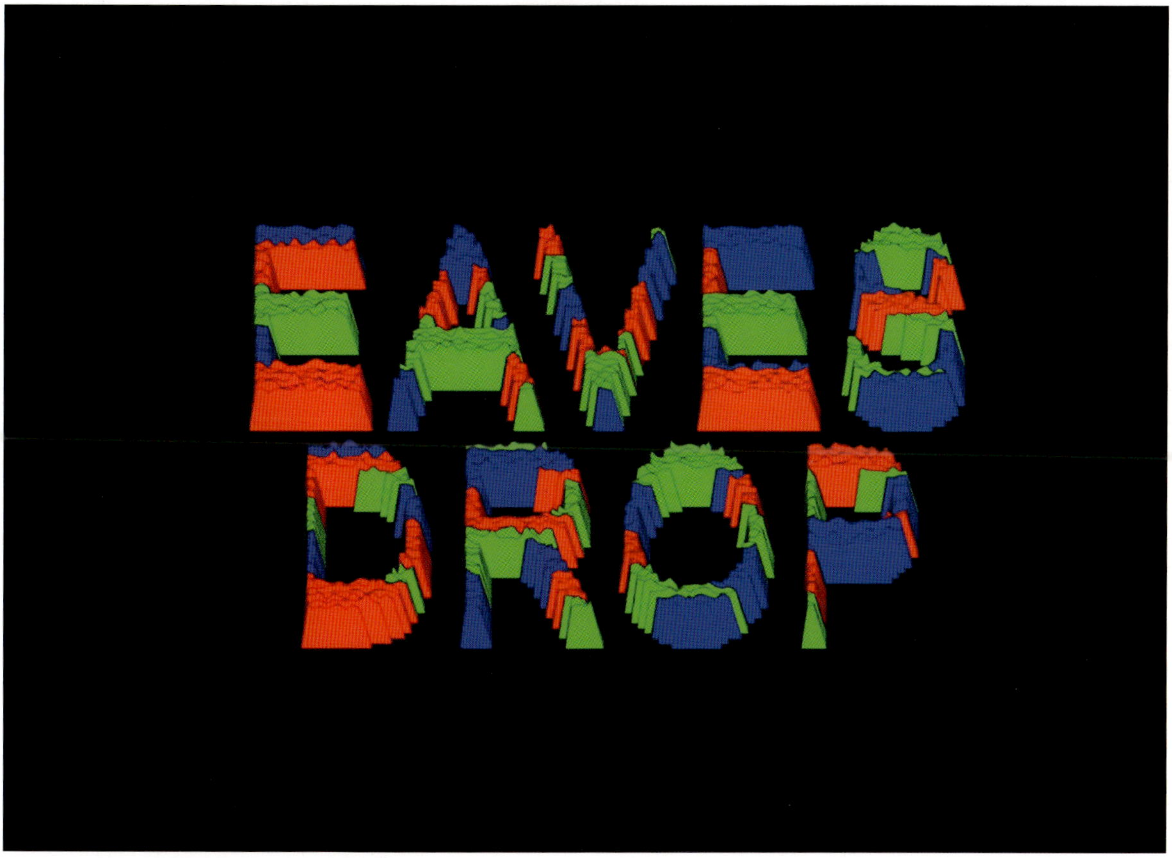

10.4. Andy Clymer's Obsidian typeface, 2015

Algorithmic type can also play an important role as a time saver in the design of type. For example, when Hoefler & Company wanted to make a three-dimensional variation of the decorative typeface Surveyor, they turned to algorithms to facilitate the process. Surveyor is a historicist type based on nineteenth-century engraved maps. The designer at Hoefler, Andy Clymer, wanted to make a shaded version but recognized that the labor involved would not be economically sensible. A company blog notes that shadowing the letters of a serpentine typeface such as Surveyor was incredibly arduous by hand (in the sense of hand and RoboFont software), as an "ampersand alone would require the designer to draw and coordinate 284 different curves, defined by placing more than 1,100 points." Coded in Python (a programming language first written in the late eighties by Guido van Rossum), algorithms were able to dramatically cut the amount of time necessary to produce the new font. This is not to say that the new typeface was simply spit out by a machine, but rather that the hundreds of hours saved in processing the basic forms allowed Clymer to devote himself to the finer details of the letters. The resulting work, called Obsidian (figure 10.4, 2015), quickly became available as a large character set that supports more than one hundred languages. Marian Bantjes opined in a review, "This is the typeface you want to sit next to at a dinner table."

No artist or designer has built a more intimate relationship with AI than the composer and computer scientist Holly Herndon. Born in the United States but based today in Berlin, Herndon considers her most recent album, *PROTO* (2019), to be a collaborative effort that includes her AI "baby" Spawn. Herndon refers to Spawn with female pronouns, speaking of the neural network as if she were part of the human group—producers, programmers, and chorus members—that worked on the album. Through machine learning, Spawn has been taught to recognize and respond to the human voices on the recording. *PROTO*'s electronic folk sound can be haunting and even uncanny, especially if a listener attempts to parse out the human and machine contributions. The title of the album refers to protocols in the digital sense as the algorithmic building blocks that facilitate communication. Herndon wants to communicate the human side of technology through Spawn, noting, "There's a pervasive narrative of technology as dehumanizing,... I don't want to live in a world where humans are automated off stage. I want an AI to be raised to appreciate and interact with that beauty."

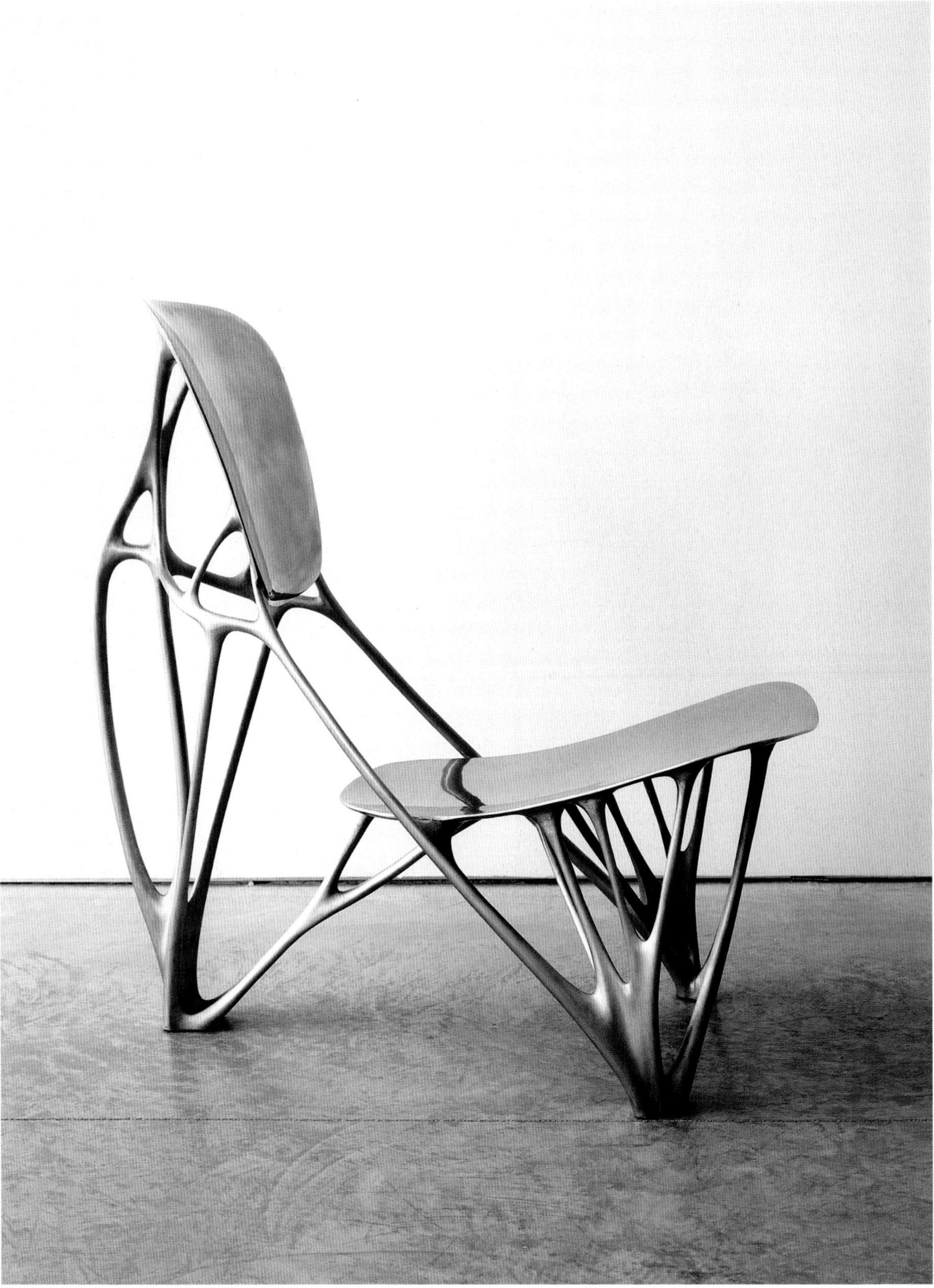

10.5. Joris Laarman, *Bone Chair*, 2006

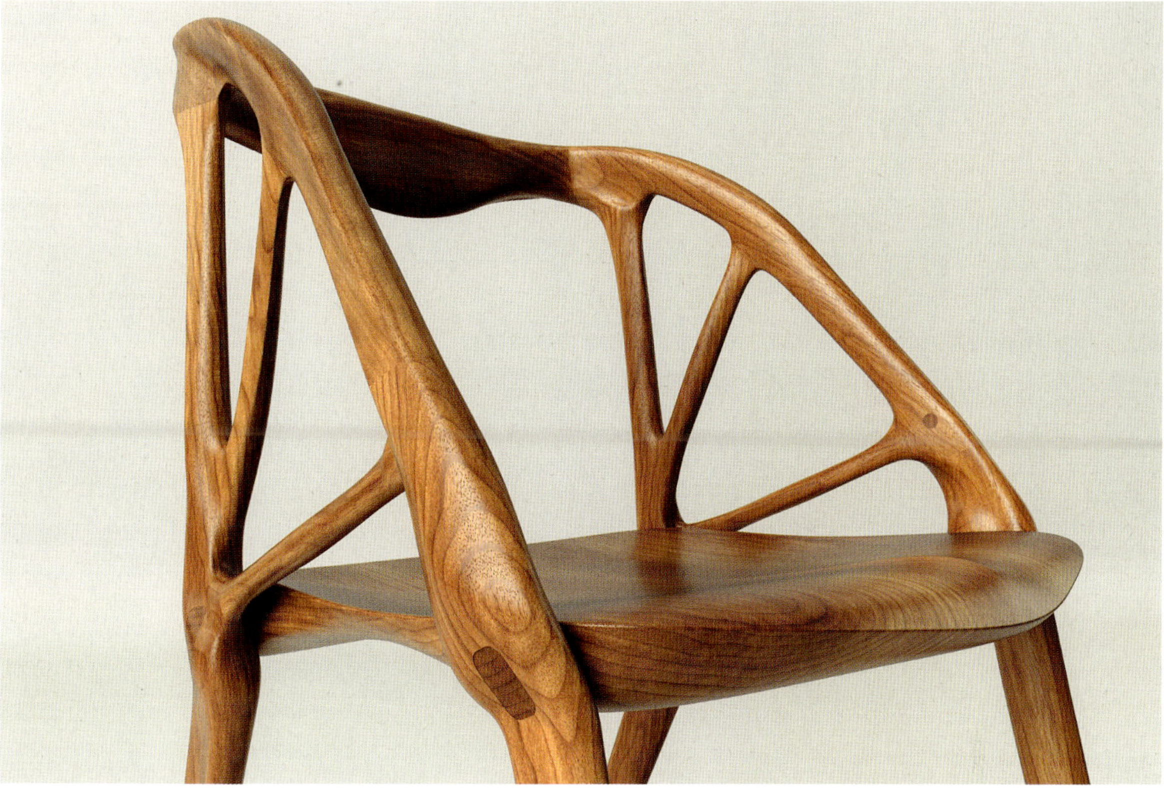

10.6. Arthur Harsuvanakit and Brittany Presten, *Elbo Chair*, 2016

In the field of industrial design, probably the most influential breakthrough regarding algorithmic, or generative, creation came through Joris Laarman's 2006 *Bone Chair* (figure 10.5). As has often been the case, Laarman created this work through adapting an algorithmic process first used by industry to design automobile parts. Specifically, he became aware of how the German company Adam Opel used algorithms to find out what was the most efficient shape for a given mechanical part. The company had sought to find the optimal blend of strength and weight for certain car parts. In pursuit of this outcome, Adam Opel used algorithms to identify superfluous material that could be cut out of the part without compromising its integrity. In emulating this process, Laarman used a parametric strategy whereby he defined certain points—the basic chair shape of seat and back and three legs—and allowed the algorithm to complete the design.

One way in which Laarman's *Bone Chair* transcends the realm of industry and enters a more conceptual space is through his recognition that this specific algorithm emulated the natural process of bone formation. The *Bone Chair* hybridizes technical sophistication and the biological traits of living organisms. For Laarman, this placed the chair firmly in the historical context of modern design. Just as artisans of the nineteenth century and art nouveau sought to emulate the beauty of natural forms, Laarman sought to digitally encode a natural process into his work.

The advances in software of recent years now allow pretty much any designer to outsource the design to a machine. In 2006 Laarman, like Frank Gehry before him in the architectural context, had to rely on access to specialized industrial software to complete his work. In 2016, Arthur Harsuvanakit and Brittany Presten could pursue the same sort of parametric project with an off-the-shelf CAD program. Harsuvanakit and Presten work for Autodesk, and their *Elbo Chair* (figure 10.6) represented a demonstration of that company's Dreamcatcher program. Dreamcatcher is a beta "generative design" program, meaning that the designers input a few parameters and then allow algorithms to complete the work. Autodesk offers the program as not just a tool but a creative partner, suggesting that the software may assist designers who finds themselves short on ideas: "design alternatives—many that you'd never think of on your own."

Both the *Bone* and the *Elbo* chairs point to a limiting factor in digital furniture design; the desire to execute projects in metal (*Bone Chair*) or wood (*Elbo Chair*). Neither of these pieces could

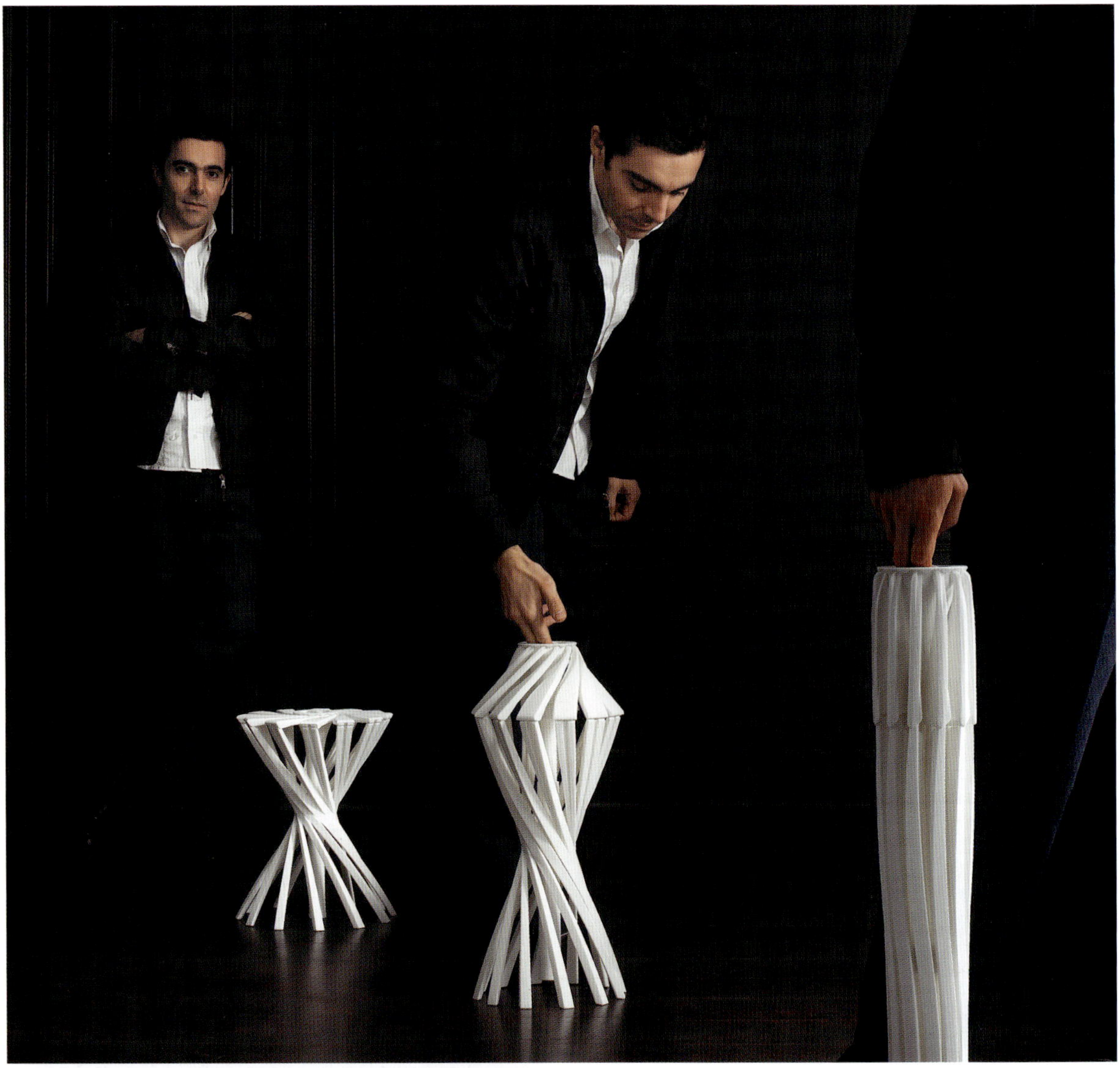

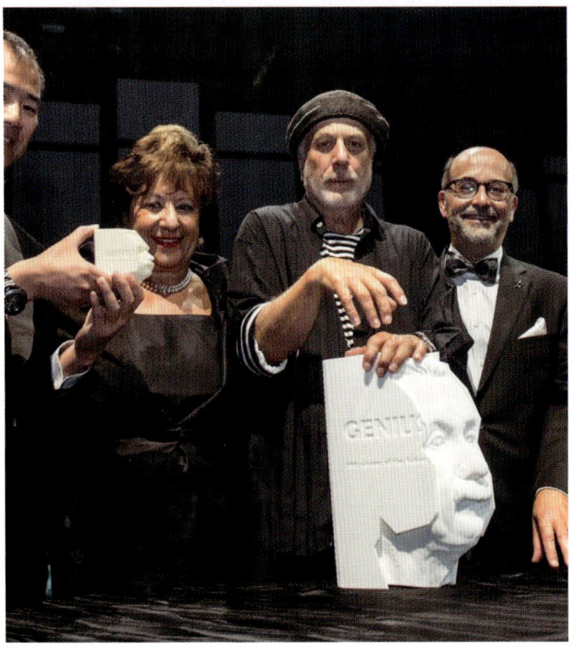

10.7. Patrick Jouin, *One Shot Stool*, 2006
10.8. Ron Arad's 3D-printed *Genius: 100 Visions of the Future*, 2017

be manufactured with a 3D printer, the logical, economical final step. The *Bone Chair* was cast by hand in aluminum, while the *Elbo* was carved out of wood using a CNC machine. Although the laser sintering process can print with metal, it is still mainly an industrial technique that is extremely costly. Sintering of polyamide resins to form plastic, however, has been successfully implemented in the work of Patrick Jouin. His *One Shot Stool* (figure 10.7, 2006) highlighted how 3D printing could simplify the productions of complex compositions. It was formed as just one piece yet can be folded along hinged elements integrated into the work. The *One Shot Stool* was created as part of the MGX project at Materialise, a company devoted to bringing 3D printing to the consumer market. While the technology is admirable, to a certain degree it has stalled out because of materials; few people want furniture made out of nylon resin as opposed to wood or metal. In addition, using 3D printing for invisible parts of furniture—in, for example, a structure finished with cloth or leather—makes little economic sense as yet because conventional manufacturing is less costly and widely available. Works like the *One Shot Stool* are aimed at the high-end design trade, not the broader consumer market, as the piece retails today for over $2,500 despite the relatively low cost of its manufacture.

As 3D printing became a hot, stylish process in the 2010s, at times it has looked like a solution seeking a problem. For example, in 2017 legendary industrial design Ron Arad was commissioned to design a 3D-printed book. The book, a compendium of visionary projections titled *Genius: 100 Visions of the Future* (figure 10.8), was not a commercial product per se but a limited-edition object created in celebration of the centenary of Albert Einstein's general theory of relativity. As a physical object, the book was shaped so that the unbound edge forms a likeness of Einstein's face.

Computational design has also affected the design of running shoes. Nike has taken to using algorithms to make size-specific alterations to its sneakers. The algorithms can be programmed to tweak the sole for any number of combinations of speed, stability, traction, and so forth. In a strategy similar to that pursued by Laarman for his *Bone Chair*, the algorithm can also remove material that it recognizes as superfluous to the shoe's performance goals. For a company that has been estimated to sell twenty-five pairs of shoes per second, the cost savings and related environmental advantages of removing a small amount of material are immense. This type of algorithmic customization is currently ramping up, and soon individuals will be able to wear bespoke trainers that have been computationally designed.

Another striking example of the potential outcome of generative designers using, in this case, Ben Fry's algorithmic Processing system came in the form of the experimental project Komorebi (figure 10.9). Representing the graduate work of designer Leslie Nooteboom, Komorebi consists of a programmable digital projector mounted on a base. In urban homes where natural sunlight may be at a premium, Komorebi is able to provide a variable simulation of natural light. Users would be able to program specific light effects, evoking, for example, the dappled sunlight of a forest scene. This is another example of computer technology that is personable and seeks to clasp rather than distance people from the digital.

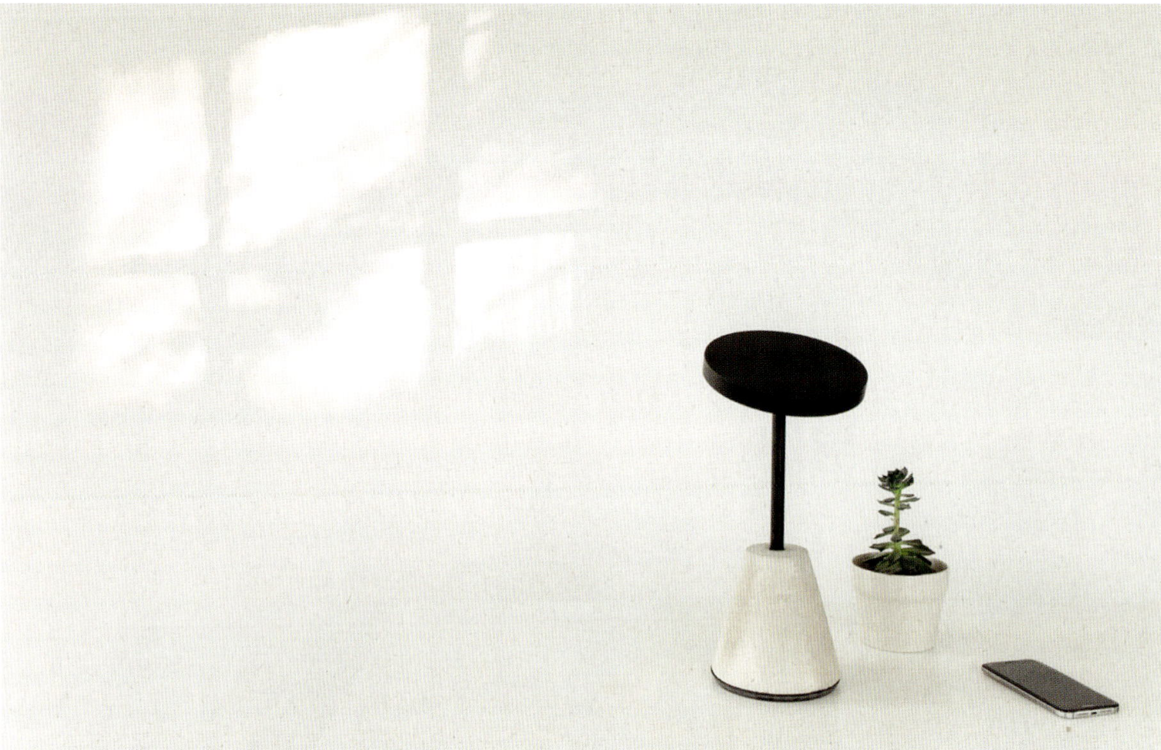

10.9. Leslie Nooteboom, Komorebi lamp, 2017

Algorithms that can distribute light or design a chair and shoes have also caught the attention of the art world. In 2018, the three-person collective Obvious presented their machine-learning piece *Portrait of Edmond de Belamy* (figure 10.10). Part of a larger series of portraits of the imaginary Belamy family designed by a generative process, *Portrait of Edmond de Belamy* looks like any of thousands of relatively indistinguishable portraits of the moneyed elite one might find in an obscure national gallery. It could be a representative example of art from any number of European countries of the past few centuries. The Paris-based members of Obvious have explained that the work was generated by a pair of algorithms. The first crunched the data—scans of thousands of European portrait paintings. The second algorithm was tasked with combing through the result. The resulting *Portrait of Edward de Belamy* is not signed by the artists but by the machine: "min G max D EX [log (D(x))] + Ez [log(1 – D (G(z)))]."

The artificial intelligence behind this project is called a generative adversarial network (GAN), and the code was first released in 2014 by Google engineer Ian Goodfellow. A GAN can be used for advanced machine learning, and is one of the components in the creation of "deepfakes," digitally derived photographs that cannot be recognized as such by the human eye. *Portrait of Edward de Belamy* is in a sense a deepfake of an oil painting, as it was printed and framed so that it appears to be a rough, unfinished study for a portrait. Google has also dabbled in the algorithmic art space, with projects that include DeepDream, which creates new artworks out of fluid, surreal mash-ups of photographs. DeepDream, part of the Google Magenta experimental lab, is an example of a "deep neural network," a biological metaphor that refers to advanced machine learning using discriminative algorithms to essentially check the work of the generative ones, teaching the GAN to better its capabilities through critical feedback. Another Magenta program, David Ha's modestly titled Sketch-RNN, features a deep neural network that has learned to draw after analyzing big data, in this case a series of human-created artworks.

One factor that unites both Silicon Valley and the upper echelon of the art world is the ability to market and monetize innovation. While Google has employed GAN for its facial recognition and sorting capabilities to improve the company's photo apps and Google Assistant, the members of Obvious have tapped into the cash stream channeled by contemporary art auctions. In October 2018, *Portrait of Edmond de Belamy* was offered for sale in New York City at Christie's, and it sold for $432,500, hundreds of thousands of dollars above its initial estimate. Notably, the portrait's success is based on how it elegantly conflated cutting-edge technology and a tangible product—it is a painting

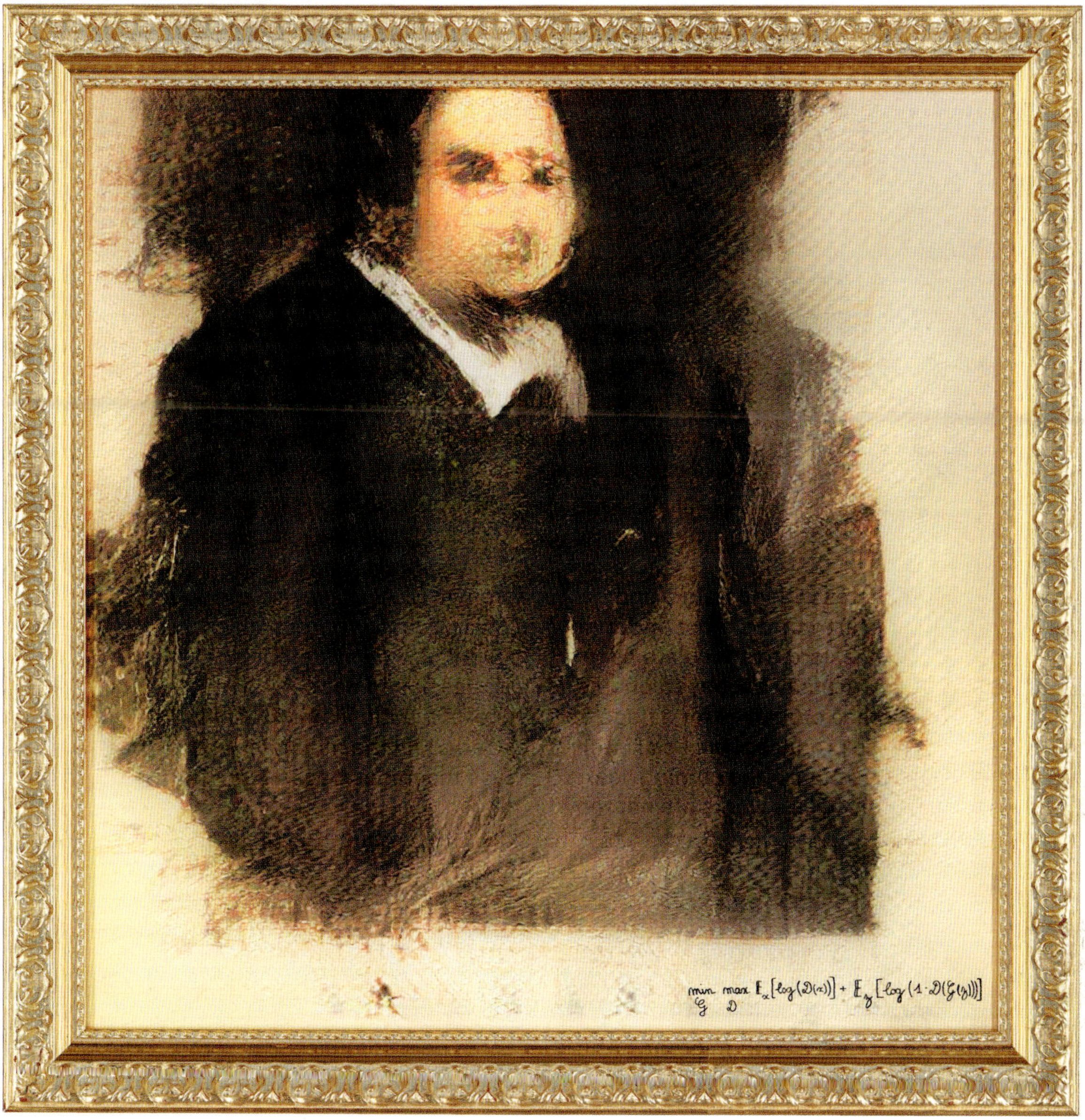

10.10. Obvious, *Portrait of Edmond de Belamy*, 2018

after all—that resonates with nostalgia and has proved to be the art world's most enduring commodity. While it is hard to speculate as to what the future of AI art may be, based on this result, we should brace ourselves for a flood of works branded as the product of artificial intelligence to appear at auction in the coming years. DALL-E's and Sketch-RNN's works are not too far behind.

Another dimension of generative design—interrogating identity—appears in the work of Yeohyun Ahn. A professor of graphic design at the University of Wisconsin, Ahn's algorithmic typography responds to "her sense of invisibility as a woman of color and as an immigrant." Ahn began her series *Selfie + Code* in 2015, using Processing and Ricard Marxer's Geomerative library to blend the ubiquitous selfie with expressive typography. The works' deconstructed, calligraphic lines blur the designer's identity while projecting diverse emotional states.

Digital design, with its complex technical demands, would seem in many ways to spell the demise of the amateur, DIY lifestyle. While analog crafts such as woodworking offer obvious space for the hobbyist, digital design demands specialized software that is built to serve professionals. The will to create has overcome these obstacles, however, and today a thriving culture of DIY design makes use of new digital tools. Probably the breakthrough product was the consumer 3D printer, a device that is understandable to anyone with basic computer skills. The key technology behind many 3D printers is stereolithography, an additive process whereby a three-dimensional form is built up out of thin layers. It was first patented in the eighties. Stereolithographic printers (known by the acronym SLA) make use of photopolymers, liquid acrylics that harden on exposure to ultraviolet light. A rival system, also invented in the eighties, fused deposition modeling uses a spool of plastic filament that is melted and extruded by the machine. About a decade ago, these machines became financially and technologically accessible to hobbyists. Costing as little as a few hundred dollars, the craft world's "makerspaces" today feature a sea afloat with millions of iterations of 3DBenchy (for "benchmark"), the little boat that many 3D printers use for initial calibration. For those who desire a more complex machine and have deeper pockets, companies such as Materialise now also accept paid commissions from DIY designers.

Beyond basic 3D printing, DIY culture has spawned an ecosystem of hardware and software services that enable more advanced projects. Utilizing Creative Commons and GNU open source licensing, websites such as Thingiverse contain vast repositories of design templates. The DIY community in many ways still embraces the inspirational, even utopian spirit, of the early computer age—think GeoCities—so designs and ideas are freely communicated, disrupting the "monetization" at the heart of Silicon Valley culture. It is common in the digital hobbyist world to admire a template or block of code online and ask the author to add something new to their design. In this way, people with different skill levels and experience can be a part of the scene, be they veteran coders, designers, or rank novices.

Autodesk, the company known for its CAD software, has been a willing partner of the DIY community. Their free web-based app Tinkercad is an accessible way to get involved in DIY

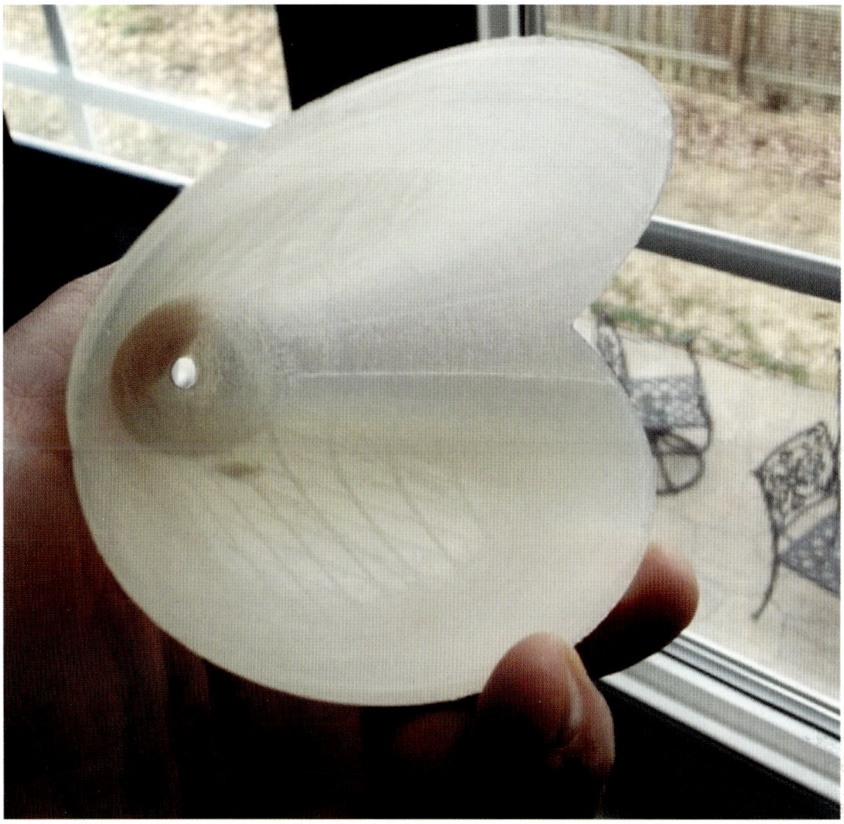

10.11. Gary Walker, Bauhaus-inspired USB lamp on Thingiverse, 2019

design. Tinkercad is widely used in schools as a way of introducing students to coding and CAD. For more advanced hobbyists, Autodesk also offers free licenses of its sophisticated Fusion360 software. Fusion360 is a cloud-based program used mainly by industry professionals and runs the gamut of acronyms: CAD, CAE (engineering), and CAM (manufacturing). For those capable of mastering its intricacies, a basement workshop can have the same tools as a professional design studio.

Finally, one of the essential products of digital DIY culture is the Arduino, a micro controller that is paired with open source software. The Arduino hardware was first invented around 2003 by Italian university students seeking an inexpensive controller for their digital projects. Since the initial board was released a few years later, a global community of hobbyists has built a countless number of sensors, motors, and the like, while others have produced vast amounts of code. Today web platforms such as GitHub—founded in 2008 and acquired by Microsoft in 2018—are replete with libraries and code that are freely downloadable and allow hobbyists to use an Arduino as the basis for an astonishing range of projects.

Putting all these tools together, a DIY designer can, for example, design a lamp from scratch: First, download templates from Thingiverse, design an additional part with Tinkercad, and print all the parts on a 3D device. Next, download code from GitHub for the Arduino, attach the board to a bank of LEDs, and, voilà, you have fabricated a Bauhaus-inspired USB lamp (figure 10.11). In essence, digital hobbyists today are far closer to simulating the realm of, say, Jonathan Ive at Apple than they ever could have been in the predigital industrial age. The internet has facilitated access to design strategies and technical knowledge in a way never before thought possible. The designer of the aforementioned lamp on Thingiverse goes by the screen name gewalker (né Gary Walker), and his description of the project offers an inside look at the supportive, human-centered element of digital DIY culture. “This is still very, very much a work in progress. I like to share my source code early, though, and give interested people a chance to mess with it themselves. This is inspired by, but cannot honestly be said to be based on Serge Mouille’s 1957 Tripod Lamp design. Eventually, I hope to have a full kit with links to the electrical parts I’ll use. Update: decided on electronics. The round panel is intended for mounting an Arduino/Adafruit Gemma [a Gemma is a small Arduino-compatible controller] and an array of addressable LEDs on the reverse side.”

Bethany Koby began her career in digital design as a graphic designer and creative director, but she entered the world of digital DIY through a

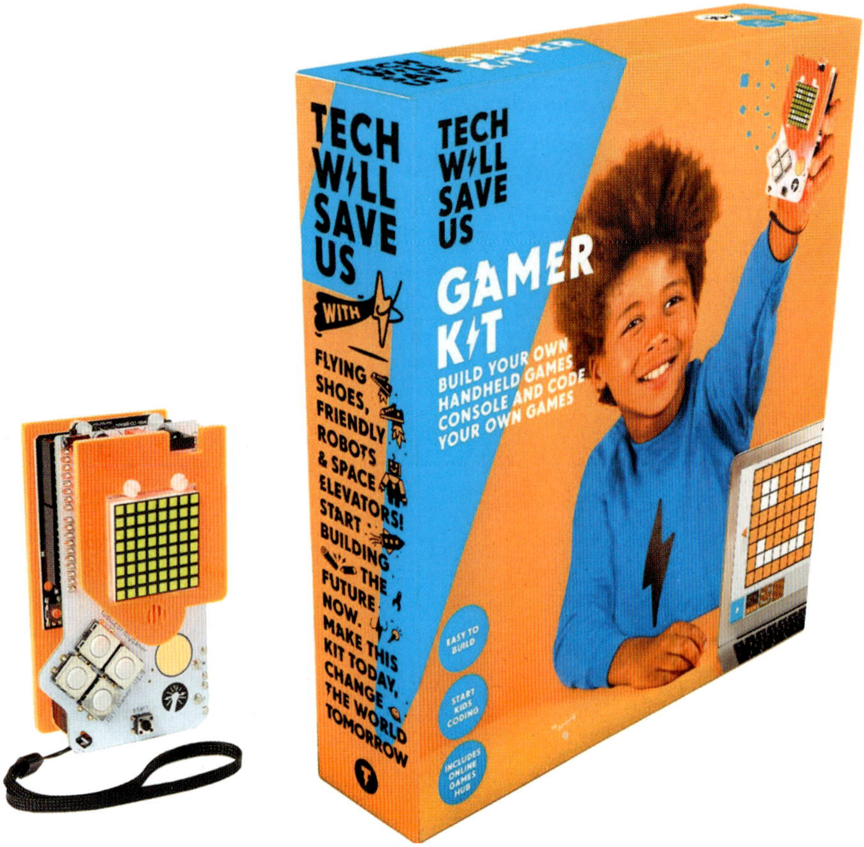

10.12. Bethany Koby's Gamer Kit, 2013

personal experience. Frustrated with the toy industry's offerings for her son, she decided to build a new company that would make technologically sophisticated kits for children. In 2012 she cofounded Technology Will Save Us, a London-based firm whose products attempt to channel technology into a more creative direction. Koby decries the "consumptive experience" that most children have with technology, mesmerized and immersed in screens. Technology Will Save Us makes DIY kits that allow children to assemble electronic components through hands-on techniques such as soldering, while also learning the basics of computer coding. For example, the Gamer Kit (figure 10.12), first released in 2013, combines making and programming, as well as two preloaded video games as well as the tools and instructions to build one's own. In a collaboration with the BBC, Technology Will Save Us—whether the company name holds an ironic undertone is unclear—played a large role in the creation of the micro:bit, an Arduino-like board that can serve as the basis for coding projects. Part of the BBC's Make It Digital campaign, the micro:bit was designed to foster a hands-on understanding of digital technology for students whom Koby has termed the advancing "creator generation."

In Roland Barthes's 1957 critique of consumer culture in *Mythologies*, he opined, "I think that cars today are almost the exact equivalent of the great Gothic cathedrals; I mean the supreme creation of an era, conceived with passion by unknown artists, and consumed in image if not in usage by a whole population which appropriates them as a purely magical object." While automobile companies in the aggregate have been at the forefront of digital design for decades, no brand has fired the imagination of the digerati more than Tesla. Founded in 2003 by digital celebrity and cofounder of PayPal Elon Musk, Tesla successfully sought to make electric vehicles sexy and glamorous with the release of a sporty roadster in 2008. Since that time, the company's sleek vehicles and a cult of personality around Musk have created one of the most powerful digital brands, even though only a tiny sliver of consumers can afford its products.

Barthes was referring to engineers and industrial workers as the passionate "unknown artists" who designed cars at midcentury, but today that anonymous group is joined by the faceless computations of big data and the algorithms that manage them. Tesla cars represent today's apogee of data collection and machine learning (figure 10.13). Especially as the

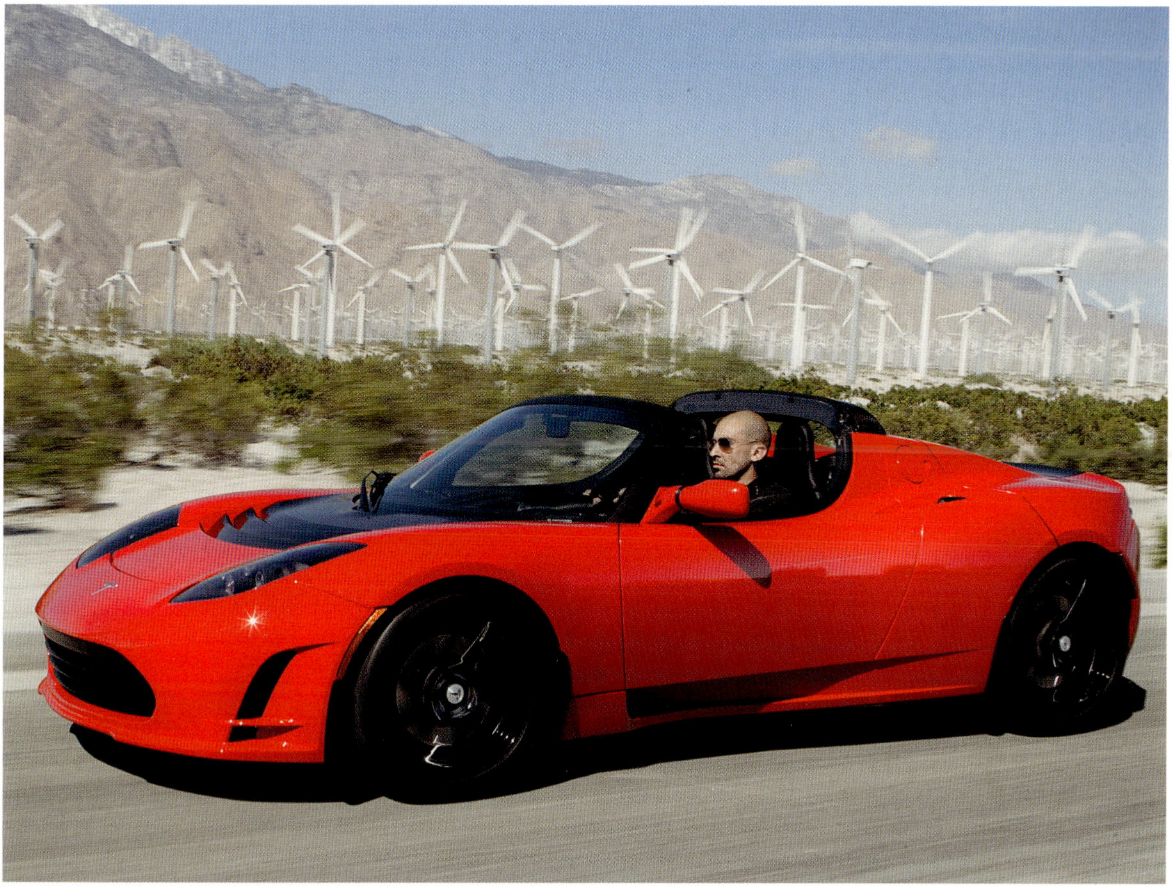

10.13. Tesla Roadster, 2008

company works toward the goal of autonomous vehicles, the myriad sensors on a Tesla collect continual streams of data that are automatically uploaded back to the firm. Front-facing cameras, radar, and other sensors record every mile driven. These networked cars foment machine learning on a massive scale, as algorithmic intelligence works to better the cars' ability to navigate without human input. In pursuit of machine perfection, a Tesla vehicle works more like an app on a smartphone than a conventional product: it is not finished when you drive it off the dealer's lot but will receive software updates continually throughout its useful life.

Perhaps inadvertently, Teslas, like the whole range of smart devices and social media services, have developed the wherewithal to become part of a dystopian surveillance machine. Most consumers choose to ignore the fact that many digital conveniences are based on the collection of big data, and—if they so choose—the machines can record who you are, where you are, and what you are doing moment by moment. Take Google's Clips camera, released in early 2018 (figure 10.14). An elegant little device that looks like the Instagram icon has been made actual, the square video camera "learns to recognize familiar faces." It essentially surveils your pets and family, gradually learning who you interact with the most. As Google emphasized, "it gets smarter over time," which may have been a promise or a threat. The camera was quietly discontinued in 2019. Clips exemplifies the trend toward machine surveillance that is abstract and nebulous for most people; of course, data today are freely given and anonymized when bought and sold, but nonetheless it casts something of a pall over big technology that the digital industries must confront as technology advances. In the autumn of 2018, none other than the CEO of Apple, Tim Cook, came out strongly in favor of greater privacy protections for consumers. "Our own information—from the everyday to the deeply personal—is being weaponized against us with military efficiency. Today, that trade has exploded into a data-industrial complex." Many critics argue that some sort of tipping point that will spark a backlash against data culture is within sight, although complacency continues to rule the day.

Facial recognition is yet another surveillance technology that combines big data and algorithmic processing. The American artist Zach Blas has created works that investigate the impact of facial recognition with a special focus on how vulnerable groups can be targeted

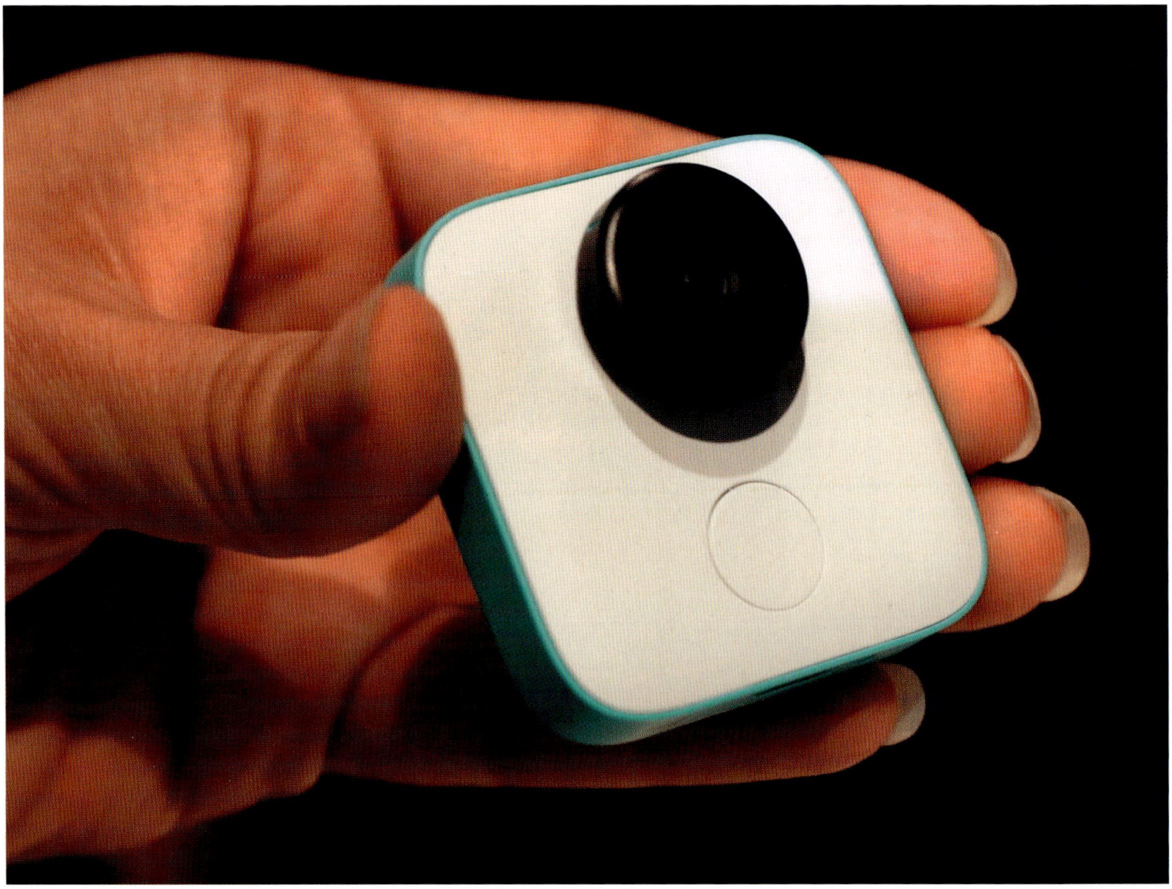

10.14. Google, Clips camera, 2018

by the machines. For example, his *Facial Weaponization Suite* (2011–14) is a meditation on how biometrics can be an instrument of power. Blas subverts recognition by creating masks out of aggregated faces of different groups. His *Fag Face Mask* of 2012 (figure 10.15) consists of a pastiche of queer men's faces that have been digitally scanned; then a CNC machine was used to carve out the work. The resulting mask is purposely grotesque and unreadable via biometric recognition, defying the scientific research that has attempted to link sexual identity to facial features. Of course, masking one's face to resist authority has both a long history and a contemporary presence, as it has been conspicuously revived by self-styled anarchists who favor the Guy Fawkes mask to conceal their identity.

Algorithmic processing is also at the heart of blockchain cryptocurrencies such as Bitcoin (2008) and Ether (2018). The mining of the coins, the "proof-of-work" that verifies the system, and the recording of transactions all depend on algorithmic calculations. Remember that while a blockchain—a type of shared digital ledger book—is mainly associated with exotic virtual currency, it can be easily coded and can be used to catalog the value of just about anything. Combine this fact with the immense semivirtual fortunes that people amassed in the blockchain bubble of 2017–18, and strange and wonderful designs are one result. Such was the case after the launch and stratospheric rise of Ether, a currency tied to the Ethereum blockchain assembled by Vitalik Buterin and launched in 2015.

Cryptocurrency has found itself at the center of the ongoing debate about the environmental impact of the digital world. Virtual currencies, like so much of the digital, seemingly free people from the pollution of industrial manufacturing and landfills. The virtual world's energy consumption, however, is unheralded in the history of new technologies. While estimates vary, the blockchain today uses more than 100 terawatts of electricity per year, a massive amount of power for a technology that has yet to develop a strong raison d'être outside building speculative fortunes for a few early adopters. The digital world is in fact replete with screen-based experiences that feel sustainable but are in fact powered by vast server farms with huge carbon footprints.

As Ether exploded in value as a part of cryptomania, legions of newly minted millionaires and billionaires reveled in their piles of what

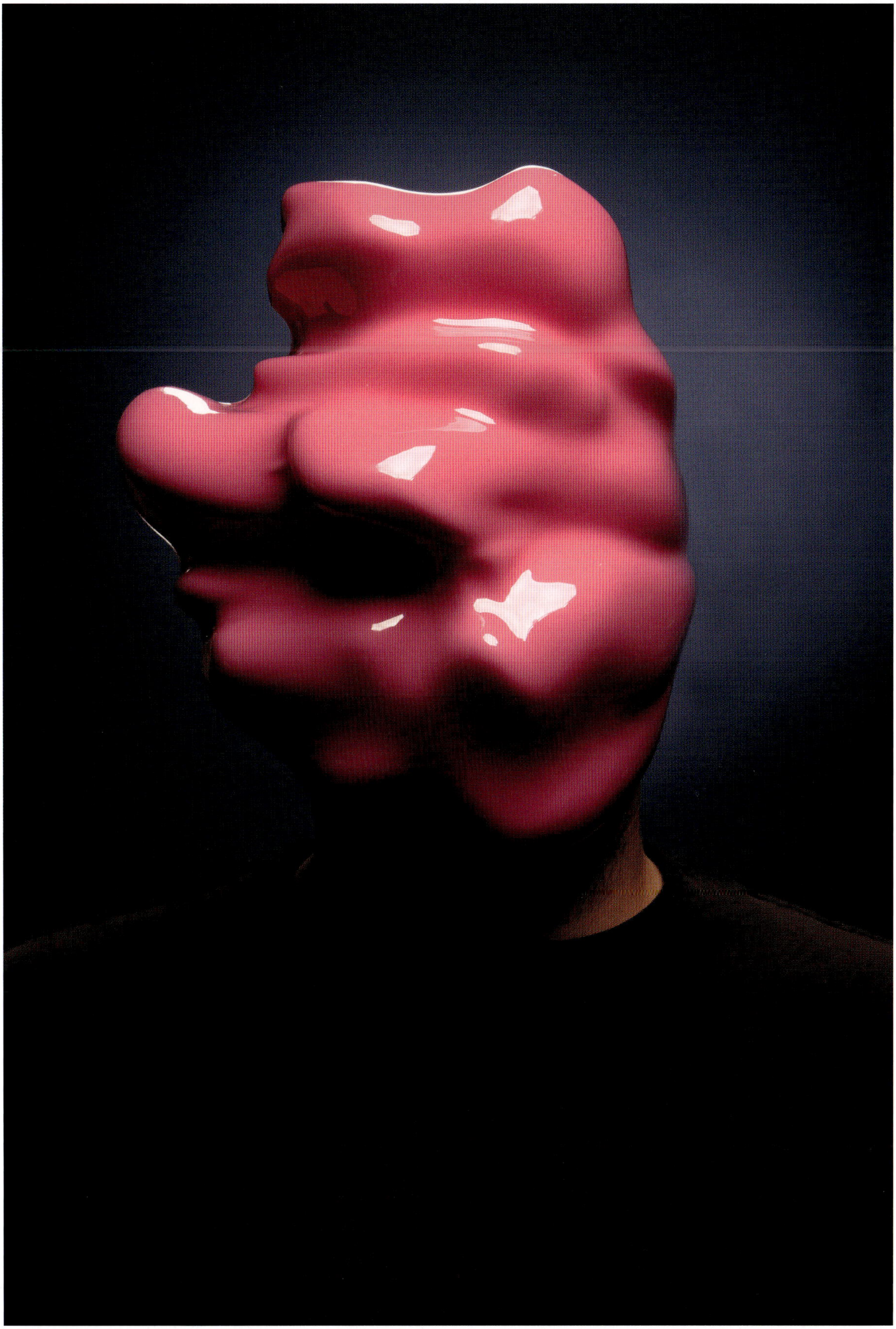

10.15. Zach Blas, *Fag Face Mask*, part of *Facial Weaponization Suite*, 2012

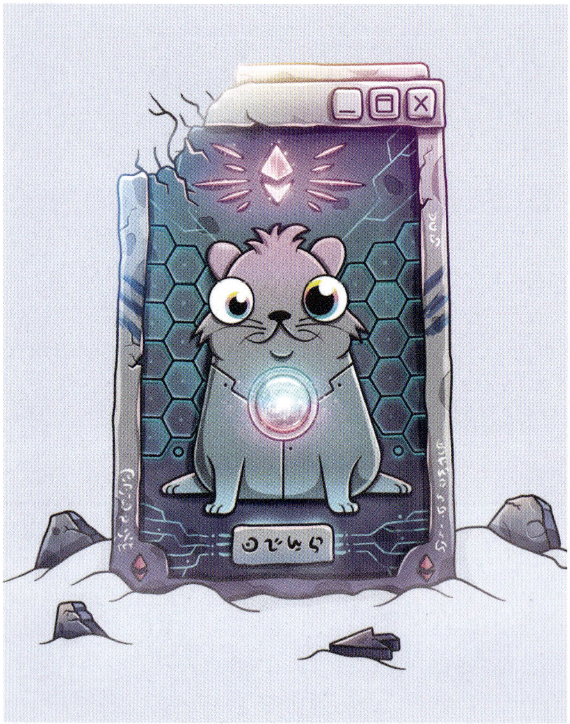

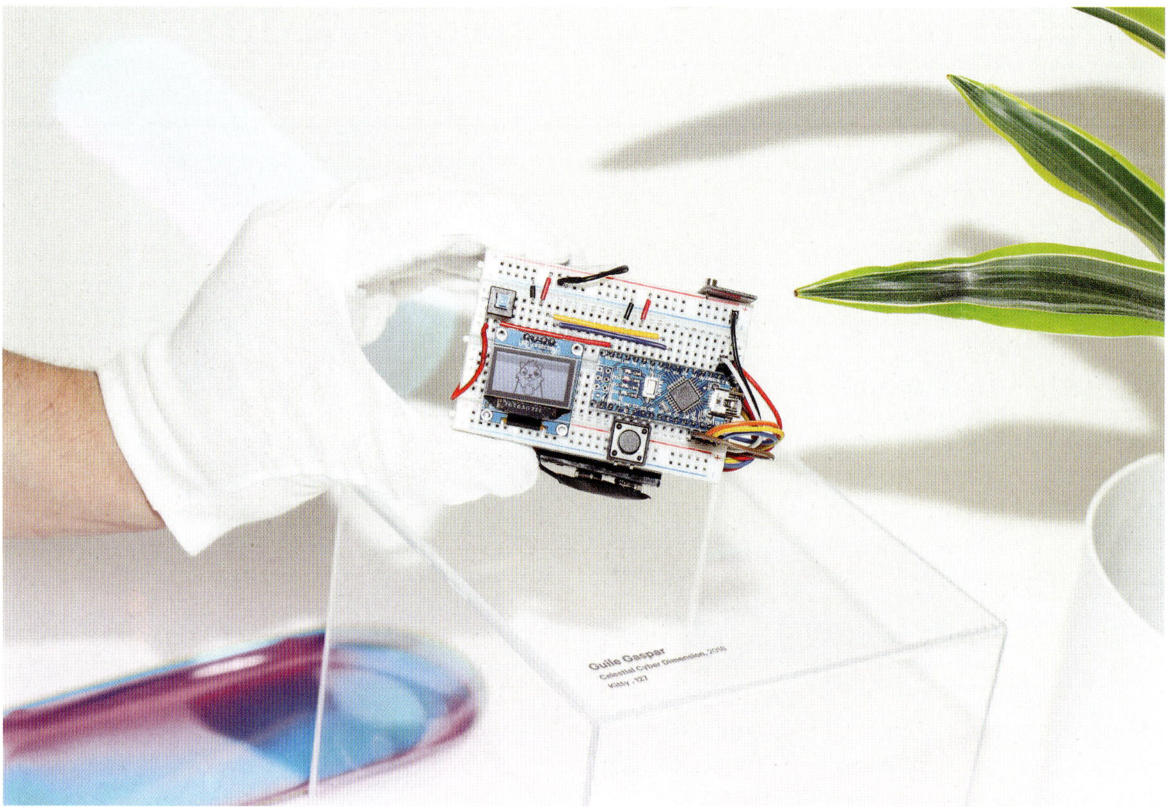

10.16. Guile Gaspar, Celestial Cyber Dimension, 2018
10.17. Guile Gaspar, NFT hardware for Celestial Cyber Dimension, 2018

surely felt somewhat like the house's money. Additionally, they felt loyalty to the blockchain that had enriched them. And CryptoKitties was born. As one of the cofounders of the feline-themed blockchain explained, "We're just like, man, people want cats." Within a few months the CryptoKitties blockchain had recorded over $20 million in Ether transactions of virtual cats, some costing more than $100,000. Unlike their not-so-distant digital ancestor, the Tamagotchi, CryptoKitties are not demanding, just cute. While feline, CryptoKitties can also be bred like racehorses, and certain early, desirable cats have garnered stud fees of more than $20,000.

In what appeared at one time as peak hubris in the cryptocurrency boom, in the spring of 2018 a CryptoKitty sold at a charity auction for $140,000. Designed by the art director at CryptoKitties, Guilherme Twardowski (aka Guile Gaspar), the work once again showed how virtual designs often betray a hunger for hardware. The virtual pet, called Celestial Cyber Dimension, is purple and as wide eyed as an anime character, wearing a glowing orb necklace (figure 10.16). But Celestial is not just virtual, as the auction offered a piece of hardware complete with an ERC-721 token, essentially a physical repository of the code that records the cat's place in the kitty blockchain (figure 10.17). A thumbnail screen shows Celestial looking out at you from the circuit board in which ($)he is entrapped for eternity.

Of course, CryptoKitties turned out to be just the point of the NFT spear. These so-called non-fungible tokens—powered by blockchain smart contracts—exploded into the mainstream in 2021, as everything from basketball highlights and artworks (Beeple!) to music and colors can be marketed as NFTs. Major corporations have immediately jumped on this hotter-than-hot market, while celebrities have found new ways to monetize themselves: Canadian musician Claire Boucher, aka Grimes, sold almost $6 million worth of her NFTs in a short span of 2021. NFTs have also powered a new wave of designer-artists like Brendan Dawes (see chapter 7), a Flash artist whose abstract graphics have been reenergized through the blockchain. As of this writing, the entire crypto universe has teetered on the brink of collapse as many question its utility—even its entire raison d'être—amid a spasm of financial scandals.

One last point about algorithmic culture: How will future historians make sense of social networks that are ruled by personalized computations? Would it ever be possible to understand the experience of a photostream or newsfeed that is tailored to the individual in real time? Additionally, the simple quantity of posts, memes, and snaps seem likely to bedevil even the most assiduous student of the digital past.

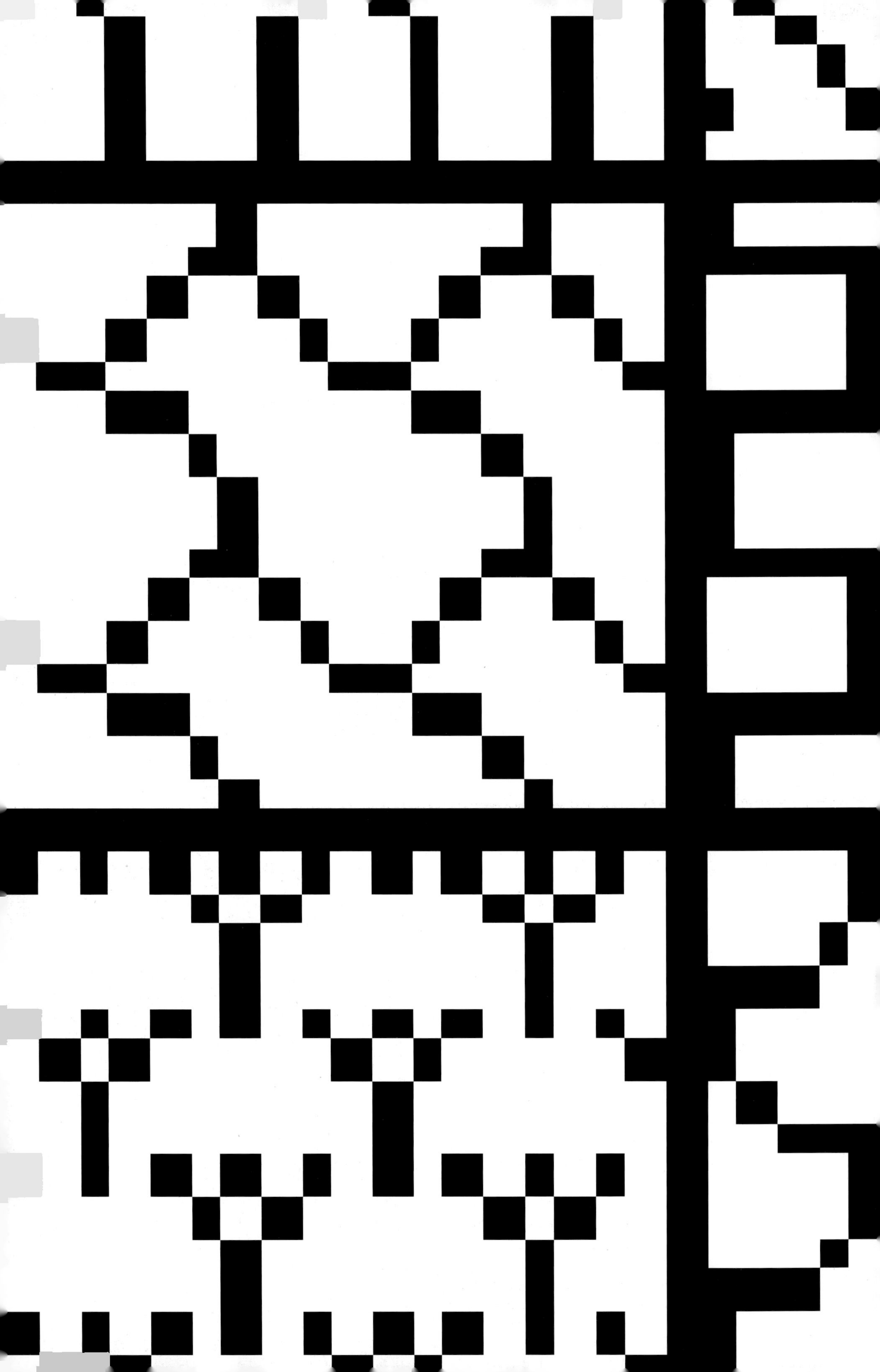

11.1. Joseph Priestley, *A New Chart of History*, 1769

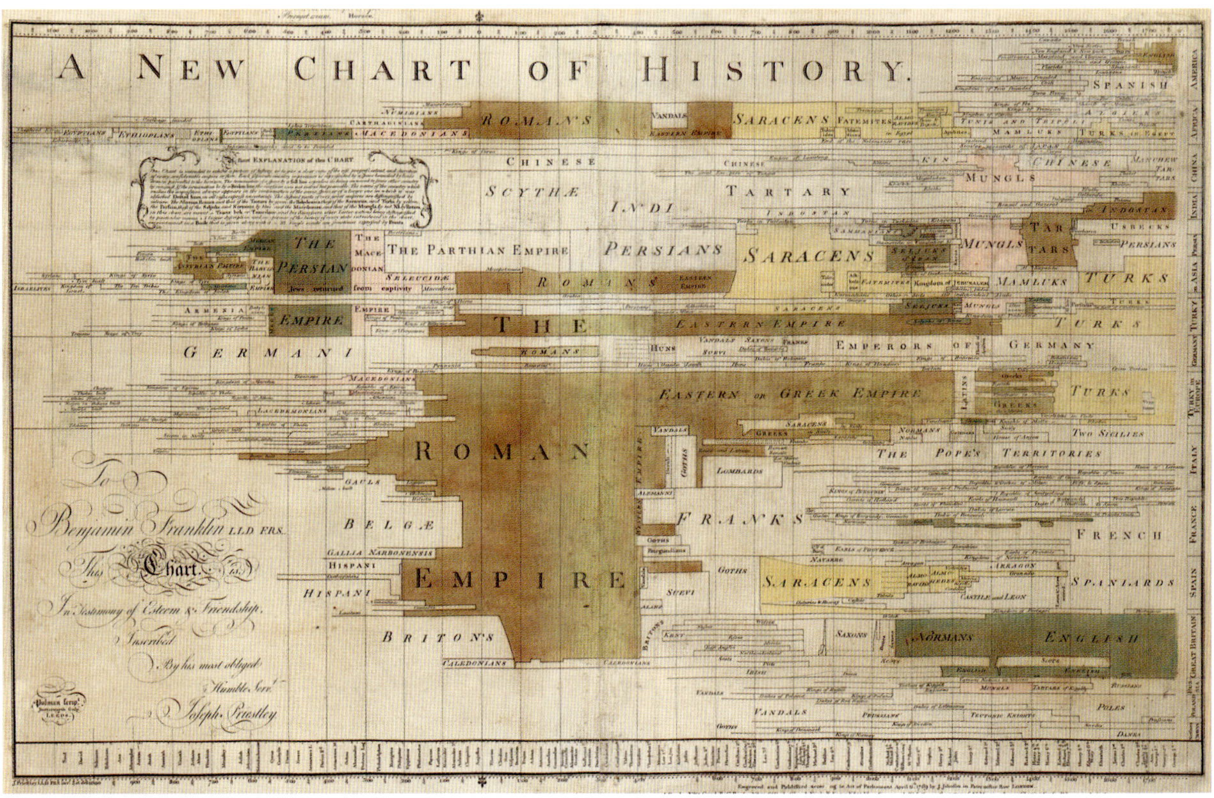

Eleven. Data Visualization

One of the greatest challenges of the digital age has been to make sense of data; in recent years, a critical mass of designers has worked to make this ubiquitous digital product visible and comprehensible. The impulse to collect data and use them to understand the world, however, is not some new function of the digital age, as it has a history almost as long as human civilization. On the walls of caves, our oldest ancestors marked their surroundings and the stars in the sky. Sumerians in ancient Mesopotamia invented astronomical instruments, and indigenous peoples like the Lakota studied the sky.

Perhaps the closest analog to the communication of big data through visual means arose from cartographic history. An important tipping point in the mapping endeavor came about in the person of Claudius Ptolemy, a Greco-Roman polymath who lived in the second century. A Roman citizen who lived in that empire's Egyptian province in the city of Alexandria, Ptolemy produced a treaty called *Geographia* that combined the accepted wisdom of generations of mainly Greek observers with several of Ptolemy's new insights into understanding the geography of the world.

Like the exabytes and zettabytes of today's internet, the world of Ptolemy's time was perceived as immeasurably big and scarcely quantifiable. Ptolemy became the first cartographer to attempt to communicate locations in an accurate, repeatable manner. While many maps from antiquity aimed for a hierarchical scale based on economic status, Ptolemy sought to show the viewer where cities and natural features were located relative to one another. His "graticule," a grid that relied on the established understanding of latitude and longitude, combined with two types of conic projections (yes, it was understood in antiquity that the earth was round) to create one of the clearest visualizations of the known world ever recorded. In a curious twist of fate, Western mapmaking entered over a millennium of stasis after Ptolemy's death around 150 CE and would only be reinvigorated by the cultural currents of the European Renaissance.

From the 1500s onward, cartography followed a fairly clear trajectory of making maps that were incrementally more accurate geographically while also introducing new datasets to the visualizations. In this regard, the first atlas was published in Flanders late in the sixteenth century—Abraham Ortelius's *Theatrum Orbis Terrarum*—although it was soon supplanted by the superior compendium produced by Gerardus Mercator. The Enlightenment obsession with data resulted in an expansion of mapmaking to include charts that cataloged weather data, populations, and the like. Atlases moved

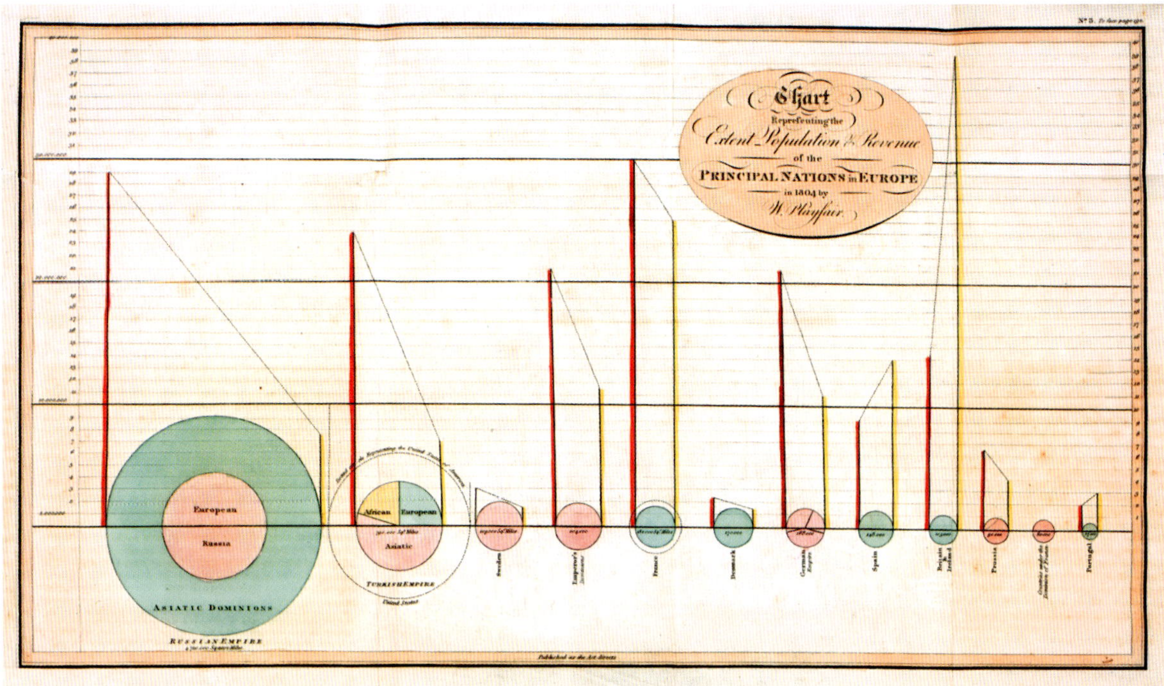

11.2. William Playfair, *The Statistical Breviary*, 1786

from being bound books of maps to broader summations of knowledge about the world and its peoples.

During the Enlightenment era, the impulse for understanding new and more complex types of data led to the organic development of a new type of visualization, the timeline. Up until the eighteenth century the march of time was most often communicated through lists. For example, a dataset of biographical information would be shown through a column of birth years. Then, in 1765, English theologian and erstwhile scientist Joseph Priestley published *A Chart of Biography*, which displayed the lifetimes of famous men through a proportional system of overlapping bars. Time flowed from left to right across the page so that this visualization allowed someone at a glance to understand the sequence of the lifespans of more than two thousand male influencers, dating all the way back to the second millennium BCE. While dotted lines indicated uncertainty and full lines confidence, a viewer could quickly grasp whose lives had overlapped without having to perform any mental calculations. The timeline was born.

Excited by the success of his biographical visualization, Priestley next turned to an even grander dataset, calling his next work *A New Chart of History*, or, more specifically, *A View of the principal Revolutions of Empire That have taken place in the world* [*sic*] (figure 11.1). This new visualization—available as a large poster for half a guinea—was based on a timeline of global governments. But Priestly also added a second element, scale, so that the relative land area of the Roman versus Persian empires could be quickly understood through blocks of color. "Time here flows uniformly, from the beginning to the end of the tablet. It is also represented as flowing *laterally*, like a river, and not as falling in a perpendicular stream." Priestley fixed in print (and in many people's minds) the Enlightenment view of time as an arbiter of steady progress in a world that can be mastered by data.

Less than twenty years after the publication of Priestley's *A New Chart of History*, another British citizen, this time a Scot named William Playfair, published the two works that would make him legendary in the realm of data viz. Playfair had a varied career and worked at times as an engineer, an economist, and even as a British secret agent. Perhaps his most important training as a data scientist came at the behest of James Watt, for whom Playfair worked as a draftsman, producing intricate engineering plans. Later, in 1786, Playfair published his *Commercial and Political Atlas*, a work that was based on available data regarding European economies. In the *Atlas*, Playfair introduced both line and bar charts, the latter perhaps an adaptation of the bars that represented lifespans in Priestley's popular work. Playfair further enhanced the toolset available to the data-minded public in 1801, when he published a follow-up assessment of European society called *The Statistical Breviary* (figure 11.2) In this book, Playfair created a new type of visualization, the

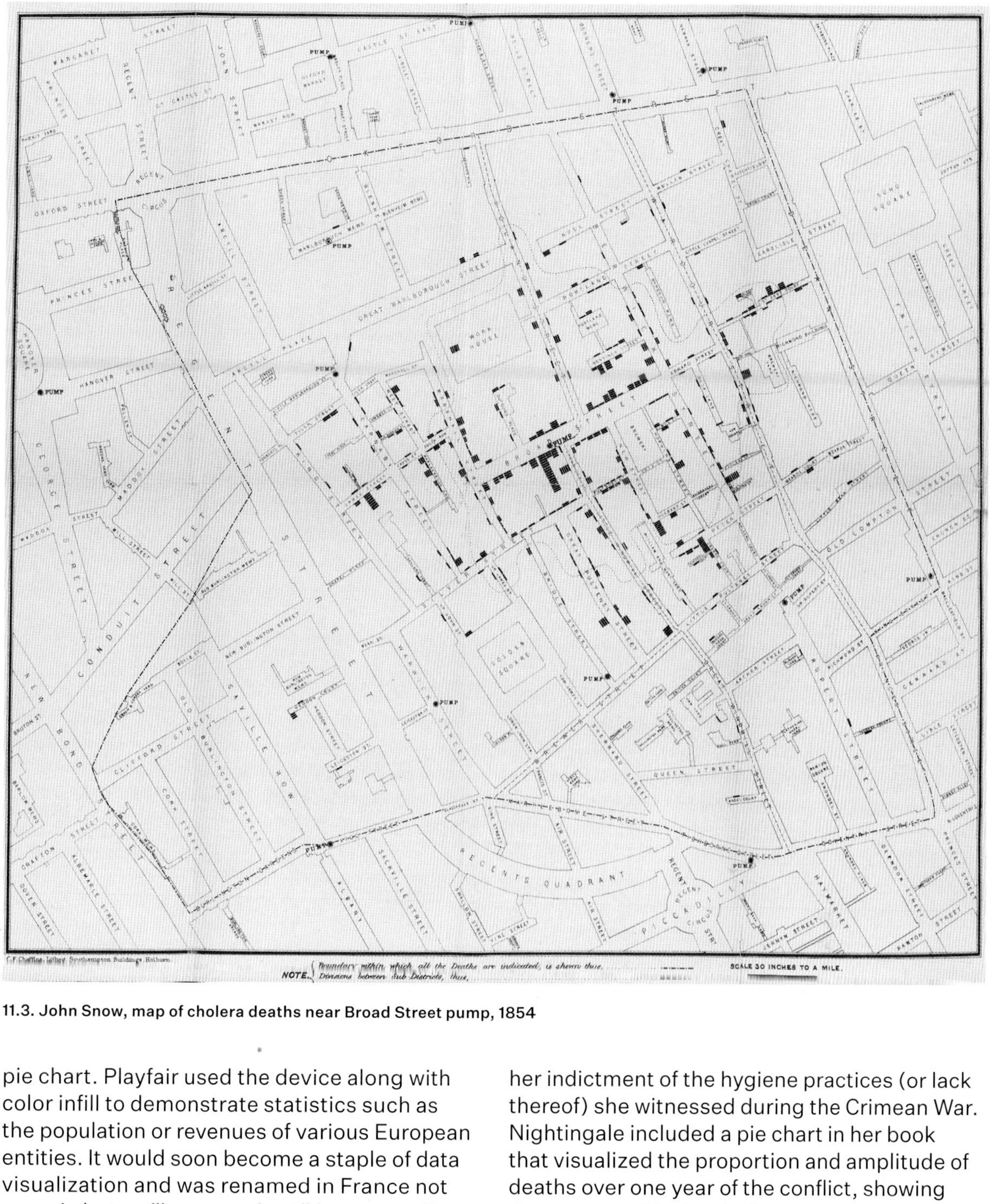

11.3. John Snow, map of cholera deaths near Broad Street pump, 1854

pie chart. Playfair used the device along with color infill to demonstrate statistics such as the population or revenues of various European entities. It would soon become a staple of data visualization and was renamed in France not as a pie but as "le camembert" because of its resemblance to a wheel of cheese.

Data maps, as opposed to geographic maps, experienced two heroic moments in the 1850s. First, in 1854, Dr. John Snow ended a London cholera epidemic because he recognized that the victims lived in a cluster around the infamous Broad Street water pump. As a data visualization, Snow's nineteenth-century map was manageable, a simple collection of dots overlaid on a London street guide (figure 11.3). Next, in 1858, Florence Nightingale published *Notes on Matters Affecting the Health, Efficiency and Hospital Administration of the British Army*, her indictment of the hygiene practices (or lack thereof) she witnessed during the Crimean War. Nightingale included a pie chart in her book that visualized the proportion and amplitude of deaths over one year of the conflict, showing that preventable deaths far outweighed combat as a source of casualties.

While most analog data visualizations were viewed in a singular format like a map or bound in books, in a few instances, designers created large installations akin to today's huge digital displays. Such was the case with W.E.B. Du Bois's visualizations of Black America. Some context: at the behest of Thomas J. Calloway and Booker T. Washington, the US government had agreed to sponsor an exhibit on postslavery Black life in America (figure 11.4). This exhibit, *Exposition des Nègres d'Amerique*, was installed at the 1900 Paris Exposition Universelle.

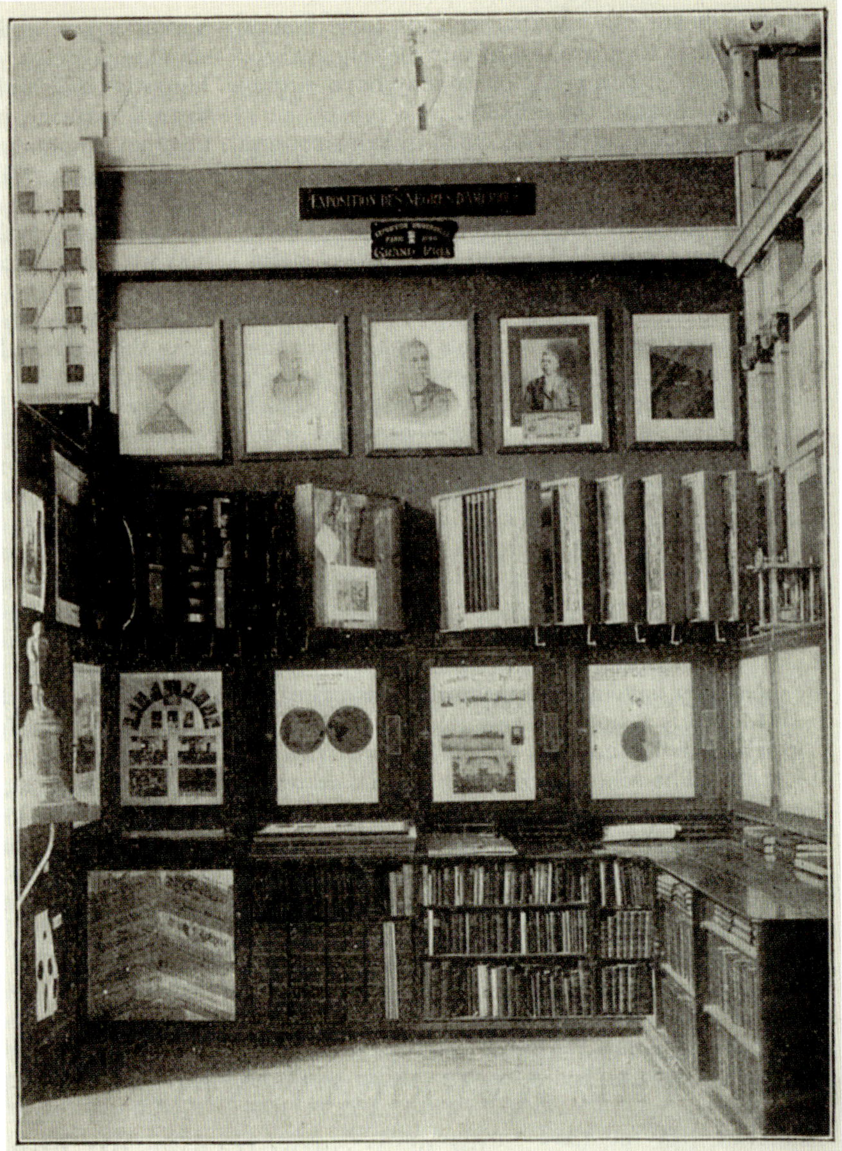

EXHIBIT OF AMERICAN NEGROES AT THE PARIS EXPOSITION.

11.4. W.E.B. Du Bois, *Exposition des Nègres d'Amerique*, Exposition Universelle, Paris, 1900

Calloway convinced Du Bois, the latter an esteemed sociologist at Atlanta University, to create two sets of infographics that would highlight the recent successes of Black Americans. Du Bois designed two sets of charts for the exhibit, one focused on Black Georgians and the other more broadly titled "A Series of Statistical Charts Illustrating the Condition of the Descendants of Former African Slaves Now in Residence in the United States of America." The resulting hand-drawn charts are straightforward and informative; their installation as a larger data environment was most notable. While some of the visualizations and related images were placed flat on a wall, many were attached to a series of angled display racks that could be moved and browsed, creating a level of interactivity that prefigures clicking through a digital space.

In a parallel to advances in charts, cartographers continued their work making the urban world knowable and traversable. For example, in the thirties, Harry Beck's amateur map of the London Underground pioneered a sophisticated type of simplification in the face of a large dataset, the intertwined railroads of London. But not until the second half of the twentieth century did the accelerating volume of data collected and produced by scientists, analysts, and bureaucrats of all kinds reach a tipping point and begin to overwhelm both conventional visualization strategies and the people who try to make sense of them. Data, which for centuries served as a conduit that made the world more knowable, were gradually becoming unwieldy in both quantity and variety. A whole vocabulary begins to emerge as early as the forties: the information "explosion," "overload," and "revolution."

In the 1957 book *The Landmarks of Tomorrow*, management theorist Peter Drucker introduced the concept of the "knowledge worker," signaling a massive economic shift to a postindustrial economy in much of the West. "Every engineer, every chemist, every accountant, every market analyst immediately creates the opportunity and the need for more men who can apply knowledge and concepts, both in his own field and all around it. This may sound obvious. But it is so new that it is not yet recognized." Drucker expounded on the new postmodern economy and its reliance on data analysis throughout his long career. His influential book *The Age of Discontinuity: Guidelines to Our Changing Society* was actually included in Stewart Brand's epochal 1971 *Whole Earth Catalog*, the latter tome serving as a sort of atlas to the new cultural threads that had been arising in American society. It might seem curious to find a corporate strategist such as Drucker touted in the *Whole Earth Catalog*, but in fact the authors and compilers of the catalog espoused a unique blend of counterculture sympathies and technological utopianism that has resonated in the digital age. Actually, Drucker's *Age of Discontinuity* shared with the *Catalog* the same sensibility that a near cosmic shift in Western culture was underway. For Drucker, data were at the heart of this new enterprise. "What we still have to create is the conceptual understanding of information. . . . We have to have a 'notation,' comparable to the one St. Ambrose invented 1,600 years ago to record music, that can express words and thoughts in symbols appropriate to electronic pulses."

In the same year that Drucker received mention in the *Whole Earth Catalog*, other thinkers were recognizing the emerging threat that digital data held for privacy. In 1971 legal scholar Arthur Miller published *The Assault on Privacy*, a book that today appears to be remarkably prescient. Miller decried the fact that computers could facilitate the creation of individual dossiers filled with data that would never be erased. Because of its "insatiable appetite for information," the computer would naturally lead to a "surveillance system that will turn society into a transparent world in which our homes, our finances, and our associations will be bared to a wide range of casual observers, including the morbidly curious and the maliciously or commercially intrusive." Decades before social media would alter the landscape of individual privacy, data were already gradually accumulating and being aggregated all over the digital world.

Not only business and legal thinkers responded to this new torrent of flowing information: artists felt the change as well. Korean-born American Nam June Paik, for example, continually explored the impact of technology on American society after immigrating to New York City in 1964. Paik had a paradoxical set of values, incorporating in his work some of the subversive tendencies of the Fluxus-era counterculture alongside the anarchic-utopian outlook that guided so much of the computer age's thinkers. After decades of work in manipulating video and creating experimental wearable tech, Paik's outsider role coalesced with the digital mainstream around the onset of the web age in the middle nineties. At that time, he had been experimenting for a few years with installations of stacked televisions in varied arrangements and diverse themes. Then, in 1995, Paik created *Electronic Superhighway: Continental U.S., Alaska, Hawaii* (figure 11.5), a work that made the new internet age relatable, its flow of data equivalent to the flow of

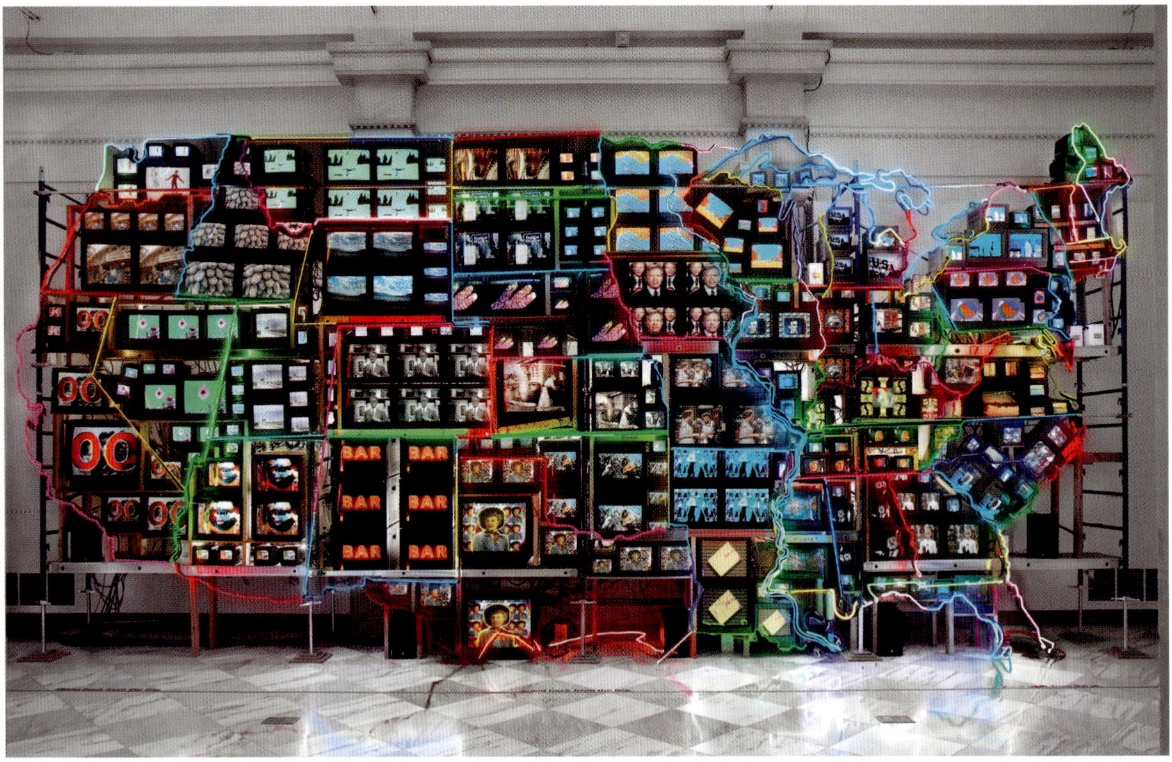

11.5. Nam June Paik, *Electronic Superhighway: Continental U.S., Alaska, Hawaii*, 1995

automobiles on the interstate highway system of the 1950s. Using more than three hundred televisions framed by neon lights like those on a roadside sign, this massive work—forty feet wide—shows data flowing with energy and verve. In a manner that recalls the spirit of nineteenth-century landscape paintings and their celebration of the colonization of the American West through railroads and telegraphs, Paik shows simultaneously highways and "electronic superhighways"—a phrase he coined—connecting the country from coast to coast. A sort of electronic Manifest Destiny is at work here, as disparate data feeds articulate the different regional cultures of the United States. *Electronic Superhighway* featured fifty-one channels of video playing on DVDs, showcasing wry, appropriated bits of popular culture: a clip from *The Wizard of Oz* in Kansas, for example. On the *Electronic Superhighway*, data flow creates the same sense of autonomy and freedom that made car travel such a magical part of the American experience. Embracing his adopted country and leaving most of his youthful subversion in the past, Paik's *Electronic Superhighway* naturally entered the collection of the Smithsonian American Art Museum in 2002.

Giant installations of digitally networked monitors that abounded with data were not just in the realm of experimental art but were also breaking into the commercial mainstream in the late nineties. The year after Paik completed *Electronic Superhighway*, the Nasdaq stock exchange debuted the first iteration of its own pathbreaking video wall. This fifty-five-foot-wide installation of more than one hundred screens was an attempt to create a physical stage set that communicated the exchange's technological sophistication. Twenty-five years ago the Nasdaq—the first digitally automated stock exchange—was plagued by a weak brand that had been degraded by multiple scandals. Known mainly for its easily manipulatable penny stocks, the Nasdaq was seeking to compete with the hoary grandeur of the New York Stock Exchange (NYSE), which had been poaching some of Nasdaq's more reputable clients. Part of the Nasdaq's branding problem was that there was no relatable way for people and the media to engage with an exchange that was entirely virtual, especially in contrast to camera shots of the NYSE's legendary trading floor and opening bell rostrum.

In a move akin to the decades-later Bitcoin visualization via a golden doubloon, the studio run by Matt and Chris Enock (since 2006 known as Percepted) devised the idea of a towering video wall to symbolize the virtual market of Nasdaq: the monitors displayed the flow of capital through the financial system. Arrows and colors indicated daily stock winners and

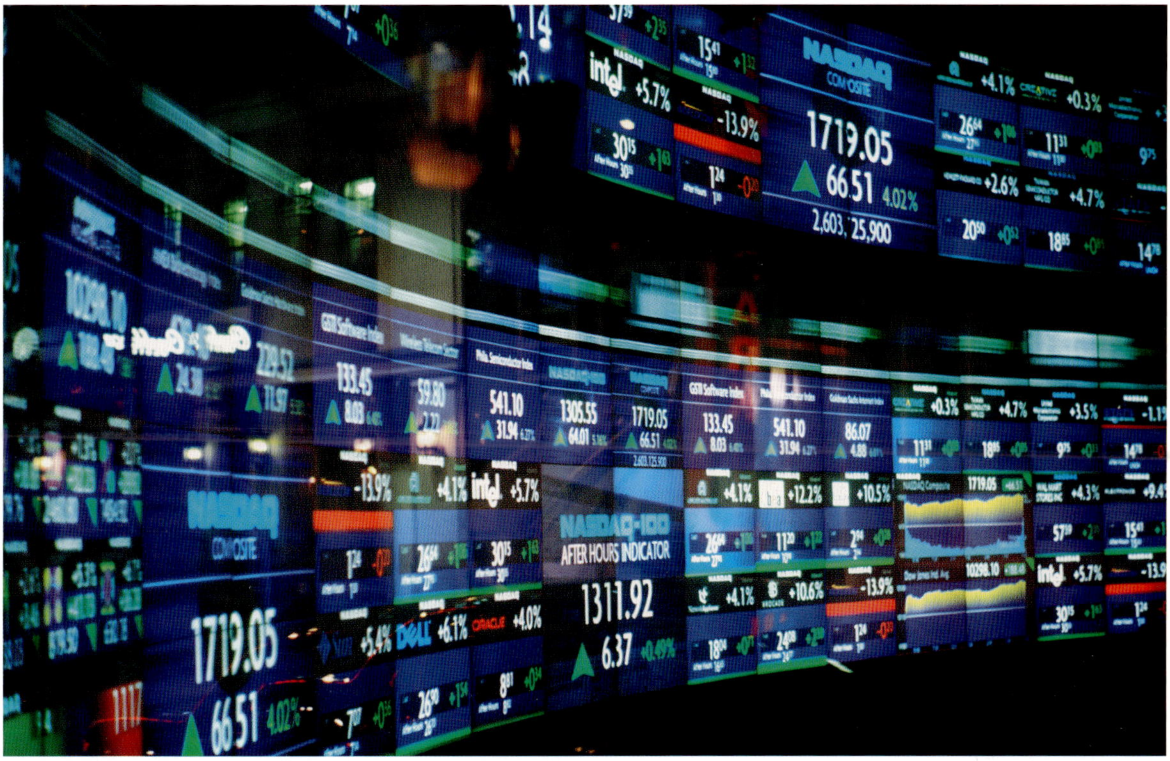

11.6. Matt Enock and Chris Enock's Nasdaq data wall, 1996

losers, while smartly displaying the actual logos of companies as opposed to the sometimes obscure stock symbols (figure 11.6). Other monitors could be programmed for newsfeeds and the like. This matrix of information gave the Nasdaq a presence that was both tangible (the MarketSite, as it became known, is a background for a television studio) and virtual, signifying that the Nasdaq was at the forefront of the digital age. At the same time, the Nasdaq was focusing its identity on like-minded technology companies, as it transformed from a seedy, smallish player to the heart of big technology, including Microsoft, Apple, Intel, Amazon, and later Google and Facebook. The MarketSite video wall has gone through several upgrades since the late nineties, with the current version made by the video wall specialist supplier Barco. Located in Times Square, the video wall is now complemented by an exterior tower festooned with 19 million LED lights.

Pentagram designer Eddie Opara has often emphasized the joyous spectacle that a brilliant display can provide for urban pedestrians. Opara was creative director for a stunning example of this type of display: the one-thousand-square-meter digital façade on the Mahanakhon Cube, a seven-story entertainment venue in Bangkok, Thailand. This massive screen is divided into a six-by-twenty-four grid of rectangles that are configured to display a range of information—temperature, time, advertising—that is synchronized to the natural world as well as to the arrival of local commuter trains (figure 11.7). Using an iridescent trixel system, the façade truly rules the night, while an upper-level skybridge allows people to actually walk through the screen (it is the entrance to a nightclub), a physical embodiment of human–computer interaction.

The mapping impulse that first propelled data visualization has maintained a prominent role in the digital age. Digital tools and newly accessible datasets have allowed for more and greater experimentation. While Harry Beck's thirties map of the London Tube had changed the manner in which people understood and navigated that subterranean world, today's freely available datasets allow for far more complex understandings of what the Underground means for culture and society writ large. For example, Oliver O'Brien, a geographer at the University of Central London, has layered data from multiple sources, including Transport for London and OpenStreetMap, to produce a series of visualizations of different aspects of life in the city at his website Tube Creature. One of his most compelling tube maps, *Tube Tongues*, shows the different languages spoken across London (figure 11.8). Using data from a 2011 census, this bubble map shows what is the most common language (excepting English) used near each

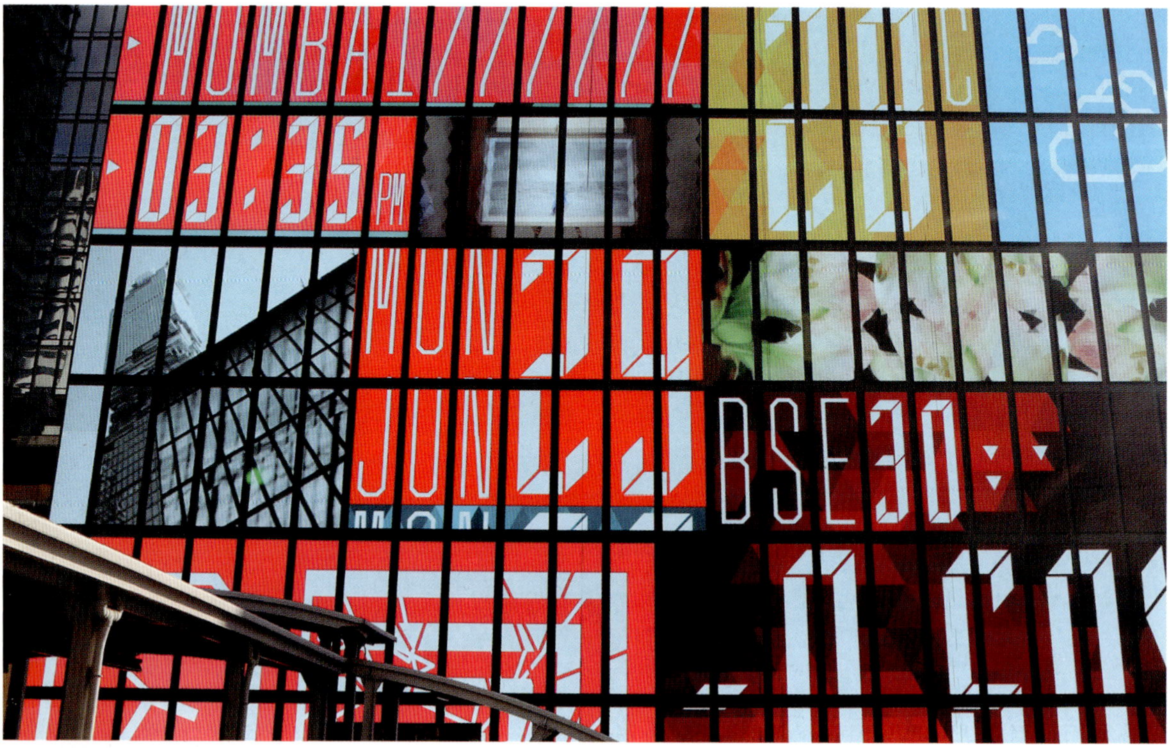

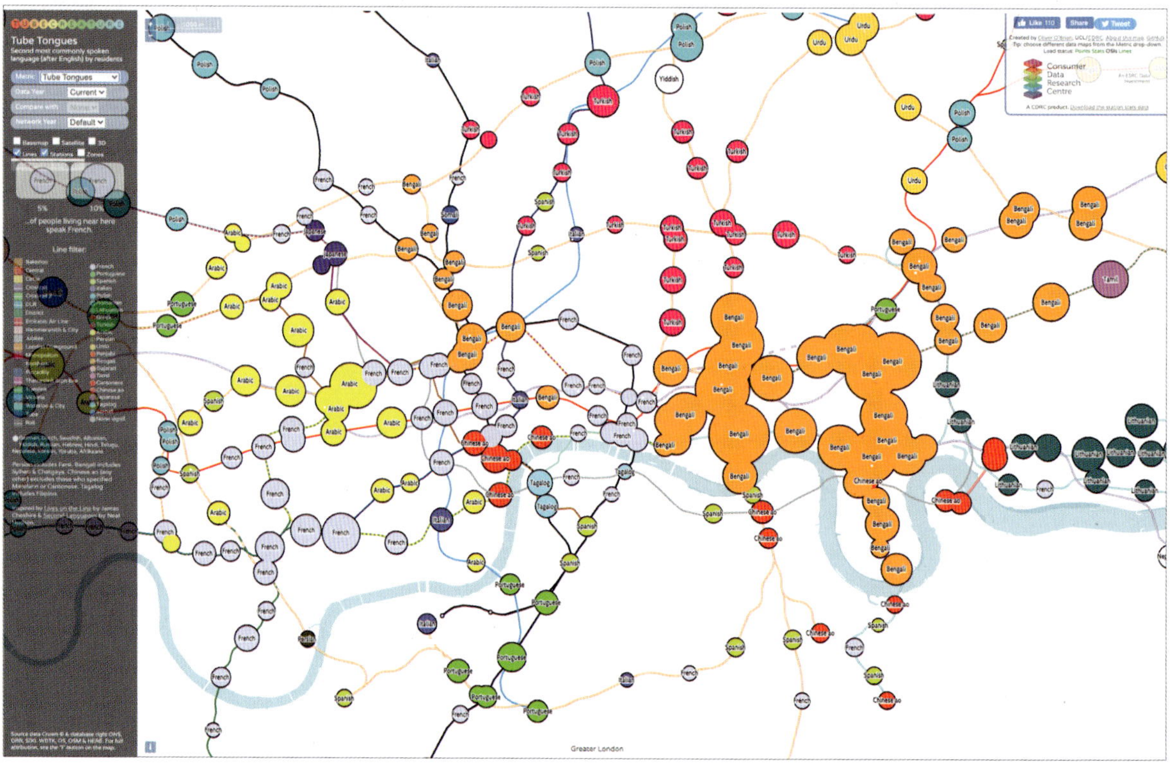

11.7. Eddie Opara and Pentagram, digital signage at Mahanakhon, 2018
11.8. Oliver O'Brien, *Tube Tongues*, 2014

tube stop. The bubble design and familiar Underground map creates a proportional view of the data that is instantly understandable despite involving an enormous amount of documentation. O'Brien told the *Guardian* in 2014, "Conventional maps of demographic data can be quite abstract to look at—they can be quite hard to relate to where people live," explains O'Brien. "By combining statistical data from the census with the familiar lines of the London Underground network, the graphic becomes more relatable to a city where everyone knows their nearest tube station."

Since the dawn of the internet age, an entire cottage industry has developed around attempts to estimate how much digital data permeate contemporary life. In this era of big data—a term that first appeared around the year 2000—the numbers are far from pleasant and manageable. In the cartographic realm from whence it all began, Google Maps alone offers many petabytes of imagery (a petabyte is a million billion bytes). That number of course pales at the storage capacity of the entire internet, which is estimated at somewhere over a million exabytes (an exabyte is 1 billion billion bytes), while internet traffic is measured now in zettabytes (1,000 exabytes each). Yottabytes and xenottabytes are out there on the horizon. While these numbers prove bewildering to most, a simple television commercial from 1999 probably did more to imprint the promise of big data on a generation of digital designers. The advertisement was created by the venerable ad agency J. Walter Thompson and featured a hot, weary traveler arriving at a roadside hotel amid a dust storm. He queries the disinterested clerk about the accommodations—which are spartan—and receives only staccato responses. When he asks about entertainment, however, the clerk makes eye contact and states, "All rooms have every movie ever made in every language anytime, day or night." Twenty years ago, this promise of flowing data seemed impossibly aspirational, at a time when narrow bandwidth meant that many servers could barely push a few GIFs onto a desktop computer.

While computers fomented this new age of data, design has been tasked with grappling with the overwhelming supply of information, a supply that has proved to be both a blessing and a curse. While John Snow had mapped 578 deaths around 13 public wells, today's flow of data is more immeasurable than the earth was in Ptolemy's time. Data visualization in the digital age is indebted to the work of Edward Tufte, whose iconic book from 1983, *The Visual Display of Quantitative Information*, is still a major touchstone in the field. In his book, Tufte coined the still functioning term "chartjunk" in reference to datasets that were inaccurately or confusingly presented. He objected strenuously to visualizations that caused the viewer to confuse the signal for the noise produced by datasets. His critique of contemporary data visualization broached into the mainstream in the nineties, when he asserted that the space shuttle *Challenger* explosion of 1986 had been a result of poor data visualization. In a subsequent book, *Visual Explanations: Images and Quantities, Evidence and Narrative* (1997), Tufte contrasted the efficacy of the map of the Broad Street pump with the charts used unsuccessfully by engineers to convince NASA to cancel the launch because of unusually cold temperatures. While some critics have contested his reasoning and subsequent fame, Tufte has inarguably inspired a new generation of digital designers to explore data in exciting new ways. And oh, is there so much data to visualize today.

As big data exploded onto the scene in the late nineties, Ben Fry was working on his graduate degrees at the Aesthetics + Computation Group, part of MIT's Media Lab. At the Media Lab, Fry worked with John Maeda and others in an attempt to grapple with techniques for displaying data. At MIT Fry initially began exploring the visualization of dynamic datasets, a field that was on the cusp of breaking into the mainstream. Around 2000, in the midst of his doctoral work (he received his PhD in 2004), Fry started to focus on the overall problems of dealing with huge amounts of data. In his dissertation précis, he wrote, "Fields such as information visualization, data mining and graphic design are employed [to understand data], each solving an isolated part of the specific problem, but failing in a broader sense: there are too many unsolved problems in the visualization of complex data." Fry sought to integrate these disparate disciplines in a holistic endeavor he called computational information design.

One of Fry's experimental implementations of computational information design involved understanding one of the most vast examples of data: the human genome. The Human Genome Project—an international collaboration dedicated to mapping our DNA—had captured the public's imagination in the late nineties as it neared completion. In naming this series of works *Genomic Cartography*, Fry nodded toward the mapping impulse that is the historical basis of the field. Fry's genomic project also takes up a subject that—like so many others—ends up in a place where digital technology interacts with the poignant, existential thread of human life. The work illustrated here, *Genomic Cartography: Chromosome 21* (figure 11.9), visualizes a small part of the 50-odd million DNA bases indicated by letters. Subtle changes in value demarcate different parts of chromosome 21.

The medium of this work is Processing software, an online tool developed by Fry and his colleague Casey Reas. The idea behind Processing was to make computer programming more accessible to the design community by providing an intuitive interface. Just as the GUI facilitated complex interactions that were inaccessible during the command-line era, Fry and Reas hoped that Processing—essentially a Java-based open source programming language paired with a digital sketchbook—would make coding something that designers could creatively embrace. Fry wrote in his dissertation, "For designers, to make *Processing* more visually engaging from the outset, the idea is to first make things happen, and use that to drive curiosity into learning how it works, and how to do more."

Somewhere around the turn of the millennium, the internet entered the dynamic phase popularly called Web 2.0. The term generally refers to the expansion of animated, interactive content—think Flash—but can also be tied to the increasing potential of big data. Two aspects of the technological backend have played key roles in collecting, categorizing, and communicating data across the web: SQLs and APIs. The former, short for Structured Query Language, is a coding format that dates back to the seventies and allows for the management of large digital databases. As data have become so important to the internet, some thinkers have argued that

11.9. Ben Fry, *Genomic Cartography: Chromosome 21*, 2001

Web 2.0 should be viewed as the moment when SQL became an indispensable part of the infrastructure. As a forward-thinking advertisement from Oracle put it as early as 1997, "Data is the foundation of every visionary web site." Equally important to Web 2.0, in the year 2000, the first API—application-programming interface—was loaded on the internet. Today, APIs invisibly run most web-based experiences. They are invisible to end users because API programs are software-to-software interfaces. In facilitating data queries and transactions across the web, APIs are what allow a user to, for example, find what restaurants in a certain zip code have availability for a group of ten patrons an hour from now. Together these two programming standards allowed data to become available to all, but it takes designers to visualize those data accessibly.

An extensive demonstration of how big data can be made understandable through design can be viewed through the No Ceilings project (figure 11.10). Funded by the Gates and Clinton Foundations, the initiative is focused on fostering global gender equality. In 2015, Fathom Information Design—a Boston studio founded by Ben Fry in 2010—released a digital interactive website and mobile app devoted to visualizing the data behind the project. This design needed to make sense of more than 850,000 data points drawn from scores of studies produced over two decades. A complex series of maps, animated charts, and interactive web pages created a comprehensible frame through which this vast dataset could be understood. "Female entrepreneurs are on the rise. Particularly in Sub-Saharan Africa and Latin America, women are making large contributions to the surge of entrepreneurial activity in their countries." The page illustrated here shows how one narrow slice of data—global female entrepreneurship—can be visualized in a manner that is effective and visually engaging. Fathom made the website the design's focus, but also scaled up the visualizations for smart screen use with large groups. This installation was complemented by a mobile app for individuals that featured a globe as its visual focus, using WebGL (a JavaScript API) to render the spinning planet in 3D.

A key part of the No Ceilings design was the use of animated charts, a development that has hugely energized the data visualization field over the last decade. Gone are the static charts embedded in PowerPoint that defined digital presentations in Web 1.0, as dynamic renderings have given even the dullest statistics lecture at least a little visual verve. While not the inventor of animated charts by any means, the Swedish physician and public health statistician Hans Rosling had a huge impact in jumpstarting the era of dynamic visualizations. A professor of global health at the Karolinska Institute in Stockholm, in 2006 Rosling delivered a TED talk for the ages. Called "The Best Stats You've Ever Seen," Rosling spent his twenty minutes surveying trends in global health, a topic that could be dry and, frankly, boring. The key to Rosling's presentation was his employment of animated, zoomable bubble charts that flowed across the screen. Rosling conducted the transitions and animations while he talked, as entertaining as Mickey Mouse-as-sorcerer's apprentice controlling the world in *Fantasia* (1940). Rosling's dynamic charts were complemented by his enthusiastic speaking style, and the synthesis of personality and technology lay at the core of his success.

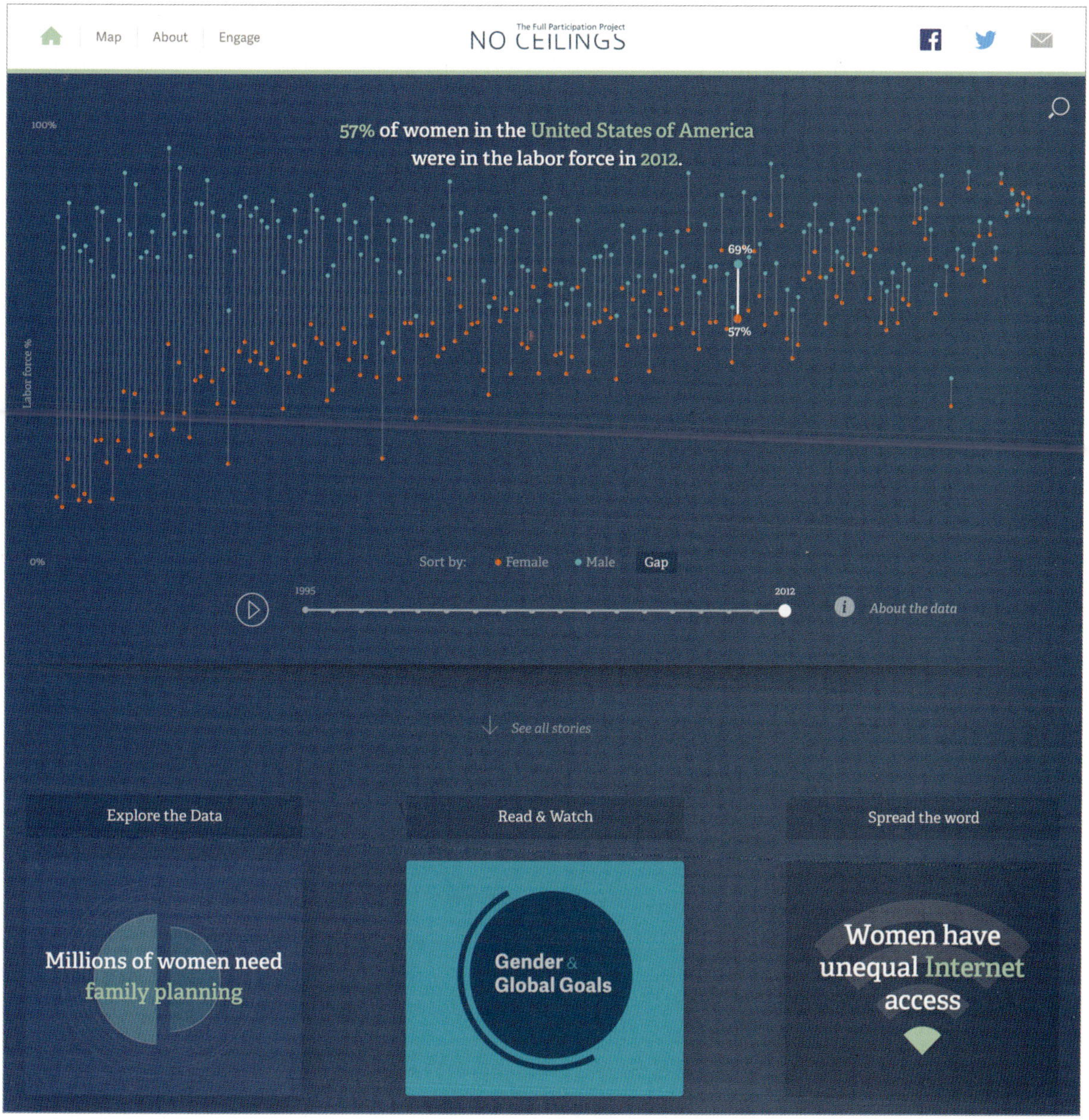

11.10. Fathom Information Design, No Ceilings, 2015

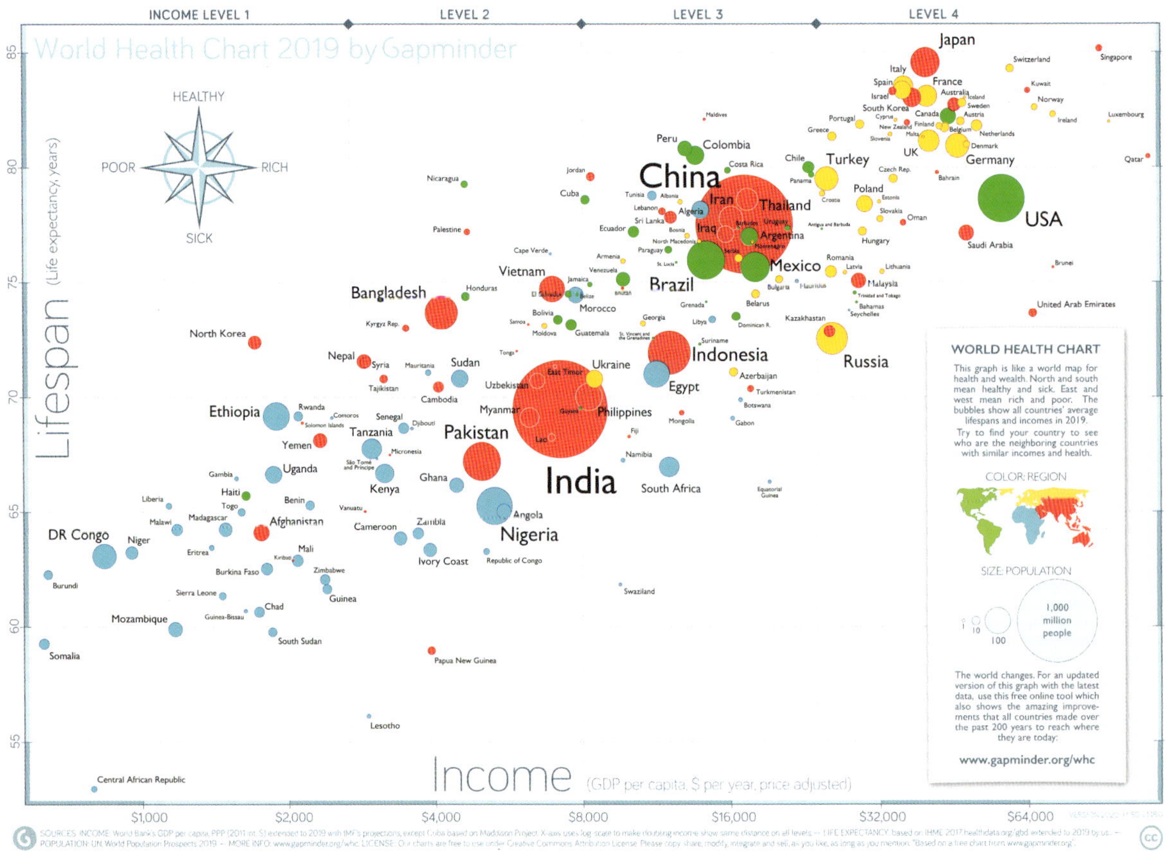

11.11. World Health Chart 2019 by Gapminder

Rosling used a Flash-based software program called Trendalyzer for his lecture, which had been developed at the Gapminder foundation he created with his children in 2005 (figure 11.11). After his breakthrough TED talk—to date it has been viewed more than 12 million times—Rosling retired from his university position to devote more time to Gapminder. Trendalyzer was acquired by Google in 2007, where the program was refined and updated. In 2010, Google released a new variation called Public Data Explorer. Although Rosling died in 2017, Gapminder continues to use data to advance knowledge about global development. "For the first time in human history reliable statistics exist. There's data for almost every aspect of global development." Gapminder has long recognized that big data can be a force for good in the world if only it can be visualized effectively; projects like No Ceilings were partly inspired by Rosling's example.

Like all things digital, the collection and analysis of big data has its dystopian side. As *Bloomberg* put it bluntly in the title of a 2018 article, "Palantir Knows Everything About You," Palantir Technologies—a data analytics firm named after a crystal ball used by wizards in *The Lord of the Rings*—became one of the leaders in the big data industry thanks to intelligence work for the US government. More recently, it has opened new divisions that seek to monetize data analytics for clients in pursuit of commerce. Their visualizations are as secret and shadowy as the company itself.

Animated big data also makes for compelling television spectacles. The video wall engineered by Nasdaq in the nineties has since launched thousands of like-minded installations, and today they are a staple of television studios across the globe. No longer able to impress with simple graphics, today's digital designers need to invent something truly stunning to stand out and catch the public's attention. Such was the case in the late summer of 2018, when the Weather Channel rolled out a new data visualization as part of their coverage of Hurricane Florence. Created in league with the Future Group, a studio that describes its work as "Interactive Mixed Reality," the Weather Channel used a towering video wall to immerse their hosts in a type of augmented reality. The visualization used data from the National Hurricane Center (NHC) to show an overlay of possible flooding on a camera shot of a city street. The wall of water rose to three, then six, and finally nine feet, giving viewers a stark, visceral view of the reality of the situation: something that simple color-coded flood maps could never communicate. The data from the NHC were interpreted and transmitted in near real time. Importantly, the code behind this data visualization was a version of the Unreal Engine, as video game software's ability to produce high-resolution virtual worlds was used to depict an all-too-real potential catastrophe.

While Rosling and others brought performative, animated visualizations into the mainstream, the *New York Times* has developed a reputation over the last few years for dynamic graphic storytelling sans narrator. In 2016, the *Times* produced a series of vignettes called the Fine Line, which delved into the minutiae of several Olympic sports. Focused on American athletes such as Simone Biles and Ryan Lochte, the series used a multimedia combination of text, image, video, and motion capture to create a rich user experience. As a *Times* press release put it, "These series will continue the tradition at The Times of pioneering innovative, never-before-seen interactive video experiences powered by data, insights and ideas." Importantly, the Fine Line was adapted for mobile and was designed to emulate the storytelling mode pioneered by Snapchat but is now a pervasive part of all social media.

While animated, the Fine Line was not substantially interactive, as the viewer only controls what is essentially pagination, swiping on their phone or using the arrow keys on a desktop to move through the different set pieces. Actually, complex interactivity has proved to be something of a quagmire for data visualizations, as outside a performative or research-based context, many readers apparently want to be entertained by animation without having to actively control the experience. Viewers are happy to watch Hans Rosling or to delve deeply into data for investigative purposes (writing a Wikipedia entry based on the No Ceilings site, for example), but not much else. Arthur Tse, deputy graphics editor at the *Times*, noted in 2016 that interactive elements were often ignored by readers. In a talk titled "Why We Are Doing Fewer Interactives," Tse related how the *Times* had learned that "Readers just want to scroll." In offering advice on visual storytelling, he wrote (on a static PowerPoint slide), "If you make a tooltip or rollover, assume no one will ever see it" (CSS tooltips are usually small text tags on a graphic that open up additional visualizations when the cursor hovers). Tse also pointed out that the expense of creating a cross-platform interactive was another barrier to the practice, and so only truly engaging projects—ones that could likely overcome interactive friction—justified such expense.

In September 2018, Sahil Chinoy and Jessia Ma published a dynamic data viz for the *Times* with a balance of information and entertainment that warranted its expense. "Entertainment" is a key term here, as somewhere in the last few years, data visualization has shifted from a dry, actuarial-like field focused on explicating facts to one where readers also expect an enjoyable diversion. Titled "Why Songs of the Summer Sound the Same," the piece used data from the Spotify and Billboard APIs to visualize the musical structure of summertime pop hits. A key part of our algorithmic musical culture, streaming companies such as Spotify use this type of sonic fingerprint to make recommendations, for example, "If you like Claude Debussy you should try Maurice Ravel." The *Times* essay was based on an easily graspable radar chart that recorded five variables: loudness, energy, danceability

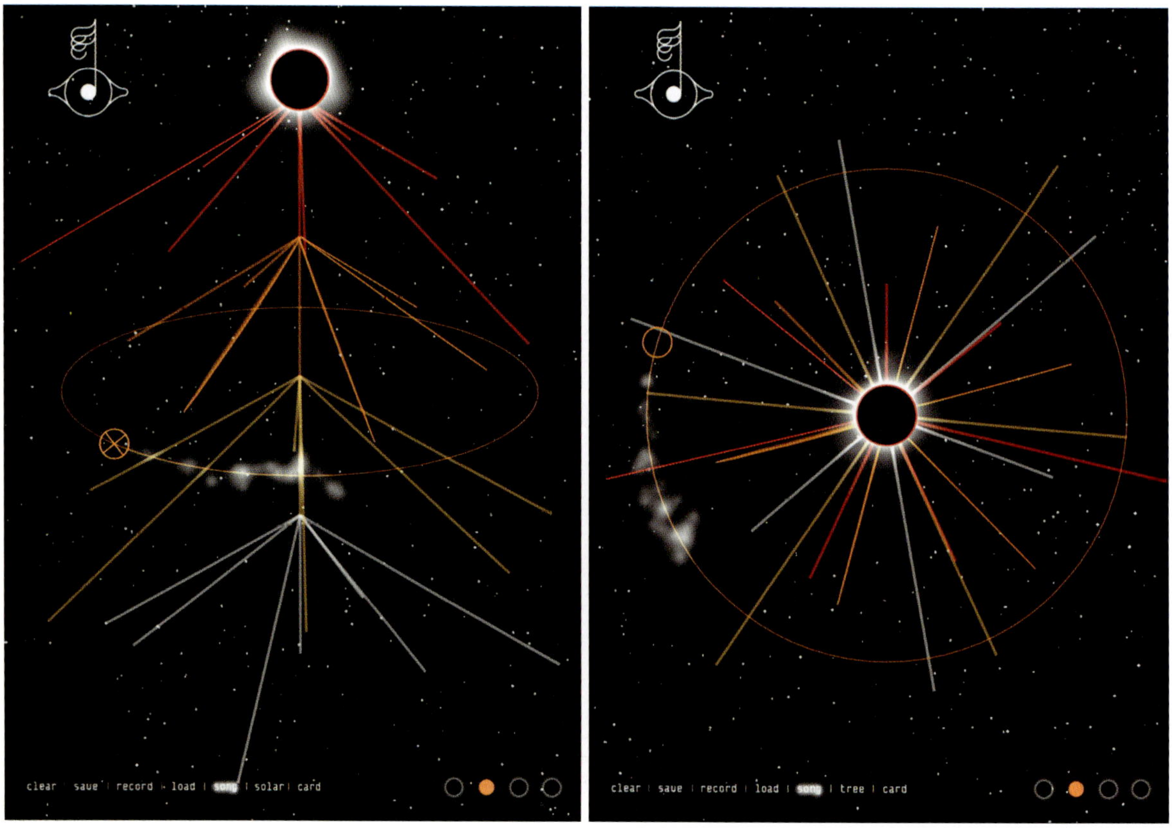

11.12. "Solstice" interface from Björk, *Biophilia*, 2011

(the beat), acoustic instrumentation, and valence (corresponds to cheerfulness). By using a radar chart, the authors created a blob-like shape for each song covered in the piece. These acoustic shapes could be overlaid to illuminate the major thread of the visualization, that recent summers had experienced a greater musical homogeneity than was common a few decades ago. Readers interacted only through a minimalist tap interface, allowing them to page back and forth without having to navigate complicated tooltips and the like.

A key part of the reason "Why Songs of the Summer" connected with readers was the music itself. Using an audio player, the radar chart was matched up to a looped snippet of each pop tune. From Def Leppard's 1988 "Pour Some Sugar on Me" to Post Malone's "Psycho" (2018), the visceral impact of the songs carried the viewer along with remembered hits. This feature points back to the success of Rosling's TED performance, as there the graphics were enlivened by his enthusiastic delivery. Like other types of motion graphics, visualizations without a meaningful soundtrack may dazzle the eyes but seem not to stir the soul. Last, note that works by both Rosling and Chinoy/Ma presented clear narrative arcs, be they global epidemiology or popular music.

If one considers music à la Spotify as an immense data trove, it is clear that interpreting sound in many ways represents another type of data visualization. While Chinoy and Ma took an analytical approach to visualizing music, many digital designers have created analogous works that focused more on the subjective, emotional aspects of sounds. As noted above in another context, music visualization that focuses on translating the subjective, emotional content of the acoustic data—think Oskar Fischinger—has a substantial predigital history. Though working with analog technology, artists such as Fischinger and Thomas Wilfred were notably in many ways on the same track as digital artists, because they believed that cutting-edge technology (electric lights, color film) could be made relatable and inspiring through artistic processes. Wilfred, for example, made near constant reference to natural phenomenon, comparing his colorful projections to polychromatic sunsets.

Many of the contemporary trends in musical data visualization appeared in Björk's 2011 app-album *Biophilia* (figure 11.12). This creation combined ten songs from the Icelandic singer with ten apps, each of which visualized one of the tracks. Like Wilfred and his sunsets, the entire suite of apps is arranged to reflect a natural order, in this case a view of the cosmos.

Collaboration is at the heart of the enterprise: in a blog post about MoMA's 2014 acquisition of *Biophilia*, Paola Antonelli touched on the diverse formulations of digital design. "The multidimensional nature of her art—in which sound and music are the spine, but never the confines, for multimedia performances that also encompass graphic and digital design, art, cinema, science, illustration, philosophy, fashion, and more—is a testament to her curiosity and desire to learn and team up with diverse experts and creators." The song "Solstice" is a telling example. Based on a Christmas poem by Sjón, it is played on an experimental gravity harp built at the MIT Media Lab by Andy Cavatorta. The app, in turn, was authored by interface designer Max Weisel, who combines the cosmic theme of the solstice with Christmas imagery. Specifically, the basic form of the app starts as a sun but morphs branches that lend it the shape of a holiday tree.

The difference between this artistic visualization of music and earlier attempts at the same lies in the element of interactivity. A Fischinger film was made strictly for passive viewing. But most of the apps in the *Biophilia* galaxy are structured so that users can use the design as an outlet for their own creative drive. With "Solstice," for example, viewers can simply experience the song in "sound mode," or they can clear the song and experiment with making their own collection of melodies using the app interface. This element of interaction is unusually deep, as other similar apps—Radiohead's *Polyfauna* (2014, Universal Everything Studio) comes to mind—have generally relied on simple touch that does not allow the user to reconfigure the music. It would be interesting to see the app data and determine whether the interactive element garnered significant attention from consumers. Did they play and create extensively or dabble a bit and then just listen to music? When designers at the *New York Times* have backed away from interactivity for the sake of interactivity, it makes one wonder if the drive for active consumption is as strong as some have postulated.

While *Biophilia* aimed for an intimate iPad-in-hand experience, Japanese sound artist Ryoji Ikeda has become known for huge installations that seem to channel a flow of big data into sound and light. In *Code-Verse* (2018, Centre Georges Pompidou) Ikeda composed digital music that highlights a relentless, buzzing texture broken up by the occasional high-pitched sequence (figure 11.10). This stream of aural data is matched with kinetic graphics that fly over and around the viewer's field of vision to create an immersive experience. The minimalist sound and black-and-white graphics intertwine to project either a sense of data flowing through a benevolent universe in a manner akin to the high-frequency whine of one's own nervous system, or, more sinisterly, the loss of autonomy as one's life is recorded and analyzed by commercial and government interests. Interpreted in the context of recent assaults on digital privacy, Ikeda's matrix of data veers away from the warm and relatable.

Often the most compelling digital design projects are composed at the intersection of multiple technologies. Neri Oxman, the Israeli American leader of the Mediated Matter Group—part of the MIT Media Lab—has become known for her research combining materials science with sophisticated computational analyses. She favors a biological metaphor for her digital work,

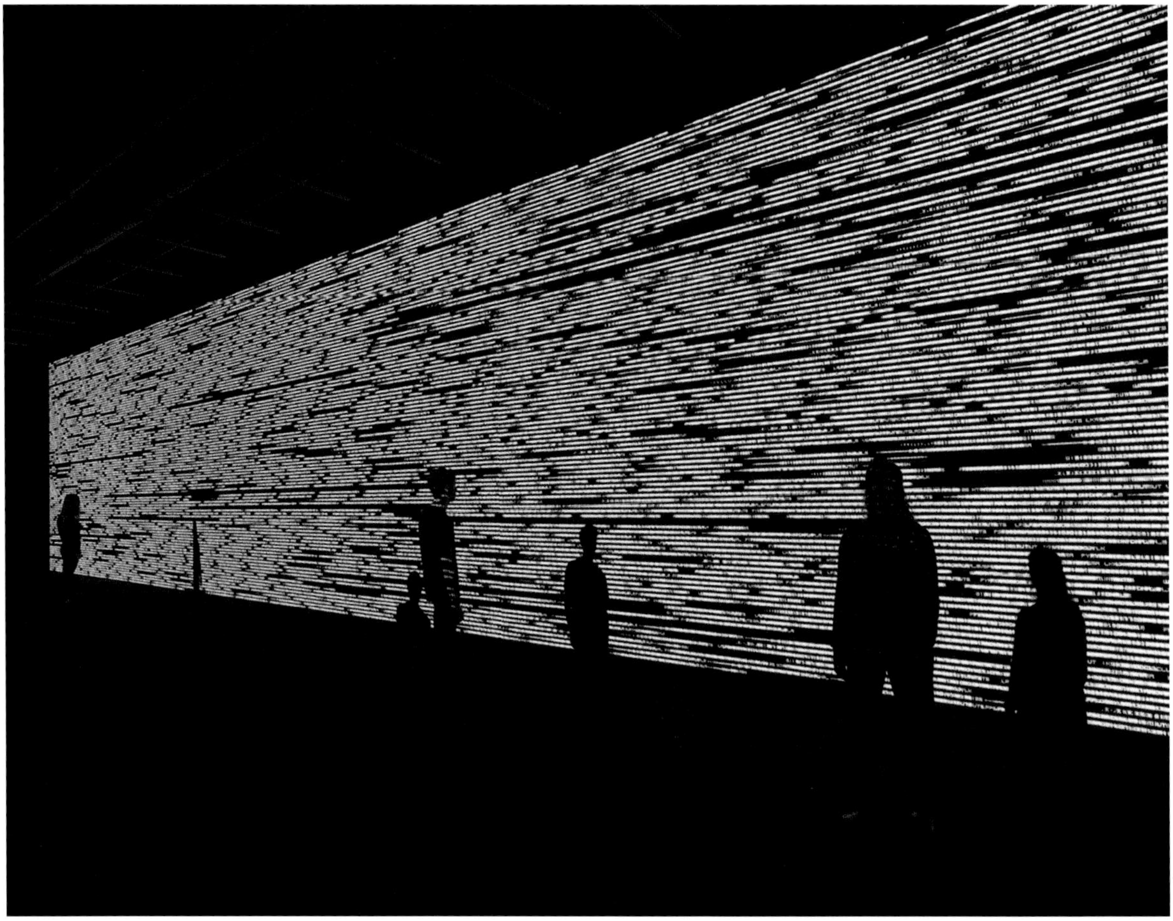

11.13. Ryoji Ikeda, *Code-Verse*, 2018

one that declaims her interest in using technology to bridge the at times artificial divide between humanity and nature. One recent research thread has delved into the problems inherent in the 2D representation of 3D digital data. For example, many 3D medical scans such as MRIs are visualized for the radiologist as a series of 2D snapshots. While it would be possible to print this type of data in three dimensions, the rasterization strategies of current 3D printers will distort the dataset. Oxman's lab has therefore worked to create a different digital map based on horizontal slices of voxels, which are 3D pixels. This voxel-based dataset could then be printed through advanced stereolithography, with different colors indicative of different structures.

David McCandless has established himself as an important creator and popularizer of contemporary data viz. His website, Information is Beautiful, has been complemented by print books, including *Information Is Beautiful* (2009, in the United States it was titled *The Visual Miscellaneum*) and a sequel in 2014, *Knowledge Is Beautiful*. These titles point to one of the most intriguing developments in the data viz world: the fact that a pronounced aesthetic drive is now behind many visualizations, as designers seek to combine engineering-like clarity with pure visual pleasure. It would seem that today's digital designers are aware of the danger posed by data that William Playfair warned of back in 1801: "No study is less alluring or more dry and tedious than statistics, unless the mind and imagination are set to work." McCandless has been instrumental in advocating on behalf of big data; he demonstrates time and again that data are not just weaponized tools of faceless bureaucrats and predatory corporations, but they can be intellectually enlightening while also being quirky and fun. While McCandless has produced plenty of serious visualizations, his ironic 2009 pyramid chart, *The Hierarchy of Digital Distractions*, traced the trajectory of digital notifications while establishing their priority based on a subjective, personal dataset. The main axis of the chart records distractibility, and one finds "any kind of actual work" at the bottom with the then two-year-old iPhone near the top, where it is only transcended by "device failure," which leads to "Dark Night" and "Digital Pain."

A large following has congregated around Information is Beautiful, and in his second book

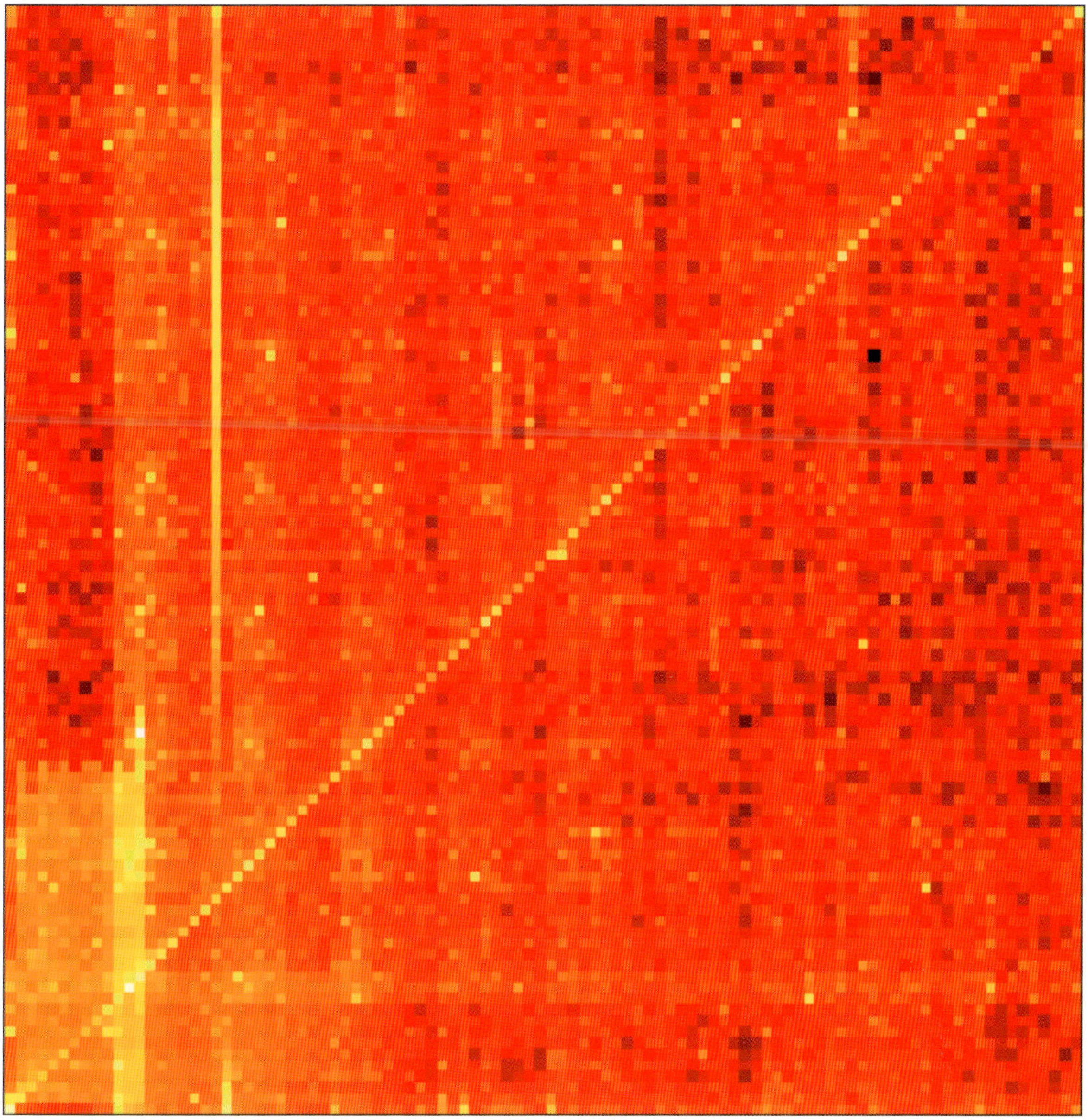

11.14. Nick Berry and DataGenetics, heat map of PINs, 2014

McCandless included a selection of essentially crowd-sourced work that he had come across. One compelling example came from Nick Berry of DataGenetics, and it features a heat map—a strategy through which data are projected via color warmth—of people's PINs (figure 11.14). Berry describes himself as "passionate about data privacy," and this visualization of four-digit numbers is gorgeous while also demonstrating how PINs can be all too predictable. "Patterns in PIN Numbers" has a vertical axis for the first two digits and a horizontal one for the last two. Note the strong diagonal down the middle that represents people's love of repetition. Berry also showed how the lower left corner is lit up because of the tendency to use a month/day format and to start a PIN with 0 or 1; of course, there are also lots of 19s, as people use years for their PIN. Berry also made note of some of the global implications of this data. For example, Koreans favor the number 1004 because it is a homophone for the word "angel." As it turns out, 8068 is the least common PIN in the dataset, but Berry warns his readers not to use it as "Hackers can read too!"

In 2012, McCandless established the Kantar Information is Beautiful Awards in collaboration with the creative director of Kantar, Aziz Cami (Kantar is the data unit of the London advertising and public relations behemoth WPP). Every year this competition, which is partly judged by a crowd-sourced vote, showcases a wealth of stunning visualizations. While some of the work is excellent yet predictable, the artistic side of data design also comes out. In 2018, for example, Mieka West and Dr. Sheelagh Carpendale of the University of

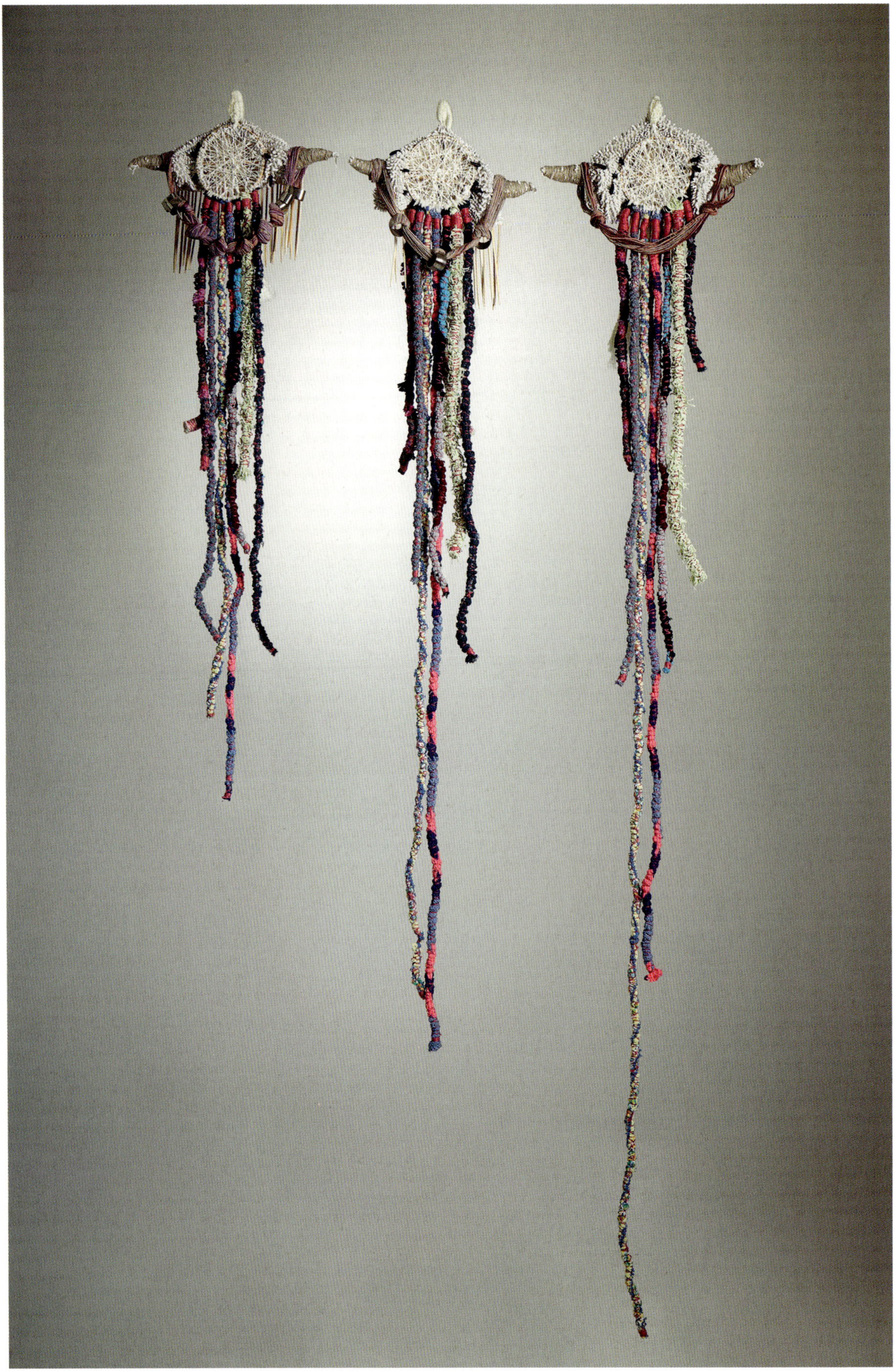

11.15. Mieka West and Dr. Sheelagh Carpendale, *Anthropocene Footprints*, 2018

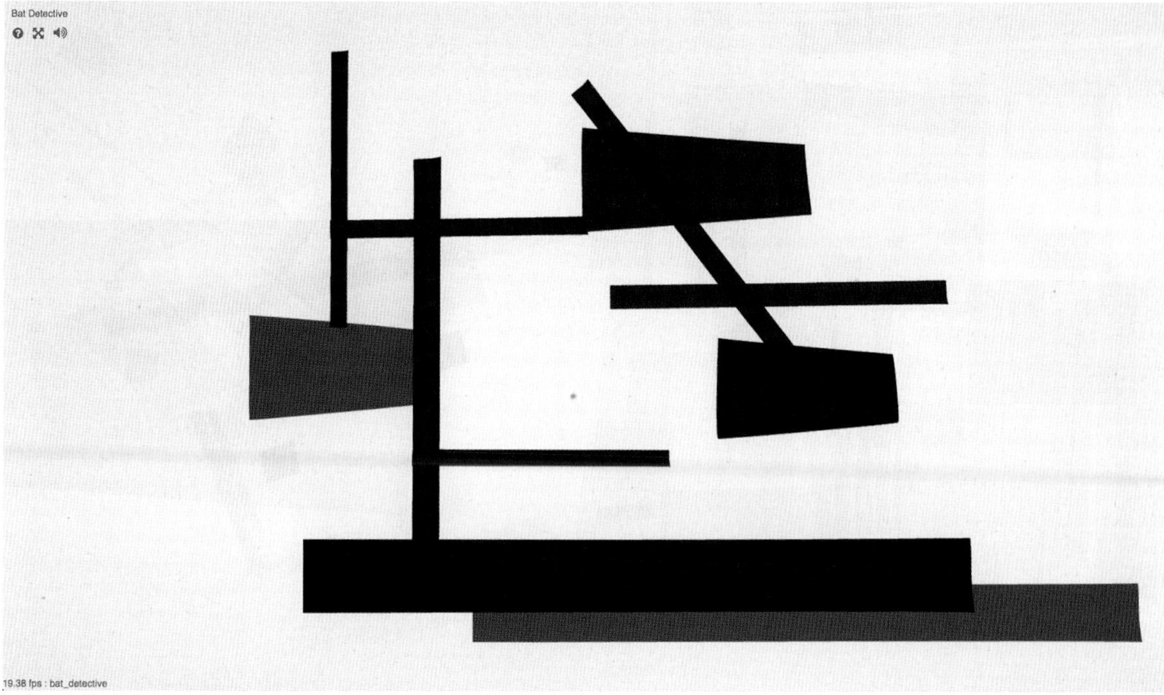

11.16. Julie Freeman, still frame from *Gravity Spy*, part of *We Need Us*, 2014–18

Calgary exhibited a climate-change piece called *Anthropocene Footprints* (figure 11.15) that transforms digital data into handicraft. "Anthropocene" is a proposed scientific term for the era in earth's history during which humans have made massive changes to the planet. The three wearable quipus act as three bars on a graph and correspond to Canada's greenhouse gas emissions of 1990, 2010, and 2030 (projected). Quipus are record-keeping devices closely associated with the height of Incan civilization around 1500, and the strategy draws attention to the arc of history and the impact of human civilization.

As one of the general goals of digital culture is to create a fluid interface between different practices, it is useful to note that there is a fine art corollary to data visualization. While *Anthropocene Footprints* still has a desire to convey empirical information at its core, artists are freer to pursue subjective interpretations of data and their meaning. For example, artist Julie Freeman's 2014–18 web-based project, *We Need Us*, feeds off the world of big data without providing any definite conclusions. The data for *We Need Us* were imported from Zooniverse, the internet portal that crowd-sources scientific research to the general public. The Zooniverse slogan is "people-powered research," a reference to the fact that even in our age of algorithms, artificial intelligence, and machine learning, the human eye still rules certain types of interpretation. One of the threads in *We Need Us* is called *Gravity Spy*, which was a project whereby users identified and classified glitches in the astrophysical data captured by the Laser Interferometer Gravitational-Wave Observatory. Freeman used data from the project as her raw material, manipulating them to create abstract visions of color and shape not unlike visualizations of music (figure 11.16). Her work is human centered, as the overall title plaintively announces. Freeman's actual subject is not necessarily the research itself but the people who are drawn to this digital realm. As she told an interviewer for TED, "What do they click on? When do they click on it? Where are they from?"

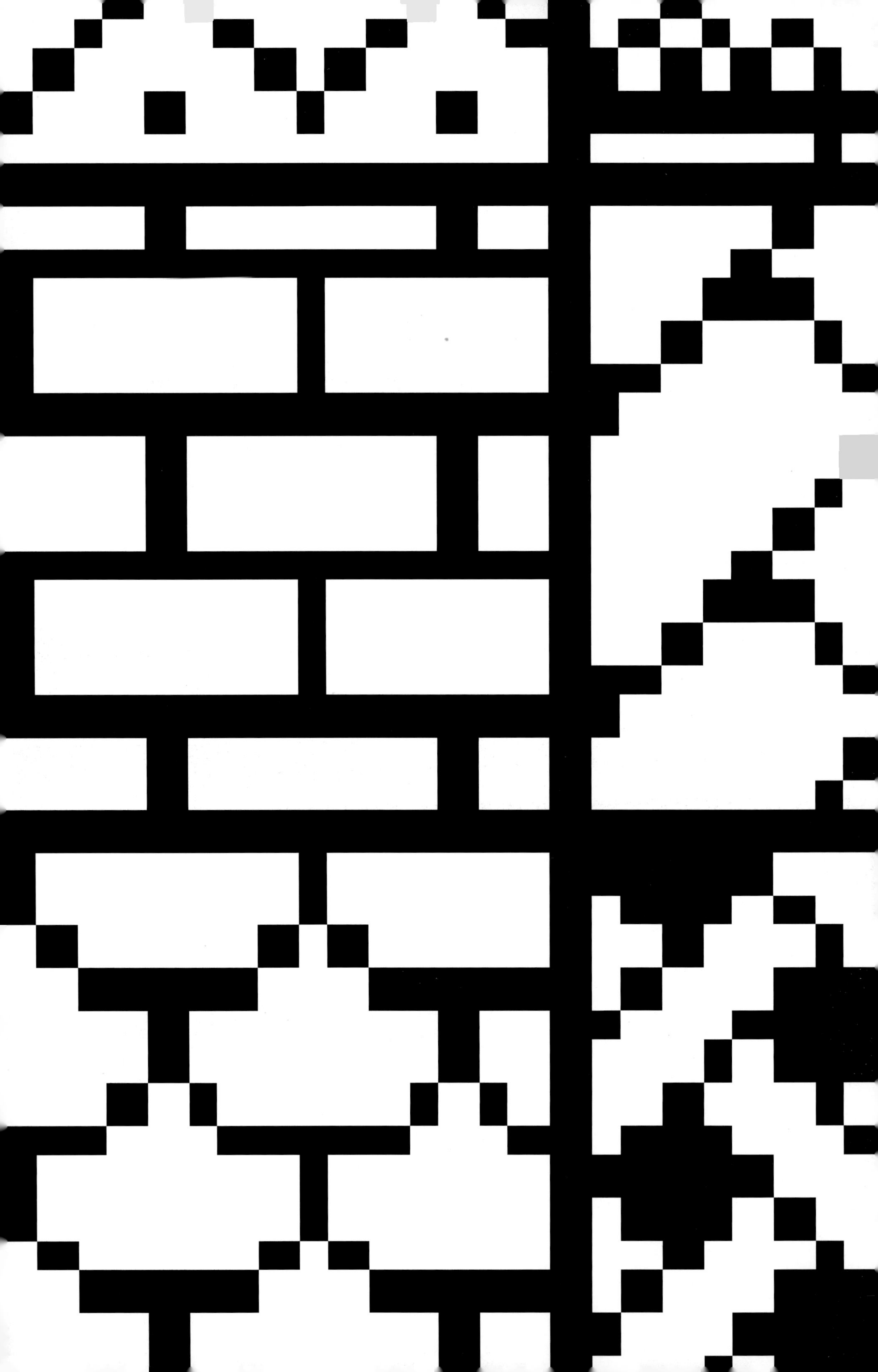

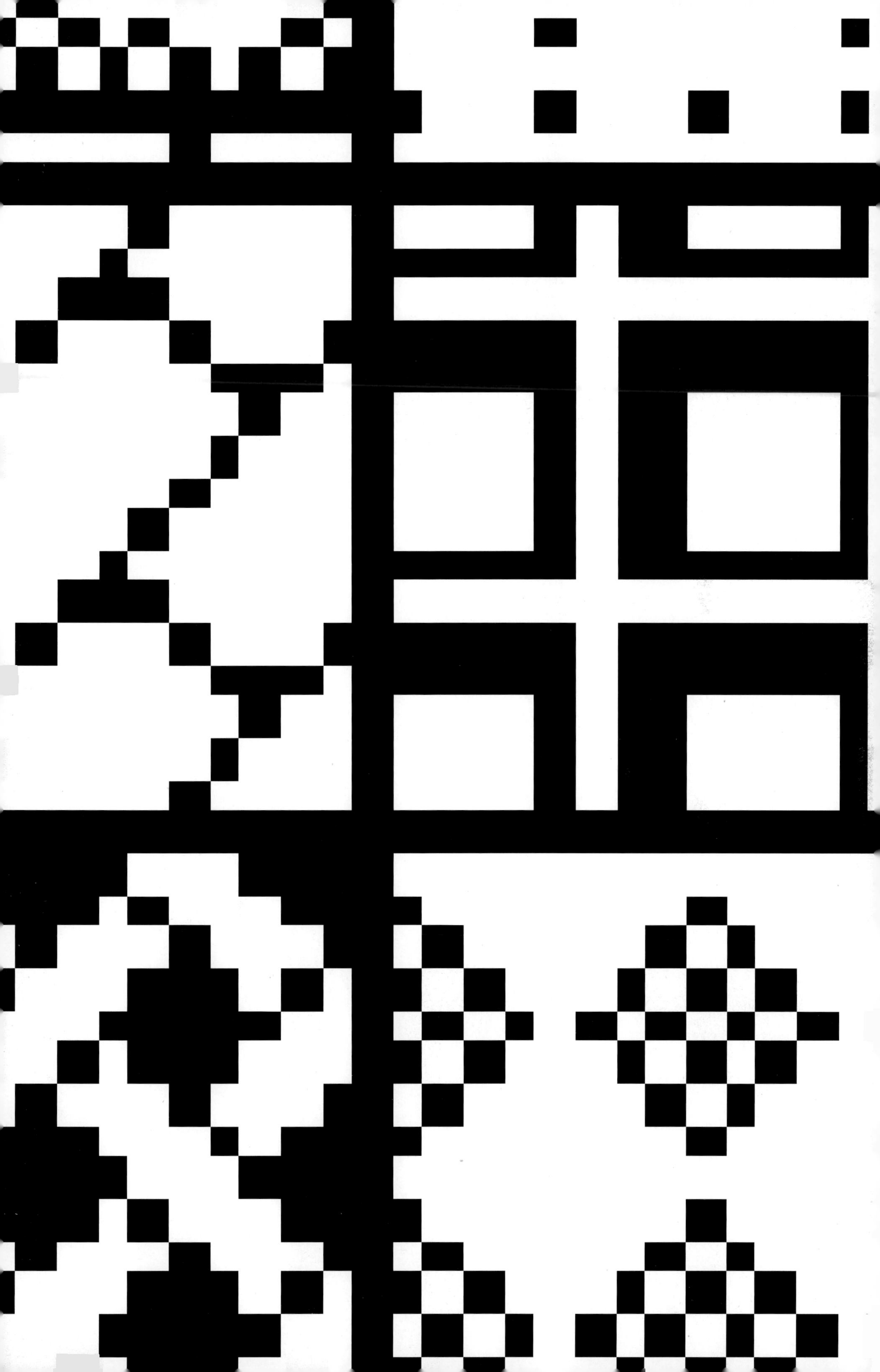

12.1. Paul Philippoteaux, *Cyclorama of the Battle of Gettysburg*, 1883

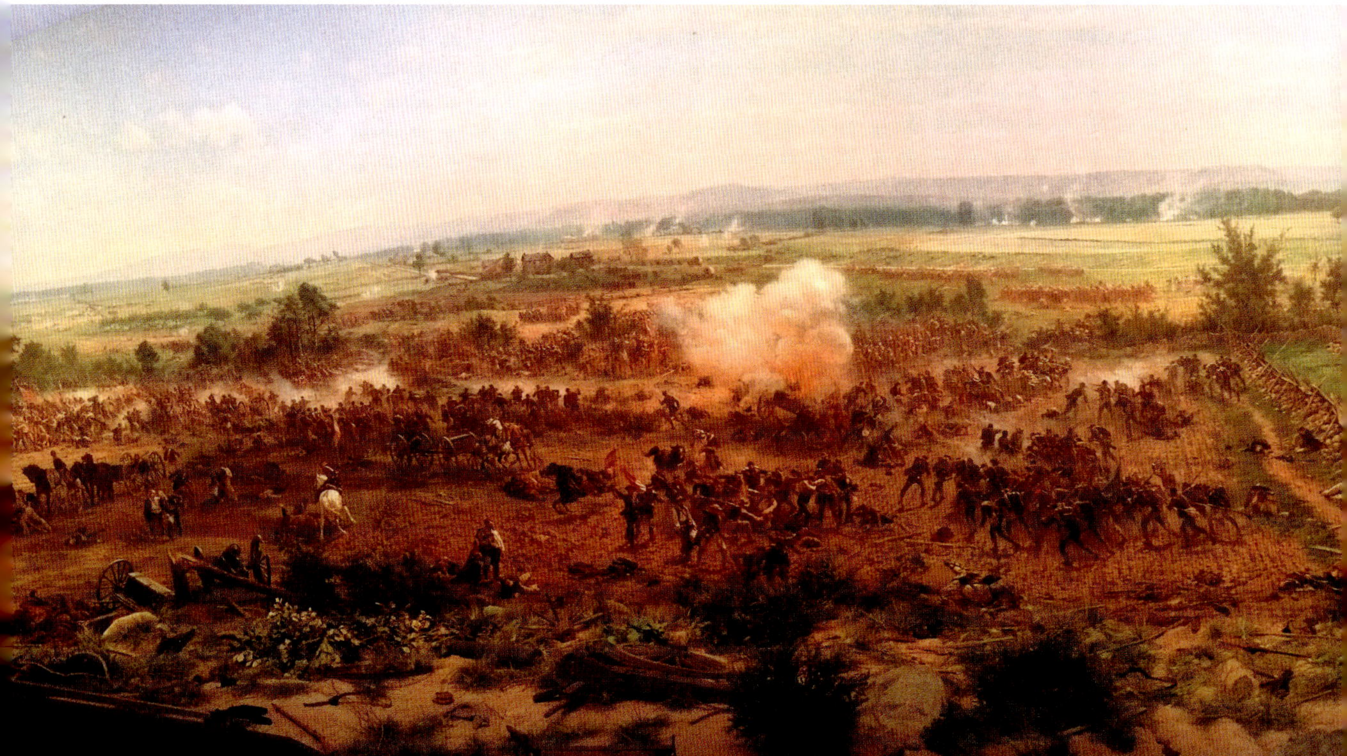

Twelve. Virtual Reality

Perhaps the most buzzworthy trends in digital design over the last few years have involved advances in virtual reality. As the technology has progressed and the excitement increased, something of a meme among web content providers (aka journalists) is to declare some phenomenon or another from the analog past to be "virtual reality before there was virtual reality." There is something viable behind these assertions, as VR, like so much of digital design, is more embedded in history and precedent than many of its purveyors acknowledge. Perhaps the fifteenth-century

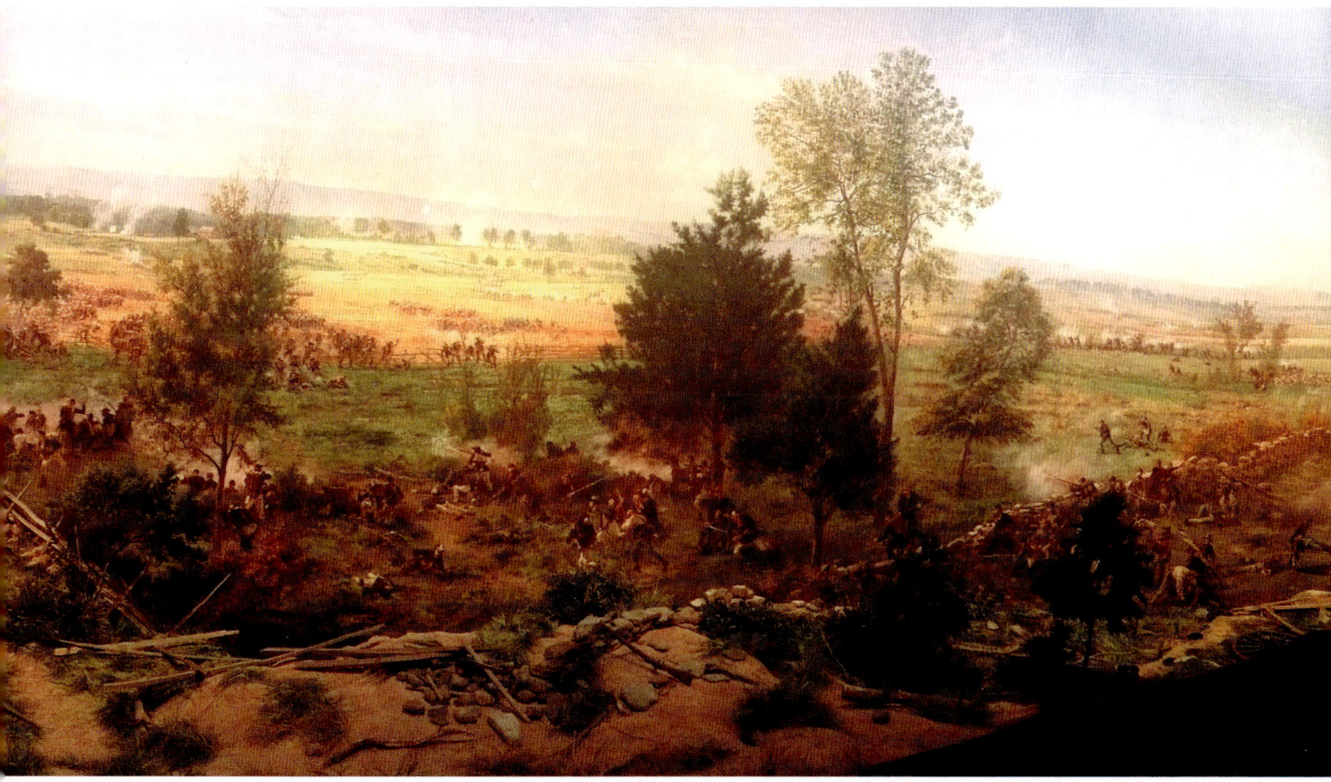

invention of linear perspective drawing is the most obvious historical precursor to today's virtual reality. Around six hundred years ago, architect Filippo Brunelleschi famously produced a perspective rendering of Florence's Baptistery and invited people to stand in front of the building and compare the real thing with his simulated reality. Brunelleschi made the experience into something of a spectacle, as he added a flourish by having spectators first peer at the actual Baptistery through a hole in the back of the painting, and then the architect would raise a mirror and dramatically reveal his virtual rendering.

A more sophisticated form of Brunelleschi's gambit was brought to the wider European public centuries later in the form of the panorama painting. Panoramas are huge pictures—some hundreds of feet wide—which are designed to immerse the viewer in an all-encompassing scene. The word "panorama" was coined in the late 1700s by Robert Barker, an Edinburgh-based painter and entrepreneur. Barker's original panorama—the word is based on the Greek roots for "all view"—showed a vista of the Scottish city where he had made his home. Barker's invention was an immediate success, and in the 1790s he built the first dedicated cylindrical building in London (its shape the root of the term "cyclorama"). With a viewing platform at the center of the space, the patron was situated in an all-seeing position as the master of a panopticon. This type of installation is important to the notion of panoramas as virtual reality, as it can eliminate distractions and allows viewers to lose themselves more thoroughly in the picture. Also, a Londoner who views an Edinburgh cityscape is transported into a different location, a simulation of a city far away. Panoramas became a crowd-pleasing juggernaut of mass entertainment in the 1800s, and today's purveyors of virtual reality can only hope that their technology will captivate the public's attention in similar fashion.

In the United States, the most famous iteration of the spectacle is the *Cyclorama of the Battle of Gettysburg*, which was painted in 1883 at a time when the wounds of the Civil War (1861–65) were still mostly fresh in the minds of the American people (figure 12.1). Commissioned as a business venture, the backers hired French artist Paul Philippoteaux to render an almost four-hundred-foot-wide view of the iconic 1863 battle. Dramatic views of armed conflict became a staple of the cyclorama business, and Philippoteaux completed at least three more views of Gettysburg, while other artists produced another half dozen. The degree of illusion was enhanced in the nineteenth century by the introduction of three-dimensional painted scenery in the space between the viewing platform and the panoramic painting, adding an element akin to today's augmented reality, whereby a "real" photo is blended with digital effects.

Another nineteenth-century mass entertainment with obvious kinship to virtual reality was the stereoscope. While Charles Wheatstone discovered the concept of tricking the brain into perceiving three dimensions through viewing two carefully calibrated images of the same scene (one through each eye), the eminent British physicist David Brewster created the first stereoscopic headset. Like virtual reality goggles or a bespoke cyclorama building, the stereoscope relied on shutting out the real world in favor of a simulation. The stereoscope also reconfigured the virtual reality experience from a social one—visiting a panorama in groups—to an individual one, as each viewer becomes lost, alone, in a scene of Tower Bridge, Buckingham Palace, or the like. By the end of the 1850s the London Stereoscopic and Photographic Company offered more than a million separate scenes as stereoscope mania swept across Europe and the United States.

Of course, theater and film continually brush up against the notion of virtual reality insomuch as they provide an immersive experience through which the viewer can lose themselves for an hour or two. Through scenery and background cycloramas, a virtual place could also be conjured, although one that is sharply demarcated from the realm of the viewer. Notably, in early twentieth-century theater there developed a clear precedent for virtual reality in the form of a more holistic type of theatrical simulation of actual reality. Some directors and scenic designers envisioned a play where the actors and viewers inhabited the same theatrical space. Rather than having a seating area sharply separated from the imaginary world of the play, the audience would become an integral part of the mise-en-scène. A fine example of this strategy opened at the Century Theater in New York City on January 15, 1924. This was director Max Reinhardt's revival of *The Miracle*, a play by Karl Vollmöller and staged by Reinhardt in 1912. Reinhardt's *Miracle* was a pantomime, or wordless play, based on the mystical and emotional journey of a medieval nun. Without dialogue, the simulated environment of a cathedral (the main set) became a more significant vehicle of communication.

The cathedral setting of *The Miracle* was not separated from the audience's space; rather, the entire auditorium had been transformed into a spectacular church (figure 12.2). With the orchestra and choir removed to the balcony, the audience sat in the pews of this imaginary world, with members of the cast circulating among them. As John Corbin reported for the *New York Times*, "To provide setting for 'The Miracle' a preliminary miracle was wrought in the Century Theatre. Inside the red and gold auditorium of the big playhouse on Central Park West has been set up the solid similitude of a Gothic Cathedral, its soaring columns and groined arches filling the stage and masking the interior of the house as far back as the balcony. . . . Nothing like it has ever been done in a New York theatre and probably nothing quite like it anywhere else in the world."

Reinhardt's simulated reality had been brought to fruition by the noted American industrial designer Norman Bel Geddes. In the early 1920s, Bel Geddes had established himself in New York as an innovative stage designer, and his atmospheric use of light was deemed especially noteworthy. Several factors in the set design of *The Miracle* would later resonate in the digital world of virtual reality, and illumination is near the top of that list. Just as it was crucial for Bel Geddes to create a light environment that unified the scene, so with virtual reality, convincing light that knits the simulated world together is one of the most significant technological challenges. Furthermore, Bel Geddes designed not just the walls and ceiling to appear as a cathedral, but the floor was also made to appear as faux stone. In contemporary VR, the floor is considered an element of the utmost importance to the user's sense of presence;

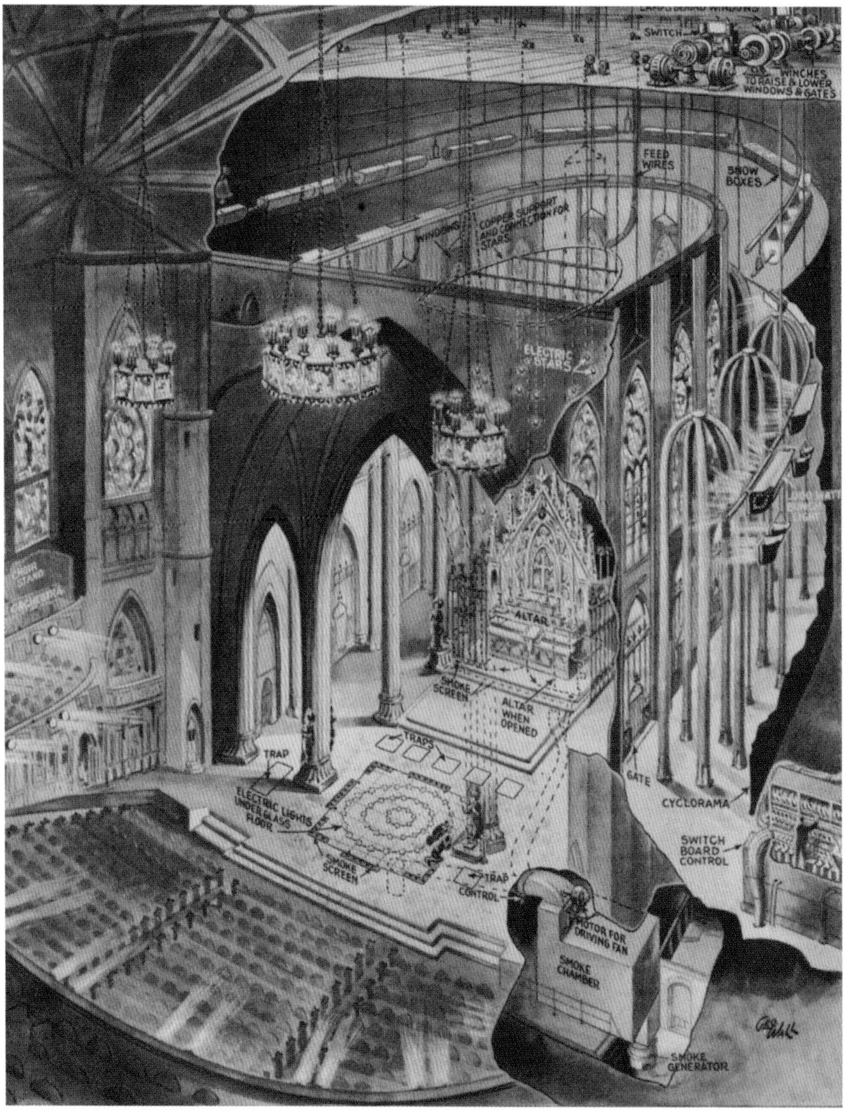

12.2. Set for *The Miracle*, directed by Max Reinhardt, 1924

watch anyone first put on a virtual reality headset, and they will invariably quickly look at the floor to establish that they are "truly" in a completely new realm. Last, a great deal of coverage about *The Miracle* and its staging concerned the technical complexity and great expense of the production. In a similar vein (discussed below), virtual reality aficionados are known for their obsession with the actual gear as much as or even more than their simulated experience. With both the theater and virtual reality, the goal is to make the world disappear, but paradoxically, the powerful technology that (possibly) accomplishes this feat becomes an object of fascination and desire that outshines the simulation.

Of course, entering the immersive environment is the most obvious forerunner to the virtual reality experience. The connection became closer in the 1920s, an era when set designers began experimenting with a novel range of visual effects. One of the icons of film in this regard was Fritz Lang's 1927 epic melodrama *Metropolis*. Produced by Universum Film, this early blockbuster enjoyed one of the most substantial budgets in film history up to that point. While the convoluted story—a combination of dystopian social commentary, religious allegory, and romantic drama—might seem to have priority, in fact even Director Lang was known to remark that the urban setting was the focus of the film. In this regard, the skyline of the title city represented one of the most iconic shots, and the city served as a character of sorts more than as a background (figure 12.3). The setting was designed by Otto Hunte, Erich Kettelhut, and Karl Vollbrecht, who worked alongside Lang to visualize a set of towers that loomed menacingly over the crowded streets and highways of Metropolis. Like a cyclorama, the cityscape was simulated through a combination of painted backdrops and three-dimensional objects. Lang used stop-action photography to animate the scene with moving vehicles as well as to show roving spotlights on the buildings, this

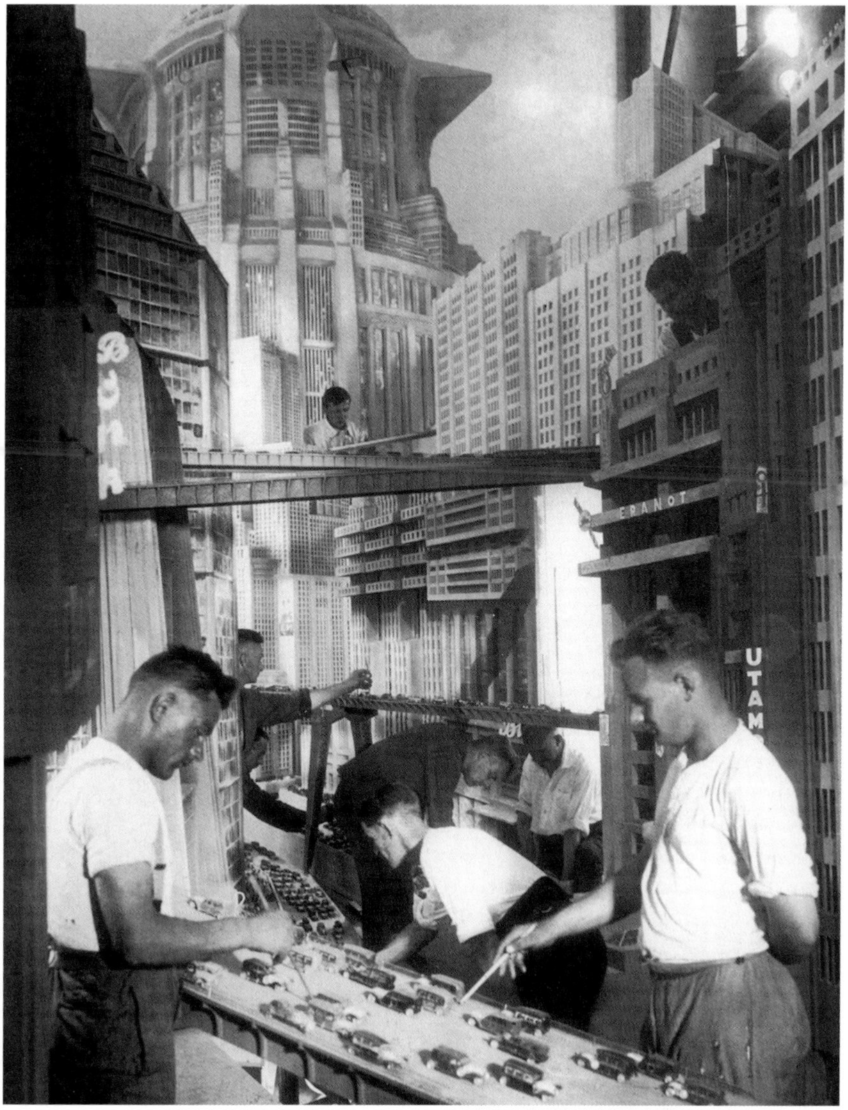

12.3. Set for *Metropolis*, directed by Fritz Lang, 1927

latter effect requiring the "lights" to be ingeniously painted on the buildings sequentially. These visual effects allowed Lang to create a vision of future dystopia, a society that viewers could lose themselves in despite the vagaries of the plot.

From analog to digital, dystopia to utopia, one can travel today in their mind's eye from Metropolis to Wakanda. In the 2018 film *Black Panther*, the futuristic setting also played an outsized role in the narrative. *Black Panther* is a superhero movie that features a compelling backstory, set in a sophisticated African society untouched by contact with the rest of the world and thus spared the predations of colonialism. Wakandan society is not just advanced, but technologically far superior to the rest of the globe. The capital of Wakanda, called the Golden City, best captures the Afrofuturist tone and feel of the production, as it blends traditional African forms with modern structures. Afrofuturism is a fluid design style that combines elements of science fiction—arguably going as far back as W.E.B. Du Bois's 1920 short story "The Comet"—with mysticism, technology, and history. Octavia Butler's 1979 novel *Kindred*, which combines time travel with America's antebellum history, is often cited as a key influence on the Afrofuturist genre. The production designer of *Black Panther*, Hannah Beachler, along with many of the visual effects supervisors, traveled to various African countries to devise the look of the film. Beachler et al. combined elements of everything from historic Malian pyramids to contemporary Ugandan skyscrapers to create a pan-African virtual world. She also culled forms from outside Africa, noting that the fluid digital architecture of Zaha Hadid played into the overall design.

While the skyline of Metropolis had been created by a small team of designers, the six miles of computer graphic imagery (CGI) that make up the Golden City required multiple effects studios and hundreds of artists to complete. Much of the work on the city was contracted to Industrial Light and Magic, where Craig Hammack was the overall visual effects supervisor. Metropolis had been hand painted in a workshop, while the creators of the Golden City relied mainly on three CGI programs. The central piece of software was Autodesk's 3ds Max, an animation and three-dimensional modeling program widely used in the video game and film industries. It was supplemented in places by Chaos Group's V-Ray and also RenderMan, the latter a CGI rendering program originally developed at George Lucas's Industrial Light and Magic, later spun into Pixar. (RenderMan dominates the VFX side of the movie industry, as fully 90 percent of the winners of the Academy Award for Best Visual Effects has used the software since its release). Importantly, RenderMan greatly reduced the amount of laborious frame-by-frame drawing that had made feature-length animated movies a difficult proposition. Algorithmic technology comes into play, as the elements of the Golden City were located through the process known as "procedural scattering," which creates a natural-looking dispersion of buildings and people. Although digitally driven, this sort of production still requires much artistic labor; in the end, every one of almost sixty thousand buildings need to be created on a computer by a digital designer. The question comes to the fore, is the experience of this highly realistic digital virtual world of 2018 materially different from that of 1927, or have the details and production values advanced while the overarching filmic encounter remains the same?

As technology continued to become more central to the world of mass entertainment in the later twentieth century, various inventors, and eccentrics, have sought to bring virtual reality into the mainstream through various gadgets and contraptions. Perhaps the most successful entrepreneur of this type was Morton Heilig, whose sixties Sensorama Simulator exemplified the drive to bring tactile and olfactory stimuli to a movie-watching experience (figure 12.4). With a stereoscopic film as the main element, the Sensorama enveloped the user in a virtual environment. That the Sensorama never became a sustained entertainment is not really that surprising, as it required one to stick their head into an imposing machine. Clearly, not for the claustrophobic. Nonetheless, the Sensorama represented a prototype for many of today's arcade video games, whereby a rumble seat and an enclosed capsule puts the player in a simulated environment.

Of course, the world of video games fomented the first mainstream acceptance of digital simulations, as well as acting as the proving ground for one of the originators of virtual reality. Jaron Lanier, the widely acknowledged godfather of virtual reality, spent the early eighties developing video games independently and at Atari. Then, in 1984, he founded VPL Research along with Thomas Zimmerman, establishing the first start-up dedicated to the commercial marketing of virtual reality technology. In the eighties, VPL worked to devise some of the first VR products, including the Data Glove (figure 12.5) for motion capture and one of the earliest head-mounted displays. While the Data Glove was their most successful venture (it retailed for $8,800 in 1989), VPL also created a futuristic data suit, the sensors on which would capture the motion of one's entire body. Of course, this hardware was enabled by continually evolving software that aimed to increase fluidity and frame rate as the available processing power advanced.

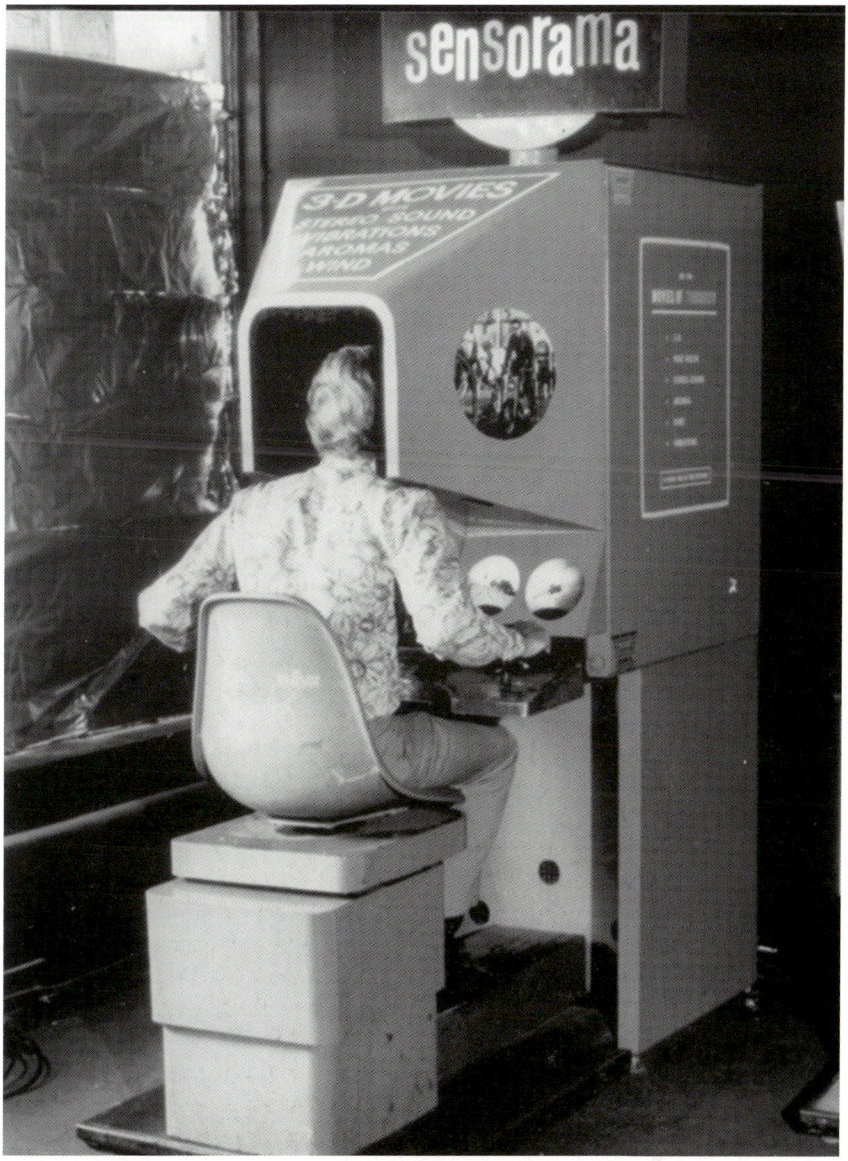

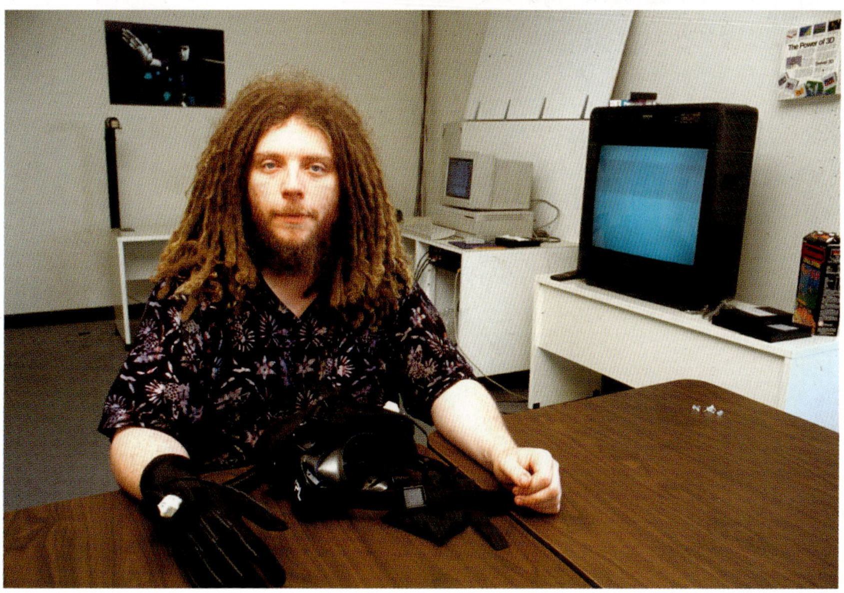

12.4. Morton Heilig, Sensorama Simulator, 1962
12.5. Jaron Lanier, Data Glove, 1989

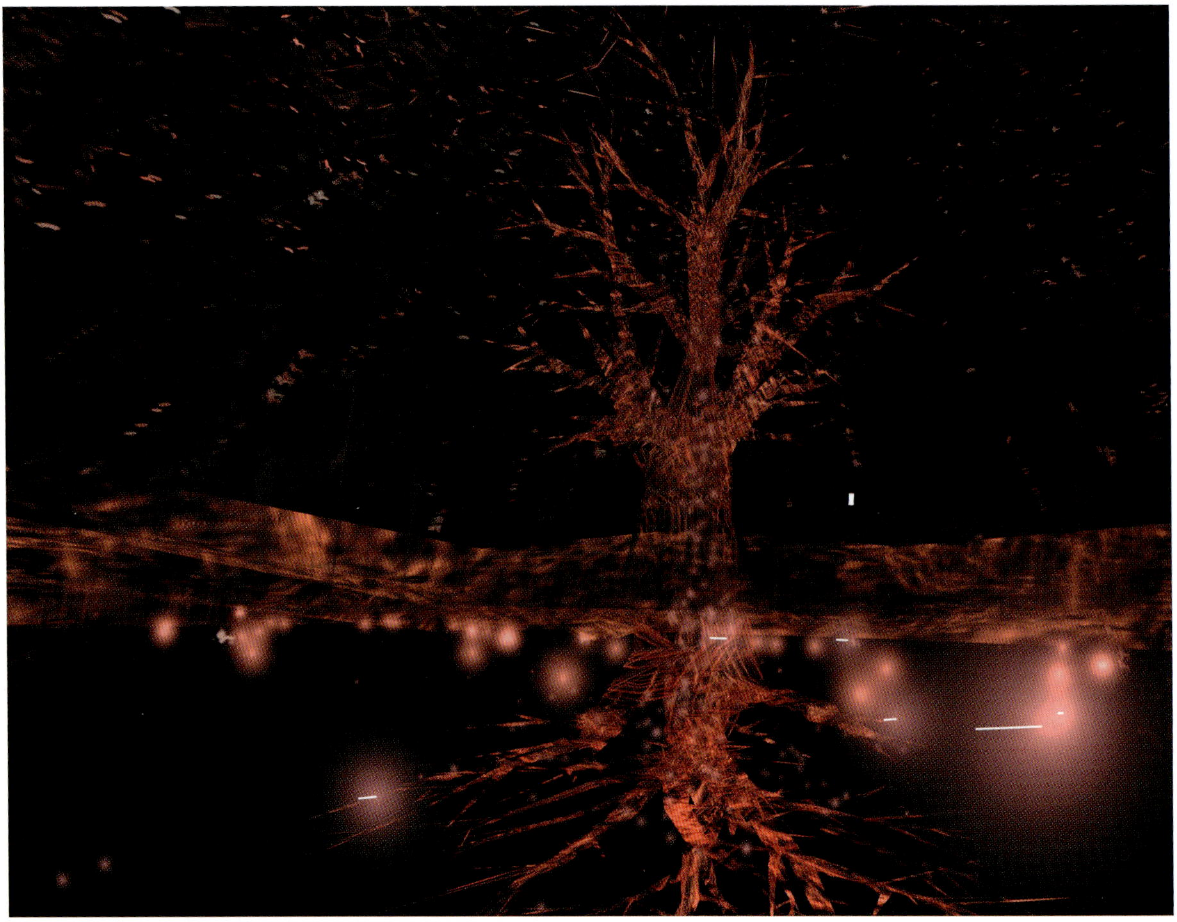

12.6. Char Davies, *Osmose*, 1995

As one of the leaders at VPL, Lanier gradually proved to be more than just a company CEO, but also a VR visionary of sorts. In the eighties a slew of terms was making the rounds—artificial realities and virtual environments among them—and Lanier is generally credited with establishing the term virtual reality while also promoting his vision of a technology that could heighten human interactions. This is the key point: for Lanier, virtual reality was about not making a human connection to a machine, but rather to enhance the intimacy of real relationships. He extolled this view to a reporter for the *New York Times* in 1989, envisioning a virtual environment where "You and your lover trade eyes so that you're responsible for each other's point of view. It's an amazingly profound thing." Lanier was aspirational in his dreams for virtual reality as expressed at the time, as one element that has been the greatest barrier to VR has been the fact that the user is alone in the simulated environment. Hybrid platforms such as the browser-based virtual world *Second Life* provide social interactions for one's avatar, but true virtual reality puts the human into a solitary existence. That Lanier dreamed of uniting with a lover in new, soulful ways shows that, like so many digital designers, he was a romantic at heart, and he hoped to enhance human connections through virtual reality, but in the eighties the technology was not there yet. In 1990, VPL filed for bankruptcy, and for the time being, virtual reality reverted to the realm of gimmickry like the Sensorama in an arcade.

While the nineties was uneventful in terms of the commercial advancement of virtual reality, the decade did see the creation of one of the most compelling VR artworks. In 1995, Char Davies created *Osmose* (figure 12.6), a virtual reality installation that sought to provide the same type of immersive, emotional experience that Lanier had envisioned. *Osmose* was designed as a full-body experience that used both a headset and a motion-tracking vest. The experience was based on exploration, as the user could travel between twelve different natural worlds: pond, tree, subterranean, abyss, and so on. In uniting the body, mind, and natural world, *Osmose* resonated with the sentiment of other analog, experiential earthworks such as Ana Mendieta's *Tree of Life* series. Importantly, navigation within *Osmose* was modeled on scuba diving, and movement in the virtual worlds was controlled by breathing and shifting one's weight. As in scuba, inflating one's lungs made the user more buoyant, and they would float upward in the virtual space, while breathing out had the opposite effect.

The environment in *Osmose* made a virtue out of low-resolution graphics, as the worlds were misty and evocative, suggesting rather than delineating a detailed landscape. The purpose of *Osmose*, however, was for the user to eventually turn inward, not outward: a calm and contemplative sense of self. Like other virtual reality pioneers, Davies hoped the technology would allow for a more profound connection between human and computer. She argued, "Traditional interface boundaries between machine and human can be transcended. . . . Immersive virtual space, when stripped of its conventions, can provide an intriguing spatio-temporal context in which to explore the self's subjective experience of 'being-in-the-world'—as embodied consciousness in an enveloping space where boundaries between inner/outer, and mind/body dissolve." Of course, this speculative merging of machine and self continues today as an unresolved, aspirational focus of human–computer interaction.

Perhaps it was inevitable that virtual reality, which had been essentially tabled for around two decades, would return with new gear in recent years. The timeline of the company Oculus VR, a maker of headsets and hand controllers, tells the story of this latest surge in interest. The founder, Palmer Luckey, started working on prototype headsets about a decade ago, working as an amateur who was something of an obsessive collector of VR gadgets. As he continued to work on his own device, he decided to form a company to facilitate a Kickstarter business plan. Oculus VR was founded in 2012, and that same year Luckey's headsets started gaining attention in gamer culture, appearing at conferences and on bulletin boards like Reddit. While the Kickstarter campaign was a brilliant success, it did not compare to the fact that Oculus VR was acquired by Facebook in 2014 for about $2 billion, setting the stage for its rapid expansion.

Finally (in accelerated Silicon Valley terms), the first headset, the Oculus Rift (figure 12.7), was released in 2016, the same year as its major competitor, the HTC Vive. Compared to older equipment, both the Rift and the Vive offered much faster frame rates, larger fields of view, and reduced lag; they were technologically superior in every way. While the gadgets themselves cost a pricey five hundred to eight hundred dollars, to work, they needed to be tethered to powerful desktop computers at much greater expense. In 2016, few laptops on the market could effectively power the graphical load of virtual reality. While other companies have offered many less expensive solutions—notably Google Cardboard paired with a smartphone—only these expensive machines provide anything close to an immersive, rich experience for the user. Despite their limitations, the release of the Rift and the Vive powered new money and energy to pour into the field, and there has been a gold rush, much of it recorded for posterity in TED talks, of entrepreneurs promising new and better technology.

In what has always been a paradox in the VR world, expensive hardware continues to rule the virtual. While in the eighties a virtual reality setup cost as much as $200,000, today's headsets are still something of a gaming luxury. Meta's—née Facebook's—$299 Oculus Quest 2, released in 2020, has lately garnered the largest

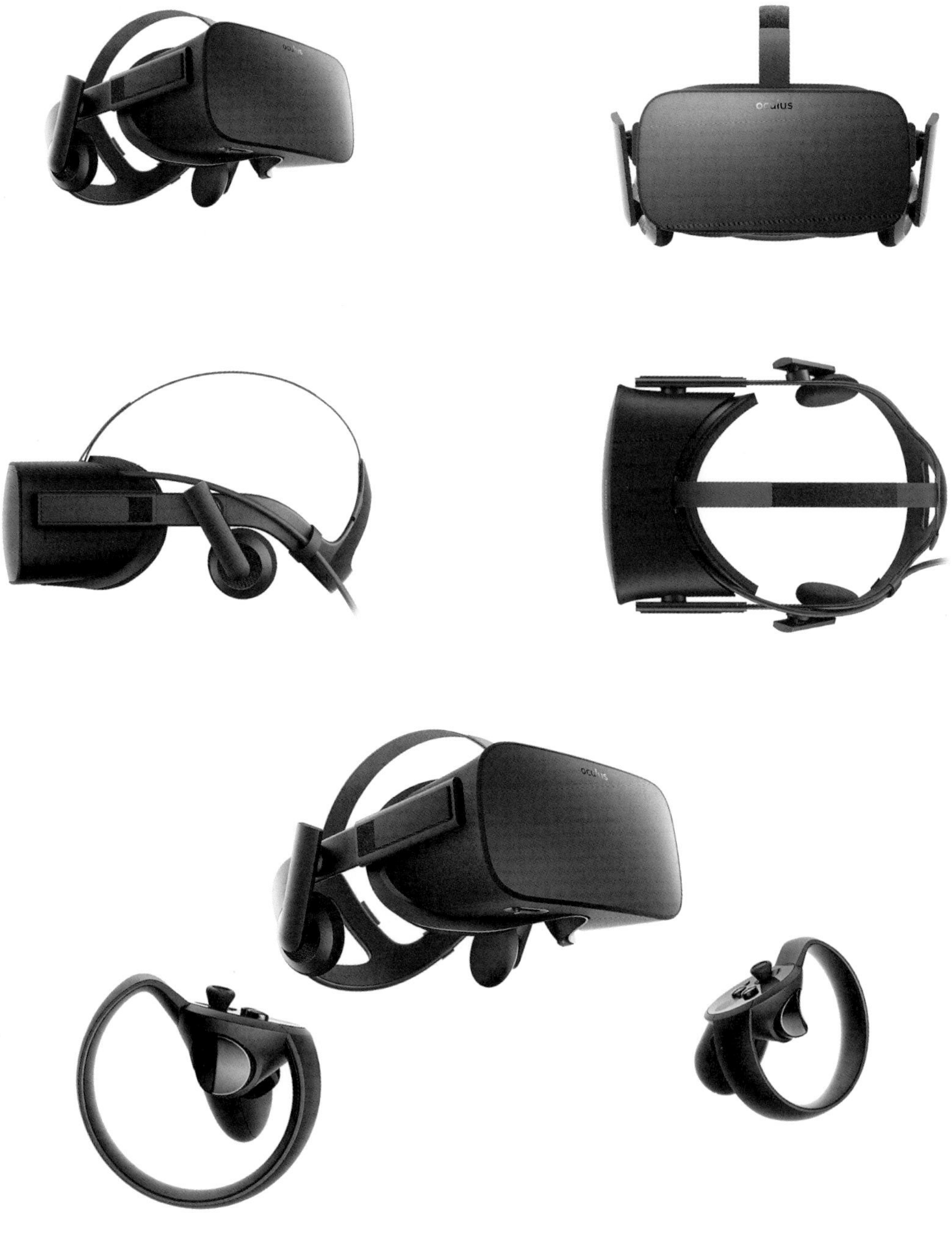

12.7. Oculus VR, Oculus Rift headset, 2016

market share. Devices such as the Quest 2 have captured the public's imagination, and what should be in theory the most immersive and seamless digital experience has actually begotten the need to gear up like a fighter pilot. Both the Quest and the Vive are designed with this in mind, as neither is particularly stylish outside a generalized high-tech shape. None of the headsets has a strong design personality, and they look close to interchangeable.

While all this sleek plastic has given virtual reality a futuristic, cyborg vibe that attracts users, especially gamers, the hardware has also been the source of enduring physical limitations. Because the hardware is not virtual, it can be heavy and is cumbersome to wear. The goggles can chafe, and necks can ache. Furthermore, while science-fiction movies such as *Ready Player One* imagine a contraption that will allow for unconstrained physical movement, virtual reality today requires a large, actual unobstructed space for a user to move around without injury; and, of course, there is something mildly comical about watching a friend

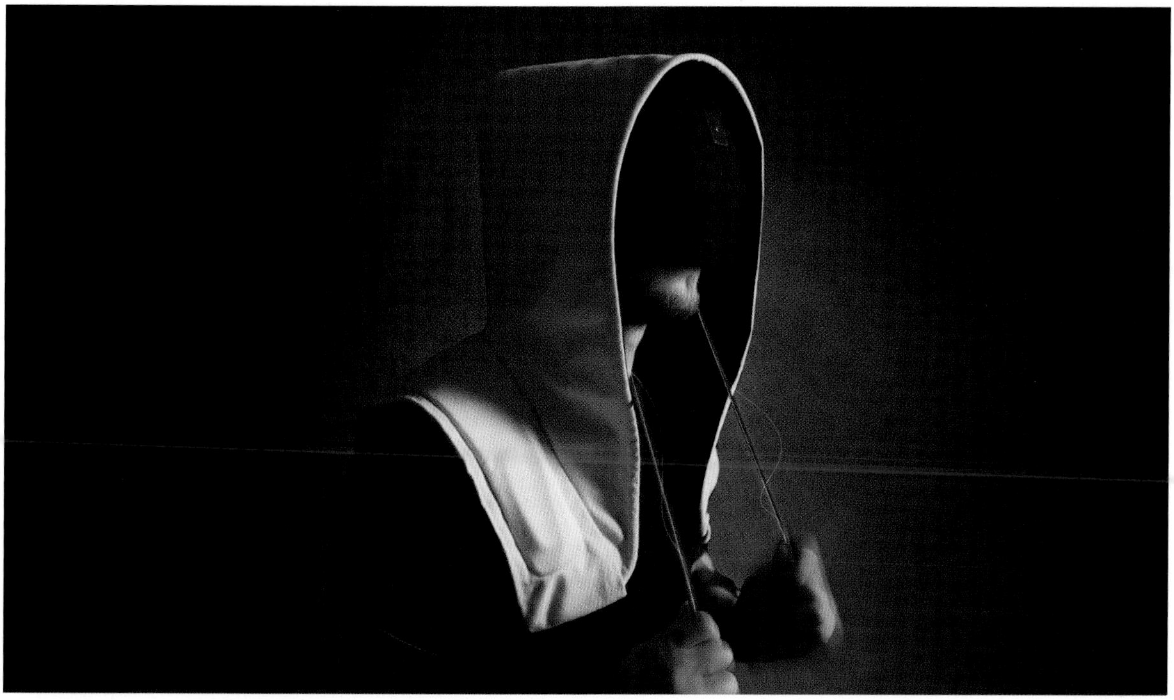

12.8. Artefact Design, Shadow VR wearables, 2019

twist and swerve, a factor that somewhat erodes the technical cool of the gear.

For the last couple of years, the design of virtual reality gear has recalled Henry Ford's century-old opinion on the styling of his company's flagship product, the Model T: "Any customer can have a car painted any color that he wants so long as it is black." Ford had focused solely on quality and functionality back in 1909 and saw styling of all sorts as a frivolous pursuit. As of late, multiple industrial designers have applied themselves to create a design breakthrough in VR, using color or shape to whet consumer desire for a device that exudes sophistication, not PlayStation. But VR gear design is not just about visual pleasure; it also seeks to address the inherently uncomfortable process of adjusting and wearing the current class of headsets and hand controllers. For example, Seattle-based Artefact Group has introduced the Shadow wearables collection (figure 12.8) as part of their experimental VR2020 project. Founded in Seattle in 2006 by Rob Girling and Gavin Kelly, Artefact has successfully navigated multiple waves of technological change, including VR. The overarching design theme of the Shadow is the ubiquitous hoodie sweatshirt, which in this case is matched with a knit cap concealing a headset and sleeves full of sensors. The Shadow ensemble is not about colors that pop—it is still mainly black with a white hood—but about an understated street credibility that is also an ergonomic success.

Additionally, the Shadow offers features that address some of the limitations of virtual reality while setting the stage for future developments. For example, a small screen on the hoodie would allow friends to see what the user is viewing. Artefact also proposes the use of cameras or smart fabric to record facial expressions that can then be transmitted to one's avatar in the manner of motion capture CGI. The sleeves are designed to provide greater haptic feedback.

In a similar vein, Branko Lukic, founder of Nonobject, has sought to improve the experience of using VR gear. Sounding a theme propounded by many in the field, Lukic has decried the overall approach embedded in many digital designs. He told Mark Wilson of *Fast Company* in 2017, "As we look around, we see our industry doing what it does time and time again. It gets into tech gadgets driven by technology, not thinking about the human. . . . A 'wearable' is not just something you strap on your head." Nonobject has recently offered up a series of what they call VR.ables, which are more human centered in their design. These projects seek to address several ergonomic drawbacks currently in play: for example, one headset splits between the eyes so that it does not tangle and muss people's hair. Another is shaped like a baseball cap, a familiar wearable that could lower resistance to wearing an awkward-looking headset. While it would seem that the ergonomic and comfort issues are solvable, it is not at all clear that Nonobject—or any other design studio for that matter—can climb the real mountain: making

VR gear look "cool" in public. Regardless of how human centered the take, the notorious social failure of Google Glasses was possibly a warning that VR industrial designers ignore at their peril: people do not want other people distracted and inhabiting another world while in their company, virtual or otherwise. It is hard to imagine broad acceptance of one's friend sitting in a coffee shop and suddenly putting on their VR ball cap. I think most of us would get up and leave.

Today multiple companies are also working to make the gear disappear completely. One of the biggest design challenges in this regard has been the hand controllers that allow users to interact through gesture. One strategy has been to eliminate them entirely. For example, Leap Motion has shifted its focus to VR in recent years and now offers its hand controllers as an accessory to the dominant headsets. The Leap Motion Controller is really a set of digital cameras that watch and track what your hands are doing and relay the motion to the VR system. Users can interact with a virtual world through flowing gestures and do not need to hold on to a physical object (most hand control systems require you to hold what looks like a pair of video game controllers). But for Leap Motion, the problem is haptics; it is disconcerting to grab and touch objects in a simulated world but never feel them. Other design firms such as Nonobject have tried to split the difference, creating the Air Hand, a tangible, haptic controller that is attached to the hand through elastic bands that distribute its weight evenly and less perceptibly than most.

In terms of functionality that has been brought to market, the Oculus Quest 2 has freed the user from the hassle and expense of the desktop tether (aspirational gear such as the Shadow hoodie are also intended to fold the CPU into the wearable). Truly, at this point, the technology for the most part remains part of gamer culture more than anything else—Amazon lists them under the category "video game VR headsets"—and the question remains as to whether virtual reality will ever break out of the entertainment realm and make a meaningful impact on design and culture.

Perhaps the most compelling personal narrative that tracks the emergence of both VR and the internet writ large is the career of Jaron Lanier, introduced above as a pioneer of virtual reality. As it happens, Lanier is perhaps the greatest apostate Silicon Valley has ever known. In the eighties he had dreamed of a simulated world that enhanced human relationships and in later years became a prophet of digital disillusion. His most cogent indictment of digital culture came in the 2010 book aptly titled *You Are Not a Gadget: A Manifesto*. In this work, Lanier argues that the internet is currently degrading human interactions, as locked-in technology channels individuality into homogeneous ruts. Rather than using technology as a tool that enhances relationships, people are becoming atomized extensions of the technology. "It's early in the twenty-first century, and that means that these words will mostly be read by nonpersons—automatons or numb mobs composed of people who are no longer acting as individuals. . . . [These words] will be copied millions of times by algorithms designed to send an advertisement to some person somewhere who happens to resonate with some fragment of what I say." Clearly, one of his major targets is social media, which he feels is dehumanizing as it reduces interaction to addictive but rather mindless likes and staged selfies. Decrying this dystopic "lifeless world of pure information," Lanier hoped through his book to break through via print and reach actual people.

Lanier hopes for reform, but he is not a Luddite (actually, the Luddites were not Luddites, as they embraced technology but had understandable objections to early nineteenth-century labor practices). So, in fact, Lanier is a Luddite in the accurate sense, as he still hopes that the internet can be harnessed to improve human experience. This impulse had led him back to virtual reality. During the era in which he wrote *You Are Not a Gadget*, Lanier was consulting with Microsoft on their motion control system Kinect. This Xbox peripheral was designed to use tracking cameras that would allow for more natural movement and richer interaction with the virtual world. In an opinion piece for the *Wall Street Journal*, Lanier argued that Kinect could enable what he called "somatic cognition," the flow state whereby one's body reacts before the person is aware they are acting: Lanier used skilled piano playing as an example. Speculating as the futurist he has always been, Lanier imagined a simulation that allowed people to assume virtual identities in a way that could lead to new understandings and intimacies. The Kinect system was initially one of the most successful gaming peripherals of all time, but like many virtual reality products, it suffered both by promising more than it could deliver and by a lack of support from outside software developers. Microsoft suspended the product in 2017, although some of the technology has been rolled into contemporary VR and AR products, and Microsoft has suggested they will soon reintroduce it. Today, Lanier is still hopeful about virtual reality's ability to humanize the internet. He told a reporter at *Wired* in 2017, "Virtual reality is a future trajectory where people get better and better at communicating more and more things in more fantastic and aesthetic ways that becomes this infinite adventure without end that's more interesting than seeking power and destroying everything."

Nonny de la Peña and Chris Milk are two designers of VR experiences who share some of the same aspirations as Lanier, mainly in the sense that digital technology will enhance human—not machine—connectivity. Between 2012 and 2014, de la Peña and her Santa Monica studio Emblematic worked on a commission from the World Economic Forum to create a VR experience that would truly communicate the plight of Syrian refugees, as their struggles exist mainly as an abstraction to people in wealthy developed societies. Focused on the devastation of Aleppo, de la Peña sought to invoke VR as an "empathy machine" that would connect with viewers on an emotional level. She realized at one point that the hardware she was using, an early version of the Oculus headset (notably, Palmer Luckey had interned for her at the University of Southern California Institute for Creative Technologies), was simply not immersive enough. Over the next few months, de la Peña built her own custom headset to fulfill the commission. Her combination of design, software, hardware, and filmmaking skills speaks to the complexity of working in the nascent field of virtual reality. But the goal of all this expertise is a simple one: connecting people. As she told a *Wall Street Journal* reporter in 2018, "If you and I were facing each other in the virtual world, would we begin to at least try to understand each other? Would we listen? Maybe. Probably. Yes."

Milk is likewise adamant that virtual reality “is not a video game peripheral” but rather a tool for igniting human emotion. In 2015, he partnered with the United Nations Virtual Reality (UNVR) project and Director Gabo Arora to tell the story of a twelve-year-old girl named Sidra who lived in a Jordanian refugee camp (figure 12.9). Sidra proves to be a poignant narrator, as her voiceover relates anecdotes about her current situation as well as her hopes for the future. Milk argues that VR technology makes Sidra’s plight more real to viewers because they feel present in a way that connects them to her. As mentioned above, a key factor in creating this enveloping sense of presence is the part most people overlook: the ground under one’s feet. When you look at the floor of the family’s tent or the dusty road outside through VR—even though that is not where the story is happening—you feel immersed in a new world. Like Lanier’s original vision of people who are able to look through one another’s eyes, one can feel a stronger bond with the refugees in the camp. Milk spoke aspirationally about UNVR at a TED conference in 2015: “So, it’s a machine. But through this machine we become more compassionate. We become more empathetic and we become more connected and, ultimately, we become more human.”

Because of its utility as an experiential, storytelling medium, virtual reality has become pervasive in the commercial design business. As yet, however, it does not have a staple, bread-and-butter role to play, but rather often serves brand building as part of an ephemeral, performative strategy. Advertisers often hope for a halo effect from this type of work. Optimist Design (OD), the Los Angeles firm founded by Tino Schaedler, is one of many that produces events and performances. Schaedler has a multidisciplinary background, having trained and worked as an architect in Germany before shifting his focus to production design and digital effects for the film industry. Optimist is similarly cross-disciplinary in its work, creating everything from print to spectacular launch parties. For example, OD designed the futuristic setting for the 2010 premiere of *Tron Legacy*. Of course, the original 1982 movie, *Tron*, is an oft-cited science-fiction thriller rooted in virtual reality. The setting for the 2010 premiere of the sequel was in fact the inverse of VR, as it was an actual environment that simulated a virtual world.

Many design studios use VR to build their own brands, reassuring clients that they are on the cutting edge of the field. For example, many design firms employ the halo effect of having a virtual reality section on their websites, regardless of whether there is a market for substantial VR work. Optimist Design’s 2015 contribution to the London Design Festival is a case in point. A collaboration between OD, United Realities (a partner firm that has designed VR music videos), and the music production studio Nordmeister, Odyssey, as it was called, offered a unique multisensory VR experience. It started with a tangible object, the construction of a jet engine that the user could mount. This was combined with a VR video shown through Oculus Rift that allowed the viewer to feel that they are taking off and soaring into the sky. The effect was enhanced by a vest that vibrated with the low-frequency rumble of a turbine.

Perhaps the most important element of the Odyssey experience was the sound. The audio was “spatial,” meaning that it created a sensation of dimension and multiple sources. The

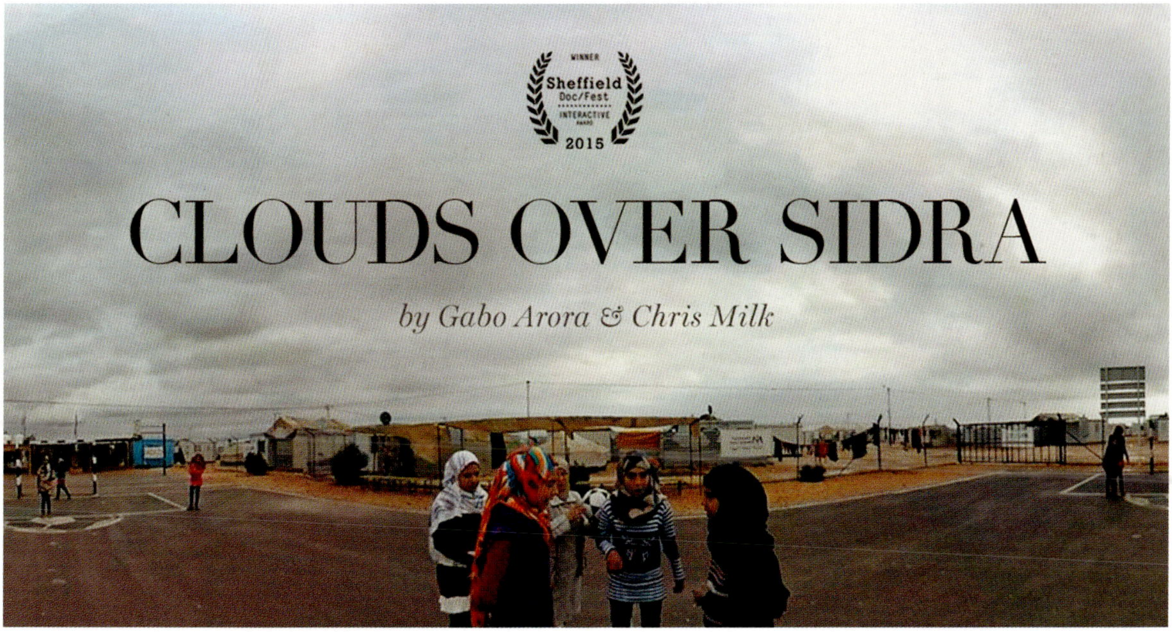

12.9. Gabo Arora and Chris Milk, dirs., *Clouds Over Sidra*, United Nations Virtual Reality project, 2015

most sophisticated type of spatial audio creates the illusion of a 360-degree soundscape that responds to movements of the viewer's head. While most people think of virtual reality as primarily a visual experience, the employment of complex digital audio files can truly determine how real the user's sensation actually feels. Most VR soundscapes involve static audio that does not respond to the user's movements, creating a significant disconnect on an intuitive level. Also, as so many VR designers seek to transmit an affecting message, it is imperative that the audio function accordingly. There is a parallel here with most abstract motion graphics, the viewing of which on mute conveys little emotional impact; try watching *Fantasia* with the sound off. Finally, it is worth noting how the tactile element of Odyssey combined with VR audio and video to create a Sensorama-like experience, reminding one how VR is rooted in play.

While virtual reality has established a beachhead in many of the established design disciplines, some of the most practical work has come in the architectural realm. Obviously, architecture deals in real space in a way that makes it more interconnected to technology that replaces the real world with a virtual simulacrum. Architecturally, virtual reality has affected the building professions both in the form of a design tool and as a key element of contemporary presentation strategies. In this latter domain, virtual reality has made an impact on architectural illustration, as it promises to enable new modes of experiencing unbuilt projects. Remember that virtual reality is part of a historical continuum of myriad practices that seek to simulate the actual built world, and it should not be understood only in the current narrow sense of wearing goggles that block out the ambient environment.

Appraising the impact of virtual reality on architectural rendering, which like many digital design disciplines at times features perhaps more rhetoric than substance, in terms of the trajectory of the field over the last century is illuminating. The architect Marion Mahony Griffin is arguably the most significant designer of presentation drawings of the twentieth century. One of the first women to acquire an architectural degree, she completed her bachelor's in architecture at the Massachusetts Institute of Technology in 1894. Back in Chicago, she became the first employee at the solo practice established by Frank Lloyd Wright after he had left Adler & Sullivan. Mahony would continue to work for Wright over the next decade and a half, as a designer and a draftswoman. She made a vital contribution to the studio, particularly in how she rendered examples of Wright's renowned Prairie houses (figure 12.10). Using mainly watercolor and ink, Mahony developed a style whose Japanese roots echoed the design principles of the architecture itself. Flat, decorative areas of color enlivened the drawings, while Mahony found a perfect balance between realistic detail and artistic flourish. Mahony and Wright developed a frankly cheerful style in these drawings, one that conveyed an upbeat marketing message. The drawings were

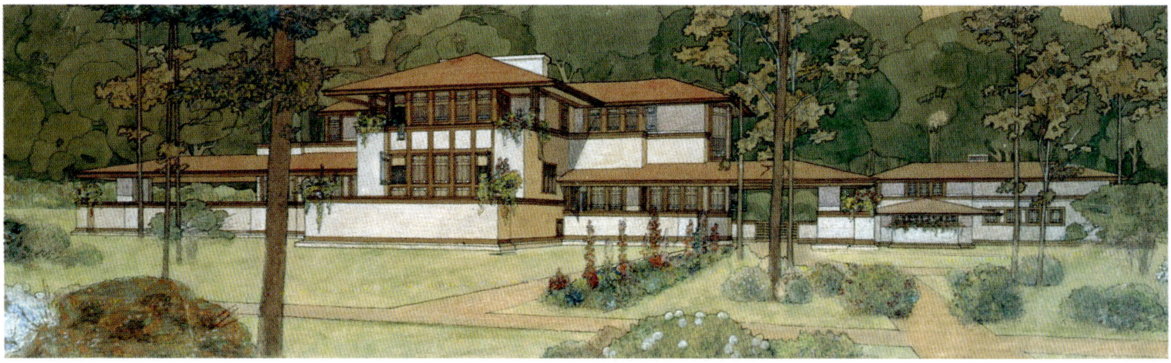

12.10. Marion Mahony Griffin, *Willits House*, from Frank Lloyd Wright's Wasmuth Portfolio, watercolor and ink, 1909

personable and romantic. Whether these renderings led to any given commission is impossible to know, but it would be foolish to overlook the impact these virtual buildings would have made on a Ward Willits or Frederick Robie.

When Wright closed up shop and left for a sojourn in Europe in 1909, Mahony was left in charge of wrapping up his existing projects. In Germany, Wright would next oversee the publication of what was perhaps his most important work, the *Ausgeführte Bauten und Entwürfe*, commonly known as the Wasmuth portfolio. This two-volume compendium of around one hundred renderings would serve Wright well for decades, as it became the basis for his European reputation and, in his view, was the catalyst for the overall invention of modern architecture. It is estimated that Mahony had created around half of the images displayed in the Wasmuth portfolio. Mahony later joined forces with her husband, another Wright studio alum, named Walter Griffin. In 1912 her artful renderings of a proposal for the federal capital of Canberra, Australia, led to her husband winning the high-profile project. Of course, like so many women architects, Mahony's work was subsumed first into that of her employer and later that of her husband, leaving her contribution scarcely visible during her lifetime.

Hugh Ferriss, a St. Louis native and graduate of the architectural school at Washington University, would design the other noteworthy set of architectural renderings produced in the first half of the twentieth century. In the 1920s, Ferriss devised a moody, expressionist style that suppressed the detail in buildings in favor of a dramatic atmosphere. His chiaroscuro renderings of towering skyscrapers caught the public's imagination, and Ferriss became highly sought after by architects pitching additions to the New York City skyline. He found his wheelhouse in depictions of fashionable stepped-back art deco skyscrapers. For example, a 1927 brochure touting the fifty-six-story Chanin Building (figure 12.11) starting construction in Midtown Manhattan featured a smoky, sculptural view of the future headquarters of the noted construction and real estate development company. The brochure echoed the atmosphere created by Ferriss in the rendering, stating that the building would be the "*mise en scene* for the romantic drama of American business."

Ferriss's evocative, emotional drawings came to inhabit a realm that was part real and part virtual. In 1929 Ferriss published his utopian-flavored book *The Metropolis of Tomorrow*, which was initiated by his earlier set of illustrations based on New York's new zoning laws in 1916. While ostensibly a study of how setbacks could allow for greater sunlight on city streets, the zoning work led Ferriss to visualizing the future, and part 3 of his new book was titled "An Imaginary Metropolis." In introducing this speculative set of renderings, Ferriss sounded much like a virtual reality publicist, enjoining the viewer to imagine: "It is again dawn, with an early mist completely enveloping the scene. . . . As the mists begin to disperse, there comes into view, one by one, the summits of what must be quite lofty tower-buildings." While lacking the photorealistic qualities of virtual reality, the combination of prose and image may well create a more powerful scene in the reader's mind than a digital rendering sans poetic text.

Even before digital rendering came on the scene in the nineties, the modern movement had a

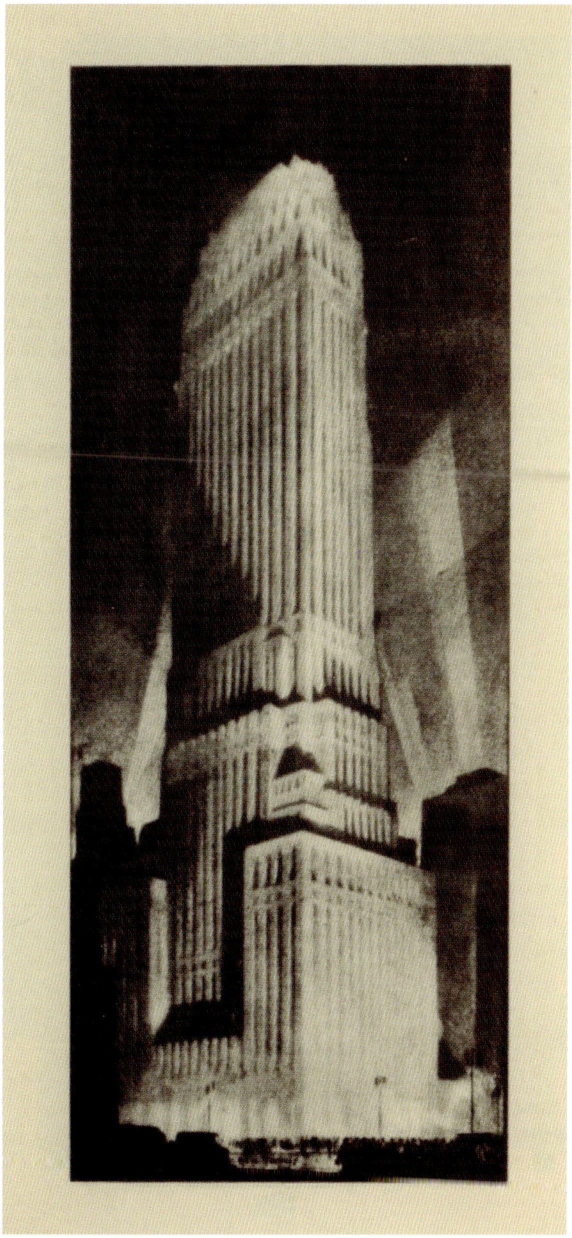

12.11. Hugh Ferriss, drawing of Chanin Building, 1927

huge impact in terms of stripping the personality out of a rendering; the rich emotion of a Mahony or Ferriss drawing was often suppressed. Postwar modern culture valorized a view of the designer as engineer, someone whose analytical eye triumphed over any emotional response. The resulting work was depersonalized, crisp and smooth; the design writer Maud Lavin has referred to this work as proffering a "clean new world." In the decades after the Second World War, the formerly radical, experimental styles of the 1920s avant-garde were whitewashed and domesticated. They reemerged during the formative years of digital design as "Bauhaus style," a shorthand that elides a great deal of complexity and political strife. Corporations used the style to project efficiency and regularity, a break with the "romance" promised by Ferriss's renderings. Just as the style has been collapsed into the seamless, glittering face of an iPhone (2007), so the history has been smoothed over and effaced.

A review of the past projects that are chronologically ordered as a gallery on the SOM website gives a clear sense of the trajectory that architectural visualization has taken over the span of the modern movement. SOM—formerly known as Skidmore, Owings, and Merrill—was founded in the thirties with a focus on government work. After designing a series of buildings for New York's 1939 World's Fair, SOM became known for its military work during the Second World War. Strikingly modernist structures by Gordon Bunshaft, such as the Hostess House at Great Lakes Naval Training Center (Illinois), established the firm as a domestic producer of the International style. During these midcentury

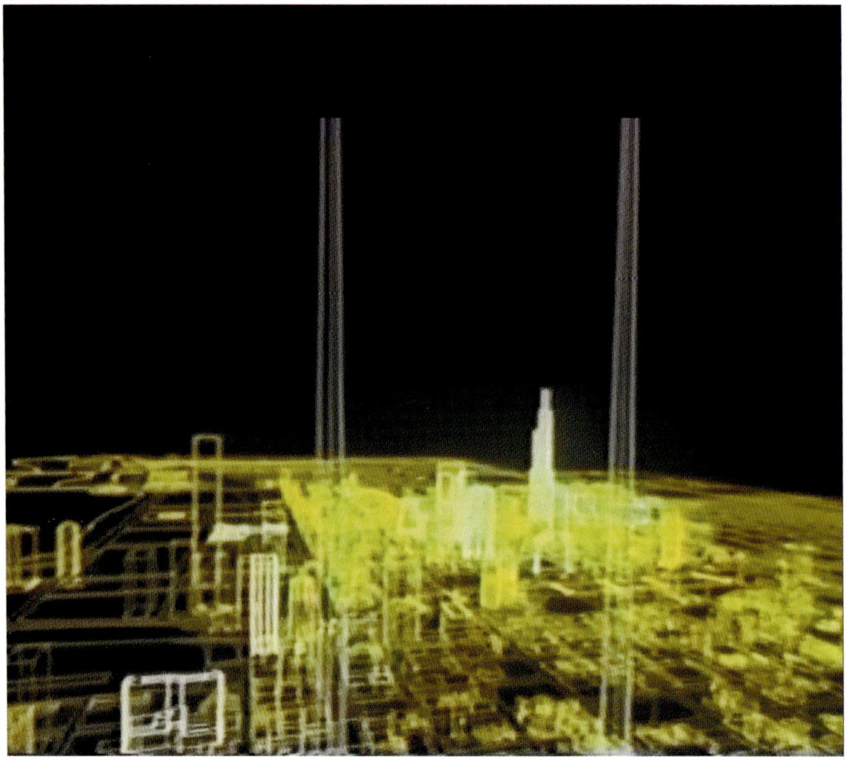

12.12. SOM, wireframe flyover of Chicago, 1980

years, SOM relied on presentation drawings and "final models" to display its proposals to clients. In the predigital era, models were a key part of the effort to communicate a virtual image of the building. Like many firms of this era, SOM built some models in-house but also relied on Theodore Conrad, a consultant known as the "Dean of Models." Conrad made many presentation models for SOM, including a sprawling one for the Air Force Academy (Walter Netsch, 1954–62) in Colorado, which featured thousands of tiny cadet figurines on the virtual campus. Notably, Conrad also made all the models for the 1950 exhibition at the Museum of Modern Art that helped to secure SOM's reputation as a cutting-edge firm.

A huge firm such as SOM, with its substantial resources, was able to employ digital technology for promotional purposes at a much faster rate than the average design studio. As early as 1980, the firm proffered wireframe flyovers (figure 12.12) of major American cities, including Chicago; these animated shorts were created from the CAD files of iconic buildings such as Inland Steel and the Sears Tower. Today on SOM's corporate website, these past projects are shown in black-and-white photographs, and no trace of the presentation drawings and models appear. Eventually in the seventies the photos turned to color, and then around the turn of the millennium, digital visualizations begin to accrue. For example, the page documenting the 2004 Time Warner Center (figure 12.13) features both color photographs of the completed building and several digital renderings from the presentation phase. Like the drawings and models that preceded them, some of the digital images were subcontracted out, in Time Warner's case to Neoscape, an architectural visualization firm. With the arrival of digital illustration in the nineties, the characteristic smooth, technological look clearly represented a tool that perfectly matched the prevailing aesthetic.

Notably, the glittering digital images from the commissioning phase of SOM's Time Warner project are still included in their corporate gallery, whereas drawings and models of projects from the predigital age have been swept away. One obvious reason for this development is that photorealistic virtual simulations remain in many ways better than the real. An architectural model is no more than a dusty curiosity that becomes sidelined and fairly irrelevant upon the completion of a finished structure. A digital visualization, however, like a selfie run through an algorithmic Snapchat filter that "tunes" one's face, remains in some fashion superior to the messy real world. The allure of the digital seems at times to have trumped visions of the actual. In a piece for the *Guardian* decrying the state of architectural education in the UK, Oliver Wainwright related an anecdote about the diploma projects he had seen while visiting universities. Many of these renderings seemed to represent a techno-utopian end in themselves, featuring fantasies born out of digital effects

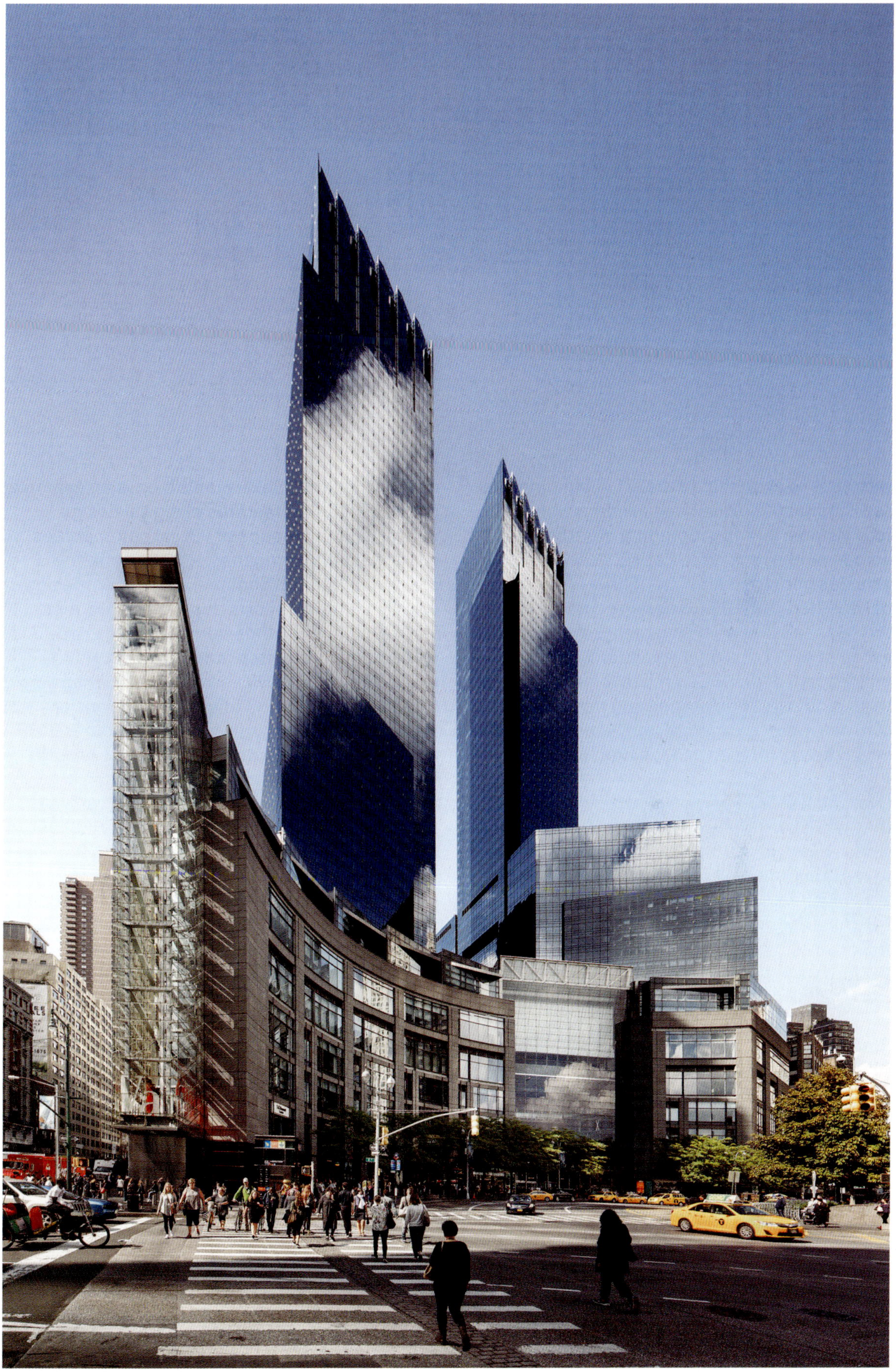

12.13. SOM and Neoscape, visualization of Time Warner Center, 2004

with little relationship to the art of building. He saw "immaculate drawings of impossibly elaborate visions: airships dragging contraptions across moon-rock landscapes, fleets of hover vehicles gliding to and fro." There is a strong parallel here with the generalized adoption of the "Bauhaus" style by big tech; both proffer an escapist world of digital splendor. Like a symbolist poem of the 1880s that allowed the reader to shut out the deprivations and depredations of urban industrial culture, so the digital renderings of today offer an escape from the real.

Over the last few years, digital rendering firms—they often use the hip term "archviz" for their work—have shifted from a series of static images to narrative simulations that rival Hollywood special effects, such as those seen in *Black Panther*. For example, John Portman and Associates' presentation of the Shanghai redevelopment project called Yangpu Ba Dai Tou featured an eight-minute CGI video that flew viewers over and around some of the virtual buildings like a ship landing in Wakanda's Golden City. Anticipated decades ago by SOM's wireframe animation, today's productions make use of video game and filmmaking software. Neoscape produced the Yangpu Ba Dai Tou video, using a combination of live action and CGI effects created with V-Ray and 3ds Max. While not, strictly speaking, an example of virtual reality, this presentation piece displays stereoscopic 3D and 4K animation in a manner that immerses the viewer in a corresponding way: plus, no goggles.

Based in Tel Aviv, the archviz specialist Ronen Bekerman has created one of the most substantial sites devoted to teaching and learning about 3D archviz. Cofounder of the archviz studio called The Craft, Bekerman's blog is an example of one of the best features of digital design writ large, the creation of virtual communities devoted to nurturing the field while offering resources for both beginner and expert designers. The internet allows this diverse group to learn about renderings from all over the world. Bekerman's blog often features guest renderers, who get to showcase their work while also offering detailed, technical breakdowns of their process. For example, in November 2018 the site featured Pedro Fernandes of Arqui9 Visualisation of London, who demonstrated the strategies he used to visualize a railway station in Riyadh, Saudi Arabia (figure 12.14). Screenshots of working pages using V-Ray and Photoshop walk the reader through complex software settings, demonstrating how light and texture affect the rendering. While the Bekerman site focuses on archviz, most digital design threads have benefited from these types of communities. For example, aspiring graphic designers can seek out Brand New, a subpage of the website Under Consideration that is maintained by Armin Vit and Bryony Gomez-Palacio. On Brand New, the designers critically analyze corporate identity projects, and the community chimes in on both the work and the review, often generating lively discussions about design.

In a sense, architectural renderings using virtual reality technology up to the present represent more of an incremental advance in the digital world than a transformative change. As new cloud-based software such as OTOY's Octane Render has come on the market, photorealistic images have become par for the course. Developed based on gaming and filmmaking CGI technology, Octane Render can create a 3D image from a Revit file in a matter of seconds.

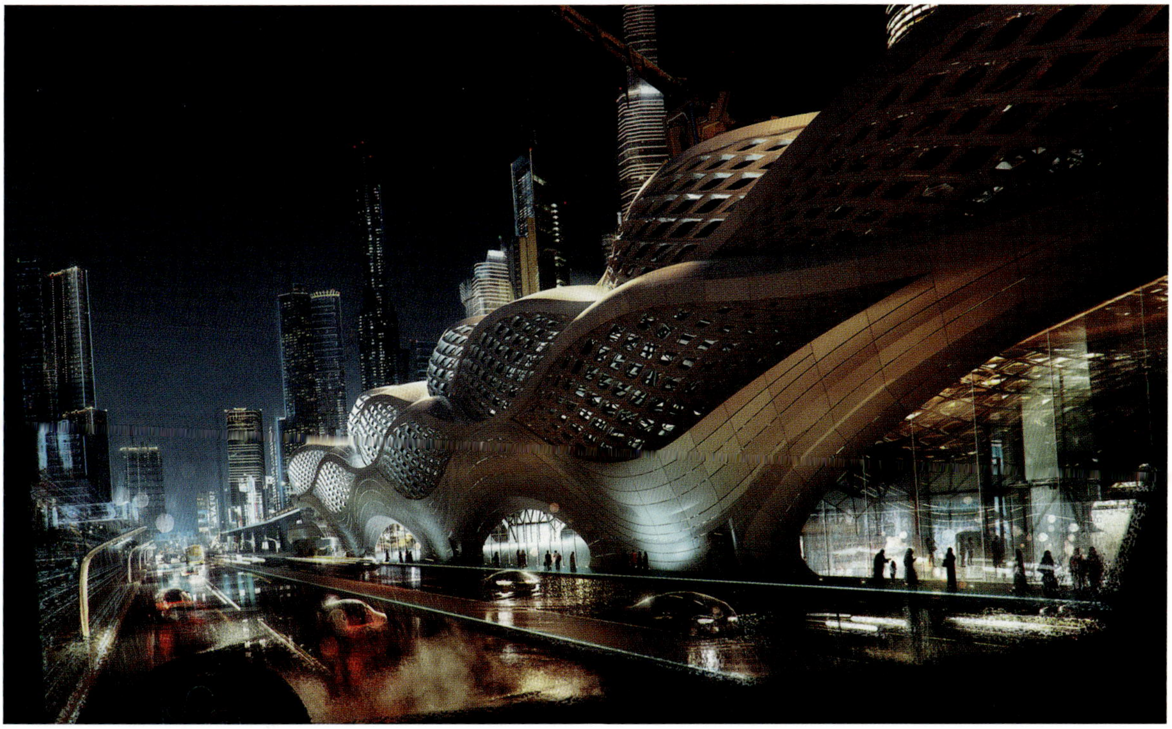

12.14. Pedro Fernandes, Arqui9, and Newtecnic, visualization on Ronen Bekerman's Architectural Visualization Hub, 2018

Mark Bassett at Gensler has explained the ramp-up in rendering technology: "To put it into perspective, when Pixar was developing the movie 'Cars 2,' its average rendering time per frame was 11.5 hours,... We're rendering at seven seconds a frame using Octane. It changes everything." Rather than spend hundreds of hours laboriously Photoshopping an image, architects today can quickly create a polished-looking drawing.

Take a typical example, the 2016 proposal for a pool complex at the Turnberry Place development in Las Vegas. Designed by Brian Thornton, he contracted the rendering out to the Chicago studio Sonny+Ash. The resulting VR illustration does an excellent job of visualizing the space in three dimensions but is not so different from viewing various three-dimensional stills. The viewer can get a good sense of how the pool would look in terms of color and materials as well as the pathways between areas and overall sense of space. While more sophisticated than earlier renderings in terms of texture and surface, it still is a video-game-like simulacrum of glittering smoothness. Studios offer this type of VR work as "interactive, immersive and engaging experiences," which is true insomuch as the depopulated world is often strictly virtual and bears little connection to the warmth or messiness that characterizes human existence. One's interaction is strictly with a machine, as an almost dystopic emptiness comes to the fore.

Digital rendering has also allowed for the realistic visualization of historic examples of "paper architecture," unbuilt projects by noted designers. While Frank Lloyd Wright's Wasmuth portfolio was an analog collection along these lines, recent digital renderings of his work have brought new attention to long ago inspiring unbuilt designs. In a collaboration with the Wright Foundation, architect David Romero has created virtual renderings of several buildings, including the plan for the Gordon Strong Automobile Objective (figure 12.15). A tourist attraction designed in 1924, the Objective featured an early example of the type of spiral form Wright employed decades later at the Guggenheim Museum. Romero reviewed the historic drawings of the structure, and then used AutoCAD with 3ds Max to create a convincing visualization. From Mahony to Romero, much of Wright's work is known through the artistic interpretations of others. The evocative power of digital renderings should not be underestimated, as contemporary technology—Vladimir Tatlin's Monument to the Third International (1920) on the Saint Petersburg skyline is a great example—has allowed historians to get a much more detailed sense of how iconic paper buildings would have fit into the fabric of the site.

There has been an inevitable backlash of sorts against digital rendering in the last few years, as some architects have turned to quirky,

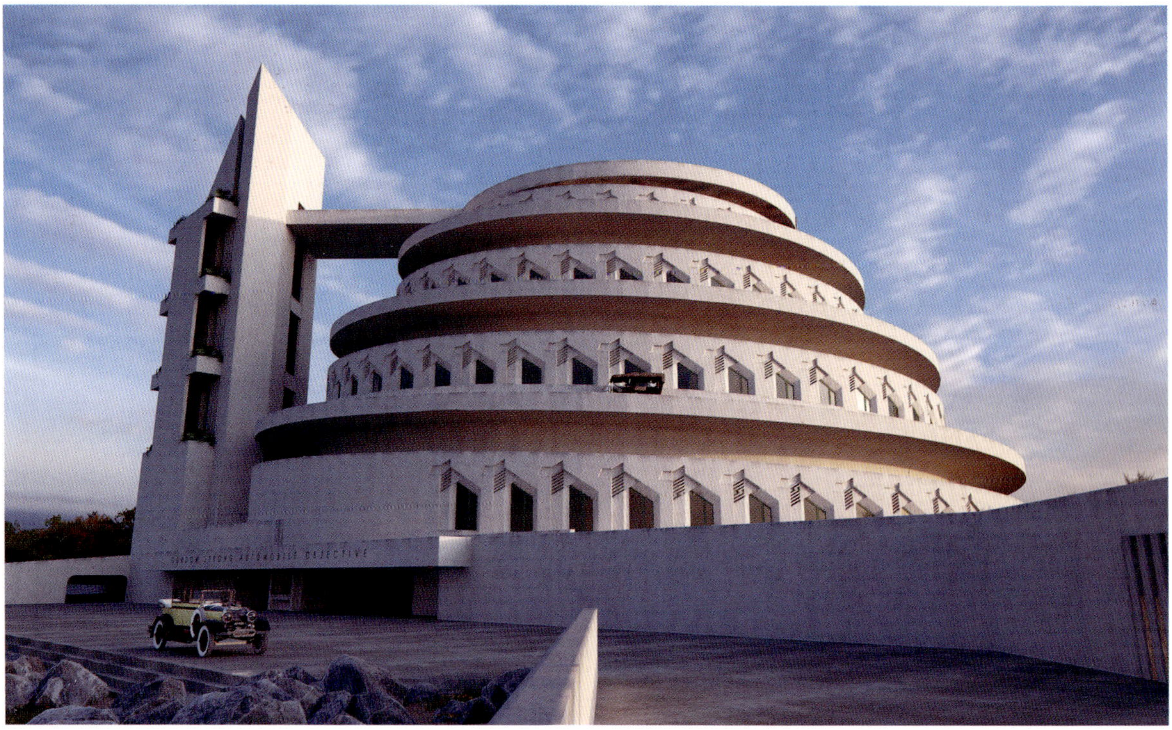

12.15. David Romero, visualization of Frank Lloyd Wright's Gordon Strong Automobile Objective [1924], 2018

subjective styles. As Sam Jacob explained in *Metropolis* magazine in 2017, "Instead of striving for pseudo-photo-realism, this new cult of the drawing explores and exploits its artificiality, making us as viewers aware that we are looking at space as a fictional form of representation. This is in strict opposition to the digital rendering's desire to make the fiction seem 'real.'" Drawing by hand represents one of the many manifestations of the "revenge of the analog," a contemporary impulse—think vinyl records—to rediscover and explore tangible technologies of a predigital era.

Some designers have also begun to point out the unrealistic coldness of VR and other digital renderings of buildings. Digital designer Stephanie Davidson has cheekily started posting renderings that have been subverted by added signs of human habitation. Essentially, she adds garbage; now the pool deck is cluttered with toys, and a stack of trash bags are piled around the corner. There is a larger issue here: the manner in which digital design thrives on novelty and incremental technological improvement. Virtual reality images share the same sleek digital aesthetic as the latest laptop or iPhone. For example, Apple's product launch in 2021 was titled "Unleashed," a word that poetically captures the excitement of the new. But for every product launch another piece of old hardware heads to the closet or the drawer, which is only a whistle-stop on its way to the landfill.

Virtual reality has also demonstrated its usefulness to architects working on the technical details of buildings. By combining VR renderings with the fruits of big data and associated visualizations, architects can better predict how certain parts of a building will function in the real world. Ennead Architects is one studio that has been experimenting with this type of multidisciplinary approach to data-driven VR in architecture. In their view, "VR is the first immersive technology that draws an immediate connection between the virtual model and the completed space, between data, design process, and visceral experience." Ennead refers to this strategy as "immersive data analytics" and has employed it in projects such as the Shanghai Planetarium, which opened in 2020. In the planning stage for the building, Ennead collected data using Ladybug Tools, an open source collection of plug-ins and applications designed to facilitate environmental studies in pursuit of green architecture. Ennead collected solar and thermal comfort data of the inverted dome that covers the central atrium. This multistory space with a spiraling ramp is one of the visual centerpieces of the building, and understanding the impact of sunlight was important from both an environmental and an experiential viewpoint. The data on vectors and solar gain were uploaded into Grasshopper 3D, which is an algorithmic editor that is integrated with the overall Rhino 3D ecosystem. Data, algorithm, virtual reality: the final step was to merge the data with a VR rendering through IrisVR. The final result allowed the architects to get a much fuller sense of how the building would respond to different daylight conditions. Ennead VR specialist Brian Hopkins told *Metropolis*, "It makes the quantifiable qualitative. We start to describe light in ways that are actually closer to metaphor than data analytics. We're humanizing the data." The planetarium project is a success story in the overall attempt by big technology workers to make the digital relatable and human centered: it is the type of project that fulfills Lanier's original goal of virtual reality that adds rather than subtracts from human experience.

Perhaps the most powerful impact of virtual reality will come through its hybrid cousin, augmented reality. Whereas VR shuts out the tangible world with blackout goggles, AR uses clear lenses or other screens to integrate the analog world with the digital. While compelling games such as *Pokémon Go!* brought AR into the mainstream through play, technologists see it becoming the strategy that could immerse people in the internet. This futuristic AR experience has been called the "mirror world," a term that refers to the fact that we have been gradually developing a digital twin to our actual environment. With BIM software, Google Maps and Streetview, vacuums that map domestic spaces: byte by byte, a 1:1 scale digital model of the whole world is on the not-so-distant horizon. Kevin Kelly recently wrote about it in *Wired*, noting, "Someday soon, every place and thing in the real world—every street, lamppost, building, and room—will have its full-size digital twin in the Mirrorworld." Kelly also pointed out that NASA had pioneered this strategy in analog fashion, keeping exact copies of space vehicles on hand so that they could analyze engineering problems on a distant craft through its doppelganger in real time. In a dystopic twist, Facebook promised in 2021 to build its own "Metaverse," an AR space that will surely collect copious amounts of marketable data on its inhabitants. The question still exists as to how these AR experiences will jibe with the actual world, or if eventually people will choose to escape the real: perhaps we will find, as did the creator of *Second Life* years ago, that all we really want is Malibu and supercars.

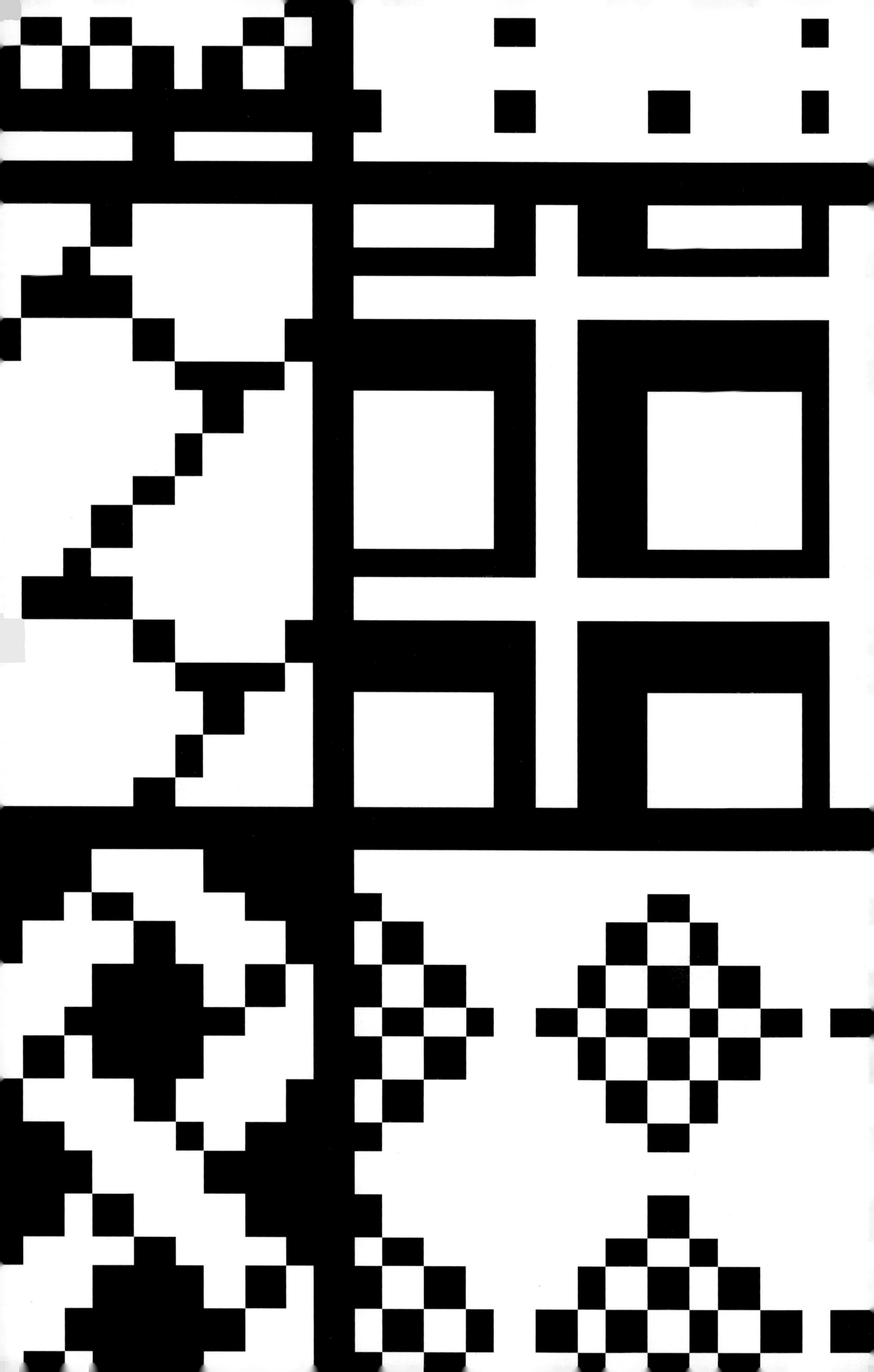

13.1. Zach Blas, Icosahedron, 2019

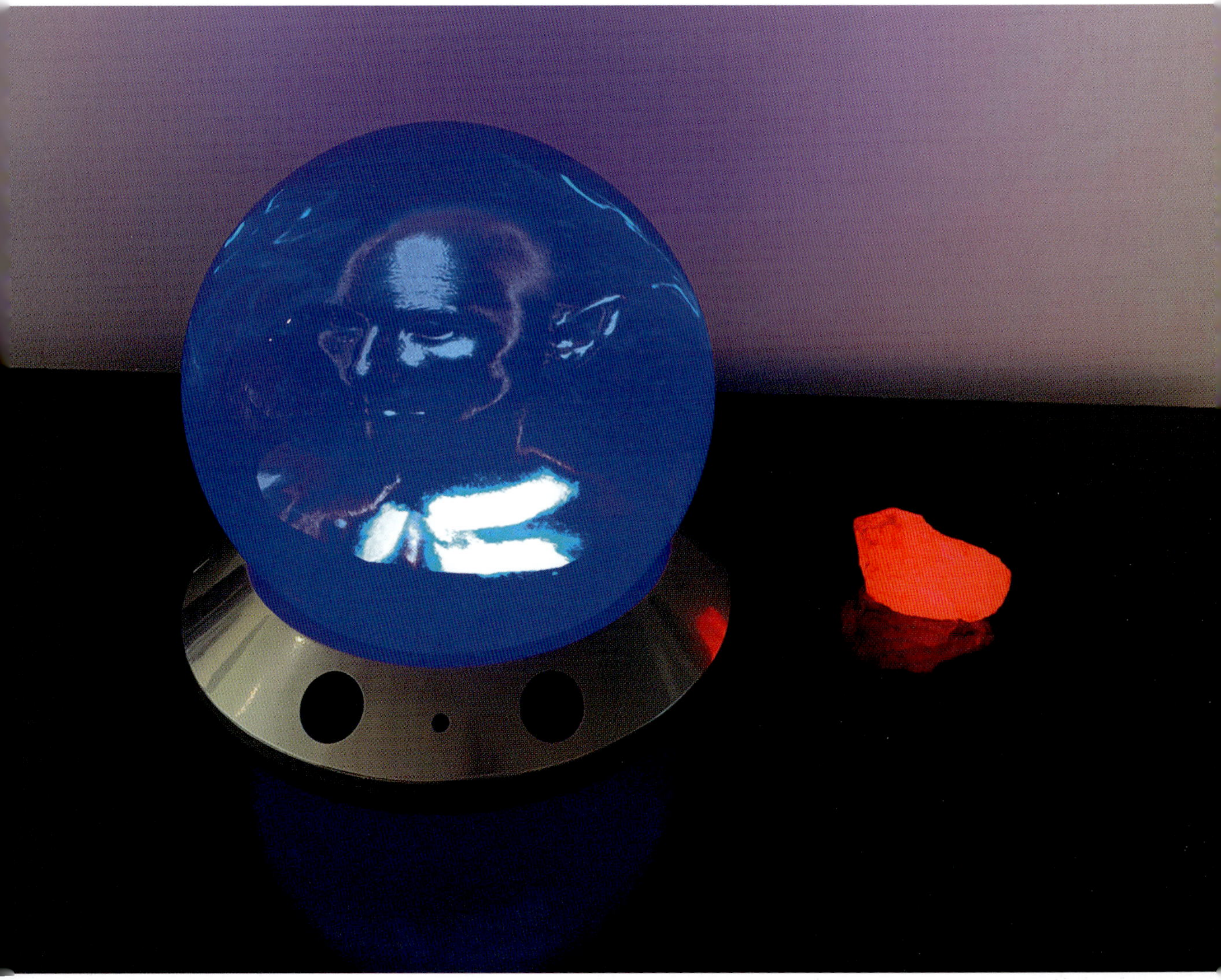

Coda. The Digital Future

Whereas Stanley Kubrick's HAL provided an earlier generation's first and only taste of human–machine interaction, today discussions with relatable assistants have become part of the mundane fabric of life. Two of the most pervasive interlocutors are barely a decade old: Apple's Siri came on the scene in 2011, followed by Amazon's Alexa in 2014. Neither really crossed the threshold of mainstream utilization until the last few years.

As digital assistants like Alexa continue updating and evolving, making them warm and personable has become a central goal of their designers. While HAL was voiced by the Shakespearean actor Douglas Rain, Alexa is a synthetic voice that uses natural language processing algorithms to drive a text-to-speech system. Machine learning of this sort has its limits, and Amazon wants to avoid even the hint of a robot voice. For this reason, Amazon has sought out a nontraditional group of professionals to give personality to the device. As *Wired* put it in a 2017 article, "Our Robots Are Powered by Poets and Musicians." The title refers to three women who collaborate in the creation of Alexa's persona. Farah Houston has a background in psychology and helps mold the humanness of Alexa. A writer, Michelle Riggen-Ransom, writes the basic responses. Beth Holmes, a mathematician, also contributes to the content and texture of the machine's personas. A fourth woman, Susan Kaplan, is the voice actress. In this regard, Alexa represents a type of "affective computing," a term coined by Rosalind Picard in the late nineties. Picard's current research is aimed at "enabling robots and computers to receive natural emotional feedback and improve human experiences," and eventually allowing computers to "have" emotions.

Alexa and Siri's original female voices also bring up the issue of gender and ethnicity in digital culture. The age of computer design began at a time of entrenched sexism, with women excluded from the fields that launched the digital age. Anecdotally, the difficulties that women faced are evident in the career of Poppy Northcutt. A mathematician, Northcutt was one of the only women computer scientists that worked on both the Gemini and Apollo programs at NASA. She was often presented as exemplary of the agency's forward-leaning culture for publicity purposes and made note of the paradox implicit in her role at NASA. On the one hand, she felt that computer programming offered a gender-free environment: "The nature of this business doesn't lend itself to discrimination. If you write a computer program, it either works or it doesn't. There's no opportunity for anyone to be subjective about your work." On the other hand, however, she has marveled in recent years over how her role was defined at NASA. Northcutt recounted to *Time* in 2019 that her official title was "Computress." She remembers pondering the awkward sexism of this job description: "Not only do they think I'm a computer, but they think I'm a gendered computer."

Another way of interpreting people's relationship to voice assistants like Alexa is through the history of brands. Corporations started the widespread use of brands in the nineteenth century as a way of establishing trust and a sense of reliability with consumers who had, until recently, bought most of their products from people personally known to them. In large industrial cities, purveyors of mass-produced items, especially foodstuffs, pioneered intentionally designed brand representatives—personifications of otherwise faceless industrial companies—to establish an emotional connection with their customers.

One of the most prominent early brand ambassadors was a character called Aunt Jemima. In 1890, the Davis Milling Company purchased a pancake mix named after the minstrel song "Old Aunt Jemima." The song had been composed in the 1870s—the beginnings of the Jim Crow era—by Billy Kersands, one of the most popular Black entertainers of the time. Importantly, the owners of Davis Milling decided to enhance the Aunt Jemima brand by hiring a real person to act as a live-action character in promotional settings. The first actor to take on the role was Nancy Green, a fifty-six-year-old woman who had been born enslaved in Kentucky. She continued to act as Aunt Jemima until her death in 1923. Over the ensuing decades a series of actors took on the role: Ana Robinson, Anna Harrington, Aylene Lewis, Edith Wilson, Ethel Harper, and Rosie Hall. The Aunt Jemima character was of course a racist stereotype aimed at white people who casually accepted plantation-era representations of Black Americans. Although Quaker Oats started downplaying the brand in the sixties, and in the eighties modernized the character to appear more like an affluent housewife, it did not retire the character and brand name until 2021.

In 2014, Amazon had introduced its own virtual, live-action digital assistant: Alexa. For six years the two brand ambassadors overlapped, seeming to symbolize the societal advances of a new age. Alexa acts as a branding personality for the retailer and by extension a simulacrum of the digital world itself, warm, helpful, and relatable. In some ways, her partly synthesized voice attempts to represent a clean, new digital world apparently washed of biases and inequities of any sort: a postracial, postbias utopia of gleaming efficiency. The virtual environment branded by big tech, however, often seems decidedly racialized, and Alexa speaks with what most people take to be the pitch and cadences of a white woman. And woe to the nonwhite person who converses with the digital; research at Stanford University has shown significant disparities in the ability of speech recognition software to correctly understand Black voices.

Digital assistants may put an engaging voice on an unequal world, but their work is mainly symbolic. The most intractable societal problems are hidden in the machines. Behind Alexa's warm tones lies a treacherous world of analog human behavior and structural bias. It has become clear that the combination of big data and artificial intelligence behind so much of our digital world is imbued with the same problems that have plagued the analog world. As computers using machine learning perform more and more of society's hiring and firing, lending and incarcerating, the problem of algorithmic bias is emerging as a vital threat to digital culture.

The Digital Future

The question remains as to where the digital age will go next. Visionaries still abound. Philosopher Yuval Noah Harari has asserted that humanity will soon attempt to attain superhuman powers through algorithmic processes: each of us our own Alexa, a Homo Deus dominating the mirror world. Or the future may be depersonalized by AI, our texts written by chatbots and our self-images by DALL-E. But, of course, this future is all quite unknowable, and in the digital age even more so than before. Harari has noted, "Centuries ago human knowledge increased slowly, so politics and economics changed at a leisurely pace too. Today our knowledge is increasing at breakneck speed, and theoretically we should understand the world better and better. But the very opposite is happening. Our new-found knowledge leads to faster economic, social, and political changes; in an attempt to understand what is happening, we accelerate the accumulation of knowledge, which leads only to faster and greater upheavals."

Digital artist Zach Blas has added his own whimsical take on the digital future through his Icosahedron (figure 13.1), a contemporary update of midcentury's twenty-sided Magic 8-Ball, which could playfully "predict" the future. Blas has loaded his work with twenty visionary texts, and through machine learning, the AI in Icosahedron will offer its predictions for the future. The original Magic 8-Ball offered ten positive responses and only five in the negative, so one can hope that the digital version will maintain that optimistic bias. As Blas has written, "Skip the TED Talk: to find out what's shaping the future, ask Icosahedron."

Acknowledgments

There are many people to thank. It has been a longish journey, and Michelle Komie at Princeton University Press has been there from the first, providing guidance and support. She was ably assisted by Kenneth Guay and Annie Miller. Also at PUP, Karen Carter and Jessica Massabrook have been instrumental in the book's production, while freelance copyeditor Melanie Mallon did an excellent job getting the text into shape. Picture research on this book was a real struggle, and Amanda Russell did a superb job tracking down images. Eileen Clancy assisted with some of the preliminary picture research. The peer reviewers, #1 and #2, offered excellent suggestions that greatly improved the text. I would also like to thank the designers who were generous with their work, especially John Maeda, Scott Snibbe, Daniel Brown, Liat Berdugo, Rudy VanderLans, Luke Turner, David Carson, Michael Hansmeyer, April Greiman, and Andi Watson. At Eastern Illinois University, chair of Art + Design Chris Kahler was continually supportive of this project, and Robert Petersen first suggested that I should write this book.

Index

Picture Credits

Figure 0.1, illustration by Grafiker61, CC BY-SA 4.0
Figure 1.1, courtesy of the estate of Marshall McLuhan
Figure 2.1, photo by Klugschnacker, CC BY-SA 3.0
Figure 2.2, photo by Ivan Sutherland, CC BY-SA 3.0
Figure 2.3, Figure 2.4, and Figure 2.5, reprint courtesy of IBM Corporation
Figure 2.6, photo by Bernard Gotfryd, Library of Congress, Prints and Photographs Division, LC-DIG-gtfy-01855
Figure 2.7, © Apple Computer, Inc.
Figure 2.8, Fine Art Images / Bridgeman Images, © 2022 Artists Rights Society, New York
Figure 2.9, © Apple Computer, Inc.
Figure 2.10, © John Knoll
Figure 3.1 and
Figure 3.2, © Emigre
Figure 3.3, courtesy of Bigelow & Holmes, Inc.
Figure 3.4 © TfL from the London Transport Museum
Figure 3.5, photo by Cethegus, CC BY-SA 3.0
Figure 3.6, photo by Lelikron, CC BY-SA 3.0
Figure 3.7, © AF Fotografie / Bridgeman Images
Figure 3.8, Zürcher Hochschule der Künste / Museum für Gestaltung Zürich / Grafiksammlung Donation: Schweizerische Stiftung Schrift und Typografie
Figure 3.9, reprinted courtesy of the MIT Press
Figure 3.10, © Apple Computer, Inc.
Figure 3.11, Roboto typeface, 2011, is a trademark of Google LLC, and this book is not endorsed by or affiliated with Google in any way
Figure 3.12, Alamy
Figure 3.13, photo by Yiğit Ali Atasoy / Unsplash
Figure 3.14, Google's corporate identity is a trademark of Google LLC, and this book is not endorsed by or affiliated with Google in any way
Figure 4.1, Visible Language Workshop archive, MIT Art, Culture and Technology Program Special Collections (01CooperVLW1985)
Figure 4.2, © 2021 John Maeda
Figure 4.3, © Fischinger Trust
Figure 4.4, reprint courtesy of IBM Corporation
Figure 4.5, photo by Katie Friesema, courtesy of Andi Watson
Figure 4.6, © Scott Snibbe
Figure 4.7, photo by Joi Ito
Figure 4.8, photo by Evan-Amos, CC BY-SA 3.0
Figure 4.9, photo by Chris Rand, CC BY-SA 3.0
Figure 4.10, © Chris Crawford
Figure 4.11, ArcadeImages / Alamy
Figure 4.12, © Bethesda Softworks
Figure 4.13, courtesy Electronic Arts Intermix (EAI), New York
Figure 4.14, photo by Linden Lab
Figure 5.1 and Figure 5.2, © April Greiman
Figure 5.3, © David Carson
Figure 5.4, © Citibank
Figure 5.5, © 1994–2022 CERN
Figure 5.6, Alta Vista
Figure 5.7, courtesy of David Siegel
Figure 5.8, ©1996 Ron Lussier / Burning Pixel Productions
Figure 5.9, MTAA, CC0 1.0
Figure 5.10, Courtesy Hotwire Productions LLC, Bridget Donahue Gallery (NY), Altman Siegel Gallery (SF)
Figure 5.11, David Bohnett and John Rezner
Figure 6.1, photo by Bernard Spragg, CC0 1.0
Figure 6.2, © Tony Hisgett
Figure 6.3, photo by Irving Penn for *Vogue*, © 2022 Austrian Frederick and Lillian Kiesler Private Foundation, Vienna
Figure 6.4, photo by Americasroof, CC BY-SA 2.5
Figure 6.5, Enric Ruiz-Geli, Cloud 9
Figure 6.6, photo by Marion Schneider and Christoph Aistleitner
Figure 7.1, © Brendan Dawes
Figure 7.2, © Luke Turner
Figure 7.3, © NEC Corporation 2004, all rights reserved
Figure 7.4, © Nike, Inc.
Figure 7.5, by kind permission of eBoy
Figure 7.6, Whitney Museum of American Art, New York
Figure 7.7, *Bejeweled* v1.23 by PopCap Games
Figure 7.8, screenshot from Newgrounds.com
Figure 7.10, © Apple Computer, Inc.
Figure 7.11, © Daniel Brown
Figure 7.12 and
Figure 7.13, photos courtesy of Amaze
Figure 8.1 and Figure 8.2, photos by Iwan Baan
Figure 8.3, © Helene Binet
Figure 8.4, © UNStudio
Figure 8.5, © Christian Richters
Figure 8.6, © Trey Trahan
Figure 8.7, © Luis Quinones, Stahl
Figure 8.8, Michael Hansmeyer and Benjamin Dillenburger
Figure 8.9, Michael Hansmeyer
Figure 8.10, © Farid Khayrulin
Figure 8.11, photo by Scarlet Green, CC BY 2.0
Figure 8.12, David Parker / Alamy
Figure 8.13, © Steve Hall
Figure 8.14, © Jose Sanchez
Figure 8.15, photo © Iwan Baan, courtesy of SHoP
Figure 8.16, courtesy of Mercedes-Benz Classics
Figure 8.17, © Baskerville
Figure 8.18, © Gramazio Kohler Research, ETH Zurich
Figure 8.19, WATG
Figure 8.20, Shoei Yoh Archive, Kyushu University
Figure 8.21, photo © James C. Weaver, reproduced courtesy of Chuck Hoberman and Katia Bertholdi
Figure 9.1, © The Museum of Modern Art, licensed by SCALA / Art Resource, NY
Figure 9.2, © Apple Computer, Inc.
Figure 9.3, © Alan Kay
Figure 9.4, © Cooper Hewitt, Smithsonian Design Museum / Art Resource, NY
Figure 9.5, photo by Ashley Pomeroy, CC BY-SA 4.0
Figure 9.6, Retro AdArchives / Alamy
Figure 9.7, © Ettore Sottsass
Figure 9.8, Reuters / Alamy
Figure 9.9, © Techcrunch
Figure 9.10, © 2012 Tangible Media Groups /s MIT Media Lab
Figure 9.11, photo by Mike McGregor, CC BY 2.5
Figure 9.12, Fuseproject
Figure 9.13, Reuters / Alamy
Figure 9.14, Image © 2022 New-York Historical Society
Figure 9.15, © Vivint

Figure 10.1, reprint courtesy of IBM Corporation
Figure 10.2, The Grid.io
Figure 10.3, © Adelia Lim
Figure 10.4, © 2015, Andy Clymer, Hoefler&Co. (a Monotype Company)
Figure 10.5, © Joris Laarman
Figure 10.6, Arthur Harsuvanakit and Brittany Presten, Autodesk
Figure 10.7, photo © Thomas Duval, Patrick Jouin iD, MGX by Materialise
Figure 10.8, © Ron Arad
Figure 10.9, © Leslie Nooteboom
Figure 10.10, public domain as a work of computer algorithm
Figure 10.11, Gewalker, CC BY-SA 3.0
Figure 10.12, © Bethany Kober / Fam Studio
Figure 10.13, Tesla Motors
Figure 10.14, Clips camera is a trademark of Google LLC, and this book is not endorsed by or affiliated with Google in any way
Figure 10.15, courtesy of Zach Blas
Figure 10.16 and Figure 10.17, © Guilherme Twardowski
Figure 11.1, © Stanford University
Figure 11.2, *Chart Representing the Extent, Population & Revenue of the Principal Nations in Europe in 1804*, plate 2 (labeled No. 3) from Playfair (1805), courtesy of the Thomas Fisher Rare Book Library, University of Toronto
Figure 11.3, Wellcome Collection, University of London
Figure 11.4, Prints and Photographs Division, Library of Congress
Figure 11.5, © Nam June Paik Estate
Figure 11.6, Cosmo Condina / Alamy
Figure 11.7, Eddie Opara and Pentagram
Figure 11.8, © Oliver O'Brien
Figure 11.9, © Ben Fry
Figure 11.10, © Ben Fry and Fathom
Figure 11.11, Gapminder, www.gapminder.org
Figure 11.12, "Solstice" interface design by Björk and Max Weisel
Figure 11.13, photo by Patrick Gries, © Ryoji Ikeda and Éditions Xavier Barral
Figure 11.14, © Nick Berry and Data Genetics
Figure 11.15, © Mieka West and Sheelagh Carpendale
Figure 11.16, © Julie Freeman
Figure 12.1, Paul Philippoteaux
Figure 12.2, Harry Ransom Center, the University of Texas at Austin
Figure 12.3, Everett Collection / Alamy Stock Photo
Figure 12.4, Sensorama, Inc. CC BY 4.0
Figure 12.5, © Shutterstock, photographer unknown
Figure 12.6, © Char Davies
Figure 12.7, © HK Strategies
Figure 12.8, © Artefact Group
Figure 12.9, © Gabo Arora and Chris Milk
Figure 12.10, © 2023 Frank Lloyd Wright Foundation, Scottsdale, AZ
12.11, Hugh Ferriss and Ives Washburn
Figure 12.12, Courtesy of SOM / © SOM
Figure 12.13, Courtesy of SOM / © James Ewing
Figure 12.14, Pedro Fernandes of Arqui9 for Newtecnic
Figure 12.15, David Romero, © Frank Lloyd Wright Foundation, Scottsdale, AZ
Figure 13.1, © Zach Blas.